# Chrysler PT Cruiser Automotive Repair Manual

**by Robert Maddox and John H Haynes**

Member of the Guild of Motoring Writers

**Models covered:**

All Chrysler PT Cruiser models
2001 through 2010

*(25035 - 5S10)*

AB

**Haynes Publishing Group**
Sparkford Nr Yeovil
Somerset BA22 7JJ England

**Haynes North America, Inc**
861 Lawrence Drive
Newbury Park
California 91320 USA

## Acknowledgements

We are grateful to the Chrysler Corporation for providing technical information, wiring diagrams and certain illustrations. Technical writers who contributed to this project include Bob Henderson, Mike Stubblefield, Larry Warren and Ralph Rendina. Technical consultants include Jamie Sarté, Jr. and Brad Conn.

---



---

**A book in the Haynes Automotive Repair Manual Series**

---

**Printed in the U.S.A.**

---



---

**ISBN-13: 978-1-56392-963-2**
**ISBN-10: 1-56392-963-5**

---

**Library of Congress Control Number 2011943389**

---



---

11-320

# Contents

**Haynes mechanic, author and photographer with a 2001 PT Cruiser**

# About this manual

### Its purpose

The purpose of this manual is to help you get the best value from your vehicle. It can do so in several ways. It can help you decide what work must be done, even if you choose to have it done by a dealer service department or a repair shop; it provides information and procedures for routine maintenance and servicing; and it offers diagnostic and repair procedures to follow when trouble occurs.

We hope you use the manual to tackle the work yourself. For many simpler jobs, doing it yourself may be quicker than arranging an appointment to get the vehicle into a shop and making the trips to leave it and pick it up. More importantly, a lot of money can be saved by avoiding the expense the shop must pass on to you to cover its labor and overhead costs. An added benefit is the sense of satisfaction and accomplishment that you feel after doing the job yourself.

### Using the manual

The manual is divided into Chapters. Each Chapter is divided into numbered Sections, which are headed in bold type between horizontal lines. Each Section consists of consecutively numbered paragraphs.

At the beginning of each numbered Section you will be referred to any illustrations which apply to the procedures in that Section. The reference numbers used in illustration captions pinpoint the pertinent Section and the Step within that Section. That is, illustration 3.2 means the illustration refers to Section 3 and Step (or paragraph) 2 within that Section.

Procedures, once described in the text, are not normally repeated. When it's necessary to refer to another Chapter, the reference will be given as Chapter and Section number. Cross references given without use of the word "Chapter" apply to Sections and/or paragraphs in the same Chapter. For example, "see Section 8" means in the same Chapter.

References to the left or right side of the vehicle assume you are sitting in the driver's seat, facing forward.

Even though we have prepared this manual with extreme care, neither the publisher nor the author can accept responsibility for any errors in, or omissions from, the information given.

### NOTE

A **Note** provides information necessary to properly complete a procedure or information which will make the procedure easier to understand.

### CAUTION

A **Caution** provides a special procedure or special steps which must be taken while completing the procedure where the Caution is found. Not heeding a Caution can result in damage to the assembly being worked on.

### WARNING

A **Warning** provides a special procedure or special steps which must be taken while completing the procedure where the Warning is found. Not heeding a Warning can result in personal injury.

# Introduction to the Chrysler PT Cruiser

The PT Cruiser is only available in a four-door, liftgate-type body style.

The four-cylinder engine is equipped with Dual Overhead Camshafts (DOHC) and is transversely mounted. All models are equipped with sequential multi-port fuel injection. A turbocharged version was offered beginning with the 2003 model year.

The engine transmits power to the front wheels through either a five-speed manual transaxle or a four-speed automatic transaxle via independent driveaxles.

The PT Cruiser features MacPherson strut-type suspension at the front and a semi-independent torsion beam type axle using coil springs and shock absorbers at the rear. The rack-and-pinion steering unit is mounted behind the engine with power-assist available as standard equipment.

All models have a power-assisted brake system with disc brakes at the front and either disc or drum brakes at the rear. An Anti-lock Brake System is available as an option.

# Vehicle identification numbers

Modifications are a continuing and unpublicized process in vehicle manufacturing. Since spare parts manuals and lists are compiled on a numerical basis, the individual vehicle numbers are essential to correctly identify the component required.

## *Vehicle Identification Number (VIN)*

This very important identification number is located on a plate attached to the dashboard inside the windshield on the driver's side of the vehicle **(see illustration)**. The VIN also appears on the Vehicle Certificate of Title and Registration. It contains information such as where and when the vehicle was manufactured, the model year and the body style.

## *VIN engine and model year codes*

Two particularly important pieces of information found in the VIN are the engine code and the model year code. Counting from the left, the engine code letter designation is the 8th digit and the model year code designation is the 10th digit.

**On the models covered by this manual the engine codes are:**

8 .......................... 2.4L HO Turbo
9 .......................... 2.0L
B .......................... 2.4L
E .......................... 2.4L Turbo
G .......................... 2.4L Turbo
S .......................... 2.4L HO Turbo
X .......................... 2.4L

**On the models covered by this manual the model year codes are:**

1 .................................. 2001
2 .................................. 2002
3 .................................. 2003
4 .................................. 2004
5 .................................. 2005
6 .................................. 2006
7 .................................. 2007
8 .................................. 2008
9 .................................. 2009
A .................................. 2010

## *Body Code Plate*

The Body Code Plate is a stamped metal plate attached to right (passenger's) side of the firewall in the engine compartment **(see illustration)**. It contains more specific information about the manufacturing of the vehicle such as the paint code, trim code and vehicle order number, as well as the VIN.

## *Vehicle Safety Certification label*

The Vehicle Safety Certification label is attached to the end of the driver's side door. The label contains the name of the manufacturer, the month and year of production, the Gross Vehicle Weight Rating (GVWR), the Gross Axle Weight Rating (GAWR) and the certification statement.

## *Engine identification numbers*

The engine identification numbers can be found stamped on a pad on either the left rear of the cylinder block, behind the starter (2.0L engine) or on the rear of the cylinder block (2.4L engines) **(see illustrations).**

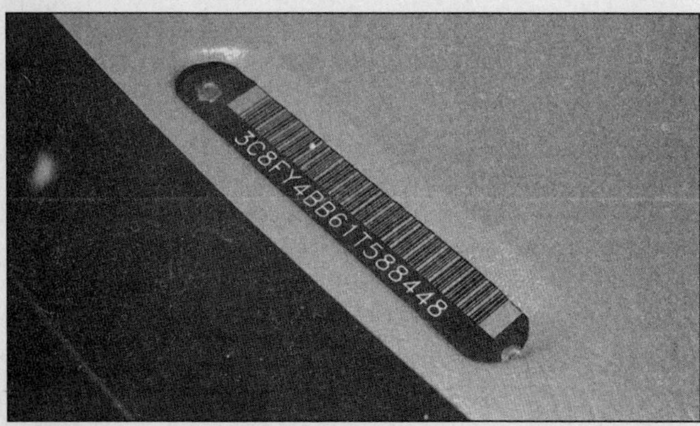


**The Vehicle Identification Number (VIN) is stamped into a metal plate fastened to the dashboard on the driver's side - it's visible through the windshield**

**The Body Code Plate is fastened to the right side of the firewall**

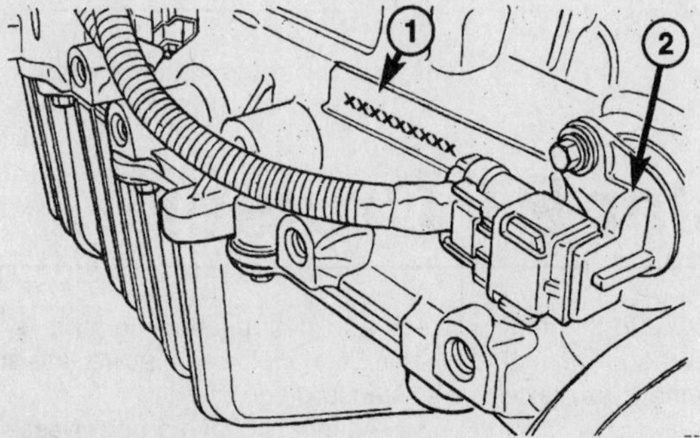


**The engine identification number (1) on the 2.0L engine is located on the front side of the engine block, near the crankshaft position sensor (2)**

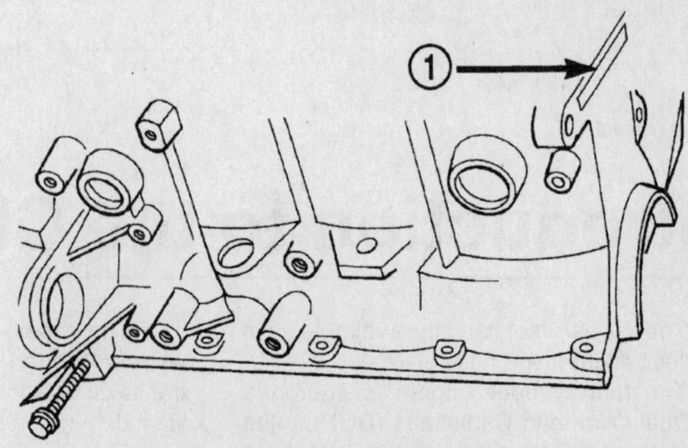


**The engine identification number (1) on the 2.4L engines is located at the rear of the cylinder block**

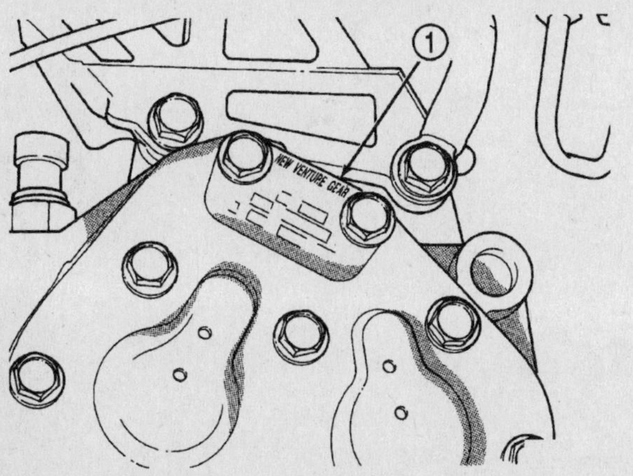


**The identification number on the T350 manual transaxle is located on a tag on the transaxle's end cover**

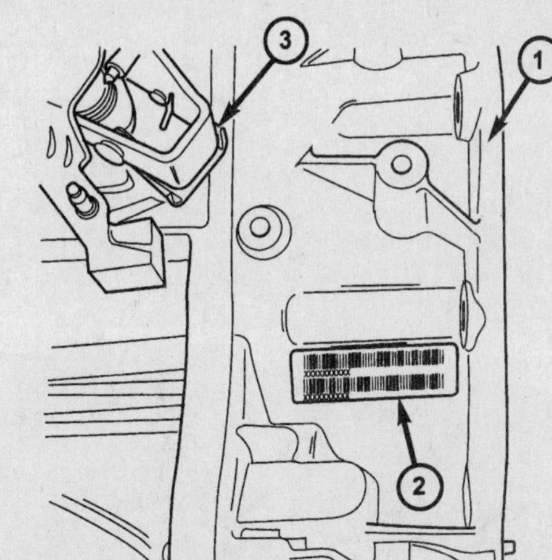


**The identification number on the G288 manual transaxle is located on a label affixed to the transaxle bellhousing**

*1 Bellhousing*
*2 Identification label*
*3 Transaxle shift lever*

### *Transaxle identification numbers*

The transaxle identification information can be found on either a stamped plate or a bar code label, depending on the type of transaxle **(see illustration)**.

### *Vehicle Emissions Control Information (VECI) label*

The emissions control information label is found under the hood, normally on the radiator support or the bottom side of the hood. This label contains information on the emissions control equipment installed on the vehicle, as well as tune-up specifications (see Chapter 6).

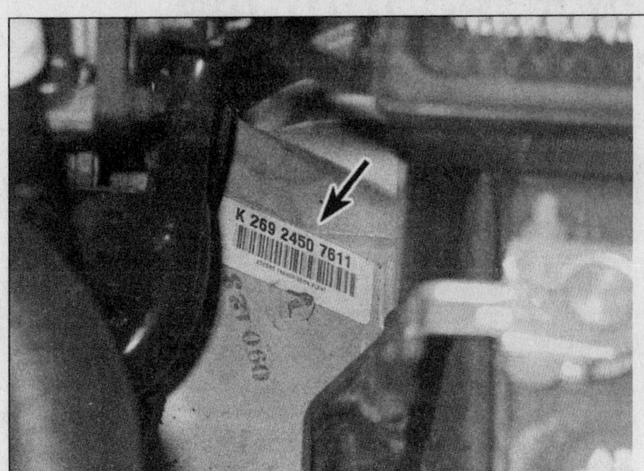


**The identification number on the automatic transaxle is located on a label affixed to the transaxle torque converter housing**

# Buying parts

Replacement parts are available from many sources, which generally fall into one of two categories - authorized dealer parts departments and independent retail auto parts stores. Our advice concerning these parts is as follows:

***Retail auto parts stores:*** Good auto parts stores will stock frequently needed components which wear out relatively fast, such as clutch components, exhaust systems, brake parts, tune-up parts, etc. These stores often supply new or reconditioned parts on an exchange basis, which can save a considerable amount of money. Discount auto parts stores are often very good places to buy materials and parts needed for general vehicle maintenance such as oil, grease, filters, spark plugs, belts, touch-up paint, bulbs, etc. They also usually sell tools and general accessories, have convenient hours, charge lower prices and can often be found not far from home.

***Authorized dealer parts department:*** This is the best source for parts which are unique to the vehicle and not generally available elsewhere (such as major engine parts, transmission parts, trim pieces, etc.).

***Warranty information:*** If the vehicle is still covered under warranty, be sure that any replacement parts purchased - regardless of the source - do not invalidate the warranty!

To be sure of obtaining the correct parts, have engine and chassis numbers available and, if possible, take the old parts along for positive identification.

# Maintenance techniques, tools and working facilities

## *Maintenance techniques*

There are a number of techniques involved in maintenance and repair that will be referred to throughout this manual. Application of these techniques will enable the home mechanic to be more efficient, better organized and capable of performing the various tasks properly, which will ensure that the repair job is thorough and complete.

### Fasteners

Fasteners are nuts, bolts, studs and screws used to hold two or more parts together. There are a few things to keep in mind when working with fasteners. Almost all of them use a locking device of some type, either a lockwasher, locknut, locking tab or thread adhesive. All threaded fasteners should be clean and straight, with undamaged threads and undamaged corners on the hex head where the wrench fits. Develop the habit of replacing all damaged nuts and bolts with new ones. Special locknuts with nylon or fiber inserts can only be used once. If they are removed, they lose their locking ability and must be replaced with new ones.

Rusted nuts and bolts should be treated with a penetrating fluid to ease removal and prevent breakage. Some mechanics use turpentine in a spout-type oil can, which works quite well. After applying the rust penetrant, let it work for a few minutes before trying to loosen the nut or bolt. Badly rusted fasteners may have to be chiseled or sawed off or removed with a special nut breaker, available at tool stores.

If a bolt or stud breaks off in an assembly, it can be drilled and removed with a special tool commonly available for this purpose. Most automotive machine shops can perform this task, as well as other repair procedures, such as the repair of threaded holes that have been stripped out.

Flat washers and lockwashers, when removed from an assembly, should always be replaced exactly as removed. Replace any damaged washers with new ones. Never use a lockwasher on any soft metal surface (such as aluminum), thin sheet metal or plastic.

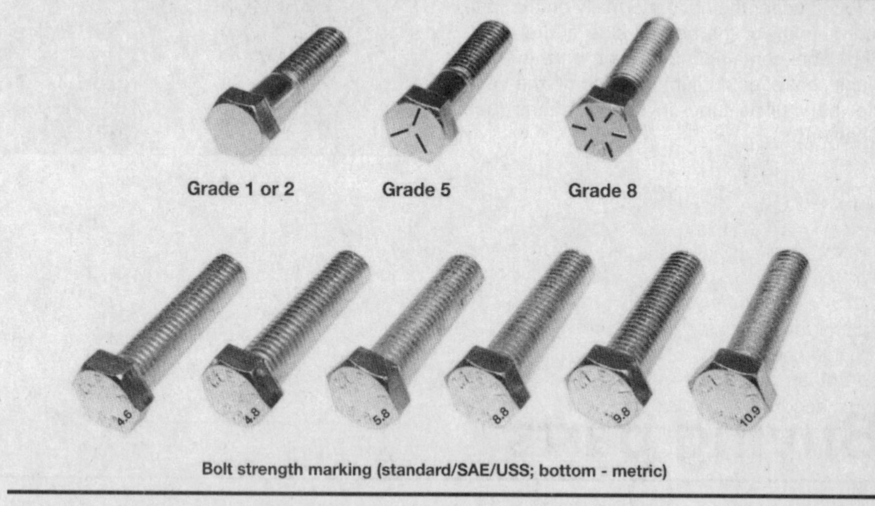


Bolt strength marking (standard/SAE/USS; bottom - metric)

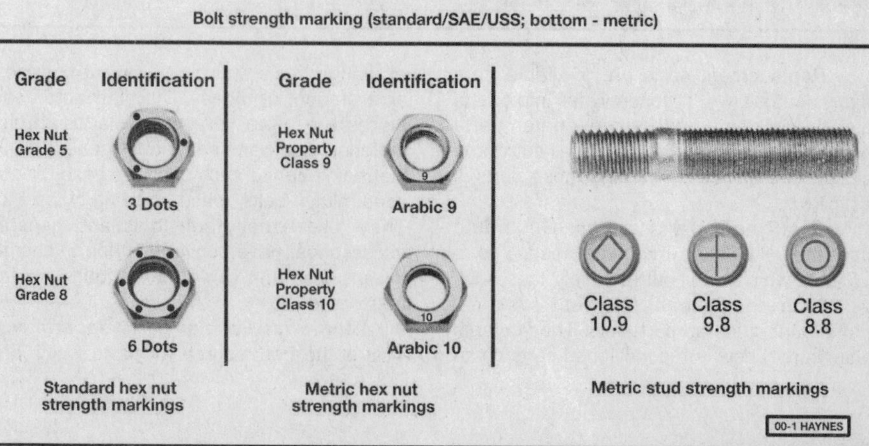


Standard hex nut strength markings

Metric hex nut strength markings

Metric stud strength markings

## Fastener sizes

For a number of reasons, automobile manufacturers are making wider and wider use of metric fasteners. Therefore, it is important to be able to tell the difference between standard (sometimes called U.S. or SAE) and metric hardware, since they cannot be interchanged.

All bolts, whether standard or metric, are sized according to diameter, thread pitch and length. For example, a standard 1/2 - 13 x 1 bolt is 1/2 inch in diameter, has 13 threads per inch and is 1 inch long. An M12 - 1.75 x 25 metric bolt is 12 mm in diameter, has a thread pitch of 1.75 mm (the distance between threads) and is 25 mm long. The two bolts are nearly identical, and easily confused, but they are not interchangeable.

In addition to the differences in diameter, thread pitch and length, metric and standard bolts can also be distinguished by examining the bolt heads. To begin with, the distance across the flats on a standard bolt head is measured in inches, while the same dimension on a metric bolt is sized in millimeters (the same is true for nuts). As a result, a standard wrench should not be used on a metric bolt and a metric wrench should not be used on a standard bolt. Also, most standard bolts have slashes radiating out from the center of the head to denote the grade or strength of the bolt, which is an indication of the amount of torque that can be applied to it. The greater the number of slashes, the greater the strength of the bolt. Grades 0 through 5 are commonly used on automobiles. Metric bolts have a property class (grade) number, rather than a slash, molded into their heads to indicate bolt strength. In this case, the higher the number, the stronger the bolt. Property class numbers 8.8, 9.8 and 10.9 are commonly used on automobiles.

Strength markings can also be used to distinguish standard hex nuts from metric hex nuts. Many standard nuts have dots stamped into one side, while metric nuts are marked with a number. The greater the number of dots, or the higher the number, the greater the strength of the nut.

Metric studs are also marked on their ends according to property class (grade). Larger studs are numbered (the same as metric bolts), while smaller studs carry a geometric code to denote grade.

It should be noted that many fasteners, especially Grades 0 through 2, have no distinguishing marks on them. When such is the case, the only way to determine whether it is standard or metric is to measure the thread pitch or compare it to a known fastener of the same size.

Standard fasteners are often referred to as SAE, as opposed to metric. However, it should be noted that SAE technically refers to a non-metric fine thread fastener only. Coarse thread non-metric fasteners are referred to as USS sizes.

Since fasteners of the same size (both standard and metric) may have different strength ratings, be sure to reinstall any bolts, studs or nuts removed from your vehicle in their original locations. Also, when replacing a fastener with a new one, make sure that the new one has a strength rating equal to or greater than the original.

| Metric thread sizes | Ft-lbs | Nm |
|---|---|---|
| M-6 | 6 to 9 | 9 to 12 |
| M-8 | 14 to 21 | 19 to 28 |
| M-10 | 28 to 40 | 38 to 54 |
| M-12 | 50 to 71 | 68 to 96 |
| M-14 | 80 to 140 | 109 to 154 |
| **Pipe thread sizes** | | |
| 1/8 | 5 to 8 | 7 to 10 |
| 1/4 | 12 to 18 | 17 to 24 |
| 3/8 | 22 to 33 | 30 to 44 |
| 1/2 | 25 to 35 | 34 to 47 |
| **U.S. thread sizes** | | |
| 1/4 - 20 | 6 to 9 | 9 to 12 |
| 5/16 - 18 | 12 to 18 | 17 to 24 |
| 5/16 - 24 | 14 to 20 | 19 to 27 |
| 3/8 - 16 | 22 to 32 | 30 to 43 |
| 3/8 - 24 | 27 to 38 | 37 to 51 |
| 7/16 - 14 | 40 to 55 | 55 to 74 |
| 7/16 - 20 | 40 to 60 | 55 to 81 |
| 1/2 - 13 | 55 to 80 | 75 to 108 |

**Standard (SAE and USS) bolt dimensions/grade marks**

- *G* *Grade marks (bolt strength)*
- *L* *Length (in inches)*
- *T* *Thread pitch (number of threads per inch)*
- *D* *Nominal diameter (in inches)*

**Metric bolt dimensions/grade marks**

- *P* *Property class (bolt strength)*
- *L* *Length (in millimeters)*
- *T* *Thread pitch (distance between threads in millimeters)*
- *D* *Diameter*

## Tightening sequences and procedures

Most threaded fasteners should be tightened to a specific torque value (torque is the twisting force applied to a threaded component such as a nut or bolt). Overtightening the fastener can weaken it and cause it to break, while undertightening can cause it to eventually come loose. Bolts, screws and studs, depending on the material they are made of and their thread diameters, have specific torque values, many of which are noted in the Specifications at the beginning of each Chapter. Be sure to follow the torque recommendations closely. For fasteners not assigned a specific torque, a general torque value chart is presented here as a guide. These torque values are for dry (unlubricated) fasteners threaded into steel or cast iron (not aluminum). As was previously mentioned, the size and grade of a fastener determine the amount of torque that can safely be applied to it. The figures listed here are approximate for Grade 2 and Grade 3 fasteners. Higher grades can tolerate higher torque values.

Fasteners laid out in a pattern, such as cylinder head bolts, oil pan bolts, differential cover bolts, etc., must be loosened or tightened in sequence to avoid warping the com-

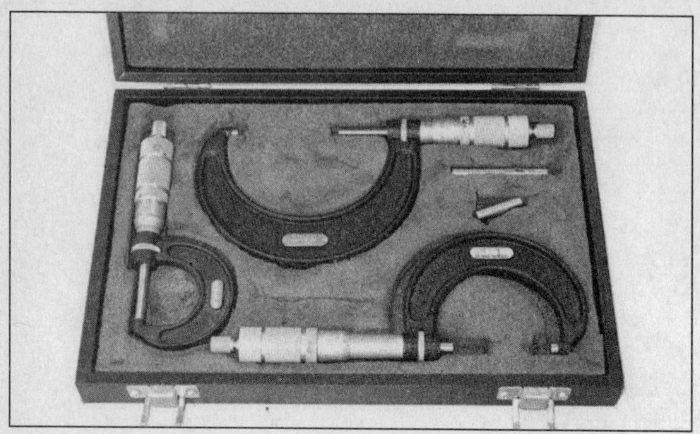

Micrometer set

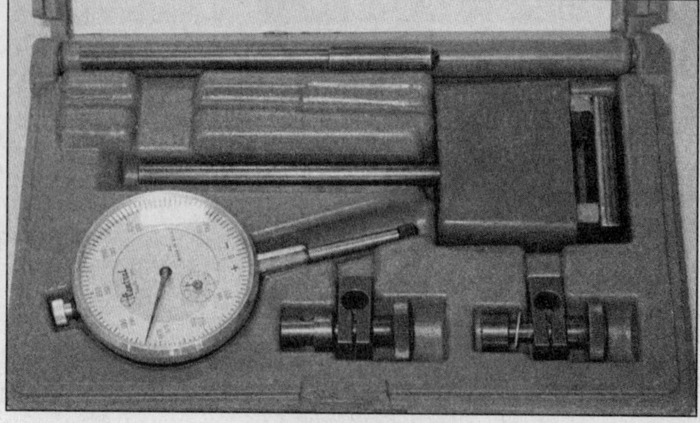

Dial indicator set

ponent. This sequence will normally be shown in the appropriate Chapter. If a specific pattern is not given, the following procedures can be used to prevent warping.

Initially, the bolts or nuts should be assembled finger-tight only. Next, they should be tightened one full turn each, in a criss-cross or diagonal pattern. After each one has been tightened one full turn, return to the first one and tighten them all one-half turn, following the same pattern. Finally, tighten each of them one-quarter turn at a time until each fastener has been tightened to the proper torque. To loosen and remove the fasteners, the procedure would be reversed.

## Component disassembly

Component disassembly should be done with care and purpose to help ensure that the parts go back together properly. Always keep track of the sequence in which parts are removed. Make note of special characteristics or marks on parts that can be installed more than one way, such as a grooved thrust washer on a shaft. It is a good idea to lay the disassembled parts out on a clean surface in the order that they were removed. It may also be helpful to make sketches or take instant photos of components before removal.

When removing fasteners from a component, keep track of their locations. Sometimes threading a bolt back in a part, or putting the washers and nut back on a stud, can prevent mix-ups later. If nuts and bolts cannot be returned to their original locations, they should be kept in a compartmented box or a series of small boxes. A cupcake or muffin tin is ideal for this purpose, since each cavity can hold the bolts and nuts from a particular area (i.e. oil pan bolts, valve cover bolts, engine mount bolts, etc.). A pan of this type is especially helpful when working on assemblies with very small parts, such as the carburetor, alternator, valve train or interior dash and trim pieces. The cavities can be marked with paint or tape to identify the contents.

Whenever wiring looms, harnesses or connectors are separated, it is a good idea to identify the two halves with numbered pieces of masking tape so they can be easily reconnected.

## Gasket sealing surfaces

Throughout any vehicle, gaskets are used to seal the mating surfaces between two parts and keep lubricants, fluids, vacuum or pressure contained in an assembly.

Many times these gaskets are coated with a liquid or paste-type gasket sealing compound before assembly. Age, heat and pressure can sometimes cause the two parts to stick together so tightly that they are very difficult to separate. Often, the assembly can be loosened by striking it with a soft-face hammer near the mating surfaces. A regular hammer can be used if a block of wood is placed between the hammer and the part. Do not hammer on cast parts or parts that could be easily damaged. With any particularly stubborn part, always recheck to make sure that every fastener has been removed.

Avoid using a screwdriver or bar to pry apart an assembly, as they can easily mar the gasket sealing surfaces of the parts, which must remain smooth. If prying is absolutely necessary, use an old broom handle, but keep in mind that extra clean up will be necessary if the wood splinters.

After the parts are separated, the old gasket must be carefully removed and the gasket surfaces cleaned. If you're working on cast iron or aluminum parts, stubborn gasket material can be soaked with rust penetrant or treated with a special chemical to soften it so it can be easily scraped off. **Caution:** *Never use gasket removal solutions or caustic chemicals on plastic or other composite components.* A scraper can be fashioned from a piece of copper tubing by flattening and sharpening one end. Copper is recommended because it is usually softer than the surfaces to be scraped, which reduces the chance of gouging the part. Some gaskets can be removed with a wire brush, but regardless of the method used, the mating surfaces must be left clean and smooth. If for some reason the gasket surface is gouged, then a gasket sealer thick enough to fill scratches will have to be used during reassembly of the components. For most applications, a non-drying (or semi-drying) gasket sealer should be used.

## Hose removal tips

**Warning:** *If the vehicle is equipped with air conditioning, do not disconnect any of the A/C hoses without first having the system depressurized by a dealer service department or a service station.*

Hose removal precautions closely parallel gasket removal precautions. Avoid scratching or gouging the surface that the hose mates against or the connection may leak. This is especially true for radiator hoses. Because of various chemical reactions, the rubber in hoses can bond itself to the metal spigot that the hose fits over. To remove a hose, first loosen the hose clamps that secure it to the spigot. Then, with slip-joint pliers, grab the hose at the clamp and rotate it around the spigot. Work it back and forth until it is completely free, then pull it off. Silicone or other lubricants will ease removal if they can be applied between the hose and the outside of the spigot. Apply the same lubricant to the inside of the hose and the outside of the spigot to simplify installation.

As a last resort (and if the hose is to be replaced with a new one anyway), the rubber can be slit with a knife and the hose peeled from the spigot. If this must be done, be careful that the metal connection is not damaged.

If a hose clamp is broken or damaged, do not reuse it. Wire-type clamps usually weaken with age, so it is a good idea to replace them with screw-type clamps whenever a hose is removed.

# *Tools*

A selection of good tools is a basic requirement for anyone who plans to maintain and repair his or her own vehicle. For the owner who has few tools, the initial investment might seem high, but when compared to the spiraling costs of professional auto maintenance and repair, it is a wise one.

To help the owner decide which tools are needed to perform the tasks detailed in this manual, the following tool lists are offered: *Maintenance and minor repair, Repair/overhaul* and *Special.*

The newcomer to practical mechanics should start off with the *maintenance and minor repair* tool kit, which is adequate for

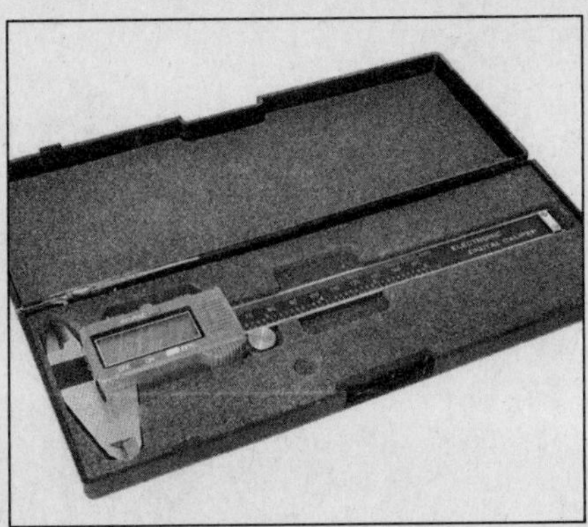

Dial caliper

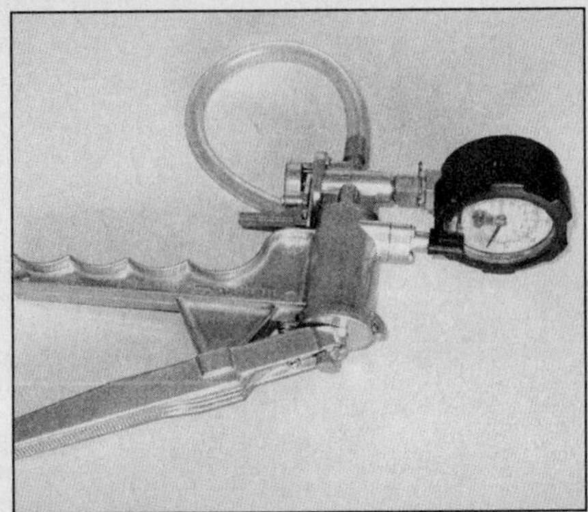

Hand-operated vacuum pump

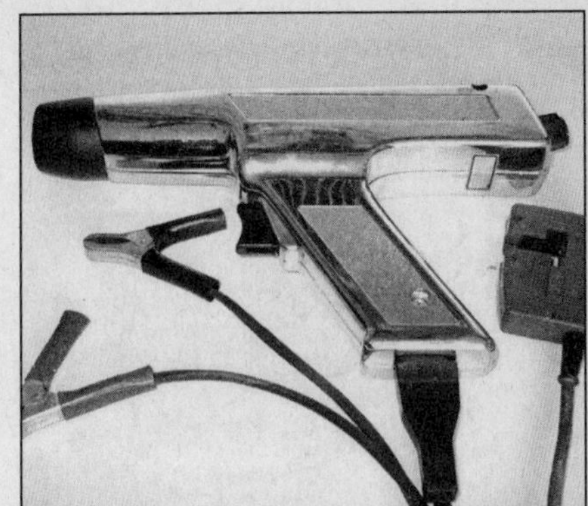

Timing light

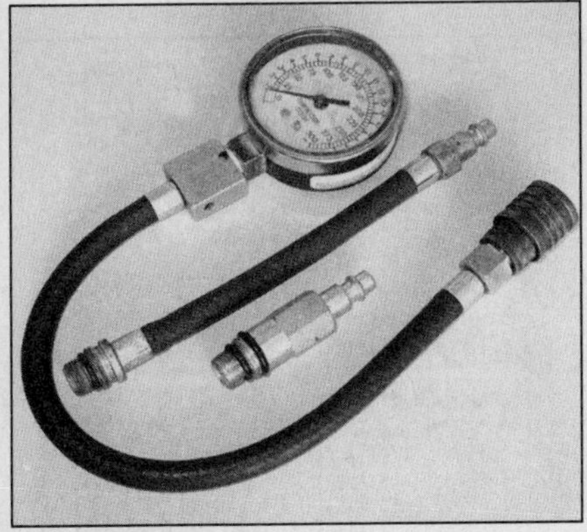

Compression gauge with spark plug hole adapter

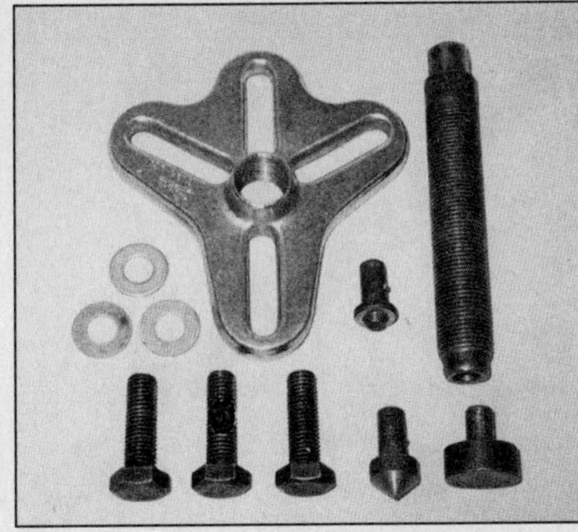

Damper/steering wheel puller

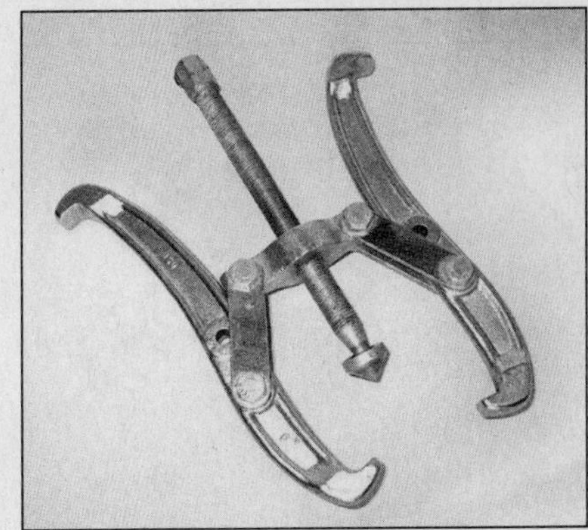

General purpose puller

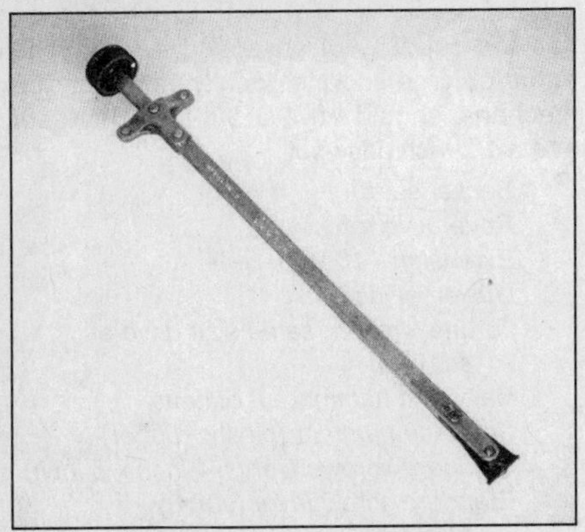

Hydraulic lifter removal tool

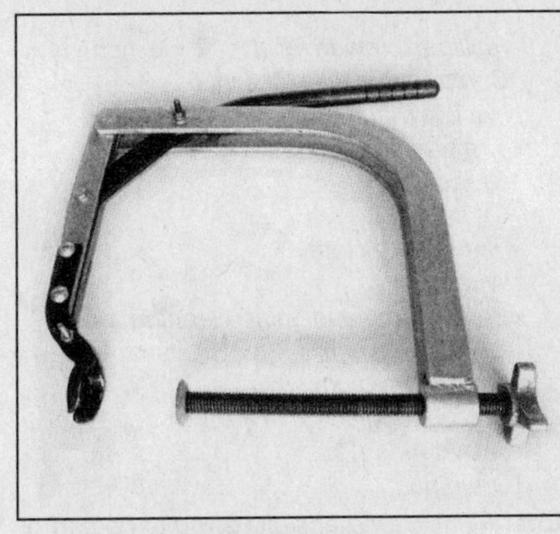

Valve spring compressor

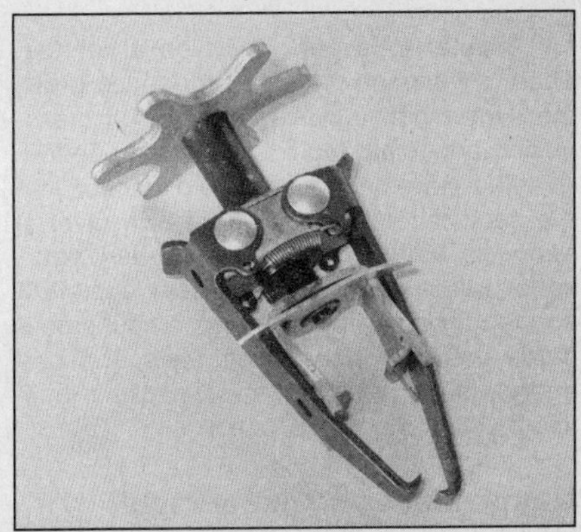

Valve spring compressor

Ridge reamer

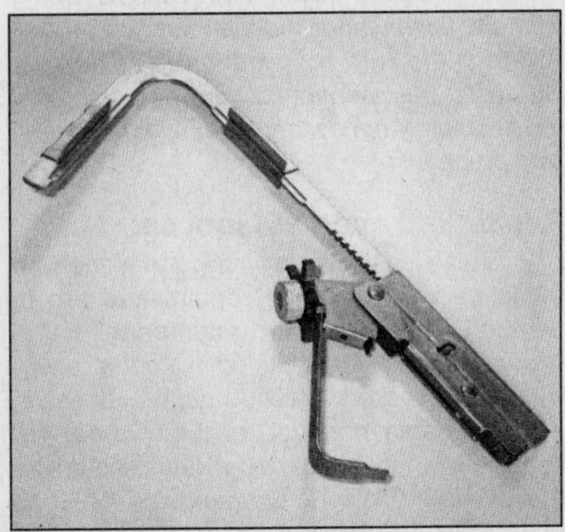

Piston ring groove cleaning tool

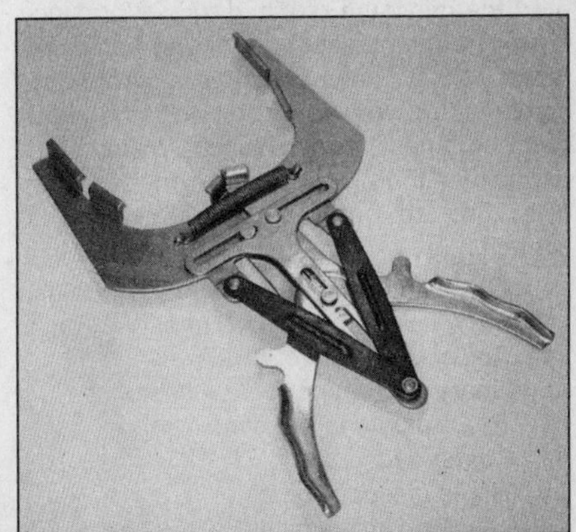

Ring removal/installation tool

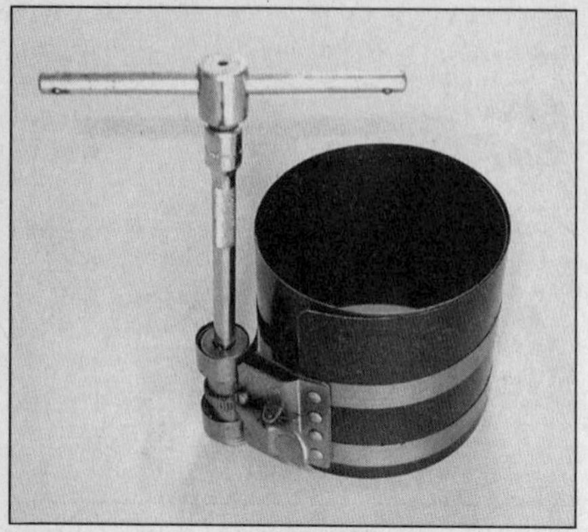
Ring compressor

Cylinder hone

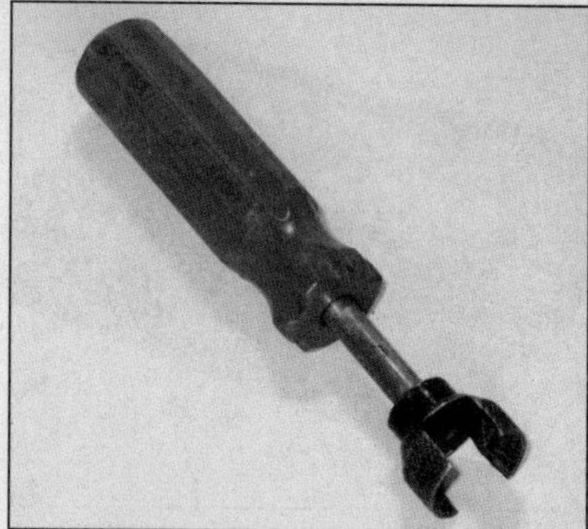
Brake hold-down spring tool

Torque angle gauge

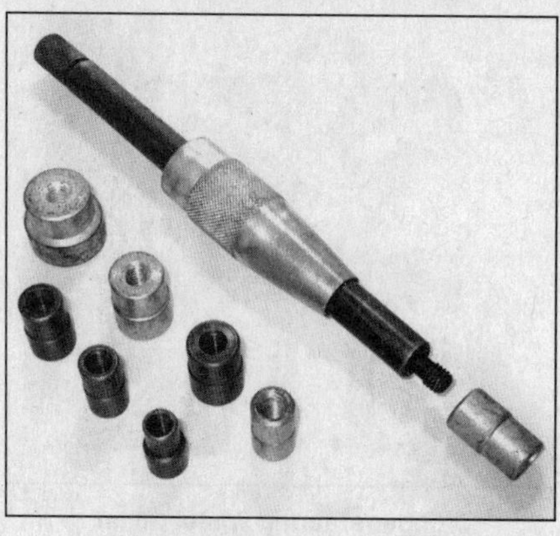
Clutch plate alignment tool

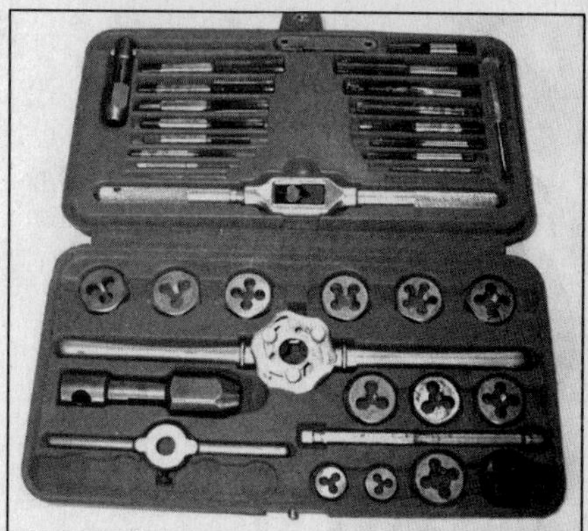
Tap and die set

the simpler jobs performed on a vehicle. Then, as confidence and experience grow, the owner can tackle more difficult tasks, buying additional tools as they are needed. Eventually the basic kit will be expanded into the *repair and overhaul* tool set. Over a period of time, the experienced do-it-yourselfer will assemble a tool set complete enough for most repair and overhaul procedures and will add tools from the special category when it is felt that the expense is justified by the frequency of use.

## Maintenance and minor repair tool kit

The tools in this list should be considered the minimum required for performance of routine maintenance, servicing and minor repair work. We recommend the purchase of combination wrenches (box-end and open-end combined in one wrench). While more expensive than open end wrenches, they offer the advantages of both types of wrench.

*Combination wrench set (1/4-inch to 1 inch or 6 mm to 19 mm)*
*Adjustable wrench, 8 inch*
*Spark plug wrench with rubber insert*
*Spark plug gap adjusting tool*
*Feeler gauge set*
*Brake bleeder wrench*
*Standard screwdriver (5/16-inch x 6 inch)*
*Phillips screwdriver (No. 2 x 6 inch)*
*Combination pliers - 6 inch*
*Hacksaw and assortment of blades*
*Tire pressure gauge*
*Grease gun*
*Oil can*
*Fine emery cloth*
*Wire brush*
*Battery post and cable cleaning tool*
*Oil filter wrench*
*Funnel (medium size)*
*Safety goggles*
*Jackstands (2)*
*Drain pan*

**Note:** *If basic tune-ups are going to be part of routine maintenance, it will be necessary to purchase a good quality stroboscopic timing light and combination tachometer/dwell meter. Although they are included in the list of special tools, it is mentioned here because they are absolutely necessary for tuning most vehicles properly.*

## Repair and overhaul tool set

These tools are essential for anyone who plans to perform major repairs and are in addition to those in the maintenance and minor repair tool kit. Included is a comprehensive set of sockets which, though expensive, are invaluable because of their versatility, especially when various extensions and drives are available. We recommend the 1/2-inch drive over the 3/8-inch drive. Although the larger drive is bulky and more expensive, it has the capacity of accepting a very wide range of large sockets. Ideally, however, the mechanic should have a 3/8-inch drive set and a 1/2-inch drive set.

*Socket set(s)*
*Reversible ratchet*
*Extension - 10 inch*
*Universal joint*
*Torque wrench (same size drive as sockets)*
*Ball peen hammer - 8 ounce*
*Soft-face hammer (plastic/rubber)*
*Standard screwdriver (1/4-inch x 6 inch)*
*Standard screwdriver (stubby - 5/16-inch)*
*Phillips screwdriver (No. 3 x 8 inch)*
*Phillips screwdriver (stubby - No. 2)*
*Pliers - vise grip*
*Pliers - lineman's*
*Pliers - needle nose*
*Pliers - snap-ring (internal and external)*
*Cold chisel - 1/2-inch*
*Scribe*
*Scraper (made from flattened copper tubing)*
*Centerpunch*
*Pin punches (1/16, 1/8, 3/16-inch)*
*Steel rule/straightedge - 12 inch*
*Allen wrench set (1/8 to 3/8-inch or 4 mm to 10 mm)*
*A selection of files*
*Wire brush (large)*
*Jackstands (second set)*
*Jack (scissor or hydraulic type)*

**Note:** *Another tool which is often useful is an electric drill with a chuck capacity of 3/8-inch and a set of good quality drill bits.*

### Special tools

The tools in this list include those which are not used regularly, are expensive to buy, or which need to be used in accordance with their manufacturer's instructions. Unless these tools will be used frequently, it is not very economical to purchase many of them. A consideration would be to split the cost and use between yourself and a friend or friends. In addition, most of these tools can be obtained from a tool rental shop on a temporary basis.

This list primarily contains only those tools and instruments widely available to the public, and not those special tools produced by the vehicle manufacturer for distribution to dealer service departments. Occasionally, references to the manufacturer's special tools are included in the text of this manual. Generally, an alternative method of doing the job without the special tool is offered. However, sometimes there is no alternative to their use. Where this is the case, and the tool cannot be purchased or borrowed, the work should be turned over to the dealer service department or an automotive repair shop.

*Valve spring compressor*
*Piston ring groove cleaning tool*
*Piston ring compressor*
*Piston ring installation tool*
*Cylinder compression gauge*
*Cylinder ridge reamer*
*Cylinder surfacing hone*
*Cylinder bore gauge*
*Micrometers and/or dial calipers*
*Hydraulic lifter removal tool*
*Balljoint separator*
*Universal-type puller*
*Impact screwdriver*
*Dial indicator set*
*Stroboscopic timing light (inductive pick-up)*
*Hand operated vacuum/pressure pump*
*Tachometer/dwell meter*
*Universal electrical multimeter*
*Cable hoist*
*Brake spring removal and installation tools*
*Floor jack*

### Buying tools

For the do-it-yourselfer who is just starting to get involved in vehicle maintenance and repair, there are a number of options available when purchasing tools. If maintenance and minor repair is the extent of the work to be done, the purchase of individual tools is satisfactory. If, on the other hand, extensive work is planned, it would be a good idea to purchase a modest tool set from one of the large retail chain stores. A set can usually be bought at a substantial savings over the individual tool prices, and they often come with a tool box. As additional tools are needed, add-on sets, individual tools and a larger tool box can be purchased to expand the tool selection. Building a tool set gradually allows the cost of the tools to be spread over a longer period of time and gives the mechanic the freedom to choose only those tools that will actually be used.

Tool stores will often be the only source of some of the special tools that are needed, but regardless of where tools are bought, try to avoid cheap ones, especially when buying screwdrivers and sockets, because they won't last very long. The expense involved in replacing cheap tools will eventually be greater than the initial cost of quality tools.

### Care and maintenance of tools

Good tools are expensive, so it makes sense to treat them with respect. Keep them clean and in usable condition and store them properly when not in use. Always wipe off any dirt, grease or metal chips before putting them away. Never leave tools lying around in the work area. Upon completion of a job, always check closely under the hood for tools that may have been left there so they won't get lost during a test drive.

Some tools, such as screwdrivers, pliers, wrenches and sockets, can be hung on a panel mounted on the garage or workshop wall, while others should be kept in a tool box or tray. Measuring instruments, gauges, meters, etc. must be carefully stored where they cannot be damaged by weather or impact from other tools.

When tools are used with care and stored properly, they will last a very long time. Even with the best of care, though, tools will wear out if used frequently. When a tool is damaged or worn out, replace it. Subsequent jobs will be safer and more enjoyable if you do.

## *How to repair damaged threads*

Sometimes, the internal threads of a nut or bolt hole can become stripped, usually from overtightening. Stripping threads is an all-too-common occurrence, especially when working with aluminum parts, because aluminum is so soft that it easily strips out.

Usually, external or internal threads are only partially stripped. After they've been cleaned up with a tap or die, they'll still work. Sometimes, however, threads are badly damaged. When this happens, you've got three choices:

1) *Drill and tap the hole to the next suitable oversize and install a larger diameter bolt, screw or stud.*
2) *Drill and tap the hole to accept a threaded plug, then drill and tap the plug to the original screw size. You can also buy a plug already threaded to the original size. Then you simply drill a hole to the specified size, then run the threaded plug into the hole with a bolt and jam nut. Once the plug is fully seated, remove the jam nut and bolt.*
3) *The third method uses a patented thread repair kit like Heli-Coil or Slimsert. These easy-to-use kits are designed to repair damaged threads in straight-through holes and blind holes. Both are available as kits which can handle a variety of sizes and thread patterns. Drill the hole, then tap it with the special included tap. Install the Heli-Coil and the hole is back to its original diameter and thread pitch.*

Regardless of which method you use, be sure to proceed calmly and carefully. A little impatience or carelessness during one of these relatively simple procedures can ruin your whole day's work and cost you a bundle if you wreck an expensive part.

## *Working facilities*

Not to be overlooked when discussing tools is the workshop. If anything more than routine maintenance is to be carried out, some sort of suitable work area is essential.

It is understood, and appreciated, that many home mechanics do not have a good workshop or garage available, and end up removing an engine or doing major repairs outside. It is recommended, however, that the overhaul or repair be completed under the cover of a roof.

A clean, flat workbench or table of comfortable working height is an absolute necessity. The workbench should be equipped with a vise that has a jaw opening of at least four inches.

As mentioned previously, some clean, dry storage space is also required for tools, as well as the lubricants, fluids, cleaning solvents, etc. which soon become necessary.

Sometimes waste oil and fluids, drained from the engine or cooling system during normal maintenance or repairs, present a disposal problem. To avoid pouring them on the ground or into a sewage system, pour the used fluids into large containers, seal them with caps and take them to an authorized disposal site or recycling center. Plastic jugs, such as old antifreeze containers, are ideal for this purpose.

Always keep a supply of old newspapers and clean rags available. Old towels are excellent for mopping up spills. Many mechanics use rolls of paper towels for most work because they are readily available and disposable. To help keep the area under the vehicle clean, a large cardboard box can be cut open and flattened to protect the garage or shop floor.

Whenever working over a painted surface, such as when leaning over a fender to service something under the hood, always cover it with an old blanket or bedspread to protect the finish. Vinyl covered pads, made especially for this purpose, are available at auto parts stores.

# Jacking and towing

## Jacking

**Warning:** *The jack supplied with the vehicle should only be used for changing a tire or placing jackstands under the frame. Never work under the vehicle or start the engine while this jack is being used as the only means of support.*

The vehicle should be on level ground. Place the shift lever in Park, if you have an automátic, or Reverse if you have a manual transaxle. Block the wheel diagonally opposite the wheel being changed. Set the parking brake.

Remove the jack and wrench from their stowage area in the luggage compartment. Remove the small trim cover at the right side of the luggage compartment opening and, using the wrench, unscrew the nut to lower the spare tire from under the vehicle.

Remove the wheel cover and trim ring (if so equipped) with the tapered end of the lug nut wrench by inserting and twisting the handle and then prying against the back of the wheel cover. Loosen the wheel lug nuts about 1/4-to-1/2 turn each.

Place the scissors-type jack under the side of the vehicle and adjust the jack height until it engages the jacking point. There is a front and rear jacking point on each side of the vehicle **(see illustration)**; at the front, the jack head fits over the rocker panel flange, in the area between the two raised darts. At the rear, the jack head engages the trailing arm bracket.

Turn the jack handle clockwise until the tire clears the ground. Remove the lug nuts and pull the wheel off. Install the spare.

Install the lug nuts with the beveled edges facing in. Tighten them snugly. Don't attempt to tighten them completely until the vehicle is lowered or it could slip off the jack. Turn the jack handle counterclockwise to lower the vehicle. Remove the jack and tighten the lug nuts in a diagonal pattern.

Install the cover (and trim ring, if used) and be sure it's snapped into place all the way around.

Place the tire in the luggage compartment and secure it with the strap provided in the jack bag and the hooks on either side of the floor. Stow the jack and wrench. Unblock the wheel.

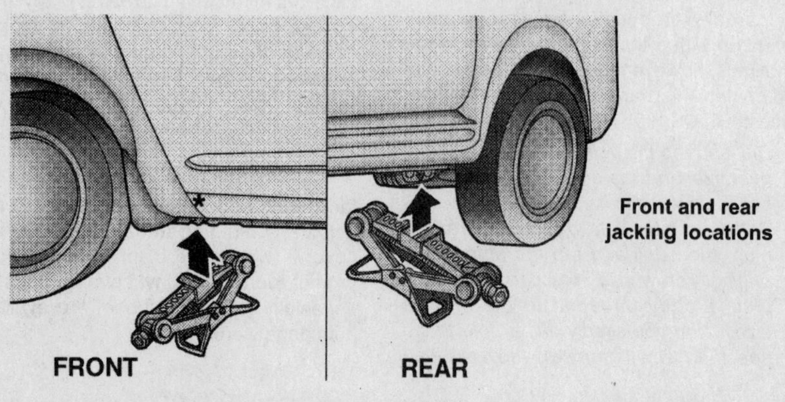


**Front and rear jacking locations**

## Towing

As a general rule, the vehicle should be towed with the front (drive) wheels off the ground. If they can't be raised, place them on a dolly. The ignition key must be in the ACC position, since the steering lock mechanism isn't strong enough to hold the front wheels straight while towing.

Vehicles equipped with an automatic transaxle can be towed from the front only with all four wheels on the ground, provided that speeds don't exceed 44 mph and the distance is not over 100 miles. Before towing, check the transmission fluid level (see Chapter 1). If the level is below the HOT line on the dipstick, add fluid or use a towing dolly.

**Caution:** *Never tow a vehicle with an automatic transaxle from the rear with the front wheels on the ground.*

When towing a vehicle equipped with a manual transaxle with all four wheels on the ground, be sure to place the shift lever in neutral and release the parking brake.

Equipment specifically designed for towing should be used. It should be attached to the main structural members of the vehicle, not the bumpers or brackets. The preferred way to tow a vehicle is with a flatbed type tow truck. Never have this vehicle towed with a sling-type tow truck.

Safety is a major consideration when towing and all applicable state and local laws must be obeyed. A safety chain system must be used at all times.

# Booster battery (jump) starting

The remote positive battery terminal is located next to the left (driver's side) strut tower

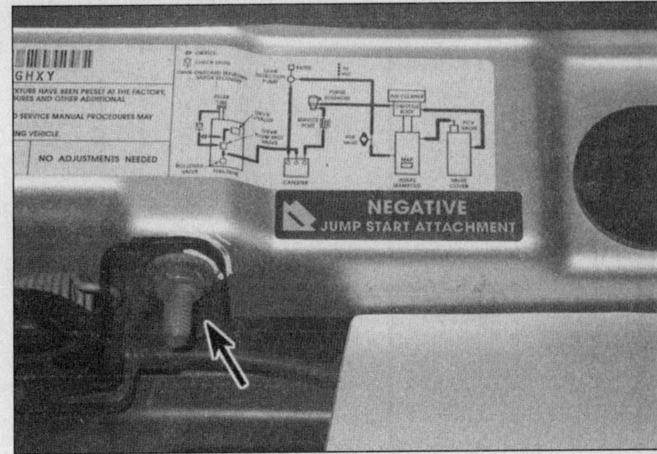


The remote negative terminal is located at the hood latch stud

Observe these precautions when using a booster battery to start a vehicle:

- a) *Before connecting the booster battery, make sure the ignition switch is in the OFF position.*
- b) *Turn off the lights, heater and other electrical loads.*
- c) *Your eyes should be shielded. Safety goggles are a good idea.*
- d) *Make sure the booster battery is the same voltage as the dead one in the vehicle.*
- e) *The two vehicles MUST NOT TOUCH each other!*
- f) *Make sure the transaxle is in Neutral (manual) or Park (automatic).*
- g) *If the booster battery is not a maintenance-free type, remove the vent caps and lay a cloth over the vent holes.*

The battery on these vehicles is located under the air filter housing. Due to the lack of accessibility, remote battery connections are provided inside the engine compartment for jump-starting **(see illustrations)**.

Connect the red colored jumper cable to the positive (+) terminal of booster battery and the other end to the positive (+) remote terminal inside the engine compartment. Then connect the black colored jumper cable to the negative (-) terminal of the booster battery and other end of the cable to the negative (-) remote terminal **(see illustration)**.

Start the engine using the booster battery, then, with the engine running at idle speed, disconnect the jumper cables in the reverse order of connection.

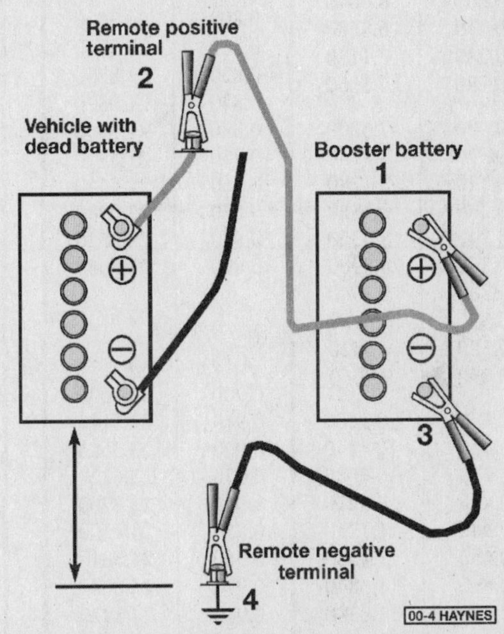


Make the booster cable connections in the numerical order shown

## DECIMALS to MILLIMETERS

| Decimal | mm | Decimal | mm |
|---|---|---|---|
| 0.001 | 0.0254 | 0.500 | 12.7000 |
| 0.002 | 0.0508 | 0.510 | 12.9540 |
| 0.003 | 0.0762 | 0.520 | 13.2080 |
| 0.004 | 0.1016 | 0.530 | 13.4620 |
| 0.005 | 0.1270 | 0.540 | 13.7160 |
| 0.006 | 0.1524 | 0.550 | 13.9700 |
| 0.007 | 0.1778 | 0.560 | 14.2240 |
| 0.008 | 0.2032 | 0.570 | 14.4780 |
| 0.009 | 0.2286 | 0.580 | 14.7320 |
| 0.010 | 0.2540 | 0.590 | 14.9860 |
| 0.020 | 0.5080 | 0.600 | 15.2400 |
| 0.030 | 0.7620 | 0.610 | 15.4940 |
| 0.040 | 1.0160 | 0.620 | 15.7480 |
| 0.050 | 1.2700 | 0.630 | 16.0020 |
| 0.060 | 1.5240 | 0.640 | 16.2560 |
| 0.070 | 1.7780 | 0.650 | 16.5100 |
| 0.080 | 2.0320 | 0.660 | 16.7640 |
| 0.090 | 2.2860 | 0.670 | 17.0180 |
| 0.100 | 2.5400 | 0.680 | 17.2720 |
| 0.110 | 2.7940 | 0.690 | 17.5260 |
| 0.120 | 3.0480 | 0.700 | 17.7800 |
| 0.130 | 3.3020 | 0.710 | 18.0340 |
| 0.140 | 3.5560 | 0.720 | 18.2880 |
| 0.150 | 3.8100 | 0.730 | 18.5420 |
| 0.160 | 4.0640 | 0.740 | 18.7960 |
| 0.170 | 4.3180 | 0.750 | 19.0500 |
| 0.180 | 4.5720 | 0.760 | 19.3040 |
| 0.190 | 4.8260 | 0.770 | 19.5580 |
| 0.200 | 5.0800 | 0.780 | 19.8120 |
| 0.210 | 5.3340 | 0.790 | 20.0660 |
| 0.220 | 5.5880 | 0.800 | 20.3200 |
| 0.230 | 5.8420 | 0.810 | 20.5740 |
| 0.240 | 6.0960 | 0.820 | 21.8280 |
| 0.250 | 6.3500 | 0.830 | 21.0820 |
| 0.260 | 6.6040 | 0.840 | 21.3360 |
| 0.270 | 6.8580 | 0.850 | 21.5900 |
| 0.280 | 7.1120 | 0.860 | 21.8440 |
| 0.290 | 7.3660 | 0.870 | 22.0980 |
| 0.300 | 7.6200 | 0.880 | 22.3520 |
| 0.310 | 7.8740 | 0.890 | 22.6060 |
| 0.320 | 8.1280 | 0.900 | 22.8600 |
| 0.330 | 8.3820 | 0.910 | 23.1140 |
| 0.340 | 8.6360 | 0.920 | 23.3680 |
| 0.350 | 8.8900 | 0.930 | 23.6220 |
| 0.360 | 9.1440 | 0.940 | 23.8760 |
| 0.370 | 9.3980 | 0.950 | 24.1300 |
| 0.380 | 9.6520 | 0.960 | 24.3840 |
| 0.390 | 9.9060 | 0.970 | 24.6380 |
| 0.400 | 10.1600 | 0.980 | 24.8920 |
| 0.410 | 10.4140 | 0.990 | 25.1460 |
| 0.420 | 10.6680 | 1.000 | 25.4000 |
| 0.430 | 10.9220 | | |
| 0.440 | 11.1760 | | |
| 0.450 | 11.4300 | | |
| 0.460 | 11.6840 | | |
| 0.470 | 11.9380 | | |
| 0.480 | 12.1920 | | |
| 0.490 | 12.4460 | | |

## FRACTIONS to DECIMALS to MILLIMETERS

| Fraction | Decimal | mm | Fraction | Decimal | mm |
|---|---|---|---|---|---|
| 1/64 | 0.0156 | 0.3969 | 33/64 | 0.5156 | 13.0969 |
| 1/32 | 0.0312 | 0.7938 | 17/32 | 0.5312 | 13.4938 |
| 3/64 | 0.0469 | 1.1906 | 35/64 | 0.5469 | 13.8906 |
| 1/16 | 0.0625 | 1.5875 | 9/16 | 0.5625 | 14.2875 |
| 5/64 | 0.0781 | 1.9844 | 37/64 | 0.5781 | 14.6844 |
| 3/32 | 0.0938 | 2.3812 | 19/32 | 0.5938 | 15.0812 |
| 7/64 | 0.1094 | 2.7781 | 39/64 | 0.6094 | 15.4781 |
| 1/8 | 0.1250 | 3.1750 | 5/8 | 0.6250 | 15.8750 |
| 9/64 | 0.1406 | 3.5719 | 41/64 | 0.6406 | 16.2719 |
| 5/32 | 0.1562 | 3.9688 | 21/32 | 0.6562 | 16.6688 |
| 11/64 | 0.1719 | 4.3656 | 43/64 | 0.6719 | 17.0656 |
| 3/16 | 0.1875 | 4.7625 | 11/16 | 0.6875 | 17.4625 |
| 13/64 | 0.2031 | 5.1594 | 45/64 | 0.7031 | 17.8594 |
| 7/32 | 0.2188 | 5.5562 | 23/32 | 0.7188 | 18.2562 |
| 15/64 | 0.2344 | 5.9531 | 47/64 | 0.7344 | 18.6531 |
| 1/4 | 0.2500 | 6.3500 | 3/4 | 0.7500 | 19.0500 |
| 17/64 | 0.2656 | 6.7469 | 49/64 | 0.7656 | 19.4469 |
| 9/32 | 0.2812 | 7.1438 | 25/32 | 0.7812 | 19.8438 |
| 19/64 | 0.2969 | 7.5406 | 51/64 | 0.7969 | 20.2406 |
| 5/16 | 0.3125 | 7.9375 | 13/16 | 0.8125 | 20.6375 |
| 21/64 | 0.3281 | 8.3344 | 53/64 | 0.8281 | 21.0344 |
| 11/32 | 0.3438 | 8.7312 | 27/32 | 0.8438 | 21.4312 |
| 23/64 | 0.3594 | 9.1281 | 55/64 | 0.8594 | 21.8281 |
| 3/8 | 0.3750 | 9.5250 | 7/8 | 0.8750 | 22.2250 |
| 25/64 | 0.3906 | 9.9219 | 57/64 | 0.8906 | 22.6219 |
| 13/32 | 0.4062 | 10.3188 | 29/32 | 0.9062 | 23.0188 |
| 27/64 | 0.4219 | 10.7156 | 59/64 | 0.9219 | 23.4156 |
| 7/16 | 0.4375 | 11.1125 | 15/16 | 0.9375 | 23.8125 |
| 29/64 | 0.4531 | 11.5094 | 61/64 | 0.9531 | 24.2094 |
| 15/32 | 0.4688 | 11.9062 | 31/32 | 0.9688 | 24.6062 |
| 31/64 | 0.4844 | 12.3031 | 63/64 | 0.9844 | 25.0031 |
| 1/2 | 0.5000 | 12.7000 | 1 | 1.0000 | 25.4000 |

# Conversion factors

### *Length (distance)*

| | | | | | |
|---|---|---|---|---|---|
| Inches (in) | X 25.4 | = Millimeters (mm) | X 0.0394 | = Inches (in) |
| Feet (ft) | X 0.305 | = Meters (m) | X 3.281 | = Feet (ft) |
| Miles | X 1.609 | = Kilometers (km) | X 0.621 | = Miles |

### *Volume (capacity)*

| | | | | |
|---|---|---|---|---|
| Cubic inches (cu in; $in^3$) | X 16.387 | = Cubic centimeters (cc; $cm^3$) | X 0.061 | = Cubic inches (cu in; $in^3$) |
| Imperial pints (Imp pt) | X 0.568 | = Liters (l) | X 1.76 | = Imperial pints (Imp pt) |
| Imperial quarts (Imp qt) | X 1.137 | = Liters (l) | X 0.88 | = Imperial quarts (Imp qt) |
| Imperial quarts (Imp qt) | X 1.201 | = US quarts (US qt) | X 0.833 | = Imperial quarts (Imp qt) |
| US quarts (US qt) | X 0.946 | = Liters (l) | X 1.057 | = US quarts (US qt) |
| Imperial gallons (Imp gal) | X 4.546 | = Liters (l) | X 0.22 | = Imperial gallons (Imp gal) |
| Imperial gallons (Imp gal) | X 1.201 | = US gallons (US gal) | X 0.833 | = Imperial gallons (Imp gal) |
| US gallons (US gal) | X 3.785 | = Liters (l) | X 0.264 | = US gallons (US gal) |

### *Mass (weight)*

| | | | | |
|---|---|---|---|---|
| Ounces (oz) | X 28.35 | = Grams (g) | X 0.035 | = Ounces (oz) |
| Pounds (lb) | X 0.454 | = Kilograms (kg) | X 2.205 | = Pounds (lb) |

### *Force*

| | | | | |
|---|---|---|---|---|
| Ounces-force (ozf; oz) | X 0.278 | = Newtons (N) | X 3.6 | = Ounces-force (ozf; oz) |
| Pounds-force (lbf; lb) | X 4.448 | = Newtons (N) | X 0.225 | = Pounds-force (lbf; lb) |
| Newtons (N) | X 0.1 | = Kilograms-force (kgf; kg) | X 9.81 | = Newtons (N) |

### *Pressure*

| | | | | |
|---|---|---|---|---|
| Pounds-force per square inch (psi; $lbf/in^2$; $lb/in^2$) | X 0.070 | = Kilograms-force per square centimeter ($kgf/cm^2$; $kg/cm^2$) | X 14.223 | = Pounds-force per square inch (psi; $lbf/in^2$; $lb/in^2$) |
| Pounds-force per square inch (psi; $lbf/in^2$; $lb/in^2$) | X 0.068 | = Atmospheres (atm) | X 14.696 | = Pounds-force per square inch (psi; $lbf/in^2$; $lb/in^2$) |
| Pounds-force per square inch (psi; $lbf/in^2$; $lb/in^2$) | X 0.069 | = Bars | X 14.5 | = Pounds-force per square inch (psi; $lbf/in^2$; $lb/in^2$) |
| Pounds-force per square inch (psi; $lbf/in^2$; $lb/in^2$) | X 6.895 | = Kilopascals (kPa) | X 0.145 | = Pounds-force per square inch (psi; $lbf/in^2$; $lb/in^2$) |
| Kilopascals (kPa) | X 0.01 | = Kilograms-force per square centimeter ($kgf/cm^2$; $kg/cm^2$) | X 98.1 | = Kilopascals (kPa) |

### *Torque (moment of force)*

| | | | | |
|---|---|---|---|---|
| Pounds-force inches (lbf in; lb in) | X 1.152 | = Kilograms-force centimeter (kgf cm; kg cm) | X 0.868 | = Pounds-force inches (lbf in; lb in) |
| Pounds-force inches (lbf in; lb in) | X 0.113 | = Newton meters (Nm) | X 8.85 | = Pounds-force inches (lbf in; lb in) |
| Pounds-force inches (lbf in; lb in) | X 0.083 | = Pounds-force feet (lbf ft; lb ft) | X 12 | = Pounds-force inches (lbf in; lb in) |
| Pounds-force feet (lbf ft; lb ft) | X 0.138 | = Kilograms-force meters (kgf m; kg m) | X 7.233 | = Pounds-force feet (lbf ft; lb ft) |
| Pounds-force feet (lbf ft; lb ft) | X 1.356 | = Newton meters (Nm) | X 0.738 | = Pounds-force feet (lbf ft; lb ft) |
| Newton meters (Nm) | X 0.102 | = Kilograms-force meters (kgf m; kg m) | X 9.804 | = Newton meters (Nm) |

### *Vacuum*

| | | | | |
|---|---|---|---|---|
| Inches mercury (in. Hg) | X 3.377 | = Kilopascals (kPa) | X 0.2961 | = Inches mercury |
| Inches mercury (in. Hg) | X 25.4 | = Millimeters mercury (mm Hg) | X 0.0394 | = Inches mercury |

### *Power*

| | | | | |
|---|---|---|---|---|
| Horsepower (hp) | X 745.7 | = Watts (W) | X 0.0013 | = Horsepower (hp) |

### *Velocity (speed)*

| | | | | |
|---|---|---|---|---|
| Miles per hour (miles/hr; mph) | X 1.609 | = Kilometers per hour (km/hr; kph) | X 0.621 | = Miles per hour (miles/hr; mph) |

### *Fuel consumption**

| | | | | |
|---|---|---|---|---|
| Miles per gallon, Imperial (mpg) | X 0.354 | = Kilometers per liter (km/l) | X 2.825 | = Miles per gallon, Imperial (mpg) |
| Miles per gallon, US (mpg) | X 0.425 | = Kilometers per liter (km/l) | X 2.352 | = Miles per gallon, US (mpg) |

### *Temperature*

Degrees Fahrenheit = (°C x 1.8) + 32

Degrees Celsius (Degrees Centigrade; °C) = (°F - 32) x 0.56

***It is common practice to convert from miles per gallon (mpg) to liters/100 kilometers (l/100km), where mpg (Imperial) x l/100 km = 282 and mpg (US) x l/100 km = 235***

# Safety first!

Regardless of how enthusiastic you may be about getting on with the job at hand, take the time to ensure that your safety is not jeopardized. A moment's lack of attention can result in an accident, as can failure to observe certain simple safety precautions. The possibility of an accident will always exist, and the following points should not be considered a comprehensive list of all dangers. Rather, they are intended to make you aware of the risks and to encourage a safety conscious approach to all work you carry out on your vehicle.

## Essential DOs and DON'Ts

**DON'T** rely on a jack when working under the vehicle. Always use approved jackstands to support the weight of the vehicle and place them under the recommended lift or support points.

**DON'T** attempt to loosen extremely tight fasteners (i.e. wheel lug nuts) while the vehicle is on a jack - it may fall.

**DON'T** start the engine without first making sure that the transmission is in Neutral (or Park where applicable) and the parking brake is set.

**DON'T** remove the radiator cap from a hot cooling system - let it cool or cover it with a cloth and release the pressure gradually.

**DON'T** attempt to drain the engine oil until you are sure it has cooled to the point that it will not burn you.

**DON'T** touch any part of the engine or exhaust system until it has cooled sufficiently to avoid burns.

**DON'T** siphon toxic liquids such as gasoline, antifreeze and brake fluid by mouth, or allow them to remain on your skin.

**DON'T** inhale brake lining dust - it is potentially hazardous (see **Asbestos** below).

**DON'T** allow spilled oil or grease to remain on the floor - wipe it up before someone slips on it.

**DON'T** use loose fitting wrenches or other tools which may slip and cause injury.

**DON'T** push on wrenches when loosening or tightening nuts or bolts. Always try to pull the wrench toward you. If the situation calls for pushing the wrench away, push with an open hand to avoid scraped knuckles if the wrench should slip.

**DON'T** attempt to lift a heavy component alone - get someone to help you.

**DON'T** rush or take unsafe shortcuts to finish a job.

**DON'T** allow children or animals in or around the vehicle while you are working on it.

**DO** wear eye protection when using power tools such as a drill, sander, bench grinder, etc. and when working under a vehicle.

**DO** keep loose clothing and long hair well out of the way of moving parts.

**DO** make sure that any hoist used has a safe working load rating adequate for the job.

**DO** get someone to check on you periodically when working alone on a vehicle.

**DO** carry out work in a logical sequence and make sure that everything is correctly assembled and tightened.

**DO** keep chemicals and fluids tightly capped and out of the reach of children and pets.

**DO** remember that your vehicle's safety affects that of yourself and others. If in doubt on any point, get professional advice.

## Steering, suspension and brakes

These systems are essential to driving safety, so make sure you have a qualified shop or individual check your work. Also, compressed suspension springs can cause injury if released suddenly - be sure to use a spring compressor.

## Airbags

Airbags are explosive devices that can **CAUSE** injury if they deploy while you're working on the vehicle. Follow the manufacturer's instructions to disable the airbag whenever you're working in the vicinity of airbag components.

## Asbestos

Certain friction, insulating, sealing, and other products - such as brake linings, brake bands, clutch linings, torque converters, gaskets, etc. - may contain asbestos or other hazardous friction material. Extreme care must be taken to avoid inhalation of dust from such products, since it is hazardous to health. If in doubt, assume that they do contain asbestos.

## Fire

Remember at all times that gasoline is highly flammable. Never smoke or have any kind of open flame around when working on a vehicle. But the risk does not end there. A spark caused by an electrical short circuit, by two metal surfaces contacting each other, or even by static electricity built up in your body under certain conditions, can ignite gasoline vapors, which in a confined space are highly explosive. Do not, under any circumstances, use gasoline for cleaning parts. Use an approved safety solvent.

Always disconnect the battery ground (-) cable at the battery before working on any part of the fuel system or electrical system. Never risk spilling fuel on a hot engine or exhaust component. It is strongly recommended that a fire extinguisher suitable for use on fuel and electrical fires be kept handy in the garage or workshop at all times. Never try to extinguish a fuel or electrical fire with water.

## Fumes

Certain fumes are highly toxic and can quickly cause unconsciousness and even death if inhaled to any extent. Gasoline vapor falls into this category, as do the vapors from some cleaning solvents. Any draining or pouring of such volatile fluids should be done in a well ventilated area.

When using cleaning fluids and solvents, read the instructions on the container carefully. Never use materials from unmarked containers.

Never run the engine in an enclosed space, such as a garage. Exhaust fumes contain carbon monoxide, which is extremely poisonous. If you need to run the engine, always do so in the open air, or at least have the rear of the vehicle outside the work area.

## The battery

Never create a spark or allow a bare light bulb near a battery. They normally give off a certain amount of hydrogen gas, which is highly explosive.

Always disconnect the battery ground (-) cable at the battery before working on the fuel or electrical systems.

If possible, loosen the filler caps or cover when charging the battery from an external source (this does not apply to sealed or maintenance-free batteries). Do not charge at an excessive rate or the battery may burst.

Take care when adding water to a non maintenance-free battery and when carrying a battery. The electrolyte, even when diluted, is very corrosive and should not be allowed to contact clothing or skin.

Always wear eye protection when cleaning the battery to prevent the caustic deposits from entering your eyes.

## Household current

When using an electric power tool, inspection light, etc., which operates on household current, always make sure that the tool is correctly connected to its plug and that, where necessary, it is properly grounded. Do not use such items in damp conditions and, again, do not create a spark or apply excessive heat in the vicinity of fuel or fuel vapor.

## Secondary ignition system voltage

A severe electric shock can result from touching certain parts of the ignition system (such as the spark plug wires) when the engine is running or being cranked, particularly if components are damp or the insulation is defective. In the case of an electronic ignition system, the secondary system voltage is much higher and could prove fatal.

## Hydrofluoric acid

This extremely corrosive acid is formed when certain types of synthetic rubber, found in some O-rings, oil seals, fuel hoses, etc. are exposed to temperatures above 750-degrees F (400-degrees C). The rubber changes into a charred or sticky substance containing the acid. *Once formed, the acid remains dangerous for years. If it gets onto the skin, it may be necessary to amputate the limb concerned.*

When dealing with a vehicle which has suffered a fire, or with components salvaged from such a vehicle, wear protective gloves and discard them after use.

# Automotive chemicals and lubricants

A number of automotive chemicals and lubricants are available for use during vehicle maintenance and repair. They include a wide variety of products ranging from cleaning solvents and degreasers to lubricants and protective sprays for rubber, plastic and vinyl.

## Cleaners

***Carburetor cleaner and choke cleaner*** is a strong solvent for gum, varnish and carbon. Most carburetor cleaners leave a dry-type lubricant film which will not harden or gum up. Because of this film it is not recommended for use on electrical components.

***Brake system cleaner*** is used to remove brake dust, grease and brake fluid from the brake system, where clean surfaces are absolutely necessary. It leaves no residue and often eliminates brake squeal caused by contaminants.

***Electrical cleaner*** removes oxidation, corrosion and carbon deposits from electrical contacts, restoring full current flow. It can also be used to clean spark plugs, carburetor jets, voltage regulators and other parts where an oil-free surface is desired.

***Demoisturants*** remove water and moisture from electrical components such as alternators, voltage regulators, electrical connectors and fuse blocks. They are non-conductive and non-corrosive.

***Degreasers*** are heavy-duty solvents used to remove grease from the outside of the engine and from chassis components. They can be sprayed or brushed on and, depending on the type, are rinsed off either with water or solvent.

## Lubricants

***Motor oil*** is the lubricant formulated for use in engines. It normally contains a wide variety of additives to prevent corrosion and reduce foaming and wear. Motor oil comes in various weights (viscosity ratings) from 0 to 50. The recommended weight of the oil depends on the season, temperature and the demands on the engine. Light oil is used in cold climates and under light load conditions. Heavy oil is used in hot climates and where high loads are encountered. Multi-viscosity oils are designed to have characteristics of both light and heavy oils and are available in a number of weights from 0W-20 to 20W-50.

***Gear oil*** is designed to be used in differentials, manual transmissions and other areas where high-temperature lubrication is required.

***Chassis and wheel bearing grease*** is a heavy grease used where increased loads and friction are encountered, such as for wheel bearings, balljoints, tie-rod ends and universal joints.

***High-temperature wheel bearing grease*** is designed to withstand the extreme temperatures encountered by wheel bearings in disc brake equipped vehicles. It usually contains molybdenum disulfide (moly), which is a dry-type lubricant.

***White grease*** is a heavy grease for metal-to-metal applications where water is a problem. White grease stays soft under both low and high temperatures (usually from -100 to +190-degrees F), and will not wash off or dilute in the presence of water.

***Assembly lube*** is a special extreme pressure lubricant, usually containing moly, used to lubricate high-load parts (such as main and rod bearings and cam lobes) for initial start-up of a new engine. The assembly lube lubricates the parts without being squeezed out or washed away until the engine oiling system begins to function.

***Silicone lubricants*** are used to protect rubber, plastic, vinyl and nylon parts.

***Graphite lubricants*** are used where oils cannot be used due to contamination problems, such as in locks. The dry graphite will lubricate metal parts while remaining uncontaminated by dirt, water, oil or acids. It is electrically conductive and will not foul electrical contacts in locks such as the ignition switch.

***Moly penetrants*** loosen and lubricate frozen, rusted and corroded fasteners and prevent future rusting or freezing.

***Heat-sink grease*** is a special electrically non-conductive grease that is used for mounting electronic ignition modules where it is essential that heat is transferred away from the module.

## Sealants

***RTV sealant*** is one of the most widely used gasket compounds. Made from silicone, RTV is air curing, it seals, bonds, waterproofs, fills surface irregularities, remains flexible, doesn't shrink, is relatively easy to remove, and is used as a supplementary sealer with almost all low and medium temperature gaskets.

***Anaerobic sealant*** is much like RTV in that it can be used either to seal gaskets or to form gaskets by itself. It remains flexible, is solvent resistant and fills surface imperfections. The difference between an anaerobic sealant and an RTV-type sealant is in the curing. RTV cures when exposed to air, while an anaerobic sealant cures only in the absence of air. This means that an anaerobic sealant cures only after the assembly of parts, sealing them together.

***Thread and pipe sealant*** is used for sealing hydraulic and pneumatic fittings and vacuum lines. It is usually made from a Teflon compound, and comes in a spray, a paint-on liquid and as a wrap-around tape.

## Chemicals

***Anti-seize compound*** prevents seizing, galling, cold welding, rust and corrosion in fasteners. High-temperature ant-seize, usually made with copper and graphite lubricants, is used for exhaust system and exhaust manifold bolts.

***Anaerobic locking compounds*** are used to keep fasteners from vibrating or working loose and cure only after installation, in the absence of air. Medium strength locking compound is used for small nuts, bolts and screws that may be removed later. High-strength locking compound is for large nuts, bolts and studs which aren't removed on a regular basis.

***Oil additives*** range from viscosity index improvers to chemical treatments that claim to reduce internal engine friction. It should be noted that most oil manufacturers caution against using additives with their oils.

***Gas additives*** perform several functions, depending on their chemical makeup. They usually contain solvents that help dissolve gum and varnish that build up on carburetor, fuel injection and intake parts. They also serve to break down carbon deposits that form on the inside surfaces of the combustion chambers. Some additives contain upper cylinder lubricants for valves and piston rings, and others contain chemicals to remove condensation from the gas tank.

## Miscellaneous

***Brake fluid*** is specially formulated hydraulic fluid that can withstand the heat and pressure encountered in brake systems. Care must be taken so this fluid does not come in contact with painted surfaces or plastics. An opened container should always be resealed to prevent contamination by water or dirt.

***Weatherstrip adhesive*** is used to bond weatherstripping around doors, windows and trunk lids. It is sometimes used to attach trim pieces.

***Undercoating*** is a petroleum-based, tar-like substance that is designed to protect metal surfaces on the underside of the vehicle from corrosion. It also acts as a sound-deadening agent by insulating the bottom of the vehicle.

***Waxes and polishes*** are used to help protect painted and plated surfaces from the weather. Different types of paint may require the use of different types of wax and polish. Some polishes utilize a chemical or abrasive cleaner to help remove the top layer of oxidized (dull) paint on older vehicles. In recent years many non-wax polishes that contain a wide variety of chemicals such as polymers and silicones have been introduced. These non-wax polishes are usually easier to apply and last longer than conventional waxes and polishes.

# Troubleshooting

## Contents

This section provides an easy reference guide to the more common problems which may occur during the operation of your vehicle. These problems and their possible causes are grouped under headings denoting various components or systems, such as Engine, Cooling system, etc. They also refer you to the chapter and/or section which deals with the problem.

Remember that successful troubleshooting is not a mysterious art practiced only by professional mechanics. It is simply the result of the right knowledge combined with an intelligent, systematic approach to the problem. Always work by a process of elimination, starting with the simplest solution and working through to the most complex - and never overlook the obvious. Anyone can run the gas tank dry or leave the lights on overnight, so don't assume that you are exempt from such oversights.

Finally, always establish a clear idea of why a problem has occurred and take steps to ensure that it doesn't happen again. If the electrical system fails because of a poor connection, check the other connections in the system to make sure that they don't fail as well. If a particular fuse continues to blow, find out why - don't just replace one fuse after another. Remember, failure of a small component can often be indicative of potential failure or incorrect functioning of a more important component or system.

## Engine

### 1 Engine will not rotate when attempting to start

1 Battery terminal connections loose or corroded (Chapter 1).
2 Battery discharged or faulty (Chapter 1).
3 Automatic transaxle not completely engaged in Park (Chapter 7B) or clutch pedal not completely depressed (Chapter 8).
4 Broken, loose or disconnected wiring in the starting circuit (Chapters 5 and 12).
5 Starter motor pinion jammed in flywheel ring gear (Chapter 5).
6 Starter solenoid faulty (Chapter 5).
7 Starter motor faulty (Chapter 5).
8 Ignition switch faulty (Chapter 12).
9 Starter pinion or flywheel teeth worn or broken (Chapter 5).
10 Defective fusible link (see Chapter 12).
11 Theft deterrent system.

### 2 Engine rotates but will not start

1 Fuel tank empty.
2 Battery discharged (engine rotates slowly) (Chapter 5).
3 Battery terminal connections loose or corroded (Chapter 1).
4 Leaking fuel injector(s), faulty fuel pump, pressure regulator, etc. (Chapter 4).
5 Broken or stripped timing belt (Chapter 2).
6 Ignition components damp or damaged (Chapter 5).
7 Worn, faulty or incorrectly gapped spark plugs (Chapter 1).
8 Broken, loose or disconnected wiring in the starting circuit (Chapter 5).
9 Broken, loose or disconnected wires at the ignition coils or faulty coils (Chapter 5).
10 Defective crankshaft sensor or PCM (see Chapter 6).

### 3 Engine hard to start when cold

1 Battery discharged or low (Chapter 1).
2 Malfunctioning fuel system (Chapter 4).
3 Faulty coolant temperature sensor or intake air temperature sensor (Chapter 6).
4 Fuel injector(s) leaking (Chapter 4).
5 Faulty ignition system (Chapter 5).
6 Defective MAP sensor (see Chapter 6).

### 4 Engine hard to start when hot

1 Air filter clogged (Chapter 1).
2 Fuel not reaching the fuel injection system (Chapter 4).
3 Corroded battery connections, especially ground (Chapter 1).
4 Faulty coolant temperature sensor or intake air temperature sensor (Chapter 6).

### 5 Starter motor noisy or excessively rough in engagement

1 Pinion or flywheel gear teeth worn or broken (Chapter 5).
2 Starter motor mounting bolts loose or missing (Chapter 5).

### 6 Engine starts but stops immediately

1 Loose or faulty electrical connections at ignition coil (Chapter 5).
2 Insufficient fuel reaching the fuel injector(s) (Chapters 4).
3 Vacuum leak at the gasket between the intake manifold/plenum and throttle body (Chapter 4).
4 Fault in the engine control system (Chapter 6).
5 Intake air leaks, broken vacuum lines (see Chapter 4).
6 Theft deterrent system.

### 7 Oil puddle under engine

1 Oil pan gasket and/or oil pan drain bolt washer leaking (Chapter 2).
2 Oil pressure sending unit leaking (Chapter 2).
3 Valve covers leaking (Chapter 2).
4 Engine oil seals leaking (Chapter 2).

### 8 Engine lopes while idling or idles erratically

1 Vacuum leakage (Chapters 2 and 4).
2 Leaking EGR valve (Chapter 6).
3 Air filter clogged (Chapter 1).
4 Fuel pump not delivering sufficient fuel to the fuel injection system (Chapter 4).
5 Leaking head gasket (Chapter 2).
6 Timing belt worn (Chapter 2).
7 Camshaft lobes worn (Chapter 2).

### 9 Engine misses at idle speed

1 Spark plugs worn or not gapped properly (Chapter 1).
2 Faulty spark plug wires (Chapter 1).
3 Vacuum leaks (Chapters 2 and 4).
4 Faulty ignition coil (Chapter 5).
5 Uneven or low compression (Chapter 2).
6 Faulty fuel injector(s) (Chapter 4).

### 10 Engine misses throughout driving speed range

1 Fuel filter clogged and/or impurities in the fuel system (Chapter 1).
2 Low fuel output at the fuel injector(s) (Chapter 4).
3 Faulty or incorrectly gapped spark plugs (Chapter 1).
4 Leaking spark plug wires (Chapter 1 or 5).
5 Faulty emission system components (Chapter 6).
6 Low or uneven cylinder compression pressures (Chapter 2).
7 Burned valves (Chapter 2).
8 Weak or faulty ignition system (Chapter 5).
9 Vacuum leak in fuel injection system, throttle body, intake manifold or vacuum hoses (Chapter 4).

### 11 Engine stumbles on acceleration

1 Spark plugs fouled (Chapter 1).
2 Problem with fuel injection system (Chapter 4).
3 Fuel filter clogged (Chapters 1 and 4).
4 Fault in the engine control system (Chapter 6).
5 Intake manifold air leak (Chapters 2 and 4).
6 EGR system malfunction (Chapter 6).

### 12 Engine surges while holding accelerator steady

1 Intake air leak (Chapter 4).
2 Fuel pump or fuel pressure regulator faulty (Chapter 4).

3 Problem with fuel injection system (Chapter 4).
4 Problem with the emissions control system (Chapter 6).

### 13 Engine stalls

1 Fuel filter clogged and/or water and impurities in the fuel system (Chapter 4).
2 Ignition components damp or damaged (Chapter 5).
3 Faulty emissions system components (Chapter 6).
4 Faulty or incorrectly gapped spark plugs (Chapter 1).
5 Faulty spark plug wires (Chapter 1).
6 Vacuum leak in the fuel injection system, intake manifold or vacuum hoses (Chapters 2 and 4).

### 14 Engine lacks power

1 Worn camshaft lobes (Chapter 2).
2 Burned valves or incorrect valve timing (Chapter 2).
3 Faulty spark plug wires or faulty coil (Chapters 1 and 5).
4 Faulty or incorrectly gapped spark plugs (Chapter 1).
5 Problem with the fuel injection system (Chapter 4).
6 Plugged air filter (Chapter 1).
7 Brakes binding (Chapter 9).
8 Automatic transaxle fluid level incorrect (Chapter 1).
9 Clutch slipping (Chapter 8).
10 Fuel filter clogged and/or impurities in the fuel system (Chapters 1 and 4).
11 Emission control system not functioning properly (Chapter 6).
12 Low or uneven cylinder compression pressures (Chapter 2).
13 Restricted exhaust system (Chapters 4 and 6).

### 15 Engine backfires

1 Emission control system not functioning properly (Chapter 6).
2 Faulty spark plug wires or coil(s) (Chapter 5).
3 Problem with the fuel injection system (Chapter 4).
4 Vacuum leak at fuel injector(s), intake manifold or vacuum hoses (Chapters 2 and 4).
5 Burned valves or incorrect valve timing (Chapter 2).

### 16 Pinging or knocking engine sounds during acceleration or uphill

1 Incorrect grade of fuel.
2 Problem with the engine control system (Chapter 6).
3 Fuel injection system faulty (Chapter 4).
4 Improper or damaged spark plugs or wires (Chapter 1).
5 EGR valve not functioning (Chapter 6).
6 Vacuum leak (Chapters 2 and 4).

### 17 Engine runs with oil pressure light on

1 Low oil level (Chapter 1).
2 Idle rpm below specification (Chapter 1).
3 Short in wiring circuit (Chapter 12).
4 Faulty oil pressure sender (Chapter 2).
5 Worn engine bearings and/or oil pump (Chapter 2).

### 18 Engine diesels (continues to run) after switching off

1 Idle speed too high (Chapter 1).
2 Excessive engine operating temperature (Chapter 3).
3 Excessive carbon deposits on valves and pistons (see Chapter 2)

## Engine electrical system

### 19 Battery will not hold a charge

1 Alternator drivebelt defective or not adjusted properly (Chapter 1).
2 Battery electrolyte level low (Chapter 1).
3 Battery terminals loose or corroded (Chapter 1).
4 Alternator not charging properly (Chapter 5).
5 Loose, broken or faulty wiring in the charging circuit (Chapter 5).
6 Short in vehicle wiring (Chapter 12).
7 Internally defective battery (Chapters 1 and 5).

### 20 Alternator light fails to go out

1 Faulty alternator or charging circuit (Chapter 5).
2 Alternator drivebelt defective or out of adjustment (Chapter 1).
3 Alternator voltage regulator inoperative (Chapter 5).

### 21 Alternator light fails to come on when key is turned on

1 Warning light bulb defective (Chapter 12).
2 Fault in the printed circuit, dash wiring or bulb holder (Chapter 12).

## Fuel system

### 22 Excessive fuel consumption

1 Dirty or clogged air filter element (Chapter 1).
2 Emissions system not functioning properly (Chapter 6).
3 Fuel injection system not functioning properly (Chapter 4).
4 Low tire pressure or incorrect tire size (Chapter 1).

### 23 Fuel leakage and/or fuel odor

1 Leaking fuel feed or return line (Chapters 1 and 4).
2 Tank overfilled.
3 Evaporative canister filter clogged (Chapters 1 and 6).
4 Problem with fuel injection system (Chapter 4).

## Cooling system

### 24 Overheating

1 Insufficient coolant in system (Chapter 1).
2 Water pump defective (Chapter 3).
3 Radiator core blocked or grille restricted (Chapter 3).
4 Thermostat faulty (Chapter 3).
5 Electric coolant fan inoperative or blades broken (Chapter 3).
6 Cooling system pressure cap not maintaining proper pressure (Chapter 3).

### 25 Overcooling

1 Faulty thermostat (Chapter 3).
2 Inaccurate temperature gauge sending unit (Chapter 3)

### 26 External coolant leakage

1 Deteriorated/damaged hoses; loose clamps (Chapters 1 and 3).
2 Water pump defective (Chapter 3).
3 Leakage from radiator core or coolant reservoir bottle (Chapter 3).
4 Engine drain or water jacket core plugs leaking (Chapter 2).

### 27 Internal coolant leakage

1 Leaking cylinder head gasket (Chapter 2).
2 Cracked cylinder bore or cylinder head (Chapter 2).

### 28 Coolant loss

1 Too much coolant in system (Chapter 1).
2 Coolant boiling away because of overheating (Chapter 3).
3 Internal or external leakage (Chapter 3).
4 Faulty pressure cap (Chapter 3).

### 29 Poor coolant circulation

1 Inoperative water pump (Chapter 3).
2 Restriction in cooling system (Chapters 1 and 3).
3 Thermostat sticking (Chapter 3).

## Clutch

### 30 Pedal travels to floor - no pressure or very little resistance

1 Broken or disconnected clutch cable (Chapter 8).
2 Broken release bearing or fork (Chapter 8).

### 31 Unable to select gears

1 Faulty transaxle (Chapter 7).
2 Faulty clutch disc or pressure plate (Chapter 8).
3 Faulty release lever or release bearing (Chapter 8).
4 Faulty shift lever assembly or rods (Chapter 8).

### 32 Clutch slips (engine speed increases with no increase in vehicle speed)

1 Clutch plate worn (Chapter 8).
2 Clutch plate is oil soaked by leaking rear main seal or transaxle input shaft seal (Chapter 8).
3 Clutch plate not seated (Chapter 8).
4 Warped pressure plate or flywheel (Chapter 8).
5 Weak diaphragm springs (Chapter 8).
6 Clutch plate overheated. Allow to cool.

### 33 Grabbing (chattering) as clutch is engaged

1 Oil on clutch plate lining, burned or glazed facings (Chapter 8).
2 Worn or loose engine or transaxle mounts (Chapters 2 and 7).
3 Worn splines on clutch plate hub (Chapter 8).
4 Warped pressure plate or flywheel (Chapter 8).
5 Burned or smeared resin on flywheel or pressure plate (Chapter 8).

### 34 Transaxle rattling (clicking)

1 Release fork loose (Chapter 8).
2 Low engine idle speed (Chapter 1).

### 35 Noise in clutch area

Faulty release bearing (Chapter 8).

### 36 Clutch pedal stays on floor

1 Broken release bearing or fork (Chapter 8).
2 Broken or disconnected clutch cable (Chapter 8).

### 37 High pedal effort

1 Binding clutch cable (Chapter 8).
2 Pressure plate faulty (Chapter 8).

## Manual transaxle

### 38 Knocking noise at low speeds

1 Worn driveaxle constant velocity (CV) joints (Chapter 8).
2 Worn side gear shaft counterbore in differential case (Chapter 7A).*

### 39 Noise most pronounced when turning

Differential gear noise (Chapter 7A).*

### 40 Clunk on acceleration or deceleration

1 Loose engine or transaxle mounts (Chapters 2 and 7A).
2 Worn differential pinion shaft in case.*
3 Worn side gear shaft counterbore in differential case (Chapter 7A).*
4 Worn or damaged driveaxle inboard CV joints (Chapter 8).

### 41 Clicking noise in turns

Worn or damaged outboard CV joint (Chapter 8).

### 42 Vibration

1 Rough wheel bearing (Chapters 1 and 10).
2 Damaged driveaxle (Chapter 8).
3 Out of round tires (Chapter 1).
4 Tire out of balance (Chapters 1 and 10).
5 Worn CV joint (Chapter 8).

### 43 Noisy in neutral with engine running

1 Damaged input gear bearing (Chapter 7A).*
2 Damaged clutch release bearing (Chapter 8).

### 44 Noisy in one particular gear

1 Damaged or worn constant mesh gears (Chapter 7A).*
2 Damaged or worn synchronizers (Chapter 7A).*
3 Bent reverse fork (Chapter 7A).*
4 Damaged fourth speed gear or output gear (Chapter 7A).*
5 Worn or damaged reverse idler gear or idler bushing (Chapter 7A).*

### 45 Noisy in all gears

1 Insufficient lubricant (Chapter 7A).
2 Damaged or worn bearings (Chapter 7A).*
3 Worn or damaged input gear shaft and/or output gear shaft (Chapter 7A).*

### 46 Slips out of gear

1 Worn or improperly adjusted linkage (Chapter 7A).
2 Transaxle loose on engine (Chapter 7A).
3 Shift linkage does not work freely, binds (Chapter 7A).
4 Input gear bearing retainer broken or loose (Chapter 7A).*
5 Dirt between clutch cover and engine housing (Chapter 7A).
6 Worn shift fork (Chapter 7A).*

### 47 Leaks lubricant

1 Driveshaft seals worn (Chapter 7A).
2 Excessive amount of lubricant in transaxle (Chapters 1 and 7A).
3 Loose or broken input gear shaft bearing retainer (Chapter 7A).*
4 Input gear bearing retainer O-ring and/or lip seal damaged (Chapter 7A).*
5 Vehicle speed sensor O-ring leaking (Chapter 7A).

### 48 Hard to shift

Shift linkage loose or worn (Chapter 7A).

** Although the corrective action necessary to remedy the symptoms described is beyond the scope of this manual, the above information should be helpful in isolating the cause of the condition so that the owner can communicate clearly with a professional mechanic.*

### Automatic transaxle

**Note:** *Due to the complexity of the automatic transaxle, it is difficult for the home mechanic to properly diagnose and service this component. For problems other than the following, the vehicle should be taken to a dealer or transaxle shop.*

#### 49 Fluid leakage

1 Automatic transaxle fluid is a deep red color. Fluid leaks should not be confused with engine oil, which can easily be blown onto the transaxle by air flow.

2 To pinpoint a leak, first remove all built-up dirt and grime from the transaxle housing with degreasing agents and/or steam cleaning. Then drive the vehicle at low speeds so air flow will not blow the leak far from its source. Raise the vehicle and determine where the leak is coming from. Common areas of leakage are:

*a) Pan (Chapters 1 and 7)*
*b) Dipstick tube (Chapters 1 and 7)*
*c) Transaxle oil lines (Chapter 7)*
*d) Speed sensor (Chapter 7)*
*e) Driveaxle oil seals (Chapter 7).*

#### 50 Transaxle fluid brown or has a burned smell

Transaxle fluid overheated (Chapter 1).

#### 51 General shift mechanism problems

1 Chapter 7, Part B, deals with checking and adjusting the shift linkage on automatic transaxles. Common problems which may be attributed to poorly adjusted linkage are:

*a) Engine starting in gears other than Park or Neutral.*
*b) Indicator on shifter pointing to a gear other than the one actually being used.*
*c) Vehicle moves when in Park.*

2 Refer to Chapter 7B for the shift linkage adjustment procedure.

#### 52 Transaxle will not downshift with accelerator pedal pressed to the floor

The transaxle is electronically controlled. This type of problem - which is caused by a malfunction in the control unit, a sensor or solenoid, or the circuit itself - is beyond the scope of this book. Take the vehicle to a dealer service department or a competent automatic transmission shop.

#### 53 Engine will start in gears other than Park or Neutral

Neutral start switch out of adjustment or malfunctioning (Chapter 7B).

#### 54 Transaxle slips, shifts roughly, is noisy or has no drive in forward or reverse gears

There are many probable causes for the above problems, but the home mechanic should be concerned with only one possibility - fluid level. Before taking the vehicle to a repair shop, check the level and condition of the fluid as described in Chapter 1. Correct the fluid level as necessary or change the fluid and filter if needed. If the problem persists, have a professional diagnose the cause.

### Driveaxles

#### 55 Clicking noise in turns

Worn or damaged outboard CV joint (Chapter 8).

#### 56 Shudder or vibration during acceleration

1 Excessive toe-in (Chapter 10).
2 Incorrect spring heights (Chapter 10).
3 Worn or damaged inboard or outboard CV joints (Chapter 8).
4 Sticking inboard CV joint assembly (Chapter 8).

#### 57 Vibration at highway speeds

1 Out-of-balance front wheels and/or tires (Chapters 1 and 10).
2 Out-of-round front tires (Chapters 1 and 10).
3 Worn CV joint(s) (Chapter 8).

### Brakes

**Note:** *Before assuming that a brake problem exists, make sure that:*

*a) The tires are in good condition and properly inflated (Chapter 1).*
*b) The front end alignment is correct (Chapter 10).*
*c) The vehicle is not loaded with weight in an unequal manner.*

#### 58 Vehicle pulls to one side during braking

1 Incorrect tire pressures (Chapter 1).
2 Front end out of alignment (have the front end aligned).
3 Front, or rear, tire sizes not matched to one another.
4 Restricted brake lines or hoses (Chapter 9).
5 Malfunctioning drum brake or caliper assembly (Chapter 9).
6 Loose suspension parts (Chapter 10).
7 Excessive wear of brake shoe or pad material or disc/drum on one side.

#### 59 Noise (high-pitched squeal when the brakes are applied)

Front and/or rear disc brake pads worn out. The noise comes from the wear sensor rubbing against the disc (does not apply to all vehicles). Replace pads with new ones immediately (Chapter 9).

#### 60 Brake roughness or chatter (pedal pulsates)

1 Excessive lateral runout (Chapter 9).
2 Uneven pad wear (Chapter 9).
3 Defective disc (Chapter 9).

#### 61 Excessive brake pedal effort required to stop vehicle

1 Malfunctioning power brake booster (Chapter 9).
2 Partial system failure (Chapter 9).
3 Excessively worn pads or shoes (Chapter 9).
4 Piston in caliper or wheel cylinder stuck or sluggish (Chapter 9).
5 Brake pads or shoes contaminated with oil or grease (Chapter 9).
6 Brake disc grooved and/or glazed (Chapter 1).
7 New pads or shoes installed and not yet seated. It will take a while for the new material to seat against the disc or drum.

#### 62 Excessive brake pedal travel

1 Partial brake system failure (Chapter 9).
2 Insufficient fluid in master cylinder (Chapters 1 and 9).
3 Air trapped in system (Chapters 1 and 9).

#### 63 Dragging brakes

1 Incorrect adjustment of brake light switch

(Chapter 9).
2 Master cylinder pistons not returning correctly (Chapter 9).
3 Restricted brakes lines or hoses (Chapters 1 and 9).
4 Parking brake adjuster malfunctioning.

### 64 Grabbing or uneven braking action

1 Malfunction of proportioning valve (Chapter 9).
2 Malfunction of power brake booster unit (Chapter 9).
3 Binding brake pedal mechanism (Chapter 9).

### 65 Brake pedal feels spongy when depressed

1 Air in hydraulic lines (Chapter 9).
2 Master cylinder mounting bolts loose (Chapter 9).
3 Master cylinder defective (Chapter 9).

### 66 Brake pedal travels to the floor with little resistance

1 Little or no fluid in the master cylinder reservoir caused by leaking caliper piston(s) (Chapter 9).
2 Loose, damaged or disconnected brake lines (Chapter 9).

### 67 Parking brake does not hold

Parking brake automatic adjuster or rear drum brake automatic adjuster not working properly (Chapter 9).

## Suspension and steering systems

**Note:** *Before attempting to diagnose the suspension and steering systems, perform the following preliminary checks:*

- *a) Tires for wrong pressure and uneven wear.*
- *b) Steering universal joints from the column to the rack and pinion for loose connectors or wear.*
- *c) Front and rear suspension and the rack and pinion assembly for loose or damaged parts.*
- *d) Out-of-round or out-of-balance tires, bent rims and loose and/or rough wheel bearings.*

### 68 Vehicle pulls to one side

1 Mismatched or uneven tires (Chapter 10).
2 Broken or sagging springs (Chapter 10).
3 Wheel alignment out-of-specifications (Chapter 10).
4 Front brake dragging (Chapter 9).

### 69 Abnormal or excessive tire wear

1 Wheel alignment out-of-specifications (Chapter 10).
2 Sagging or broken springs (Chapter 10).
3 Tire out-of-balance (Chapter 10).
4 Worn strut damper (Chapter 10).
5 Overloaded vehicle.
6 Tires not rotated regularly.

### 70 Wheel makes a thumping noise

1 Blister or bump on tire (Chapter 10).
2 Improper strut damper action (Chapter 10).

### 71 Shimmy, shake or vibration

1 Tire or wheel out-of-balance or out-of-round (Chapter 10).
2 Loose or worn wheel bearings (Chapters 1, 8 and 10).
3 Worn tie-rod ends (Chapter 10).
4 Worn lower balljoints (Chapters 1 and 10).
5 Excessive wheel runout (Chapter 10).
6 Blister or bump on tire (Chapter 10).

### 72 Hard steering

1 Lack of lubrication at balljoints, tie-rod ends and rack and pinion assembly (Chapter 10).
2 Front wheel alignment out-of-specifications (Chapter 10).
3 Low tire pressure(s) (Chapters 1 and 10).

### 73 Poor returnability of steering to center

1 Binding in balljoints or tie-rod ends (Chapter 10).
2 Binding in steering column (Chapter 10).
3 Lack of lubricant in steering gear assembly (Chapter 10).
4 Front wheel alignment out-of-specifications (Chapter 10).

### 74 Abnormal noise at the front end

1 Balljoints or tie-rod ends worn (Chapter 10).
2 Damaged strut mounting (Chapter 10).
3 Worn control arm bushings or tie-rod ends (Chapter 10).
4 Loose stabilizer bar (Chapter 10).
5 Loose wheel nuts (Chapters 1 and 10).
6 Loose suspension bolts (Chapter 10)

### 75 Wander or poor steering stability

1 Mismatched or uneven tires (Chapter 10).
2 Lack of lubrication at balljoints and tie-rod ends (Chapters 1 and 10).
3 Worn strut assemblies (Chapter 10).
4 Loose stabilizer bar (Chapter 10).
5 Broken or sagging springs (Chapter 10).
6 Wheels out of alignment (Chapter 10).

### 76 Erratic steering when braking

1 Wheel bearings worn (Chapter 10).
2 Broken or sagging springs (Chapter 10).
3 Leaking wheel cylinder or caliper (Chapter 10).
4 Warped rotors or drums (Chapter 10).

### 77 Excessive pitching and/or rolling around corners or during braking

1 Loose stabilizer bar (Chapter 10).
2 Worn strut dampers or mountings (Chapter 10).
3 Broken or sagging springs (Chapter 10).
4 Overloaded vehicle.

### 78 Suspension bottoms

1 Overloaded vehicle.
2 Worn strut dampers or shock absorbers (Chapter 10).
3 Incorrect, broken or sagging springs (Chapter 10).

### 79 Cupped tires

1 Front wheel or rear wheel alignment out-of-specifications (Chapter 10).
2 Worn strut dampers (Chapter 10).
3 Wheel bearings worn (Chapter 10).
4 Excessive tire or wheel runout (Chapter 10).
5 Worn balljoints (Chapter 10).

### 80 Excessive tire wear on outside edge

1 Inflation pressures incorrect (Chapter 1).
2 Excessive speed in turns.
3 Front end alignment incorrect (excessive toe-in). Have professionally aligned.
4 Suspension arm bent or twisted (Chapter 10).

### 81 Excessive tire wear on inside edge

1 Inflation pressures incorrect (Chapter 1).

2 Front end alignment incorrect (toe-out). Have professionally aligned.
3 Loose or damaged steering components (Chapter 10).

## 82 Tire tread worn in one place

1 Tires out-of-balance.
2 Damaged or buckled wheel. Inspect and replace if necessary.
3 Defective tire (Chapter 1).

## 83 Excessive play or looseness in steering system

1 Wheel bearing(s) worn (Chapter 10).
2 Tie-rod end loose (Chapter 10).
3 Steering gear loose (Chapter 10).
4 Worn or loose steering intermediate shaft (Chapter 10).

## 84 Rattling or clicking noise in steering gear

1 Steering gear loose (Chapter 10).
2 Steering gear defective.

# Chapter 1
# Tune-up and routine maintenance

## Contents



## Specifications

### Recommended lubricants and fluids

Engine oil

| | |
|---|---|
| Type | API "Certified for gasoline engines" |
| Viscosity | See accompanying chart |

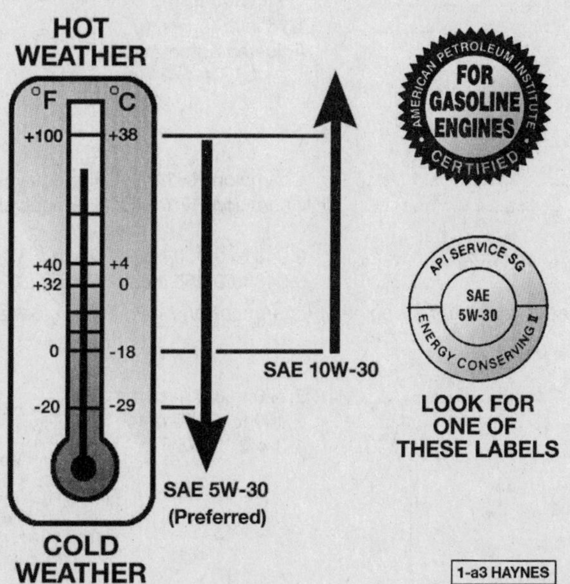

Recommended engine oil viscosity

## Recommended lubricants and fluids (continued)

| | |
|---|---|
| Manual transaxle lubricant | |
| 2001 models | Mopar manual transaxle fluid type MS 9417 or equivalent |
| 2002 models | |
| North American models | Mopar manual transaxle fluid type MS 9417 or equivalent |
| All others | Mopar ATF +4 automatic transmission fluid (type MS 9602), or equivalent |
| 2003 and later models | Mopar ATF +4 automatic transmission fluid (type MS 9602), or equivalent |
| Automatic transaxle fluid | Mopar ATF +4 automatic transmission fluid (type MS 9602), or equivalent |
| Power steering fluid | |
| 2001 models | Mopar power steering fluid, or equivalent |
| 2002 and later models | Mopar ATF +4 automatic transmission fluid (type 9602), or equivalent |
| Brake and clutch fluid | DOT type 3 brake fluid |
| Engine coolant | 50/50 mixture of Mopar 5 year/100,000 mile Formula (MS-9769) anti-freeze/coolant with HOAT (Hybrid Organic Additive Technology) and water* |
| Door and liftgate latch | Multi-purpose grease |
| Fuel filler door remote control latch mechanism | Multi-purpose grease |
| Hood, door and liftgate hinge lubricant | Engine oil |
| Key lock cylinder lubricant | Graphite spray |
| Parking brake mechanism grease | Mopar Spray White Lube or equivalent |

**These vehicles are filled with a 50/50 mixture of Mopar 5 year/100,000 mile coolant that shouldn't be mixed with other coolants. Refer to the coolant reservoir label under the hood to determine what type coolant you have. Always refill with the correct coolant.*

## Capacities*

| | |
|---|---|
| Engine oil (including filter) | |
| 2.0L engine | 4.5 quarts (4.3 liters) |
| 2.4L engine | 5.0 quarts (4.8 liters) |
| Automatic transaxle (drain and refill)** | 4.0 quarts (3.8 liters) |
| Manual transaxle | |
| NVT-350 transaxle | 2.5 to 2.8 quarts (2.4 to 2.7 liters) |
| G288 transaxle (turbo models) | 1.9 quarts (1.8 liters) |
| Cooling system*** | |
| 2002 and earlier models | 7.4 quarts (7.0 liters) |
| 2003 and later models | 6.5 quarts (6.2 liters) |

** All capacities approximate. Add as necessary to bring to appropriate level.*

*** The best way to determine the amount of fluid to add during a routine fluid change is to measure the amount drained. It's important to not overfill the transaxle.*

**** Includes heater and coolant reservoir.*

## Brakes

| | |
|---|---|
| Disc brake pad wear limit | 1/8 inch (3 mm) |
| Drum brake shoe wear limit | 1/16 inch (1.5 mm) |
| Parking brake lever travel | Adjusted automatically |

## Ignition system

| | |
|---|---|
| Spark plug type and gap* | |
| Type | |
| 2.0L engine | Champion RE14MCC5 or equivalent |
| 2.4L engine | Champion RE14MCC5 or equivalent |
| Gap | |
| 2.0L engine | 0.048 to 0.053 inch (1.24 to 1.37 mm) |
| 2.4L engine | 0.048 to 0.053 inch (1.24 to 1.37 mm) |

**Refer to the Vehicle Emission Control Information label in the engine compartment and follow the information on the label if it differs from that shown here.*

| | |
|---|---|
| Spark plug wire resistance (approximate) | |
| Wire numbers 1 and 4 | 2,970 to 8,910 ohms |
| Wire numbers 2 and 3 | 2,360 to 7,070 ohms |
| Firing order | 1-3-4-2 |

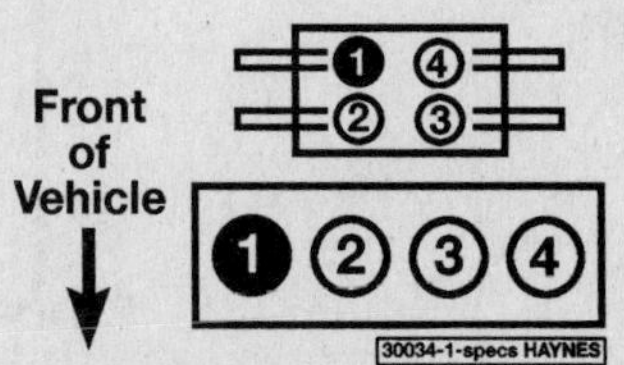


**Cylinder numbering and coil terminal locations**

## Torque specifications

| | Ft-lbs (unless otherwise indicated) | Nm |
|---|---|---|
| **Note:** *One foot-pound (ft-lb) of torque is equivalent to 12 inch-pounds (in-lbs) of torque. Torque values below approximately 15 foot-pounds are expressed in inch-pounds, because most foot-pound torque wrenches are not accurate at these smaller values.* | | |
| Automatic drivebelt tensioner | | |
| Mounting bolt | 40 | 54 |
| Pulley bolt | 20 | 27 |
| Automatic transaxle fluid pan bolts | 165 in-lbs | 19 |
| Engine oil drain plug | 20 | 27 |
| Manual transaxle drain plug | | |
| T350 transaxle | 21 | 28 |
| G288 transaxle (turbo models) | 29 | 39 |
| Manual transaxle fill plug (G288 transaxle) | 29 | 39 |
| Spark plugs | 156 in-lbs | 17.5 |
| Wheel lug nuts | 100 | 135 |

**Engine compartment layout (left-hand drive with a 2.4L engine)**

1. *Brake fluid reservoir*
2. *Air filter housing*
3. *Battery (under air filter housing)*
4. *Radiator hose*
5. *PCV valve*
6. *Automatic transaxle fluid dipstick*
7. *Engine oil dipstick*
8. *Cooling system pressure cap*
9. *Engine oil filler cap*
10. *Spark plug/wire*
11. *Power steering fluid reservoir*
12. *Windshield/rear window washer fluid reservoir*
13. *Coolant reservoir*

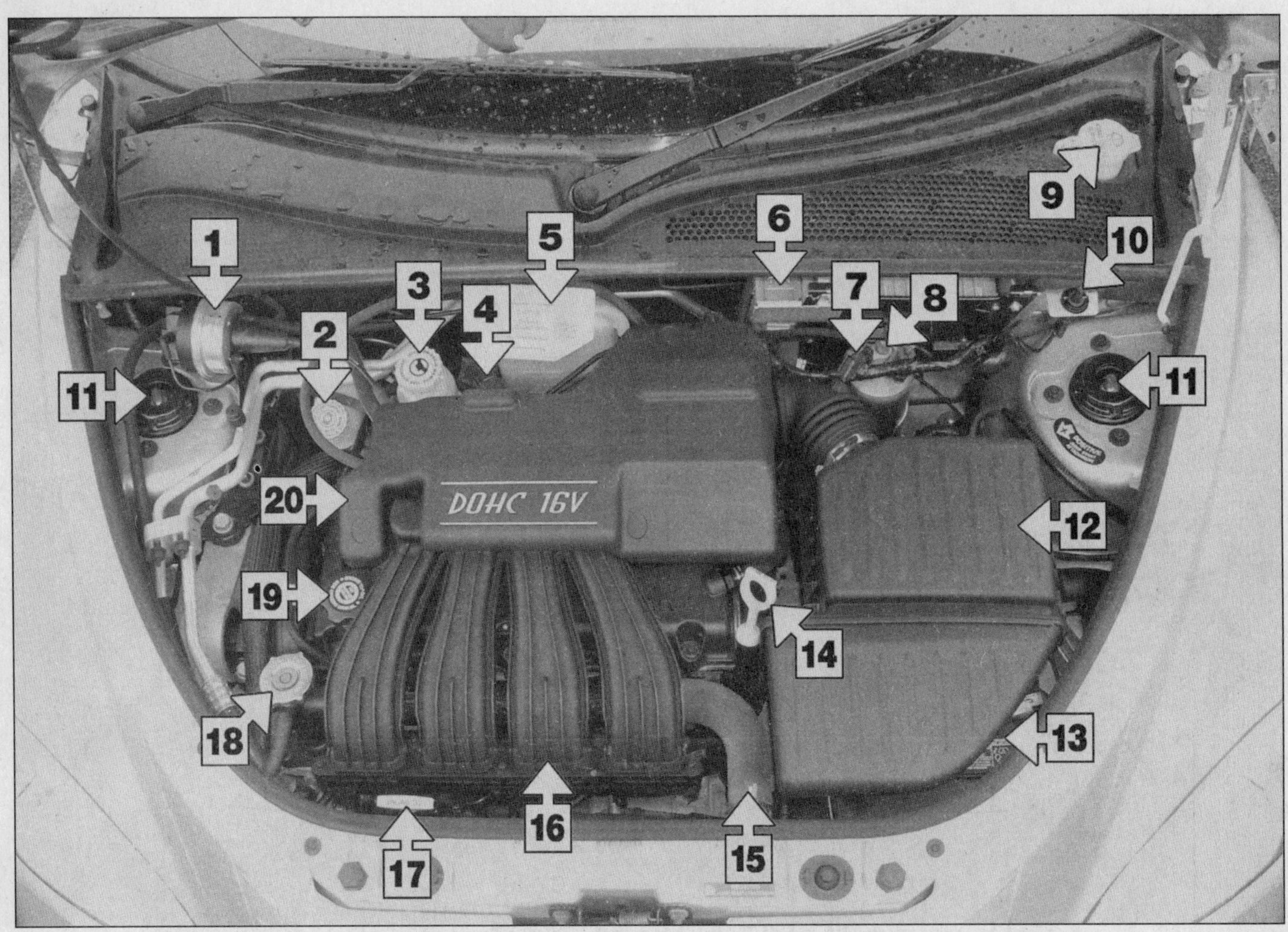


**Engine compartment layout (right-hand drive with a 2.0L engine)**

1. *Cruise control servo unit*
2. *Brake fluid reservoir*
3. *Power steering fluid reservoir*
4. *MAP sensor*
5. *Coolant reservoir*
6. *Powertrain control module (PCM)*
7. *Intake Air Temperature sensor*
8. *Air conditioning system accumulator (receiver/dryer)*
9. *Windshield/rear window washer fluid reservoir*
10. *Hood-open switch - alarm system*
11. *Suspension strut top mounting*
12. *Air filter housing*
13. *Battery*
14. *Automatic transmission fluid dipstick*
15. *Radiator hose*
16. *Upper intake manifold*
17. *Engine oil dipstick*
18. *Cooling system pressure cap*
19. *Engine oil filler cap*
20. *Engine cover*

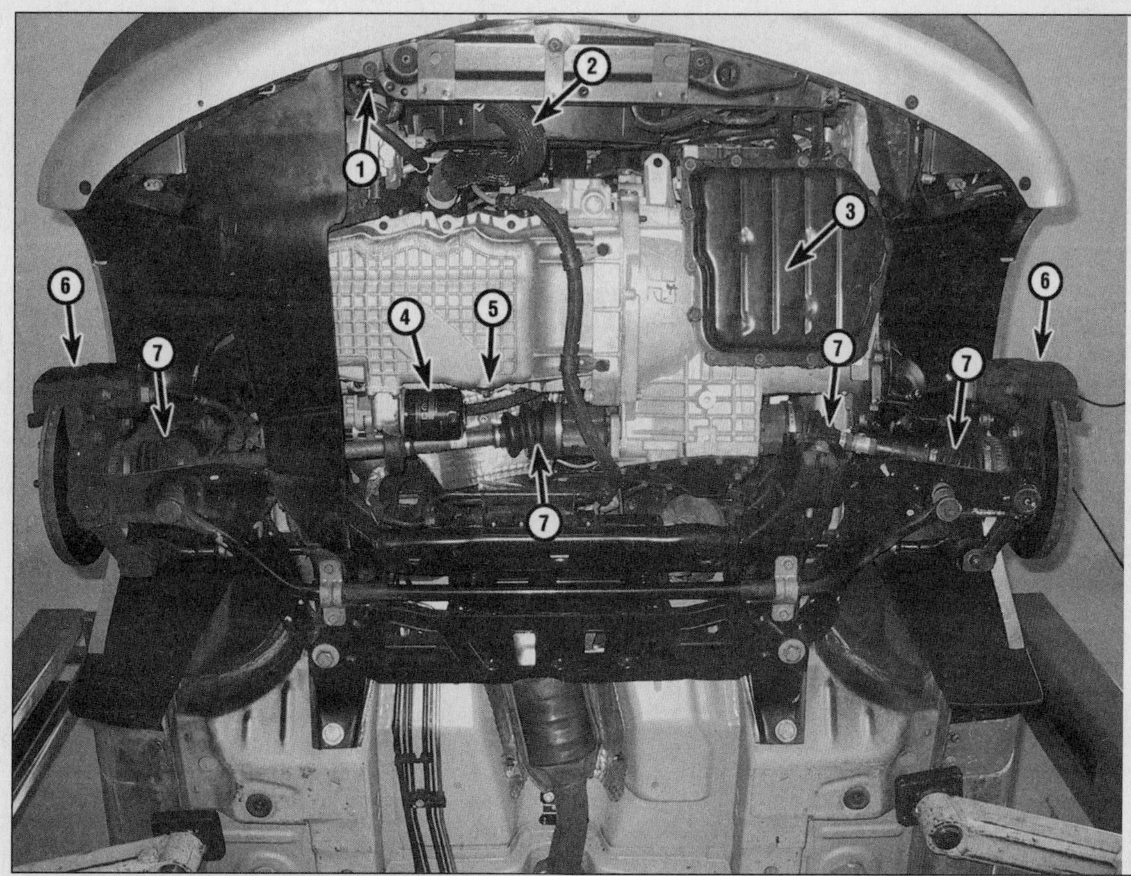


**Engine compartment underside components**

1. *Radiator drain fitting*
2. *Lower radiator hose*
3. *Automatic transaxle fluid pan*
4. *Engine oil filter*
5. *Engine oil drain plug*
6. *Brake caliper*
7. *Driveaxle boot*

**Rear underside components**

1. *Muffler*
2. *Fuel filler hose*
3. *Brake caliper*
4. *Coil spring*
5. *Fuel tank*

# 1 PT Cruiser Maintenance schedule

The following maintenance intervals are based on the assumption that the vehicle owner will be doing the maintenance or service work, as opposed to having a dealer service department do the work. Although the time/mileage intervals are loosely based on factory recommendations, most have been shortened to ensure, for example, that such items as lubricants and fluids are checked/changed at intervals that promote maximum engine/driveline service life. Also, subject to the preference of the individual owner interested in keeping his or her vehicle in peak condition at all times, and with the vehicle's ultimate resale in mind, many of the maintenance procedures may be performed more often than recommended in the following schedule. We encourage such owner initiative.

When the vehicle is new it should be serviced initially by a factory authorized dealer service department to protect the factory warranty. In many cases the initial maintenance check is done at no cost to the owner (check with your dealer service department for more information).

## Every 250 miles or weekly, whichever comes first

Check the engine oil level (see Section 4)
Check the engine coolant level (see Section 4)
Check the windshield washer fluid level (see Section 4)
Check the brake and clutch fluid level (see Section 4)
Check the tires and tire pressures (see Section 5)
Check the automatic transaxle fluid level (see Section 6)
Check the power steering fluid level (see Section 7)
Check the operation of all lights
Check the horn operation

## Every 3,000 miles or 3 months, whichever comes first

Change the engine oil and filter (see Section 8)*

## Every 7,500 miles or 6 months, whichever comes first

Check and clean the battery and terminals (see Section 9)
Check the cooling system hoses and connections for leaks and damage (see Section 10)
Check the condition of all underhood hoses and connections (see Section 11)
Check the wiper blade condition (see Section 12)
Rotate the tires (see Section 13)
Check for freeplay in the steering linkage and balljoints (see Section 14)
Check the suspension components (see Section 14)
Check the exhaust pipes and hangers (see Section 15)
Check the manual transaxle lubricant level (see Section 16)
Check the driveaxle boots (see Section 17)

## Every 15,000 miles or 12 months, whichever comes first

*All items listed above, plus:*

Check the brake system (see Section 18)
Check the fuel system hoses and connections for leaks and damage (see Section 19)
Check the drivebelts and adjust if necessary (see Section 20)
Replace the cabin air filter (see Chapter 3)

## Every 30,000 miles or 24 months, whichever comes first

*All items listed above, plus:*

Lubricate the body hinges and locks (see Section 21)*
Replace the air filter element (see Section 22)*
Change the automatic transaxle fluid and filter (see Section 23)*
Change the manual transaxle lubricant (see Section 24)*
Drain and replace the engine coolant (unless filled with Mopar 5 year/100,000 mile coolant) (see Section 25)
Check the fuel evaporative emission control system and hoses (see Section 26)
Replace the spark plugs (non-platinum type) (see Section 27)

## Every 60,000 miles or 48 months, whichever comes first

*All items listed above, plus:*

Replace the drivebelts (see Section 20)
Replace spark plug wires (see Section 28)
Check and replace, if necessary, the PCV valve (see Section 29)*

## Every 60 months (regardless of mileage)

Service the cooling system (drain, flush and refill) (Section 25)

## Every 90,000 miles or 72 months, whichever comes first

Replace the timing belt (see Chapter 2A)

## Every 100,000 miles or 84 months, whichever comes first

Replace the spark plugs (platinum or iridium spark plugs) (see Section 27)*

**This item is affected by "severe" operating conditions as described below. If the vehicle in question is operated under "severe" conditions, perform all maintenance procedures marked with an asterisk (*) at the intervals specified by the mileage headings below.*

*Consider the conditions "severe" if most driving is done . . .*

In dusty areas

Towing a trailer

Idling for extended periods and/or low-speed operation

When outside temperatures remain below freezing and most trips are less than four miles

In heavy city traffic where outside temperatures regularly reach 90-degrees F or higher

## Every 15,000 miles

Check and replace, if necessary, the air filter element (see Section 22)

Change the automatic transaxle fluid and filter (see Section 23)

Change the manual transaxle lubricant (see Section 24)

## Every 30,000 miles

Check and replace, if necessary, the PCV valve (see Section 29)

## Every 48,000 miles

Change the brake fluid by bleeding the complete system until the fluid being bled is clear (see Chapter 9 for the bleeding procedure).

## Every 75,000 miles

Replace the spark plugs (platinum or iridium-type plugs) (see Section 27)

## 2 Introduction

This Chapter is designed to help the home mechanic maintain the PT Cruiser with the goals of maximum performance, economy, safety and reliability in mind.

Included is a master maintenance schedule, followed by procedures dealing specifically with each item on the schedule. Visual checks, adjustments, component replacement and other helpful items are included. Refer to the accompanying illustrations of the engine compartment and the underside of the vehicle for the locations of various components.

Adhering to the mileage/time maintenance schedule and following the step-by-step procedures, which is simply a preventive maintenance program, will result in maximum reliability and vehicle service life. Keep in mind that it's not possible for this comprehensive program to produce the same results if you maintain some items at the specified intervals but not others.

As you service the vehicle, you'll discover that many of the procedures can - and should - be grouped together because of the nature of the particular procedure you're performing or because of the close proximity of two otherwise unrelated components to one another.

For example, if the vehicle is raised, you should inspect the exhaust, suspension, steering and fuel systems while you're under the vehicle. When you're rotating the tires, it makes good sense to check the brakes, since the wheels are already removed. Finally, let's suppose you have to borrow or rent a torque wrench. Even if you only need it to tighten the spark plugs, you might as well check the torque of as many critical fasteners as time allows.

The first step in this maintenance program is to prepare before the actual work begins. Read through all the procedures you're planning, then gather together all the parts and tools needed. If it looks like you might run into problems during a particular job, seek advice from a mechanic or an experienced do-it-yourselfer.

### *Owner's Manual and VECI label information*

Your vehicle owner's manual was written for your year and model and contains very specific information on component locations, specifications, fuse ratings, part numbers, etc. The Owner's Manual is an important resource for the do-it-yourselfer to have; if one was not supplied with your vehicle, it can generally be ordered from a dealer parts department.

Among other important information, the Vehicle Emissions Control Information (VECI) label contains specifications and procedures for applicable tune-up adjustments and, in some instances, spark plugs (see Chapter 6 for more information on the VECI label). The information on this label is the exact maintenance data recommended by the manufacturer. This data often varies by intended operating altitude, local emissions regulations, month of manufacture, etc.

This Chapter contains procedural details, safety information and more ambitious maintenance intervals than you might find in manufacturer's literature. However, you may also find procedures or specifications in your Owner's Manual or VECI label that differ with what's printed here. In these cases, the Owner's Manual or VECI label can be considered correct, since it is specific to your particular vehicle.

## 3 Tune-up general information

The term "tune-up" is used in this manual to represent a combination of individual operations rather than one specific procedure.

The engine will be kept in relatively good running condition and the need for additional work will be minimized if the routine maintenance schedule is followed closely and frequent checks are made of fluid levels and high wear items, as suggested throughout this manual from the time the vehicle is new.

More likely than not, however, there will be times when the engine is running poorly due to lack of regular maintenance. This is even more likely if a used vehicle, which hasn't received regular and frequent maintenance checks, is purchased. In such cases, an engine tune-up will be needed outside of the regular routine maintenance intervals.

The first step in any tune-up or diagnostic procedure to help correct a poor running engine is a cylinder compression check. A compression check (see Chapter 2, Part B) will help determine the condition of internal engine components and should be used as a guide for tune-up and repair procedures. For instance, if a compression check indicates serious internal engine wear, a conventional tune-up will not improve the performance of the engine and would be a waste of time and money. Because of its importance, someone with the right equipment and the knowledge to use it properly should do the compression check.

The following procedures are those most often needed to bring a generally poor running engine back into a proper state of tune:

4.2 The engine oil dipstick is located at the front of the engine and is clearly marked

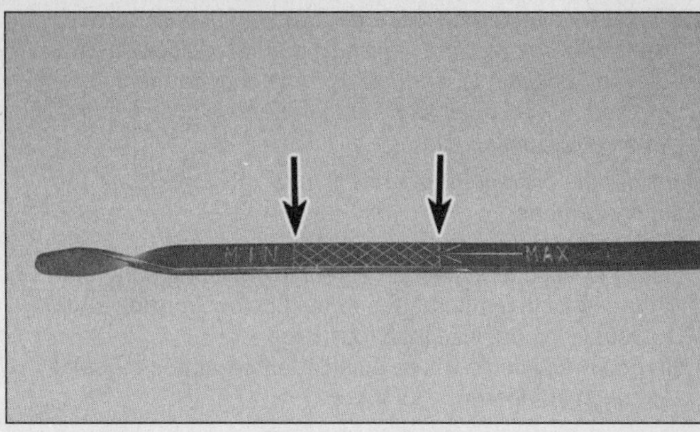


4.4 The oil level should be between the MIN and MAX marks, near the top of the cross-hatched area on the dipstick - if it isn't, add enough oil to bring the level up to or near the upper mark (do not overfill)

## Minor tune-up

Check all engine related fluids (see Section 4)
Clean and inspect the battery (see Section 9)
Check all underhood hoses (see Section 11)
Check and adjust the drivebelts (see Section 20)
Check the air filter (see Section 22)
Service the cooling system (see Section 25)
Replace the spark plugs (see Section 27)
Check the PCV valve (see Section 29)

## Major tune-up

*All items listed under Minor tune-up plus . . .*

Check the fuel system (see Section 19)
Replace the air filter (see Section 22)
Replace the spark plug wires (see Section 28)
Check the charging system (see Chapter 5)

## 4 Fluid level checks (every 250 miles or weekly)

**Note:** *The following are fluid level checks to be done on a 250 mile or weekly basis. Additional fluid level checks can be found in specific maintenance procedures that follow. Regardless of the intervals, develop the habit of checking under the vehicle periodically for evidence of fluid leaks.*

1 Fluids are an essential part of the lubrication, cooling, brake and window washer systems. Because the fluids gradually become depleted and/or contaminated during normal operation of the vehicle, they must be replenished periodically. See *Recommended lubricants and fluids* at the beginning of this Chapter before adding fluid to any of the following components. **Note:** *The vehicle must be on level ground when fluid levels are checked.*

### Engine oil

*Refer to illustrations 4.2, 4.4 and 4.5*

2 Engine oil level is checked with a dipstick that is located on the side of the engine facing the front of the vehicle **(see illustration)**. The dipstick extends through a tube and into the oil pan at the bottom of the engine.

3 The oil level should be checked before the vehicle has been driven, or about 5 minutes after the engine has been shut off. If the oil is checked immediately after driving the vehicle, some of the oil will remain in the upper engine components, resulting in an inaccurate reading on the dipstick.

4 Pull the dipstick out of the tube and wipe all the oil off the end with a clean rag or paper towel. Insert the clean dipstick all the way back into the tube, then pull it out again. Note the oil level at the end of the dipstick. Add oil as necessary to bring the oil level to the top of the cross-hatched area, or MAX mark **(see illustration)**.

5 Oil is added to the engine after removing a cap located on the valve cover **(see illustration)**. The cap will be marked "Engine oil". Use a funnel to prevent spills as the oil is added.

6 Don't allow the level to drop below the MIN mark on the dipstick or engine damage may occur. On the other hand, don't overfill the engine by adding too much oil - it may result in oil aeration and loss of oil pressure and also could result in oil fouled spark plugs, oil leaks or seal failures.

7 Checking the oil level is an important

4.5 Turn the oil filler cap counterclockwise to remove it

4.9 Maintain the coolant level near the FULL HOT mark on the reservoir

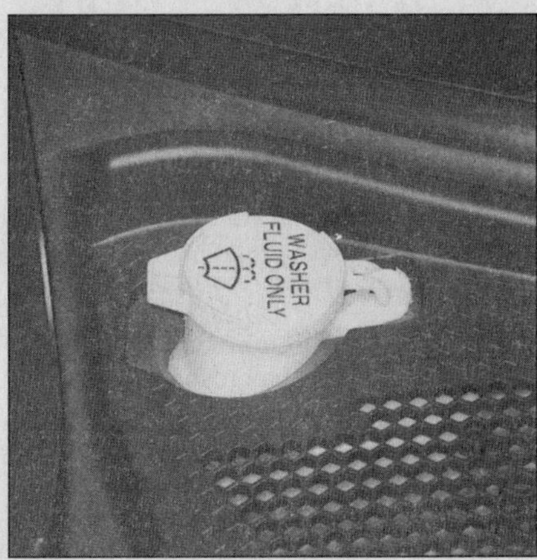


**4.14 Flip up the cap to add washer fluid**

**4.17 Brake fluid level, indicated on the translucent white plastic brake fluid reservoir, should be kept at the upper (FULL) mark**

preventive maintenance step. A consistently low oil level indicates oil leakage through damaged seals, defective gaskets or past worn rings or valve guides. If the oil looks milky in color or has water droplets in it, the block or head may be cracked and leaking coolant is entering the crankcase. The engine should be checked immediately. The condition of the oil should also be checked. Each time you check the oil level, slide your thumb and index finger up the dipstick before wiping off the oil. If you see small dirt or metal particles clinging to the dipstick, the oil should be changed (see Section 8).

## Engine coolant

*Refer to illustration 4.9*

**Warning:** *Do not allow antifreeze to come in contact with your skin or painted surfaces of the vehicle. Flush contaminated areas immediately with plenty of water. Don't store new coolant or leave old coolant lying around where it's accessible to children or pets – they're attracted by its sweet smell. Ingestion of even a small amount of coolant can be fatal! Wipe up garage floor and drip pan spills immediately. Keep antifreeze containers covered and repair cooling system leaks as soon as they're noticed.*

8 All vehicles covered by this manual are equipped with a pressurized coolant recovery system. A white plastic coolant reservoir is located at the rear of the engine compartment, on the center of the firewall.

9 The coolant level in the reservoir should be checked regularly. **Warning:** *Do not remove the cooling system pressure cap to check the coolant level when the engine is warm!* The level in the reservoir varies with the temperature of the engine. When the engine is cold, the coolant level should be slightly above the ADD mark on the reservoir. Once the engine has warmed up, the level should be at or near the FULL HOT mark. If it isn't, allow the engine to cool, then remove the cap from the tank and add a 50/50 mixture of ethylene glycol based antifreeze and water **(see illustration)**.

10 Drive the vehicle and recheck the coolant level. If only a small amount of coolant is required to bring the system up to the proper level, water can be used. However, repeated additions of water will dilute the antifreeze and water solution. In order to maintain the proper ratio of antifreeze and water, always top up the coolant level with the correct mixture. Don't use rust inhibitors or additives. An empty plastic milk jug or bleach bottle makes an excellent container for mixing coolant.

11 If the coolant level drops consistently, there may be a leak in the system. Inspect the radiator, hoses, filler cap, drain plugs and water pump (see Section 10). If no leaks are noted, have the pressure cap pressure tested by a service station.

12 If you have to remove the pressure cap, wait until the engine has cooled completely, then wrap a thick cloth around the cap and turn it to the first stop. If coolant or steam escapes, or if you hear a hissing noise, let the engine cool down longer, then remove the cap.

13 Check the condition of the coolant as well. It should be relatively clear. If it's brown or rust colored, the system should be drained, flushed and refilled. Even if the coolant appears to be normal, the corrosion inhibitors wear out, so it must be replaced at the specified intervals.

## Windshield and rear window washer fluid

*Refer to illustration 4.14*

14 The fluid for the windshield and rear window washer system is stored in a plastic reservoir. The reservoir level should be maintained about one inch (25 mm) below the filler cap. The reservoir is accessible after opening the hood and is located behind the right (passenger's) side of the engine compartment, under the cowl grille screen **(see illustration)**.

15 In milder climates, plain water can be used in the reservoir, but it should be kept no more than two-thirds full to allow for expansion if the water freezes. In colder climates, use windshield washer system antifreeze, available at any auto parts store, to lower the freezing point of the fluid. Mix the antifreeze with water in accordance with the manufacturer's directions on the container. **Caution:** *DO NOT use cooling system antifreeze - it will damage the vehicle's paint. To help prevent icing in cold weather, warm the windshield with the defroster before using the washer.*

## Brake and clutch fluid

*Refer to illustration 4.17*

16 The brake fluid reservoir is located on top of the brake master cylinder on the driver's side of the engine compartment near the firewall. The clutch fluid reservoir is mounted on the firewall, next to the brake master cylinder.

17 The fluid level should be maintained at the upper (FULL or MAX) mark on either reservoir **(see illustration)**.

18 If additional fluid is necessary to bring the level up, use a rag to clean all dirt off the top of the reservoir to prevent contamination of the system. Also, make sure all painted surfaces around the reservoir are covered, since brake fluid will ruin paint. Carefully pour new, clean brake fluid obtained from a sealed container into the reservoir. Be sure the specified fluid is used; mixing different types of brake fluid can cause damage to the system. See *Recommended lubricants and fluids* at the beginning of this Chapter or your owner's manual.

19 At this time the fluid and the master cylinder should be inspected for contamination. Normally the brake hydraulic system won't need periodic draining and refilling, but if rust deposits, dirt particles or water droplets are observed in the fluid, the system should be dismantled, cleaned and refilled with fresh fluid. Over time brake fluid will absorb moisture from the air. Moisture in the fluid lowers the fluid boiling point; if the fluid boils, the brakes will become ineffective. Normal brake fluid is clear in color. If the brake fluid is dark brown in color, it's a good idea to replace it (see Chapter 9).

20 Reinstall the fluid reservoir cap.

21 The brake fluid in the master cylinder will drop slightly as the brake lining material at each wheel wears down during normal operation. If the master cylinder requires repeated replenishing to maintain the correct level, there is a leak in the brake system that should be corrected immediately. Check all brake lines and connections, along with the calipers (disc brakes), wheel cylinders (drum brakes) and power brake booster (see Section 18 and Chapter 9 for more information).

22 If you discover that the reservoir is empty or nearly empty, the system should be thoroughly inspected, refilled and then bled (see Chapter 8 for clutch system bleeding and Chapter 9 for brake system bleeding).

## 5 Tire and tire pressure checks (every 250 miles or weekly)

*Refer to illustrations 5.2, 5.3, 5.4a, 5.4b and 5.8*

1 Periodic inspection of the tires may spare you the inconvenience of being stranded with a flat tire. It can also provide you with vital information regarding possible problems in the steering and suspension systems before major damage occurs.

2 Original tires on this vehicle are equipped with 1/2-inch (13 mm) wide bands that will appear when tread depth reaches 1/16-inch (1.5 mm), at which point the tires can be considered worn out. Tread wear can be monitored with a simple, inexpensive device known as a tread depth indicator **(see illustration)**.

3 Note any abnormal tread wear **(see illustration)**. Tread pattern irregularities such as cupping, flat spots and more wear on one side than the other are indications of front end alignment and/or balance problems. If any of these conditions are noted, take the vehicle to a tire shop or service station to correct the problem.

4 Look closely for cuts, punctures and embedded nails or tacks. Sometimes a tire will hold air pressure for a short time or leak down very slowly after a nail has embedded itself in the tread. If a slow leak persists, check the valve stem core to make sure it's tight **(see illustration)**. Examine the tread for an object that may have embedded itself in the tire or for a "plug" that may have begun to leak (radial tire punctures are repaired with a plug that's installed in a puncture). If a puncture is suspected, it can be easily verified by spraying a solution of soapy water onto the puncture area **(see illustration)**. The soapy solution will bubble if there's a leak. Unless the puncture is unusually large, a tire shop or service station can usually repair the tire.

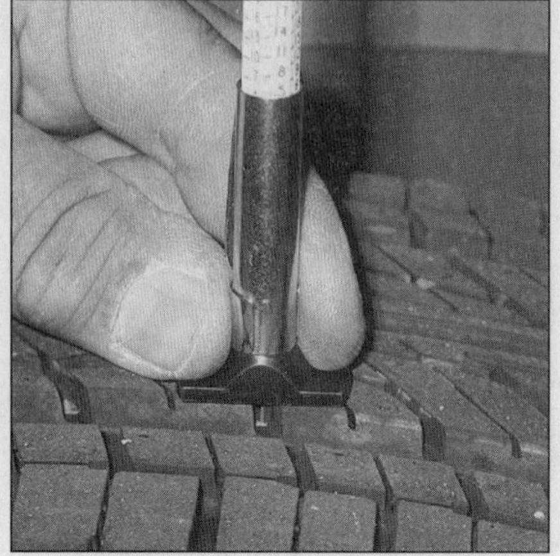

**5.2 Use a tire tread depth indicator to monitor tire wear - they are available at auto parts stores or service stations and are relatively inexpensive**

5 Carefully inspect the inner sidewall of each tire for evidence of brake fluid leakage. If you see any, inspect the brakes immediately.

6 Correct air pressure adds miles to the life span of the tires, improves mileage and enhances overall ride quality. Tire pressure cannot be accurately estimated by looking at a tire, especially if it's a radial. A tire pressure gauge is essential. Keep an accurate gauge in the vehicle. The pressure gauges attached to the nozzles of air hoses at gas stations are often inaccurate.

7 Always check tire pressure when the tires are cold. Cold, in this case, means the vehicle has not been driven over a mile in the three hours preceding a tire pressure check. A pressure rise of four to eight pounds is not uncommon once the tires are warm.

8 Unscrew the valve cap protruding from the wheel or hubcap and push the gauge firmly onto the valve stem **(see illustration)**. Compare the reading on the gauge to the recommended tire pressure shown on the placard on the end of the driver's side door.

**UNDERINFLATION**

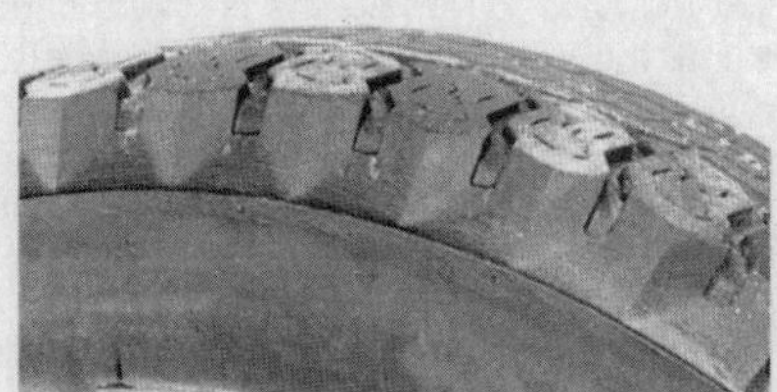

**CUPPING**

**Cupping may be caused by:**

- **Underinflation and/or mechanical irregularities such as out-of-balance condition of wheel and/or tire, and bent or damaged wheel.**
- **Loose or worn steering tie-rod or steering idler arm.**
- **Loose, damaged or worn front suspension parts.**

**OVERINFLATION**

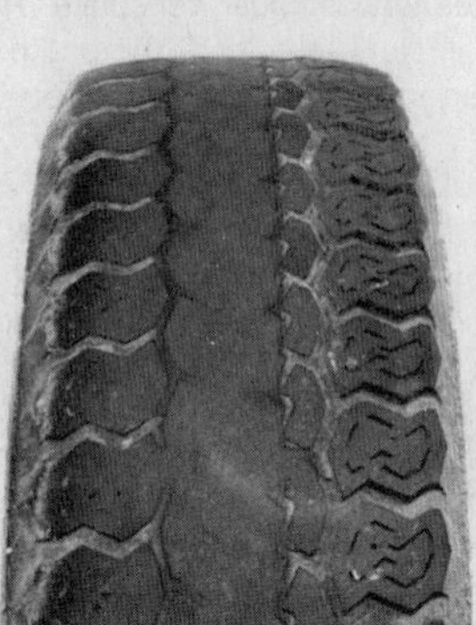

**INCORRECT TOE-IN OR EXTREME CAMBER**

**FEATHERING DUE TO MISALIGNMENT**

**5.3 This chart will help you determine the condition of the tires, the probable cause(s) of abnormal wear and the corrective action necessary**

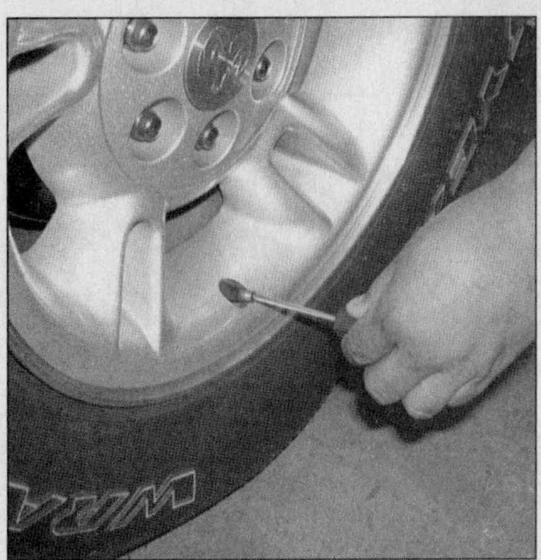
5.4a If a tire loses air on a steady basis, check the valve stem core first to make sure it's snug (special inexpensive wrenches are commonly available at auto parts stores)

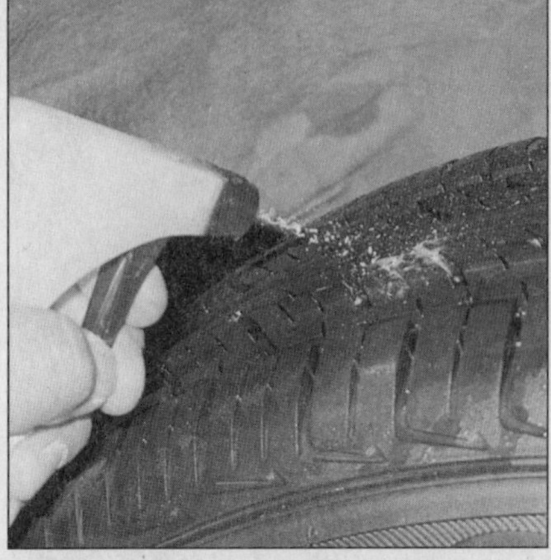
5.4b If the valve stem core is tight, raise the corner of the vehicle with the low tire and spray a soapy water solution onto the tread as the tire is turned slowly - leaks will cause small bubbles to appear

5.8 To extend the life of the tires, check the air pressure at least once a week with an accurate gauge (don't forget the spare!)

Be sure to reinstall the valve cap to keep dirt and moisture out of the valve stem mechanism. Check all four tires and, if necessary, add enough air to bring them up to the recommended pressure.

9 Don't forget to keep the spare tire inflated to the specified pressure (refer to your owner's manual or the tire sidewall). Note that the pressure recommended for the compact spare is higher than for the tires on the vehicle.

## 6 Automatic transaxle fluid level check (every 250 miles or weekly)

*Refer to illustrations 6.3 and 6.4*

1 Fluid inside the transaxle should be at normal operating temperature to get an accurate reading on the dipstick. This is done by driving the vehicle for several miles, making frequent starts and stops to allow the transaxle to shift through all gears.

2 Park the vehicle on a level surface and apply the parking brake. With the engine running, apply the brakes and place the gear selector lever momentarily in Reverse, then Drive and repeat the sequence again ending with the gear selector in the Park position.

3 With the engine still running, locate the transaxle fluid dipstick near the air filter housing. The dipstick marked "TRANS FLUID" **(see illustration)**. Remove the dipstick and wipe the fluid from the end with a clean rag.

4 Insert the dipstick back into the transaxle until the cap seats completely. Remove the dipstick again and note the fluid level on the end. The level should be in the area marked HOT **(see illustration)**. If the fluid isn't hot (temperature approximately 100-degrees F), the level should be in the area marked WARM.

5 If the fluid level is at or below the ADD mark on the dipstick, add just enough of the specified fluid (see *Recommended lubricants and fluids* at the beginning of this Chapter) to raise the level to within the marks indicated for the appropriate temperature. Fluid should be slowly added into the dipstick tube, using a funnel to prevent spills.

6 DO NOT overfill the transaxle. Never allow the fluid level to go above the upper end of the cross-hatched area on the dipstick - it could cause internal transaxle damage. The best way to prevent overfilling is to add fluid a little at a time, driving the vehicle and checking the level between additions.

7 Use only transaxle fluid specified by the manufacturer. This information can be found in the *Recommended lubricants and fluids* Section at the beginning of this Chapter or in your owner's manual.

8 The condition of the fluid should also be checked along with the level. If it's a dark reddish-brown color, or if it smells burned, it should be changed. If you're in doubt about the condition of the fluid, purchase some new fluid and compare the two for color and odor.

## 7 Power steering fluid level check (every 250 miles or weekly)

*Refer to illustrations 7.2 and 7.5*

1 Unlike manual steering, the power steering system relies on hydraulic fluid that may, over a period of time, require replenishing.

6.3 The automatic transaxle dipstick is located at the left end of the engine, near the air filter housing, and is clearly marked

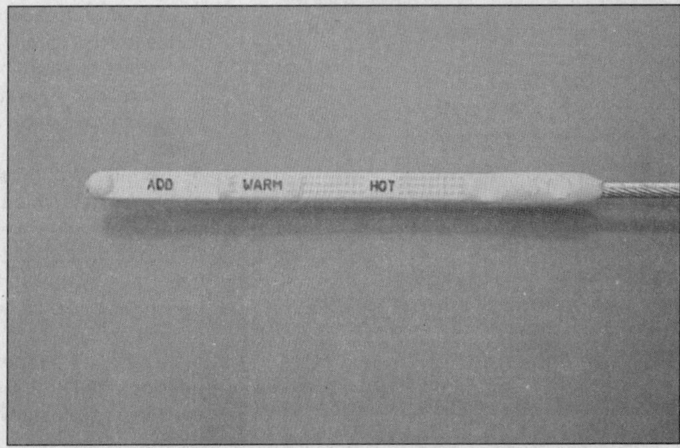

6.4 Check the fluid with the transaxle at normal operating temperature - the level should be kept in the HOT range

7.2 The power steering fluid reservoir is located on the right (passenger's) side of the engine compartment

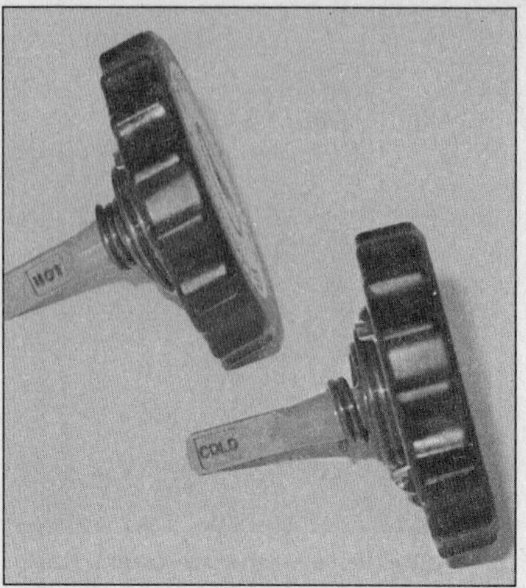


7.5 The power steering fluid dipstick is marked on both sides for checking the fluid level cold or hot

2 The fluid reservoir for the power steering pump is located on the right (passenger's) side of the engine compartment **(see illustration)**.

3 The power steering fluid level can be checked with the engine either hot or cold; one side of the dipstick is marked HOT, and the other side is marked COLD.

4 With the engine off, use a rag to clean the reservoir cap and the area around the cap. This will help prevent dirt from falling into the reservoir when the cap is removed.

5 Turn and pull out the reservoir cap, which has a dipstick attached to it. Wipe the fluid off the dipstick with a clean rag. Reinstall the cap, then remove it again and note the fluid level. It should be at the appropriate mark on the dipstick in relation to the fluid temperature **(see illustration)**.

6 If additional fluid is required, pour the specified type fluid (see *Recommended lubricants and fluids* at the beginning of this Chapter or your owner's manual) directly into the reservoir using a funnel to prevent spills.

7 If the reservoir requires frequent topping up, all power steering hoses, hose connections, the power steering pump and the steering gear should be carefully examined for leaks.

8.8 To avoid rounding off the corners, use the correct size box-end wrench or a socket to remove the engine oil drain plug

## 8 Engine oil and filter change (every 3,000 miles or 3 months)

*Refer to illustrations 8.3, 8.8, 8.13 and 8.18*

1 Frequent oil changes are the most important preventive maintenance procedures that can be performed by the home mechanic. When engine oil ages, it gets diluted and contaminated, which ultimately leads to premature engine wear.

2 Although some sources recommend oil filter changes every other oil change, a new filter should be installed every time the oil is changed.

3 Gather together all necessary tools and materials before beginning this procedure **(see illustration)**. **Note:** *To avoid rounding off the corners of the drain plug, use a box-end type wrench or socket.* In addition, you should have plenty of clean rags and newspapers handy to mop up any spills.

4 Raise the front of the vehicle and support it securely on jackstands. **Warning:** *Never work under a vehicle that is supported only by a jack!*

5 If this is your first oil change on the vehicle, familiarize yourself with the locations of the oil drain plug and the oil filter. Since the engine and exhaust components will be warm during the actual work, it's a good idea to figure out any potential problems beforehand.

6 Allow the engine to warm up to normal operating temperature. If oil or tools are needed, use the warm-up time to gather everything necessary for the job. The correct type of oil to buy for your application can be found in the *Recommended lubricants and fluids* Section at the beginning of this Chapter or your owner's manual.

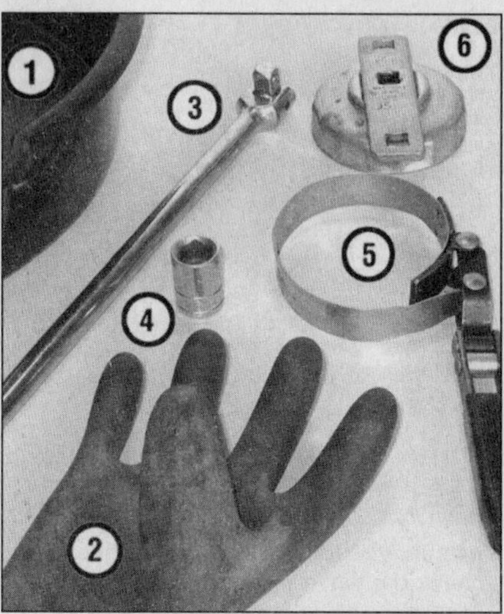


8.3 These tools are required when changing the engine oil and filter

*1* ***Drain pan*** *- It should be fairly shallow in depth, but wide to prevent spills and capable of holding at least 5 quarts*
*2* ***Rubber gloves*** *- When removing the drain plug and filter, you will get oil on your hands (the gloves will prevent burns)*
*3* ***Breaker bar*** *- Sometimes the oil drain plug is tight, and a long breaker bar is needed to loosen it*
*4* ***Socket*** *- To be used with the breaker bar or a ratchet (must be the correct size to fit the drain plug - six-point preferred)*
*5* ***Filter wrench*** *- This is a metal band-type wrench, which requires clearance around the filter to be effective*
*6* ***Filter wrench*** *- This type fits on the bottom of the filter and can be turned with a ratchet or breaker bar (different size wrenches are available for different types of filters)*

7 Move all necessary tools, rags and newspapers under the vehicle. Place a drain pan capable of holding at least 5 quarts under the drain plug. Keep in mind that the oil will initially flow from the engine with some force, so position the pan accordingly.

8 Being careful not to touch any of the hot exhaust components, use the breaker bar and socket or box-end wrench to remove the drain plug **(see illustration)**. Depending on how hot the oil is, you may want to wear gloves while unscrewing the plug the final few turns.

9 Allow the oil to drain into the pan. It may be necessary to move the pan further under the engine when the oil flow slows to a trickle.

10 After all the oil has completely drained, clean the plug thoroughly with a rag. Small metal particles may cling to it and would immediately contaminate the new oil.

11 Clean the area around the drain plug opening and reinstall the plug. Tighten it to the torque listed in this Chapter's Specifications.

12 Next, carefully move the drain pan into position under the oil filter.

8.13 Since the oil filter is probably very tight, you'll need a special wrench for removal

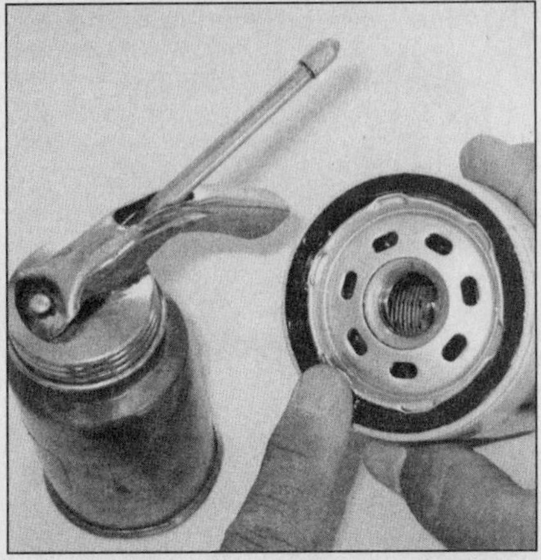

8.18 Lubricate the oil filter gasket with clean engine oil before installing the filter on the engine

13 Now use the filter wrench to loosen the oil filter in a counterclockwise direction **(see illustration)**.

14 Sometimes the oil filter is on so tight it cannot be loosened, or it's positioned in an area inaccessible with a conventional filter wrench. Other type of tools which fit over the end of the filter and turned with a ratchet or breaker bar are available and may be better for removing the filter.

15 Completely unscrew the old filter. Be careful, it's full of oil. Empty the old oil inside the filter into the drain pan.

16 Compare the old filter with the new one to make sure they're identical.

17 Use a clean rag to remove all oil, dirt and sludge from the area where the oil filter seals on the engine. Check the old filter to make sure the rubber gasket isn't stuck to the engine mounting surface.

18 Apply a light coat of clean engine oil to the rubber gasket on the new oil filter **(see illustration)**.

19 Attach the new filter to the engine, following the tightening directions printed on the filter canister or packing box. Most filter manufacturers recommend against using a filter wrench due to the possibility of overtightening and damage to the seal.

20 Remove all tools and materials from under the vehicle, being careful not to spill the oil in the drain pan. Lower the vehicle.

21 Working inside the engine compartment, locate and remove the oil filler cap from the engine valve cover **(see illustration 4.5)**.

22 Using a funnel to prevent spills, pour the specified type and amount of new oil required (see this Chapter's Specifications) into the engine. Wait a few minutes to allow the oil to drain down to the pan, then check the level on the dipstick (see Section 4 if necessary). If the oil level is at or above the lower mark on the dipstick, start the engine and allow the new oil to circulate.

23 Run the engine for only about a minute, then shut it off. Immediately look under the vehicle and check for leaks at the oil pan drain plug and around the oil filter. If either one is leaking, tighten it with a bit more force.

24 With the new oil circulated and the filter now completely full, wait a few minutes for the oil to drain back down into the pan then recheck the oil level on the dipstick. If necessary, add enough oil to bring the level to the upper mark on the dipstick. DO NOT overfill!

25 During the first few trips after an oil change, make it a point to check for leaks and keep a close watch on the oil level.

26 The old oil drained from the engine cannot be reused in its present state and should be disposed of. Check with your local auto parts store, disposal facility or environmental agency to see if they will accept the oil for recycling. After the oil has cooled it can be drained into a container (capped plastic jugs, topped bottles, milk cartons, etc.) for transport to one of these disposal sites. Don't dispose of the oil by pouring it on the ground or down a drain!

## 9 Battery check, maintenance and charging (every 7,500 miles or 6 months)

**Warning:** *Certain precautions must be followed when checking and servicing the battery. Hydrogen gas, which is highly explosive, is produced by the battery. Keep lighted tobacco, open flames, bare light bulbs or other possible sources of ignition away from the battery. Furthermore, the electrolyte inside the battery is sulfuric acid which is highly corrosive and can burn your skin and cause severe injury to your eyes. Always wear eye protection! It will also destroy clothing and ruin painted surfaces.*

### Servicing

*Refer to illustrations 9.1, 9.5, 9.6, 9.7a, 9.7b and 9.8*

1 A routine preventive maintenance program for the battery in your vehicle is the only way to ensure quick and reliable starts. But before performing any battery maintenance, make sure that you have the proper equipment necessary to work safely around the battery **(see illustration)**.

2 Prior to servicing the battery always turn the engine and all accessories off and disconnect the cable from the negative terminal of the battery.

3 The battery is located in the left side of the engine compartment, under the front part of the air filter housing. To gain access to the battery, remove the cover from the air filter housing (see Section 22).

4 Inspect the external condition of the bat-

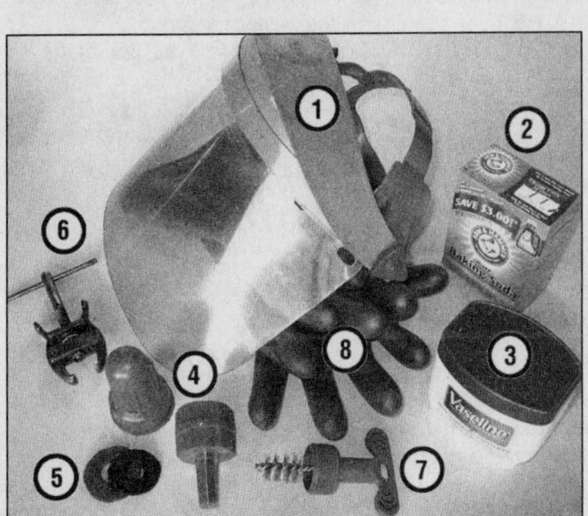


9.1 Tools and materials required for battery maintenance

1 ***Face shield/safety goggles*** *- When removing corrosion with a brush, the acidic particles can easily fly up into your eyes*
2 ***Baking soda*** *- A solution of baking soda and water can be used to neutralize corrosion*
3 ***Petroleum jelly*** *- A layer of this on the battery posts will help prevent corrosion*
4 ***Battery post/cable cleaner*** *- This wire brush cleaning tool will remove all traces of corrosion from the battery posts and cable clamps*
5 ***Treated felt washers*** *- Placing one of these on each post, directly under the cable clamps, will help prevent corrosion*
6 ***Puller*** *- Sometimes the cable clamps are very difficult to pull off the posts, even after the nut/bolt has been completely loosened. This tool pulls the clamp straight up and off the post without damage*
7 ***Battery post/cable cleaner*** *- Here is another cleaning tool which is a slightly different version of Number 4 above, but it does the same thing*
8 ***Rubber gloves*** *- Another safety item to consider when servicing the battery; remember that's acid inside the battery!*

9.5 **Battery terminal corrosion usually appears as a light, fluffy powder (typical)**

Terminal end corrosion or damage.

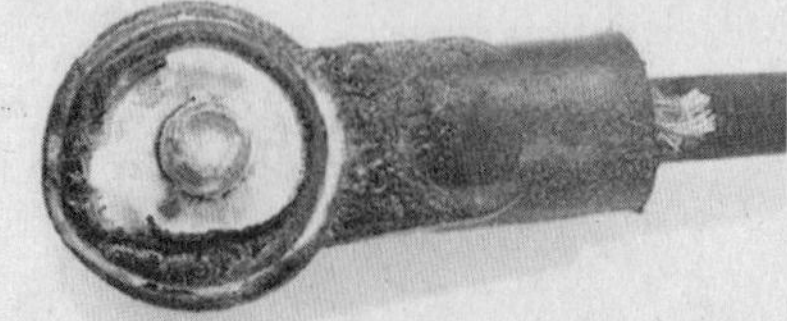

Insulation cracks.

Chafed insulation or exposed wires.

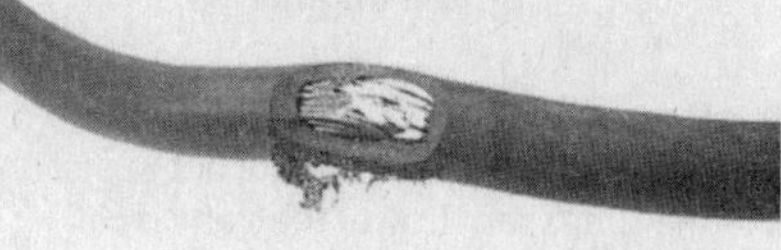

Burned or melted insulation.

**9.6 Typical battery cable problems**

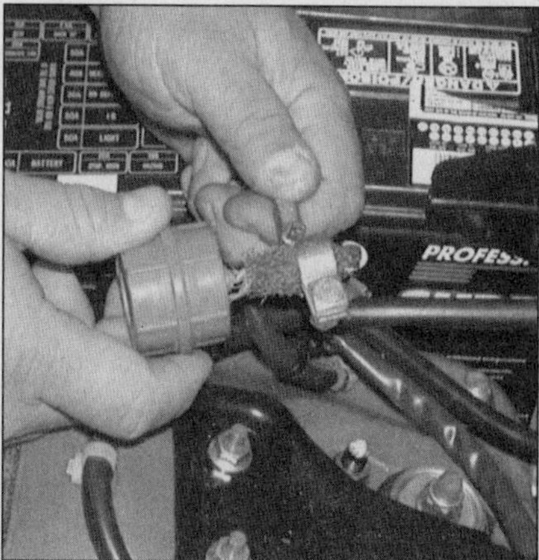

**9.7a When cleaning the cable clamps, all corrosion must be removed**

tery. Check the battery case for cracks or other damage.

5 If corrosion, which looks like white, fluffy deposits **(see illustration)** is evident, particularly around the terminals, the battery should be removed for cleaning. Loosen the cable clamp nuts, being careful to remove the ground (negative) cable first, and slide them off the terminals. Then remove the battery (see Step 8).

6 Check the entire length of each cable for cracks, worn insulation and frayed conductors **(see illustration)**.

7 Clean the cable clamps thoroughly with a battery brush **(see illustration)** and a solution of warm water and baking soda. Wash the terminals and the top of the battery case with the same solution but make sure that the solution doesn't get into the battery. When cleaning the cables, terminals and battery top, wear safety goggles and rubber gloves to prevent any solution from coming in contact with your eyes or hands. Wear old clothes too - even diluted, sulfuric acid splashed onto clothes will burn holes in them. If the terminals have been extensively corroded, clean them up with a terminal cleaner **(see illustration)**. Thoroughly wash all cleaned areas with plain water.

8 If it's necessary to remove the battery, remove the air filter housing (see Chapter 4), then loosen the clamp bolt and remove the battery from the engine compartment **(see illustration)**.

9 Inspect the battery carrier. If it's dirty or covered with corrosion, clean it with the same solution of warm water and baking soda and rinse it with clean water.

10 If the battery is a maintenance-type, it has removable cell caps which allow you to add water (use distilled water only) to the battery when the electrolyte level gets low.

11 If you are not sure what type of battery you have (some maintenance-types have recessed cell caps that resemble maintenance-free batteries), one simple way to confirm your type of battery is to look for a built-in hydrometer. Most maintenance-free batteries have built-in hydrometers that indicate the state of charge by the color displayed in the hydrometer window, since measuring the specific gravity of the electrolyte is not possible. Also check for cut-outs near the cell caps - if the caps can be removed, cut-outs are usually provided to assist with prying off the caps.

12 If your battery is a maintenance-type,

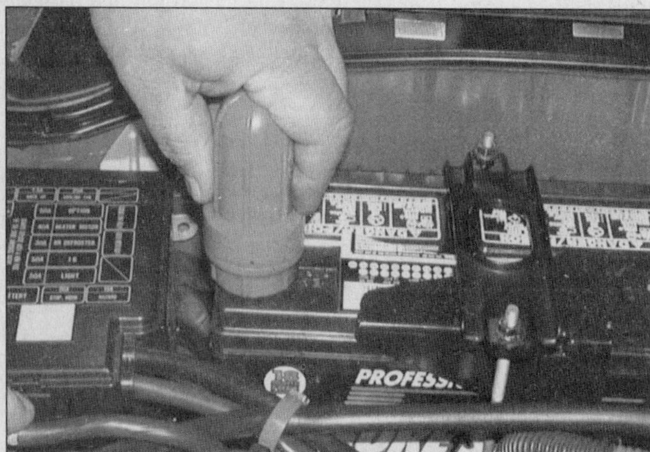

**9.7b Regardless of the type of tool used on the battery post, a clean, shiny surface should be the result (the inside of the clamp is tapered to match the taper on the post, so don't remove too much material**

**9.8 The battery is secured by a clamp at its base - to remove the battery, loosen the bolt, slide the clamp back and lift the battery out**

remove the cell caps and check the level of the electrolyte. It should be up to the split-ring inside the battery. If the level is low, add distilled water (distilled water is mineral-free, tap water contains minerals that will shorten the life of your battery) to bring the electrolyte up to the proper level.
13 Install the battery (see Chapter 5).

## Charging

**Warning:** *When batteries are being charged, hydrogen gas, which is very explosive and flammable, is produced. Do not smoke or allow open flames near a charging or a recently charged battery. Wear eye protection when near the battery during charging. Also, make sure the charger is unplugged before connecting or disconnecting the battery from the charger.*
14 Slow-rate charging is the best way to restore a battery that's discharged to the point where it will not start the engine. It's also a good way to maintain the battery charge in a vehicle that's only driven a few miles between starts. Maintaining the battery charge is particularly important in the winter when the battery must work harder to start the engine and electrical accessories that drain the battery are in greater use.
15 It's best to use a one or two-amp battery charger (sometimes called a "trickle" charger). They are the safest and put the least strain on the battery. They are also the least expensive. For a faster charge, you can use a higher amperage charger, but don't use one rated more than 1/10th the amp/hour rating of the battery. Rapid boost charges that claim to restore the power of the battery in one to two hours are hardest on the battery and can damage batteries not in good condition. This type of charging should only be used in emergency situations.
16 The average time necessary to charge a battery should be listed in the instructions that come with the charger. As a general rule, a trickle charger will charge a battery in 12 to 16 hours.
17 Remove the cover from the air filter housing for access to the battery (see Section 22).
18 On maintenance-type batteries, remove the cell caps. Make sure the electrolyte level is OK before beginning to charge the battery. Cover the holes with a clean cloth to prevent spattering electrolyte.
19 On batteries with the terminals located on the side, install bolts (with the appropriate thread size and pitch) in the terminals so the charger can be attached.
20 Connect the battery charger leads to the battery posts (positive to positive, negative to negative), then plug in the charger. Make sure it is set at 12 volts if it has a selector switch. If the battery charger does not have a built-in timer, it's a good idea to use one in case you forget - so you won't over charge the battery.
21 If you're using a charger with a rate higher than two amps, check the battery regularly during charging to make sure it doesn't overheat. If you're using a trickle charger, you can safely let the battery charge overnight after you've checked it regularly for the first couple of hours.
22 If the battery has removable cell caps, measure the specific gravity with a hydrometer every hour during the last few hours of the charging cycle. Hydrometers are available inexpensively from auto parts stores - follow the instructions that come with the hydrometer. Consider the battery charged when there's no change in the specific gravity reading for two hours and the electrolyte in the cells is outgassing (bubbling) freely. The specific gravity reading from each cell should be very close to the others. If not, the battery probably has a bad cell(s).
23 Most batteries with sealed tops have built-in hydrometers on the top that indicate the state of charge by the color displayed in the hydrometer window. Normally, a bright-colored hydrometer indicates a full charge and a dark hydrometer indicates the battery still needs charging. Check the battery manufacturer's instructions to be sure you know what the colors mean. **Note:** *It may be necessary to jiggle the battery to bring the test indicator fluid into view.*
24 If the battery has a sealed top and does not have a built-in hydrometer, you can hook up a voltmeter across the battery terminals to check the charge. A fully charged battery should read approximately 12.6 volts or higher.
25 Further information on the battery and jump starting can be found in Chapter 5 and at the front of this manual, respectively.

**Check for a chafed area that could fail prematurely.**

**Check for a soft area indicating the hose has deteriorated inside.**

**Overtightening the clamp on a hardened hose will damage the hose and cause a leak.**

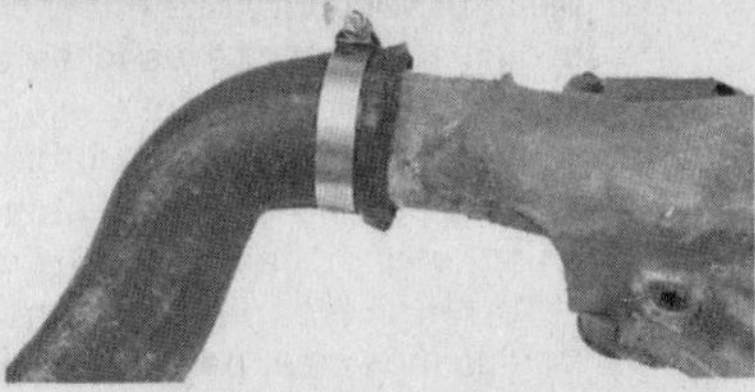

**Check each hose for swelling and oil-soaked ends. Cracks and breaks can be located by squeezing the hose.**

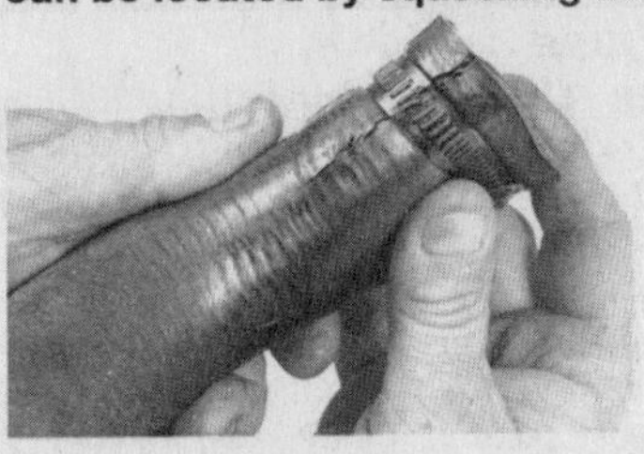

**10.4 Hoses, like drivebelts, have a habit of failing at the worst possible time - to prevent the inconvenience of a blown radiator or heater hose, inspect them carefully as shown here**

## 10 Cooling system check (every 7,500 miles or 6 months)

*Refer to illustration 10.4*

**Warning:** *The electric cooling fan(s) on these models can activate at any time the ignition switch is in the ON position. Make sure the ignition is OFF when working in the vicinity of the fan(s).*
1 Many major engine failures can be attributed to a faulty cooling system. If the vehicle is equipped with an automatic transaxle, a transmission fluid cooler is incorporated inside the radiator side tank.
2 The cooling system should be checked with the engine cold. Do this before the vehicle is driven for the day or after it has been shut off for three or four hours and the upper radiator hose feels cool to the touch.
3 Remove the cooling system pressure cap **(see the underhood photo at the beginning of this Chapter)** and thoroughly clean the cap with water. Also clean the filler neck. All traces of corrosion should be removed.
4 Carefully check the upper and lower radiator hoses along with the smaller diameter heater hoses. Inspect the entire length of each hose, replacing any that are cracked, swollen or deteriorated **(see illustration)**. Cracks may become more apparent when a hose is squeezed.
5 Also check that all hose connections are tight. If the vehicle came equipped with spring-type hose clamps which lose their tension over time, replace them with the more reliable screw-type clamps when new hoses are installed. A leak in the cooling system will usually show up as white or rust-colored deposits on the areas adjoining the leak.
6 Use compressed air, water or a soft brush to remove bugs, leaves, and other debris from the front of the radiator or air conditioning condenser. Be careful not to damage the delicate cooling fins, or cut yourself on them.
7 Finally, have the cap and system pressure tested. If you do not have a pressure tester available, most gas stations and repair shops will do this for a minimal charge.

**12.3 Remove the cap and check the wiper arm mounting nut for tightness**

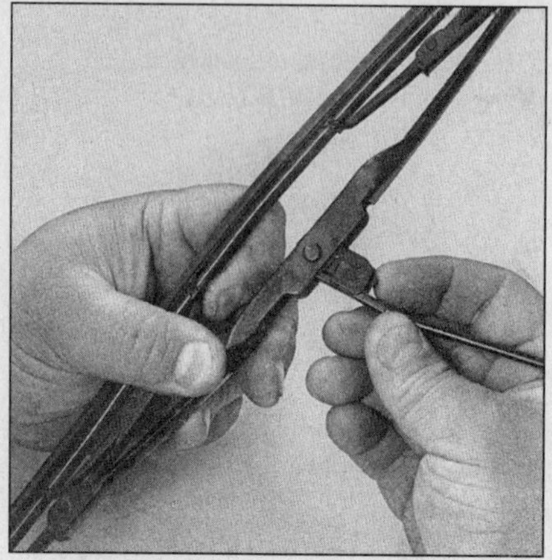

**12.5a Depress the release lever . . .**

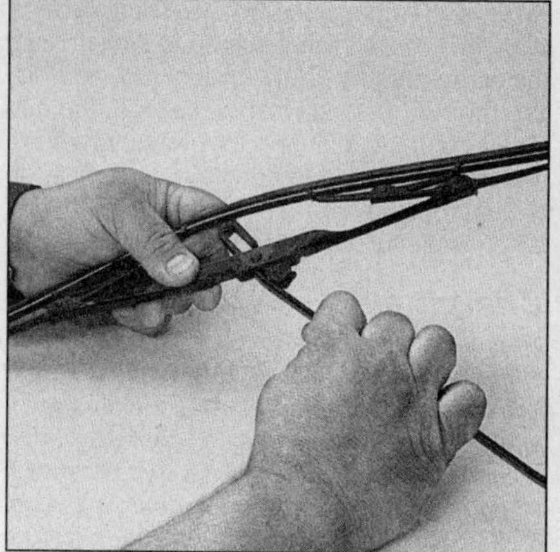

**12.5b . . . then slide the wiper element down and out of the hook in the end of the arm**

## 11 Underhood hose check and replacement (every 7,500 miles or 6 months)

**Warning:** *Replacement of air conditioning hoses must be left to a dealer service department or air conditioning shop equipped to depressurize the system safely. Never remove air conditioning components or hoses until the system has been depressurized.*

### General

1 High temperatures under the hood can cause the deterioration of the rubber and plastic hoses used for engine, accessory and emission systems operation. Periodic inspection should be made for cracks, loose clamps, material hardening and leaks.

2 Information specific to the cooling system hoses can be found in Section 10.

3 Some hoses use clamps to secure the hoses to fittings. Where clamps are used, check to be sure that they haven't lost their tension, allowing the hose to leak. Where clamps are not used, make sure the hose hasn't expanded and/or hardened where it slips over the fitting, allowing it to leak.

### Vacuum hoses

4 It's quite common for vacuum hoses, especially those in the emissions system, to be color coded or identified by colored stripes molded into the hose. Various systems require hoses with different wall thickness, collapse resistance and temperature resistance. When replacing hoses, make sure the new ones are made of the same material as the original.

5 Often the only effective way to check a hose is to remove it completely from the vehicle. Where more than one hose is removed, be sure to label the hoses and their attaching points to insure proper reattachment.

6 Include plastic T-fittings in the check of vacuum hoses. Check the fittings for cracks and the hose where it fits over the fitting for enlargement, which could cause leakage.

7 A small piece of vacuum hose (1/4-inch [6 mm] inside diameter) can be used as a stethoscope to detect vacuum leaks. Hold one end of the hose to your ear and probe around vacuum hoses and fittings, listening for the "hissing" sound characteristic of a vacuum leak. **Warning:** *When probing with the vacuum hose stethoscope, be careful not to allow your body or the hose to come into contact with moving engine components such as the drivebelt, cooling fan, etc.*

### Fuel hose

**Warning:** *Gasoline is extremely flammable, so take extra precautions when you work on any part of the fuel system. Don't smoke or allow open flames or bare light bulbs near the work area, and don't work in a garage where a gas-type appliance (such as a water heater or clothes dryer) is present. If you spill any fuel on your skin, rinse it off immediately with soap and water. When you perform any kind of work on the fuel system, wear fuel-resistant gloves and safety glasses, and have a Class B type fire extinguisher on hand. Before working on any part of the fuel system, relieve the fuel system pressure* (see Chapter 4).

8 Check all rubber fuel hoses for damage and deterioration. Check especially for cracks in areas where the hose bends and just before quick-connect fittings (see Chapter 4).

9 High quality fuel line, specifically designed for fuel injection systems, must be used for fuel line replacement. **Warning:** *Never use vacuum line, clear plastic tubing or water hose for fuel lines.*

### Brake hoses

10 The hoses used to connect the brake calipers or wheel cylinders to the metal lines are subject to extreme working conditions. They must endure high hydraulic pressures, heat and still maintain flexibility. The brake hoses typically can be inspected without removing the wheels. Carefully examine each hose for leakage, cracks, bulging, delaminating and damage. If any damage is found, the hose must be replaced immediately (see Chapter 9).

### Fuel and brake system metal lines

11 Sections of metal line are often used for fuel line between the fuel tank and fuel injection system. Carefully check to be sure the line has not been bent and crimped and that no cracks have started in the line.

12 If a section of metal fuel line must be replaced, only seamless steel tubing should be used, since copper and aluminum tubing do not have the strength necessary to withstand normal engine operating vibration.

13 Check the metal brake lines where they enter the master cylinder and ABS unit (if equipped) for cracks in the lines or loose fittings. Any sign of brake fluid leakage calls for an immediate thorough inspection of the brake system.

## 12 Windshield wiper blade inspection and replacement (every 7,500 miles or 6 months)

*Refer to illustrations 12.3, 12.5a and 12.5b*

1 The windshield wiper blade elements should be checked periodically for cracks and deterioration.

2 Road film can build up on the wiper blades and affect their efficiency, so they should be washed regularly with a mild detergent solution.

3 The action of the wiping mechanism can loosen the wiper arm retaining nuts, so they should be checked and tightened at the same time the wiper blades are checked **(see illustration)**.

4 Lift the wiper blade away from the windshield.

5 Press the release lever and slide the blade assembly out of the hook in the end of the wiper arm **(see illustrations)**. Carefully rest the wiper arm on the windshield.

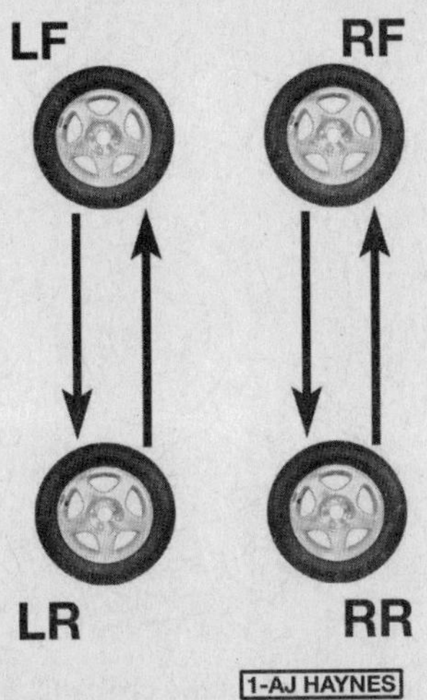


13.2a The recommended rotation pattern for *directional* radial tires

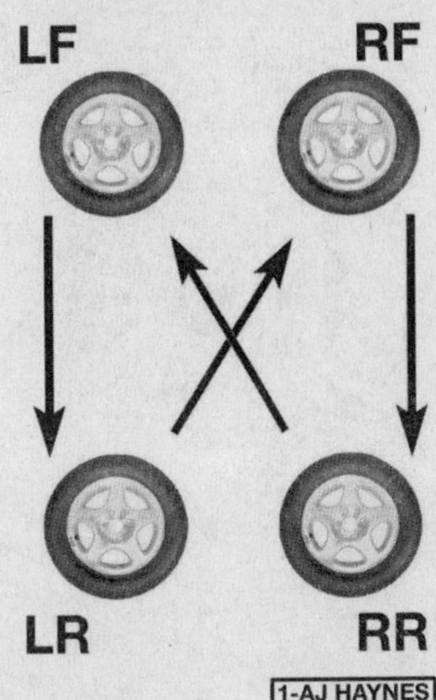


13.2b The recommended rotation pattern for *non-directional* radial tires

6 The rubber wiper element is secured to the blade assembly at one end of the blade element channel. Compress the locking feature on the element so it clears the tangs on the blade assembly channel claw and then slide the element out of the frame.

7 Installation is the reverse of removal. Make sure the rubber element and blade assembly is securely attached.

## 13 Tire rotation (every 7,500 miles or 6 months)

*Refer to illustrations 13.2a and 13.2b*

1 The tires should be rotated at the specified intervals and whenever uneven wear is noticed. Since the vehicle will be raised and the tires removed, this is a good time to check the brakes also (see Section 18).

2 Radial tires must be rotated in a specific pattern **(see illustrations)**. **Note:** *Most vehicles are sold with non-directional radial tires, but some performance tires are directional, and have an arrow on the sidewall indicating the direction they must turn when mounted on the vehicle.*

3 See the information in *Jacking and towing* at the front of this manual for the proper procedures to follow when raising the vehicle and changing a tire; however, if the brakes are to be checked, don't apply the parking brake as stated. Make sure the tires are blocked to prevent the vehicle from rolling. **Note:** *Prior to raising the vehicle, loosen all lug nuts a quarter turn.*

4 Preferably, the entire vehicle should be raised at the same time. This can be done on a hoist or by jacking up each corner of the vehicle and lowering it onto jackstands. Always use jackstands and make sure the vehicle is safely supported. **Warning:** *Never work under a vehicle that is supported only by a jack!*

5 After the tire rotation, check and adjust the tire pressures as necessary and tighten the wheel lug nuts to the torque listed in this Chapter's Specifications.

## 14 Steering and suspension check (every 7,500 miles or 6 months)

**Note:** *The steering linkage and suspension components should be checked periodically. Worn or damaged suspension and steering components can result in excessive and abnormal tire wear, poor ride quality and vehicle handling and reduced fuel economy. For detailed illustrations of the steering and suspension components, refer to Chapter 10.*

### Shock absorber/strut check

1 Park the vehicle on level ground, turn the engine off and set the parking brake. Check the tire pressures.

2 Push down at one corner of the vehicle, then release it while noting the movement of the body. It should stop moving and come to rest in a level position within one or two bounces.

3 If the vehicle continues to move up-and-down or if it fails to return to its original position, a worn or weak shock absorber or strut assembly is probably the reason.

4 Repeat the above check at each of the three remaining corners of the vehicle.

5 Raise the vehicle and support it securely on jackstands.

6 Check the shock absorbers/struts for evidence of fluid leakage. A light film of fluid is no cause for concern. Make sure that any fluid noted is from the shocks and not from some other source. If leakage is noted, replace the shocks/struts as a set.

7 Check the shocks/struts to be sure that they are securely mounted and undamaged. Check the upper mounts for damage and wear. If damage or wear is noted, replace the shocks/struts as a set (front or rear).

8 If the shocks or struts must be replaced, refer to Chapter 10 for the procedure.

### Suspension and steering check

9 Raise the vehicle and support it securely on jackstands. **Warning:** *Never work under a vehicle that is supported only by a jack!* Visually inspect the steering and suspension components (front and rear) for damage and distortion. Look for damaged seals, boots and bushings and leaks of any kind. Examine the bushings where the lower control arm meets the chassis and on the stabilizer bar connections.

10 Grasp each front tire at the front and rear edges, push in at the front, pull out at the rear and feel for play in the steering system components. If any freeplay is noted, check the tie-rod ends for looseness.

11 Lower the vehicle and check the balljoints using the procedure described in Chapter 10.

12 Additional steering and suspension system information and illustrations can be found in Chapter 10.

13 Inspect the steering gear boots for cracks as well as loose clamps. If you notice lubricant leaking from the boots, the rack seals have failed, in which case the steering gear will have to be replaced with a new or rebuilt unit, or overhauled by an automotive service technician.

## 15 Exhaust system check (every 7,500 miles or 6 months)

*Refer to illustrations 15.3a and 15.3b*

**Note:** *Perform the following procedure with the engine cold.*

1 Raise the vehicle and support it securely on jackstands. **Warning:** *Never work under a vehicle that is supported only by a jack!*

2 With the engine cold (at least three hours after the vehicle has been driven), check the complete exhaust system from its starting point at the engine to the end of the tailpipe.

3 Check the pipes and connections for signs of leakage and/or corrosion indicating a

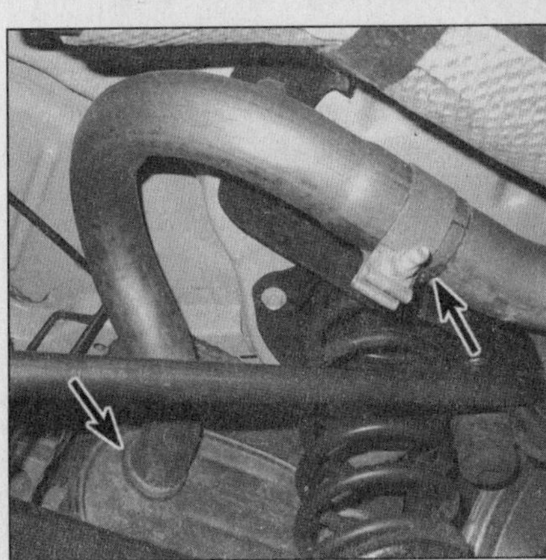

15.3a Check the exhaust system connections, clamps and welds for damage

15.3b Also check the exhaust system rubber hangers for cracks and deterioration

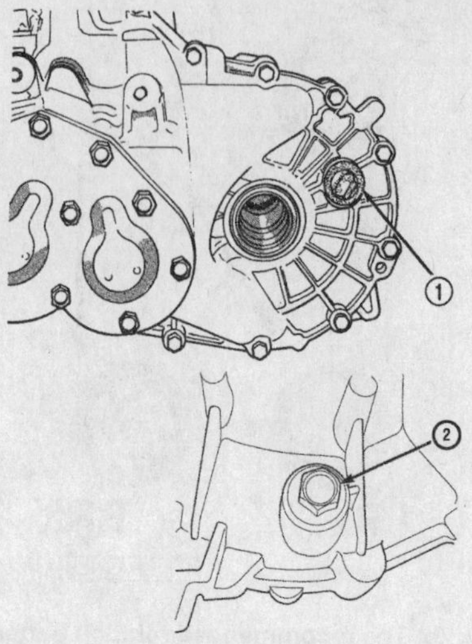


16.3a On the T350 transaxle, the check/fill plug (1) is located on the left side of the transaxle case; the drain plug (2) is located on the right side

16.3b Location of the check/fill plug (1) and the drain plug (2) on the G288 transaxle

17.3 Check the inner and outer boot on each driveaxle for cracks and/or leaking grease

potential failure. Make sure that all brackets and hangers are in good condition and tight **(see illustrations)**.

4 At the same time, inspect the underside of the body for holes, corrosion and open seams which may allow exhaust gases to enter the passenger compartment. Seal all body openings with silicone sealant or body putty.

5 Rattles and other noises can often be traced to the exhaust system, especially the mounts and hangers. Try to move the pipes, muffler and catalytic converter. If the components can come into contact with the body, secure the exhaust system with new mounts.

6 This is also an ideal time to check the running condition of the engine by inspecting the very end of the tailpipe. The exhaust deposits here are an indication of the engine's state-of-tune. If the pipe is black and sooty or coated with white deposits, the engine may be in need of a tune-up (including a thorough fuel injection system inspection).

## 16 Manual transaxle lubricant level check (every 7,500 miles or 6 months)

*Refer to illustrations 16.3a and 16.3b*

1 Manual transaxles do not have a fluid dipstick. The lubricant level is checked by removing the plug from the side of the transaxle case. The lubricant level should be checked with the engine cold and the vehicle level.

2 Raise the vehicle and support it securely on jackstands in a level position. **Warning:** *Never work under a vehicle that is supported only by a jack!*

3 Locate the metal or rubber plug on the side of the transaxle differential near the driveaxle shaft **(see illustrations)**. Use a rag to clean it and the surrounding area.

4 Use a socket or wrench (metal plug), or pliers or a screwdriver (rubber plug) to remove the plug. If oil begins to run out, let it find its own level (presuming the vehicle is relatively level). If oil does not run out, insert your finger to feel the lubricant level. It should be within 3/16-inch (5 mm) of the bottom of the plug hole.

5 If the transaxle requires additional lubricant, use a funnel with a rubber tube or a syringe to pour or squeeze the recommended lubricant into the plug hole to restore the level. If you overfill it, let the fluid run out until it is level with the plug hole. **Caution:** *Use only the specified transaxle lubricant - see* Recommended lubricants and fluids *at the beginning of this Chapter or your owner's manual.* **Note:** *Most auto parts stores sell pumps that screw into the oil containers which make this job much easier and less messy.*

6 Install the plug, tighten it securely and lower the vehicle. Test drive it and check for leaks.

## 17 Driveaxle boot check (every 7,500 miles or 6 months)

*Refer to illustration 17.3*

1 If the driveaxle boots are damaged, letting grease out and water and dirt in, serious (not to mention costly) damage can occur to the CV joints. The boots should be inspected very carefully at the recommended intervals or anytime the vehicle is raised.

2 Raise the front of the vehicle and support it securely on jackstands. **Warning:** *Never work under a vehicle that is supported only by a jack!*

3 Place the transaxle in Neutral. While rotating the wheels, inspect the four driveaxle boots (two on each driveaxle) very carefully for cracks, tears, holes, deteriorated rubber and loose or missing clamps **(see illustration)**. If the boots are dirty, wipe them clean before beginning the inspection.

4 If damage or deterioration is evident, replace the boots and check the CV joints for damage (see Chapter 8).

5 Place the transaxle in Park or in gear as applicable and lower the vehicle.

## 18 Brake system check (every 15,000 miles or 12 months)

**Warning:** *Dust created by the brake system is harmful to your health. Never blow it out with compressed air and don't inhale any of it. An approved filtering mask should be worn when working on the brakes. Do not, under any circumstances, use petroleum-based solvents to clean brake parts. Use brake system cleaner only!*

**Note:** *For detailed photographs of the brake system, refer to Chapter 9.*

1 In addition to the specified intervals, the brakes should be inspected every time the wheels are removed or whenever a defect is

18.6 With the wheel off, check the thickness of the pads through the inspection hole

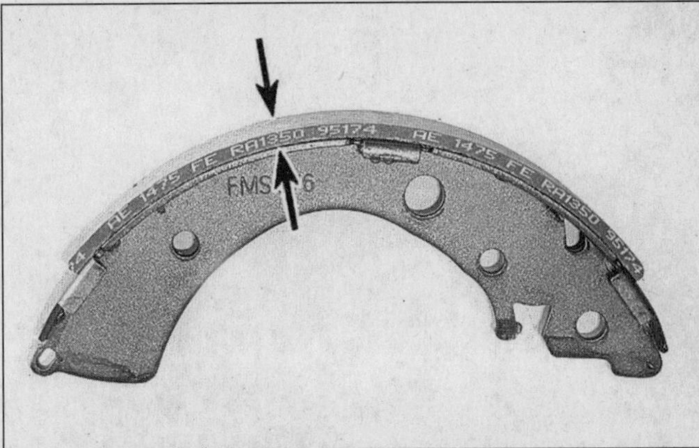

18.14 If the lining is bonded to the brake shoe, measure the lining thickness from the outer surface to the metal shoe; if the lining is riveted to the shoe, measure from the lining outer surface to the rivet head

suspected. Any of the following symptoms could indicate a potential brake system defect: The vehicle pulls to one side when the brake pedal is depressed; the brakes make squealing or dragging noises when applied; brake travel is excessive; the pedal pulsates; brake fluid leaks, usually onto the inside of the tire or wheel.

2 The front disc brake pads have built-in wear indicators will make a high-pitched squealing or scraping noise when they are worn to the replacement point. When you hear this noise, replace the pads immediately or expensive damage to the discs can result.

3 Loosen the wheel lug nuts.

4 Raise the vehicle and place it securely on jackstands.

5 Remove the wheels (see *Jacking and towing* at the front of this book, or your owner's manual, if necessary).

## Disc brakes

*Refer to illustration 18.6*

6 There are two pads - an outer and an inner - in each caliper. The pads are visible through small inspection holes in each caliper **(see illustration)**.

7 Check the pad thickness by looking at each end of the caliper and through the inspection hole in the caliper body. If the lining material is less than the thickness listed in this Chapter's Specifications, replace the pads. **Note:** *Keep in mind that the lining material is riveted or bonded to a metal backing plate and the metal portion is not included in this measurement.*

8 If it is difficult to determine the exact thickness of the remaining pad material by the above method, or if you are at all concerned about the condition of the pads, remove the caliper(s), then remove the pads from the calipers for further inspection (see Chapter 9).

9 Once the pads are removed from the calipers, clean them with brake cleaner and re-measure them.

10 Measure the disc thickness with a micrometer to make sure that it still has service life remaining. If any disc is thinner than the specified minimum thickness, replace it (refer to Chapter 9). Even if the disc has service life remaining, check its condition. Look for scoring, gouging and burned spots. If these conditions exist, remove the disc and have it resurfaced (see Chapter 9).

11 Before installing the wheels, check all brake lines and hoses for damage, wear, deformation, cracks, corrosion, leakage, bends and twists, particularly in the vicinity of the rubber hoses at the calipers.

12 Check the clamps for tightness and the connections for leakage. Make sure that all hoses and lines are clear of sharp edges, moving parts and the exhaust system. If any of the above conditions are noted, repair, reroute or replace the lines and/or fittings as necessary (see Chapter 9).

## Rear drum brakes

*Refer to illustrations 18.14 and 18.16*

13 Refer to Chapter 9 and remove the rear brake drums.

14 Note the thickness of the lining material on the rear brake shoes **(see illustration)** and look for signs of contamination by brake fluid and grease. If the lining material is within 1/16-inch (1.5 mm) of the recessed rivets or metal shoes, replace the brake shoes with new ones. The shoes should also be replaced if they are cracked, glazed (shiny lining surfaces) or contaminated with brake fluid or grease. See Chapter 9 for the replacement procedure.

15 Check the shoe return and hold-down springs and the adjusting mechanism to make sure they're installed correctly and in good condition. Deteriorated or distorted springs, if not replaced, could allow the linings to drag and wear prematurely.

16 Check the wheel cylinders for leakage by carefully peeling back the rubber boots **(see illustration)**. If brake fluid is noted behind the boots, the wheel cylinders must be replaced (see Chapter 9).

17 Check the drums for cracks, score marks, deep scratches and hard spots, which

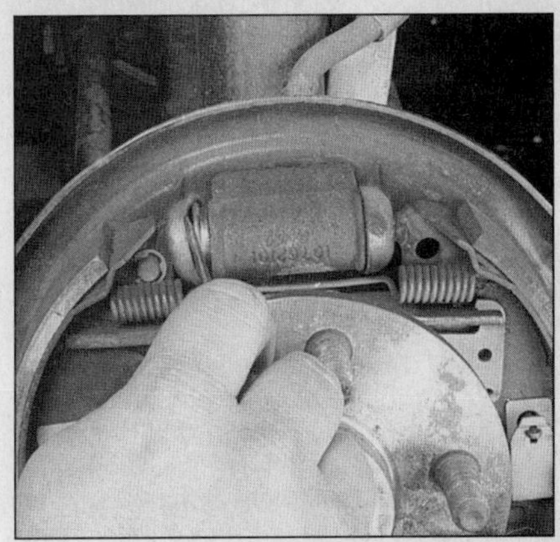

18.16 Pull the boot away from the cylinder and check for fluid leakage

will appear as small discolored areas. If imperfections cannot be removed with emery cloth, the drums must be resurfaced by an automotive machine shop (see Chapter 9 for more detailed information).

18 Install the brake drums.

19 Install the wheels and lug nuts.

20 Remove the jackstands and lower the vehicle.

21 Tighten the wheel lug nuts to the torque listed in this Chapter's Specifications.

## Brake booster check

22 Sit in the driver's seat and perform the following sequence of tests.

23 With the brake fully depressed, start the engine - the pedal should move down a little when the engine starts.

24 With the engine running, depress the brake pedal several times- the travel distance should not change.

25 Depress the brake, stop the engine and hold the pedal in for about 30 seconds - the pedal should neither sink nor rise.

26 Restart the engine, run it for about a minute and turn it off. Then firmly depress the brake several times - the pedal travel should decrease with each application.

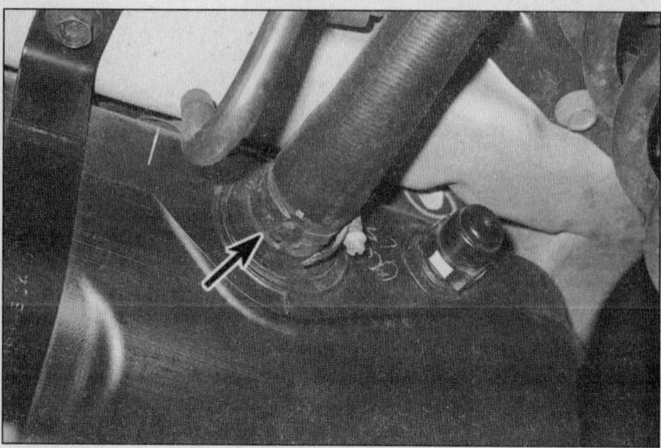

19.5 Check the fuel filler neck-to-tank hose and clamp

20.2 Remove these fasteners and detach the drivebelt splash shield

27 If your brakes do not operate as described above when the preceding tests are performed, the brake booster has failed. Refer to Chapter 9 for the replacement procedure.

## 19 Fuel system hoses and connections check (every 15,000 miles or 12 months)

*Refer to illustration 19.5*

**Warning:** *Gasoline is extremely flammable, so take extra precautions when you work on any part of the fuel system. Don't smoke or allow open flames or bare light bulbs near the work area, and don't work in a garage where a gas-type appliance (such as a water heater or clothes dryer) is present. If you spill any fuel on your skin, rinse it off immediately with soap and water. When you perform any kind of work on the fuel system, wear fuel-resistant gloves and safety glasses, and have a Class B type fire extinguisher on hand. Before working on any part of the fuel system, relieve the fuel system pressure (see Chapter 4).*

1 If the smell of gasoline is noticed while driving, or after the vehicle has been parked in the sun, the fuel system and evaporative emissions control system (see Section 26) should be thoroughly inspected immediately.

2 The fuel system is under pressure even when the engine is off. Consequently, the fuel system must be depressurized before servicing the system (see Chapter 4). Even after depressurization, if any fuel lines are disconnected for servicing, be prepared to catch some fuel as it spills out. Plug all disconnected fuel lines immediately.

3 Remove the fuel tank filler cap and check for damage, corrosion and a proper sealing imprint on the gasket. Replace the cap with a new one if necessary.

4 Raise the vehicle and support it securely on jackstands. **Warning:** *Never work under a vehicle that is supported only by a jack!*

5 Inspect the fuel tank and filler neck for punctures, cracks and other damage. The hose connection between the filler neck and the tank is especially critical **(see illustration)**. Sometimes the filler neck hose will leak due to loose clamps or deteriorated rubber; problems a home mechanic can usually rectify.

6 Carefully inspect all rubber hoses and metal lines leading to-and-from the fuel tank. Check for loose connections, deteriorated hoses, crimped lines and damage of any kind. Follow the lines up to the front of the vehicle, carefully inspecting them all the way. Repair or replace damaged sections as necessary (see Chapter 4).

## 20 Drivebelt check, adjustment and replacement (every 15,000 miles or 12 months)

**Warning:** *The electric cooling fan(s) on these models can activate at any time the ignition switch is in the ON position. Make sure the ignition is OFF when working in the vicinity of the fan(s).*

### Check

*Refer to illustrations 20.2, 20.3 and 20.5*

1 The drivebelts are located at the front of the engine and play an important role in the operation of the vehicle and its components. Due to their function and material makeup, the belts are prone to failure after a period of time and should be inspected periodically to prevent major damage. The alternator drivebelt is adjustable, while the power steering pump and air conditioning compressor (if equipped) drivebelt is adjusted by an automatic tensioner.

2 The drivebelts are very difficult to see from above. Apply the parking brake, loosen the right (passenger's side) front wheel lug nuts, raise the front of the vehicle and support it securely on jackstands. Remove the wheel, then remove the drivebelt splash shield **(see illustration)**.

3 Use a flashlight to carefully check each belt. Check for a severed core, separation of the adhesive rubber on both sides of the core

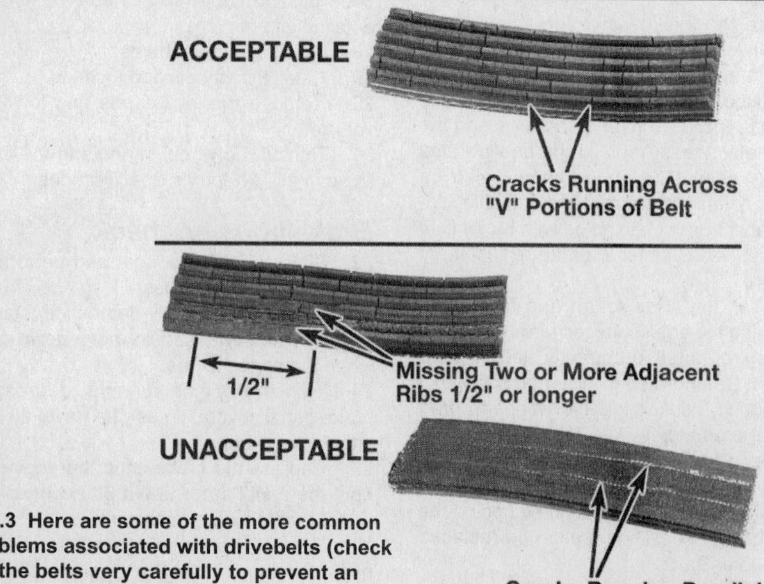


20.3 Here are some of the more common problems associated with drivebelts (check the belts very carefully to prevent an untimely breakdown)

**20.5 Details of the power steering pump/air conditioning compressor drivebelt tensioner**

1 *Belt length indicator*
2 *Maximum length (belt worn out)*
3 *Normal length*
4 *Minimum length*

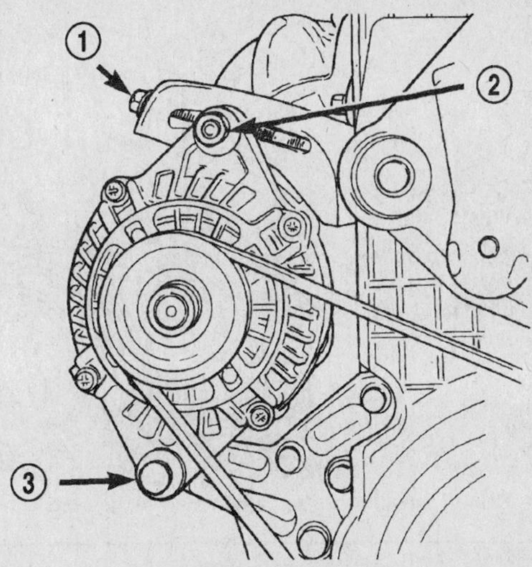


**20.6 Alternator belt adjustment details**

1 *Adjusting bolt*
2 *Lock nut*
3 *Pivot bolt*

and for core separation from the belt side. Inspect the ribs for separation from the adhesive rubber and for cracking or separation of the ribs, torn or worn ribs or cracks in the inner ridges of the ribs **(see illustration)**. Also check for fraying and glazing, which gives the belt a shiny appearance. Inspect both sides of the belt by twisting the belt to check the underside. Use your fingers to feel the belt where you can't see it. If any of the above conditions are evident, replace the belt(s).

4 The tension of the alternator drivebelt is checked by pushing on it at a distance halfway between the pulleys. Apply about 10 pounds of force with your thumb and see how much the belt moves (deflects); the belt should deflect about 1/4-inch (6 mm).

5 The tension of the power steering pump/air conditioning compressor drivebelt is adjusted by an automatic tensioner. Look at the wear indicator on the tensioner **(see illustration)**. The marks should be within the specified range; if not, the belt will have to be replaced.

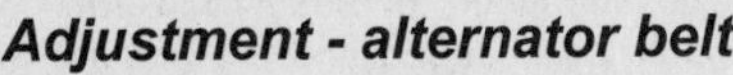

## *Adjustment - alternator belt*

*Refer to illustration 20.6*

6 Loosen the pivot bolt and lock nut, then turn the adjusting bolt clockwise to tighten the belt or counterclockwise to loosen the belt **(see illustration)**. When you have obtained the desired tension, tighten the lock nut and pivot bolt securely.

## *Replacement*

**Note:** *Since belts tend to wear out more or less at the same time, it's a good idea to replace both of them at the same time.*

7 Apply the parking brake, loosen the right (passenger's side) front wheel lug nuts, raise the front of the vehicle and support it securely on jackstands. Remove the wheel, then remove the drivebelt splash shield **(see illustration 20.2)**.

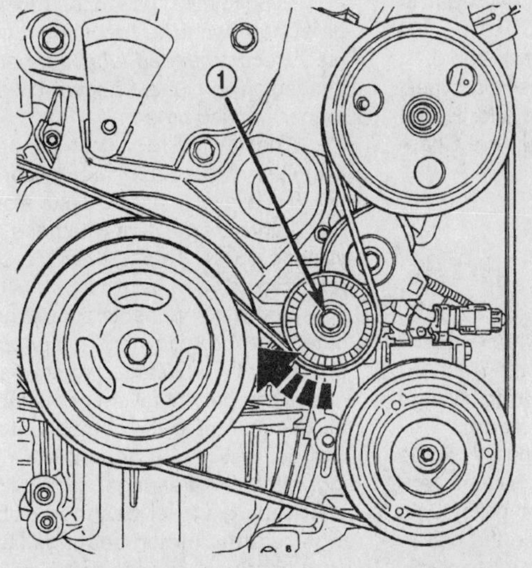


**20.8 Rotate the drivebelt tensioner (1) clockwise to release tension on the belt**

### Power steering pump/air conditioning compressor belt

*Refer to illustrations 20.8 and 20.9*

8 The automatic tensioner must be released to allow drivebelt replacement. Place a wrench or a socket on the tensioner pulley bolt and rotate it clockwise until the belt can be removed **(see illustration)**. Remove the belt and slowly release the tensioner. Install the new belt then rotate the tensioner clockwise to allow the belt to slip over it, then release the tensioner slowly until it contacts the drivebelt.

9 When installing the belt, make sure the belt is centered on the pulleys **(see illustration)**.

10 Install the drivebelt splash shield, wheel and lug nuts. Lower the vehicle and tighten the lug nuts to the torque listed in this Chapter's Specifications.

### Alternator belt

11 Remove the power steering pump/air

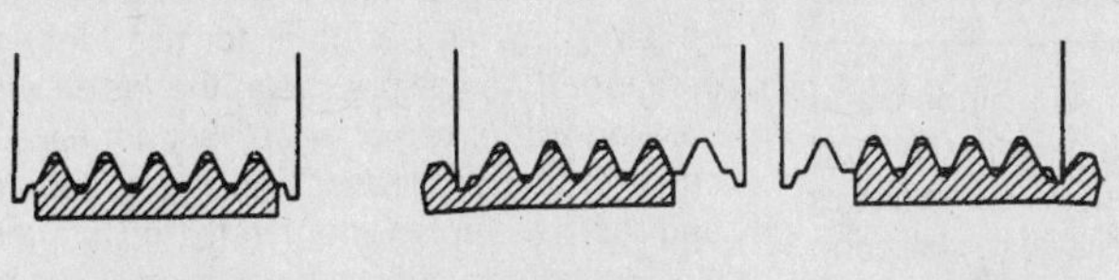


**20.9 When installing a drivebelt, make sure it is centered - it must not overlap either edge of the pulley**

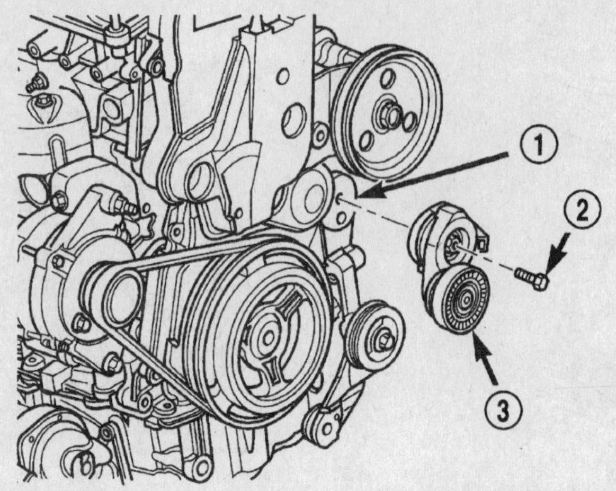


**20.17 Drivebelt tensioner details**

1 *Torque strut bracket*
2 *Bolt*
3 *Automatic tensioner assembly*

**22.2a To remove the air filter, release the latches securing the cover to the air filter housing . . .**

**22.2b . . . then raise the cover and remove the filter element from the housing**

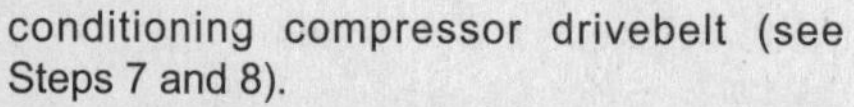

conditioning compressor drivebelt (see Steps 7 and 8).

12 Follow Step 6 for drivebelt adjustment, but slip the belt off the pulleys and remove it.

13 When installing the belt, make sure the belt is centered on the pulleys **(see illustration 20.9)**.

14 Adjust the belt as described in Step 6.

15 Install the drivebelt splash shield, wheel and lug nuts. Lower the vehicle and tighten the lug nuts to the torque listed in this Chapter's Specifications.

### Automatic tensioner replacement

*Refer to illustration 20.17*

16 Remove the power steering/air conditioning compressor drivebelt (see Steps 7 and 8).

17 Unscrew the tensioner mounting bolt and remove the tensioner **(see illustration)**.

18 If necessary, the tensioner pulley can be replaced individually. To do so, mount the tensioner in a vise and unscrew the pulley bolt. Install the new pulley and tighten the bolt to the torque listed in this Chapter's Specifications.

19 Install the tensioner assembly by reversing the removal procedure. Tighten the mounting bolt to the torque listed in this Chapter's Specifications.

20 Install the drivebelt as described previously in this Section.

21 Install the drivebelt splash shield, wheel and lug nuts. Lower the vehicle and tighten the lug nuts to the torque listed in this Chapter's Specifications.

## 21 Body hinge and lock lubrication (every 30,000 miles or 24 months)

1 Regular lubrication of the hinges and locks will keep them working smoothly and from wearing out prematurely. A container of multi-purpose grease, graphite spray, silicone spray and an oil can filled with engine oil will be required to lubricate the hinges, latches and locks.

2 Open the hood and smear a little multi-purpose grease on the hood latch mechanism and striker. Have an assistant pull the hood release lever from inside the vehicle as you lubricate the cable at the latch.

3 Lubricate all the hinges (door, hood, liftgate, etc.) with the recommended lubricant (see *Recommended lubricants and fluids* at the beginning of this Chapter) to keep them in proper working order.

4 The key lock cylinders can be lubricated with spray-type graphite or silicone lubricant which is available at auto parts stores.

5 Lubricate the door weather-stripping with silicone spray. This will reduce chafing and retard wear.

6 Some components should not be lubricated for the following reasons. Some are permanently lubricated, some lubricants will cause component failure or the lubricants will be detrimental to the component's operating characteristics. Do not lubricate the following: alternator bearings, drivebelts, drivebelt idler pulley, wheel bearings, rubber bushings, starter motor bearings, suspension strut bearings, or accelerator or cruise control cables.

## 22 Air filter replacement (every 30,000 miles or 24 months)

*Refer to illustrations 22.2a and 22.2b*

1 The air filter element is located in a housing on the driver's side of the engine compartment.

2 Unclip the latches securing the top cover of the air filter housing, raise the cover, then lift the filter element out **(see illustrations)**.

3 Inspect the inside of the air cleaner housing, top and bottom, for dirt, debris or damage. If necessary, clean the inside of the housing with a rag or shop vacuum as applicable. If the air cleaner housing is damaged and requires replacement, refer to Chapter 4.

4 Install the filter, making sure it properly engages the housing, then lower the cover and push the latches into position.

## 23 Automatic transaxle fluid and filter change (every 30,000 miles or 24 months)

*Refer to illustrations 23.4 and 23.5*

1 The automatic transaxle fluid and filter should be changed and the magnet (if equipped) cleaned at the recommended intervals.

2 Raise the front of the vehicle and support it securely on jackstands. **Warning:** *Never work under a vehicle that is supported only by a jack!*

3 Position a container capable of holding at least 5 quarts under the transaxle oil pan.

4 Since the transaxle drain pan does not have a drain plug, this procedure can get a bit messy, so you should have plenty of clean rags and newspapers handy to mop up any spills that may occur. If the drain pan you're using isn't very large in diameter, place it on a piece of plastic such as a trash bag to catch any splashing oil. Loosen, but don't remove, the pan bolts. Now remove the bolts on each side of the pan leaving two bolts loosely in place on the upper and lower sides of the pan

**23.4 To drain the transaxle fluid, first loosen the bolts, then remove all the bolts except for two on the high side and two on the low side - after breaking the pan seal, remove the two bolts on the lower side and let the pan hang down to drain further**

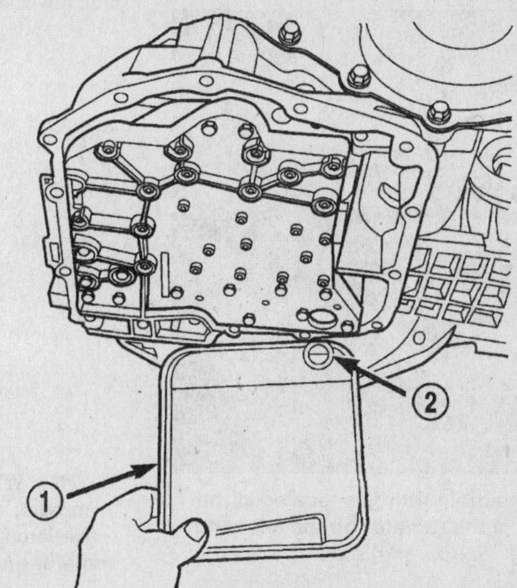


**23.5 Remove the transaxle fluid filter (1) and O-ring (2)**

**(see illustration)**. Tap the corners of the pan using a soft-faced mallet to break the seal and allow the fluid to drain into the container (the remaining bolts will prevent the pan from completely separating from the transaxle). Remove the 2 bolts from the lower side of the pan and let it hang down to drain further. After the pan has finished draining, remove the remaining bolts and detach the pan.

5 Remove the filter by pulling it straight down. Also remove the O-ring seal **(see illustration)**.

6 Carefully remove all traces of old sealant from the pan, transaxle body (be careful not to nick or gouge the sealing surfaces) and the bolts.

7 Clean the pan and the magnet located inside the pan with a clean, lint-free cloth moistened with solvent. Don't forget to place the magnet back in its proper location at the bottom of the pan.

8 Fit the new filter in place, with a new O-ring installed, on the transaxle valve body.

9 Apply a 1/8-inch (3 mm) bead of RTV sealant to the pan sealing surface (stay on the inboard side of the bolt holes) and to the underside of each bolt head.

10 Position the pan on the transaxle and install the bolts. Tighten them to the torque listed in this Chapter's Specifications following a criss-cross pattern. Work up to the final torque in three or four steps. Allow the RTV sealant time to dry according to the manufacturer's instructions.

11 Lower the vehicle and add four quarts of the specified fluid (see *Recommended lubricants and fluids* at the beginning of this Chapter) to the transaxle (see Section 6 if necessary). Start the engine and allow it to idle for at least two minutes while checking for leakage around the pan.

12 With the engine running and the brakes applied, move the shift lever through each of the gear positions and ending in Park. Check the fluid level on the dipstick. The level should be just up to the ADD mark. If necessary, add more fluid (a little at a time) until the level is just at the ADD mark (be careful not to overfill it).

13 Drive the vehicle until it reaches normal operating temperature. Recheck the fluid level and add as necessary until the fluid reaches the HOT range on the dipstick (see Section 6).

14 The old fluid drained from the transaxle cannot be reused in its present state and should be disposed of. Check with your local auto parts store, disposal facility or environmental agency to see if they will accept the fluid for recycling. After the fluid has cooled it can be drained into a container (capped plastic jugs, topped bottles, milk cartons, etc.) for transport to one of these disposal sites. Don't dispose of the fluid by pouring it on the ground or down a drain!

## 24 Manual transaxle lubricant change (every 30,000 miles or 24 months)

1 Raise the vehicle and support it securely on jackstands in a level position. **Warning:** *Never work under a vehicle that is supported only by a jack!*

2 Remove the drain plug **(see illustrations 16.3a and 16.3b)**. Drain the fluid into a suitable container capable of holding at least four quarts.

3 After the fluid has completely drained, install the drain plug and tighten it to the torque given in this Chapter's Specifications.

4 Fill the transaxle with the recommended lubricant (see Section 16).

5 The old oil drained from the transaxle cannot be reused in its present state and should be disposed of. Check with your local auto parts store, disposal facility or environmental agency to see if they will accept the oil for recycling. After the oil has cooled it can be drained into a container (capped plastic jugs, topped bottles, milk cartons, etc.) for transport to one of these disposal sites. Don't dispose of the oil by pouring it on the ground or down a drain!

## 25 Cooling system servicing (draining, flushing and refilling) (refer to the Maintenance schedule for service interval)

**Warning:** *Do not allow coolant (antifreeze) to come in contact with your skin or painted surfaces of the vehicle. Flush contaminated areas immediately with plenty of water. Do not store new coolant or leave old coolant lying around where it's accessible to children or pets - they're attracted by its sweet smell. Ingestion of even a small amount of coolant can be fatal! Wipe up garage floor and drip pan spills immediately. Keep antifreeze containers covered and repair cooling system leaks as soon as they're noticed. Check with local authorities about the disposal of used antifreeze. Many communities have collection centers which will see that antifreeze is disposed of properly.*

**Warning:** *The electric cooling fan(s) on these models can activate at any time the ignition switch is in the ON position. Make sure the ignition is OFF when working in the vicinity of the fan(s).*

**Note:** *These vehicles are originally filled with Mopar 5 year/100,000 mile coolant that shouldn't be mixed with other coolants. Check the coolant reservoir under the hood to determine what type coolant you have. Always refill with the correct coolant.*

1 Periodically, the cooling system should be drained, flushed and refilled to replenish the coolant (antifreeze) mixture and prevent formation of rust and corrosion, which can impair the performance of the cooling system and cause engine damage.

25.5 The drain fitting is located at the bottom of the radiator on the left hand (driver's) side

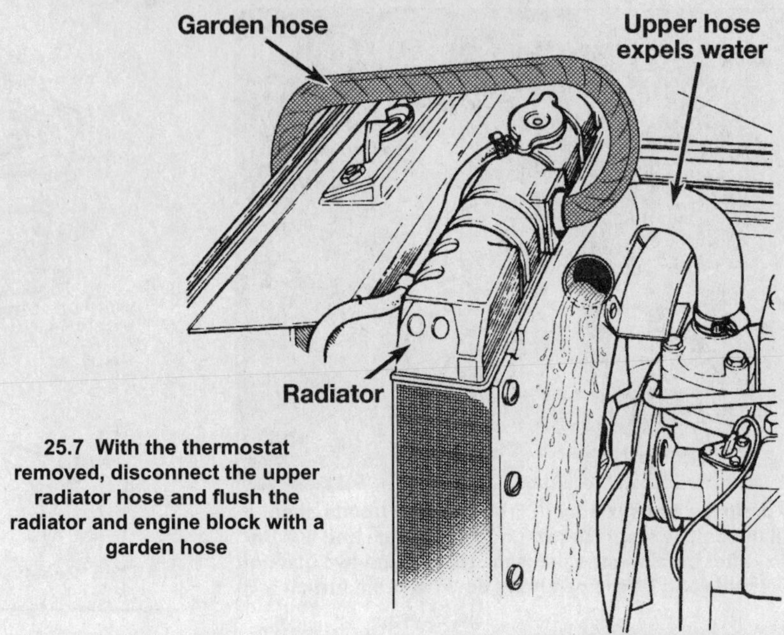


25.7 With the thermostat removed, disconnect the upper radiator hose and flush the radiator and engine block with a garden hose

2 At the same time the cooling system is serviced, all hoses and the radiator (pressure) cap should be inspected, tested and replaced if faulty (see Section 10).

## Draining

*Refer to illustration 25.5*

**Warning:** *Wait until the engine is completely cool before beginning this procedure.*

3 With the engine cold, remove the pressure cap and set the heater control to maximum heat.

4 Move a large container capable of holding at least 12 quarts under the radiator drain fitting to catch the coolant mixture as it's drained.

5 Open the drain fitting located at the bottom of the radiator **(see illustration)**. Allow the coolant to completely drain out.

## Flushing

*Refer to illustration 25.7*

6 Once the system is completely drained, remove the thermostat from the engine (see Chapter 3). Then reinstall the thermostat housing without the thermostat. This will allow the system to be thoroughly flushed.

7 Disconnect the upper radiator hose from the radiator, then place a garden hose in the upper radiator inlet and flush the system until the water runs clear at the upper radiator hose **(see illustration)**.

8 Severe cases of radiator contamination or clogging will require removing the radiator (see Chapter 3) and reverse flushing it. This involves inserting the hose in the bottom radiator outlet to allow the clean water to run against the normal flow, draining out through the top. A radiator repair shop should be consulted if further cleaning or repair is necessary.

9 When the coolant is regularly drained and the system refilled with the correct coolant mixture there should be no need to employ chemical cleaners or descalers.

10 Disconnect the coolant reservoir hose, remove the reservoir from the vehicle and flush it with clean water (see Chapter 3). Inspect it for damage and replace if necessary.

## Refilling

*Refer to illustration 25.13*

11 Install the thermostat, the thermostat housing and reconnect the radiator hose (see Chapter 3).

12 Install the coolant reservoir, reconnect the hose and close the radiator drain fitting.

13 Attach a length of tubing to the coolant bleed valve, direct the end of the hose into a container, then loosen the bleed valve **(see illustration)**. **Note:** *The use of the hose will prevent coolant from bubbling out and spilling on the drivebelts and air conditioning compressor.*

14 Remove the cooling system pressure cap. Add the correct mixture of the proper type of antifreeze/coolant and water in the ratio specified on the antifreeze container or in this Chapter's Specifications through the filler neck until it reaches the pressure cap seat and a steady bubble-free stream of coolant flows from the bleed valve bolt (if equipped). Tighten the bleed valve securely.

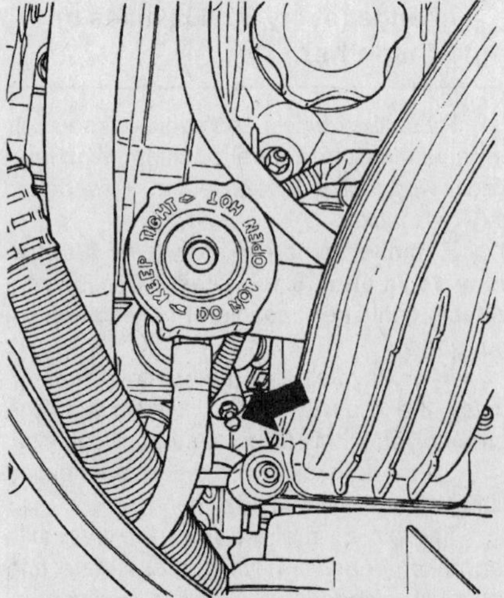

25.13 The cooling system bleed valve is located on the thermostat housing

15 Add the same coolant mixture to the reservoir until the level is between the FULL HOT and ADD marks. Install the pressure cap.

16 Run the engine until normal operating temperature is reached (the fans will cycle on, then off), then allow the engine to cool. With the engine cold, add coolant as necessary to bring it up to the correct level.

17 Keep a close watch on the coolant level and the various cooling system hoses during the first few miles of driving and check for any coolant leaks. Tighten the hose clamps and add more coolant mixture as necessary.

## 26 Evaporative emissions control system check (every 30,000 miles or 24 months)

1 The function of the evaporative emissions control system is to prevent fuel vapors from escaping the fuel system and being released into the atmosphere. Vapors from the fuel tank are temporarily stored in a charcoal canister. The Powertrain Control Module (PCM) monitors the system and allows the vapors to be drawn into the intake manifold when the engine reaches normal operating temperature.

2 The charcoal canister is located above the fuel tank. The canister is maintenance-free and should last the life of the vehicle.

3 The most common symptom of a fault in the evaporative emissions system is a strong fuel odor at the rear (or inside of) the vehicle,

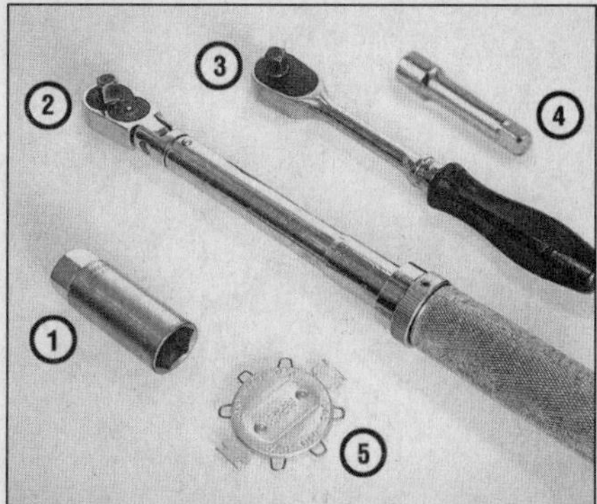


**27.2 Tools required for changing spark plugs**

1 ***Spark plug socket*** *- This will have special padding inside to protect the spark plug's porcelain insulator*
2 ***Torque wrench*** *- Although not mandatory, using this tool is the best way to ensure the plugs are tightened properly*
3 ***Ratchet*** *- Standard hand tool to fit the spark plug socket*
4 ***Extension*** *- Depending on model and accessories, you may need special extensions and universal joints to reach one or more of the plugs*
5 ***Spark plug gap gauge*** *- This gauge for checking the gap comes in a variety of styles. Make sure the gap for your engine is included*

or raw fuel leaking from the canister. These indications are usually more prevalent in hot temperatures. All systems are pressurized by a Leak Detection Pump (LDP). If normal system pressure cannot be achieved by the LDP, which indicates a leak, the PCM will store the appropriate fault code and illuminate the CHECK ENGINE light on the instrument panel. The most common cause of system pressure loss is a loose or poor-sealing gas cap.

4 For more information and replacement procedures see Chapter 6.

## 27 Spark plug check and replacement (see Maintenance schedule for intervals)

*Refer to illustrations 27.2, 27.5a, 27.5b, 27.10, 27.12 and 27.13*

1 The spark plugs are located in the center of the cylinder head.

2 In most cases the tools necessary for spark plug replacement include a spark plug socket which fits onto a ratchet (this special socket is padded inside to protect the porcelain insulators on the new plugs and hold them in place), various extensions and a feeler gauge to check and adjust the spark plug gap **(see illustration)**. Since these engines are equipped with an aluminum cylinder head, a torque wrench should be used when tightening the spark plugs.

**27.5a Spark plug manufacturers recommend using a wire-type gauge when checking the gap - if the wire does not slide between the electrodes with a slight drag, adjustment is required**

3 The best approach when replacing the spark plugs is to purchase the new spark plugs beforehand, adjust them to the proper gap and then replace each plug one at a time. When buying the new spark plugs, be sure to obtain the correct plug for your specific engine. This information can be found in the Specification Section at the front of this Chapter, in your owner's manual or on the Vehicle Emissions Control Information (VECI) label located under the hood. If differences exist between the sources, purchase the spark plug type specified on the VECI label as it was printed for your specific engine.

4 Allow the engine to cool completely before attempting to remove any of the plugs. During this cooling off time, each of the new spark plugs can be inspected for defects and the gaps can be checked.

5 The gap is checked by inserting the proper thickness gauge between the electrodes at the tip of the plug **(see illustration)**. The gap between the electrodes should be as listed in this Chapter's Specifications or in your owner's manual. The wire should touch each of the electrodes. If the gap is incorrect, use the adjuster on the thickness gauge body to bend the curved side electrode slightly until the proper gap is obtained **(see illustration)**. **Caution:** *The manufacturer recommends against checking the gap on platinum-tipped spark plugs; the platinum coating could be scraped off.* Also, at this time check for cracks in the spark plug body (if any are found, the plug must not be used). If the side electrode is not exactly over the center one, use the adjuster to align the two.

6 Cover the fender to prevent damage to the paint. Fender covers are available from auto parts stores but an old blanket will work just fine.

7 It will be necessary to remove the upper intake manifold for access to the spark plugs (see Chapter 2A). **Note:** *To prevent dirt or other foreign debris from entering the engine, place duct tape over the openings in the lower*

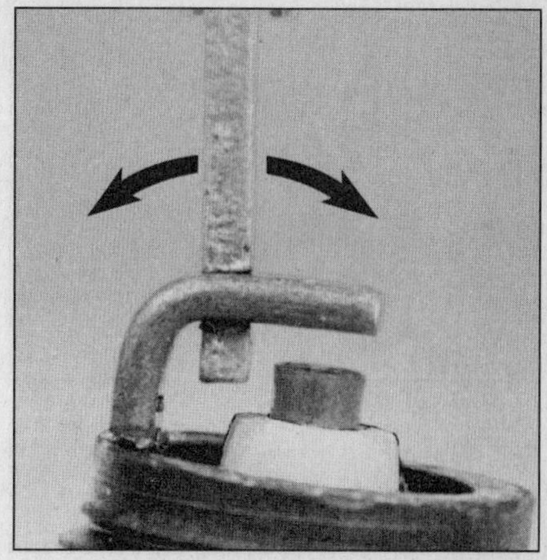

**27.5b To change the gap, bend the side electrode only, as indicated by the arrows, and be very careful not to crack or chip the porcelain insulator surrounding the center electrode**

*intake manifold or plug them with rags.*

8 Using a twisting motion, detach one of the spark plug boots/wires from the ignition coil, then withdraw the boot/wire from the valve cover. Pull only on the boot at the end of the wire; don't pull on the wire. **Note:** *Due to the short length of the spark plug wire, always disconnect the spark plug wire from the ignition coil pack first.*

9 If compressed air is available, use it to blow any dirt or foreign material away from the spark plug area. **Warning:** *Wear eye protection!* The idea here is to eliminate the possibility of material falling into the cylinder through the spark plug hole as the spark plug is removed.

10 Place the spark plug socket over the plug and remove it from the engine by turning it in a counterclockwise direction **(see illustration)**.

11 Compare the spark plug with the chart on the inside back cover of this manual to get an indication of the overall running condition of the engine.

**27.10 Use a ratchet and extension to remove the spark plugs**

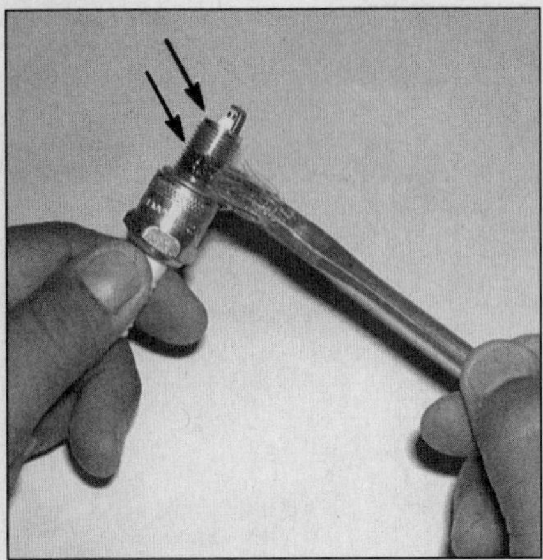

**27.12 Apply a thin coat of anti-seize compound to the spark plug threads - DO NOT get any on the electrodes!**

**27.13 A length of snug-fitting rubber hose will save time and prevent damaged threads when installing the spark plugs**

**29.2 The PCV valve is located in the valve cover**

12 It's a good idea to lightly coat the threads of the spark plugs with an anti-seize compound **(see illustration)** to insure that the spark plugs do not seize in the aluminum cylinder head.

13 It's often difficult to insert spark plugs into their holes without cross-threading them. To avoid this possibility, fit a piece of rubber hose over the end of the spark plug **(see illustration)**. The flexible hose acts as a universal joint to help align the plug with the plug hole. Should the plug begin to cross-thread, the hose will slip on the spark plug, preventing thread damage. Install the spark plug and tighten it to the torque listed in this Chapter's Specifications.

14 Attach the plug wire to the new spark plug, again using a twisting motion on the boot until it is firmly seated on the end of the spark plug. Attach the other end to the ignition coil pack.

15 Follow the above procedure for the remaining spark plugs, replacing them one at a time to prevent mixing up the spark plug wires.

18 Install the upper intake manifold (see Chapter 2A).

## 28 Spark plug wire check and replacement (every 60,000 miles or 48 months)

1 The spark plug wires should be replaced at the recommended intervals and/or checked when new spark plugs are installed.

2 For access to the spark plug wires, remove the upper intake manifold (see Chapter 2A).

3 Disconnect the spark plug wire from the ignition coil pack. Pull only on the boot at the end of the wire; don't pull on the wire itself. Use a twisting motion to free the boot/wire from the coil. Disconnect the same spark plug wire from the spark plug, using the same twisting method while pulling on the boot.

4 Check inside the boot for corrosion, which will look like a white, crusty powder (don't mistake the white dielectric grease used on some plug wire boots for corrosion protection).

5 Now push the wire and boot back onto the end of the spark plug. It should be a tight fit on the plug end. If not, remove the wire and use a pair of pliers to carefully crimp the metal connector inside the wire boot until the fit is snug.

6 Now push the wire and boot back into the end of the ignition coil terminal. It should be a tight fit in the terminal. If not, remove the wire and use a pair of pliers to carefully crimp the metal connector inside the wire boot until the fit is snug.

7 Now, using a cloth, clean each wire along its entire length. Remove all built-up dirt and grease. As this is done, inspect for burned areas, cracks and any other form of damage. Bend the wires in several places to ensure that the conductive material inside hasn't hardened. Repeat the procedure for the remaining wires.

8 If you are replacing the spark plug wires, purchase a complete set for your particular engine. The terminals and rubber boots should already be installed on the wires. Replace the wires one at a time to avoid mixing up the firing order and make sure the terminals are securely seated on the coil pack and the spark plugs.

9 Attach the plug wire to the new spark plug and to the ignition coil pack using a twisting motion on the boot until it is firmly seated.

10 Reinstall the upper intake manifold.

## 29 Positive Crankcase Ventilation (PCV) valve check and replacement (every 60,000 miles or 48 months)

*Refer to illustration 29.2*

1 The PCV valve controls the amount of crankcase vapors allowed to enter the intake manifold. Inside the PCV valve is a spring loaded valve that opens in relation to intake manifold vacuum, which allows crankcase vapors to be drawn from the valve cover back into the engine combustion chamber.

2 The PCV valve is located in the valve cover **(see illustration)**.

3 To check the operation of the PCV valve, disconnect the hose from the valve, then unscrew the valve from the valve cover and reconnect the hose to it.

4 Start the engine and listen for a hissing sound coming from the PCV valve. Place your finger over the valve opening - you should feel vacuum. If there's no vacuum at the valve, check for a plugged hose, port or valve. Replace any plugged or deteriorated hoses.

5 Check the spring-loaded pintle located inside the valve for freedom of movement by using a small screwdriver or equivalent to push the valve off its seat and see that it returns to the fully seated position. If the valve is sluggish or the inside of the valve is contaminated with gum and carbon deposits, the valve must be replaced.

6 To remove the valve, see Step 3.

7 When purchasing a replacement PCV valve, make sure it's for your particular vehicle and engine size. Compare the old valve with the new one to make sure they're the same.

8 Apply thread sealant to the threads of the valve, then install it in the valve cover and tighten it securely. Reconnect the hose to the valve.

# Chapter 2 Part A
# Engines

## Contents



## Specifications

### 2.0L engine

#### General

| | |
|---|---|
| Bore | 3.445 inches (87.5 mm) |
| Stroke | 3.268 inches (83.0 mm) |
| Compression ratio | 9.6:1 |
| Compression pressure | |
| Standard | 170 to 225 psi (1172 to 1551 kPa) |
| Maximum variation between cylinders | 25 percent |
| Displacement | 122 cubic inches (2.0 liters) |
| Firing order | 1-3-4-2 |
| Oil pressure | |
| At idle speed (minimum) | 4 psi (27.5 kPa) |
| At 3000 rpm | 25 to 80 psi (172 to 552 kPa) |



**Cylinder numbering and coil terminal location (2.0L DOHC and 2.4L DOHC engines)**

#### Camshaft

| | |
|---|---|
| Bearing bore diameter | 1.024 to 1.025 inches (26.020 to 26.041 mm) |
| Bearing journal diameter | 1.021 to 1.022 inches (25.951 to 25.970 mm) |
| Bearing clearance | 0.0027 to 0.0030 inch (0.069 to 0.071 mm) |
| Endplay | 0.002 to 0.006 inch (0.05 to 0.15 mm) |
| Lobe lift | |
| Intake | 0.340 inch (8.65 mm) |
| Exhaust | 0.312 inch (7.95 mm) |

#### Cylinder head

| | |
|---|---|
| Cylinder head warpage (maximum) | |
| Head gasket surface | 0.004 inch (0.101 mm) |
| Exhaust manifold mounting surfaces | 0.006 inch (0.152 mm) |

#### Intake and exhaust manifolds

| | |
|---|---|
| Warpage limit (maximum) | 0.006 inch (0.152 mm) |

#### Oil pump

| | |
|---|---|
| Cover warpage limit | 0.003 inch (0.076 mm) |
| Inner rotor thickness (minimum) | 0.301 inch (0.301 mm) |
| Outer rotor thickness (minimum) | 0.301 inch (0.301 mm) |
| Outer rotor diameter (minimum) | 3.148 inch (79.95 mm) |
| Rotor-to-pump cover clearance (maximum) | 0.004 inch (0.10 mm) |
| Outer rotor-to-housing clearance (maximum) | 0.015 inch (0.039 mm) |
| Inner rotor-to-outer rotor lobe clearance (maximum) | 0.008 inch (0.20 mm) |

## Torque specifications (2.0L engine)

**Note:** *One foot-pound (ft-lb) of torque is equivalent to 12 inch-pounds (in-lbs) of torque. Torque values below approximately 15 foot-pounds are expressed in inch-pounds, because most foot-pound torque wrenches are not accurate at these smaller values.*

| | Ft-lbs (unless otherwise indicated) | Nm |
|---|---|---|
| Camshaft bearing cap bolts **(see illustration 10.19)** | | |
| M6 bolts | 105 in-lbs | 12 |
| M8 bolts | 20 | 28 |
| Camshaft sprocket bolt | 85 | 115 |
| Crankshaft damper bolt | 100 | 136 |
| Cylinder head bolts **(see illustration 13.14)** | | |
| Step 1 | 25 | 34 |
| Step 2 | | |
| Bolts 1 through 6 | 50 | 68 |
| Bolts 7 through 10 | 35 | 49 |
| Step 3 | | |
| Bolts 1 through 6 | 50 | 68 |
| Bolts 7 through 10 | 35 | 49 |
| Step 4 | Tighten an additional 90-degrees (1/4 turn) | |
| Exhaust manifold heat shield bolts | 105 in-lbs | 12 |
| Exhaust manifold-to-cylinder head bolts | 16 | 23 |
| Exhaust manifold-to-exhaust pipe bolts | 33 | 44 |
| Flywheel/driveplate-to-crankshaft bolts | 70 | 95 |
| Intake manifold bolts/nuts | | |
| Upper intake manifold bolts | 105 in-lbs | 12 |
| Lower intake manifold-bolts | 105 in-lbs | 12 |
| Oil pan bolts | 105 in-lbs | 12 |
| Oil pump | | |
| Oil pump mounting bolts | 20 | 28 |
| Cover screws | 105 in-lbs | 12 |
| Pick-up tube bolt | 16 | 23 |
| Relief valve cap | 30 | 42 |
| Timing belt | | |
| Cover bolts | | |
| Upper bolt | 105 in-lbs | 12 |
| Lower bolt | 105 in-lbs | 12 |
| Timing belt tensioner assembly | | |
| Timing belt tensioner bolts | | |
| 2001 and 2002 models | 23 | 31 |
| 2003 models | 22 | 30 |
| Tensioner pulley bolt | 50 | 67 |
| Structural collar-to-transaxle bolts **(see illustration 14.4a)** | 80 | 108 |
| Structural collar-to-oil pan bolts | 40 in-lbs | 4.5 |
| Torque strut bolts | 87 | 115 |
| Valve cover bolts | 105 in-lbs | 12 |

**Refer to Part B for additional torque specifications*

## 2.4L engine

### General

| | |
|---|---|
| Bore | 3.445 inches (87.5 mm) |
| Stroke | 3.976 inches (101.0 mm) |
| Compression ratio | |
| Non-turbo | 9.5:1 |
| Turbo | 8.1:1 |
| Compression pressure | |
| Standard | 170 to 225 psi |
| Maximum variation between cylinders | 25 percent |
| Displacement | 148 cubic inches (2.4 liters) |
| Firing order | 1-3-4-2 |
| Oil pressure | |
| At idle speed (minimum) | 4 psi (27.5 kPa) |
| At 3000 rpm | 25 to 80 psi (172 to 552 kPa) |

### Camshaft

| | |
|---|---|
| Bearing bore diameter | 1.024 to 1.025 inches (26.020 to 26.041 mm) |
| Bearing journal diameter | 1.021 to 1.022 inches (25.951 to 25.970 mm) |
| Bearing clearance | 0.0027 to 0.0030 inch (0.069 to 0.071 mm) |
| Endplay | 0.0019 to 0.0066 inch (0.05 to 0.17 mm) |
| Lobe lift | |
| Intake | 0.324 inch (8.25 mm) |
| Exhaust | 0.259 inch (6.60 mm) |

### Cylinder head

| | |
|---|---|
| Head gasket surface warpage limit | 0.004 inch (0.101 mm) |
| Exhaust manifold mounting surface warpage limit | 0.006 inch (0.152 mm) |

### Intake and exhaust manifolds

| | |
|---|---|
| Warpage limit | 0.006 inch (0.152 mm) |

### Oil pump

| | |
|---|---|
| Cover warpage limit | 0.001 inch (0.025 mm) |
| Inner rotor thickness (minimum) | |
| 2001 and 2002 models | 0.370 inch (9.40 mm) |
| 2003 and later models | 0.421 inch (10.699 mm) |
| Outer rotor thickness (minimum) | |
| 2001 and 2002 models | 0.370 inch (9.40 mm) |
| 2003 and later models | 0.421 inch (10.699 mm) |
| Outer rotor diameter (minimum) | |
| 2001 and 2002 models | 3.148 inch (79.95 mm) |
| 2003 and later models | 3.383 inch (85.924 mm) |
| Rotor-to-pump cover clearance (maximum) | 0.004 inch (0.101 mm) |
| Outer rotor-to-housing clearance (maximum) | 0.015 inch (0.039 mm) |
| Inner rotor-to-outer rotor lobe clearance (maximum) | 0.008 inch (0.20 mm) |

### Torque specifications (2.4L engine)

**Note:** *One foot-pound (ft-lb) of torque is equivalent to 12 inch-pounds (in-lbs) of torque. Torque values below approximately 15 foot-pounds are expressed in inch-pounds, because most foot-pound torque wrenches are not accurate at these smaller values.*

| | **Ft-lbs** (unless otherwise indicated) | **Nm** |
|---|---|---|
| Camshaft bearing cap bolts **(see illustration 10.19)** | | |
| M6 bolts | 105 in-lbs | 12 |
| M8 bolts | 20 | 28 |
| Camshaft sprocket bolt | | |
| 2001 models | 75 | 101 |
| 2002 and later models | 85 | 115 |
| Crankshaft damper bolt | 100 | 136 |
| Cylinder head bolts (2001 through 2005 models) **(see illustration 13.14)** | | |
| Step 1 | 25 | 34 |
| Step 2 | 50 | 68 |
| Step 3 | 50 | 68 |
| Step 4 | Tighten an additional 1/4 turn (90-degrees) | |
| Cylinder head bolts (2006 and later models) | | |
| Step 1 | 25 | 34 |
| Step 2 | 60 | 82 |
| Step 3 | 60 | 82 |
| Step 4 | Tighten an additional 1/4 turn (90 degrees) | |
| Driveplate-to-crankshaft bolts | 70 | 95 |
| Exhaust manifold heat shield bolts | 105 in-lbs | 12 |
| Exhaust manifold-to-cylinder head bolts | 16 | 23 |
| Exhaust manifold-to-exhaust pipe bolts | 21 | 28 |
| Intake manifold bolts | | |
| 2001 through 2003 models | | |
| Non-turbocharged models | | |
| Upper intake manifold bolts | 105 in-lbs | 12 |
| Lower intake manifold bolts | 105 in-lbs | 12 |
| Turbocharged models | | |
| Upper intake manifold bolts | 20 | 28 |
| Lower intake manifold bolts | 20 | 28 |
| 2004 models | | |
| Non-turbocharged models | | |
| Upper intake manifold bolts | 105 in-lbs | 12 |
| Lower intake manifold bolts | 105 in-lbs | 12 |
| Turbocharged models | | |
| Upper intake manifold bolts | 20 | 28 |
| Lower intake manifold bolts | 20 | 28 |
| 2005 and later models | | |
| Non-turbocharged models | | |
| Upper and lower intake manifold bolts | 105 in-lbs | 12 |
| Turbocharged models | | |
| Plastic manifolds (upper and lower) | 105 in-lbs | 12 |
| Aluminum manifolds (upper and lower) | 20 | 27 |
| Oil pan bolts | 105 in-lbs | 12 |

## 2.4L engines (continued)

### Torque specifications

| | Ft-lbs (unless otherwise indicated) | Nm |
|---|---|---|

**Note:** *One foot-pound (ft-lb) of torque is equivalent to 12 inch-pounds (in-lbs) of torque. Torque values below approximately 15 foot-pounds are expressed in inch-pounds, because most foot-pound torque wrenches are not accurate at these smaller values.*

| | Ft-lbs (unless otherwise indicated) | Nm |
|---|---|---|
| Oil pump | | |
| Attaching bolts | 20 | 28 |
| Cover screws | 118 in-lbs | 13 |
| Pick-up tube bolt | | |
| 2001 models | 20 | 28 |
| 2002 and later models | 16 | 23 |
| Relief valve cap bolt | 30 | 42 |
| Structural collar assembly | | |
| Automatic transaxle models **(see illustration 14.4b)** | | |
| Bolts 1, 2 and 3 | 75 | 101 |
| Bolts 4, 5, 6, 7 and 8 | 45 | 61 |
| Manual transaxle models **(see illustration 14.4c)** | | |
| Bolt 1 | 75 | 101 |
| Bolts 2 and 5 | 45 | 61 |
| Bolts 3 and 4 | 20 | 28 |
| Thermostat housing bolts | See Chapter 3 | |
| Timing belt | | |
| Cover bolts | | |
| 2001 models | | |
| Outer cover bolts | 40 in-lbs | 4.5 |
| Rear cover bolts | 105 in-lbs | 12 |
| 2002 models | | |
| Outer cover bolts | 80 in-lbs | 9 |
| Rear cover bolts | | |
| M6 bolts | 105 in-lbs | 12 |
| M8 bolts | 20 | 28 |
| 2003 models | | |
| Outer cover bolts | 50 in-lbs | 6 |
| Rear cover bolts | | |
| M6 bolts | 105 in-lbs | 12 |
| M8 bolts | 20 | 28 |
| Idler pulley bolt | 45 | 61 |
| Tensioner assembly | | |
| Tensioner pulley bolt | 16 | 23 |
| Tensioner bolt | | |
| 2001 and 2002 models (assembly mounting bolt) | 45 | 61 |
| 2003 models | 18 | 24 |
| Torque strut bolts | 87 | 115 |
| Valve cover bolts **(see illustration 4.9)** | | |
| Step 1 | 40 in-lbs | 4.5 |
| Step 2 | 80 in-lbs | 9 |
| Step 3 | 105 in-lbs | 12 |

**Refer to Part B for additional torque specifications*

## 1 General information

This Part of Chapter 2 is devoted to in-vehicle engine repair procedures. Information concerning engine removal and installation can be found in Part B of this Chapter.

The following repair procedures are based on the assumption that the engine is installed in the vehicle. If the engine has been removed from the vehicle and mounted on a stand, many of the steps outlined in this Part of Chapter 2 will not apply.

The Specifications included in this Part of Chapter 2 apply only to the procedures contained in this Part.

These models are equipped with either a 2.0L DOHC or 2.4L DOHC four-cylinder engine.

## 2 Repair operations possible with the engine in the vehicle

Many major repair operations can be accomplished without removing the engine from the vehicle.

Clean the engine compartment and the exterior of the engine with some type of degreaser before any work is done. It will make the job easier and help keep dirt out of the internal areas of the engine.

Depending on the components involved, it may be helpful to remove the hood to improve access to the engine as repairs are performed (refer to Chapter 11 if necessary). Cover the fenders to prevent damage to the paint. Special pads are available, but an old bedspread or blanket will also work.

If vacuum, exhaust, oil or coolant leaks develop, indicating a need for gasket or seal replacement, the repairs can generally be made with the engine in the vehicle. The intake and exhaust manifold gaskets, oil pan gasket, camshaft and crankshaft oil seals and cylinder head gasket are all accessible with the engine in place.

Exterior engine components, such as the intake and exhaust manifolds, the oil pan, the oil pump, the water pump, the starter motor, the alternator, the distributor and the fuel system components can be removed for repair with the engine in place.

Since the camshaft(s) and cylinder head can be removed without pulling the engine, valve component servicing can also be accomplished with the engine in the vehicle. Replacement of the timing belt and sprockets is also possible with the engine in the vehicle.

In extreme cases caused by a lack of necessary equipment, repair or replacement of piston rings, pistons, connecting rods and rod bearings is possible with the engine in the vehicle. However, this practice is not recommended because of the cleaning and preparation work that must be done to the components involved.

## 3 Top Dead Center (TDC) for number one piston - locating

1 Top Dead Center (TDC) is the highest point in the cylinder that each piston reaches as it travels up-and-down when the crankshaft turns. Each piston reaches TDC on the compression stroke and again on the exhaust stroke, but TDC generally refers to piston position on the compression stroke. The cast-in timing mark arrow on the crankshaft timing belt pulley installed on the front of the crankshaft is referenced to the number one piston at TDC when the arrow is straight up, or at "12 o'clock", and aligned with the cast-in timing mark arrow on the oil pump housing (see Section 7).

2 Positioning a specific piston at TDC is an essential part of many procedures such as camshaft(s) removal, rocker arm removal, timing belt and sprocket replacement.

3 In order to bring any piston to TDC, the crankshaft must be turned using one of the methods outlined below. When looking at the front of the engine, normal crankshaft rotation is clockwise. **Warning:** *Before beginning this procedure, be sure to set the parking brake, place the transmission in Park or Neutral and disable the ignition system by disconnecting the primary electrical connector from the ignition coil pack.*

*a) The preferred method is to turn the crankshaft with a large socket and breaker bar attached to the crankshaft balancer hub bolt that is threaded into the front of the crankshaft.*

*b) A remote starter switch, which may save some time, can also be used. Attach the switch leads to the S (switch) and B (battery) terminals on the starter solenoid. Once the piston is close to TDC, discontinue with the remote switch and use a socket and breaker bar as described in the previous paragraph.*

*c) If an assistant is available to turn the ignition switch to the Start position in short bursts, you can get the piston close to TDC without a remote starter switch. Use a socket and breaker bar as described in Paragraph a) to complete the procedure.*

4 Remove all spark plugs as this will make it easier to rotate the engine by hand.

5 Insert a compression gauge (screw-in type with a hose) in the number 1 spark plug hole. Place the gauge dial where you can see it while turning the crankshaft balancer hub bolt. **Note:** *The number one cylinder is located at the front (timing belt end) of the engine.*

6 Turn the crankshaft clockwise until you see compression building up on the gauge - you are on the compression stroke for that cylinder. If you did not see compression build up, continue with one more complete revolution to achieve TDC for the number one cylinder.

7 Remove the compression gauge. Through the number one cylinder spark plug hole insert a section of wooden dowel or plastic rod and slowly push it down until it reaches the top surface of the piston crown. **Caution:** *Don't insert a metal or sharp object into the spark plug hole as the piston crown may be damaged.*

8 With the dowel or rod in place on top of the piston crown, slowly rotate the crankshaft clockwise until the dowel or rod is pushed upward, stops, and then starts to move back down. At this point, rotate the crankshaft slightly counterclockwise until the dowel or rod has reached it upper most travel. At this point the number one piston is at the TDC position.

9 Remove the upper timing belt cover (see Section 7). Then check the alignment of the camshaft timing marks **(see illustrations 7.18 and 7.31)**. At this point the camshaft(s) timing marks should be aligned. If not repeat this procedure until alignment is correct.

10 After the number one piston has been positioned at TDC on the compression stroke, TDC for any of the remaining cylinders can be located by turning the crankshaft 180-degrees (1/2-turn) at a time and following the firing order (refer to the Specifications).

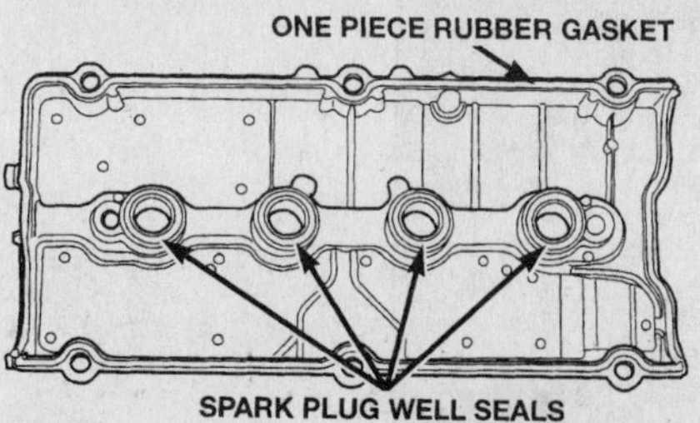

**4.8 Install a new rubber gasket and new spark plug well seals onto the valve cover**

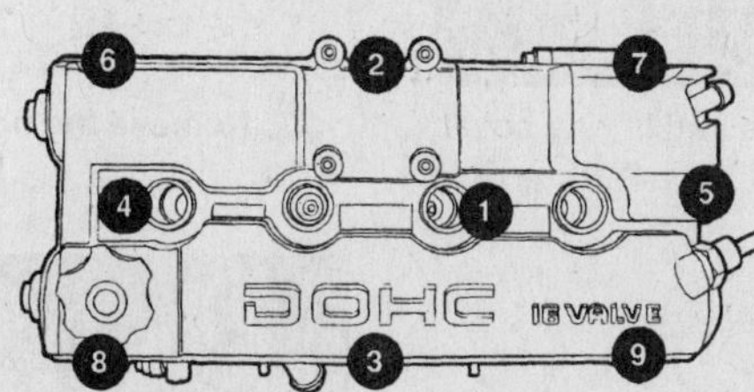

**4.10 Valve cover bolt tightening sequence**

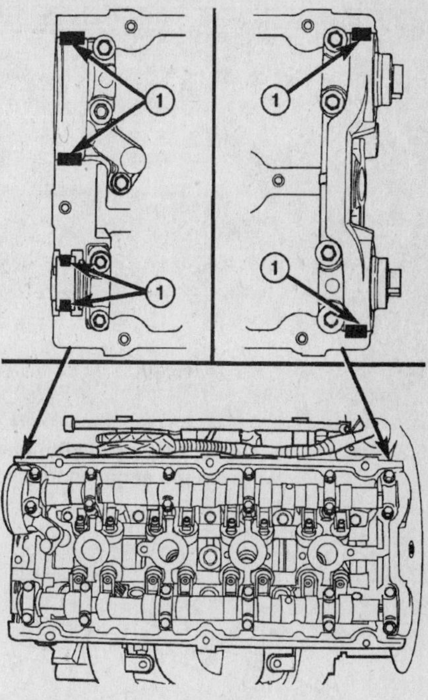

**4.9 Apply a light coat of RTV sealant onto the corners of the number 1 and the number 6 camshaft bearing caps**

## 4 Valve cover - removal and installation

### Removal

1 Disconnect the cable from the negative battery terminal (see Chapter 5).

2 Remove the upper intake manifold (see Section 5).

3 Remove the ignition coil pack from the valve cover (see Chapter 5).

4 Clearly label and detach any electrical wiring harnesses which connect to or cross over the valve cover.

5 Disconnect the PCV valve hose and breather hose from the valve cover (see Chapter 6).

6 Remove the valve cover bolts and lift off the cover. If the cover sticks to the cylinder head, tap on it with a soft-face hammer or place a wood block against the cover and tap on the wood with a hammer. **Caution:** *If you have to pry between the valve cover and the cylinder head, be extremely careful not to gouge or nick the gasket surfaces of either part. A leak could develop after reassembly.* **Note:** *Do not interchange the two center bolts with the seven perimeter bolts. The two center bolts contain a special aluminum sealing washer.*

7 Remove the valve cover perimeter rubber seal. Thoroughly clean the valve cover and remove all traces of old gasket material. Gasket removal solvents are available from auto parts stores and may prove helpful. After cleaning the surfaces, degrease them with a rag soaked in lacquer thinner or acetone.

### Installation

*Refer to illustrations 4.8, 4.9 and 4.10*

8 Inspect the spark plug tube seals **(see illustration)** for deterioration and hardness. Replace them if necessary.

9 Install a new gasket on the cover, using RTV sealant to hold it in place **(see illustration)**. Apply RTV sealant to the camshaft cap corners and the top edges of the half-round

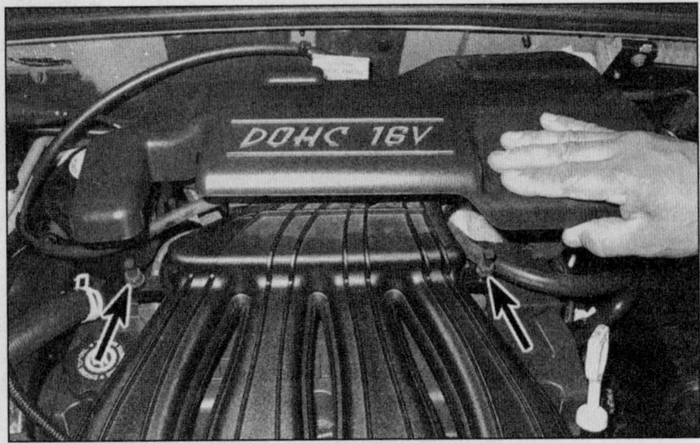


5.2 Remove the engine cover from the ballstuds and lift the cover from the engine compartment

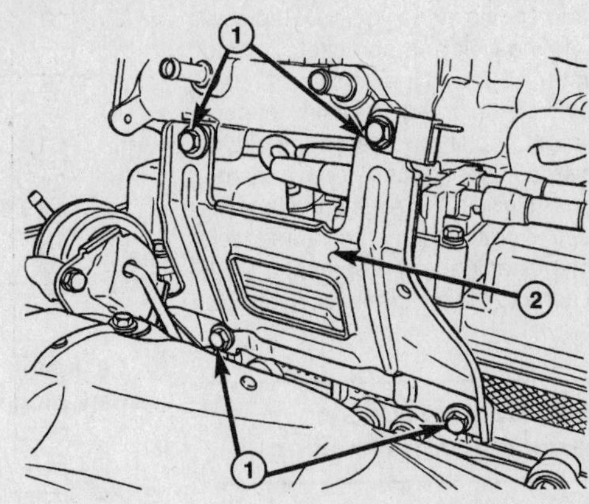


5.7 Remove the bolts (1) and then separate the intake manifold bracket (2) from the engine

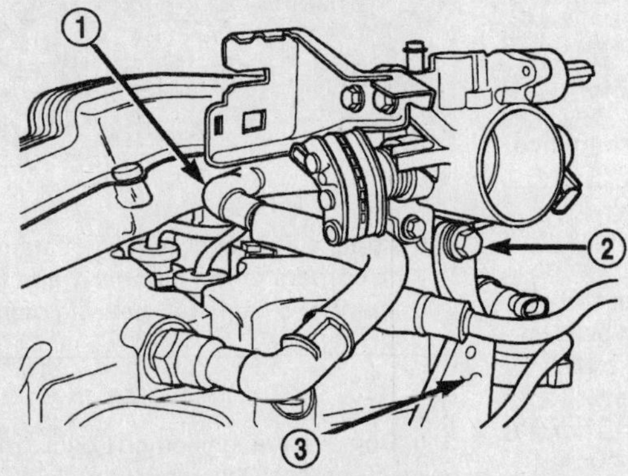


5.11 First disconnect the PCV hose (1), then remove the bracket bolt (2) from the throttle body bracket (3)

5.14 Remove the upper intake manifold mounting bolts

seal. Place the cover on the engine and install the cover bolts.

10 Tighten the bolts to the torque listed in this Chapter's Specifications **(see illustration)**.

11 Install the upper intake manifold (see Section 5).

12 The remaining steps are the reverse of removal. When finished, run the engine and check for oil leaks.

## 5 Intake manifold - removal and installation

*Refer to illustration 5.2*

1 Relieve the fuel system pressure (see Chapter 4), then disconnect the cable from the negative battery terminal (see Chapter 5).

2 Remove the engine cover **(see illustration)**.

### *Removal*

### Upper intake manifold

3 Disconnect the IAT sensor (see Chapter 6) and remove the air inlet duct (see Chapter 4).

4 Unplug the electrical connectors from the Idle Air Control (IAC) motor, the Throttle Position Sensor (TPS) and the Manifold Absolute Pressure (MAP) sensor (see Chapter 6).

### Turbocharged models

*Refer to illustration 5.7*

5 Disconnect the throttle inlet pressure (TIP) hose from the intake air duct (see Chapter 4).

6 Disconnect the charge air cooler hose at the throttle body (see Chapter 4).

7 Remove the intake manifold support bracket **(see illustration)**.

### All models

*Refer to illustrations 5.11 and 5.14*

8 Remove the air filter housing (see Chapter 4).

9 Disconnect the accelerator cable and, if equipped, the cruise control cable from the throttle lever arm (see Chapter 4).

10 Remove the purge control hoses) and the brake booster hose from the intake manifold.

11 Remove the throttle body support bracket **(see illustration)**.

12 If you're planning to *replace* or *service* the intake manifold, remove the throttle body (see Chapter 4). If you're simply removing the intake manifold to remove or service the cylinder head, it's not necessary to remove the throttle body from the intake manifold.

13 Remove the EGR pipe from the manifold (see Chapter 6), if equipped.

14 Remove the upper intake manifold fasteners **(see illustration)**, then remove the upper intake manifold.

### Lower intake manifold

*Refer to illustration 5.20*

**Warning:** *Wait until the engine is completely cool before beginning this procedure.*

15 Drain the cooling system (see Chapter 1).

16 Remove the upper radiator hose (see Chapter 3).

17 Disconnect the fuel line at the fuel rail (see Chapter 4).

18 Disconnect the electrical connectors from the fuel injectors (see Chapter 4).

19 Remove the dipstick tube brace.

20 On turbocharged models, remove the lower intake manifold brace **(see illustration)**.

21 Remove the lower intake manifold fasteners and washers and then remove the lower intake manifold and the gasket.

### Inspection

22 Using a straightedge and feeler gauge, check the intake manifold mating surface for warpage. Check the intake manifold surface on the cylinder head also. If the warpage on either surface exceeds the limit listed in this Chapter's Specifications, the intake manifold and/or the cylinder head must be resurfaced at an auto-

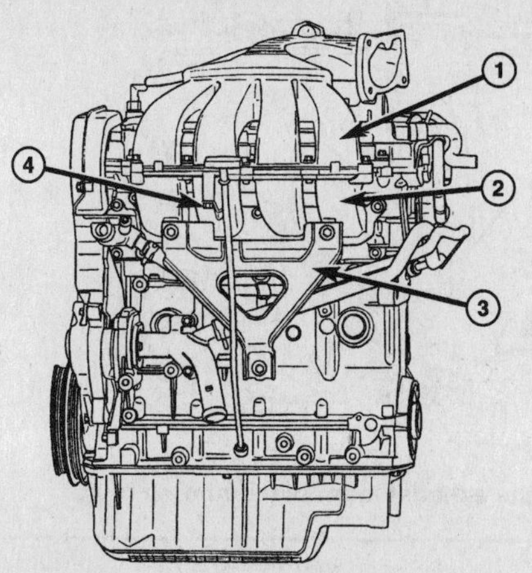


**5.20 On turbocharged models, first remove the dipstick tube (4), then remove the lower intake manifold brace mounting bolts (3) and separate it from the lower intake manifold (2)**

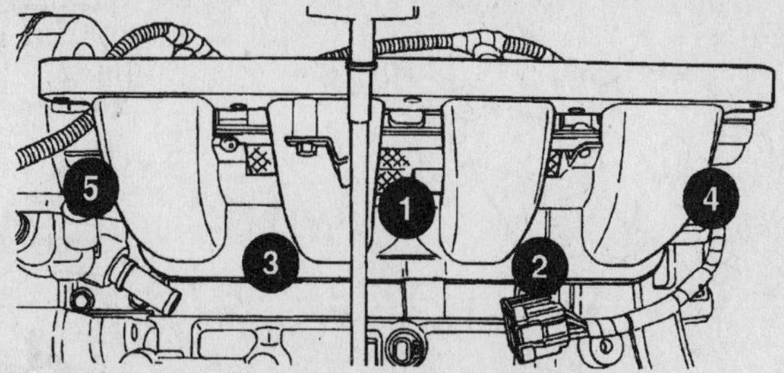


**5.24 Lower intake manifold fastener tightening sequence**

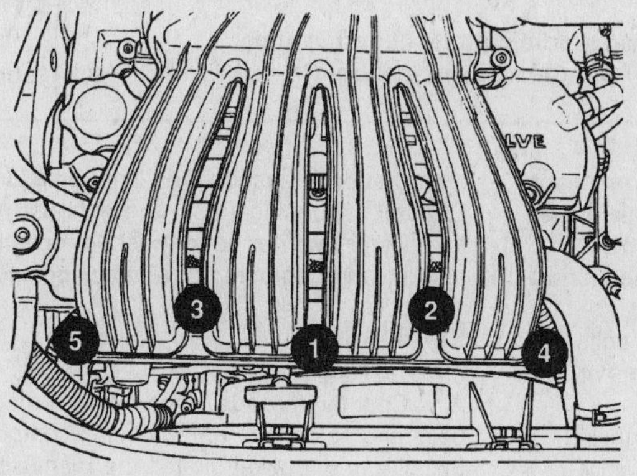


**5.26 Upper intake manifold tightening sequence**

motive machine shop or, if the warpage is too excessive for resurfacing, replaced.

## *Installation*

### Lower intake manifold

*Refer to illustration 5.24*

23 Install new seals into the lower intake manifold on non-turbocharged models or a new manifold gasket on turbocharged models.

24 Install the lower intake manifold and tighten the intake manifold fasteners gradually and evenly in the indicated sequence **(see illustration)** to the torque listed in this Chapter's Specifications.

25 Installation is otherwise the reverse of removal. Refill and bleed the cooling system as described in Chapter 1.

### Upper intake manifold

*Refer to illustration 5.26*

26 Check the condition of the manifold seals and replace them if they are damaged or hardened. Install the upper intake manifold and tighten the intake manifold fasteners gradually and evenly in the indicated sequence **(see illustration)** to the torque listed in this Chapter's Specifications.

27 Installation is otherwise the reverse of removal.

## 6 Exhaust manifold - removal and installation

*Refer to illustrations 6.9, 6.10, 6.12 and 6.14*

**Warning:** *Allow the engine to cool completely before beginning this procedure.*

**Note:** *Turbocharged models are equipped with an exhaust manifold and turbocharger assembly. If the exhaust manifold is damaged, it must be replaced as a complete unit* (see Chapter 4).

1 Disconnect the cable from the negative battery terminal (see Chapter 5).

2 Set the parking brake and block the rear wheels.

3 Raise the vehicle and support it securely on jackstands.

4 Remove the air filter housing (see Chapter 4).

5 Remove the coolant reservoir (see Chapter 3).

6 Disconnect the MAP sensor (see Chapter 6).

7 Remove the power steering fluid reservoir from the cylinder head and position it off to the side without disconnecting the fluid lines.

8 Remove the accelerator cable and the cruise control cable, if equipped (see Chapter 4).

9 Remove the upper heat shield bolts and remove the upper heat shield from the exhaust manifold **(see illustration)**.

10 Remove the exhaust manifold support bracket **(see illustration)**.

11 Working from under the vehicle, apply penetrating oil to the threads of the exhaust manifold-to-exhaust pipe studs and allow it to soak in for awhile. Then remove the exhaust pipe-to-exhaust manifold flange nuts and separate the exhaust pipe from the exhaust manifold.

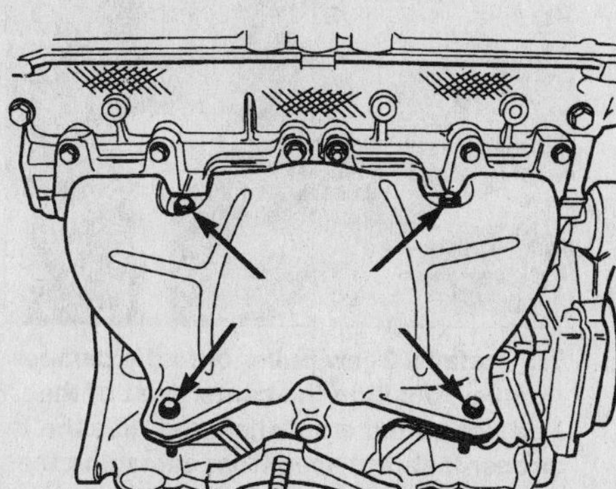

**6.9 Remove the upper heat shield mounting bolts and separate the shield from the exhaust manifold**

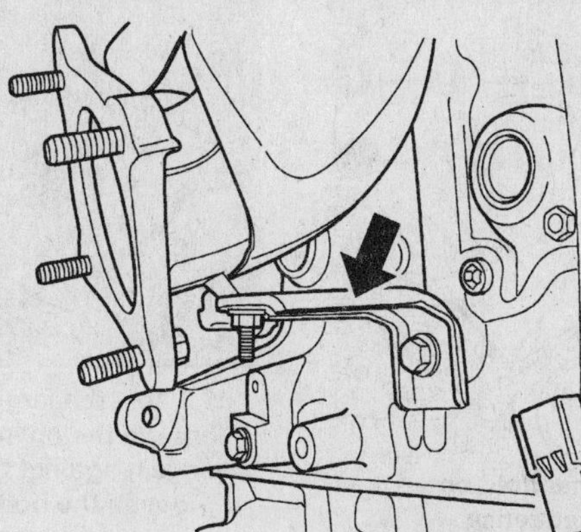

**6.10 Location of the exhaust manifold support bracket**

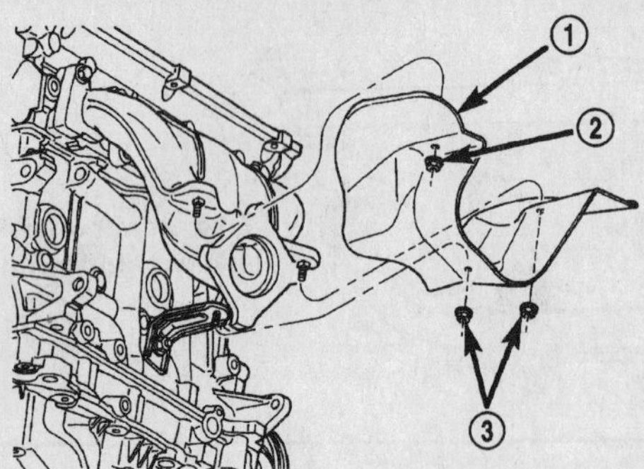


6.12 Remove the lower heat shield mounting nuts (2 and 3) and separate the heat shield (1) from the exhaust manifold

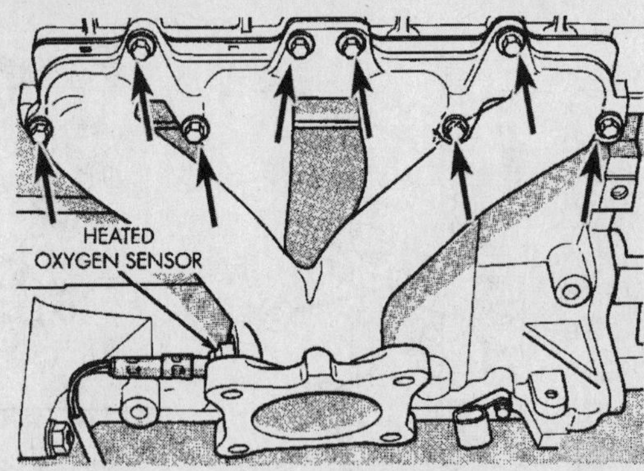


6.14 Location of the exhaust manifold mounting bolts

12 Remove the lower heat shield mounting nuts and remove the lower heat shield **(see illustration)** from the exhaust manifold.

13 Remove the oxygen sensor (see Chapter 6).

14 Remove the exhaust manifold bolts and nuts **(see illustration)** and remove the exhaust manifold.

15 Remove the exhaust manifold gasket.

### Inspection

16 Inspect the exhaust manifold for cracks and any other obvious damage. If the manifold is cracked or damaged in any way, replace it.

17 Using a wire brush, clean up the threads of the exhaust manifold bolts and inspect the threads for damage. Replace any bolts that have thread damage.

18 Using a scraper, remove all traces of gasket material from the mating surfaces and inspect them for wear and cracks. **Caution:** *When removing gasket material from any surface, especially aluminum, be very careful not to scratch or gouge the gasket surface. Any damage to the surface may leak after reassembly. Gasket removal solvents are available from auto parts stores and may prove helpful.*

19 Using a straightedge and feeler gauge, inspect the exhaust manifold mating surface for warpage. Check the exhaust manifold surface on the cylinder head also. If the warpage on any surface exceeds the limits listed in this Chapter's Specifications, the exhaust manifold and/or cylinder head must be replaced or resurfaced at an automotive machine shop.

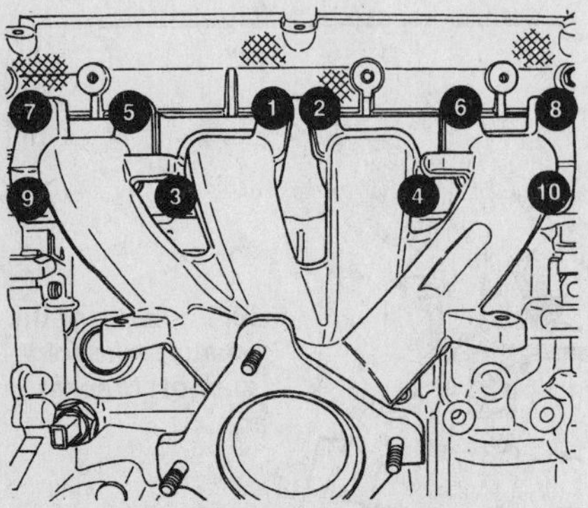

### Installation

*Refer to illustration 6.20*

20 Coat the threads of the exhaust manifold bolts and studs with an anti-seize compound. Install a new gasket, install the manifold and install the fasteners. Tighten the bolts and nuts in several stages **(see illustration)**, working from the center out, to the torque listed in this Chapter's Specifications.

21 The remainder of installation is the reverse of removal. When you're done, be sure to run the engine and check for exhaust leaks.

6.20 Exhaust manifold bolt tightening sequence

## 7 Timing belt - removal, inspection and installation

*Refer to illustrations 7.6 and 7.7*

**Warning:** *Wait until the engine is completely cool before beginning this procedure.*

**Caution 1:** *If the timing belt failed with the engine operating, damage to the valves may have occurred. Perform an engine compression check to confirm damage.*

**Caution 2:** *Do not try to turn the crankshaft with a camshaft sprocket bolt and do not rotate the crankshaft counterclockwise.*

**Caution 3:** *Do not turn the crankshaft or camshaft(s) after the timing belt has been removed. Doing so will damage the valves from contact with the pistons. Do not try to turn the crankshaft with the camshaft sprocket bolt(s) and do not rotate the crankshaft counterclockwise.*

1 Have the refrigerant discharged and recovered by an air conditioning technician.

2 Position the number one piston at Top Dead Center (see Section 3). Disconnect the cable from the negative battery terminal (see Chapter 5).

3 Remove the accessory drivebelts (see Chapter 1).

4 Set the parking brake and block the rear wheels. Raise the front of the vehicle and support it securely on jackstands.

5 Remove the right (passenger-side) inner fender splash shield, if equipped.

6 Loosen the large bolt in the center of the crankshaft damper pulley. It might be very tight; to break it loose insert a large screwdriver or bar through the opening in the pulley to keep the pulley stationary and loosen the bolt with a socket and breaker bar **(see illustration)**.

7 Install a 3-jaw puller onto the damper pulley and remove the pulley from the crank-

7.6 Insert a large screwdriver or bar through the opening in the pulley and wedge it against the engine block, then loosen the bolt with a socket and breaker bar

7.7 Install a 3-jaw puller onto the damper pulley, position the center post of the puller on the crankshaft end (use the proper insert to keep from damaging the crankshaft threads), tighten the puller and remove the pulley from the crankshaft

7.17 Remove the two lower bolts that attach the timing belt outer cover to the engine

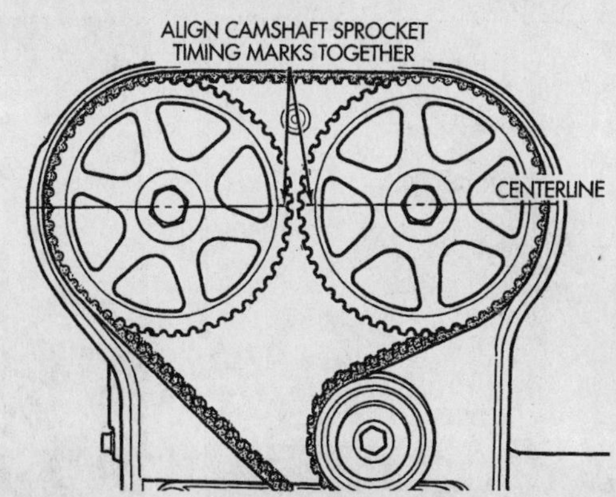


7.18 Camshaft timing mark details (2.0L DOHC models)

shaft **(see illustration)**. Use the proper insert to keep the puller from damaging the crankshaft bolt threads. If the pulley is difficult to remove, tap the center bolt of the puller with a brass mallet to break it loose. Reinstall the bolt with a spacer so you can rotate the crankshaft later.

## 2.0L models

### Removal

*Refer to illustrations 7.17, 7.18 and 7.19*

8 Remove the exhaust flange mounting bolts and separate the exhaust pipe from the exhaust manifold (see Chapter 4).

9 Disconnect the air conditioning lines at the coupling block (see Chapter 3).

10 Drain the engine coolant (see Chapter 1).

11 Remove the upper radiator support crossmember (see Chapter 3).

12 Remove the ground strap from the torque strut bracket.

13 Remove the power steering pump and the power steering pump bracket (see Chapter 10) and position it off to the side without disconnecting the fluid lines.

14 Remove the torque strut from the engine and chassis (see Section 18).

15 Support the engine with a floor jack under the oil pan. Place a wood block on the jack head to prevent the floor jack from denting or damaging the oil pan.

16 Remove the right (passenger's side) engine mount and engine mount bracket (see Section 18).

17 Remove the two lower timing belt cover bolts **(see illustration)** and the single upper bolt, then remove the timing belt cover.

18 Before removing the timing belt, make sure that the camshaft sprocket timing marks are aligned **(see illustration)**. **Note:** *If you plan to reuse the timing belt, paint an arrow on it to indicate the direction of rotation (clockwise).*

19 Release tension on the timing belt:

*a) On 2001 and 2002 models, remove the timing belt tensioner mounting bolts* **(see illustration)** *and then remove the tensioner.* **Note:** *The tensioner plunger will extend when the assembly is removed.*

*b) On 2003 models, insert a 6 mm Allen wrench into the hexagon opening located on the top plate of the belt tensioner pulley* **(see illustration 7.46b)**. *Then, loosen the tensioner bolt and, using the 6 mm Allen wrench as a lever, rotate the belt tensioner CLOCKWISE until there is slack on the timing belt.*

20 Carefully slip the timing belt off the sprockets and set it aside. If you plan to reuse the timing belt, place it in a plastic bag - do not allow the belt to come in contact with any type of oil or water as this will greatly shorten belt life.

21 If you're planning to replace a camshaft seal, it will be necessary to remove the camshaft sprockets, the timing belt tensioner pulley and the rear timing belt cover (see Section 9).

22 Inspect the crankshaft front oil seal for leaks and replace it if necessary (see Section 8).

### Inspection

*Refer to illustration 7.24*

23 Rotate the tensioner pulley and idler pulley by hand and move them side-to-side to detect roughness and excess play. Inspect the sprockets for any signs of damage and wear. Replace parts as necessary.

24 Inspect the timing belt for cracks, separation, wear, missing teeth and oil contamination. Replace the belt if it's in questionable condition **(see illustration)**. If the timing belt is excessively worn or damaged on one side, it might be due to incorrect tracking (misalignment). If the belt looks like it was misaligned, be sure to replace the belt tensioner assembly.

7.19 Timing belt tensioner mounting bolts

7.24 Carefully inspect the timing belt; bending it backwards will often make wear or damage more apparent

7.26a The tensioner pin must be compressed into the tensioner housing prior to installation

25 Check the automatic tensioner for leaks or any obvious damage to the body.

## Installation

*Refer to illustrations 7.26a, 7.26b, 7.26c, 7.28a, 7.28b, 7.28c and 7.31*

26 On 2001 and 2002 models, the tensioner pin must be compressed into the tensioner housing prior to installation. Place the tensioner in the vise so the surface with the hole faces up. Slowly compress the tensioner, then install a 5/64-inch Allen wrench or similar tool through the body to retain the plunger in this position until it is installed **(see illustrations)**. Remove the tensioner from the vise.

27 Confirm that the camshaft sprocket timing marks are aligned **(see illustration 7.18)**.

28 Position the crankshaft timing sprocket as follows **(see illustrations)**:

a) *Initially align the TDC mark on the sprocket with the arrow on the oil pump housing.*
b) *Back it off counterclockwise 3 teeth BTDC.*
c) *Rotate the crankshaft timing sprocket clockwise to 1/2-tooth BTDC.*

29 Install the timing belt as follows; first place the belt onto the crankshaft sprocket, maintaining tension on the belt, wrap it around the water pump sprocket, idler pulley and camshaft sprockets, then slip the belt onto the tensioner pulley.

30 To take the slack out of the timing belt, rotate the crankshaft timing sprocket clockwise to align the marks (TDC), make sure the camshaft sprocket timing marks remain aligned.

7.26b Place the tensioner in the vise so the hole faces up

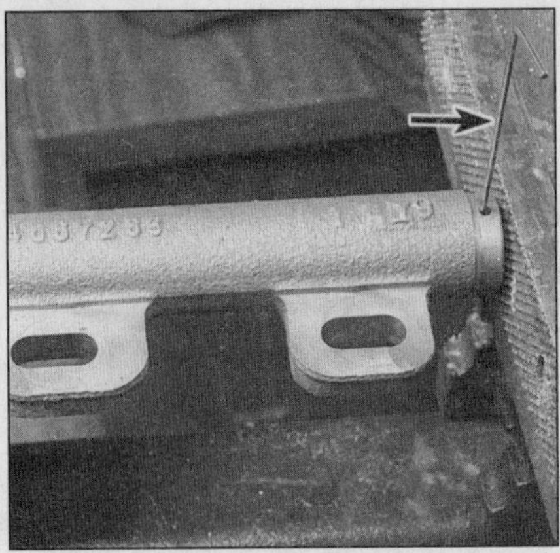

7.26c Compress the pin with the vise and place a small Allen wrench, or something similar, through the hole to keep the pin retracted for reassembly on the engine

31 Reset the tension on the timing belt:

a) *On 2001 and 2002 models, install the tensioner assembly - don't tighten the bolts at this time. Place a torque wrench on the center bolt of the tensioner pulley and apply 250 inch-lbs of torque. With the torque applied to the tensioner pulley, move the tensioner up against the tensioner pulley bracket and tighten the tensioner bolts to the torque listed in this Chapter's Specifications* **(see illustration)***. Remove the torque wrench. Release the Allen wrench or pin from the tensioner. The timing belt tension is correct when the pin can be withdrawn and reinserted easily. Double check that the timing marks on both the camshaft sprocket(s) and crankshaft sprocket are still aligned at TDC.*

7.28a Using a box-end wrench, rotate the crankshaft timing sprocket until the TDC mark on the sprocket is aligned with the arrow on the oil pump housing (arrow) . . .

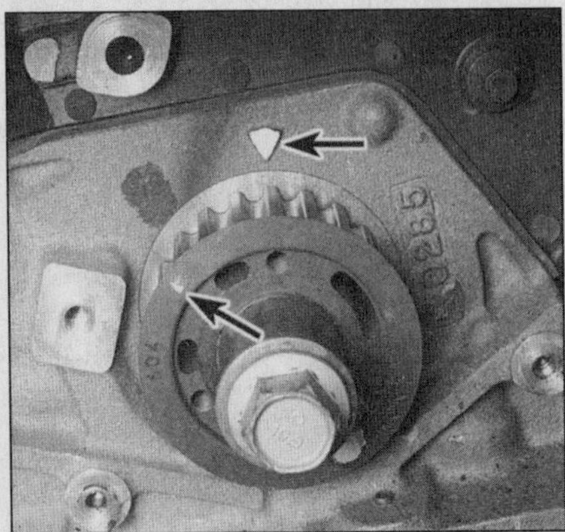

7.28b . . . then back it off counterclockwise 3 teeth BTDC (arrows)

7.28c Rotate the crankshaft timing sprocket clockwise to 1/2-tooth BTDC (arrows)

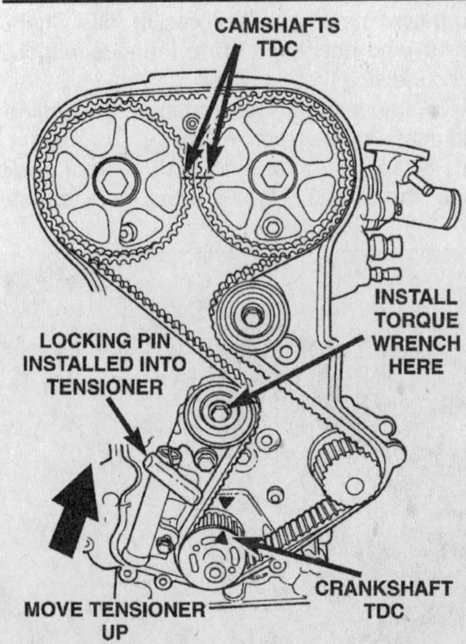


7.31 Using a torque wrench on the tensioner pulley, apply 250 inch-lbs of torque, move the tensioner up against the tensioner pulley bracket and tighten the tensioner mounting bolts

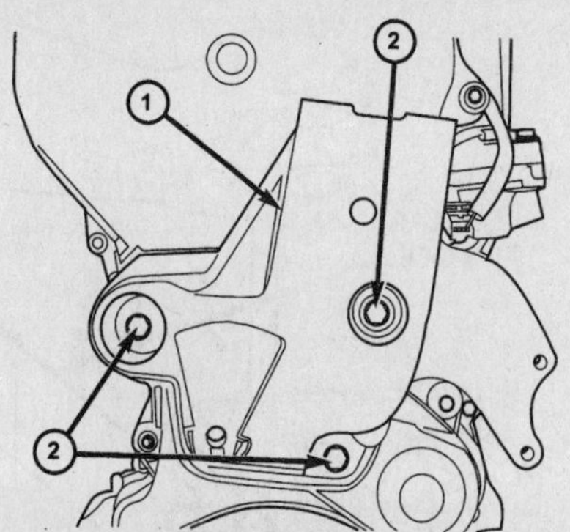


**7.43 Remove the engine support bracket**

1 *Engine support bracket*
2 *Mounting bolts*

b) *On 2003 models, insert a 6 mm Allen wrench into the hexagon opening located on the top plate of the belt tensioner pulley* **(see illustration 7.47b)**. *Then, using the 6 mm Allen wrench as a lever, rotate the belt tensioner COUNTERCLOCKWISE until there is tension on the timing belt. Continue to rotate the tension until the setting notch is aligned with the spring tang. Grip the Allen wrench to prevent the tensioner from rotating, and tighten the tensioner bolt to 22 ft-lbs. Recheck the alignment marks. If they are incorrect, loosen the bolt and repeat the procedure.*

32 Using the bolt in the center of the crankshaft sprocket, turn the crankshaft clockwise through two complete revolutions. **Caution:** *If you feel resistance while turning the crankshaft - STOP, the valves may be hitting the pistons from incorrect valve timing. Stop and re-check the valve timing.* **Note:** *The camshaft and crankshaft sprocket marks will align every two revolutions of the crankshaft.*

33 On 2003 models, check the alignment of the spring tang and the alignment notch on the tensioner. If the alignment is incorrect, repeat the above procedure.

34 Recheck the alignment of the timing marks. If the marks do not align properly, loosen the tensioner, slip the belt off the camshaft sprocket, realign the marks, reinstall the belt, and check the alignment again.

35 Reinstall the remaining parts in the reverse order of removal. Refill and bleed the cooling system as described in Chapter 1.

36 Start the engine and road test the vehicle.

## 2.4L models

### Removal

*Refer to illustrations 7.43, 7.44, 7.45, 7.46a, 7.46b, 7.47, 7.49, 7.50a, 7.50b, 7.51a and 7.51b*

37 Disconnect the air conditioning lines at the coupling block (see Chapter 3).

38 Drain the engine coolant (see Chapter 1).

39 Remove the upper radiator support crossmember (see Chapter 3).

40 Remove the ground strap from the torque strut bracket.

41 Remove the power steering pump and the power steering pump bracket (see Chapter 10) and position it off to the side without disconnecting the fluid lines.

42 Remove the torque struts from the engine and chassis (see Section 18).

43 Remove the support bracket **(see illustration)**. **Note:** *Make sure the engine is supported with a piece of wood and a floor jack placed under the oil pan. The wood will prevent the floor jack from denting or damaging the oil pan.*

44 Remove the upper and lower timing belt cover fasteners **(see illustration)** and remove the covers.

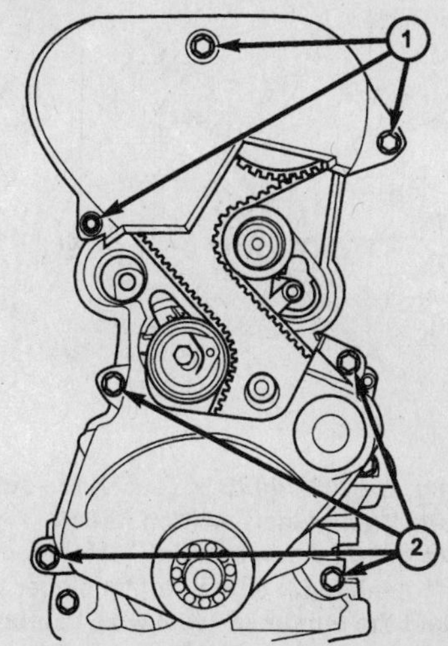


**7.44 Remove the upper (1) and lower (2) timing belt cover fasteners and then remove the covers**

45 Before removing the timing belt, make sure that the camshaft timing marks are aligned and that the TDC mark on the crankshaft timing belt sprocket is aligned with the stationary index mark on the oil pump housing **(see illustration)**. Note that the crankshaft timing belt sprocket TDC mark is located on the *trailing edge* of the sprocket tooth. If you don't align the trailing edge of the sprocket tooth with the TDC mark on the oil pump housing, the camshaft timing marks won't be aligned.

46 Release tension on the timing belt:

a) *On 2001 and 2002 models, insert a 6 mm Allen wrench into the belt tensioner and insert the long end of a 1/8-inch (3 mm) Allen wrench into the small hole*

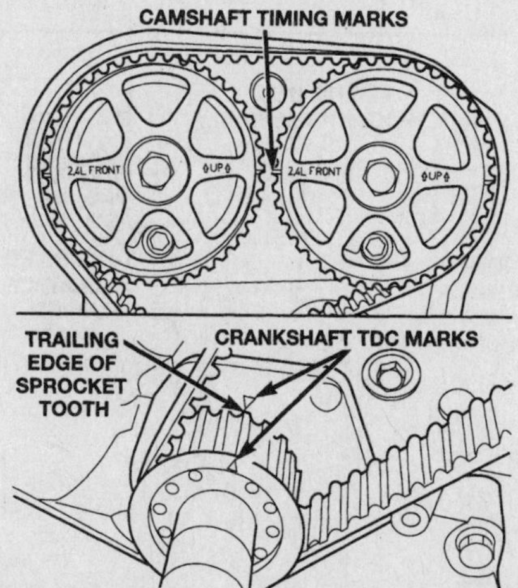


**7.45 Before removing the timing belt, make sure that the camshaft timing marks are aligned and that the TDC mark on the crankshaft timing belt sprocket is aligned with the stationary index mark on the oil pump housing (note that the crankshaft timing belt sprocket TDC mark is located on the *trailing edge* of the sprocket tooth)**

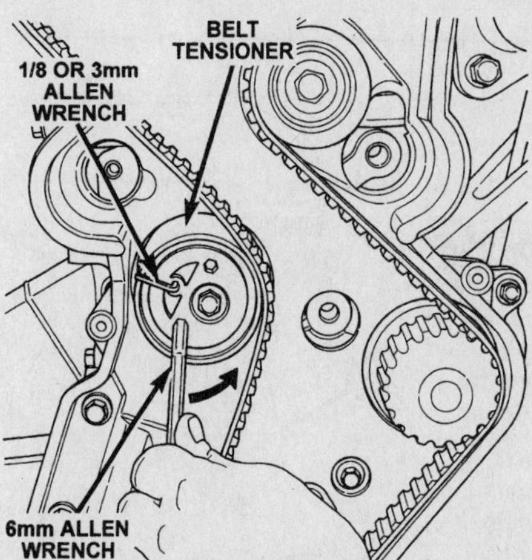


**7.46a On 2001 and 2002 models, insert a 6 mm Allen wrench into the belt tensioner and insert the long end of a 1/8-inch (3 mm) Allen wrench into the small hole located on the front of the tensioner; then, using the 6 mm Allen wrench as a lever, rotate the tensioner counterclockwise and simultaneously and lightly push in your 1/8-inch or 3 mm Allen wrench until it slides into the hole in the tensioner**

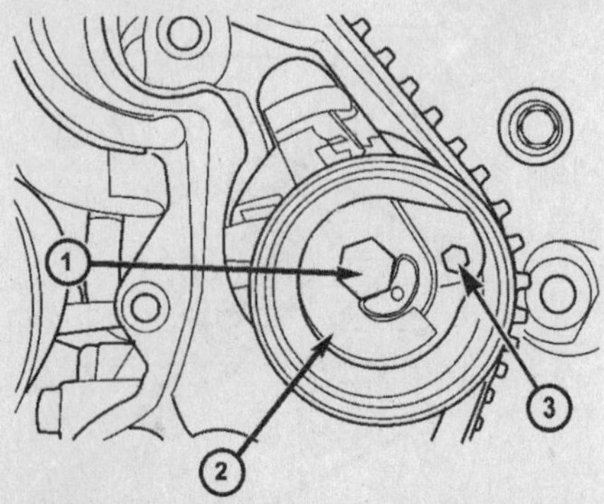

**7.46b On 2003 models, loosen the pulley bolt (1) and insert a 6 mm Allen wrench into the hexagon opening (3) located in the top plate (2) of the belt tensioner and rotate the tensioner clockwise to release tension on the timing belt**

**7.48 Timing belt idler pulley on 2003 models**

1 *Idler pulley*
2 *Bolt*

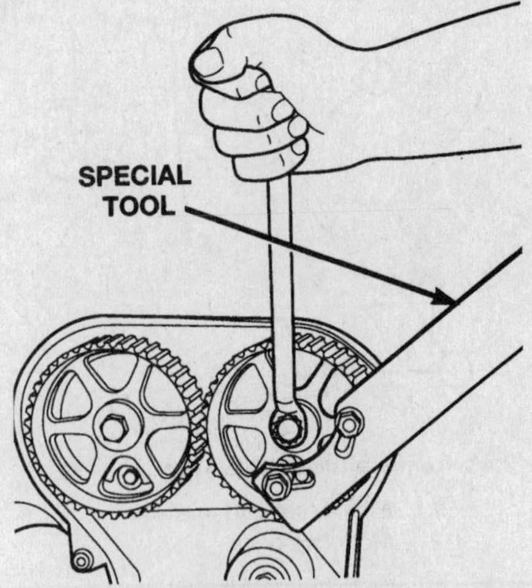

**7.49 Using a suitable holding tool, remove the camshaft sprocket bolts and then remove the camshaft sprockets; if you're unable to obtain a holding tool similar to the one shown here, use a strap wrench suitable for holding crankshaft damper pulleys**

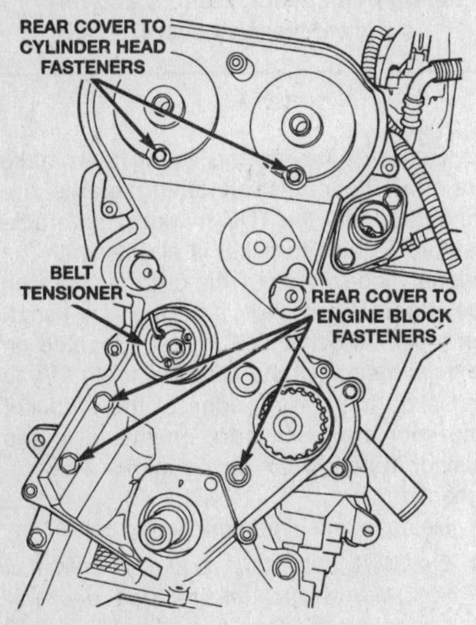

**7.50a On 2001 and 2002 models, remove the rear timing belt cover fasteners and then remove the rear cover.**

*located on the front of the tensioner* **(see illustration)**. *Then, using the 6 mm Allen wrench as a lever, rotate the tensioner COUNTERCLOCKWISE and simultaneously and lightly push in your 1/8-inch or 3 mm Allen wrench until it slides into the hole in the tensioner.*

*b) On 2003 models, insert a 6 mm Allen wrench into the hexagon opening located on the top plate of the belt tensioner pulley* **(see illustration)**. *Then, loosen the tensioner bolt and using the 6 mm Allen wrench as a lever, rotate the belt tensioner CLOCKWISE until there is slack on the timing belt.*

47 Remove the timing belt.

48 Remove the timing belt idler pulley bolt and then remove the timing belt idler pulley **(see illustration)**.

49 Using a suitable holding tool **(see illustration)**, remove the camshaft sprocket bolts and then remove the camshaft sprockets. **Note:** *If you're unable to obtain a holding tool similar to the one shown in the accompanying illustration, use a strap wrench suitable for holding crankshaft damper pulleys.*

50 Remove the rear timing belt cover fasteners **(see illustrations)** and remove the rear cover.

51 Remove the lower timing belt tensioner bolt **(see illustrations)** and remove the tensioner assembly.

## Inspection

52 Refer to Steps 23 through 25.

## Installation

*Refer to illustrations 7.58 and 7.60*

53 Place the timing belt tensioner in position on the front of the engine and then install

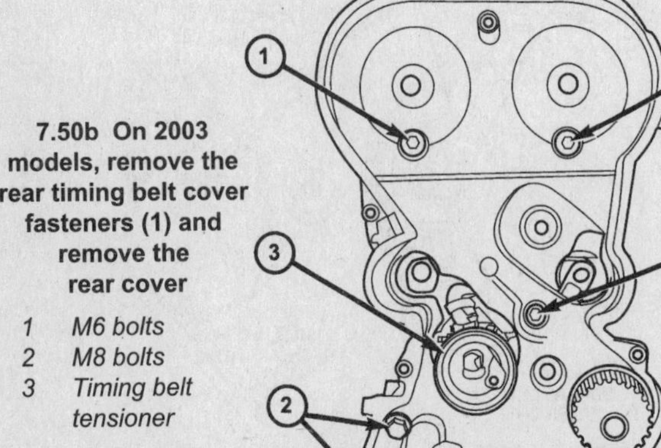

**7.50b On 2003 models, remove the rear timing belt cover fasteners (1) and remove the rear cover**

1 *M6 bolts*
2 *M8 bolts*
3 *Timing belt tensioner*

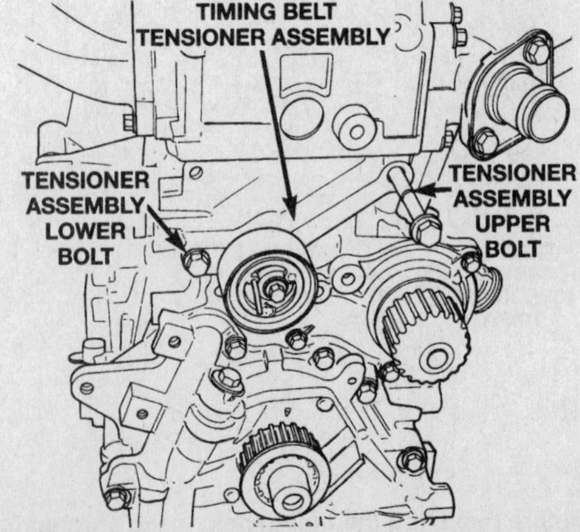

**7.51a On 2001 and 2002 models, remove the lower timing belt tensioner bolt and remove the tensioner assembly; when installing the tensioner assembly, use one of the engine support bracket M10 bolts in the upper bolt hole to position the tensioner while tightening the lower bolt**

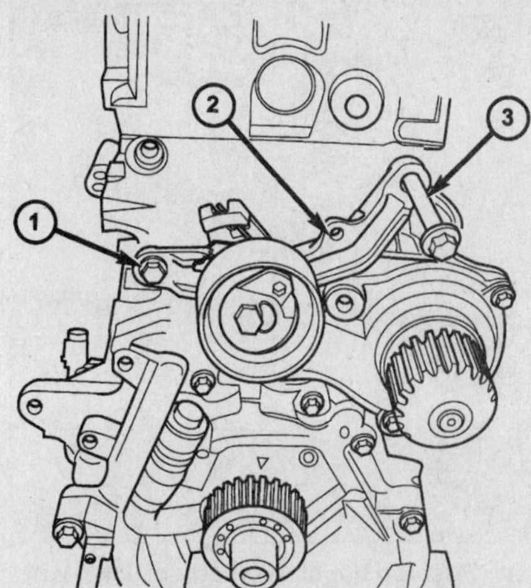


**7.51b On 2003 models, remove the tensioner bolt (1) and the tensioner (2) from the engine block; when installing the tensioner assembly, use one of the engine support bracket M10 bolts (3) in the upper bolt hole to position the tensioner while torquing the lower bolt**

the lower mounting bolt to hold it in place, but don't tighten the lower bolt yet. Install an engine bracket mounting bolt (M10) in the upper tensioner bolt hole **(see illustration 7.51a and 7.51b)** and then screw it in five to seven turns. Tighten the lower tensioner bolt to the torque listed in this Chapter's Specifications and then remove the upper bolt.

54 Install the rear timing belt cover and tighten the cover fasteners securely.

55 Install the timing belt idler pulley and then tighten the idler pulley bolt to the torque listed in this Chapter's Specifications.

56 Install the camshaft sprockets and then tighten the camshaft sprocket bolts to the torque listed in this Chapter's Specifications.

57 Make sure that the TDC mark on the crankshaft timing belt sprocket is still aligned with the stationary index mark on the oil pump housing **(see illustration 7.46)**.

58 Turn the exhaust camshaft sprocket clockwise so that the timing mark on the exhaust sprocket is slightly below the timing mark on the intake camshaft sprocket **(see illustration)**.

58 Install the timing belt as follows: Start at the crankshaft sprocket, then thread the belt onto the water pump sprocket, the idler pulley, the camshaft sprockets and then finally the tensioner **(see illustration 7.59)**. Now take up tension by moving the exhaust camshaft sprocket counterclockwise until the timing marks on the two cam sprockets are realigned.

60 Reset the tension on the timing belt:

a) *On 2001 and 2002 models, remove the Allen wrench from the tensioner. If you have installed a new tensioner assembly, remove the pull pin (new tensioners are locked in the "wound" position by a pull pin).*

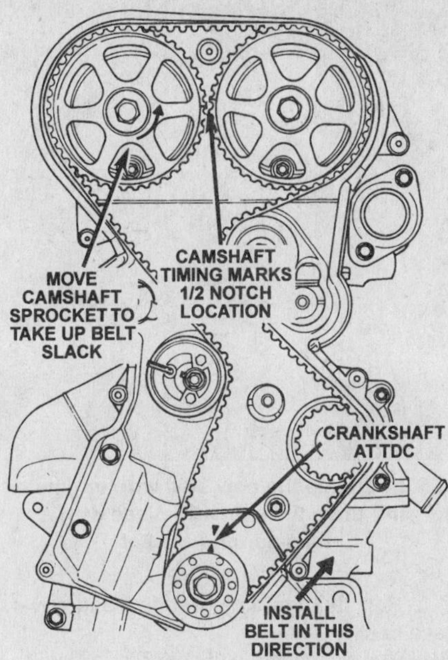


**7.58 Before installing the timing belt, turn the exhaust camshaft sprocket clockwise so that the timing mark on the exhaust sprocket is slightly below the timing mark on the intake camshaft sprocket; when installing the belt, start at the crankshaft sprocket and thread the belt around the water pump sprocket, the idler pulley, the cam sprockets and the tensioner pulley**

b) *On 2003 models, insert a 6 mm Allen wrench into the hexagon opening located on the top plate of the belt tensioner pulley* **(see illustration 7.46b)**. *Then, using the 6 mm Allen wrench as a lever, rotate the belt tensioner COUNTERCLOCKWISE until there is tension on the timing belt* **(see illustration)**. *Continue to rotate the tension until the setting notch is aligned with the spring tang. Grip the Allen wrench to prevent the tensioner from rotating, and torque the tensioner bolt to 220 in-lbs. Recheck the alignment marks. If they are incorrect, loosen the bolt and repeat the procedure.*

61 Rotate the crankshaft 720 degrees (two complete revolutions) and then verify that the TDC marks on the crankshaft sprocket and the oil pump housing are still aligned and that the timing marks on the camshaft sprockets are still aligned. If they're not, stop right here, go back to Step 60 and install the belt again.

62 Install the right engine mount and support bracket. Tighten all fasteners securely.

63 Install the upper and lower timing belt covers and tighten the fasteners to the torque listed in this Chapter's Specifications.

64 Install the alternator drivebelt idler pulley and tighten the idler pulley bolt to the torque listed in this Chapter's Specifications.

65 Install the crankshaft vibration damper pulley, install the washer and pulley bolt and then tighten the pulley bolt to the torque listed

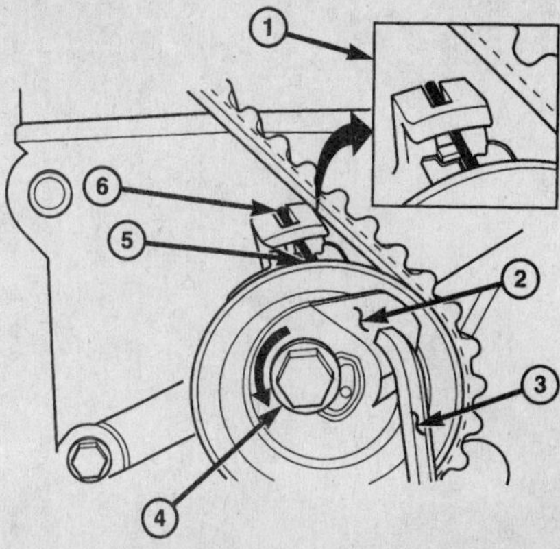


**7.60 Timing belt tensioner details on 2003 models**

1 *Align setting notch with spring tang*
2 *Top plate*
3 *6 mm Allen wrench*
4 *Lock bolt*
5 *Setting notch*
6 *Spring tang*

in this Chapter's Specifications.

66 The remainder of installation is the reverse of removal.

67 Refill and bleed the cooling system (see Chapter 1).

## 8 Crankshaft front oil seal - replacement

*Refer to illustrations 8.2, 8.3, 8.5 and 8.6*

**Caution:** *Do not rotate the camshaft(s) or crankshaft when the timing belt is removed or damage to the engine may occur.*

1 Remove the timing belt (see Section 7).

2 Measure the installed depth of the crankshaft sprocket (in relation to the end of the crankshaft or the front of the engine); this is important for proper timing belt alignment. Pull the crankshaft sprocket from the crankshaft with a bolt-type gear puller **(see illustration)**. Remove the Woodruff key.

**8.2 Attach a bolt-type gear puller to the crankshaft sprocket and remove the sprocket from the crankshaft**

8.3 Working from below the right inner fender, use the screwdriver to pry the seal out of its bore

8.5 Lubricate the new seal with engine oil and drive the seal into place with a hammer and socket

8.6 Position the crankshaft sprocket with the word FRONT facing out and install it onto the crankshaft

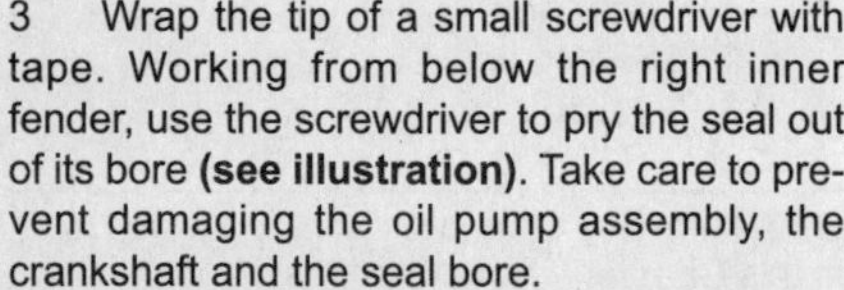

3 Wrap the tip of a small screwdriver with tape. Working from below the right inner fender, use the screwdriver to pry the seal out of its bore **(see illustration)**. Take care to prevent damaging the oil pump assembly, the crankshaft and the seal bore.

4 Thoroughly clean and inspect the seal bore and sealing surface on the crankshaft. Minor imperfections can be removed with emery cloth. If there is a groove worn in the crankshaft sealing surface (from contact with the seal), installing a new seal will probably not stop the leak.

5 Lubricate the new seal with engine oil and drive the seal into place with a hammer and an appropriate size socket **(see illustration)**.

6 The remaining steps are the reverse of removal. **Caution:** *The crankshaft sprocket depth is set to a factory specification to insure correct timing belt alignment. If available, use the special factory tool with a built-in setting to install the crankshaft sprocket or carefully push it on until it is in the same position as measured in Step 2.* **Note:** *Position the crankshaft sprocket with the word FRONT facing out* **(see illustration)**.

7 Reinstall the timing belt(s) and covers (see Section 7).

8 Run the engine and check for oil leaks.

## 9 Camshaft oil seal - replacement

*Refer to illustrations 9.5, 9.7 and 9.9*

**Caution:** *Do not rotate the camshaft(s) or crankshaft when the timing belt is removed or damage to the engine may occur.*

1 Remove the timing belt cover and timing belt (see Section 7).

2 Rotate the crankshaft counterclockwise until the crankshaft sprocket is three teeth BTDC **(see illustration 7.28b)**. This will prevent engine damage if the camshaft sprocket is inadvertently rotated during removal.

3 If the engine is equipped with a rear timing belt cover, remove the upper part (see Section 7).

4 Using a pin spanner to hold the sprocket from turning, remove the camshaft sprocket bolt(s). Then, using two large screwdrivers, lever the sprocket(s) off the camshaft.

5 Carefully pry the seal out with a small screwdriver **(see illustration)**. Don't scratch the bore or damage the camshaft in the process (if the camshaft is damaged, the new seal will end up leaking).

6 Clean the bore and coat the outer edge of the new seal with engine oil or multi-purpose grease. Also lubricate the seal lip.

7 Using a socket with an outside diameter slightly smaller than the outside diameter of the seal **(see illustration)**, carefully drive the new seal into place with a hammer. Make sure it's installed squarely and driven in so it is flush with the head. If a socket isn't available, a short section of pipe will also work.

8 If the engine is equipped with a rear timing belt cover, install the upper part (see Section 7).

9 Install the camshaft sprocket, aligning the pin in the camshaft with the hole in the sprocket **(see illustration)**. Use an appropriate tool to hold the camshaft sprocket(s) while tightening the bolt(s) to the torque listed in this Chapter's Specifications.

10 Reinstall the timing belt (see Section 7).

11 Run the engine and check for oil leaks at the camshaft seal.

9.5 Carefully pry the camshaft seal out of the bore - DO NOT nick or scratch the camshaft or seal bore

9.7 Gently tap the new seal into place with the spring side toward the engine

9.9 When installing a camshaft sprocket, make sure the pin in the camshaft is aligned with the hole in the sprocket

10.4 Note the camshaft bearing cap location numbers - they must be reinstalled in the same location in the cylinder head

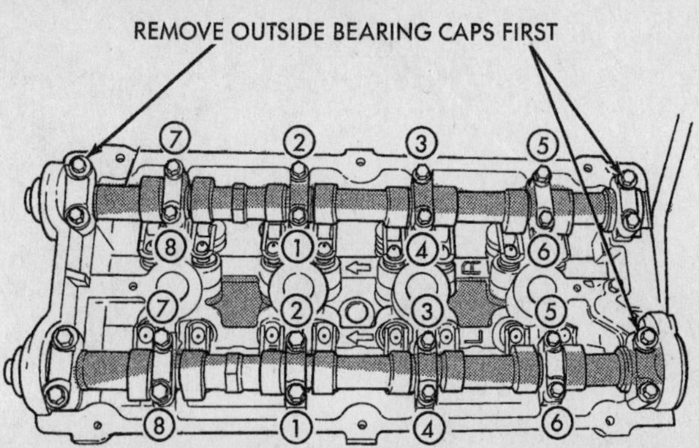


10.5 First, remove the outside bearing caps, then remove the remaining camshaft bearing caps in the sequence shown

## 10 Camshaft(s) - removal, inspection and installation

### Removal

*Refer to illustrations 10.4 and 10.5*

1 Remove the camshaft position sensor and the target magnet (see Chapter 6).

2 Remove the valve cover (see Section 4).

3 Remove the timing belt (see Section 7), remove the camshaft sprockets and the rear timing belt cover (see Section 9).

4 The camshaft bearing caps are identified with their numbered location in the cylinder head **(see illustration)**.

5 Remove the outside bearing caps at each end of the camshafts. Remove the remaining camshaft bearing caps, loosening the bolts a little at a time to prevent distorting the camshafts, in the sequence shown **(see illustration)**. When the bearing caps have all been loosened enough for removal, they may still be difficult to remove. Use the bearing cap bolts for leverage and move the cap back and forth to loosen the cap from the cylinder head. If they are still difficult to remove you can tap them gently with a soft face mallet until they can be lifted off. **Caution:** *Store them in order so they can be returned to their original locations, with the same side facing forward.*

6 Carefully lift the camshafts out of the cylinder head. Mark the camshafts INTAKE and EXHAUST so they don't get mixed-up.

7 Remove the front seal from each camshaft. **Note:** *It would be prudent to inspect the rocker arms and lash adjusters at this time* (see Section 11).

### Inspection

*Refer to illustration 10.9*

8 Clean the camshaft(s) and the gasket surface. Inspect the camshaft(s) for wear and/or damage to the lobe surfaces, bearing journals, and seal contact surfaces. Inspect the camshaft bearing surfaces in the cylinder head and bearing caps for scoring and other damage.

9 Measure the camshaft bearing journal diameters **(see illustration)**. Measure the inside diameter of the camshaft bearing surfaces in the cylinder head, using a telescoping gauge (temporarily install the bearing caps). Subtract the journal measurement from the bearing measurement to obtain the camshaft bearing oil clearance. Compare this clearance with the value listed this Chapter's Specifications. Replace worn components as required.

10 Replace the camshaft if the journals measure less than the minimum allowable diameter, or if the lobes are worn. If the oil clearance is too great but the journals are OK, the cylinder head will have to be replaced. **Note:** *If the lobes are worn, replace the rocker arms and lash adjusters along with the camshaft.* The cylinder head will also have to be replaced if the camshaft bearing surfaces in the head are damaged or excessively worn.

11 Clean and inspect the cylinder head.

### Camshaft endplay measurement

*Refer to illustration 10.14*

12 Lubricate the camshaft(s) and cylinder head bearing journals with clean engine oil.

13 Place the camshaft in its original location in the cylinder head. **Note:** *Do not install the rocker arms for this check.* Install the rear bearing cap and tighten the bolts to the torque listed in this Chapter's Specifications.

14 Install a dial indicator on the cylinder head and place the indicator tip on the camshaft at the sprocket end **(see illustration)**.

15 Use a screwdriver to carefully pry the camshaft to the fully to the rear (toward the

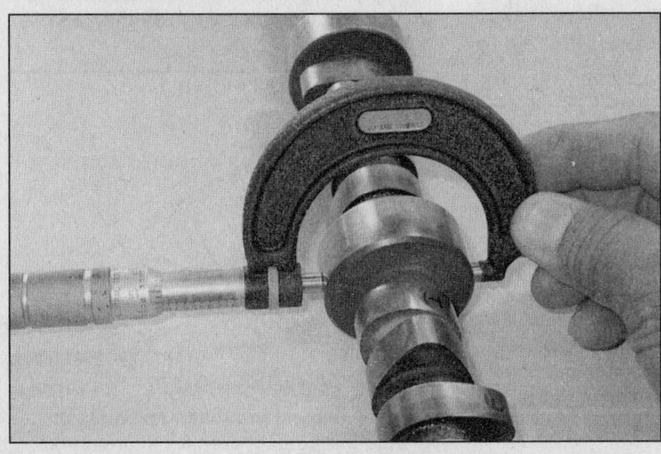

10.9 Measure the camshaft bearing journal diameters with a micrometer

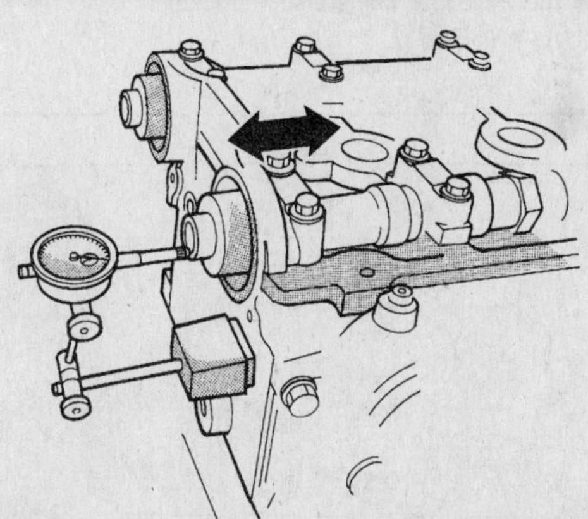

10.14 Measure the camshaft endplay with a dial indicator positioned on the sprocket end of the camshaft as shown

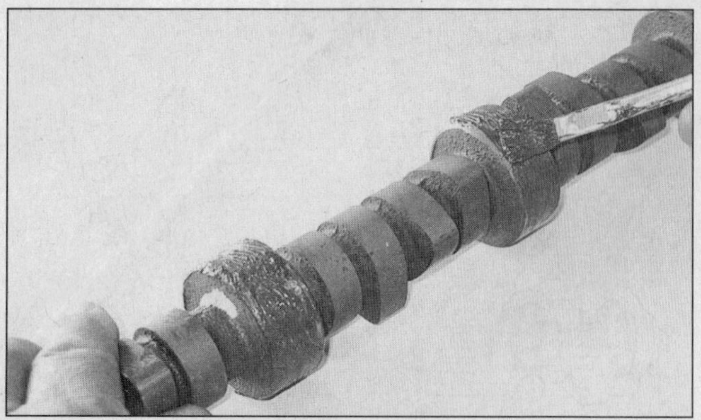

**10.17 Prior to installing each camshaft, lubricate the bearing journals, thrust surfaces and lobes with assembly lube or clean engine oil**

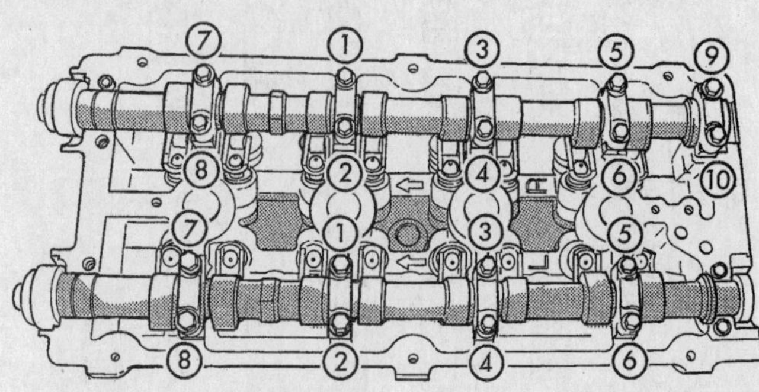


**10.19 Except for the No. 1 and No. 6 (left side) end caps, install the bearing caps and tighten in the indicated sequence**

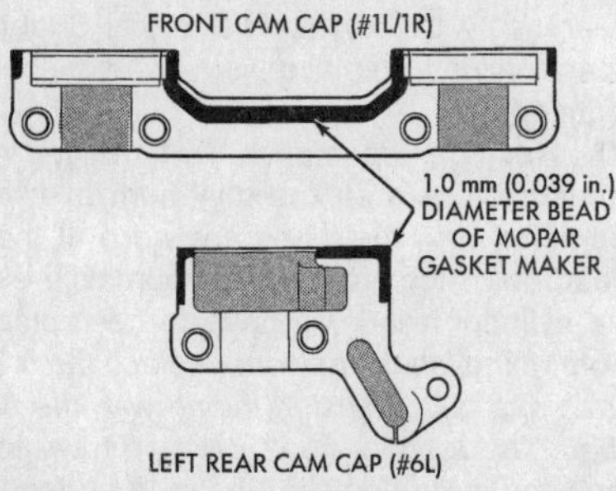


**10.20 Apply a bead of RTV sealant to the indicated areas on the No. 1 and No. 6 bearing caps, then install these bearing caps**

camshaft position sensor) until it stops. Zero the dial indicator and pry the camshaft fully to the front (toward the dial indicator end). The amount of indicator travel is the camshaft endplay. Compare the endplay with the tolerance given in this Chapter's Specifications. If the endplay is excessive, check the camshaft and cylinder head bearing journals for wear. Replace as necessary.

## Installation

*Refer to illustrations 10.17, 10.19, and 10.20*

16 Install the valve lash adjusters and rocker arms (see Section 11).

17 Clean the camshaft and bearing journals and caps. Liberally coat the journals, lobes, and thrust portions of the camshaft with assembly lube or engine oil **(see illustration)**.

18 Carefully install the camshafts in the cylinder head in their original location. Temporarily install the camshaft sprockets and rotate the camshafts so that their timing marks align **(see illustration 7.18)**. Make sure the crankshaft is positioned with the crankshaft sprocket timing mark at three notches BTDC. **Caution:** *If the pistons are at TDC when tightening the camshaft bearing caps, damage to the engine may occur.*

19 Install the bearing caps, except for the No. 1 and No. 6 (left side) end caps **(see illustration 10.4)**. Tighten the bolts in several steps, in the sequence shown to the torque listed in this Chapter's Specifications **(see illustration)**.

20 Apply a bead of RTV sealant (approximately 1/16 inch [1.5 mm]) to the No. 1 and No. 6 (left side) bearing caps **(see illustration)**. Install the bearing caps and tighten the bolts to the torque listed in this Chapter's Specifications.

21 Install new camshaft oil seals (see Section 9).

22 Install the timing belt, covers, and related components (see Section 7).

23 Install the valve cover (see Section 4).

24 Installation is the reverse of removal.

## 11 Rocker arm assembly - removal, inspection and installation

### Removal

*Refer to illustration 11.3*

1 Remove the valve cover (see Section 4).

2 Remove both camshafts (see Section 10).

3 Once the camshafts have been removed, the rocker arms can be lifted off **(see illustration)**. **Caution:** *Each rocker arm must be placed back in the same location it was removed from, so mark each rocker arm or place them in a container (such as an egg carton) so they won't get mixed up.* The lash adjusters can remain in the head at this time, unless they are being replaced (see Section 12).

### Inspection

*Refer to illustration 11.4*

4 Inspect the rocker arm tip, roller and lash adjuster pocket for wear **(see illustration)**. Replace them if evidence of wear or damage is found.

5 Carefully inspect each lash adjuster for signs of wear and damage, particularly on the ball tip that contacts the rocker arm. The lash adjusters become clogged as they age, so

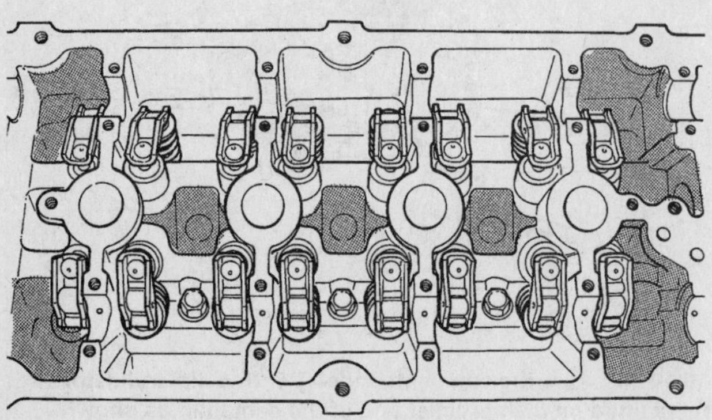

**11.3 After the camshafts have been removed, remove the rocker arms and lift off the valve lash adjusters; be sure to keep the rocker arms and lash adjusters in order so they can be returned to their original locations**

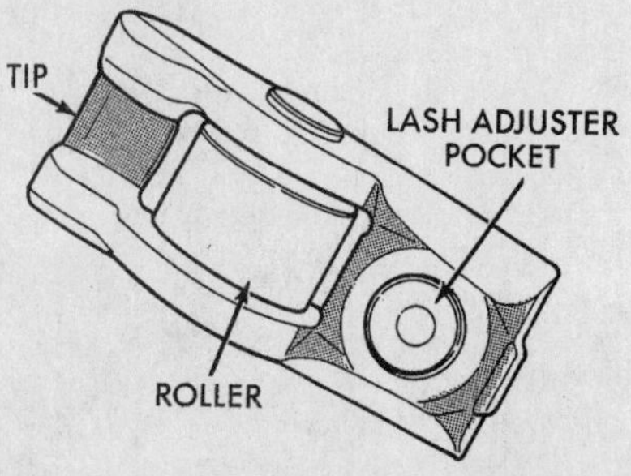


**11.4 Inspect the roller, tip and lash-adjuster contact area for score marks and pitting**

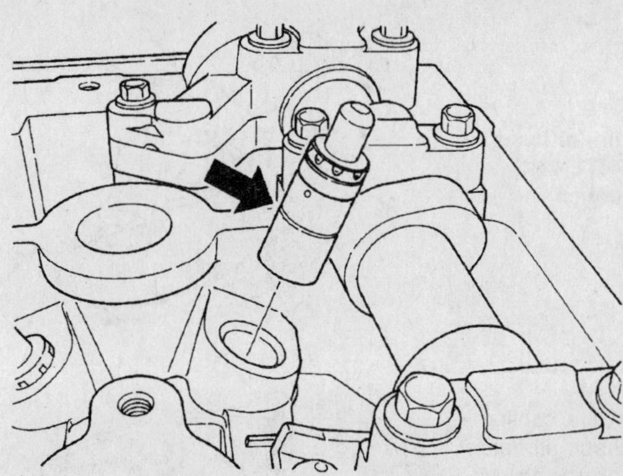

12.3 Lift the valve lash adjuster from the cylinder head

13.4 Cover the intake ports with duct tape (arrow) to keep out debris before removing the cylinder head

it's a good idea to replace them if you're concerned about their condition or if the engine is making valve "tapping" noises.

## Installation

6 Installation is the reverse of removal. When reinstalling the rocker arms, make sure that you install them at the same locations from which they were removed.

## 12 Valve lash adjusters - removal, inspection and installation

*Refer to illustration 12.3*

1 Remove the camshafts (see Section 10).
2 Remove the rocker arms (see Section 11).
3 If the lash adjusters aren't already removed from the head, lift them out now **(see illustration)**. **Caution:** *Be sure to keep the adjusters in order so they can be placed back in the same location in the cylinder head it was removed from.*
4 Inspect each adjuster carefully for signs of wear and damage, particularly on the ball tip that contacts the rocker arm. Since the lash adjusters frequently become clogged, we recommend replacing them if you're concerned about their condition or if the engine is exhibiting valve "tapping" noises.
5 The lash adjusters must be partially full of engine oil - indicated by little or no plunger action when the adjuster is depressed. If there's excessive plunger travel, place the lash adjuster into clean engine oil and pump the plunger until the plunger travel is eliminated. **Note:** *If the plunger still travels within the lash adjuster when full of oil it's defective and the lash adjuster must be replaced.*
6 When re-starting the engine after replacing the adjusters, the adjusters will normally make "tapping" noises. After warm-up, raise the speed of the engine from idle to 3,000 rpm for one minute. If the adjuster(s) do not become silent, replace the defective ones.

13.10a Carefully lift the cylinder head straight up and place the head on wood blocks to prevent damage to the sealing surfaces

## 13 Cylinder head - removal and installation

**Warning:** *Allow the engine to cool completely before beginning this procedure.*

## Removal

*Refer to illustrations 13.4, 13.10a and 13.10b*

1 Position the number one piston at Top Dead Center (see Section 3).
2 Disconnect the cable from the negative battery terminal (see Chapter 5).
3 Drain the cooling system and remove the spark plugs (see Chapter 1).
4 Remove the intake manifold (see Section 5). Cover the intake ports with duct tape to keep out debris **(see illustration)**.
5 If necessary, remove the exhaust manifold (see Section 6). **Note:** *On some models, the exhaust manifold is easier to remove after the cylinder head is removed.*
6 Remove the coil (see Chapter 5).
7 Remove the timing belt (see Section 7).
8 Remove the valve cover (see Section 4).

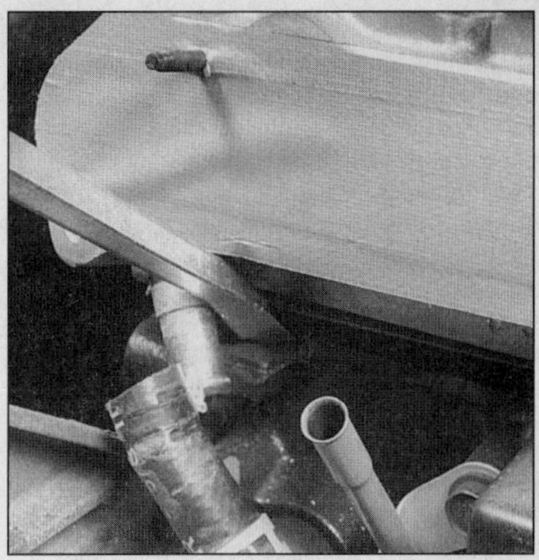

13.10b If the head sticks to the engine block, dislodge it by placing a wood block against the head casting and tapping the wood with a hammer or by prying the head with a prybar placed carefully on a casting protrusion

9 Loosen the cylinder head bolts, 1/4-turn at a time, in the reverse of the tightening sequence **(see illustration 13.14)** until they can be removed by hand. **Note:** *Write down the location of the different length bolts so they will be reinstalled in the correct location.*
10 Carefully lift the cylinder head **(see illustration)** straight up and place the head on wood blocks to prevent damage to the sealing surfaces. If the head sticks to the engine block, dislodge it by placing a wood block against the head casting and tapping the wood with a hammer or by prying the head with a prybar placed carefully on a casting protrusion **(see illustration)**. **Caution:** *The cylinder head is aluminum, so you must be very careful not to gouge the sealing surfaces.* **Note:** *It's a good idea to have the head checked for warpage, even if you're just replacing the gasket.*
11 Special gasket removal solvents that soften gaskets and make removal much easier are available at auto parts stores. Remove

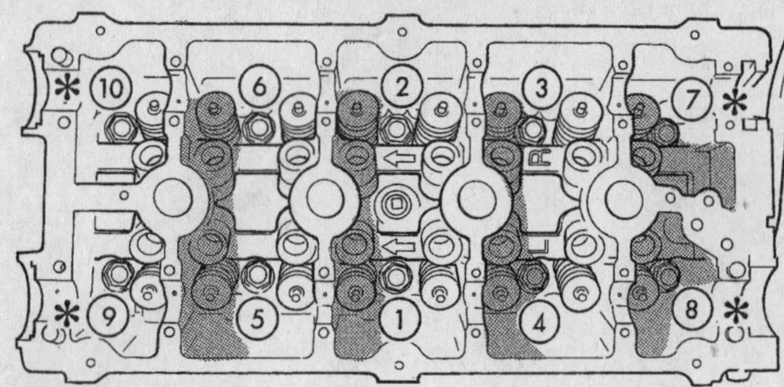


13.14 Cylinder head bolt TIGHTENING sequence

all traces of old gasket material from the block and head. Do not allow anything to fall into the engine. Clean and inspect all threaded fasteners and be sure the threaded holes in the block are clean and dry.

## Installation

*Refer to illustration 13.14*

12 Place a new gasket and the cylinder head in position on the engine block.

13 Apply clean engine oil to the cylinder head bolt threads prior to installation.

14 Tighten the cylinder head bolts in several stages in the recommended sequence **(see illustrations)** to the torque listed in this Chapter's Specifications. **Note:** *The final step in the tightening procedure requires you to tighten the bolts a specific number of degrees. An angle-torque gauge, that fits on your torque wrench, is available at most auto parts stores and is highly recommended for this procedure. If the tool is not available, paint marks on the bolt heads and tighten then in sequence until the mark is the specified number of degrees from the starting point.*

15 Reinstall the timing belt (see Section 7).

16 Reinstall the remaining parts in the reverse order of removal.

17 Be sure to refill and bleed the cooling system (see Chapter 1) and check all fluid levels. Rotate the crankshaft clockwise slowly by hand through six complete revolutions. Recheck the camshaft timing marks (see Section 7).

18 Start the engine and run it until normal operating temperature is reached. Check for leaks and proper operation.

## 14 Oil pan - removal and installation

### Removal

*Refer to illustrations 14.4a, 14.4b and 14.4c*

1 Disconnect the cable from the negative battery terminal (see Chapter 5).

2 Raise the vehicle and support it securely on jackstands. Working under the vehicle, remove the engine protection cover.

3 Drain the engine oil (see Chapter 1). Remove the oil filter adapter from the engine block on 2.0L engines or from the oil pan on 2.4L DOHC engines.

4 Remove the structural collar **(see illustrations)**.

5 Remove the lateral bending brace.

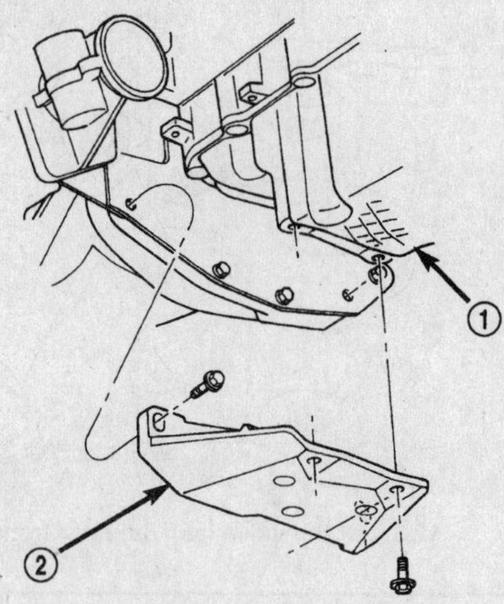


14.4a Structural collar installation details on the 2.0L DOHC engine

1 Oil pan
2 Structural collar

### Turbocharged models

6 Remove the charge air cooler hose from the turbocharger (see Chapter 4).

7 Remove the oil cooler connector bolt but do not remove the oil cooler lines (see Chapter 3). Position the oil cooler lines to the side.

### All models

*Refer to illustrations 14.10a, 14.10b, 14.10c, 14.10d, 14.11a, 14.11b and 14.12*

8 On 2.4L DOHC engines, remove the lower torque strut (see Section 18).

9 Remove the flywheel/driveplate inspection cover.

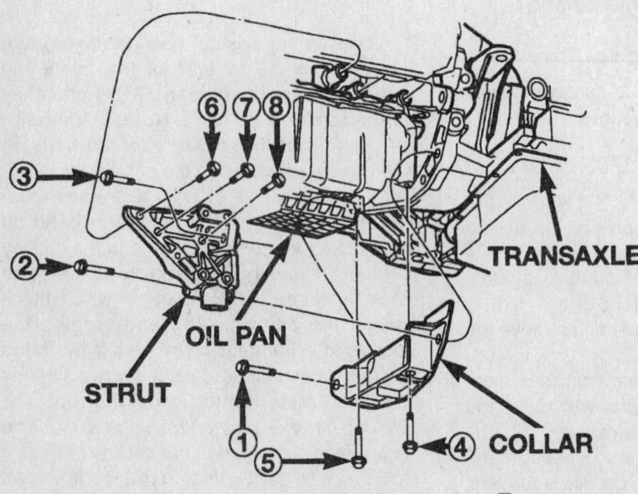


14.4b Structural collar installation details on the 2.4L DOHC engine with automatic transaxle - numbers indicate the bolt tightening sequence for reassembly

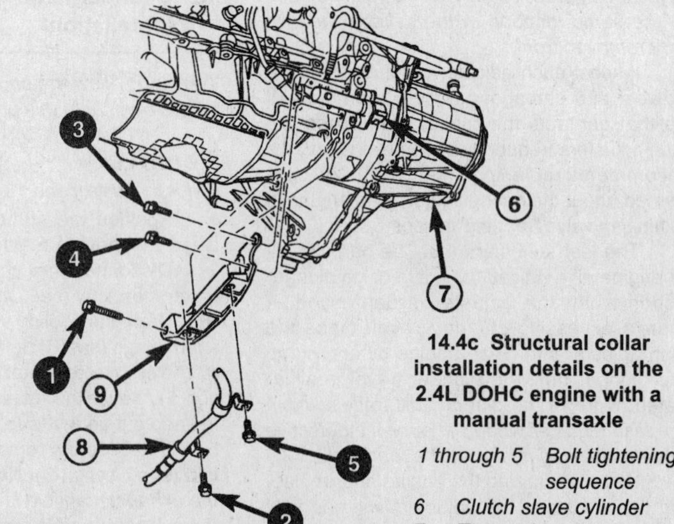


14.4c Structural collar installation details on the 2.4L DOHC engine with a manual transaxle

1 through 5 Bolt tightening sequence
6 Clutch slave cylinder
7 Transaxle
8 Power steering hose
9 Structural collar

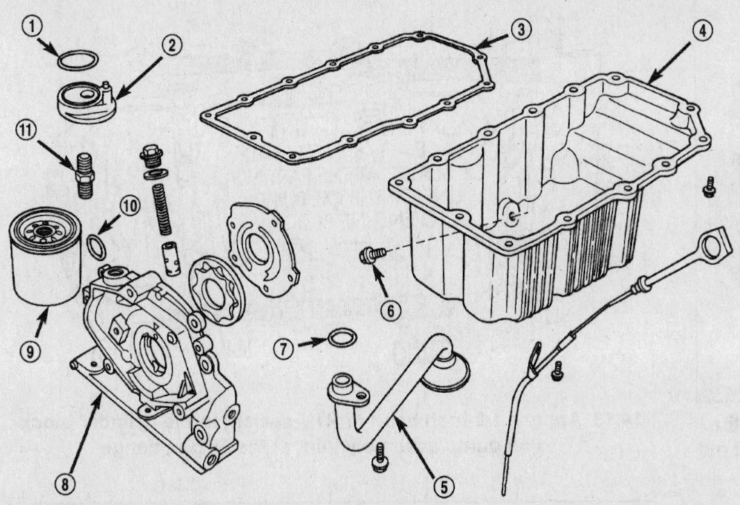


14.10a Oil pan and oil pump mounting details on the 2.0L DOHC engine

| | | | | | |
|---|---|---|---|---|---|
| 1 | O-ring | 5 | Oil pick-up tube | 9 | Oil filter |
| 2 | Oil filter adapter | 6 | Drain plug | 10 | O-ring |
| 3 | Oil pan gasket | 7 | O-ring | 11 | Nipple |
| 4 | Oil pan | 8 | Oil pump body | | |

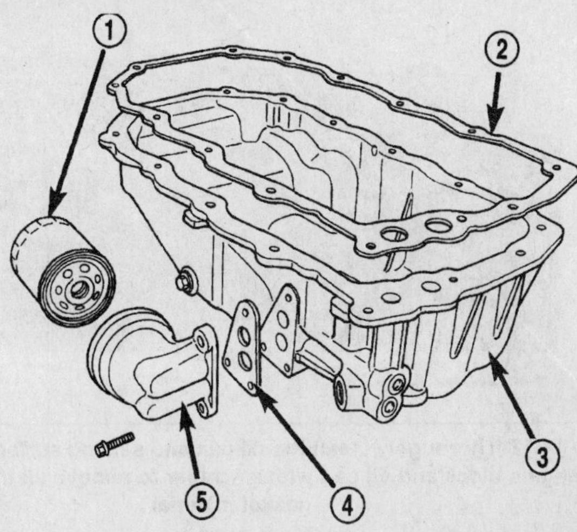


14.10b Oil pan mounting details on the 2.4L DOHC engine

| | | | |
|---|---|---|---|
| 1 | Oil filter | 4 | Oil filter adapter gasket |
| 2 | Oil pan gasket | | |
| 3 | Oil pan | 5 | Oil filter adapter |

10 Remove the mounting bolts and lower the oil pan from the vehicle **(see illustrations)**. If the pan is stuck, tap it with a soft-face hammer **(see illustration)** or place a wood block against the pan and tap the wood block with a hammer. **Caution:** *If you're wedging something between the oil pan and the engine block to separate the two, be extremely careful not to gouge or nick the gasket surface of either part; an oil leak could result.*

11 Remove the oil pump pick-up tube and screen assembly **(see illustration)** and clean both the tube and screen thoroughly. Install the pick-up tube and screen with a new seal **(see illustration)**.

12 Thoroughly clean the oil pan and sealing

14.10c Lower the pan carefully (there might still be some residual oil in the pan)

14.10d If the pan is stuck, tap it with a soft-face hammer or place a wood block against the pan and tap the wood block with a hammer

14.11a Remove the bolt and remove the oil pump pick-up tube and screen assembly - clean both the tube and screen thoroughly before reassembly

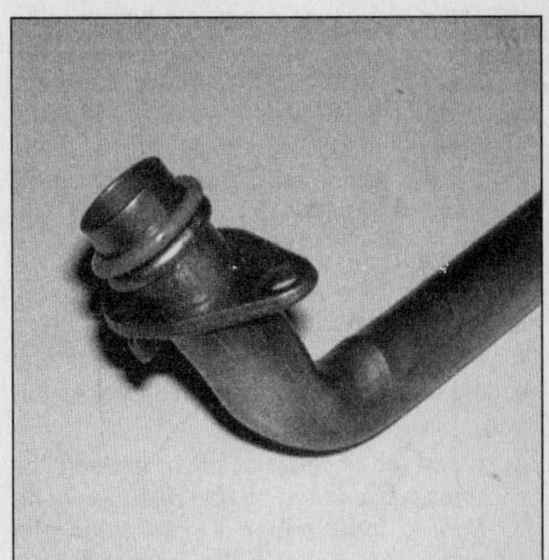

14.11b Install a new seal at the oil pump pick-up tube mounting flange

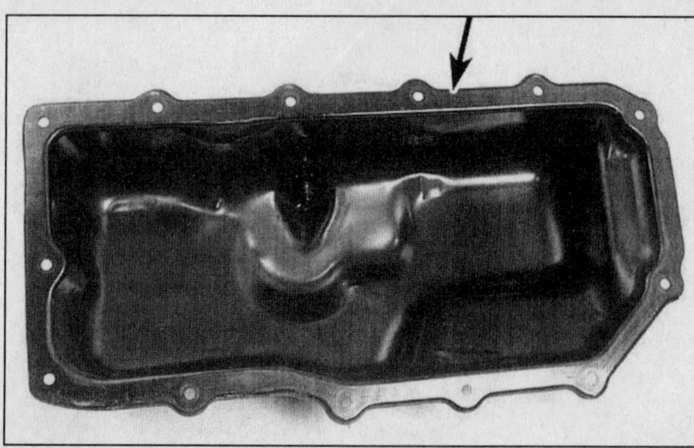

14.12 Thoroughly clean the oil pan and sealing surfaces on the engine block and oil pan with a scraper to remove all traces of old gasket material

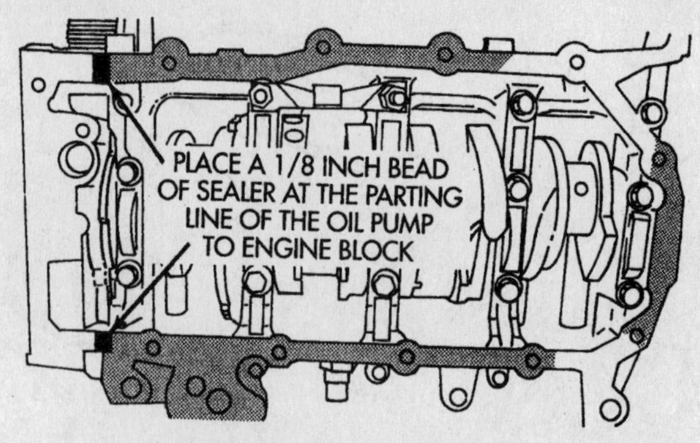


14.13 Apply a 1/8-inch bead of RTV sealant to the cylinder block-to-oil pump assembly joint at the oil pan flange

surfaces on the block and pan **(see illustration)**. Use a scraper to remove all traces of old gasket material. Gasket removal solvents are available at auto parts stores and may prove helpful. Check the oil pan sealing surface for distortion. Straighten or replace as necessary. After cleaning and straightening (if necessary), wipe the gasket surfaces of the pan and block clean with a rag soaked in lacquer thinner or acetone.

## Installation

*Refer to illustration 14.13*

13 Apply a 1/8-inch bead of RTV sealant at the cylinder block-to-oil pump assembly joint at the oil pan flange **(see illustration)**.

14 Install a new oil pan gasket.

15 Place the oil pan into position and install the bolts finger tight. Working side-to-side from the center out, tighten the bolts to the torque listed in this Chapter's Specifications.

### 2.0L engine

16 Install the structural collar and the lateral bending brace **(see illustration 14.4a)** as follows:

- *a) Place the collar in position between the transaxle and the oil pan and tighten the collar-to-oil pan bolts to about 30 in-lbs.*
- *b) Install the collar-to-transaxle bolts and then tighten them to 80 ft-lbs.*
- *c) Finally, tighten the structural collar-to-oil pan bolts to 40 in-lbs.*

### 2.4L engine

#### Automatic transaxles

17 Install the structural collar and the lateral bending brace **(see illustration 14.4b)** as follows:

- *a) Place the collar in position between the transaxle and the oil pan and then hand tighten the number 1 collar-to-oil pan bolt.*
- *b) Position the power steering hose bracket and install collar-to-oil pan bolt number 4. Hand tighten the bolt.*
- *c) Install the bending brace and hand tighten bolt number 3.*
- *d) Install bolt number 2 and hand tighten.*
- *e) Install bolt number 6 and hand tighten.*
- *f) Position the power steering hose bracket and install bolt number 5. Hand tighten bolt number 5.*
- *g) Tighten the collar-to-transaxle bolts numbers 1 through 3 to 75 ft-lbs.*
- *h) Install bolts number 7 and 8 into the collar and engine block.*
- *i) Finally, tighten the structural collar bolt numbers 4 through 8 to 45 ft-lbs.*

#### Manual transaxles

18 Install the structural collar and the lateral bending brace **(see illustration 14.4c)** as follows:

- *a) Place the collar in position between the transaxle and the oil pan and then hand tighten the number 1 collar-to-oil pan bolt.*
- *b) Position the power steering hose bracket and install collar-to-oil pan bolt number 2. Hand tighten the bolt.*
- *c) Install the clutch slave cylinder and hand tighten bolt number 3 and 4.*
- *d) Position the power steering hose bracket and install bolt number 5. Hand tighten bolt number 5.*
- *e) Tighten bolt number 1 to 75 ft-lbs.*
- *f) Tighten bolt number 2 and 5 to 45 ft-lbs.*
- *g) Tighten bolt number 3 and 4 to 20 ft-lbs.*

19 The remainder of installation is the reverse of removal.

20 Refill the crankcase with the correct quantity and grade of oil, run the engine and check for leaks.

21 Road test the vehicle and check for leaks again.

## 15 Oil pump - removal, inspection and installation

## Removal

*Refer to illustrations 15.5a, 15.5b, 15.6a, 15.6b and 15.6c*

1 Disconnect the cable from the negative battery terminal (see Chapter 5).

2 Raise the vehicle and place it securely on jackstands.

3 Remove the oil pan and pick-up tube/strainer assembly (see Section 14).

4 Remove the timing belt and the crankshaft sprocket (see Section 7).

5 Remove the bolts and detach the oil pump assembly from the engine **(see illus-**

15.5a Oil pump mounting bolts

15.5b If the pump doesn't come off by hand, tap it gently with a soft-faced hammer or pry gently on a casting protrusion

15.6a Remove the cover mounting screws . . .

15.6b . . . and the cover

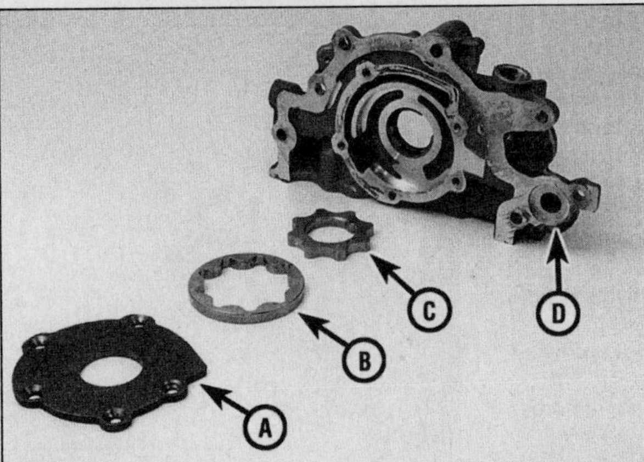


15.6c Arrangement of oil pump components

A Cover
B Outer rotor
C Inner rotor
D Oil pump body

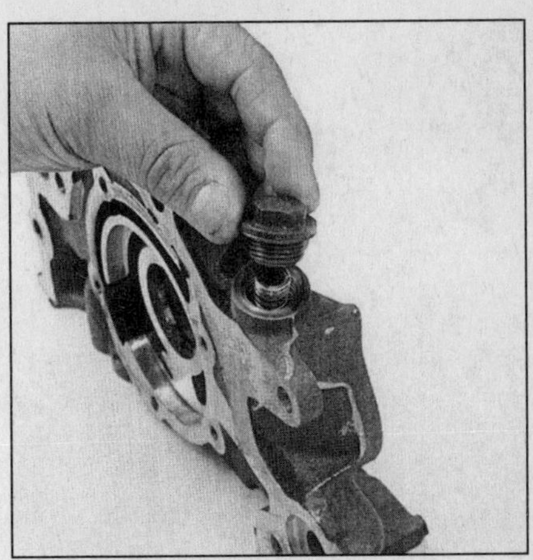

15.9a Unscrew the oil pressure relief valve cap from the body

tration). **Caution:** *If the pump doesn't come off by hand, tap it gently with a soft-faced hammer or pry on a casting boss* **(see illustration).**

6 Remove the mounting screws and remove the cover **(see illustration)**. Remove the inner and outer rotor from the body **(see illustrations)**. **Caution:** *Be very careful with these parts. Close tolerances are critical in creating the correct oil pressure. Any nicks or other damage will require replacement of the complete pump assembly.*

7 If necessary, replace the crankshaft front seal within the oil pump body (see Section 8).

## Inspection

*Refer to illustrations 15.9a, 15.9b, 15.10a, 15.10b, 15.10c, 15.10d and 15.10e*

8 Clean all components including the block surfaces with solvent, then inspect all surfaces for excessive wear and/or damage.

9 Disassemble the relief valve, unscrew the cap bolt and remove the bolt, washer, spring and relief valve **(see illustrations)**. Check the oil pressure relief valve piston sliding surface and valve spring. If either the spring or the valve is damaged, they must be replaced as a set. If no damage is found, reassemble the relief valve parts. Make sure to install the relief valve into the pump body with the grooved end going in first. Coating the parts with oil, and reinstall them in the oil pump body. Tighten the cap bolt securely.

10 Check the clearance of the oil pump components with a micrometer and a feeler gauge **(see illustrations)** and compare the results to this Chapter's Specifications.

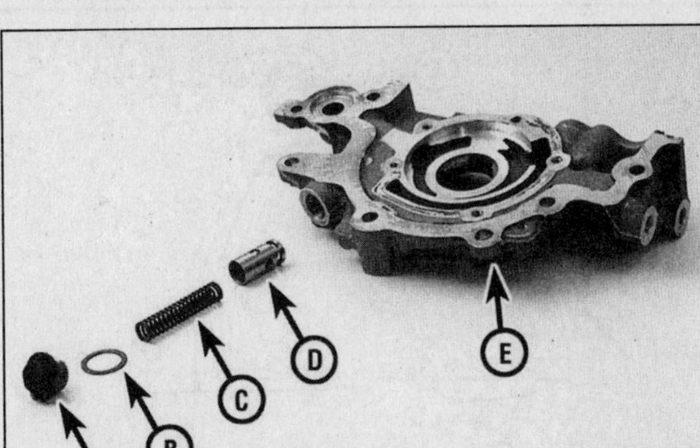


15.9b Oil pressure relief valve components

A Cap
B Gasket
C Spring
D Relief valve
E Oil pump body

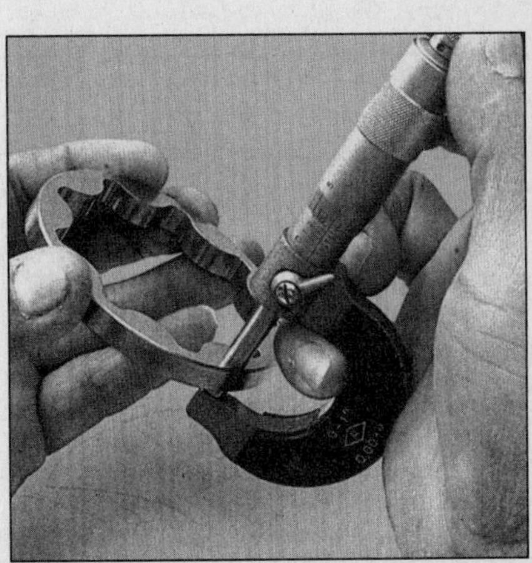

15.10a Measure the outer rotor thickness

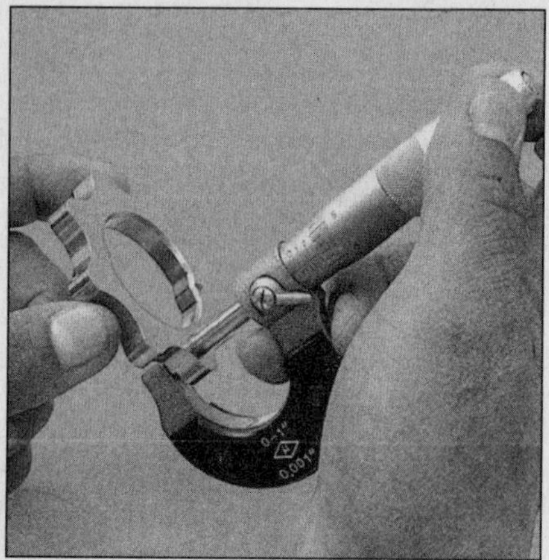

15.10b Measure the inner rotor thickness

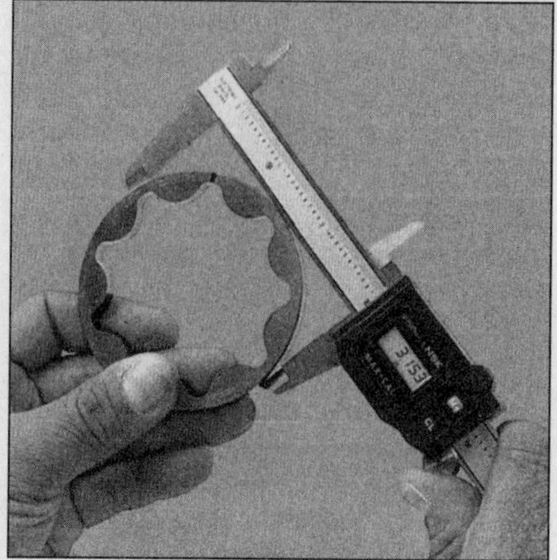

15.10c Use a dial caliper and measure the outer diameter of the outer rotor

15.10d Use a feeler gauge and measure the outer rotor-to-case clearance

15.10e Place a precision straightedge over the rotors and measure the clearance between the rotors and the cover

## Installation

*Refer to illustrations 15.12a, 15.12b and 15.12c*

11 Lubricate the housing and the inner and outer rotors with clean engine oil and install both rotors in the body. Install the cover and tighten the cover screws securely. Prime the oil pump with clean engine oil.

12 Install a new O-ring in the oil discharge passage **(see illustration)**. Apply sealant to the oil pump body **(see illustrations)**, and attach the pump to the block. Tighten the bolts to the torque listed in this Chapter's Specifications.

13 Install the crankshaft sprocket (see Section 8) and the timing belt (see Section 7).

14 Install the pick-up tube/strainer assembly and oil pan (see Section 15).

15 Install a new oil filter and engine oil (see Chapter 1).

16 Start the engine and check for oil pressure and leaks.

17 Recheck the engine oil level.

## 16 Flywheel/driveplate - removal and installation

## Removal

*Refer to illustrations 16.4 and 16.5*

1 Raise the vehicle and support it securely on jackstands, then refer to Chapter 7 and remove the transaxle assembly.

2 If the vehicle has a manual transaxle, remove the pressure plate and clutch disc (see Chapter 8). Now is a good time to check/replace the clutch components and the pilot bearing.

3 To ensure correct alignment during reinstallation, mark the position of the flywheel/driveplate to the crankshaft before removal.

4 Remove the bolts that secure the fly-

15.12a Install a new O-ring seal in the oil pump body - apply clean engine oil to the seal - 2.0L DOHC engine shown

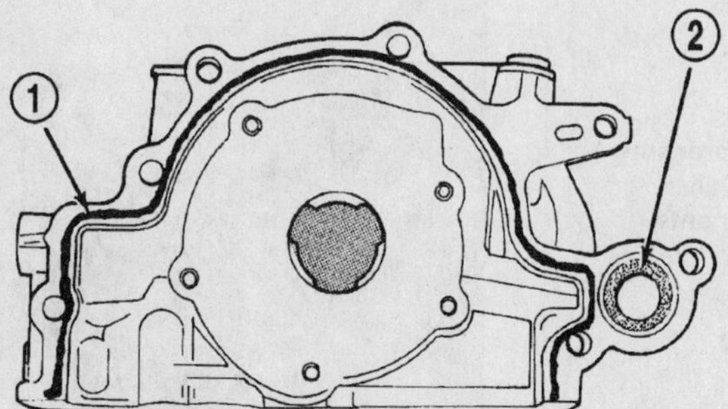


15.12b On 2.0L DOHC engines, install a new O-ring (2) and apply a bead of sealant to the housing sealing surface (1)

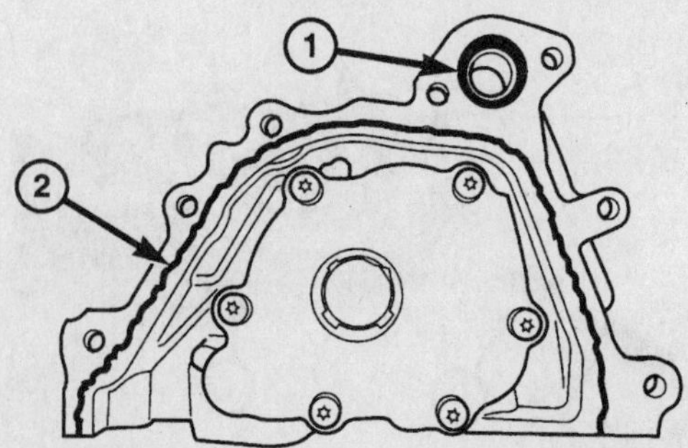


15.12c On 2.4L DOHC engines, install a new O-ring (1) and then apply a bead of sealant to the housing sealing surface (2)

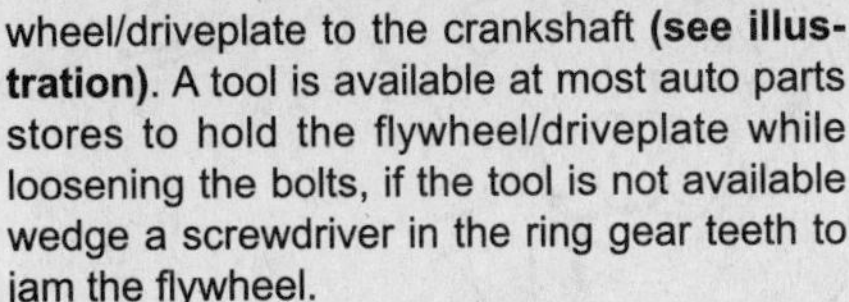

**16.4 Mark the relative position of the flywheel or driveplate to the crankshaft and, using an appropriate tool to hold the flywheel, remove the bolts**

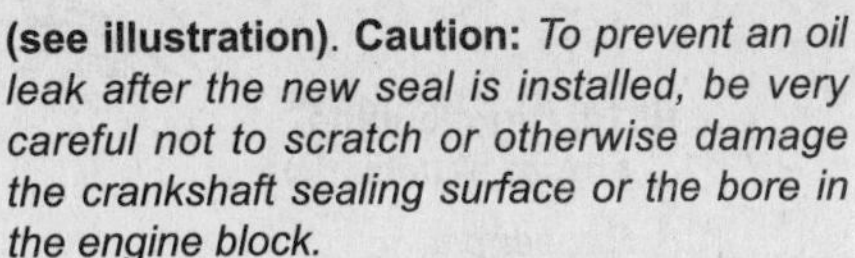

**16.5 Remove the flywheel/driveplate from the crankshaft**

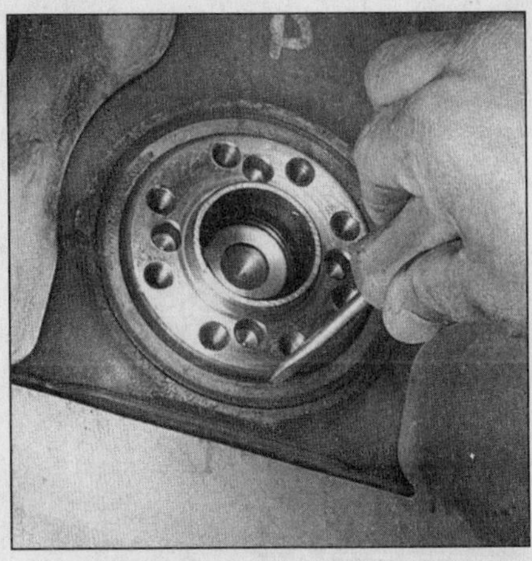

**17.2 Carefully pry the crankshaft seal out of the bore - DO NOT nick or scratch the crankshaft or seal bore**

wheel/driveplate to the crankshaft **(see illustration)**. A tool is available at most auto parts stores to hold the flywheel/driveplate while loosening the bolts, if the tool is not available wedge a screwdriver in the ring gear teeth to jam the flywheel.

5 Remove the flywheel/driveplate from the crankshaft **(see illustration)**. Since the flywheel is fairly heavy, be sure to support it while removing the last bolt.

6 Clean the flywheel to remove grease and oil. To inspect the flywheel, see Chapter 8.

7 Clean and inspect the mating surfaces of the flywheel/driveplate and the crankshaft. If the crankshaft rear main seal is leaking, replace it before reinstalling the fly-wheel/driveplate (see Section 17).

### *Installation*

8 Position the flywheel/driveplate against the crankshaft. Align the previously applied match marks. Before installing the bolts, apply thread locking compound to the threads.

9 Hold the flywheel/driveplate with the holding tool, or wedge a screwdriver in the ring gear teeth to keep the flywheel/driveplate from turning as you tighten the bolts to the torque listed in this Chapter's Specifications.

10 The remainder of installation is the reverse of the removal procedure.

## 17 Rear main oil seal - replacement

*Refer to illustrations 17.2 and 17.4*

1 The one-piece rear main oil seal is pressed into a bore machined into the rear main bearing cap and engine block. Remove the transaxle (see Chapter 7), the clutch components, if equipped (see Chapter 8) and the flywheel or driveplate (see Section 16).

2 **Note:** *The oil seal is installed flush with the outer surface of the block.* Pry out the old seal with a 3/16-inch flat blade screwdriver **(see illustration)**. **Caution:** *To prevent an oil leak after the new seal is installed, be very careful not to scratch or otherwise damage the crankshaft sealing surface or the bore in the engine block.*

3 Clean the crankshaft and seal bore in the block thoroughly and de-grease these areas by wiping them with a rag soaked in lacquer thinner or acetone.

4 Position the new seal onto the crankshaft. **Note:** *When installing the new seal, if so marked, the words THIS SIDE OUT on the seal must face out, toward the rear of the engine.* Using an appropriate size driver and pilot tool, drive the seal into the cylinder block until it is flush with the outer surface of the block **(see illustration)**. If the seal is driven in past flush, there will be a oil leak.

5 The remainder of installation is the reverse of removal.

**17.4 Position the new seal with the words THIS SIDE OUT facing out, toward the rear of the engine. Gently drive the seal into the cylinder block until it is flush with the outer surface of the block. Do not drive it past flush or there will be an oil leak**

## 18 Engine mounts - check, replacement and torque strut adjustment

1 The engine mounting system on these vehicles consists of two load carrying mounts (right and left) and two torque struts (upper and lower). This four-point system requires proper adjustment in the event of replacement. The upper and lower torque struts need to be adjusted together to properly position the engine and load. The adjustment procedure must also be performed if a torque strut bolt is loosened for engine component replacement procedures or other reasons.

2 Engine mounts seldom require attention, but broken or deteriorated mounts should be replaced immediately or the added strain placed on the driveline components may cause damage or wear.

### *Check*

3 During the check, the engine must be raised slightly to remove the weight from the mounts.

4 Raise the vehicle and support it securely on jackstands, then position a jack under the engine oil pan. Place a large wood block between the jack head and the oil pan to prevent oil pan damage, then carefully raise the engine just enough to take the weight off the mounts. **Warning:** *DO NOT place any part of your body under the engine when it's supported only by a jack!*

5 Check the mounts to see if the rubber is cracked, hardened or separated from the metal backing. Sometimes the rubber will split right down the center.

6 Check for relative movement between the mount plates and the engine or frame (use a large screwdriver or pry bar to attempt to move the mounts). If movement is noted, lower the engine and tighten the mount fasteners.

7 Rubber preservative may be applied to the mounts to slow deterioration.

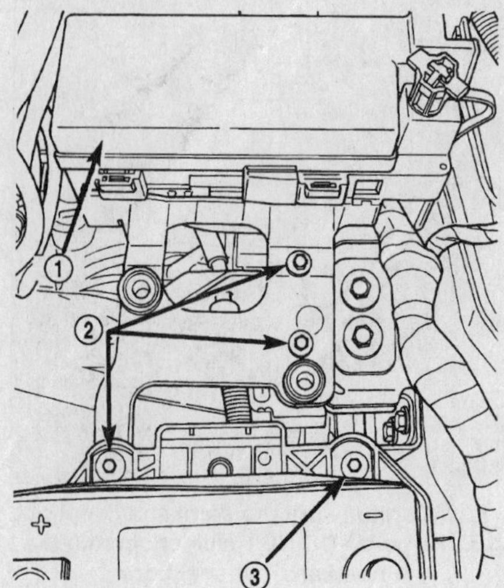


18.10 Power Distribution Center details

1 *Power Distribution Center*
2 *Bracket bolts*
3 *Battery tray mounting bolts*

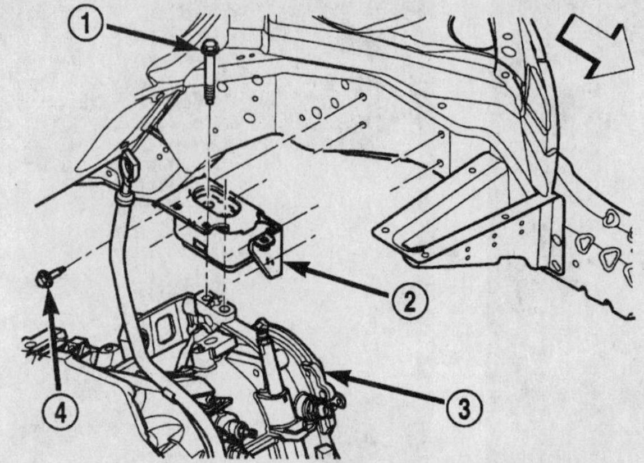


18.12 Left engine mount details

1 *Bolt*
2 *Left engine mount*
3 *Transaxle*
4 *Engine mount bolt*

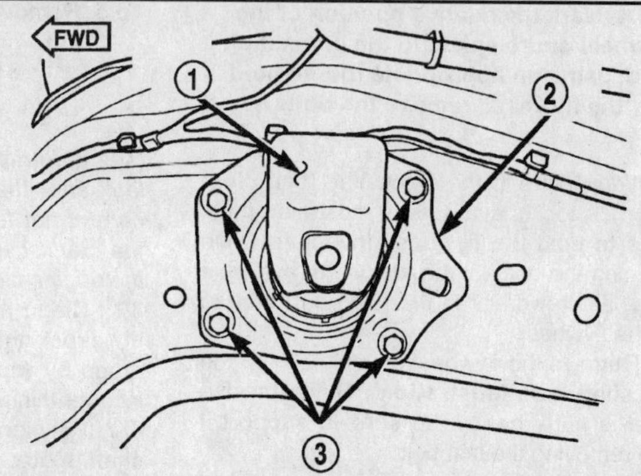


18.15 Right engine mount details

1 *Rubber pad*
2 *Right engine mount*
3 *Engine mount bolts*

## Replacement

*Refer to illustrations 18.10, 18.12, 18.15, 18.18, 18.23 and 18.24*

8 Disconnect the cable from the negative battery terminal, then raise the vehicle and support it securely on jackstands (if not already done).

9 Remove the air filter housing (see Chapter 4).

### Left engine mount

10 Remove the bolts that secure the Power Distribution Center to the left engine mount and the battery tray **(see illustration)**.

11 Place a floor jack under the transaxle (with a wood block between the jack head and the transaxle) and raise the transaxle slightly to relieve the weight from the mounts.

12 Remove the mounting bolts and separate the left engine mount from the left frame rail **(see illustration)**.

13 Installation is the reverse of removal. Use thread locking compound on the mount bolts and be sure to tighten them securely.

### Right engine mount

14 Due to extremely limited accessibility, removal of this mount is very difficult. On 1.6L models it is possible to support the engine from below with a floor jack and block of wood, remove the upper and lower torque struts, remove the access cover from the right frame rail and the mount bracket through-bolt behind it, followed by the bracket, then proceeding as described in the following Steps. On other models the manufacturer recommends removing the engine/transaxle assembly, but with a lot of patience it is possible to support the engine/transaxle assembly with a hoist (or a floor jack and block of wood from below), unbolt the torque struts and mounts, then reposition the assembly as necessary for access to the right-side mount. It also helps to remove the right-side headlight housing for access to the top mount.

15 Carefully mark the position of the right engine mount before removing any fasteners **(see illustration)**.

16 Remove the bolts and detach the mount from the frame and engine.

17 Installation is the reverse of removal. Use thread locking compound on the mount bolts and be sure to tighten them securely.

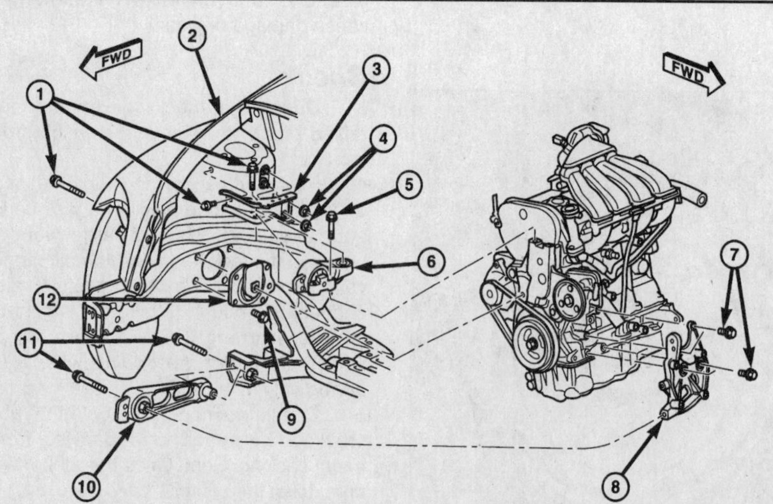


18.18 Upper and lower torque struts and surrounding components

1 *Upper mounting bolts*
2 *Right fender*
3 *Upper torque strut bracket*
4 *Mounting nuts*
5 *Mounting bolts*
6 *Upper torque strut*
7 *Lower mounting bolts*
8 *Lower torque strut bracket*
9 *Mounting bolt*
10 *Lower torque strut*
11 *Mounting bolt*
12 *Right engine mount*

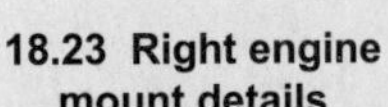

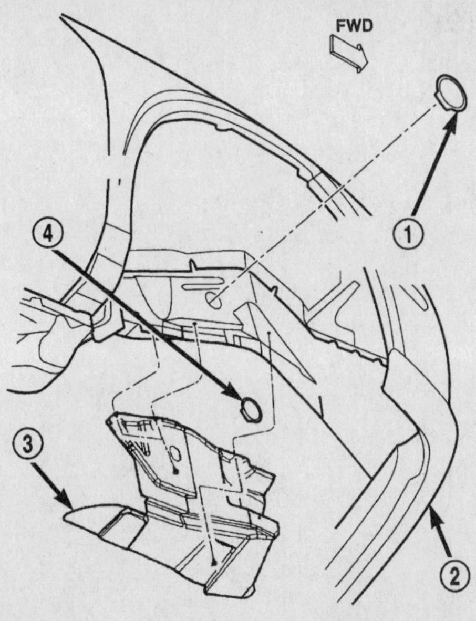


**18.23 Right engine mount details**

1. *Right engine mount bolt access plug*
2. *Fascia*
3. *Splash shield*
4. *Crankshaft bolt access plug*

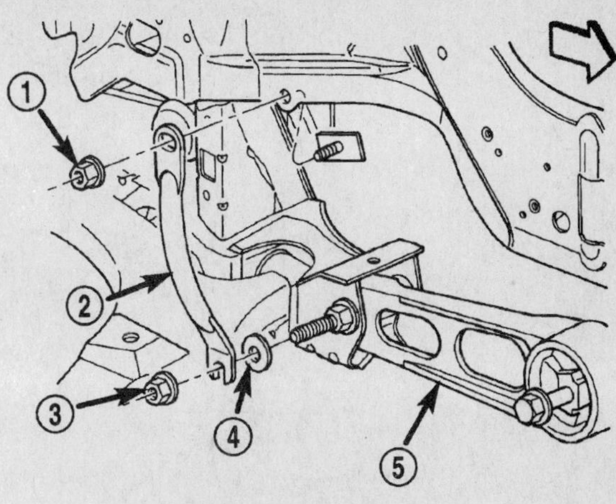


**18.24 Pencil strut details**

1. *Mounting nut*
2. *Pencil strut*
3. *Mounting nut*
4. *Flat washer*
5. *Lower torque strut*

## Upper torque strut

18 Remove the bolts that secure the upper torque strut to the shock tower bracket and engine mount bracket **(see illustration)**.

19 On vehicles equipped with air conditioning, remove the upper timing belt cover (see Section 7).

20 Separate the upper torque strut from the vehicle.

21 Installation is the reverse of removal.

22 Be sure to perform the engine torque strut adjustment procedure (see Steps 28 through 39). Use thread locking compound on the torque strut bolts and be sure to tighten them securely.

## Lower torque strut

23 Remove the splash shield from the right inner fender **(see illustration)**.

24 Remove the pencil strut **(see illustration)**.

25 Remove the lower torque strut mounting bolts and separate the torque strut from the crossmember.

26 Installation is the reverse of removal.

27 Be sure to perform the engine torque strut adjustment procedure (see Steps 28 through 38). Use thread locking compound on the torque strut bolts and be sure to tighten them securely.

## *Torque strut adjustment*

*Refer to illustrations 18.32 and 18.35*

28 Disconnect the cable from the negative battery terminal, then raise the vehicle and support it securely on jackstands (if not already done).

29 Remove the air filter housing (see Chapter 4).

30 Remove the pencil strut **(see illustration 18.24)**.

31 Loosen the upper and lower torque strut attachment bolts at the crossmember and the shock tower bracket.

32 Install a floor jack on the forward edge of the transmission bellhousing **(see illustration)**.

33 Remove the upper and lower torque strut bolts. Make sure the torque struts are free and not binding.

34 Reinstall the torque strut bolts hand tight.

35 Carefully apply upward force using the floor jack. Allow the engine to rotate to the rear and measure the distance between the engine mount bracket (point A) and the center of the hole on the shock tower bracket (point B) **(see illustration)**. This distance should be 4.70 inches.

36 With the engine in the correct position, tighten the upper and lower torque strut bolts to the Specifications listed in this Chapter.

37 Remove the floor jack.

38 Install the pencil strut **(see illustration 18.24)**.

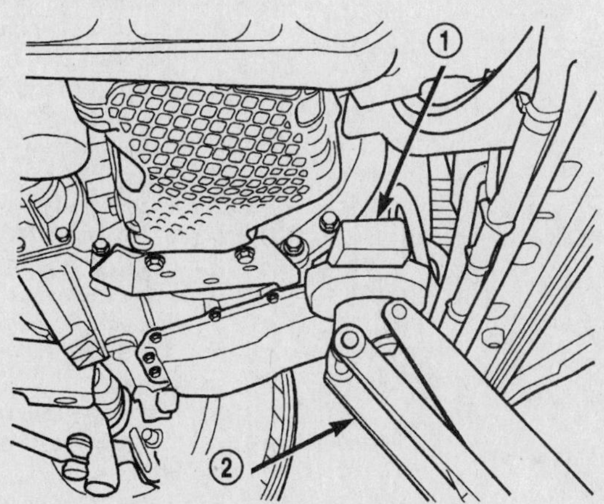


**18.32 Floor jack positioning details**

1. *Wood block*
2. *Floor jack*

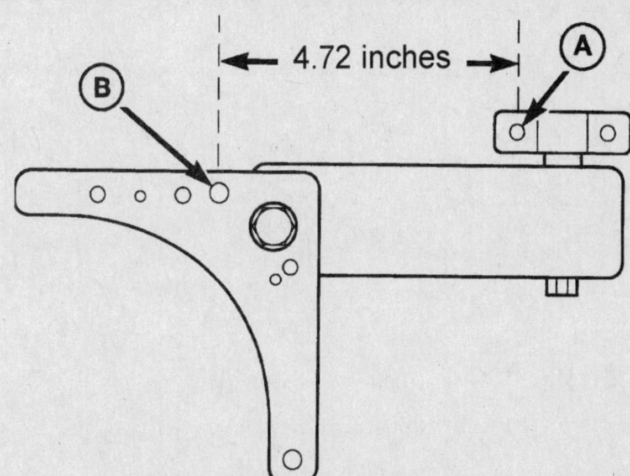


**18.35 Measure the distance from the center of the rear engine mount bolt (point A) to the center of the hole on the shock tower bracket (point B)**

# Notes

# Chapter 2 Part B
# General engine overhaul procedures

## Contents



## Specifications

### General

| | |
|---|---|
| Displacement | |
| 2.0L models | 122 cubic inches |
| 2.4L models | 148 cubic inches |
| Bore and Stroke | |
| 2.0L models | 3.445 x 3.268 inches (87.5 x 83.0 mm) |
| 2.4L models | 3.445 x 3.976 inches (87.5 x 101.0 mm) |
| Cylinder compression pressure | |
| Standard | 170 to 225 psi (1172 to 1551 kPa) |
| Maximum variation between cylinders | 25 percent |
| Oil pressure | |
| At curb idle | 4 psi (27.5 kPa) minimum |
| At 3000 rpm | 25 to 80 psi (172 to 552 kPa) |

### Torque specifications

**Note:** *One foot-pound (ft-lb) of torque is equivalent to 12 inch-pounds (in-lbs) of torque. Torque values below approximately 15 foot-pounds are expressed in inch-pounds, because most foot-pound torque wrenches are not accurate at these smaller values.*

| | **Ft-lbs** (unless otherwise indicated) | **Nm** |
|---|---|---|
| Balance shaft chain guide bolt | 105 in-lbs | 12 |
| Balance shaft chain tensioner adjustment bolt | 105 in-lbs | 12 |
| Balance shaft chain tensioner pivot bolt | 105 in-lbs | 12 |
| Balance shaft carrier cover bolts | 105 in-lbs | 12 |
| Balance shaft gear cover (double ended stud) | 105 in-lbs | 12 |
| Balance shaft sprocket bolts | 20 | 28 |
| Balance shaft carrier bolts | 40 | 54 |
| Driveplate-to-torque converter bolts | 55 | 74 |
| Connecting rod bearing cap bolts (use new bolts) | | |
| Step 1 | 20 | 27 |
| Step 2 | Tighten an additional 1/4-turn (90 degrees) | |
| Main bearing assembly | | |
| 2.0L models | | |
| Bedplate bolts | 25 | 33 |
| Main bearing cap bolts | 60 | 81 |
| 2.4L models | | |
| Bedplate bolts | | |
| Step 1 | 20 | 28 |
| Step 2 | 20 | 28 |
| Main bearing cap bolts | | |
| Step 1 | 30 | 41 |
| Step 2 | 30 | 41 |
| Step 3 | Tighten an additional 1/4-turn (90 degrees) | |
| Step 4 | 55 | 74 |

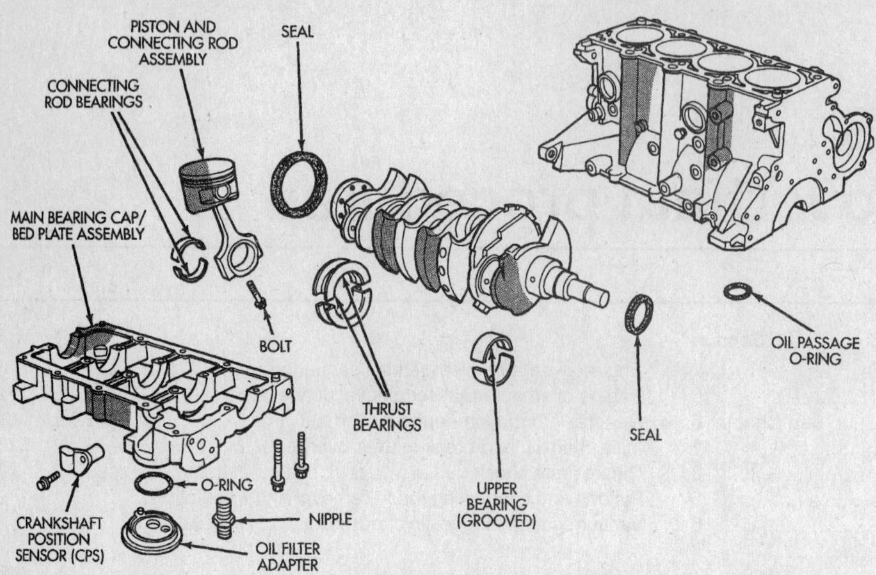


1.1a Exploded view of the engine block and components on the 2.0L DOHC engine

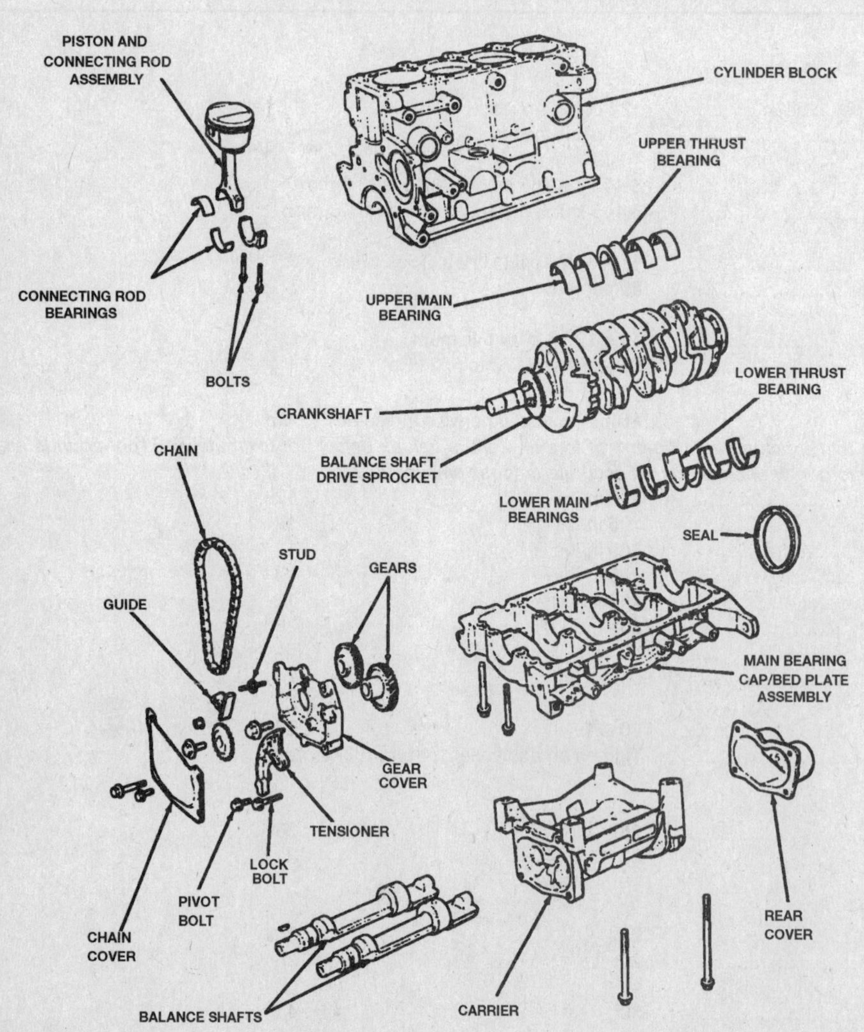


1.1b Exploded view of the engine block and components on the 2.4L DOHC engine

## 1 General information - engine overhaul

*Refer to illustrations 1.1a, 1.1b, 1.2, 1.3, 1.4, 1.5, 1.6 and 1.7*

Included in this portion of Chapter 2 are general information and diagnostic testing procedures for determining the overall mechanical condition of your engine.

The information ranges from advice concerning preparation for an overhaul and the purchase of replacement parts and/or components to detailed, step-by-step procedures covering removal and installation.

The following Sections have been written to help you determine whether your engine needs to be overhauled and how to remove and install it once you've determined it needs to be rebuilt. For information concerning in-vehicle engine repair, see Chapter 2A.

The Specifications included in this Part are general in nature and include only those necessary for testing the oil pressure and checking the engine compression. See Chapter 2A for additional engine Specifications.

It's not always easy to determine when, or if, an engine should be completely overhauled, because a number of factors must be considered.

High mileage is not necessarily an indication that an overhaul is needed, while low mileage doesn't preclude the need for an overhaul. Frequency of servicing is probably the most important consideration. An engine that's had regular and frequent oil and filter changes, as well as other required maintenance, will most likely give many thousands of miles of reliable service. Conversely, a neglected engine may require an overhaul very early in its service life.

Excessive oil consumption is an indication that piston rings, valve seals and/or valve guides are in need of attention. Make sure that oil leaks aren't responsible before deciding that the rings and/or guides are bad. Perform a cylinder compression check to determine the extent of the work required (see Section 3). Also check the vacuum readings under various conditions (see Section 4).

Check the oil pressure with a gauge installed in place of the oil pressure sending unit and compare it to this Chapter's Specifications (see Section 2). If it's extremely low, the bearings and/or oil pump are probably worn out.

Loss of power, rough running, knocking or metallic engine noises, excessive valve train noise and high fuel consumption rates may also point to the need for an overhaul, especially if they're all present at the same time. If a complete tune-up doesn't remedy the situation, major mechanical work is the only solution.

An engine overhaul involves restoring the internal parts to the specifications of a new engine **(see illustrations 1.1a and 1.1b)**. During an overhaul, the piston rings are replaced and the cylinder walls are recon-

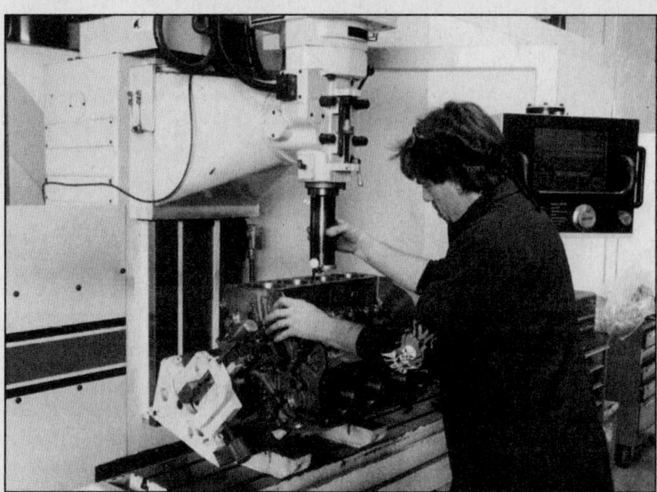

**1.2 An engine block being bored. An engine rebuilder will use special machinery to recondition the cylinder bores**

**1.3 If the cylinders are bored, the machine shop will normally hone the engine on a machine like this**

ditioned (rebored and/or honed) **(see illustrations 1.2 and 1.3)**. If a rebore is done by an automotive machine shop, new oversize pistons will also be installed. The main bearings, connecting rod bearings and camshaft bearings are generally replaced with new ones and, if necessary, the crankshaft may be reground to restore the journals **(see illustration 1.4)**. Generally, the valves are serviced as well, since they're usually in less-than-perfect condition at this point. While the engine is being overhauled, other components, such as the distributor, starter and alternator, can be rebuilt as well. The end result should be similar to a new engine that will give many trouble free miles. **Note:** *Critical cooling system components such as the hoses, drivebelts, thermostat and water pump should be replaced with new parts when an engine is overhauled. The radiator should be checked carefully to ensure that it isn't clogged or leaking* (see Chapter 3). *If you purchase a rebuilt engine or short block, some rebuilders will not warranty their engines unless the radiator has been professionally flushed. Also, we don't recommend overhauling the oil pump - always install a new one when an engine is rebuilt.*

**1.4 A crankshaft having a main bearing journal ground**

Overhauling the internal components on today's engines is a difficult and time-consuming task which requires a significant amount of specialty tools and is best left to a professional engine rebuilder **(see illustrations 1.5, 1.6 and 1.7)**. A competent engine rebuilder will handle the inspection of your old parts and offer advice concerning the reconditioning or replacement of the original engine, never purchase parts or have machine work done on other components until the block has been thoroughly inspected by a professional machine shop. As a general rule, time

**1.5 A machinist checks for a bent connecting rod, using specialized equipment**

**1.6 A bore gauge being used to check the main bearing bore**

**1.7 Uneven piston wear like this indicates a bent connecting rod**

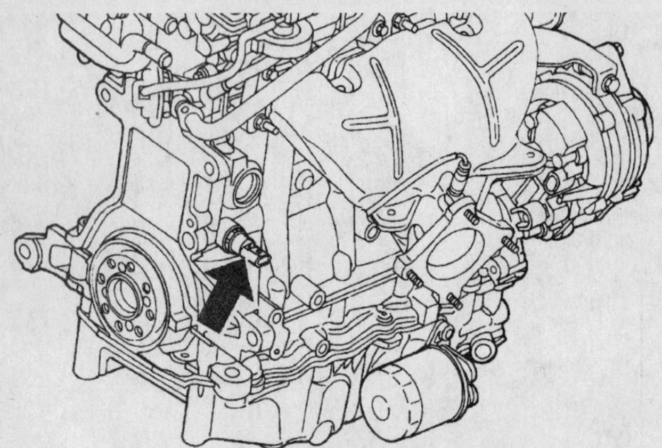

2.2 The oil pressure sending unit is located on the rear of the engine block, near the exhaust manifold

3.6 Use a compression gauge with a threaded fitting for the spark plug hole, not the type that requires hand pressure to maintain the seal

is the primary cost of an overhaul, especially since the vehicle may be tied up for a minimum of two weeks or more. Be aware that some engine builders only have the capability to rebuild the engine you bring them while other rebuilders have a large inventory of rebuilt exchange engines in stock. Also be aware that many machine shops could take as much as two weeks time to completely rebuild your engine depending on shop workload. Sometimes it makes more sense to simply exchange your engine for another engine that's already rebuilt to save time.

## 2 Oil pressure check

*Refer to illustration 2.2*

1 Low engine oil pressure can be a sign of an engine in need of rebuilding. A "low oil pressure" indicator (often called an "idiot light") is not a test of the oiling system. Such indicators only come on when the oil pressure is dangerously low. Even a factory oil pressure gauge in the instrument panel is only a relative indication, although much better for driver information than a warning light. A better test is with a mechanical (not electrical) oil pressure gauge.

2 Locate the oil pressure sending unit on the engine block. The oil pressure sending unit is located on the rear of the engine block, below the exhaust manifold **(see illustration)**.

3 Unscrew and remove the oil pressure sending unit and screw in the hose for your oil pressure gauge. If necessary, install an adapter fitting. Use Teflon tape or thread sealant on the threads of the adapter and/or the fitting on the end of your gauge's hose.

4 Connect an accurate tachometer to the engine, according to the tachometer manufacturer's instructions.

5 Check the oil pressure with the engine running (normal operating temperature) at the specified engine speed, and compare it to this Chapter's Specifications. If it's extremely low, the bearings and/or oil pump are probably worn out.

## 3 Cylinder compression check

*Refer to illustration 3.6*

1 A compression check will tell you what mechanical condition the upper end of your engine (pistons, rings, valves, head gaskets) is in. Specifically, it can tell you if the compression is down due to leakage caused by worn piston rings, defective valves and seats or a blown head gasket. **Note:** *The engine must be at normal operating temperature and the battery must be fully charged for this check.*

2 Begin by cleaning the area around the spark plugs before you remove them (compressed air should be used, if available). The idea is to prevent dirt from getting into the cylinders as the compression check is being done.

3 Remove all of the spark plugs from the engine (see Chapter 1).

4 Block the throttle wide open.

5 Disable the ignition system by unplugging the wiring harness from the ignition coil pack (see Chapter 5) and remove the fuel pump relay (see Chapter 4).

6 Install a compression gauge in the spark plug hole **(see illustration)**.

7 Crank the engine over at least seven compression strokes and watch the gauge. The compression should build up quickly in a healthy engine. Low compression on the first stroke, followed by gradually increasing pressure on successive strokes, indicates worn piston rings. A low compression reading on the first stroke, which doesn't build up during successive strokes, indicates leaking valves or a blown head gasket (a cracked head could also be the cause). Deposits on the undersides of the valve heads can also cause low compression. Record the highest gauge reading obtained.

8 Repeat the procedure for the remaining cylinders and compare the results to this Chapter's Specifications.

9 Add some engine oil (about three squirts from a plunger-type oil can) to each cylinder, through the spark plug hole, and repeat the test.

10 If the compression increases after the oil is added, the piston rings are definitely worn. If the compression doesn't increase significantly, the leakage is occurring at the valves or head gasket. Leakage past the valves may be caused by burned valve seats and/or faces or warped, cracked or bent valves.

11 If two adjacent cylinders have equally low compression, there's a strong possibility that the head gasket between them is blown. The appearance of coolant in the combustion chambers or the crankcase would verify this condition.

12 If one cylinder is slightly lower than the others, and the engine has a slightly rough idle, a worn lobe on the camshaft could be the cause.

13 If the compression is unusually high, the combustion chambers are probably coated with carbon deposits. If that's the case, the cylinder head(s) should be removed and decarbonized.

14 If compression is way down or varies greatly between cylinders, it would be a good idea to have a leak-down test performed by an automotive repair shop. This test will pinpoint exactly where the leakage is occurring and how severe it is.

## 4 Vacuum gauge diagnostic checks

*Refer to illustrations 4.4 and 4.6*

1 A vacuum gauge provides inexpensive but valuable information about what is going on in the engine. You can check for worn rings or cylinder walls, leaking head or intake manifold gaskets, incorrect carburetor adjustments, restricted exhaust, stuck or burned valves, weak valve springs, improper ignition or valve timing and ignition problems.

2 Unfortunately, vacuum gauge readings are easy to misinterpret, so they should be used in conjunction with other tests to confirm the diagnosis.

3 Both the absolute readings and the rate of needle movement are important for accurate interpretation. Most gauges measure vacuum in inches of mercury (in-Hg). The

4.4 A simple vacuum gauge can be handy in diagnosing engine condition and performance

following references to vacuum assume the diagnosis is being performed at sea level. As elevation increases (or atmospheric pressure decreases), the reading will decrease. For every 1,000 foot increase in elevation above approximately 2000 feet, the gauge readings will decrease about one inch of mercury.

4 Connect the vacuum gauge directly to the intake manifold vacuum, not to ported (throttle body) vacuum **(see illustration)**. Be sure no hoses are left disconnected during the test or false readings will result.

5 Before you begin the test, allow the engine to warm up completely. Block the wheels and set the parking brake. With the transaxle in Park, start the engine and allow it to run at normal idle speed. **Warning:** *Keep your hands and the vacuum gauge clear of the fans.*

6 Read the vacuum gauge; an average, healthy engine should normally produce about 17 to 22 in-Hg with a fairly steady needle **(see illustration)**. Refer to the following vacuum gauge readings and what they indicate about the engine's condition:

7 A low steady reading usually indicates a leaking gasket between the intake manifold and cylinder head(s) or throttle body, a leaky vacuum hose, late ignition timing or incorrect camshaft timing. Check ignition timing with a timing light and eliminate all other possible causes, utilizing the tests provided in this Chapter before you remove the timing chain cover to check the timing marks.

8 If the reading is three to eight inches below normal and it fluctuates at that low reading, suspect an intake manifold gasket leak at an intake port or a faulty fuel injector.

9 If the needle has regular drops of about two-to-four inches at a steady rate, the valves are probably leaking. Perform a compression check or leak-down test to confirm this.

10 An irregular drop or down-flick of the needle can be caused by a sticking valve or an ignition misfire. Perform a compression check or leak-down test and read the spark plugs.

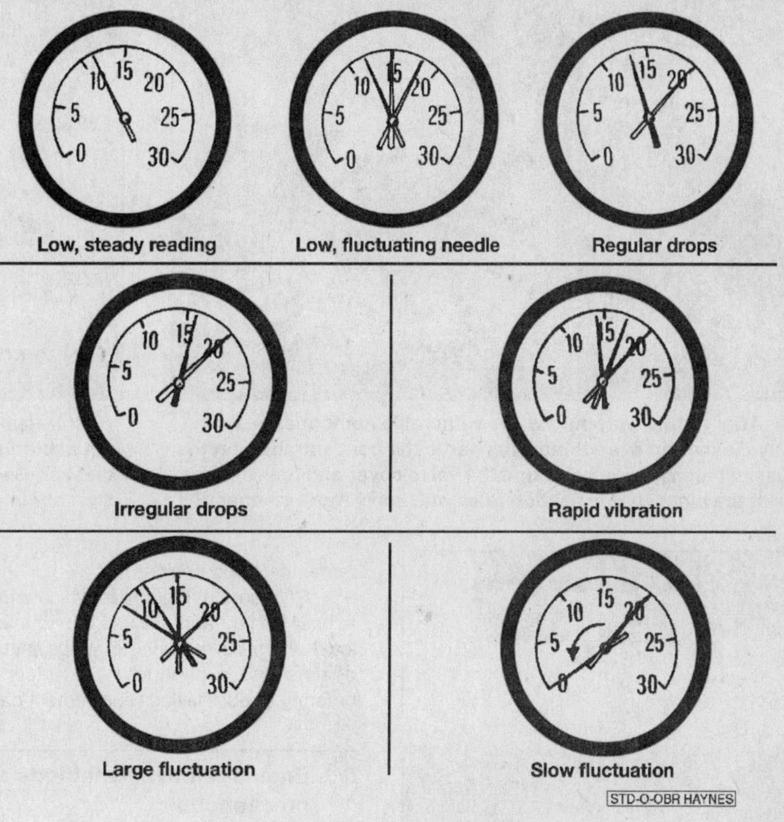


4.6 Typical vacuum gauge readings

11 A rapid vibration of about four in-Hg vibration at idle combined with exhaust smoke indicates worn valve guides. Perform a leak-down test to confirm this. If the rapid vibration occurs with an increase in engine speed, check for a leaking intake manifold gasket or head gasket, weak valve springs, burned valves or ignition misfire.

12 A slight fluctuation, say one inch up and down, may mean ignition problems. Check all the usual tune-up items and, if necessary, run the engine on an ignition analyzer.

13 If there is a large fluctuation, perform a compression or leak-down test to look for a weak or dead cylinder or a blown head gasket.

14 If the needle moves slowly through a wide range, check for a clogged PCV system, incorrect idle fuel mixture, throttle body or intake manifold gasket leaks.

15 Check for a slow return after revving the engine by quickly snapping the throttle open until the engine reaches about 2,500 rpm and let it shut. Normally the reading should drop to near zero, rise above normal idle reading (about 5 in-Hg over) and then return to the previous idle reading. If the vacuum returns slowly and doesn't peak when the throttle is snapped shut, the rings may be worn. If there is a long delay, look for a restricted exhaust system (often the muffler or catalytic converter). An easy way to check this is to temporarily disconnect the exhaust ahead of the suspected part and redo the test.

## 5 Engine rebuilding alternatives

The do-it-yourselfer is faced with a number of options when purchasing a rebuilt engine. The major considerations are cost, warranty, parts availability and the time required for the rebuilder to complete the project. The decision to replace the engine block, piston/connecting rod assemblies and crankshaft depends on the final inspection results of your engine. Only then can you make a cost effective decision whether to have your engine overhauled or simply purchase an exchange engine for your vehicle.

Some of the rebuilding alternatives include:

**Individual parts** - If the inspection procedures reveal that the engine block and most engine components are in reusable condition, purchasing individual parts and having a rebuilder rebuild your engine may be the most economical alternative. The block, crankshaft and piston/connecting rod assemblies should all be inspected carefully by a machine shop first.

**Short block** - A short block consists of an engine block with a crankshaft and piston/connecting rod assemblies already installed.

**6.1 After tightly wrapping water-vulnerable components, use a spray cleaner on everything, with particular concentration on the greasiest areas, usually around the valve cover and lower edges of the block. If one section dries out, apply more cleaner**

**6.2 Depending on how dirty the engine is, let the cleaner soak in according to the directions and then hose off the grime and cleaner. Get the rinse water down into every area you can get at; then dry important components with a hair dryer or paper towels**

**6.3 Get an engine stand sturdy enough to firmly support the engine while you're working on it. Stay away from three-wheeled models; they have a tendency to tip over more easily, so get a four-wheeled unit.**

All new bearings are incorporated and all clearances will be correct. The existing camshafts, valve train components, cylinder head and external parts can be bolted to the short block with little or no machine shop work necessary.

**Long block** - A long block consists of a short block plus an oil pump, oil pan, cylinder head, valve cover, camshaft and valve train components, timing sprockets and chain or gears and timing cover. All components are installed with new bearings, seals and gaskets incorporated throughout. The installation of manifolds and external parts is all that's necessary.

**Low mileage used engines** - Some companies now offer low mileage used engines which is a very cost effective way to get your vehicle up and running again. These engines often come from vehicles which have been in totaled in accidents or come from other countries which have a higher vehicle turn over rate. A low mileage used engine also usually has a similar warranty like the newly remanufactured engines.

Give careful thought to which alternative is best for you and discuss the situation with local automotive machine shops, auto parts dealers and experienced rebuilders before ordering or purchasing replacement parts.

## 6 Engine removal - methods and precautions

*Refer to illustrations 6.1, 6.2 and 6.3*

If you've decided that an engine must be removed for overhaul or major repair work, several preliminary steps should be taken. Read all removal and installation procedures carefully prior to committing to this job. These engines are removed by lowering to the floor, along with the transaxle, and then raising the vehicle sufficiently to slide the assembly out; this will require a vehicle hoist as well as an engine hoist.

Locating a suitable place to work is extremely important. Adequate work space, along with storage space for the vehicle, will be needed. If a shop or garage isn't available, at the very least a flat, level, clean work surface made of concrete or asphalt is required.

Cleaning the engine compartment and engine before beginning the removal procedure will help keep tools clean and organized **(see illustrations 6.1 and 6.2)**.

An engine hoist will also be necessary. Make sure the hoist is rated in excess of the combined weight of the engine and transaxle. Safety is of primary importance, considering the potential hazards involved in removing the engine from the vehicle.

If you're a novice at engine removal, get at least one helper. One person cannot easily do all the things you need to do to remove a big heavy engine and transaxle assembly from the engine compartment. Also helpful is to seek advice and assistance from someone who's experienced in engine removal.

Plan the operation ahead of time. Arrange for or obtain all of the tools and equipment you'll need prior to beginning the job **(see illustration 6.3)**. Some of the equipment necessary to perform engine removal and installation safely and with relative ease are (in addition to a vehicle hoist and an engine hoist) a heavy duty floor jack (preferably fitted with a transmission jack head adapter), complete sets of wrenches and sockets as described in the front of this manual, wooden blocks, plenty of rags and cleaning solvent for mopping up spilled oil, coolant and gasoline.

Plan for the vehicle to be out of use for quite a while. A machine shop can do the work that is beyond the scope of the home mechanic. Machine shops often have a busy schedule, so before removing the engine, consult the shop for an estimate of how long it will take to rebuild or repair the components that may need work.

## 7 Engine - removal and installation

*Refer to illustration 7.8*

**Warning 1:** *Gasoline is extremely flammable, so take extra precautions when you work on any part of the fuel system. Don't smoke or allow open flames or bare light bulbs near the work area, and don't work in a garage where a gas-type appliance (such as a water heater or a clothes dryer) is present. Since gasoline is carcinogenic, wear fuel-resistant gloves when there's a possibility of being exposed to fuel, and, if you spill any fuel on your skin, rinse it off immediately with soap and water. Mop up any spills immediately and do not store fuel-soaked rags where they could ignite. The fuel system is under constant pressure, so, if any fuel lines are to be disconnected, the fuel pressure in the system must be relieved first (see Chapter 4 for more information). When you perform any kind of work on the fuel system, wear safety glasses and have a Class B type fire extinguisher on hand.*

**Warning 2:** *The engine must be completely cool before beginning this procedure.*

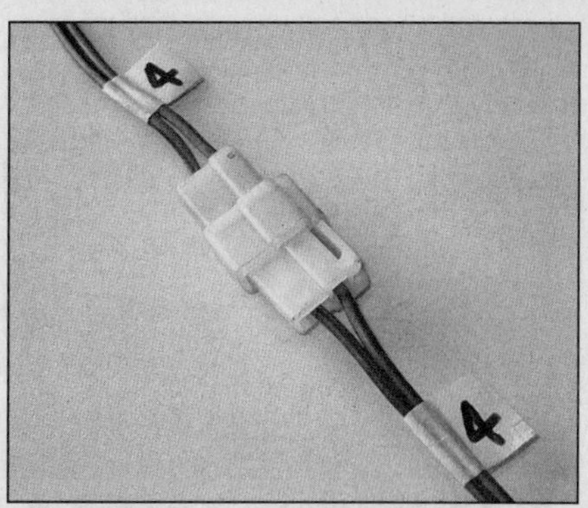


**7.8 Label both ends of each wire and hose before disconnecting it**

**Note 1:** *Engine removal on these models is a difficult job, especially for the do-it-yourself mechanic working at home. Because of the vehicle's design, the manufacturer states that the engine and transaxle have to be removed as a unit from the bottom of the vehicle, not the top. With a floor jack and jackstands the vehicle can't be raised high enough and supported safely enough for the engine/transaxle assembly to slide out from underneath. The manufacturer recommends that removal of the engine transaxle assembly only be performed on a frame-contact type vehicle hoist.*

**Note 2:** *Read through the entire Section before beginning this procedure. The engine and transaxle are removed as a unit from below and then separated outside the vehicle.*

## Removal

1 Have the air conditioning system discharged by an automotive air conditioning technician.

2 Park the vehicle on a frame-contact type vehicle hoist, then engage the arms of the hoist with the jacking points of the vehicle. Raise the hoist arms until they contact the vehicle, but not so much that the wheels come off the ground.

3 Relieve the fuel system pressure (see Chapter 4).

4 Place protective covers on the fenders and cowl and remove the hood (see Chapter 11).

5 Remove the air filter housing (see Chapter 4).

6 Disconnect the accelerator cable (and cruise control cable, if equipped) and bracket from the engine and position them aside.

7 Remove the battery and the battery tray (see Chapter 5).

8 Clearly label and disconnect all vacuum lines, emissions hoses, wiring harness connectors, ground straps and fuel lines. Masking tape and/or a touch up paint applicator work well for marking items **(see illustration)**. Take instant photos or sketch the locations of components and brackets.

9 Disconnect the electrical connectors from the PCM (see Chapter 6). Also detach any other electrical connectors between the engine and the vehicle.

10 Detach the positive cable from the engine compartment fuse/relay box and the ground cable from the vehicle. Unbolt the fuse/relay box and position it out of the way.

11 Detach the electrical connectors from the battery tray support. Also unbolt the ground cable from the right (passenger's) side strut tower.

12 Loosen the front wheel lug nuts, then raise the vehicle on the hoist. **Note:** *Keep in mind that during this procedure you'll have to adjust the height of the vehicle to perform certain operations.*

13 Drain the cooling system and engine oil and remove the drivebelts (see Chapter 1).

14 Remove the alternator and its brackets (see Chapter 5).

15 Remove the power steering pump and bracket (see Chapter 10).

16 Detach the lower radiator hose from the engine.

17 Lower the vehicle and detach the heater hoses at the firewall.

18 Detach the upper radiator hose from the thermostat housing.

19 Remove the upper radiator support crossmember.

20 Remove the cooling fan(s), shroud(s) and radiator (see Chapter 3).

21 Disconnect the shift cable(s) from the transaxle (see Chapter 7A or 7B). Also disconnect any wiring harness connectors from the transaxle.

22 Disconnect the upper air conditioning line from the condenser.

23 Disconnect the air conditioning lines at the compressor and the junction near the upper torque strut. Remove the air conditioning compressor (see Chapter 3).

24 Remove the power steering pump (see Chapter 10).

25 Raise the vehicle on the hoist. Remove the front wheels.

26 Remove the driveaxles (see Chapter 8).

27 If equipped with a manual transaxle, disconnect the quick-connect fitting at the clutch release cylinder (see Chapter 8).

28 Unplug the downstream oxygen sensor electrical connector.

29 Detach the exhaust pipe from the exhaust manifold (see Chapter 4).

30 Detach the pressure hose from the power steering gear (see Chapter 10).

31 Remove the engine lower torque strut and the structural collar (see Chapter 2A).

32 If equipped with an automatic transaxle, remove the torque converter bolts (see Chapter 7B).

33 If equipped with a manual transaxle, remove the driveplate-to-modular clutch bolts (see Chapter 8).

34 Lower the vehicle.

35 Remove the upper intake manifold (see Chapter 2A). This is to prevent possible damage to the plastic manifold.

36 Support the engine with a floor jack and a block of wood. Remove the right (passenger's) side engine mount center bolt (see Chapter 2A). Using one of the mount-to-engine bolts, attach one end of an engine lifting sling or chain to the mount boss. Tighten the bolt securely. Attach the other end of the sling or chain to other side of the engine, using one of the transaxle-to-engine bolts. Be sure the positioning of the chain or sling will support the engine and transaxle in a balanced attitude. **Note:** *The sling or chain must be long enough to allow the engine hoist to lower the engine/transaxle assembly to the ground, without letting the hoist arm contact the vehicle.*

37 Roll the hoist into position and attach the sling or chain to it. Take up the slack until there is slight tension on the hoist, then remove the jack from under the engine. Remember that the transaxle end of the engine will be heavier, so position the chain on the hoist so it balances the engine and the transaxle level with the vehicle. **Note:** *Depending on the design of the engine hoist, it may be helpful to position the hoist from the side of the vehicle, so that when the engine/transaxle assembly is lowered it will fit between the legs of the hoist.*

38 Recheck to be sure nothing except the remaining mounts are still connecting the engine to the vehicle or to the transaxle. Disconnect and label anything still remaining.

39 Remove the through-bolt on the driver's side transaxle mount and the upper engine torque strut (see Chapter 2A).

40 Slowly lower the engine/transaxle to the ground.

41 Once the powertrain is on the floor, disconnect the engine lifting hoist and raise the vehicle it clears the powertrain.

42 Reconnect the chain or sling and raise the engine and transaxle. Support the engine with blocks of wood or another floor jack, while leaving the sling or chain attached to the right-side mounting boss. Support the transaxle with another floor jack, preferably one with a transmission jack head adapter. At this point the transaxle can be unbolted and removed from the engine. Be very careful to ensure that the components are supported securely so they won't topple off their supports during disconnection.

43 Reconnect the lifting chain to the engine, then raise the engine and attach it to an engine stand.

## Installation

44 Installation is the reverse of removal, noting the following points:

*a) Check the engine/transaxle mounts. If they're worn or damaged, replace them.*

*b) On manual transaxle equipped models, inspect the clutch components (see Chapter 8) and on automatic models inspect the converter seal and bushing.*

*c) Attach the transaxle to the engine following the procedure described in Chapter 7A or 7B.*

*d) Add coolant, oil, power steering and transmission fluids as needed (see Chapter 1).*

*e) Run the engine and check for proper operation and leaks. Shut off the engine and recheck the fluid levels.*

**9.1 Before you try to remove the pistons, use a ridge reamer to remove the raised material (ridge) from the top of the cylinders**

**9.3 Checking the connecting rod endplay (side clearance)**

**9.4 If the connecting rods and caps are not marked, use permanent ink or paint to mark the caps to the rods by cylinder number (for example, this would be the No. 4 connecting rod)**

## 8 Engine overhaul - disassembly sequence

1 It's much easier to remove the external components if it's mounted on a portable engine stand. A stand can often be rented quite cheaply from an equipment rental yard. Before the engine is mounted on a stand, the flywheel/driveplate should be removed from the engine.

2 If a stand isn't available, it's possible to remove the external engine components with it blocked up on the floor. Be extra careful not to tip or drop the engine when working without a stand.

3 If you're going to obtain a rebuilt engine, all external components must come off first, to be transferred to the replacement engine. These components include:

*Clutch and flywheel (models with manual transaxle)*
*Driveplate (models with automatic transaxle)*
*Ignition system components*
*Emissions-related components*
*Engine mounts and mount brackets*
*Engine rear cover (spacer plate between flywheel/driveplate and engine block)*
*Intake/exhaust manifolds*
*Fuel injection components*
*Oil filter*
*Spark plug wires and spark plugs*
*Thermostat and housing assembly*
*Water pump*

**Note:** *When removing the external components from the engine, pay close attention to details that may be helpful or important during installation. Note the installed position of gaskets, seals, spacers, pins, brackets, washers, bolts and other small items.*

4 If you're going to obtain a short block (assembled engine block, crankshaft, pistons and connecting rods), then remove the timing belt, cylinder head, oil pan, oil pump pick-up tube, oil pump and water pump from your engine so that you can turn in your old short block to the rebuilder as a core. See *Engine rebuilding alternatives* for additional information regarding the different possibilities to be considered.

## 9 Pistons and connecting rods - removal and installation

### Removal

*Refer to illustrations 9.1, 9.3, and 9.4*

**Note:** *Prior to removing the piston/connecting rod assemblies, remove the cylinder head, oil pan and, on 2.4L engines, the balance shafts and carrier assembly* (see Chapter 2A or 2B).

1 Use your fingernail to feel if a ridge has formed at the upper limit of ring travel (about 1/4-inch down from the top of each cylinder). If carbon deposits or cylinder wear have produced ridges, they must be completely removed with a special tool **(see illustration)**. Follow the manufacturer's instructions provided with the tool. Failure to remove the ridges before attempting to remove the piston/connecting rod assemblies may result in piston breakage.

2 After the cylinder ridges have been removed, turn the engine so the crankshaft is facing up.

3 Before the main bearing cap assembly and connecting rods are removed, check the connecting rod endplay with feeler gauges. Slide them between the first connecting rod and the crankshaft throw until the play is removed **(see illustration)**. Repeat this procedure for each connecting rod. The endplay is equal to the thickness of the feeler gauge(s). Check with an automotive machine shop for the endplay service limit (a typical endplay should measure between 0.005 to 0.015-inch [0.127 to 0.369 mm]). If the play exceeds the service limit, new connecting rods will be required. If new rods (or a new crankshaft) are installed, the endplay may fall under the minimum allowable. If it does, the rods will have to be machined to restore it. If necessary, consult an automotive machine shop for advice.

4 Check the connecting rods and caps for identification marks **(see illustration)**. If they aren't plainly marked, use permanent ink or paint to make the appropriate number on each rod and cap (1, 2, 3, etc., depending on the cylinder they're associated with).

5 Loosen each of the connecting rod cap bolts 1/2-turn at a time until they can be removed by hand. **Note:** *New connecting rod cap bolts must be used when reassembling the engine, but save the old bolts for use when checking the connecting rod bearing oil clearance.*

6 Remove the number one connecting rod cap and bearing insert. Don't drop the bearing insert out of the cap.

7 Remove the bearing insert and push the connecting rod/piston assembly out through the top of the engine. Use a wooden or plastic hammer handle to push on the upper bearing surface in the connecting rod. If resistance is felt, double-check to make sure that all of the ridge was removed from the cylinder.

8 Repeat the procedure for the remaining cylinders.

9 After removal, reassemble the connecting rod caps and bearing inserts in their respective connecting rods and install the cap bolts finger tight. Leaving the old bearing inserts in place until reassembly will help prevent the connecting rod bearing surfaces from being accidentally nicked or gouged.

10 The pistons and connecting rods are now ready for inspection and overhaul at an automotive machine shop.

### Piston ring installation

*Refer to illustrations 9.13, 9.14, 9.15, 9.19a, 9.19b, 9.21 and 9.22*

11 Before installing the new piston rings, the ring end gaps must be checked. It's assumed that the piston ring side clearance has been checked and verified correct.

12 Lay out the piston/connecting rod assemblies and the new ring sets so the ring sets will be matched with the same piston and cylinder during the end gap measurement and engine assembly.

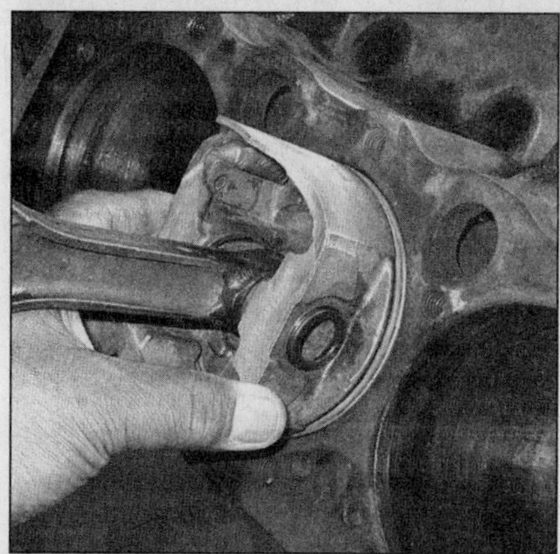
**9.13 Install the piston ring into the cylinder then push it down into position using a piston so the ring will be square in the cylinder**

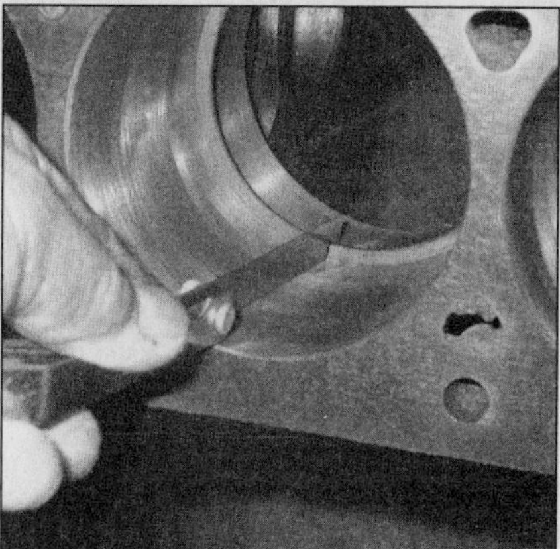
**9.14 With the ring square in the cylinder, measure the ring end gap with a feeler gauge**

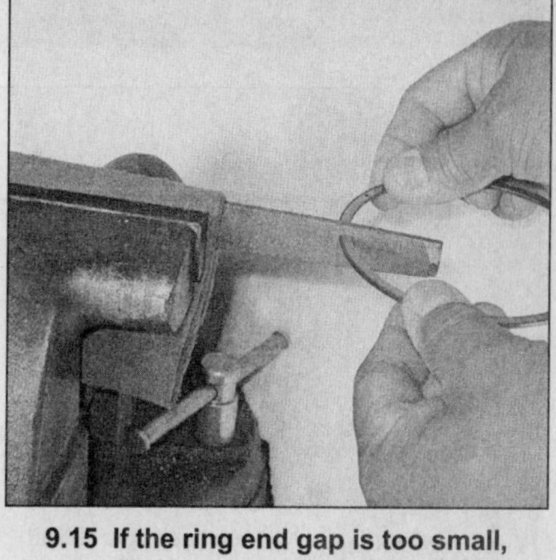
**9.15 If the ring end gap is too small, clamp a file in a vise as shown and file the piston ring ends - be sure to remove all raised material**

13 Insert the top (number one) ring into the first cylinder and square it up with the cylinder walls by pushing it in with the top of the piston **(see illustration)**. The ring should be near the bottom of the cylinder, at the lower limit of ring travel.

14 To measure the end gap, slip feeler gauges between the ends of the ring until a gauge equal to the gap width is found **(see illustration)**. The feeler gauge should slide between the ring ends with a slight amount of drag. A typical ring gap should fall between 0.010 to 0.020-inch (0.25 to 0.50 mm) for compression rings, and up to 0.030-inch (0.76) for the oil ring steel rails. If the gap is larger or smaller than specified, double-check to make sure you have the correct rings before proceeding.

15 If the gap is too small, it must be enlarged or the ring ends may come in contact with each other during engine operation, which can cause serious damage to the engine. The end gap can be increased by filing the ring ends very carefully with a fine file. Mount the file in a vise equipped with soft jaws, slip the ring over the file with the ends contacting the file face and slowly move the ring to remove material from the ends. When performing this operation, file only by pushing the ring from the outside end of the file towards the vise **(see illustration)**.

16 Excess end gap isn't critical unless it's greater than approximately 0.040-inch (1.01 mm). Again, double-check to make sure you have the correct ring type.

17 Repeat the procedure for each ring that will be installed in the first cylinder and for each ring in the remaining cylinders. Remember to keep rings, pistons and cylinders matched up.

18 Once the ring end gaps have been checked/corrected, the rings can be installed on the pistons.

19 The oil control ring (lowest one on the piston) is usually installed first. It's composed of three separate components. Slip the spacer/expander into the groove **(see illustration)**. If an anti-rotation tang is used, make sure it's inserted into the drilled hole in the ring groove. Next, install the upper side rail in the same manner **(see illustration)**. Don't use a piston ring installation tool on the oil ring side rails, as they may be damaged. Instead, place one end of the side rail into the groove between the spacer/expander and the ring land, hold it firmly in place and slide a finger around the piston while pushing the rail into the groove. Finally, install the lower side rail.

**9.19a Installing the spacer/expander in the oil ring groove**

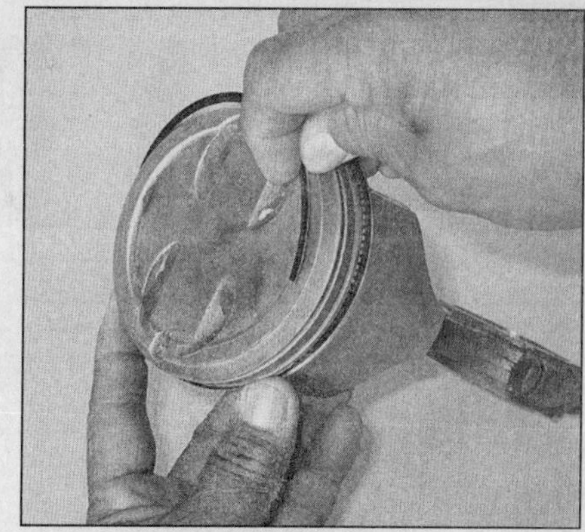
**9.19b DO NOT use a piston ring installation tool when installing the oil control side rails**

20 After the three oil ring components have been installed, check to make sure that both the upper and lower side rails can be rotated smoothly inside the ring grooves.

21 The number two (middle) ring is installed next. It's usually stamped with a mark which must face up **(see illustration)**, toward the top of the piston. Do not mix up the top and middle rings, as they have different cross-sections. **Note:** *Always follow the instructions printed on the ring package or box - different manufacturers may require different approaches.*

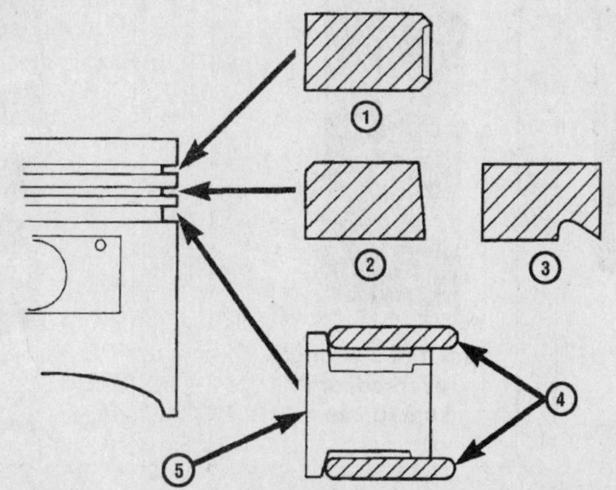

**9.21 Piston ring details**

1. *No. 1 compression ring*
2. *No. 2 compression ring - all except 2003 2.4L engines*
3. *No. 2 compression ring - 2003 2.4L engines*
4. *Oil ring side rails*
5. *Oil ring spacer/expander*

# ENGINE BEARING ANALYSIS

## Debris

Babbitt bearing embedded with debris from machinings

Microscopic detail of debris

Microscopic detail of gouges

Overplated copper alloy bearing gouged by cast iron debris

Aluminum bearing embedded with glass beads

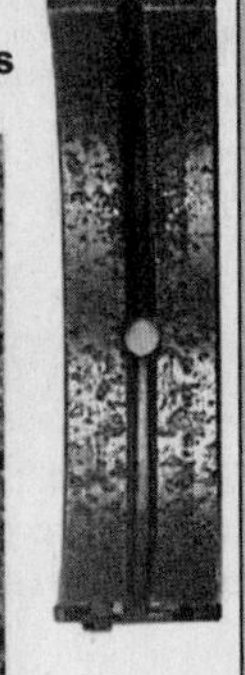

Microscopic detail of glass beads

Damaged lining caused by dirt left on the bearing back

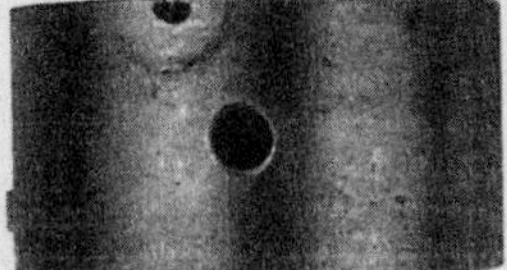

## Misassembly

Result of a lower half assembled as an upper - blocking the oil flow

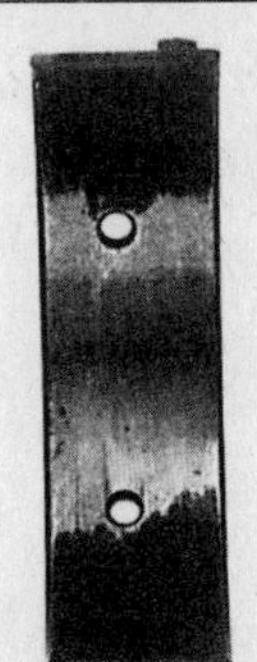

Excessive oil clearance is indicated by a short contact arc

Polished and oil-stained backs are a result of a poor fit in the housing bore

Result of a wrong, reversed, or shifted cap

## Overloading

Damage from excessive idling which resulted in an oil film unable to support the load imposed

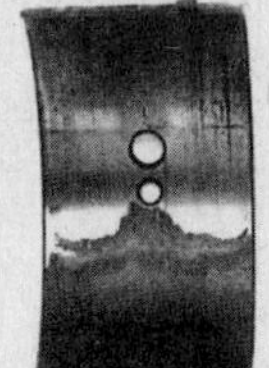

Damaged upper connecting rod bearings caused by engine lugging; the lower main bearings (not shown) were similarly affected

The damage shown in these upper and lower connecting rod bearings was caused by engine operation at a higher-than-rated speed under load

## Misalignment

A warped crankshaft caused this pattern of severe wear in the center, diminishing toward the ends

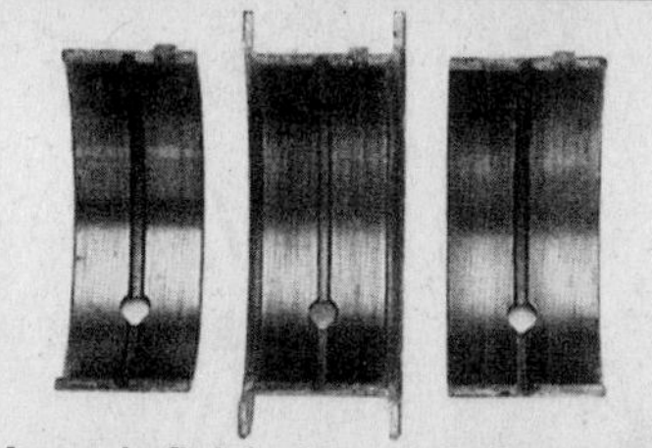

A poorly finished crankshaft caused the equally spaced scoring shown

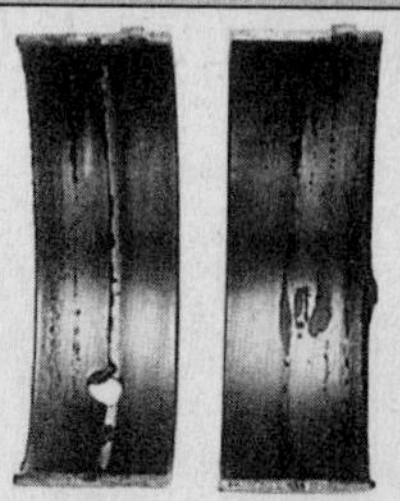

A tapered housing bore caused the damage along one edge of this pair

A bent connecting rod led to the damage in the "V" pattern

## Lubrication

Result of dry start: The bearings on the left, farthest from the oil pump, show more damage

## Corrosion

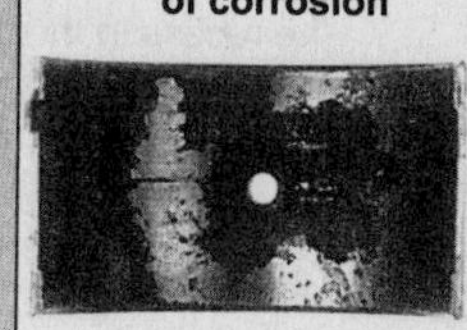

Microscopic detail of corrosion

Corrosion is an acid attack on the bearing lining generally caused by inadequate maintenance, extremely hot or cold operation, or inferior oils or fuels

Microscopic detail of cavitation

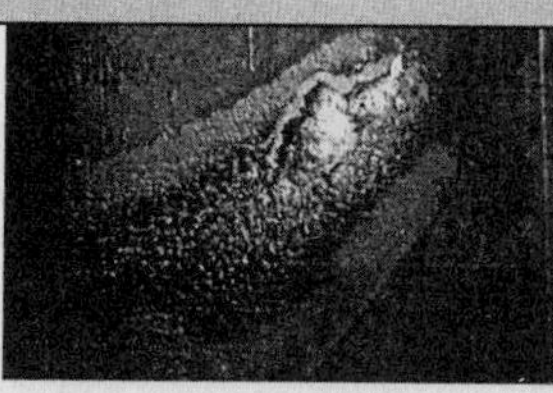

Example of cavitation - a surface erosion caused by pressure changes in the oil film

Result of a low oil supply or oil starvation

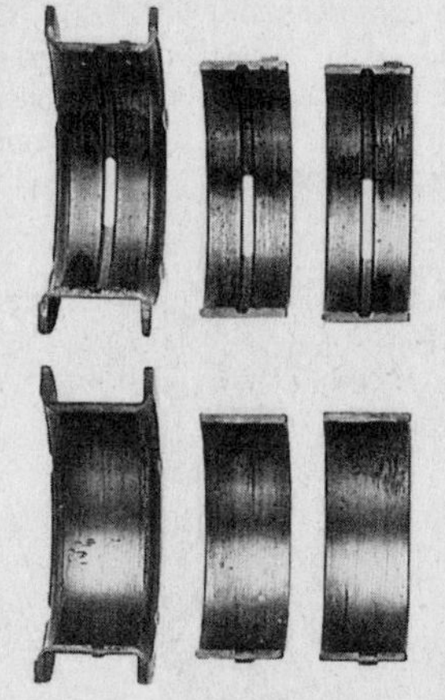

Severe wear as a result of inadequate oil clearance

Damage from excessive thrust or insufficient axial clearance

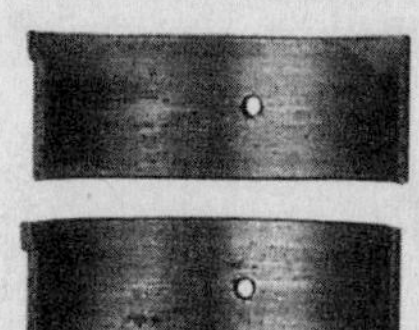

Bearing affected by oil dilution caused by excessive blow-by or a rich mixture

**9.22 Use a piston ring installation tool to install the number 2 and the number 1 (top) rings - be sure the directional mark on the piston ring(s) is facing toward the top of the piston**

22 Use a piston ring installation tool and make sure the identification mark is facing the top of the piston, then slip the ring into the middle groove on the piston **(see illustration)**. Don't expand the ring any more than necessary to slide it over the piston.

23 Install the number one (top) ring in the same manner. Make sure the mark is facing up. Be careful not to confuse the number one and number two rings **(see illustration 9.21)**.

24 Repeat the procedure for the remaining pistons and rings.

## Installation

25 Before installing the piston/connecting rod assemblies, the cylinder walls must be perfectly clean, the top edge of each cylinder bore must be chamfered, and the crankshaft must be in place.

26 Remove the cap from the end of the number one connecting rod (refer to the marks made during removal). Remove the original bearing inserts and wipe the bearing surfaces of the connecting rod and cap with a clean, lint-free cloth. They must be kept spotlessly clean.

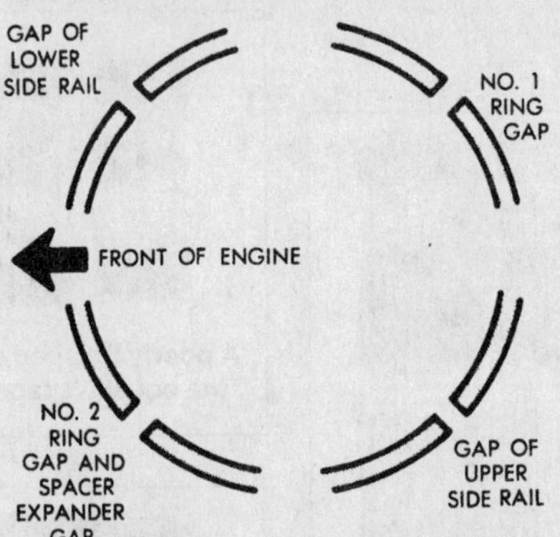


**9.30 Position the piston ring end gaps as shown**

## Connecting rod bearing oil clearance check

*Refer to illustrations 9.30, 9.33, 9.35, 9.37, 9.38 and 9.41*

27 Clean the back side of the new upper bearing insert, then lay it in place in the connecting rod.

28 Make sure the tab on the bearing fits into the recess in the rod. Don't hammer the bearing insert into place and be very careful not to nick or gouge the bearing face. Don't lubricate the bearing at this time.

29 Clean the back side of the other bearing insert and install it in the rod cap. Again, make sure the tab on the bearing fits into the recess in the cap, and don't apply any lubricant. It's critically important that the mating surfaces of the bearing and connecting rod are perfectly clean and oil free when they're assembled.

30 Position the piston ring gaps at 90-degree intervals around the piston as shown **(see illustration)**.

31 Lubricate the piston and rings with clean engine oil and attach a piston ring compressor to the piston. Leave the skirt protruding about 1/4-inch (6 mm) to guide the piston into the cylinder. The rings must be compressed until they're flush with the piston.

32 Rotate the crankshaft until the number one connecting rod journal is at BDC (bottom dead center) and apply a liberal coat of engine oil to the cylinder walls.

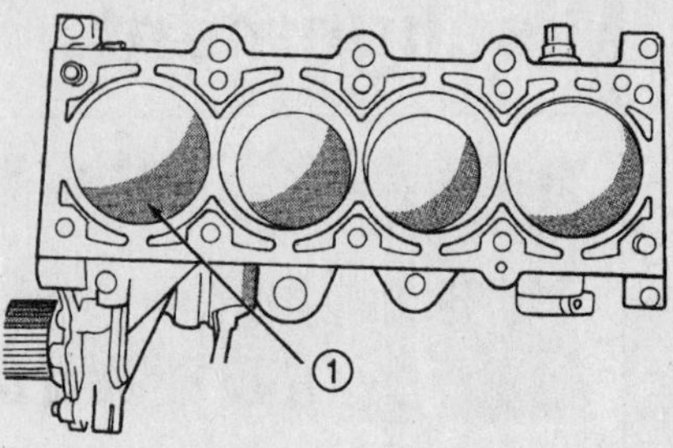


**9.33 The directional arrow (1) is marked on the top of each piston**

33 With the mark on top of the piston pointing towards the front (timing belt end) of the engine **(see illustration)**, gently insert the piston/connecting rod assembly into the number one cylinder bore and rest the bottom edge of the ring compressor on the engine block.

34 Tap the top edge of the ring compressor to make sure it's contacting the block around its entire circumference.

35 Gently tap on the top of the piston with the end of a wooden or plastic hammer handle **(see illustration)** while guiding the end of the connecting rod into place on the crankshaft journal. The piston rings may try to pop out of the ring compressor just before entering the cylinder bore, so keep some downward pressure on the ring compressor. Work slowly, and if any resistance is felt as the piston enters the cylinder, stop immediately. Find out what's hanging up and fix it before proceeding. Do not, for any reason, force the piston into the cylinder - you might break a ring and/or the piston.

36 Once the piston/connecting rod assembly is installed, the connecting rod bearing oil clearance must be checked before the rod cap is permanently installed.

37 Cut a piece of the appropriate size Plastigage slightly shorter than the width of the connecting rod bearing and lay it in place on the number one connecting rod journal, parallel with the journal axis **(see illustration)**.

38 Clean the connecting rod cap bearing

**9.35 Use a plastic or wooden hammer handle to push the piston into the cylinder**

**9.37 Place Plastigage on each connecting rod bearing journal parallel to the crankshaft centerline**

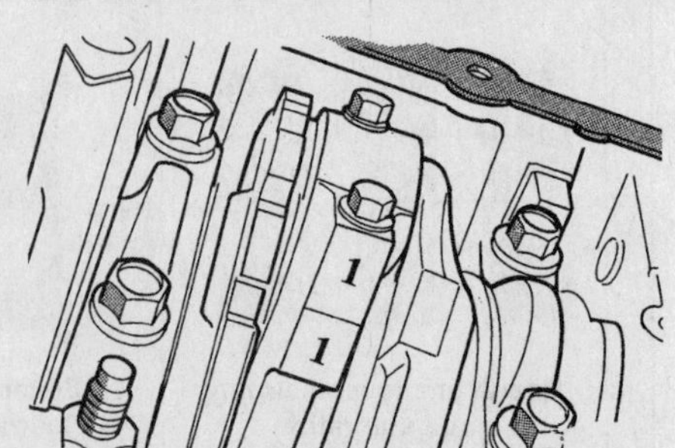


**9.38 Install the connecting rod cap making sure the cap and rod identification numbers match**

9.41 Use the scale on the Plastigage package to determine the bearing oil clearance - be sure to measure the widest part of the Plastigage and use the correct scale; it comes with both standard and metric scales

face and install the rod cap. Make sure the mating mark on the cap is on the same side as the mark on the connecting rod **(see illustration)**.

39 Install the old rod bolts at this time, and tighten them to the torque listed in this Chapter's Specifications. **Note:** *Use a thin-wall socket to avoid erroneous torque readings that can result if the socket is wedged between the rod cap and the bolt. If the socket tends to wedge itself between the fastener and the cap, lift up on it slightly until it no longer contacts the cap. DO NOT rotate the crankshaft at any time during this operation.*

40 Remove the fasteners and detach the rod cap, being very careful not to disturb the Plastigage.

41 Compare the width of the crushed Plastigage to the scale printed on the Plastigage envelope to obtain the oil clearance **(see illustration)**. The connecting rod oil clearance is usually about 0.001 to 0.002 inch. Consult an automotive machine shop for the clearance specified for the rod bearings on your engine.

42 If the clearance is not as specified, the bearing inserts may be the wrong size (which means different ones will be required). Before deciding that different inserts are needed, make sure that no dirt or oil was between the bearing inserts and the connecting rod or cap when the clearance was measured. Also, recheck the journal diameter. If the Plastigage was wider at one end than the other, the journal may be tapered. If the clearance still exceeds the limit specified, the bearing will have to be replaced with an undersize bearing. **Caution:** *When installing a new crankshaft always use a standard size bearing.*

### Final installation

43 Carefully scrape all traces of the Plastigage material off the rod journal and/or bearing face. Be very careful not to scratch the bearing - use your fingernail or the edge of a plastic card.

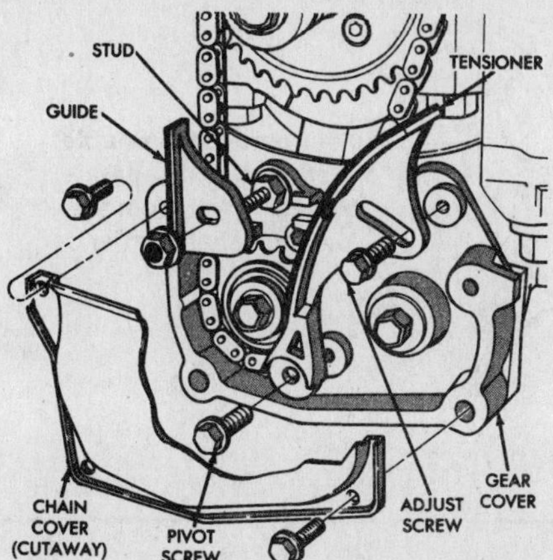


10.2 Balance shaft chain cover, guide and tensioner

44 Make sure the bearing faces are perfectly clean, then apply a uniform layer of clean moly-base grease or engine assembly lube to both of them. You'll have to push the piston into the cylinder to expose the face of the bearing insert in the connecting rod. **Caution:** *Install new connecting rod cap bolts. Do NOT reuse old bolts - they have stretched and cannot be reused.*

45 Slide the connecting rod back into place on the journal, then install the rod cap. Lubricate the threads of the new bolts with clean engine oil, then install the bolts and tighten them to the torque listed in this Chapter's Specifications.

46 Repeat the entire procedure for the remaining pistons/connecting rods.

47 The important points to remember are:

a) *Keep the back sides of the bearing inserts and the insides of the connecting rods and caps perfectly clean when assembling them.*
b) *Make sure you have the correct piston/rod assembly for each cylinder.*
c) *The mark on the piston must face the front (timing belt end) of the engine.*
d) *Lubricate the cylinder walls liberally with clean oil.*
e) *Lubricate the bearing faces when installing the rod caps after the oil clearance has been checked.*

48 After all the piston/connecting rod assemblies have been correctly installed, rotate the crankshaft a number of times by hand to check for any obvious binding.

49 As a final step, check the connecting rod endplay again.

50 Compare the measured endplay to the tolerance listed in this Chapter's Specifications to make sure it's acceptable. If it was correct before disassembly and the original crankshaft and rods were reinstalled, it should still be correct. If new rods or a new crankshaft were installed, the endplay may be inadequate. If so, the rods will have to be removed and taken to an automotive machine shop for resizing.

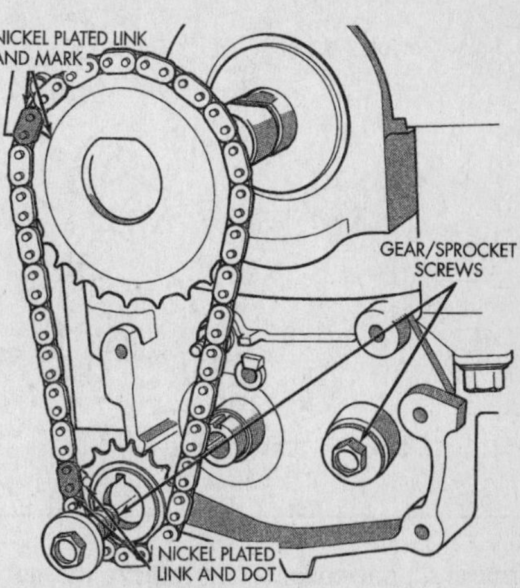


10.4 Remove the balance shaft chain sprocket, chain, and crankshaft bolts

## 10 Balance shafts and carrier assembly (2.4L models) - removal, inspection and installation

**Note:** *This procedure assumes that the engine has been removed from the vehicle and the driveplate, timing belt, oil pan and oil pump have also been removed (see Chapter 2A).*

**Caution:** *With the timing belt removed, do not rotate the crankshaft unless the camshafts have first been removed (see Chapter 2A); valve damage may occur.*

### Removal

*Refer to illustrations 10.2, 10.4, 10.5 and 10.6*

1 The balance shafts are installed in a carrier mounted to the main bearing cap/bedplate on the lower part of the engine block. The shafts are connected through two gears which rotate them in opposite directions. These gears are driven by a chain from the crankshaft and are designed to rotate at a 2:1 ratio with the crankshaft (one turn of the crankshaft equals two turns of the balance shafts), which counterbalances reciprocating masses within the engine.

2 Remove the chain cover, guide and tensioner from the engine block **(see illustration)**.

3 Keep the crankshaft from rotating and remove the balance shaft bolts. **Note:** *A block of wood placed tightly between the engine block and the crankshaft counterbalance weight will prevent crankshaft rotation.*

4 Remove the balance shaft chain sprocket, chain, and crankshaft chain sprocket **(see illustration)**. Use two prybars to work the sprocket back and forth until it is free from the crankshaft. **Note:** *The carrier assembly may be removed from the main bearing cap/bedplate at this time, if balance shaft removal is not required.*

5 Remove the special stud (double-ended)

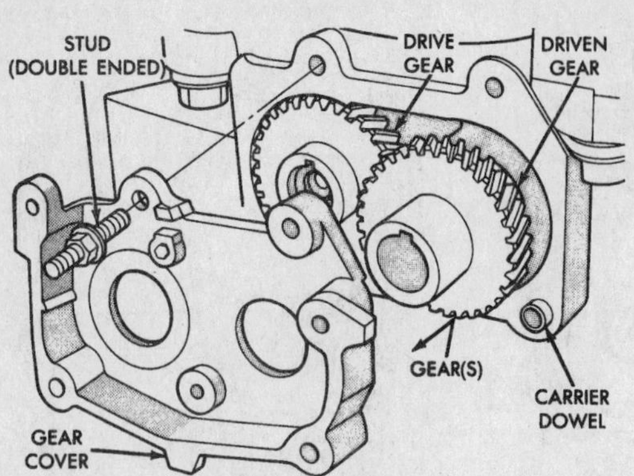


**10.5 Remove the double ended stud and separate the gear cover from the balance shaft carrier**

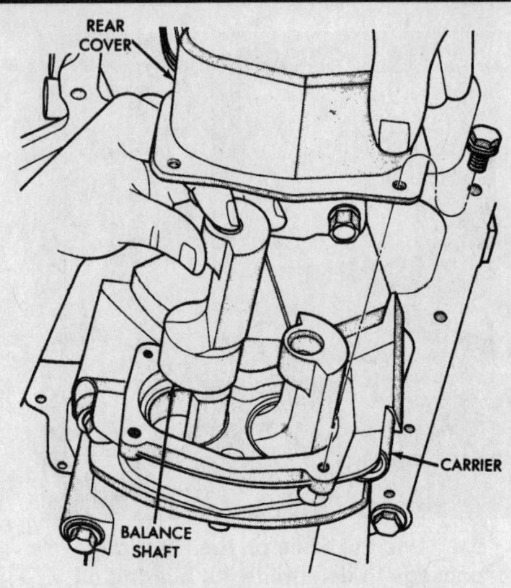


**10.6 Remove the rear cover from the carrier and pull out the balance shafts**

from the gear cover. Then remove the gear cover and balance shaft gears **(see illustration)**.

6 Remove the rear cover from the carrier and pull out the balance shafts **(see illustration)**.

7 Remove the bolts that hold the carrier to the main bearing cap/bedplate, and separate the carrier from the engine.

## Cleaning and inspection

8 Clean all components with solvent and dry thoroughly. Inspect all components for damage and wear. Pay close attention to the chain, sprocket and gear teeth and the bearing surfaces of the carrier and balance shafts. Replace defective parts as necessary.

## Installation

*Refer to illustrations 10.12 and 10.15*

9 Install the balance shaft carrier on the main bearing cap/bedplate and tighten the bolts to the torque in this Chapter's Specifications.

10 Lubricate the balance shafts with clean engine oil and insert them into the carrier.

11 Install the rear cover and tighten the bolts to the torque in this Chapter's Specifications.

12 Rotate the balance shafts until both shaft keyways are parallel and face the crankshaft. Install the short hub drive gear on the sprocket driven shaft and the long hub gear on the gear driven shaft. After installation, the timing marks (dots) should be together and the keyways positioned as shown **(see illustration)**.

13 Install the gear cover and tighten the double-ended stud to the torque in this Chapter's Specifications.

14 Install the sprocket on the crankshaft with the timing mark facing out, be careful not to cock the sprocket as its being installed.

15 Position the crankshaft so the timing mark on the chain sprocket is lined up with the parting line on the left side of the number 1 main bearing cap **(see illustration)**.

16 Place the chain on the crankshaft sprocket so that the nickel plated link of the chain is located at the timing mark on the crankshaft sprocket **(see illustration 10.15)**.

17 Install the balance shaft sprocket in the chain so that the timing mark on the sprocket (yellow dot) mates with the nickel plated link on the chain (8 links from the upper nickel plated link) **(see illustration 10.15)**.

18 Slide the balance shaft sprocket on the balance shaft. If the sprocket is difficult to install, it may be necessary to loosen the rear cover and push the balance shaft slightly out of the carrier to ease sprocket installation. **Note:** *The timing mark on the balance shaft sprocket and the nickel plated link should align with the notch on the side of the gear cover* **(see illustration 10.15)**.

19 Install the balance shaft bolts. Keep the crankshaft from rotating and tighten the balance shaft bolts to the torque in this Chapter's Specifications. **Note:** *A block of wood placed tightly between the engine block and the crankshaft counterbalance will prevent crankshaft rotation.*

## Chain tensioning

*Refer to illustration 10.20*

20 Install the chain tensioner loosely. Place a 0.039 x 2.75 inch shim (a feeler gauge cut

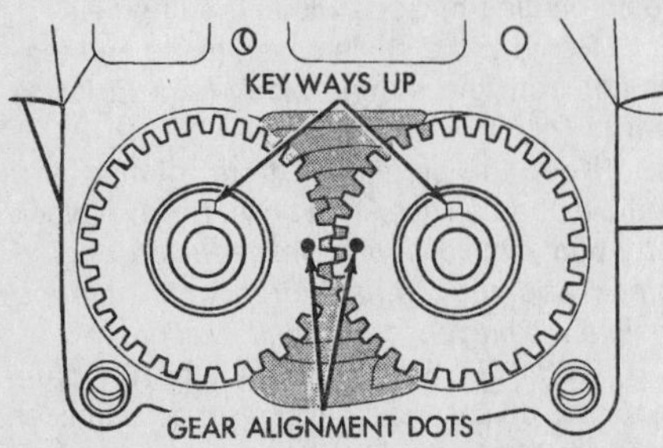


**10.12 After gear installation, the balance shaft keyways should be parallel and facing the crankshaft, and the gear alignment dots should be together as shown**

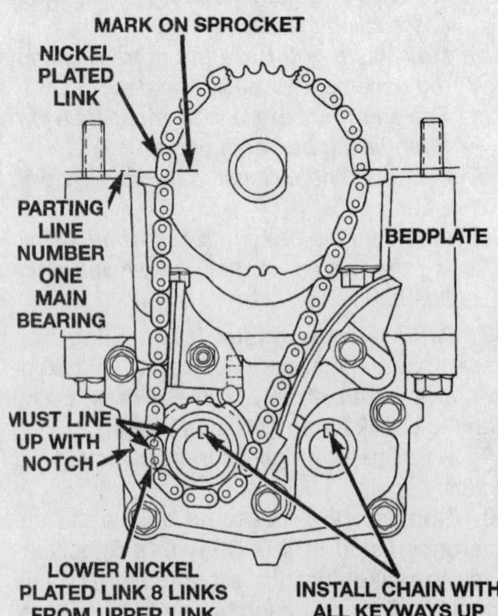


**10.15 The timing mark on the crankshaft sprocket, nickel plated links, notch and the yellow dot on the balance shaft sprocket must be aligned for correct timing**

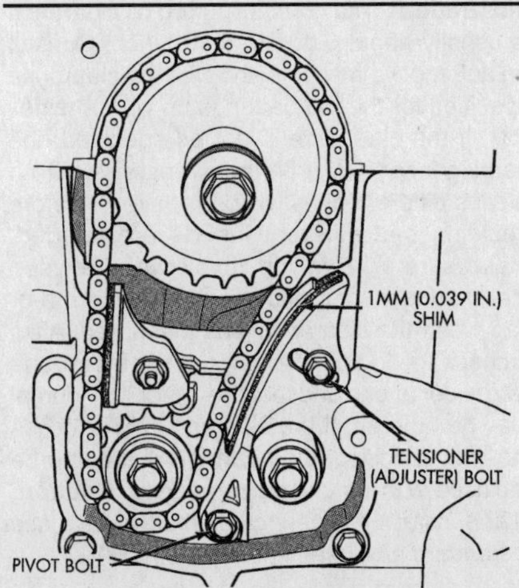


**10.20 With the shim in place, apply approximately 5.5 to 6.5 lbs of pressure to the chain tensioner and tighten the bolt to the torque listed in this Chapter's Specifications**

**11.1 Checking crankshaft endplay with a dial indicator**

to the appropriate size can be used) between the tensioner and the chain **(see illustration)**. Push the tensioner against the chain. Apply pressure (approximately 5.5 to 6.5 lbs) directly behind the adjustment slot to remove the slack.

21 With pressure applied, tighten the top tensioner bolt first then the bottom pivot bolt. Tighten the bolts to the torque in this Chapter's Specifications. Remove the shim.

22 Place the chain guide on the double-ended stud making sure the tab on the guide fits into the slot on the gear cover. Tighten the nut to the torque in this Chapter's Specifications.

23 Install the chain cover and tighten the bolts securely.

## 11 Crankshaft - removal and installation

### Removal

*Refer to illustrations 11.1 and 11.3*

**Note:** *The crankshaft can be removed only after the engine has been removed from the vehicle. It's assumed that the flywheel or driveplate, crankshaft pulley, timing belt, oil pan, oil pump body, oil filter, balance shafts and carrier assembly and piston/connecting rod assemblies have already been removed. The rear main oil seal retainer must be unbolted and separated from the block before proceeding with crankshaft removal.*

1 Before the crankshaft is removed, measure the endplay. Mount a dial indicator with the indicator in line with the crankshaft and touching the end of the crankshaft **(see illustration)**.

2 Pry the crankshaft all the way to the rear and zero the dial indicator. Next, pry the crankshaft to the front as far as possible and check the reading on the dial indicator. The distance traveled is the endplay. A typical crankshaft endplay will fall between 0.003 to 0.010-inch (0.076 to 0.254 mm). If it's greater than that, check the crankshaft thrust surfaces for wear after it is removed. If no wear is evident, new main bearings should correct the endplay.

3 If a dial indicator isn't available, feeler gauges can be used. Gently pry the crankshaft all the way to the front of the engine. Slip feeler gauges between the crankshaft and the front face of the thrust bearing or washer to determine the clearance **(see illustration)**.

4 Loosen the main bearing cap assembly bolts 1/4-turn at a time each, until they can be removed by hand.

5 Gently tap the main bearing cap assembly with a soft-face hammer around the perimeter of the assembly. Pull the main bearing cap assembly straight up and off the cylinder block. Try not to drop the bearing inserts if they come out with the assembly.

6 Carefully lift the crankshaft out of the engine. It may be a good idea to have an assistant available, since the crankshaft is quite heavy and awkward to handle. With the bearing inserts in place inside the engine block and main bearing caps, reinstall the main bearing cap assembly onto the engine block and tighten the bolts finger tight. Make sure you install the main bearing cap assembly with the arrow facing the front end of the engine.

**11.3 Checking crankshaft endplay with feeler gauges at the thrust bearing journal**

### Installation

7 Crankshaft installation is the first step in engine reassembly. It's assumed at this point that the engine block and crankshaft have been cleaned, inspected and repaired or reconditioned.

8 Position the engine block with the bottom facing up.

9 Remove the mounting bolts and lift off the main bearing cap assembly.

10 If they're still in place, remove the original bearing inserts from the block and from the main bearing cap assembly. Wipe the bearing surfaces of the block and main bearing cap assembly with a clean, lint-free cloth. They must be kept spotlessly clean. This is critical for determining the correct bearing oil clearance.

### Main bearing oil clearance check

*Refer to illustrations 11.11a, 11.11b, 11.11c, 11.11d, 11.17, 11.19a, 11.19b and 11.21*

11 Without mixing them up, clean the back sides of the new upper main bearing inserts (with grooves and oil holes) and lay one in each main bearing saddle in the block. Each upper bearing has an oil groove and oil hole in it. **Caution:** *The oil holes in the block must*

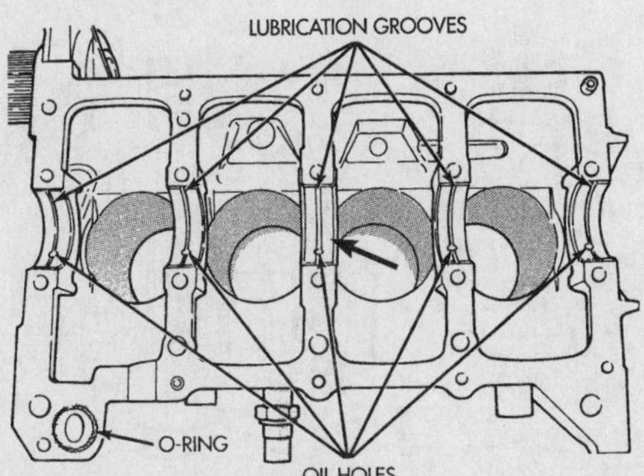


**11.11a Be sure the lubrication grooves (1) and the oil holes (2) are positioned correctly**

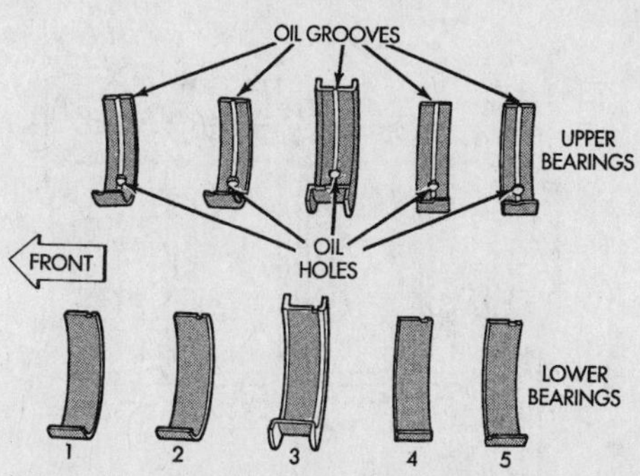


**11.11b On 2.0L engines, the upper bearings with the oil holes are installed into the engine block while the lower bearings without the oil holes are installed in the crankshaft bedplate (main bearing assembly)**

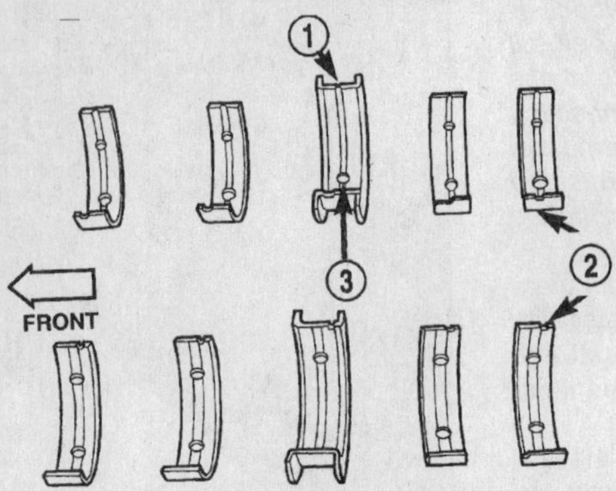

11.11c On 2.4L non-turbocharged models, the upper bearings with the oil holes vary slightly than the lower bearings in the crankshaft bedplate (main bearing assembly)

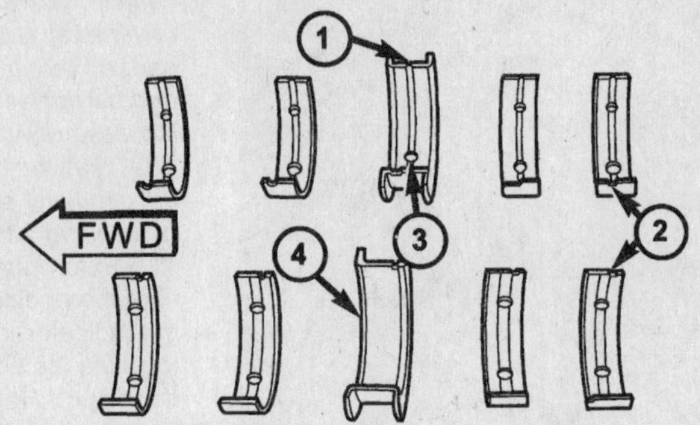

11.11d On turbocharged models, the upper thrust bearing with the oil hole is installed into the engine block while the lower thrust bearing without the oil hole is installed in the crankshaft bedplate (main bearing assembly)

*line up with the oil holes in the upper bearing inserts.* The thrust washer or thrust bearing insert must be installed in the number 3 crankshaft journal **(see illustration)**. Clean the back sides of the lower main bearing inserts and lay them in the corresponding location in the main bearing cap assembly. Make sure the tab on the bearing insert fits into the recess in the block or main bearing cap assembly. **Caution:** *Do not hammer the bearing insert into place and don't nick or gouge the bearing faces. DO NOT apply any lubrication at this time.*

- a) *On 2.0L models, the upper bearings with the oil holes are installed into the engine block while the lower bearings without the oil holes are installed in the crankshaft bedplate (main bearing assembly)* **(see illustration)**.
- b) *On 2.4L non-turbocharged models, the upper bearings with the oil holes vary slightly than the lower bearings in the crankshaft bedplate (main bearing assembly)* **(see illustration)**.
- c) *On turbocharged models, the upper thrust bearing with the oil hole is installed into the engine block while the lower thrust bearing without the oil hole is installed in the crankshaft bedplate (main bearing assembly)* **(see illustration)**.

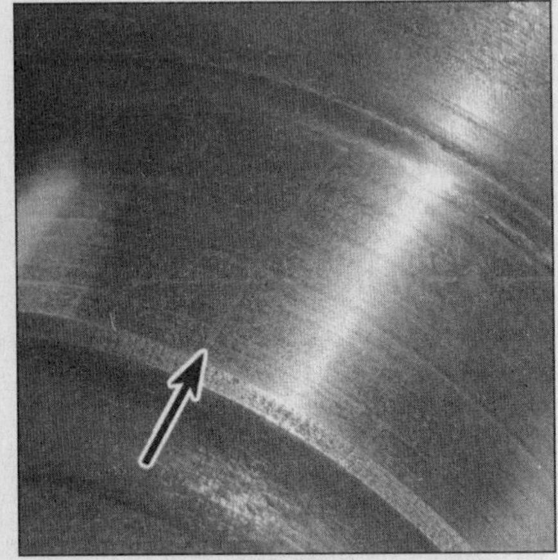
11.17 Place the Plastigage onto the crankshaft bearing journal as shown

12 Clean the faces of the bearing inserts in the block and the crankshaft main bearing journals with a clean, lint-free cloth.

13 Check or clean the oil holes in the crankshaft, as any dirt here can go only one way - straight through the new bearings.

14 Once you're certain the crankshaft is clean, carefully lay it in position in the cylinder block.

15 Before the crankshaft can be permanently installed, the main bearing oil clearance must be checked.

16 Cut several strips of the appropriate size of Plastigage. They must be slightly shorter than the width of the main bearing journal.

17 Place one piece on each crankshaft main bearing journal, parallel with the journal axis as shown **(see illustration)**.

18 Clean the faces of the bearing inserts in the main bearing cap assembly. Hold the bearing inserts in place and install the assembly onto the crankshaft and cylinder block. DO NOT disturb the Plastigage. Make sure you install the main bearing cap assembly with the arrow facing the front (timing belt end) of the engine.

19 Apply clean engine oil to all bolt threads prior to installation, then install all bolts finger-tight. Tighten main bearing cap assembly bolts in the sequence shown **(see illustrations)** progressing in two steps, to the torque listed in this Chapter's Specifications. DO NOT rotate the crankshaft at any time during this operation. **Note:** *On 2.0L DOHC engines, be sure the three locating dowels are in place in the engine block. Their locations are indicated by the stars.*

20 Remove the bolts in the *reverse* order of the tightening sequence and carefully lift the main bearing cap assembly straight up and

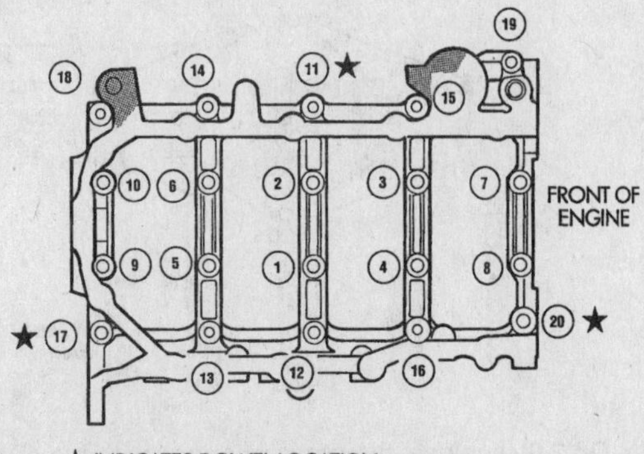

11.19a Main bearing cap bolt and bedplate bolts tightening sequence (2.0L models)

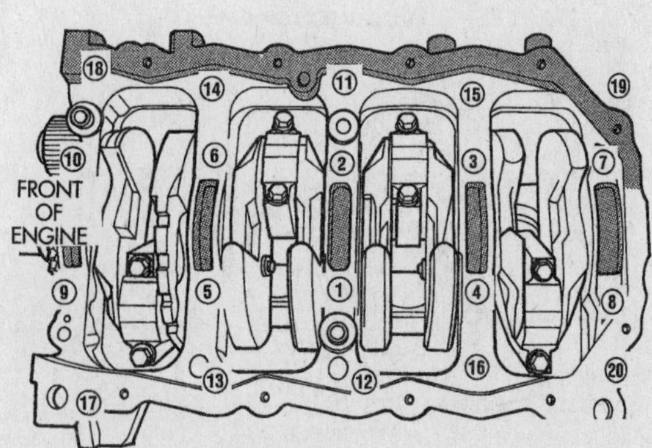

11.19b Main bearing cap bolt and bedplate bolt tightening sequence (2.4L models)

11.21 Use the scale on the Plastigage package to determine the bearing oil clearance - be sure to measure the widest part of the Plastigage and use the correct scale; it comes with both standard and metric scales

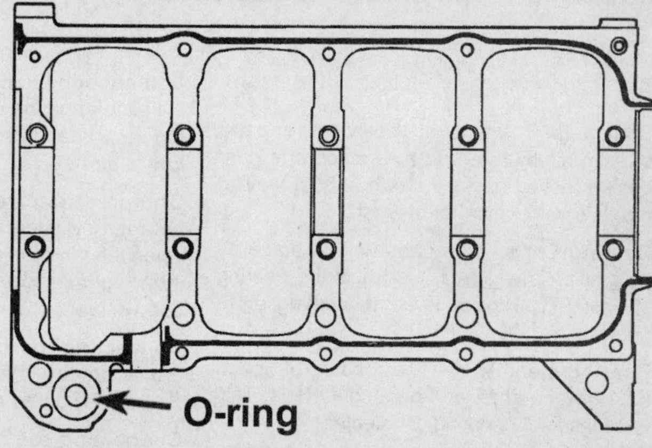

11.27 Apply a 1.5 to 2.0 mm bead of special bedplate sealant (or equivalent anaerobic sealant). Also install a new O-ring in the oil passage recess

off the block. Do not disturb the Plastigage or rotate the crankshaft. If the main bearing cap assembly is difficult to remove, tap it gently from side-to-side with a soft-face hammer to loosen it.

21 Compare the width of the crushed Plastigage on each journal to the scale printed on the Plastigage envelope to determine the main bearing oil clearance **(see illustration)**. A typical main bearing oil clearance should fall between 0.0015 to 0.0023-inch (0.03 to 0.05 mm). Check with an automotive machine shop for the oil clearance for your engine.

22 If the clearance is not as specified, the bearing inserts may be the wrong size (which means different ones will be required). Before deciding if different inserts are needed, make sure that no dirt or oil was between the bearing inserts and the cap assembly or block when the clearance was measured. If the Plastigage was wider at one end than the other, the crankshaft journal may be tapered. If the clearance still exceeds the limit specified, the bearing insert(s) will have to be replaced with an undersize bearing insert(s). **Caution:** *When installing a new crankshaft always install a standard bearing insert set.*

23 Carefully scrape all traces of the Plastigage material off the main bearing journals and/or the bearing insert faces. Be sure to remove all residue from the oil holes. Use your fingernail or the edge of a plastic card - don't nick or scratch the bearing faces.

## Final installation

*Refer to illustration 11.27*

24 Carefully lift the crankshaft out of the cylinder block.

25 Clean the bearing insert faces in the cylinder block, then apply a thin, uniform layer of moly-base grease or engine assembly lube to each of the bearing surfaces. Be sure to coat the thrust faces as well as the journal face of the thrust bearing.

26 Make sure the crankshaft journals are clean, then lay the crankshaft back in place in the cylinder block.

27 Clean the bearing insert faces and then apply the same lubricant to them. **Note:** *On 2.0L DOHC engines, make sure the three locating dowels are installed in the engine block, and make sure to replace any O-ring seals between the cap assembly and the engine block, if equipped.* **Note:** *Clean the engine block and the bedplate thoroughly. The surfaces must be free of oil residue. Apply a 1/16-inch bead of anaerobic sealant (Mopar Torque Cure Gasket Maker or equivalent) to the engine block* **(see illustration)**.

28 Hold the bedplate (main bearing assembly) and bearings in place and install the main bearing assembly onto the crankshaft and cylinder block. On 2.0L DOHC engines, install the main bearing assembly until the dowels lock together with the assembly.

29 Prior to installation, apply clean engine oil to all bolt threads wiping off any excess, then install all bolts finger-tight.

30 On 2.0L engines, tighten the main bearing cap assembly as follows **(see illustration 11.19a)**:

a) *Tighten bolts 11, 17 and 20 until the assembly contacts the engine block.*
b) *Tighten bolts 1 through 10 in the sequence shown, to the torque listed in this Chapter's Specifications.*
c) *Tighten bolts 11 through 20 in the sequence shown to the torque listed in this Chapter's Specifications. Be sure the baffle studs are located in bolts 12, 13 and 16.*

31 On 2.4L four-cylinder engines, tighten the main bearing cap assembly as follows **(see illustration 11.19b)**:

a) *Tighten bolts 11, 17 and 20 until the assembly contacts the engine block.*
b) *To ensure correct thrust bearing alignment, rotate the crankshaft until the No. 4 piston is at TDC.*
c) *Carefully pry the crankshaft all the way towards the rear of the block and then towards the front of the block.*
d) *Wedge an appropriate tool such as a block of wood, between the engine block and the crankshaft counterweight to hold the crankshaft in the most forward position.* ***DO NOT*** *drive the wedge between the main bearing cap assembly and the crankshaft.*
e) *Tighten bolts 1 through 10 in the sequence shown, in 3 steps to the torque listed in this Chapter's Specifications.*
g) *Tighten bolts 11 through 20 in the sequence shown in two steps to the torque listed in this Chapter's Specifications.*

32 Recheck crankshaft endplay with a feeler gauge or a dial indicator. The endplay should be correct if the crankshaft thrust faces aren't worn or damaged and if new bearings have been installed.

33 Rotate the crankshaft a number of times by hand to check for any obvious binding. It should rotate with a running torque of 50 in-lbs (5.6 Nm) or less (without the pistons and connecting rods installed). If the running torque is too high, correct the problem at this time.

34 Install the new rear main oil seal (see Chapter 2A).

## 12 Engine overhaul - reassembly sequence

1 Before beginning engine reassembly, make sure you have all the necessary new parts, gaskets and seals as well as the following items on hand:

*Common hand tools*
*A 1/2-inch drive torque wrench*
*New engine oil*
*Gasket sealant*
*Thread locking compound*

2 If you obtained a short block it will be necessary to install the cylinder head, the oil pump and pick-up tube, the oil pan, the water pump, the timing belt and timing cover, and the valve cover (see Chapter 2A or 2B). In order to save time and avoid problems, the

# COMMON ENGINE OVERHAUL TERMS

## B

**Backlash** - The amount of play between two parts. Usually refers to how much one gear can be moved back and forth without moving the gear with which it's meshed.

**Bearing Caps** - The caps held in place by nuts or bolts which, in turn, hold the bearing surface. This space is for lubricating oil to enter.

**Bearing clearance** - The amount of space left between shaft and bearing surface. This space is for lubricating oil to enter.

**Bearing crush** - The additional height which is purposely manufactured into each bearing half to ensure complete contact of the bearing back with the housing bore when the engine is assembled.

**Bearing knock** - The noise created by movement of a part in a loose or worn bearing.

**Blueprinting** - Dismantling an engine and reassembling it to EXACT specifications.

**Bore** - An engine cylinder, or any cylindrical hole; also used to describe the process of enlarging or accurately refinishing a hole with a cutting tool, as to bore an engine cylinder. The bore size is the diameter of the hole.

**Boring** - Renewing the cylinders by cutting them out to a specified size. A boring bar is used to make the cut.

**Bottom end** - A term which refers collectively to the engine block, crankshaft, main bearings and the big ends of the connecting rods.

**Break-in** - The period of operation between installation of new or rebuilt parts and time in which parts are worn to the correct fit. Driving at reduced and varying speed for a specified mileage to permit parts to wear to the correct fit.

**Bushing** - A one-piece sleeve placed in a bore to serve as a bearing surface for shaft, piston pin, etc. Usually replaceable.

## C

**Camshaft** - The shaft in the engine, on which a series of lobes are located for operating the valve mechanisms. The camshaft is driven by gears or sprockets and a timing chain. Usually referred to simply as the cam.

**Carbon** - Hard, or soft, black deposits found in combustion chamber, on plugs, under rings, on and under valve heads.

**Cast iron** - An alloy of iron and more than two percent carbon, used for engine blocks and heads because it's relatively inexpensive and easy to mold into complex shapes.

**Chamfer** - To bevel across (or a bevel on) the sharp edge of an object.

**Chase** - To repair damaged threads with a tap or die.

**Combustion chamber** - The space between the piston and the cylinder head, with the piston at top dead center, in which air-fuel mixture is burned.

**Compression ratio** - The relationship between cylinder volume (clearance volume) when the piston is at top dead center and cylinder volume when the piston is at bottom dead center.

**Connecting rod** - The rod that connects the crank on the crankshaft with the piston. Sometimes called a con rod.

**Connecting rod cap** - The part of the connecting rod assembly that attaches the rod to the crankpin.

**Core plug** - Soft metal plug used to plug the casting holes for the coolant passages in the block.

**Crankcase** - The lower part of the engine in which the crankshaft rotates; includes the lower section of the cylinder block and the oil pan.

**Crank kit** - A reground or reconditioned crankshaft and new main and connecting rod bearings.

**Crankpin** - The part of a crankshaft to which a connecting rod is attached.

**Crankshaft** - The main rotating member, or shaft, running the length of the crankcase, with offset throws to which the connecting rods are attached; changes the reciprocating motion of the pistons into rotating motion.

**Cylinder sleeve** - A replaceable sleeve, or liner, pressed into the cylinder block to form the cylinder bore.

## D

**Deburring** - Removing the burrs (rough edges or areas) from a bearing.

**Deglazer** - A tool, rotated by an electric motor, used to remove glaze from cylinder walls so a new set of rings will seat.

## E

**Endplay** - The amount of lengthwise movement between two parts. As applied to a crankshaft, the distance that the crankshaft can move forward and back in the cylinder block.

## F

**Face** - A machinist's term that refers to removing metal from the end of a shaft or the face of a larger part, such as a flywheel.

**Fatigue** - A breakdown of material through a large number of loading and unloading cycles. The first signs are cracks followed shortly by breaks.

**Feeler gauge** - A thin strip of hardened steel, ground to an exact thickness, used to check clearances between parts.

**Free height** - The unloaded length or height of a spring.

**Freeplay** - The looseness in a linkage, or an assembly of parts, between the initial application of force and actual movement. Usually perceived as slop or slight delay.

**Freeze plug** - See Core plug.

## G

**Gallery** - A large passage in the block that forms a reservoir for engine oil pressure.

**Glaze** - The very smooth, glassy finish that develops on cylinder walls while an engine is in service.

## H

**Heli-Coil** - A rethreading device used when threads are worn or damaged. The device is installed in a retapped hole to reduce the thread size to the original size.

## I

**Installed height** - The spring's measured length or height, as installed on the cylinder head. Installed height is measured from the spring seat to the underside of the spring retainer.

## J

**Journal** - The surface of a rotating shaft which turns in a bearing.

## K

**Keeper** - The split lock that holds the valve spring retainer in position on the valve stem.

**Key** - A small piece of metal inserted into matching grooves machined into two parts fitted together - such as a gear pressed onto a shaft - which prevents slippage between the two parts.

**Knock** - The heavy metallic engine sound, produced in the combustion chamber as a result of abnormal combustion - usually detonation. Knock is usually caused by a loose or worn bearing. Also referred to as detonation, pinging and spark knock. Connecting rod or main bearing knocks are created by too much oil clearance or insufficient lubrication.

## L

**Lands** - The portions of metal between the piston ring grooves.

**Lapping the valves** - Grinding a valve face and its seat together with lapping compound.

**Lash** - The amount of free motion in a gear train, between gears, or in a mechanical assembly, that occurs before movement can begin. Usually refers to the lash in a valve train.

**Lifter** - The part that rides against the cam to transfer motion to the rest of the valve train.

## M

**Machining** - The process of using a machine to remove metal from a metal part.

**Main bearings** - The plain, or babbit, bearings that support the crankshaft.

**Main bearing caps** - The cast iron caps, bolted to the bottom of the block, that support the main bearings.

## O

**O.D.** - Outside diameter.

**Oil gallery** - A pipe or drilled passageway in the engine used to carry engine oil from one area to another.

**Oil ring** - The lower ring, or rings, of a piston; designed to prevent excessive amounts of oil from working up the cylinder walls and into the combustion chamber. Also called an oil-control ring.

**Oil seal** - A seal which keeps oil from leaking out of a compartment. Usually refers to a dynamic seal around a rotating shaft or other moving part.

**O-ring** - A type of sealing ring made of a special rubberlike material; in use, the O-ring is compressed into a groove to provide the sealing action.

**Overhaul** - To completely disassemble a unit, clean and inspect all parts, reassemble it with the original or new parts and make all adjustments necessary for proper operation.

## P

**Pilot bearing** - A small bearing installed in the center of the flywheel (or the rear end of the crankshaft) to support the front end of the input shaft of the transmission.

**Pip mark** - A little dot or indentation which indicates the top side of a compression ring.

**Piston** - The cylindrical part, attached to the connecting rod, that moves up and down in the cylinder as the crankshaft rotates. When the fuel charge is fired, the piston transfers the force of the explosion to the connecting rod, then to the crankshaft.

**Piston pin (or wrist pin)** - The cylindrical and usually hollow steel pin that passes through the piston. The piston pin fastens the piston to the upper end of the connecting rod.

**Piston ring** - The split ring fitted to the groove in a piston. The ring contacts the sides of the ring groove and also rubs against the cylinder wall, thus sealing space between piston and wall. There are two types of rings: Compression rings seal the compression pressure in the combustion chamber; oil rings scrape excessive oil off the cylinder wall.

**Piston ring groove** - The slots or grooves cut in piston heads to hold piston rings in position.

**Piston skirt** - The portion of the piston below the rings and the piston pin hole.

**Plastigage** - A thin strip of plastic thread, available in different sizes, used for measuring clearances. For example, a strip of plastigage is laid across a bearing journal and mashed as parts are assembled. Then parts are disassembled and the width of the strip is measured to determine clearance between journal and bearing. Commonly used to measure crankshaft main-bearing and connecting rod bearing clearances.

**Press-fit** - A tight fit between two parts that requires pressure to force the parts together. Also referred to as drive, or force, fit.

**Prussian blue** - A blue pigment; in solution, useful in determining the area of contact between two surfaces. Prussian blue is commonly used to determine the width and location of the contact area between the valve face and the valve seat.

## R

**Race (bearing)** - The inner or outer ring that provides a contact surface for balls or rollers in bearing.

**Ream** - To size, enlarge or smooth a hole by using a round cutting tool with fluted edges.

**Ring job** - The process of reconditioning the cylinders and installing new rings.

**Runout** - Wobble. The amount a shaft rotates out-of-true.

## S

**Saddle** - The upper main bearing seat.

**Scored** - Scratched or grooved, as a cylinder wall may be scored by abrasive particles moved up and down by the piston rings.

**Scuffing** - A type of wear in which there's a transfer of material between parts moving against each other; shows up as pits or grooves in the mating surfaces.

**Seat** - The surface upon which another part rests or seats. For example, the valve seat is the matched surface upon which the valve face rests. Also used to refer to wearing into a good fit; for example, piston rings seat after a few miles of driving.

**Short block** - An engine block complete with crankshaft and piston and, usually, camshaft assemblies.

**Static balance** - The balance of an object while it's stationary.

**Step** - The wear on the lower portion of a ring land caused by excessive side and back-clearance. The height of the step indicates the ring's extra side clearance and the length of the step projecting from the back wall of the groove represents the ring's back clearance.

**Stroke** - The distance the piston moves when traveling from top dead center to bottom dead center, or from bottom dead center to top dead center.

**Stud** - A metal rod with threads on both ends.

## T

**Tang** - A lip on the end of a plain bearing used to align the bearing during assembly.

**Tap** - To cut threads in a hole. Also refers to the fluted tool used to cut threads.

**Taper** - A gradual reduction in the width of a shaft or hole; in an engine cylinder, taper usually takes the form of uneven wear, more pronounced at the top than at the bottom.

**Throws** - The offset portions of the crankshaft to which the connecting rods are affixed.

**Thrust bearing** - The main bearing that has thrust faces to prevent excessive endplay, or forward and backward movement of the crankshaft.

**Thrust washer** - A bronze or hardened steel washer placed between two moving parts. The washer prevents longitudinal movement and provides a bearing surface for thrust surfaces of parts.

**Tolerance** - The amount of variation permitted from an exact size of measurement. Actual amount from smallest acceptable dimension to largest acceptable dimension.

## U

**Umbrella** - An oil deflector placed near the valve tip to throw oil from the valve stem area.

**Undercut** - A machined groove below the normal surface.

**Undersize bearings** - Smaller diameter bearings used with re-ground crankshaft journals.

## V

**Valve grinding** - Refacing a valve in a valve-refacing machine.

**Valve train** - The valve-operating mechanism of an engine; includes all components from the camshaft to the valve.

**Vibration damper** - A cylindrical weight attached to the front of the crankshaft to minimize torsional vibration (the twist-untwist actions of the crankshaft caused by the cylinder firing impulses). Also called a harmonic balancer.

## W

**Water jacket** - The spaces around the cylinders, between the inner and outer shells of the cylinder block or head, through which coolant circulates.

**Web** - A supporting structure across a cavity.

**Woodruff key** - A key with a radiused backside (viewed from the side).

external components must be installed in the following general order:

*Thermostat and housing cover*
*Water pump*
*Intake and exhaust manifolds*
*Fuel injection components*
*Emission control components*
*Spark plug wires and spark plugs*
*Ignition coils*
*Oil filter*
*Engine mounts and mount brackets*
*Clutch and flywheel (manual transaxle)*
*Driveplate (automatic transaxle)*

## 13 Initial start-up and break-in after overhaul

**Warning:** *Have a fire extinguisher handy when starting the engine for the first time.*

1 Once the engine has been installed in the vehicle, double-check the engine oil and coolant levels.

2 With the spark plugs out of the engine and the ignition system and fuel pump disabled, crank the engine until oil pressure registers on the gauge or the light goes out.

3 Install the spark plugs, hook up the plug wires and restore the ignition system and fuel pump functions.

4 Start the engine. It may take a few moments for the fuel system to build up pressure, but the engine should start without a great deal of effort.

5 After the engine starts, it should be allowed to warm up to normal operating temperature. While the engine is warming up, make a thorough check for fuel, oil and coolant leaks.

6 Shut the engine off and recheck the engine oil and coolant levels.

7 Drive the vehicle to an area with minimum traffic, accelerate from 30 to 50 mph (48 to 80 km/h), then allow the vehicle to slow to 30 mph (48 km/h)with the throttle closed. Repeat the procedure 10 or 12 times. This will load the piston rings and cause them to seat properly against the cylinder walls. Check again for oil and coolant leaks.

8 Drive the vehicle gently for the first 500 miles (800 kilometers) (no sustained high speeds) and keep a constant check on the oil level. It is not unusual for an engine to use oil during the break-in period.

9 At approximately 500 to 600 (800 to 970 kilometers)miles, change the oil and filter.

10 For the next few hundred miles, drive the vehicle normally. Do not pamper it or abuse it.

11 After 2000 miles (3200 kilometers), change the oil and filter again and consider the engine broken in.

# Chapter 3
# Cooling, heating and air conditioning systems

## Contents



## Specifications

### General

| | |
|---|---|
| Coolant type and capacity | See Chapter 1 |
| Radiator cap pressure rating | 14 to 18 psi |
| Thermostat rating (opening temperature) | 192 to 199 degrees F |
| Cooling system capacity | See Chapter 1 |
| Refrigerant capacity | Refer to HVAC specification tag |

### Torque specifications

**Note:** *One foot-pound (ft-lb) of torque is equivalent to 12 inch-pounds (in-lbs) of torque. Torque values below approximately 15 foot-pounds are expressed in inch-pounds, because most foot-pound torque wrenches are not accurate at these smaller values.*

| | **Ft-lbs** (unless otherwise indicated) | **Nm** |
|---|---|---|
| Oil cooler union bolt | 41 | 55 |
| Thermostat housing cover-to-housing bolts | 110 in-lbs | 12.5 |
| Thermostat housing-to-cylinder head bolts | 20 | 27 |
| Water pump mounting bolts | 105 in-lbs | 12 |

## 1 General information

### *Engine cooling system*

All vehicles covered by this manual employ a pressurized engine cooling system with thermostatically controlled coolant circulation. An impeller-type water pump mounted on the front of the engine pumps coolant through the engine. The pump mounts directly on the engine block and is driven by the timing belt. The coolant flows around the combustion chambers and toward the rear of the engine. Cast-in coolant passages direct coolant near the intake ports, exhaust ports, and spark plug areas.

A wax pellet-type thermostat is located in a housing near the right side of the engine. During warm-up, the closed thermostat prevents coolant from circulating through the radiator. As the engine nears normal operating temperature, the thermostat opens and allows hot coolant to travel through the radiator, where it's cooled before returning to the engine.

The cooling system is sealed by a pressure-type cap, which raises the boiling point of the coolant and increases the cooling efficiency of the system. If the system pressure exceeds the cap pressure relief value, the excess pressure in the system forces the spring-loaded valve inside the cap off its seat and allows the coolant to escape through the overflow tube into a coolant reservoir. When the system cools the excess coolant is automatically drawn from the reservoir back into the radiator.

The coolant reservoir serves as both the point at which fresh coolant is added to the cooling system to maintain the proper fluid level and as a holding tank for overheated coolant. This type of cooling system is known as a closed design because coolant that escapes past the pressure cap is saved and reused.

There are two different types of cooling fan systems installed on these vehicles. Non-turbocharged models are equipped with a two speed electric motor and fan assembly. Radiator fan operation is controlled by the PCM in response to signals by the ECT and VSS. Power to the fan is switched using the low or high speed relays. Turbocharged models are equipped with a variable speed electric motor and fan assembly. Radiator fan operation is controlled by the PCM using a pulse width modulated signal (variable). Fan performance is controlled over many speeds to improve cooling.

### *Heating system*

The heating system consists of a blower fan and heater core located in the heater/ventilation air conditioning (HVAC) housing, with hoses connecting the heater core to the engine cooling system. Hot engine coolant is circulated through the heater core. When the heater mode on the heater/air conditioning control panel on the instrument panel is activated, a flap door opens to expose the heater core to the passenger compartment. A fan switch on the control panel activates the blower motor, which forces air through the core, heating the air.

## *Air conditioning system*

The air conditioning system consists of a condenser mounted in front of the radiator, an evaporator mounted adjacent to the heater core, a compressor mounted on the engine, an accumulator which contains a high pressure relief valve and the plumbing connecting all of the above components.

A blower fan forces the warmer air of the passenger compartment through the evaporator core, transferring the heat from the air to the refrigerant (sort of a "radiator in reverse"). The liquid refrigerant boils off into low pressure vapor, taking the heat with it when it leaves the evaporator.

## 2 Antifreeze - general information

*Refer to illustration 2.5*

**Warning:** *Do not allow antifreeze to come in contact with your skin or painted surfaces of the vehicle. Rinse off spills immediately with plenty of water. Antifreeze is highly toxic if ingested. Never leave antifreeze lying around in an open container or in puddles on the floor; children and pets are attracted by it's sweet smell and may drink it. Check with local authorities about disposing of used antifreeze. Many communities have collection centers which will see that antifreeze is disposed of safely. Never dump used antifreeze on the ground or pour it into drains.*

**Caution:** *Do not mix coolants of different colors. Doing so might damage the cooling system and/or the engine. Read the warning label in the engine compartment for additional information.*

**Note:** *Non-toxic antifreeze is now manufactured and available at local auto parts stores, but even this type must be disposed of properly.*

The cooling system should be filled with a water/ethylene glycol based antifreeze solution, which will prevent freezing down to at least -20-degrees F (even lower in cold climates). It also provides protection against corrosion and increases the coolant boiling point. The engines in these vehicles have aluminum cylinder heads. The manufacturer recommends that the correct type of coolant be used and strongly urges that coolant types not be mixed (see Chapter 1 for the specified coolant type and mixture ratio).

Drain, flush and refill the cooling system at the service interval listed in the Chapter 1 maintenance schedule. The use of antifreeze solutions for periods longer than recommended is likely to cause damage and encourage the formation of rust and scale in the system.

Before adding antifreeze to the system, inspect all hose connections. Antifreeze can leak through very minute openings.

The exact mixture of antifreeze to water, which you should use, depends on the relative weather conditions. The mixture should contain at least 50-percent antifreeze, but should never contain more than 70-percent antifreeze. Consult the mixture ratio chart on the container before adding coolant.

Hydrometers are available at most auto parts stores to test the coolant **(see illustration)**.

**2.5 Use a hydrometer to test the coolant (typical)**

## 3 Thermostat - check and replacement

**Warning:** *Do not remove the pressure cap, drain the coolant or replace the thermostat until the engine has cooled completely.*

### *Check*

1 Before assuming the thermostat is to blame for a cooling system problem, check the coolant level, drivebelt tension (see Chapter 1) and temperature gauge operation.

2 If the engine seems to be taking a long time to warm up (based on heater output or temperature gauge operation), the thermostat is probably stuck open. Replace the thermostat with a new one.

3 If the engine runs hot, use your hand to check the temperature of the upper radiator hose. If the hose isn't hot, but the engine is, the thermostat is probably stuck closed, preventing the coolant inside the engine from escaping to the radiator. Replace the thermostat. **Caution:** *Don't drive the vehicle without a thermostat. The computer may stay in open loop and emissions and fuel economy will suffer.*

4 If the upper radiator hose is hot, it means that the coolant is flowing and the thermostat is open. Consult the *Troubleshooting* section at the front of this manual for cooling system diagnosis.

### *Replacement*

5 Disconnect the cable from the negative battery terminal (see Chapter 5).

6 Drain the cooling system (see Chapter 1). If the coolant is relatively new and still in good condition, save it and reuse it.

7 Remove the upper intake manifold (see Chapter 2A).

8 Remove the upper radiator hose from the thermostat housing cover. Detach the hose from the fitting. If it's stuck, grasp it near the end with a pair of adjustable pliers and twist it to break the seal, then pull it off. If the hose is old or if it has deteriorated, cut it off and install a new one.

9 Disconnect the coolant reservoir hose at the thermostat housing cover.

#### Turbocharged models

10 Disconnect the air conditioning suction (low side) line support bracket from the thermostat housing stud.

11 Disconnect the support bracket and position it off to the side.

#### All models

*Refer to illustrations 3.12, 3.16a, 3.16b and 3.18*

12 Remove the thermostat housing cover mounting bolts **(see illustration)**. If the housing cover is stuck, tap it with a soft-face hammer to jar it loose. Be prepared for some coolant to spill as the gasket seal is broken.

13 Check the thermostat housing cover for damage, especially in the area of the sealing surfaces. Replace the housing cover if necessary.

14 Note how it's installed (which end is facing up, or out) and then remove the thermostat.

15 Remove all traces of old gasket material and sealant from the housing and cover with a gasket scraper.

16 Install a new rubber gasket on the thermostat **(see illustration)** and install the thermostat into the housing cover, spring-end

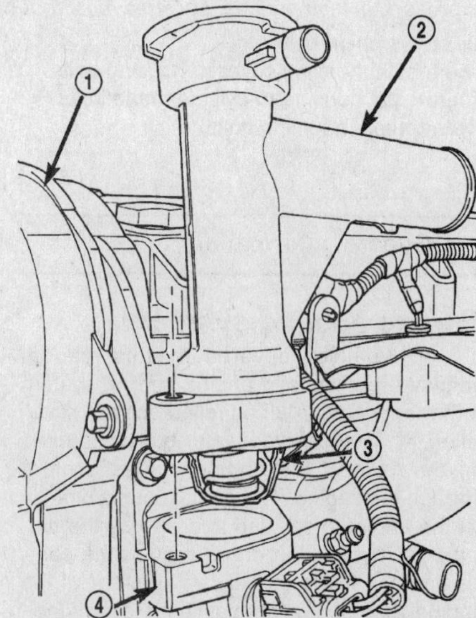


**3.12 The thermostat housing cover is located at the right (timing belt) end (1) of the cylinder head; the pressure cap, radiator outlet connector (2) and the thermostat (3) are also integral components of the thermostat housing cover. The thermostat housing (4) is located directly below the housing cover**

3.16a Be sure to install a new rubber O-ring type gasket on the thermostat

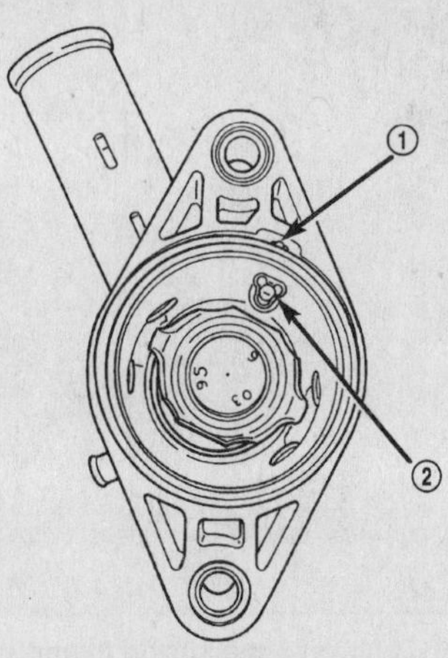


3.16b When installing the thermostat, make sure that the jiggle valve (2) is aligned with the locator notch (1) on the thermostat housing cover

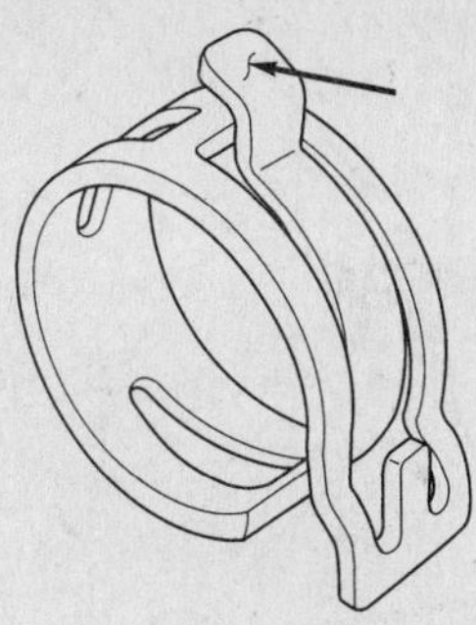

3.18 Loosen the spring clamps by squeezing the ends together with hose clamp pliers (these pliers are specially designed for this type of hose clamp, but regular pliers will also work)

out (when the housing cover is installed, the spring end of the thermostat will be pointing down, into the engine, **as in illustration 3.12**). Make sure that you install the thermostat with the "jiggle valve" aligned with the locator notch in the housing cover **(see illustration)**.

17 Install the thermostat housing cover and bolts. Tighten the bolts to the torque listed in this Chapter's Specifications.

18 Reattach the hose to the thermostat housing cover. If equipped with a spring-type clamp make sure the clamp is still tight. If it isn't, replace it. **Note:** *These models are equipped with either a worm drive hose clamp or a spring hose clamp. If the clamp is replaced, be sure to use only a factory replacement part that matches the original* **(see illustration)**.

19 Reinstall the upper intake manifold (see Chapter 2A), then refill and bleed the cooling system (see Chapter 1).

20 Start the engine and allow it to reach normal operating temperature, then check for leaks and proper thermostat operation (as described in Steps 2 through 4).

## 4 Engine cooling fans - check and replacement

**Warning:** *To avoid possible injury or damage, DO NOT operate the engine with a damaged fan. Do not attempt to repair fan blades - replace a damaged fan with a new one.*

**Note:** *Always be sure to check for blown fuses before attempting to diagnose an electrical circuit problem.*

### *Check*

#### 2001 through 2005 models

**Note:** *Turbocharged models are equipped with a cooling fan module mounted on the fan assembly. The cooling fan module controls the fan speed depending on operating conditions (engine speed, temperature, A/C activity, etc.). The following checks do not apply to the turbocharged models. In the event of cooling fan failure, have the cooling fan module and circuit checked by a dealer service department or other qualified repair facility.*

1 If the engine is overheating and the cooling fan is not coming on when the engine temperature rises to an excessive level, unplug the fan motor electrical connector **(see illustration 4.12)** and connect the motor directly to the battery with fused jumper cables. If the fan motor doesn't come on, replace the motor.

2 If the radiator fan motor is okay, but it isn't coming on when the engine gets hot, one of the fan relays might be defective, There are two cooling fan relays; the low speed fan relay and the high speed fan relay. A relay is used to control a circuit by turning it on and off in response to a control signal by the Powertrain Control Module (PCM). These control circuits are fairly complex, and checking them should be left to a dealer service department. Sometimes, the cooling fan system can be fixed by simply identifying and replacing a bad fuse and/or relay (see Chapter 12).

3 Locate the low speed and high speed fan relays in the engine compartment fuse/relay box (see Chapter 12). Test each relay (see Chapter 12).

4 If the relays are okay, check all wiring and connections to the fan motor. Refer to the wiring diagrams at the end of Chapter 12. If no obvious problems are found, the problem could be the engine coolant temperature (ECT) sensor or the Powertrain Control Module (PCM). Have the cooling fan system and circuit diagnosed by a dealer service department or repair shop with the proper diagnostic equipment.

#### 2006 and later models

5 These models are equipped with a Totally Integrated Power Module (TIPM) located behind the air filter housing. It's essentially a unitized fuse/relay box and solid-state control module. The TIPM controls many electrical functions of the vehicle, one of which is the fan speed, depending on the operating conditions (engine speed, temperature, A/C activity, etc.). Have the cooling fan system, the TIPM and circuit checked by a dealer service department or other qualified automotive repair facility.

### *Replacement*

*Refer to illustrations 4.10, 4.12, 4.13, 4.14, 4.15a and 4.15b*

**Warning:** *Wait until the engine is completely cool before beginning this procedure.*

6 Disconnect the cable from the negative battery terminal (see Chapter 5).

7 Remove the battery and the battery tray (see Chapter 5).

8 Drain the cooling system (see Chapter 1). If the coolant is relatively new and still in good condition, save it and reuse it.

9 Remove the radiator grille (see Chapter 11).

10 Remove the upper radiator crossmember and brace **(see illustration)**.

4.10 Remove the upper radiator crossmember (1) and the radiator center support bracket (2)

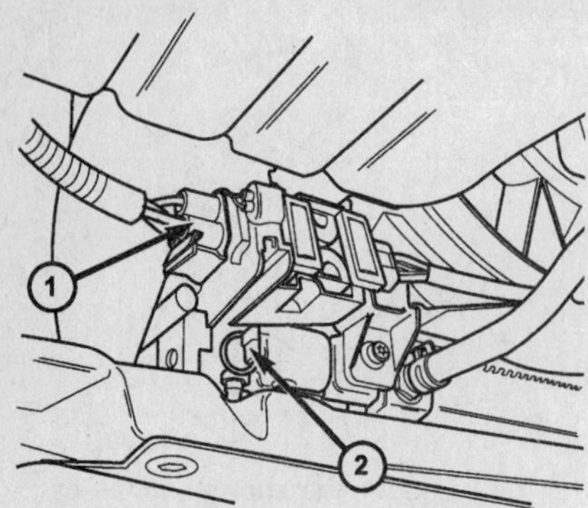

**4.12 Disconnect the cooling fan connector (1) located at the bottom of the radiator - turbocharged models shown**

1 *Radiator fan connector*
2 *Radiator drain plug*

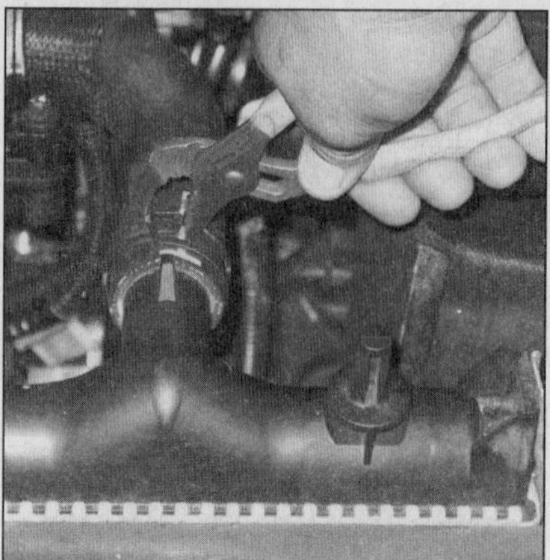
**4.13 Compress the spring clamp with pliers and remove the upper radiator hose**

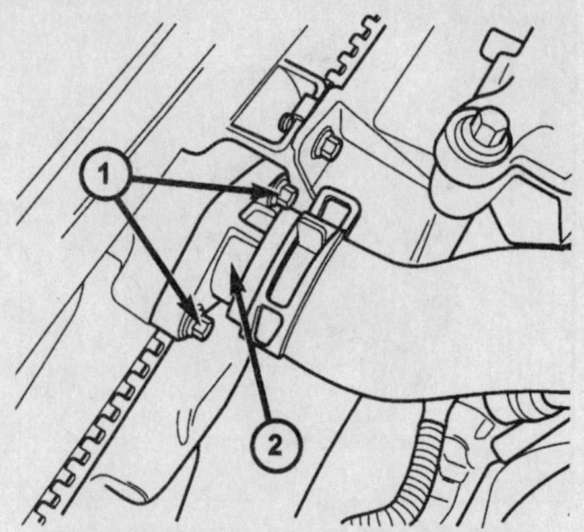

**4.14 Remove the radiator inlet neck mounting bolts (1) and separate the inlet neck (2) from the radiator**

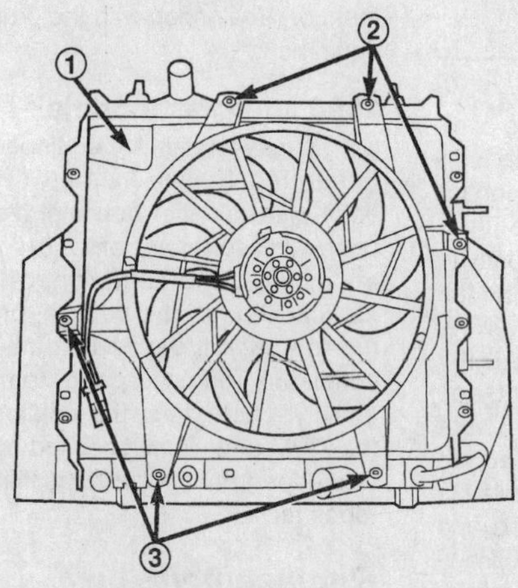

**4.15a Cooling fan mounting details - non-turbocharged model**

1 *Cooling fan shroud*
2 *Upper mounting screws*
3 *Lower mounting screws*

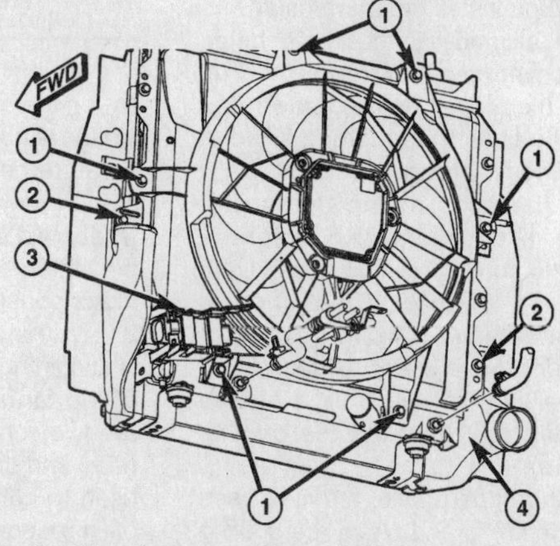

**4.15b Cooling fan mounting details - turbocharged model**

1 *Cooling fan mounting screws*
2 *Charge air cooler mounting screws*
3 *Radiator fan connector*
4 *Charge air cooler*

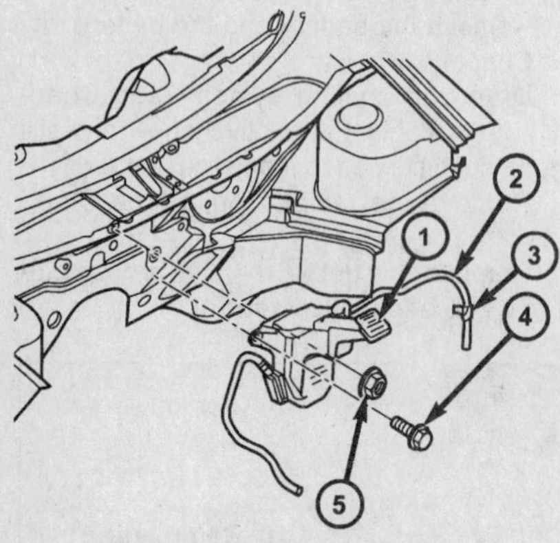

**5.3 Coolant reservoir details on a non-turbocharged model**

1 *Coolant reservoir*
2 *Vent hose*
3 *Clip*
4 *Mounting screw*
5 *Mounting nut*

11 Raise the vehicle and support it securely on jackstands.

12 Disconnect the fan motor electrical connector **(see illustration)**.

13 On non-turbocharged models, detach the upper radiator hose from the radiator **(see illustration)**. Loosen the hose clamp by squeezing the ends together. Hose clamp pliers work best, but regular pliers will work also. If the radiator hose is stuck, grasp it near the end with a pair of adjustable pliers and twist it to break the seal, then pull it off. If the hose is old or if it has deteriorated, cut it off and install a new one.

14 On turbocharged models, unbolt the radiator inlet neck and position the hose out of the way **(see illustration)**.

15 Remove the fan mounting screws **(see illustrations)**.

16 Remove the fan assembly by lifting it up and out of the engine compartment.

17 If the fan motor, fan blade or shroud requires replacement, the entire assembly must be replaced (at the time of writing, individual parts were not available).

18 Installation is the reverse of removal. **Note:** *When reinstalling the fan assembly, make sure the rubber air seals around the assembly are still in place - without them, the cooling system may not work efficiently.*

## 5 Coolant reservoir - removal and installation

1 **Warning:** *Wait until the engine is completely cool before beginning this procedure.*

2 Disconnect the coolant reservoir hose from the thermostat housing cover (see Section 3). Plug the hose to prevent leakage.

### *Non-turbocharged models*

*Refer to illustration 5.3*

3 Remove the vent hose clip from the stud on the firewall **(see illustration)**.

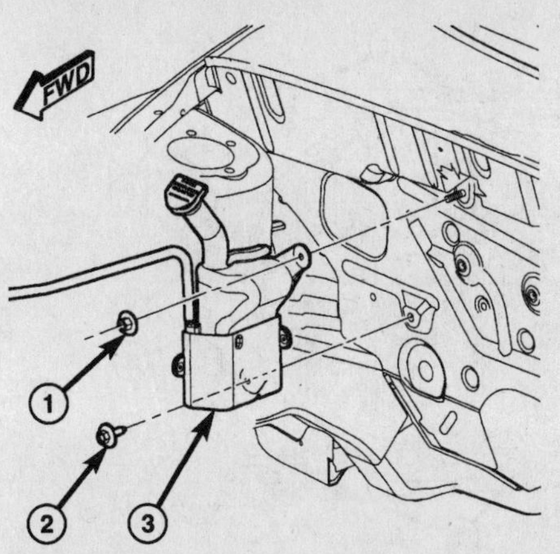


**5.10 Coolant reservoir details on a non-turbocharged model**

1. *Mounting nut*
2. *Mounting screw*
3. *Coolant reservoir*

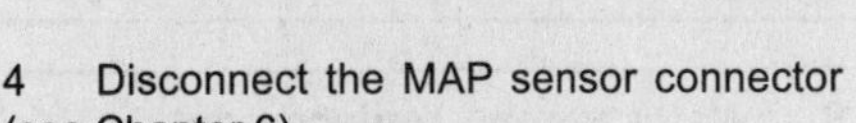

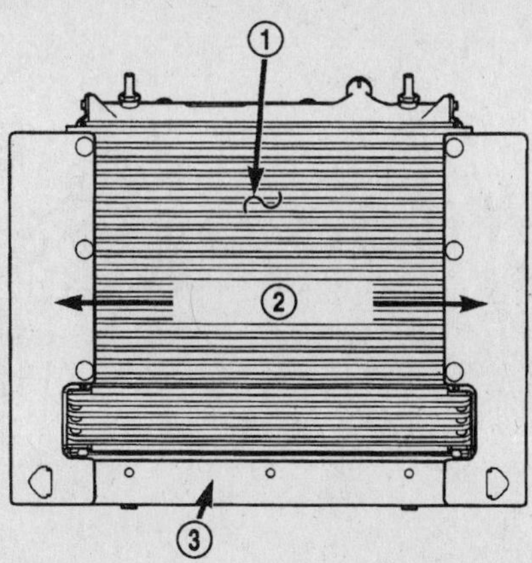


**6.7 Angle the lower seal slightly to provide extra room for radiator removal**

1. *Air conditioning condenser*
2. *Radiator side seals*
3. *Radiator lower seal*

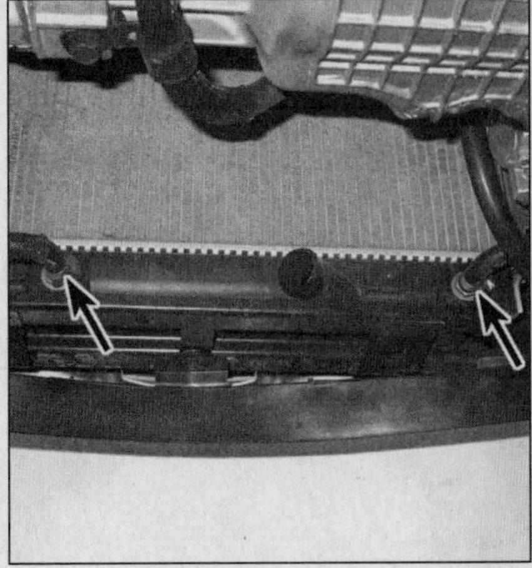

**6.8 Location of the transaxle oil cooler lines at the radiator**

4 Disconnect the MAP sensor connector (see Chapter 6).

5 Remove the power steering fluid reservoir mounting bolts and position the reservoir out of the way (see Chapter 10). Do not disconnect the power steering lines from the reservoir.

6 Remove the coolant reservoir mounting fasteners **(see illustration 5.3)** and lift the reservoir from the engine compartment.

7 Clean out the reservoir with soapy water and a brush to remove any deposits inside. Inspect the reservoir carefully for cracks. If you find a crack, replace the reservoir.

8 Installation is the reverse of removal.

## *Turbocharged models*

*Refer to illustration 5.10*

9 Raise the vehicle and secure it on jackstands.

10 Remove the lower screw that mounts the coolant reservoir to the firewall **(see illustration)**.

11 Remove the accelerator cable and the cruise control cable, if equipped, from the throttle body (see Chapter 4).

12 Remove the coolant reservoir retaining nut from the upper section of the reservoir. Lift the reservoir from the engine compartment.

13 Clean out the reservoir with soapy water and a brush to remove any deposits inside. Inspect the reservoir carefully for cracks. If you find a crack, replace the reservoir.

14 Installation is the reverse of removal.

## 6 Radiator - removal and installation

*Refer to illustrations 6.7, 6.8, 6.10, 6.11a, 6.11b and 6.14*

**Warning:** *Wait until the engine is completely cool before beginning this procedure.*

## *Removal*

1 Disconnect the cable from the negative battery terminal (see Chapter 5).

2 Drain the cooling system (see Chapter 1). If the coolant is relatively new and in good condition, save it and reuse it.

3 Remove the cooling fan (see Section 4).

4 Raise the vehicle and place it securely on jackstands.

### Turbocharged models

5 Disconnect the power steering lines from the power steering fluid reservoir and cap the lines (see Chapter 9).

6 Remove the charge air cooler-to-radiator fasteners (see Chapter 4).

### Non-turbocharged models

7 Slightly angle the lower radiator air seal from the radiator side air seals **(see illustration)** to make extra room for radiator removal.

### All models

8 On automatic transaxle models, disconnect the transmission oil cooler hoses **(see illustration)** from the radiator (see Chapter 7B).

9 On models with air conditioning, disconnect the condenser from the radiator (see Section 16).

10 Disconnect the upper and lower radiator hoses. Loosen the hose clamps by squeezing the ends together. Hose clamp pliers work best, but regular pliers will work also. If the radiator hose is stuck, grasp it near the end with a pair of adjustable pliers and twist it to break the seal, then pull it off. If the hose is old or if it has deteriorated, cut it off and install a new one.

11 Carefully lift out the radiator **(see illustrations)**. Don't spill coolant on the vehicle or scratch the paint. Make sure the rubber radiator seals or insulators that fit on the bottom of the radiator and into the sockets in the body remain in place in the body for proper reinstallation of the radiator.

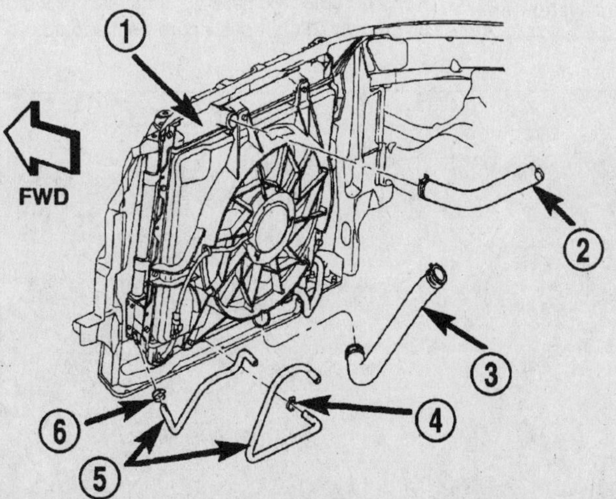


**6.10 Radiator coolant hoses, transaxle lines and surrounding components**

1. *Radiator*
2. *Radiator upper hose*
3. *Radiator lower hose*
4. *Clamp*
5. *Transaxle oil cooler hoses*
6. *Clamp*

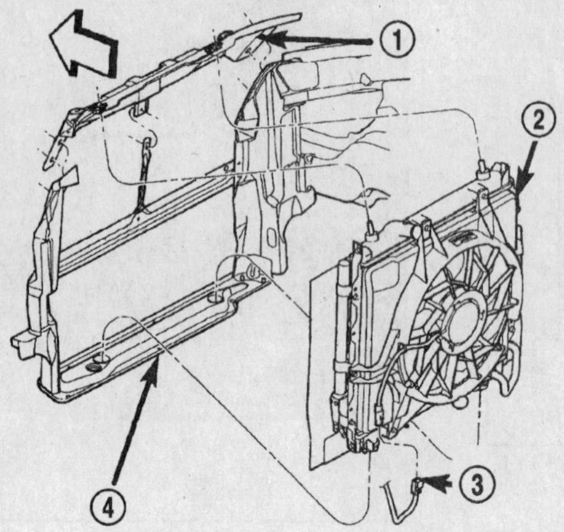

**6.11a Radiator mounting details on a non-turbocharged model**

1. *Upper radiator crossmember*
2. *Cooling fan assembly*
3. *Cooling fan electrical connector*
4. *Lower radiator crossmember*

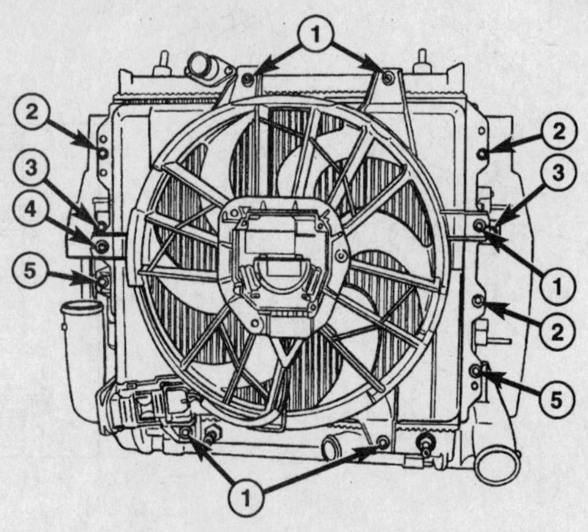

**6.11b Radiator mounting details on a turbocharged model**

1. *Cooling fan mounting screws*
2. *Condenser mounting screws*
3. *Transaxle cooler mounting screws*
4. *Cooling fan to condenser mounting screws*
5. *Charge air cooler mounting screws*

12 Remove bugs and dirt from the radiator with compressed air and a soft brush. Don't bend the cooling fins. Inspect the radiator for leaks and damage. If it needs repair, have a radiator shop or a dealer service department do the work.

13 On non-turbocharged models, remove the lower radiator side seal from the engine compartment.

### *Installation*

14 Inspect the rubber seals or insulators in the lower crossmember **(see illustration)** and upper crossmember for cracks and deterioration. Make sure that they're free of dirt and gravel. When installing the radiator, make sure that it's correctly seated on the insulators before fastening the top brackets.

15 On non-turbocharged models, install the lower seal **(see illustration 6.7)**.

16 Installation is otherwise the reverse of the removal procedure. After installation, fill (and bleed) the cooling system with the correct mixture of antifreeze and water (see Chapter 1).

17 Start the engine and check for leaks. Allow the engine to reach normal operating temperature, indicated by the upper radiator hose becoming hot. Recheck the coolant level and add more if required.

18 If you're working on an automatic transaxle equipped vehicle, check and add fluid as needed (see Chapter 1).

## 7 Water pump - check

1 A failure in the water pump can cause serious engine damage due to overheating.

2 If a failure occurs in the pump seal, coolant will leak from the front (right side) of the engine.

3 If the water pump shaft bearings fail there may be a howling sound at the front of the engine while it's running.

4 A quick water pump performance check is to put the heater on. If the pump is failing, it won't be able to efficiently circulate hot water all the way to the heater core as it should.

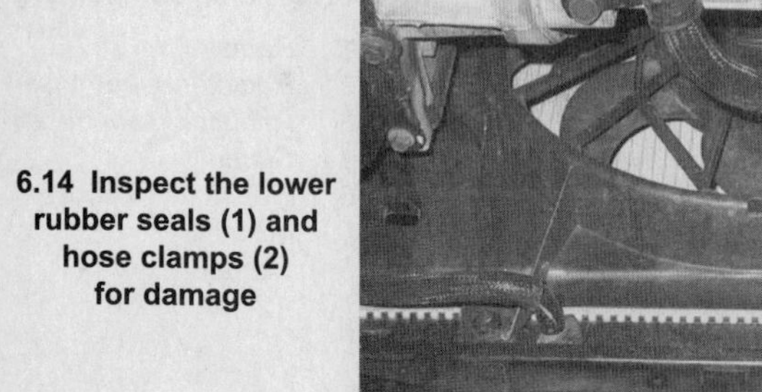

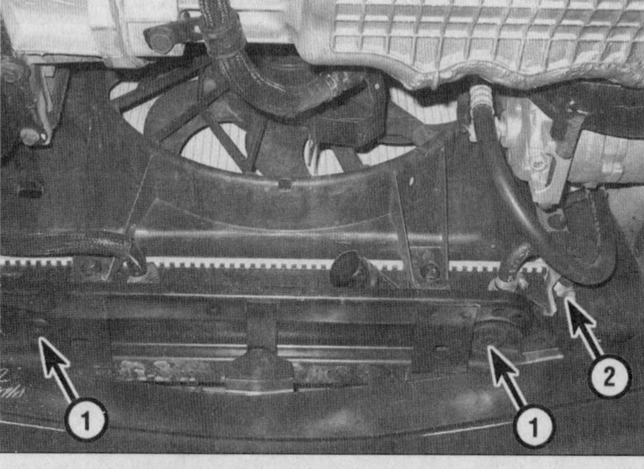

**6.14 Inspect the lower rubber seals (1) and hose clamps (2) for damage**

## 8 Water pump - replacement

*Refer to illustrations 8.5a, 8.5b and 8.8*

**Warning:** *Wait until the engine is completely cool before beginning this procedure.*

1 Disconnect the cable from the negative battery terminal (see Chapter 5).

2 Drain the cooling system (see Chapter 1).

3 Remove the accessory drivebelts (see Chapter 1).

4 Remove the timing belt cover(s), the timing belt, camshaft sprockets and the rear timing belt cover (see Chapter 2A).

5 Remove the bolts attaching the water pump to the engine block and remove the pump from the engine **(see illustrations)**. If

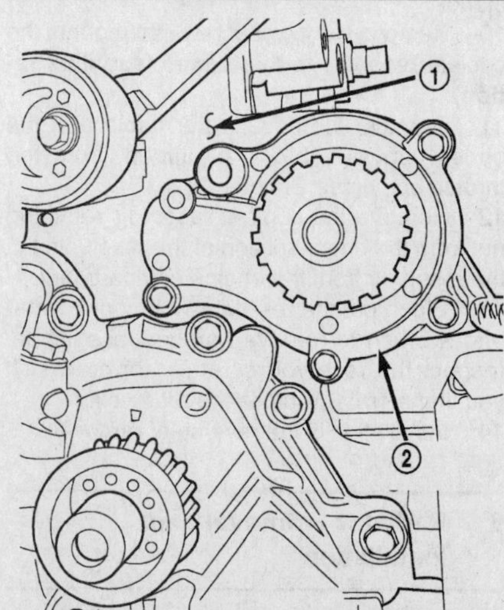

**8.5a Using a criss-cross pattern, remove the bolts securing the water pump (2) to the cylinder block (1). . .**

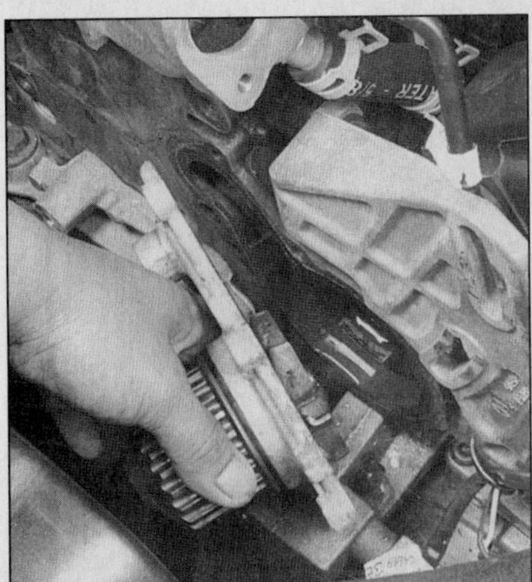

8.5b . . . then remove the water pump from the engine; if necessary, tap it gently with a soft-faced hammer to break the seal

8.8 Remove the old O-ring seal, install a new one, then apply a thin film of RTV sealant to hold the seal in place during installation; make sure that the O-ring seal is correctly seated in the water pump and that it stays in place during pump installation

the water pump is stuck, gently tap it with a soft-faced hammer to break the seal.

6 Clean the bolt threads and the threaded holes in the engine to remove the corrosion and sealant. Remove all traces of old gasket material from the sealing surfaces.

7 Compare the new pump to the old one to make sure that they're identical.

8 Install a new O-ring seal in the groove that lines the water pump body **(see illustration)**, then apply a thin film of RTV sealant to hold the seal in place during installation. **Caution:** *Make sure that the O-ring seal is correctly seated in the water pump groove to avoid a coolant leak.* Carefully mate the pump to the engine.

9 Install the water pump bolts and tighten them to the torque listed in this Chapter's Specifications. Don't overtighten the water pump bolts; doing so will damage the pump.

10 The remainder of installation is the reverse of removal. Refill and bleed the cooling system (see Chapter 1) when you're done. Then run the engine and check for leaks.

## 9 Coolant temperature sending unit - check and replacement

**Warning:** *Wait until the engine is completely cool before beginning this procedure.*

### Check

1 The coolant temperature indicator system consists of a warning light or a temperature gauge on the dash and a coolant temperature sending unit mounted on the engine. On the models covered by this manual, the Engine Coolant Temperature (ECT) sensor, which is an information sensor for the Powertrain Control Module (PCM), also functions as the coolant temperature sending unit.

2 If an overheating indication occurs, check the coolant level in the system and make sure all connectors in the wiring harness between the sending unit and the indicator light or gauge are tight.

3 When the ignition switch is turned to START and the starter motor is turning, the indicator light (if equipped) should come on. This doesn't mean the engine is overheated; it just means that the bulb is good.

4 If the light doesn't come on when the ignition key is turned to START, the bulb might be burned out, the ignition switch might be faulty or the circuit might be open.

5 As soon as the engine starts, the indicator light should go out and remain off, unless the engine overheats. If the light doesn't go out, the wire between the sending unit and the light could be grounded (see the Wiring Diagrams at the end of Chapter 12); the sending unit might be defective (have it checked by a dealer service department); or the ignition switch might be faulty (see Chapter 12).

### Replacement

6 See Chapter 6.

## 10 Blower motor resistor and blower motor - replacement

**Warning:** *These models are equipped with airbags. Always disable the airbag system before working in the vicinity of any airbag system components to avoid the possibility of accidental deployment of the airbag, which could cause personal injury (see Chapter 12).*

### Blower motor resistor

*Refer to illustration 10.4*

**Warning:** *The resistor may be very hot. Let it cool completely before removing it.*

1 Disconnect the cable from the negative battery terminal (see Chapter 5).

2 Remove the windshield wiper arms (see Chapter 12).

3 Remove the cowl grille screen from the plenum at the base of the windshield (see Chapter 11).

4 Working on the right side of the cowl plenum area, disconnect the electrical connector from the blower motor resistor **(see illustration)**.

5 Remove the blower motor resistor by carefully prying the resistor with a flat-bladed screwdriver to release the snap fit. There are two different types of resistors; an air conditioning type or non-air conditioning type. Do not interchange these two different resistors.

6 Installation is the reverse of removal.

### Blower motor

*Refer to illustrations 10.9, 10.10, 10.12 and 10.14*

7 Disconnect the cable from the negative battery terminal (see Chapter 5).

8 Remove the lower dash panel from the right side of the dashboard below the glovebox (see Chapter 11).

9 Pull back the carpet and disconnect the

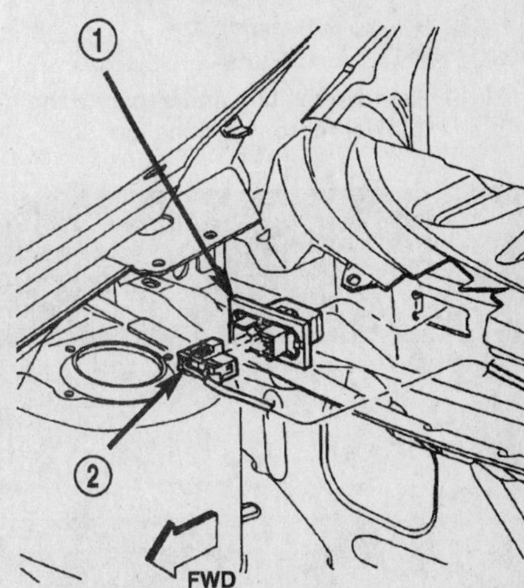


**10.4 The blower motor resistor snap-fits into engine compartment firewall**

1 *Blower motor resistor*
2 *Electrical connector*

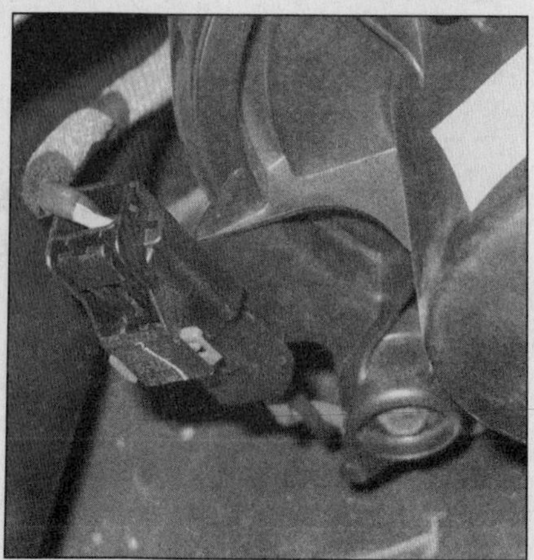

**10.9 Disconnect the electrical connector from the blower motor assembly**

blower motor electrical connector **(see illustration)**. On 2006 and later models, remove the glove box (see Chapter 11) to access the blower motor electrical connector.

### Air-conditioned models

10 Remove the blower motor mounting screws **(see illustration)**.

11 Remove the blower motor from the blower housing.

**10.14 Remove the clip and separate the blower motor from the fan**

**10.10 Remove the blower motor mounting screws (air-conditioned models)**

### Non-air-conditioned models

12 Pull the release tab down and simultaneously rotate the blower motor 1/8-turn counterclockwise **(see illustration)**.

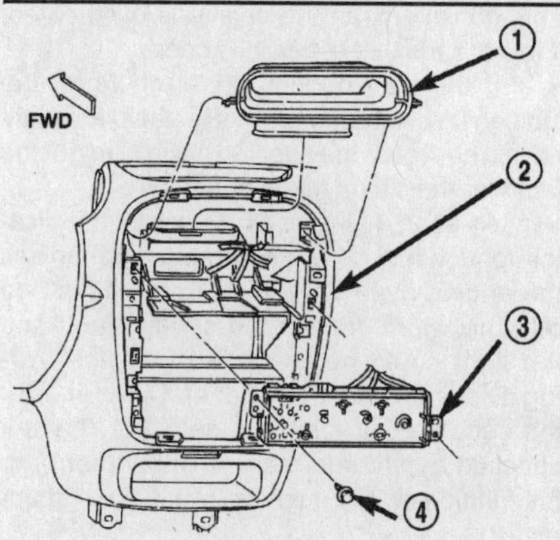


**11.3 Heater/air conditioner control assembly mounting details**

1 *Center air duct*
2 *Instrument panel*
3 *Heater/air conditioner control assembly*
4 *Mounting screws*

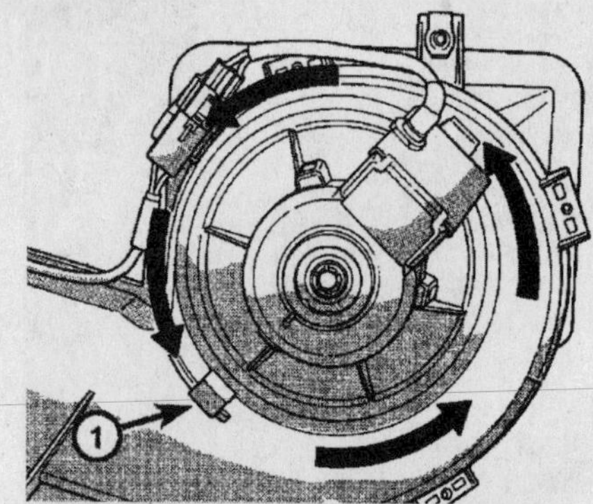


**10.12 To remove the fan from the blower motor assembly on non-air-conditioned models, pull down on the release tab and turn the assembly 1/8-turn counterclockwise**

13 Separate the blower motor from the blower housing.

### All models

14 Remove the circlip from the fan **(see illustration)** and separate the fan from the blower motor frame.

15 Installation is the reverse of removal.

## 11 Heater/air conditioner control assembly - removal and installation

*Refer to illustrations 11.3, 11.4 and 11.5*

**Warning:** *These models are equipped with airbags, always disable the airbag system before working in the vicinity of any airbag system components to avoid the possibility of accidental deployment of the airbag, which could cause personal injury* (see Chapter 12).

1 Disconnect the cable from the negative battery terminal (see Chapter 5).

2 Remove the center trim bezel (see Chapter 11).

3 Remove the center air duct **(see illustration)**.

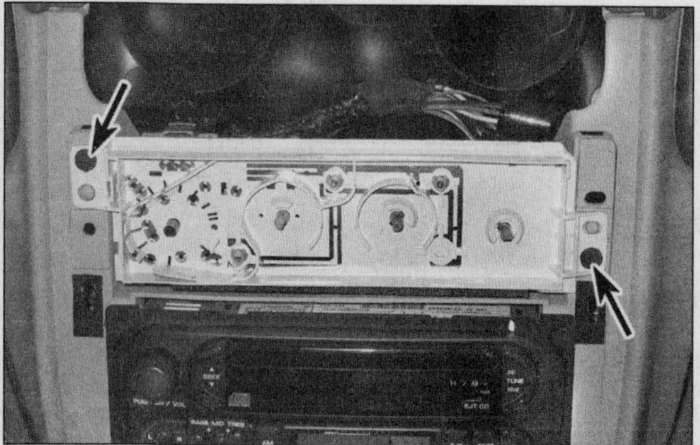

**11.4 Remove the mounting screws from the heater/air conditioner control assembly**

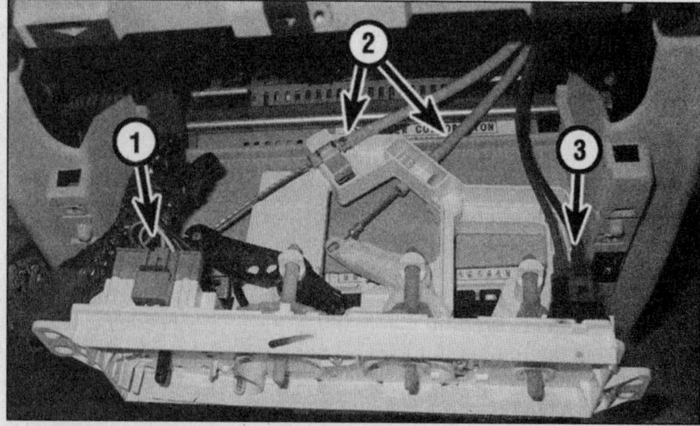


**11.5 Pull out the the heater/air conditioner control assembly, then unplug the electrical connector (1), detach the control cables (2) and the vacuum harness (3)**

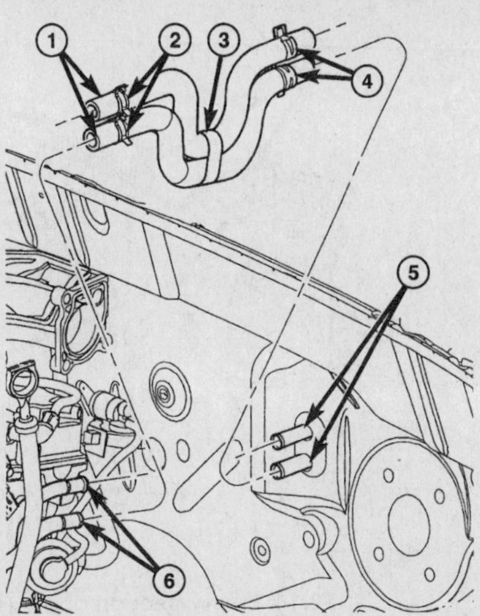


**12.2 Trace the heater hoses to the firewall, remove the hose clamps and then disconnect the hoses from the heater core pipes**

1 *Heater hoses*
2 *Heater hose clamps*
3 *Heater hose retainer*
4 *Heater hose clamps*
5 *Heater core pipes*
6 *Engine coolant pipes*

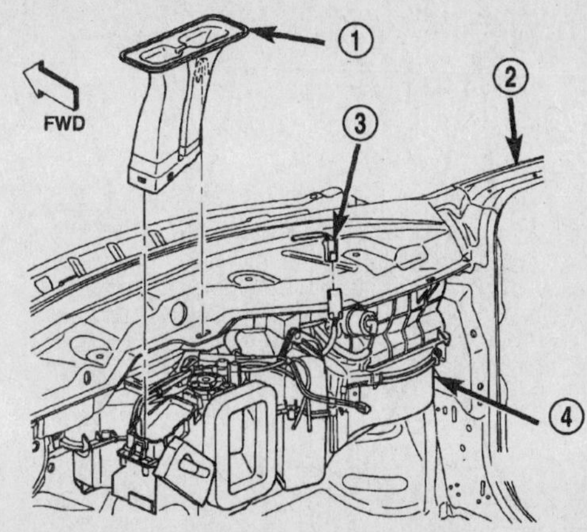


**12.9 Heater/ventilation/air conditioner (HVAC) assembly details**

1 *Defroster duct*
2 *Vehicle body*
3 *Electrical connector*
4 *HVAC assembly*

4 Remove the heater/air conditioner control assembly retaining screws **(see illustration)**.

5 Pull out the control assembly and disconnect the electrical connectors, control cables and the vacuum hoses **(see illustration)**.

6 Installation is the reverse of removal.

## 12 Heater core - replacement

*Refer to illustrations 12.2, 12.9, 12.10, 12.11, 12.13 and 12.14*

**Warning:** *All models are equipped with airbags, so to avoid the possibility of accidental deployment of the airbag, which could cause personal injury, always make sure that you disable the airbag system before working in the vicinity of any airbag system components (see Chapter 12).*

**Warning:** *The heating/ventilation/air conditioning (HVAC) housing must be removed before the heater core can be removed. Have the air conditioning system discharged by an automotive air conditioning shop BEFORE beginning this procedure. Do NOT loosen any refrigerant line fittings until the system has been discharged. The system is under high pressure and could cause a serious injury if opened while still pressurized. You will not be able to drive the vehicle to an automotive air conditioning shop to have the system discharged once you have begun this procedure because the instrument panel must be removed and the vehicle will not be driveable.*

**Warning:** *Wait until the engine is completely cool before beginning this procedure.*

1 Have the air conditioning system discharged by a dealer service department or an automotive air conditioning shop before proceeding (see **Warning 2** above).

2 Drain the cooling system (see Chapter 1) and disconnect the heater hoses from the heater core inlet and outlet pipes at the firewall **(see illustration)**. **Note:** *Although not absolutely necessary, removing the Powertrain Control Module (PCM) will make it easier to access the heater hoses* (see Chapter 6).

3 Remove the coolant reservoir (see Section 5).

4 Remove the instrument panel (see Chapter 11).

5 Working in the engine compartment, disconnect the air conditioning lines from the evaporator, if equipped.

6 Working in the engine compartment, disconnect the refrigerant line connector block **(see illustration 12.10)**.

7 Disconnect the vacuum lines from the brake power booster (see Chapter 9).

8 Working in the engine compartment, remove the drain tube from the lower section of the heater/ventilation/air conditioning (HVAC) housing **(see illustration 13.1)**.

9 Working in the passenger compartment, remove the defroster duct from the HVAC housing **(see illustration)**.

10 Working in the engine compartment, remove the HVAC mounting nuts **(see illustration)**.

11 Working in the passenger compartment, first remove the right side mounting screw from the HVAC housing **(see illustration)** then remove the remaining fasteners.

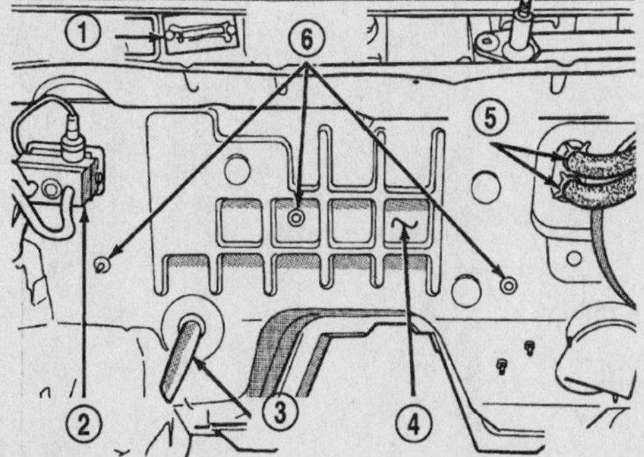


**12.10 Heater core mounting details in engine compartment**

1 *Blower motor resistor*
2 *Refrigerant line connector block*
3 *Drain tube*
4 *Firewall*
5 *Heater hoses*
6 *HVAC mounting bolts*

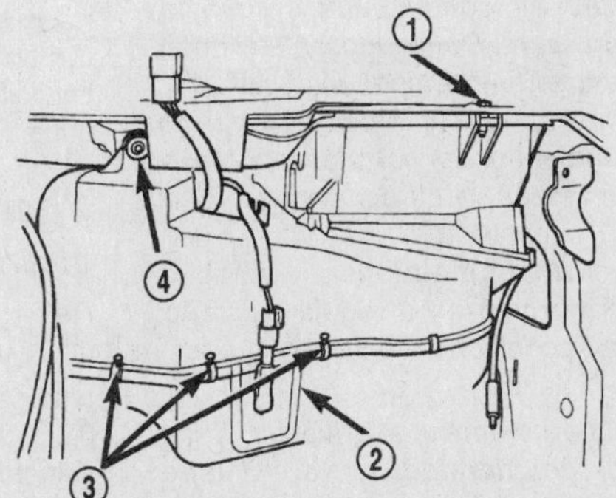


**12.11 HVAC assembly mounting details in passenger compartment**

1 *Right side retaining screw*
2 *Evaporator probe*
3 *Assembly screws*
4 *Dash panel stud with mounting nut*

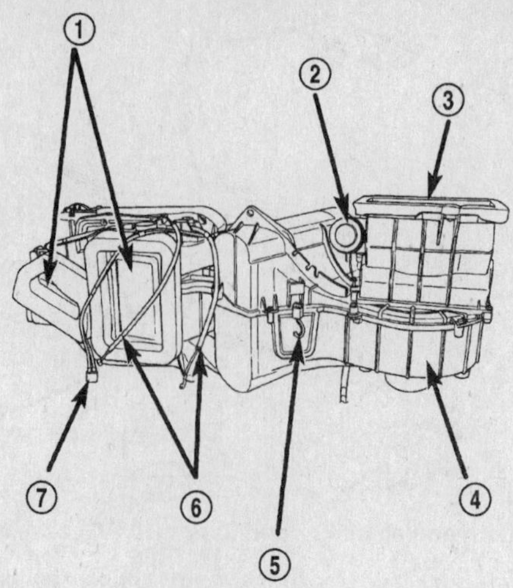


12.13 HVAC assembly details

1 *Air distribution*
2 *Blend door vacuum actuator*
3 *Air inlet*
4 *Blower motor*
5 *Evaporator probe connector*
6 *Control cables*
7 *Vacuum harness*

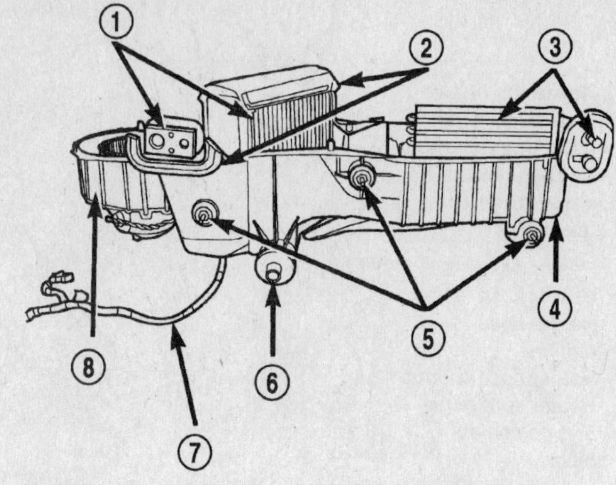


12.14 Lower section of the HVAC assembly

1 *Evaporator*
2 *Foam seals*
3 *Heater core*
4 *HVAC assembly lower section*
5 *HVAC mounting studs*
6 *Drain*
7 *Harness connector*
8 *Blower motor*

12 Lift the HVAC housing from the passenger compartment.
13 Remove the foam seal from the air distribution outlet, the evaporator lines and the heater core tubes **(see illustration)**.
14 Remove upper and lower heater case mounting screws, then pull the heater core out of the housing **(see illustration)**.
15 If the old heater core has been leaking, clean the coolant from the housing.
16 Installation is the reverse of removal. Don't forget to reconnect the heater core inlet and outlet hoses at the firewall.
17 Refill and bleed the cooling system (see Chapter 1).

## 13 Air conditioning and heating system - check and maintenance

*Refer to illustration 13.1*

**Warning:** *The air conditioning system is under high pressure. Do not loosen any hose fittings or remove any components until after the system has been discharged by a dealer service department or service station. Always wear eye protection when disconnecting air conditioning system fittings.*

1 The following maintenance checks should be performed on a regular basis to ensure the air conditioner continues to operate at peak efficiency.

a) *Check the compressor drivebelt. If it's worn or deteriorated, replace it (see Chapter 1).*
b) *Check the system hoses. Look for cracks, bubbles, hard spots and deterioration. Inspect the hoses and all fittings for oil bubbles and seepage. If there's any evidence of wear, damage or leaks, replace the hose(s).*
c) *Inspect the condenser fins for leaves, bugs and other debris. Use a "fin comb" or compressed air to clean the condenser.*
d) *Make sure the system has the correct refrigerant charge.*
e) *Check the evaporator housing drain tube* **(see illustration)** *for blockage.*

2 It's a good idea to operate the system for about 10 minutes at least once a month, particularly during the winter. Long term non-use can cause hardening, and subsequent failure, of the seals.
3 Because of the complexity of the air conditioning system and the special equipment necessary to service it, in-depth troubleshooting and repairs are not included in this manual (refer to the *Haynes Automotive Heating and Air Conditioning Repair Manual*). However, simple checks and component replacement procedures are provided in this Chapter.
4 The most common cause of poor cooling is simply a low system refrigerant charge. If a noticeable drop in cool air output occurs, the following quick check will help you determine if the refrigerant level is low.

### Checking the refrigerant charge

*Refer to illustration 13.7*

5 Warm the engine up to normal operating temperature.
6 Place the air conditioning temperature selector at the coldest setting and the blower at the highest setting. Open the doors (to make sure the air conditioning system does not cycle off as soon as it cools the passenger compartment).
7 With the compressor engaged - the clutch will make an audible click and the center of the clutch will rotate. If the compressor discharge line feels warm and the suction pipe feels cool, the system probably has a satisfactory charge **(see illustration)**.
8 Place a thermometer in the dashboard vent nearest the evaporator and operate the system until the indicated temperature is around 40 to 45-degrees F (4.5 to 7.5-de-grees C). If the ambient (outside) air temperature is very high, say 110 degrees F (43-degrees C), the duct air temperature may be as high as 60-degrees F (16-degrees C) , but generally the air conditioning is 30 to 50 degrees F (10 to 25-degrees C) cooler than the ambient air. **Note:** *Humidity of the ambient air also affects the cooling capacity of the system. Higher ambient humidity lowers the effectiveness of the air conditioning system.*

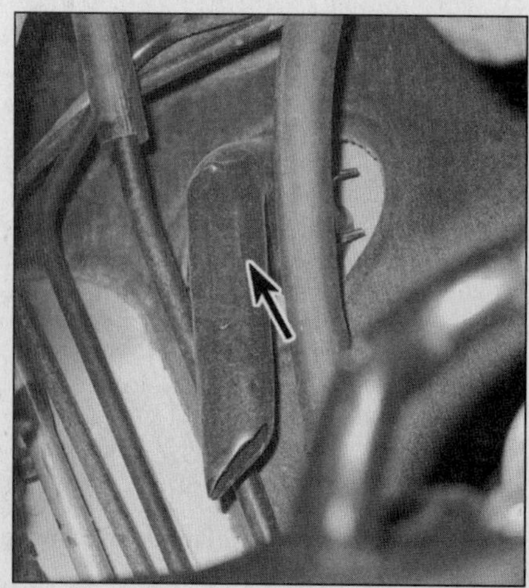

**13.1 Look for the evaporator drain hose on the firewall in the engine compartment; to remove it for cleaning, remove the hose clamp and simply pull it off**

**13.7 Location of the air conditioning discharge line (1) and suction line (2)**

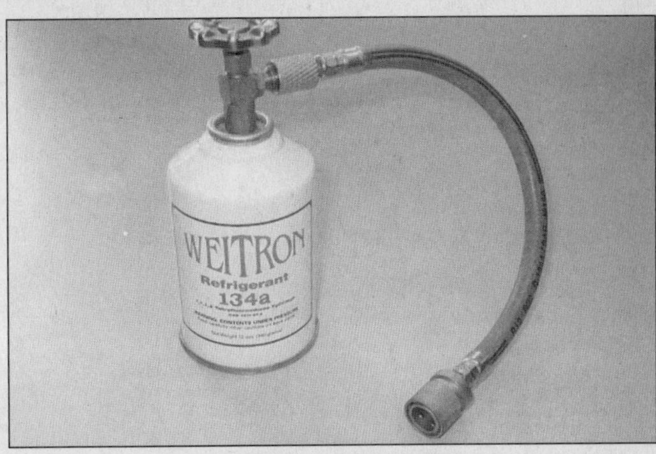


**13.12 Cans of R-134A refrigerant available at auto parts stores can be added to the low side of the air conditioning system with a simple recharging kit**

## Adding refrigerant

*Refer to illustrations 13.12 and 13.15*

9 Buy an automotive charging kit at an auto parts store. A charging kit includes a 14-ounce can of refrigerant, a tap valve and a short section of hose that can be attached between the tap valve and the system low side service valve. If you suspect a leak, make sure the can contains red refrigerant dye. If the system is leaking, the red dye will leak out with the refrigerant and help you pinpoint the location of the leak. **Caution:** *There are two types of refrigerant used in automotive systems; R-12 - which has been widely used on earlier models and the more environmentally-friendly R-134a used in all models covered by this manual. These two refrigerants (and their appropriate refrigerant oils) are not compatible and must never be mixed or components will be damaged. Use only R-134a refrigerant in the models covered by this manual.*

10 Hook up the charging kit by following the manufacturer's instructions. **Warning:** *DO NOT hook the charging kit hose to the system high side! The fittings on the charging kit are designed to fit* ***only*** *on the low side of the system.*

11 Back off the valve handle on the charging kit and screw the kit onto the refrigerant can, making sure first that the O-ring or rubber seal inside the threaded portion of the kit is in place. **Warning:** *Wear protective eyewear when dealing with pressurized refrigerant cans.*

12 Remove the dust cap from the low-side charging connection and attach the quick-connect fitting on the kit hose **(see illustration)**.

13 Warm up the engine and turn on the air conditioner. Keep the charging kit hose away from the fan and other moving parts. **Note:** *The charging process requires the compressor to be running. Your compressor may cycle off if the pressure is low due to a low charge. If the clutch cycles off, you can pull the low-pressure cycling switch plug and attach a jumper wire. This will keep the compressor ON.*

14 Turn the valve handle on the kit until the stem pierces the can, then back the handle out to release the refrigerant. You should be able to hear the rush of gas. Add refrigerant to the low side of the system until both the receiver-drier surface and the evaporator inlet pipe feel about the same temperature

15 If you have an accurate thermometer, place it in the center air conditioning vent **(see illustration)** and then note the temperature of the air coming out of the vent. A fully-charged system which is working correctly should cool down to about 40-degrees F (4.5-degrees C). Generally, an air conditioning system will put out air that is 30 to 50 degrees F (10 to 25-degrees C) cooler than the ambient air.

16 When the can is empty, turn the valve handle to the closed position and release the connection from the low-side port. Replace the dust cap. **Warning:** *Never add more than one can of refrigerant to the system.*

17 Remove the charging kit from the can and store the kit for future use with the piercing valve in the UP position, to prevent inadvertently piercing the can on the next use.

## Heating systems

18 If the carpet under the heater core is damp, or if antifreeze vapor or steam is coming through the vents, the heater core is leaking. Remove it (see Section 11) and install a new unit (most radiator shops will not repair a leaking heater core).

19 If the air coming out of the heater vents isn't hot, the problem could stem from any of the following causes:

a) *The thermostat is stuck open, preventing the engine coolant from warming up enough to carry heat to the heater core. Replace the thermostat (see Section 3).*
b) *There is a blockage in the system, preventing the flow of coolant through the heater core. Feel both heater hoses at the firewall. They should be hot. If one of them is cold, there is an obstruction in one of the hoses or in the heater core. Detach the hoses and backflush the heater core with a water hose. If the heater core is clear but circulation is impeded, remove the two hoses and flush them out with a water hose.*
c) *If flushing fails to remove the blockage from the heater core, the core must be replaced (see Section 12).*

## Eliminating air conditioning odors

*Refer to illustration 13.23*

20 Unpleasant odors that often develop in air conditioning systems are caused by the growth of a fungus, usually on the surface of the evaporator core. The warm, humid environment there is a perfect breeding ground for mildew to develop.

21 The evaporator core on most vehicles is difficult to access, and factory dealerships have a lengthy, expensive process for eliminating the fungus by opening up the evaporator case and using a powerful disinfectant and rinse on the core until the fungus is gone.

**13.15 Insert a thermometer in the center vent, turn on the air conditioning system and wait for it to cool down; depending on the humidity, the output air should be 30 to 50-degrees F (10 to 25-degrees C) cooler than the ambient air temperature**

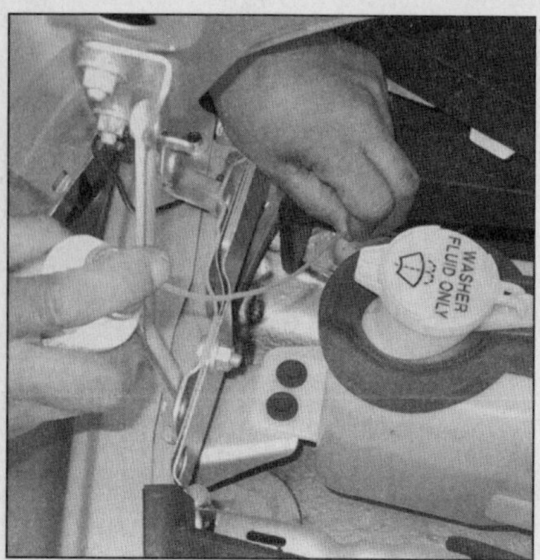


**13.23 Lift the windshield wiper cowl and insert the nozzle of the disinfectant can into the duct that leads to the evaporator housing**

**14.5 Unplug the electrical connector from the high-pressure cutout switch (arrow) and the compressor clutch electrical connector (not visible here)**

You can service your own system at home, but it takes something much stronger than basic household germ-killers or deodorizers.

22 Aerosol disinfectants for automotive air conditioning systems are available in most auto parts stores, but remember when shopping for them that the most effective treatments are also the most expensive. The basic procedure for using these sprays is to start by running the system in the RECIRCULATION mode for ten minutes with the blower on its highest speed. Use the highest heat mode to dry out the system and keep the compressor from engaging by disconnecting the wiring connector at the compressor (see Section 14).

23 Make sure that the disinfectant can comes with a long spray hose. Lift up the cowl above the windshield wiper motor (see Chapter 12) and point the nozzle so that it protrudes inside the duct that leads to the evaporator housing **(see illustration)**, and then spray according to the manufacturer's recommendations. Try to cover the whole surface of the evaporator core, by aiming the spray up, down and sideways. Follow the manufacturer's recommendations for the length of spray and waiting time between applications.

24 Once the evaporator has been cleaned, the best way to prevent the mildew from coming back again is to make sure your evaporator housing drain tube is clear **(see illustration 13.1)**.

## 14 Air conditioning compressor - removal and installation

**Warning:** *The air conditioning system is under high pressure. DO NOT disassemble any part of the system (hoses, compressor, line fittings, etc.) until after the system has been discharged by a dealer service department or an automotive air conditioning shop. Always wear eye protection when disconnecting air conditioning system components.*

**Note:** *If you're replacing the compressor, also replace the accumulator (see Section 15) and the orifice tube (see Section 18).*

### Removal

*Refer to illustrations 14.5, 14.6, 14.7a and 14.7b*

1 Have the air conditioning system discharged (see the **Warning** above).

2 Disconnect the cable from the negative battery terminal (see Chapter 5).

3 Raise the vehicle and support it securely on jackstands.

4 Remove the accessory drivebelts (see Chapter 1).

5 Unplug the electrical connector from the compressor clutch connector and the high-pressure cutout switch **(see illustration)**.

6 Disconnect the refrigerant lines from the compressor **(see illustration)**. Plug the open fittings to prevent entry of dirt and moisture. Be sure to remove and discard the old refrigerant line fitting O-rings.

7 Remove the compressor mounting bolts **(see illustrations)** and remove it from the vehicle.

### Installation

8 If a new compressor is being installed, pour out the oil from the old compressor into a graduated container and add that amount of new refrigerant oil to the new compressor. Also follow any directions included with the new compressor.

9 The clutch might have to be transferred from the original compressor to the new unit.

10 Installation is the reverse of removal. Replace all O-rings with new ones specifically made for use with R-134a refrigerant and lubricate them with R-134a-compatible refrigerant oil.

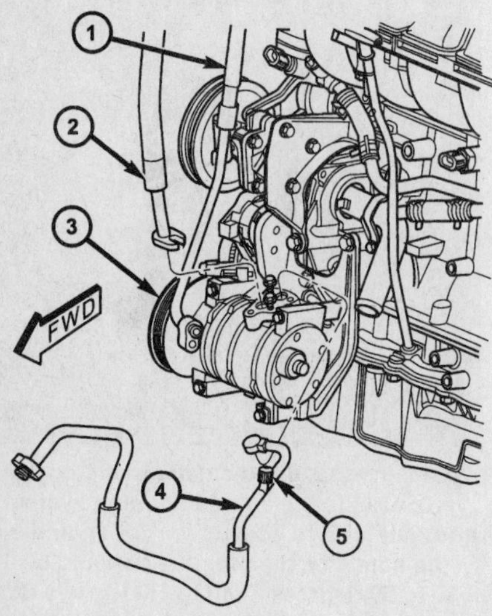


**14.6 Details of the refrigerant lines at the compressor**

1 *Liquid line (connects to condenser)*
2 *Suction line*
3 *Compressor*
4 *Discharge line*
5 *Service port*

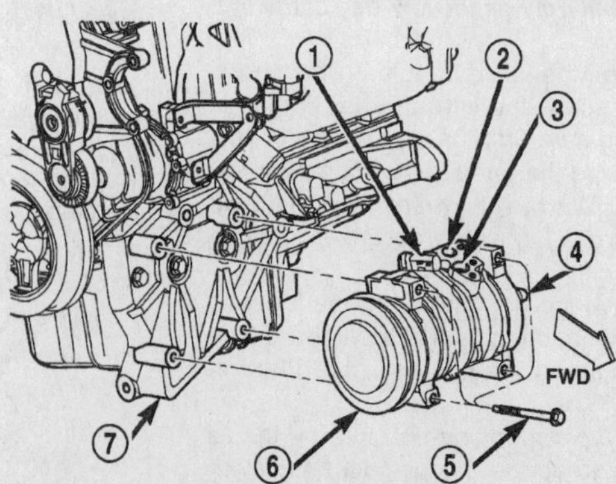


**14.7a Air conditioning compressor details on a non-turbocharged model**

1 *Compressor clutch connector*
2 *Discharge port (high side)*
3 *Suction port (low side)*
4 *High-pressure cutout switch*
5 *Mounting screw*
6 *Compressor*
7 *Bracket*

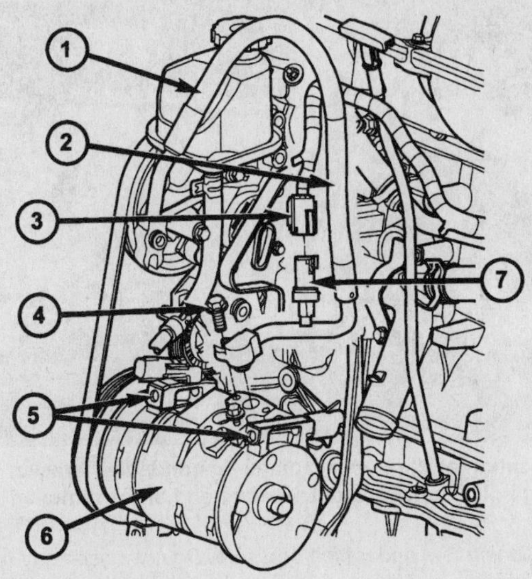


**14.7b Air conditioning compressor details on a turbocharged model**

1 *Power steering fluid reservoir*
2 *Discharge line (high side)*
3 *High-pressure cutout switch connector*
4 *Discharge line (high side) connection bolt*
5 *Compressor mounting bolts*
6 *Compressor*
7 *High-pressure cutout switch*

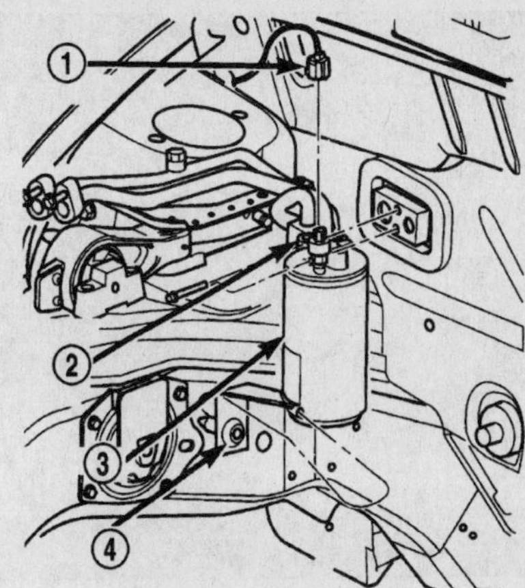


**15.5 Accumulator details**

1 *Pressure cycling switch connector*
2 *Refrigerant line block connector*
3 *Accumulator*
4 *Mounting screw*

11 Have the system evacuated, recharged and leak tested by the shop that discharged it.

## 15 Air conditioning accumulator - removal and installation

**Warning:** *The air conditioning system is under high pressure. DO NOT disassemble any part of the system (hose, compressor, line fittings, etc.) until after the system has been evacuated and the refrigerant recovered by a dealer service department or service station. Always wear eye protection when disconnecting air conditioning system components.*

**Caution:** *Replacement accumulator units are so effective at absorbing moisture that they can quickly saturate upon exposure to the atmosphere. When installing a new unit, have all tools and supplies ready for quick reassembly to avoid having the system open any longer than necessary.*

### Removal

*Refer to illustrations 15.5 and 15.6*

1 The accumulator acts as a reservoir for the system refrigerant. It's located on the right side of the engine compartment, between the evaporator outlet and the compressor suction (low side) port.

2 Have the system discharged (see the **Warning** at the beginning of this Section).

3 Remove the cruise control servo mounting bolts and position the assembly off to the side. Do not disconnect the servo components.

4 Remove the low pressure cycling switch from the accumulator (see Section 17).

5 Disconnect the refrigerant lines from the accumulator **(see illustration)**. Be sure to discard and replace the old O-rings in the fittings and then plug the open fittings to prevent entry of dirt and moisture.

6 Remove the bracket screw at the base of the accumulator **(see illustration)**.

7 Lift the accumulator from the engine compartment.

### Installation

8 Installation is the reverse of removal. If a new accumulator is being installed, add one ounce of refrigerant oil to it before installation.

9 Replace all the O-rings with new ones.

10 Take the vehicle back to the shop that discharged it. Have the system evacuated, recharged and leak tested.

## 16 Air conditioning condenser - removal and installation

**Warning:** *The air conditioning system is under high pressure. DO NOT disassemble any part of the system (hose, compressor, line fittings, etc.) until after the system has been evacuated and the refrigerant recovered by a dealer service department or service station. Always wear eye protection when disconnecting air conditioning system components.*

**Note:** *The accumulator should be replaced whenever the condenser is replaced (see Section 14).*

### Removal

*Refer to illustrations 16.5a, 16.5b, 16.5c and 16.7*

1 Have the system discharged (see the **Warning** at the beginning of this Section).

2 Disconnect the cable from the negative battery terminal (see Chapter 5).

3 Remove the battery support strut (see Chapter 5).

4 Remove the radiator cooling fan (see Section 4).

5 Remove the radiator to condenser mounting bolts **(see illustrations)**. The radia-

**15.6 Remove the accumulator mounting screw from the bracket**

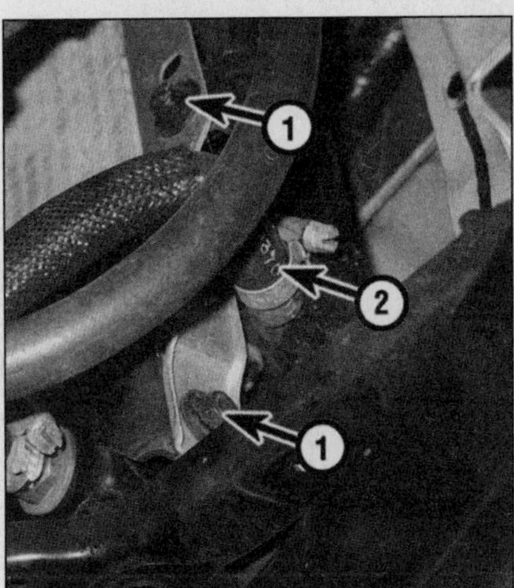


**16.5a Condenser mounting details**

1 *Lower radiator-to-condenser mounting bolts*
2 *Transaxle oil cooler line to oil cooler*

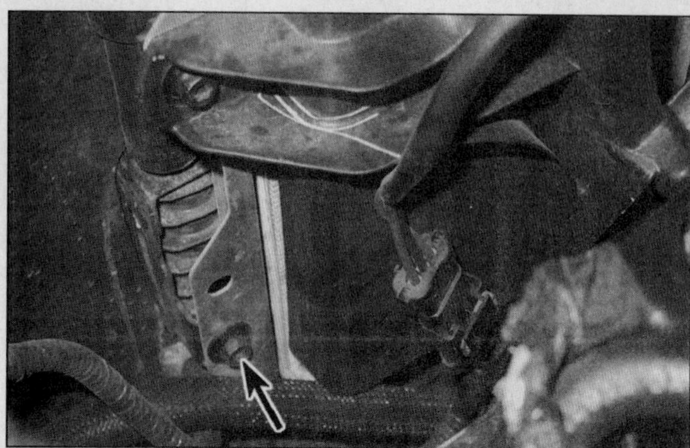

16.5b Working on the left side of the vehicle, remove the lower radiator-to-condenser bracket bolt

16.5c Location of the upper radiator-to-condenser bracket mounting bolt - radiator crossmember and brace removed

tor is supported by the condenser mounting brackets.

6 Remove the radiator (see Section 5).

7 Disconnect the refrigerant lines **(see illustration)**. Be sure to remove and discard the old O-rings.

8 Remove the condenser from the vehicle.

### Installation

9 Be sure to inspect the rubber mounting bolt insulators for cracks and deterioration. Replace them if they're worn or damaged.

10 Installation is the reverse of removal. If a new condenser is being installed add one ounce of refrigerant oil to it before installation.

11 Take the vehicle back to the shop that discharged it. Have the system evacuated, recharged and leak tested.

## 17 Air conditioning pressure cycling switch - replacement

*Refer to illustration 17.2*

**Warning:** *The air conditioning system is under high pressure. Do not loosen any hose fittings or remove any components until the system has been discharged. Air conditioning refrigerant should be properly discharged into an EPA-approved recovery/recycling unit by a dealer service department or an automotive air conditioning repair facility. Always wear eye protection when disconnecting air conditioning system fittings.*

1 Have the refrigerant discharged by an air conditioning technician.

2 Unplug the electrical connector from the pressure cycling switch **(see illustration)**.

3 Unscrew the pressure cycling switch. Be sure to use a back-up wrench to prevent deforming the pressure line.

4 Lubricate the switch O-ring with clean refrigerant oil of the correct type.

5 Screw the new switch onto the threads and tighten it securely.

6 Reconnect the electrical connector.

7 Have the system evacuated, charged and leak tested by the shop that discharged it.

## 18 Orifice tube - removal and installation

*Refer to illustrations 18.2 and 18.3*

**Warning:** *The air conditioning system is under high pressure. Do not loosen any hose fittings or remove any components until the system has been discharged. Air conditioning refrigerant should be properly discharged into an EPA-approved recovery/recycling unit by a dealer service department or an automotive air conditioning repair facility. Always wear eye protection when disconnecting air conditioning system fittings.*

**Note:** *The orifice tube is an integral part of the liquid line. The liquid line must be replaced as a complete unit when servicing the orifice tube. Consult a dealer parts department.*

1 Have the refrigerant discharged by an air conditioning technician.

2 Disconnect the refrigerant lines **(see illustration)** at the condenser.

3 Disconnect the refrigerant lines at the connector block **(see illustration)**.

4 Lift the refrigerant lines from the engine compartment.

5 Installation is the reverse of removal. Be sure to remove and discard the old O-rings.

6 Take the vehicle back to the shop that discharged it. Have the system evacuated, recharged and leak tested.

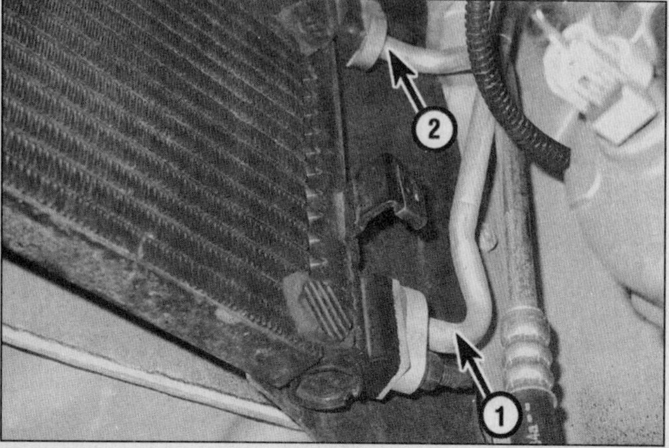


16.7 Location of the refrigerant liquid line (1) and the discharge line (2) at the condenser

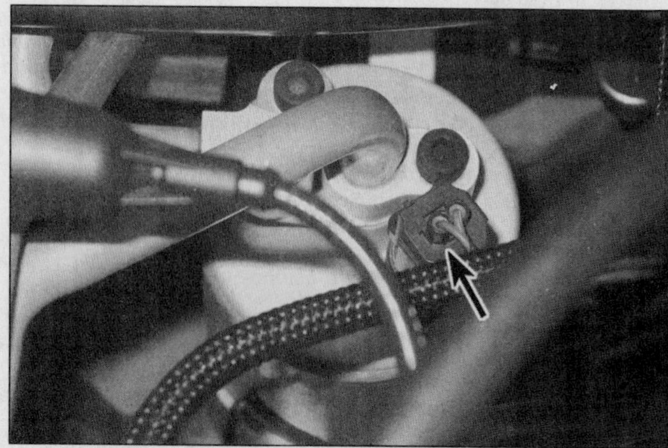

17.2 Remove the electrical connector from the pressure cycling switch

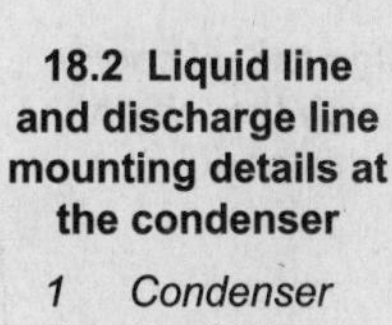

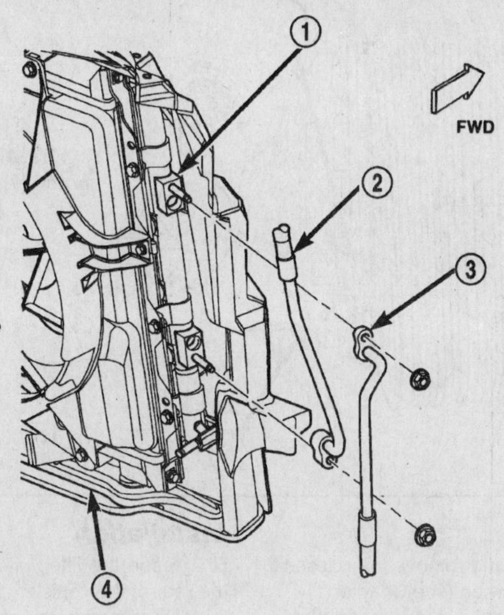


**18.2 Liquid line and discharge line mounting details at the condenser**

1 *Condenser*
2 *Liquid line*
3 *Discharge line*
4 *Cooling fan assembly*

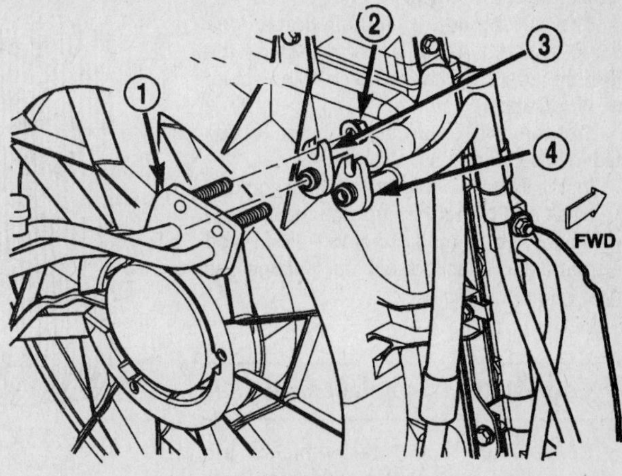


**18.3 Details of the refrigerant lines at the midline connector block**

1 *Connector block*
2 *Mounting nut*
3 *Suction line*
4 *Liquid line*

## 19 Oil cooler (turbocharged models) - removal and installation

**Warning:** *Wait until the engine is completely cool before beginning this procedure.*

### Removal

*Refer to illustrations 19.4 and 19.5*

1 Raise the vehicle and support it securely on jackstands.

2 Drain the engine oil and remove the oil filter (see Chapter 1).

3 Drain the coolant (see Chapter 1) into a container.

4 Disconnect the coolant lines from the oil cooler **(see illustration)**. Be sure to position a drain pan directly below the cooler lines.

5 Remove the union bolt **(see illustration)** and separate the oil cooler from the oil filter adapter.

### Installation

*Refer to illustrations 19.6 and 19.7*

6 Be sure to install a new O-ring onto the

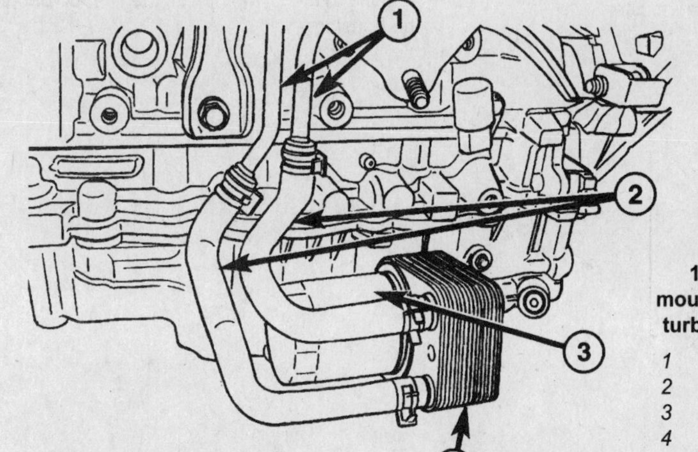


**19.4 Oil cooler mounting details on a turbocharged model**

1 *Coolant tubes*
2 *Coolant hoses*
3 *Oil filter*
4 *Oil cooler*

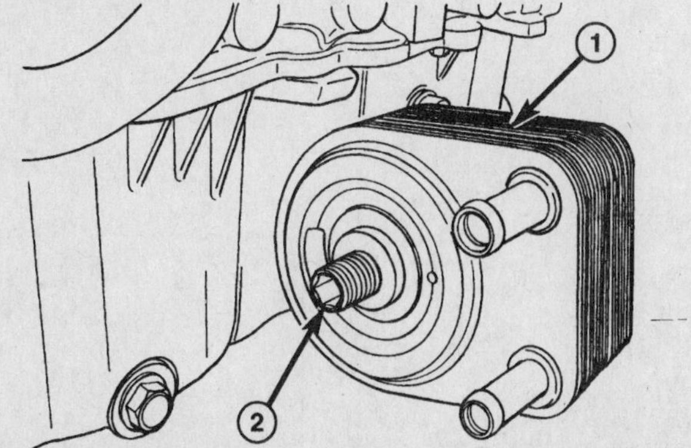


**19.5 Remove the oil cooler union bolt (2) from the oil cooler (1)**

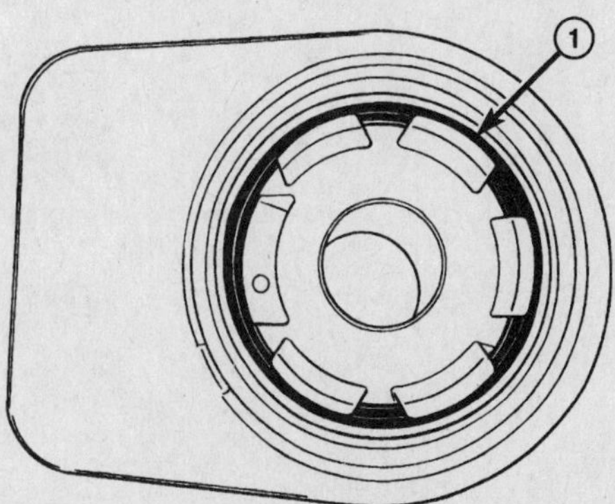


**19.6 Be sure to install a new oil cooler seal (1) before installing it onto the oil filter adapter**

oil cooler **(see illustration)**.

7 The remainder of installation is the reverse of removal but be sure to align the tab on the adapter with the notch in the cooler **(see illustration)**.

8 Tighten the union bolt to the torque listed in this Chapter's Specifications.

9 Install the coolant lines to the oil cooler.

10 Refill and bleed the cooling system, refill the engine with oil (see chapter 1), then start the engine and check for coolant leakage and proper gauge function.

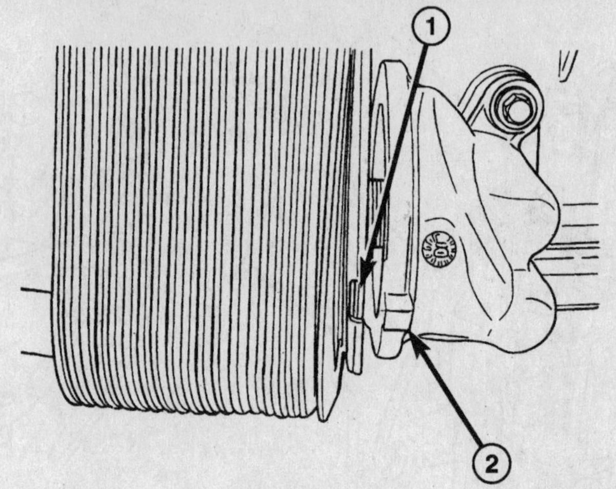


**19.7 Align the oil cooler notch (1) with the tab on the adapter (2)**

## 20 Cabin air filter - replacement

1 Some 2005 and later vehicles are equipped with a particulate air filter that filters the outside air entering the HVAC housing. The filter is mounted in the engine compartment, under the passenger side cowl grille screen. The filter should be replaced once a year or every 15,000 miles (24,000 km) and inspected when diagnosing any heating/air conditioning system performance concerns. The particulate air filter is labeled with "REAR OF VEHICLE" and an arrow to indicate air flow direction through the filter.

### *Removal*

2 Open the hood and remove the passenger side cowl grille screen (see Chapter 11).

3 Remove the windshield washer fluid reservoir bolts and relocate the reservoir away from the cabin filter housing.

4 Remove the two screws holding the filter housing to the cowl, then lift the filter up out of the housing.

### *Installation*

5 Insert the filter with the arrow indicating the rear of the vehicle.

6 Reassemble the remaining components in reverse order of removal.

7 Replace any windshield washer fluid that may have been lost during reservoir relocation.

# Chapter 4
# Fuel and exhaust systems

## Contents



## Specifications

### Fuel system

| | |
|---|---|
| Fuel system pressure | 53 to 63 psi (366 to 434 kPa) |
| Injector resistance | 11.4 to 12.6 ohms |

### Torque specifications

**Note:** *One foot-pound (ft-lb) of torque is equivalent to 12 inch-pounds (in-lbs) of torque. Torque values below approximately 15 foot-pounds are expressed in inch-pounds, because most foot-pound torque wrenches are not accurate at these smaller values.*

| | Ft-lbs (unless otherwise indicated) | Nm |
|---|---|---|
| Fuel rail bolts | | |
| Non-turbo engine | 96 in-lbs | 11 |
| Turbo engine | 16 | 22 |
| Throttle body mounting bolts | | |
| 2001 and 2002 models | 20 | 28 |
| 2003 and later models | 105 in-lbs | 12 |
| Turbocharger/exhaust manifold assembly fasteners | 20 | 28 |
| Turbocharger coolant and oil lines | | |
| Coolant supply and return line banjo bolts | 22 | 30 |
| Coolant and oil return and supply line brass fittings | 30 | 40 |

**1.1a Fuel system components (intake manifold installed)**

1 Air filter housing cover
2 Air intake duct
3 Throttle body
4 Accelerator cable
5 Air intake manifold

**1.1b Fuel system components (intake manifold and upper radiator hose removed for clarity)**

1 Power Distribution Center (PDC) (houses fuel pump fuse and fuel pump relay)
2 Air filter element
3 Fuel supply hose
4 Fuel injectors

## 1 General information

*Refer to illustrations 1.1a and 1.1b*

All models are equipped with a sequential Multi-Port Electronic Fuel Injection (MPI) system **(see illustrations)**. The fuel system consists of the following components:

*Air filter, housing and air intake duct between housing and throttle body*

*Electric fuel pump/fuel level sending unit module (located in the fuel tank)*

*Fuel pressure regulator (integrated into the fuel pump/fuel level sending unit module)*

*Fuel rail and fuel injector assembly*

*Fuel tank*

*Throttle body assembly, which includes throttle valve, Throttle Position (TP) sensor and Idle Air Control (IAC) valve (for information on the TP sensor and IAC valve, see Chapter 6)*

### Sequential Multi-Port Electronic Fuel Injection (MPI) system

Intake air is drawn through the air filter housing and air intake duct into the throttle body. Inside the throttle body, the throttle valve controls the amount of air passing into the air intake plenum and then into the cylinders. The intake port for each cylinder is equipped with its own injector. The MPI system injects fuel into the intake ports in the same sequence as the firing order of the engine. The injectors are controlled by the Powertrain Control Module (PCM). The PCM constantly monitors the operating conditions of the engine - temperature, speed, load, etc. - and then delivers the optimal amount of fuel for these conditions. The amount of fuel delivered by each injector is determined by its "on time," which the PCM can vary so quickly that two successive injectors can deliver a different amount of fuel. In other words, the PCM responds instantly to any changes in the operating conditions of the engine.

### Fuel pump

The electric fuel pump is located inside the fuel tank.

Voltage to the fuel pump circuit is supplied through the fuel pump relay, which is located inside the Power Distribution Center (PDC) which is located in the engine compartment. The fuel pump relay is controlled by the Powertrain Control Module (PCM). When the ignition key is turned to ON (but not cranked), the PCM energizes the fuel pump relay for one second, which closes the fuel pump circuit long enough to pressurize the fuel system. Then the PCM turns off the fuel pump relay.

When the ignition key is turned to START, current flows from the ignition switch to the starter relay coil and to the PCM, which also receives a signal from the Crankshaft Position (CKP) sensor. When the PCM receives these two signals (from the ignition switch and from the CKP sensor), a transistor inside the PCM that controls the fuel pump relay allows current to flow to the fuel pump relay, which allows current to flow to the fuel pump. As long as the transistor inside the PCM that controls the fuel pump relay continues to receive the CKP sensor signal, it continues to supply current to the fuel pump relay, which continues to supply current to the fuel pump.

When the engine is running, fuel is pumped by the fuel pump inside the fuel tank to the fuel rail and injectors through a metal line running along the underside of the vehicle. There is no fuel return line between the fuel rail and the fuel tank. The fuel pressure regulator, which is an integral part of the fuel pump module, maintains fuel pressure between 53 and 63 psi. If the fuel pressure exceeds this range, a fuel-return valve routes the excess fuel back to the fuel tank.

### Fuel line, fuel hoses and quick-connect fittings

The metal fuel line underneath the vehicle which carries pressurized fuel from the fuel tank to the fuel rail is connected to the fuel pump module and to the fuel rail by hoses which use special quick-connect fittings. For more information on these fittings, refer to Section 4.

### Exhaust system

The exhaust system consists of the exhaust manifold, the catalytic converter, the exhaust pipe, the muffler and the tail pipe. For information on servicing the exhaust system, refer to Section 16. The catalytic converter is an emission-control device in the exhaust system that reduces hydrocarbon (HC), carbon monoxide (CO) and oxides of nitrogen (NOx) pollutants. For more information regarding the catalytic converter, refer to Chapter 6.

## 2 Fuel pressure relief

*Refer to illustration 2.3*

**Warning:** *Gasoline is extremely flammable, so take extra precautions when you work on any part of the fuel system. Don't smoke or allow open flames or bare light bulbs near the work area, and don't work in a garage where a gas-type appliance (such as a water heater or a clothes dryer) is present. Since gasoline is carcinogenic, wear latex gloves when*

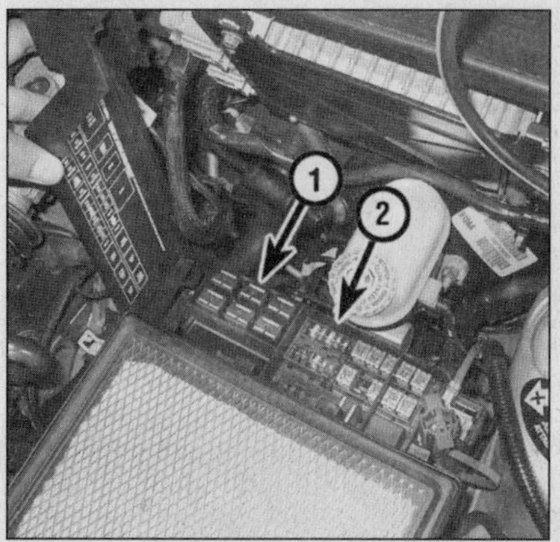


**2.3 To relieve the pressure in the fuel system, disable the electric fuel pump by removing the fuel pump relay (1); if you're checking the fuel pump electrical circuit, always check the fuel pump relay and the fuel pump fuse (2)**

*there's a possibility of being exposed to fuel, and, if you spill any fuel on your skin, rinse it off immediately with soap and water. Mop up any spills immediately and do not store fuel-soaked rags where they could ignite. The fuel system is under constant pressure, so, if any fuel lines are to be disconnected, the fuel pressure in the system must be relieved first. When you perform any kind of work on the fuel system, wear safety glasses and have a Class B type fire extinguisher on hand.*

1 Remove the fuel filler cap to relieve any pressure inside the fuel tank.

2 Remove the cover from the air filter housing (see Section 13).

3 Remove the fuel pump relay from the Power Distribution Center (PDC), the fuse and relay box located on the left side of the engine compartment, right behind and below the air filter housing **(see illustration)**.

4 Start the engine.

5 Allow the engine to run until it stops. Turn the ignition switch to OFF, then disconnect the cable from the negative terminal of the battery (see Chapter 5) before working on the fuel system.

6 The fuel system pressure is now relieved. When you're finished working on the fuel system, install the circuit opening relay and connect the negative cable to the battery.

## 3 Fuel pump/fuel pressure - check

**Warning:** *Gasoline is extremely flammable, so take extra precautions when you work on any part of the fuel system. See the* **Warning** *in Section 2.*

### General checks

1 If you suspect insufficient fuel delivery check the following items first:

a) *Check the battery and make sure that it's fully charged (see Chapter 5).*

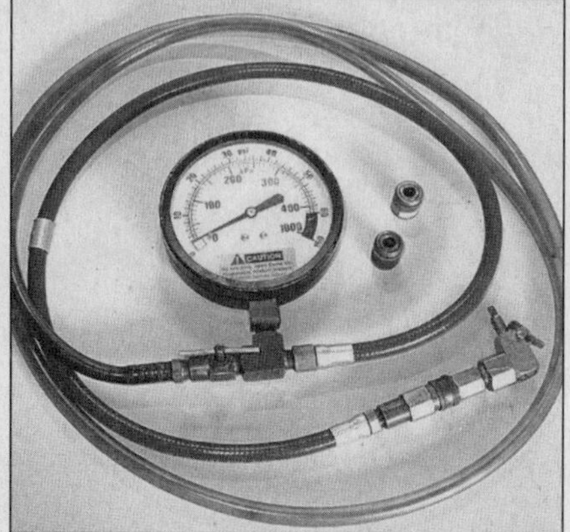

**3.4 This typical fuel pressure testing setup includes a fuel pressure gauge capable of measuring the operating pressure range of fuel injection systems and a special Schrader valve-type adapter to allow you easily connect the pressure gauge hose to the fuel rail test port**

b) *Check the fuel filter (see Section 8) for obstructions (the fuel filter is attached to the bottom of the fuel pump/fuel level sending unit module).*

c) *Inspect the fuel line, hoses and quick-connect fittings (see Section 4). Verify that the problem is not simply a leak in a line.*

2 Verify that the fuel pump actually runs. Remove the fuel filler cap and have an assistant turn the ignition switch to ON while you listen carefully for the sound of the fuel pump operating. You should hear a brief whirring noise (for about one second) as the pump comes on and pressurizes the system. If the fuel pump makes no sound, check the fuel pump electrical circuit (see the wiring diagrams at the end of Chapter 12). If the fuel pump runs, but a fuel system problem persists, proceed to the fuel pump pressure check.

### Fuel pump pressure check

*Refer to illustrations 3.4, 3.5a and 3.5b*

**Note:** *Before proceeding, make sure that you have a fuel pressure gauge capable of measuring fuel pressure up to 70 psi and an adapter suitable for connecting the fuel pressure gauge to the Schrader valve-type test port on the fuel rail.*

3 Relieve the fuel system pressure (see Section 2).

4 In addition to a fuel pressure gauge capable of reading fuel pressure up to 70 psi, you'll need a hose and an adapter suitable for hooking up to the Schrader valve-type test port on the fuel rail **(see illustration)**.

5 Unscrew the test port cap **(see illustration)** located on the left end of the fuel rail and connect the fuel pressure gauge and hose to the test port **(see illustration)**.

6 Turn off all the accessories, then start the engine and let it idle. The fuel pressure should be within the operating range listed in

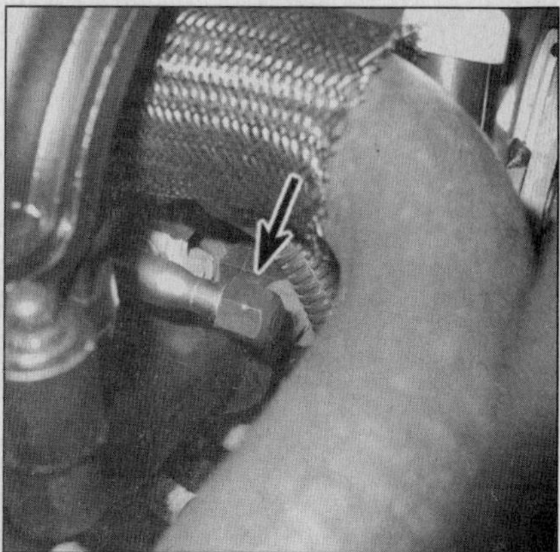

**3.5a To check the fuel pressure, unscrew this cap from the test port on the left end of the fuel rail . . .**

**3.5b . . . then hook up the fuel pressure gauge to the test port with the Schrader valve-type adapter**

this Chapter's Specifications. If the pressure reading is within the specified range, the system is operating correctly.

7 If the fuel pressure is higher than specified, replace the fuel pump module (see Section 7).

8 If the fuel pressure is lower than specified, check the fuel line, the fuel hoses, the connectors and the fuel injectors for leaks. Remove the fuel pump module and inspect the fuel strainer for restrictions. If all these components are okay, the fuel pressure regulator or the fuel pump is probably defective. Replace the fuel pump module to prevent any future fuel pressure problems.

9 After the testing is complete, relieve the fuel pressure (see Section 2), remove the fuel pressure gauge and install the cap on the test port.

### Fuel pump electrical circuit check

10 If the pump does not turn on, check the fuel pump fuse and the fuel pump relay, both of which are located in the Power Distribution Center (PDC) **(see illustration 2.3)**.

4.2 The metal fuel supply line running under the vehicle is attached to the pan by a series of clips such as this one; the clips also route the plastic EVAP lines and the electrical harness

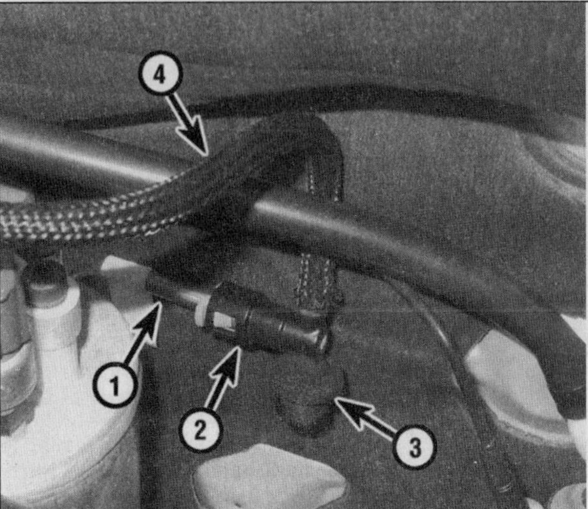


4.3 The metal fuel supply line is connected to the fuel supply hoses back at the fuel tank and in the engine compartment by quick-connect fittings; this is a typical two-tab type fitting

1 *Metal fuel supply line from fuel tank*
2 *Quick-connect fitting (two-tab type shown)*
3 *Fuel pulsation damper*
4 *Fuel supply hose (delivers fuel to fuel rail)*

11 If the fuse and relay are good and the fuel pump does not operate, check the fuel pump circuit (see wiring diagrams at the end of Chapter 12).

## 4 Fuel lines and fittings - general information

*Refer to illustrations 4.2 and 4.3*

**Warning:** *Gasoline is extremely flammable, so take extra precautions when you work on any part of the fuel system. See the* **Warning** *in Section 2.*

1 Always relieve the system fuel pressure before servicing fuel lines or fittings (see Section 2).

2 The fuel supply line extends from the fuel tank to the engine compartment. The lines are secured to the underbody with clips **(see illustration)**. Anytime you raise the vehicle for underbody service, inspect the lines underneath the vehicle for leaks, kinks and dents.

3 The fuel supply line is attached to the fuel supply hoses at the fuel tank and in the engine compartment by quick-connect fittings **(see illustration)**.

4 If evidence of dirt is found in the system during disassembly, disconnect the fuel supply line and then blow it out with compressed air. And be sure to inspect the fuel filter on the fuel pump module (see Section 8) for damage and deterioration.

### Steel tubing

5 If replacement of a fuel line or emission line is called for, use welded steel tubing meeting the manufacturer's specifications or its equivalent.

6 Don't use copper or aluminum tubing to replace steel tubing. These materials cannot withstand normal vehicle vibration.

7 Because fuel lines used on fuel-injected vehicles are under high pressure, they require special consideration.

8 Some fuel lines have threaded fittings with O-rings. Any time the fittings are loosened to service or replace components:

a) *When loosening or tightening threaded fittings, always hold the fitting on the stationary line with a wrench to prevent the line from twisting.*
b) *Check all O-rings for cuts, cracks and deterioration. Replace any that appear hardened, worn or damaged.*
c) *If the lines are replaced, always use original equipment parts, or parts that meet the original equipment standards specified in this Section.*

### Flexible hose

**Caution:** *Use only original equipment replacement hoses or their equivalent. Others may fail from the high pressures of this system.*

9 Don't route fuel hose within four inches of any part of the exhaust system or within ten inches of the catalytic converter. Metal lines and rubber hoses must never be allowed to chafe against the frame. A minimum of 1/4-inch clearance must be maintained around a line or hose to prevent contact with the frame.

10 Some models may be equipped with nylon fuel line and quick-connect fittings at the fuel filter and/or fuel pump. The quick-connect fittings cannot be serviced separately. Do not attempt to service these types of fuel lines in the event the retainer tabs or the line becomes damaged. Replace the entire fuel line as an assembly.

### Replacement

11 If a fuel line or fuel hose is damaged, replace it with factory replacement parts. Do not substitute line or hose of inferior quality; it might not be suitable for, and it might fail from, the operating pressure of this system.

12 Relieve the fuel system pressure (see Section 2).

13 Disconnect the cable from the negative terminal of the battery (see Chapter 5).

14 Remove all clamps and/or clips attaching the line to the vehicle body. Pay close attention to all clips; they not only secure the fuel line and hoses, they also route them correctly. The hoses and line must be reattached to their respective clips when reassembled.

### Quick-connect fittings

15 Various types of quick-connect fittings are used on the vehicles covered by this manual. After you locate the fitting, determine which type it is and use whichever of the following procedures that applies to that fitting to disconnect and reconnect it.

#### Single-tab type

*Refer to illustrations 4.19*

16 Squeeze the retainer tabs together then pull the quick-connect fitting and the fuel line apart. The retainer remains on the fuel line.

17 Wipe off the fuel line and the retainer with a clean shop rag, then coat the fuel line with clean engine oil.

18 Inspect the condition of the fitting. If any part is damaged, worn or broken, replace the fuel line and the fitting as an assembly.

19 Push the quick-connect fitting onto the fuel line until you hear a click, but do NOT rely upon this audible click to verify that the retainer is fully seated. The fitting has "windows" through which the retainer locking ears protrude. If the fitting is correctly attached to the fuel line, the retainer locking ears and the fuel line shoulder will be visible in this window **(see illustration)**. If they're not visible, the retainer is not fully seated.

20 Reconnect the negative battery cable, then start the engine and check the fitting for leaks.

#### Two-tab type

*Refer to illustrations 4.21a and 4.21b*

**Note:** *The retainers for this type of quick-connect fitting can be replaced separately, but not the O-rings and spacers. So this type of fitting, if damaged, cannot be repaired. Instead, replace the complete fuel line assembly.*

21 Squeeze the plastic retainer tabs against the fuel line with your fingers, then pull the fuel line and the fitting apart **(see illustra-**

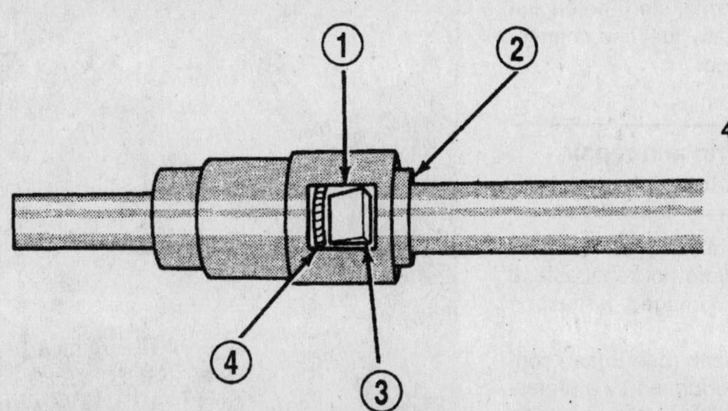

4.19 **Typical single-tab type quick-connect fitting:**

1 *Window*
2 *Tab*
3 *Ear*
4 *Shoulder*

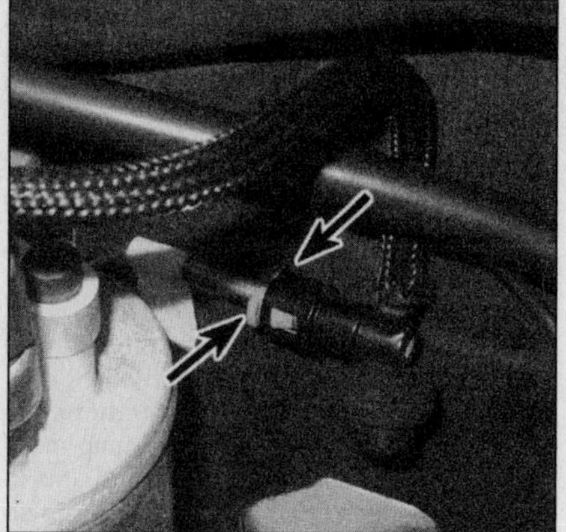

**4.21a To disconnect a two-tab type fitting, squeeze the two plastic retainer tabs together . . .**

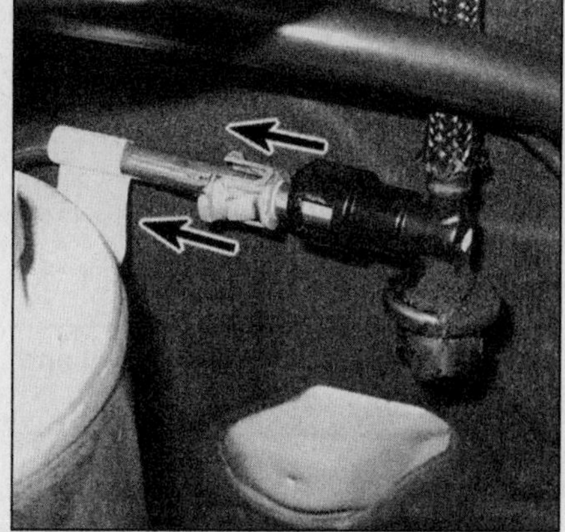

**4.21b . . . and then pull the metal line out of the quick-connect fitting**

**tions)**. The plastic retainer remains with the fuel line. The O-rings and spacer remain inside the quick-connect fitting connector body.

22 Wipe off both halves of the quick-connect fitting with a clean shop rag, then lubricate the fuel line with clean engine oil.

23 Push the quick-connect fitting onto the fuel line until you hear a click, which indicates that the retainer has seated. Verify that the two halves are locked together by trying to pull them apart.

24 Reconnect the negative battery cable, then start the engine and check the fitting for leaks.

### Plastic retainer type

*Refer to illustrations 4.26*

25 This type of fitting is distinguished by its one-piece retainer ring, which is usually black in color.

26 Firmly push the fitting toward the fuel line while simultaneously pushing the plastic retainer ring into the fitting and with the plastic ring depressed, pull the fuel line and the fitting apart **(see illustration)**. **Note:** *Press the retainer ring squarely into the fitting. If the retainer is cocked, disconnection of the fuel line and the fitting is difficult. If necessary, use a tool such as a small adjustable wrench or a small pair of pliers to push the retainer into the fitting.* After disconnection, the plastic retainer ring remains with the quick-connect fitting.

27 Wipe off the fitting and the fuel line with a clean shop rag and inspect the fitting parts for damage and wear. Replace as necessary.

28 Lubricate the fuel line with clean engine oil and insert it into the quick-connect fitting until you hear a click. Verify that the fitting is locked by trying to pull apart the line and the fitting.

29 Reconnect the negative battery cable, then start the engine and check the fitting for leaks.

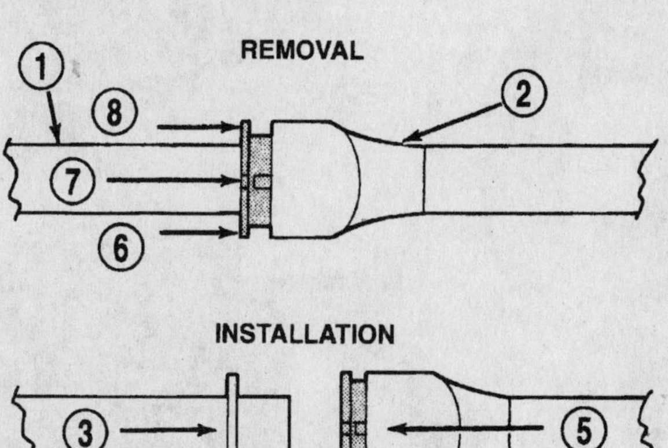


**4.26 Typical plastic retainer ring type fitting:**

1 *Fuel line*
2 *Quick-connect fitting*
3 *Push*
4 *Plastic retainer*
5 *Push*
6 *Push*
7 *Push*
8 *Push*

## 5 Fuel tank - removal and installation

**Warning:** *Gasoline is extremely flammable, so take extra precautions when you work on any part of the fuel system. See the* **Warning** *in Section 2.*

### *Removal*

*Refer to illustrations 5.4, 5.5, 5.6, 5.7 and 5.8*

1 Slowly remove the fuel filler cap to relieve fuel tank pressure, then relieve the system fuel pressure (see Section 2).

2 Disconnect the cable from the negative terminal of the battery (see Chapter 5).

3 Raise the rear of the vehicle and place it securely on jackstands.

4 Put a drain pan with a capacity of at least 16 gallons under the drain cap, unscrew the fuel tank drain cap **(see illustration)** and allow the tank to drain. When the tank is empty, install the drain cap.

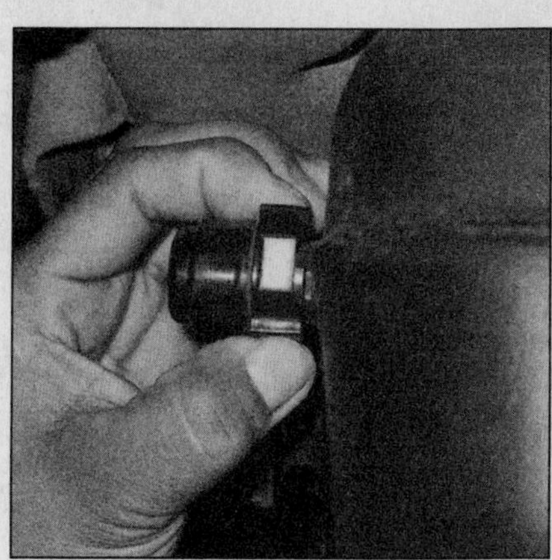

**5.4 Before removing the fuel tank, unscrew the fuel tank drain cap and drain the fuel into a drain pan with a capacity of 16 gallons**

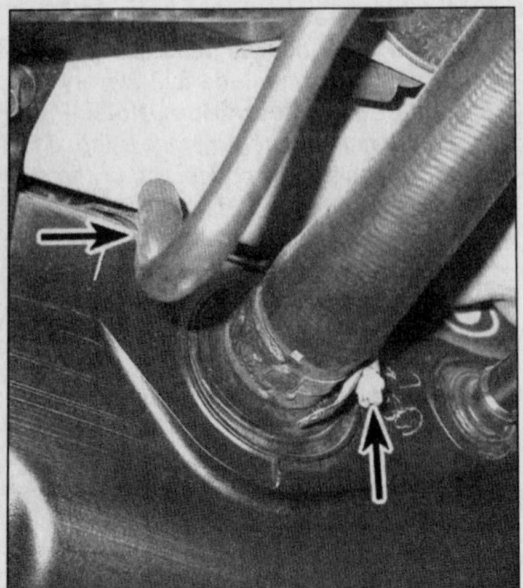

**5.5 Disconnect the vapor hose, loosen the hose clamp screw, then disconnect the fuel filler neck hose from the fuel inlet pipe**

5 Disconnect the vapor hose, loosen the screw on the fuel filler-neck hose clamp **(see illustration)** and disconnect the fuel filler-neck hose from the fuel inlet pipe.

6 Place a transmission jack or a floor jack under the fuel tank to support it **(see illustration)**. If you're going to use a floor jack, put a piece of plywood between the jack head and the tank to protect the tank.

7 Disconnect the electrical connector for the fuel pump/fuel level sending unit and for the leak detection pump. Also disconnect the EVAP line and the quick-connect fitting for the fuel supply hose **(see illustration)**.

8 Remove the bolts that secure the fuel tank straps **(see illustration)**.

9 Carefully lower the fuel tank from the vehicle.

10 Installation is the reverse of removal. Be sure to tighten the fuel tank strap bolts securely. When you're done, start the engine and check for leaks at any fuel line connectors that you disconnected.

## 6 Fuel tank cleaning and repair - general information

1 The fuel tanks installed in the vehicles covered by this manual are not repairable. If the fuel tank becomes damaged, it must be replaced.

2 Cleaning the fuel tank (due to fuel contamination) should be performed by a professional with the proper training to carry out this critical and potentially dangerous work. Even after cleaning and flushing, explosive fumes may remain inside the fuel tank.

3 If the fuel tank is removed from the vehicle, it should not be placed in an area where sparks or open flames could ignite the fumes coming out of the tank. Be especially careful inside a garage where a gas-type appliance is located.

## 7 Fuel pump module - removal and installation

*Refer to illustration 7.3a, 7.3b, 7.4, 7.5a, 7.5b and 7.6*

1 Relieve the system fuel pressure (see Section 2).

2 Remove the fuel tank (see Section 5).

3 Disconnect the fuel supply hose and the electrical connector from the fuel pump module **(see illustrations)**.

4 Before removing the fuel pump module, make an alignment mark on top of the fuel tank, right underneath the fuel outlet pipe **(see illustration)**. This mark ensures that the fuel pump module will be correctly realigned when installed again.

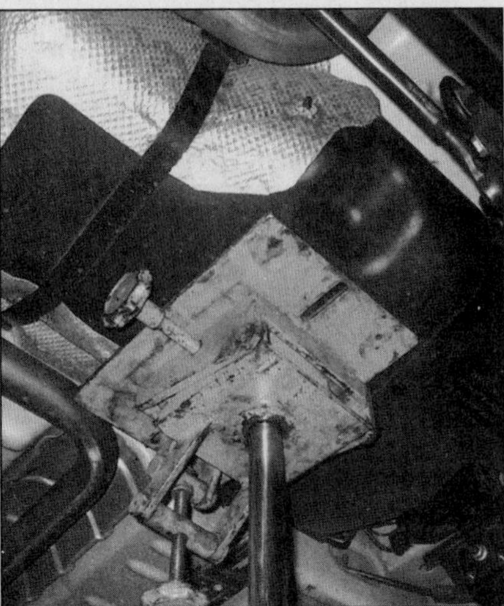

**5.6 Support the tank with a transmission jack (shown) or use a floor jack; if you use a floor jack, put a piece of plywood between the jack head and the fuel tank to protect the tank**

5 Unscrew the fuel pump module locknut with a pair of large water pump pliers or a hammer and brass drift **(see illustrations)**.

6 Carefully withdraw the fuel pump module from the fuel tank **(see illustration)**. Make sure that you don't damage the fuel pump filter or bend the sending unit float arm.

7 If you want to replace either the fuel pump or the fuel level sending unit, you'll have to separate the two components (see Section 8).

8 While the pump is removed, inspect the pump filter (see Section 8). Make sure that it's not clogged or damaged. If the filter is dirty, try washing it in clean solvent. If it's still clogged, replace it.

9 Installation is the reverse of removal. Be sure to tighten the fuel pump module locknut securely.

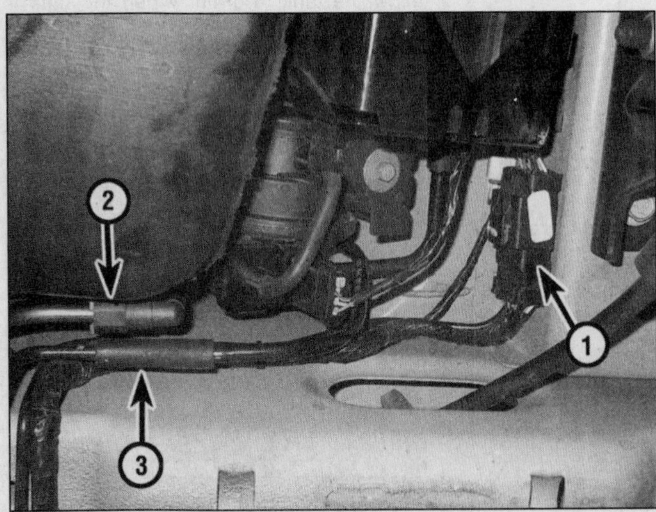


**5.7 Disconnect the electrical connector (1) for the fuel pump module and for the leak detection pump, then disconnect the fuel supply line quick-connect fitting (2) and the EVAP line (3)**

**5.8 To detach the fuel tank, remove these tank strap bolts**

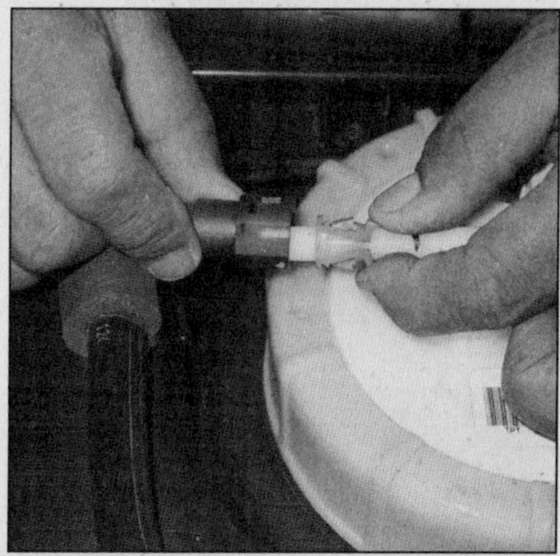

7.3a Squeeze the two locking tabs together and disconnect the fuel supply hose from the pipe on top of the fuel pump module

7.3b To unlock the electrical connector for the fuel pump module, pull out this locking tab

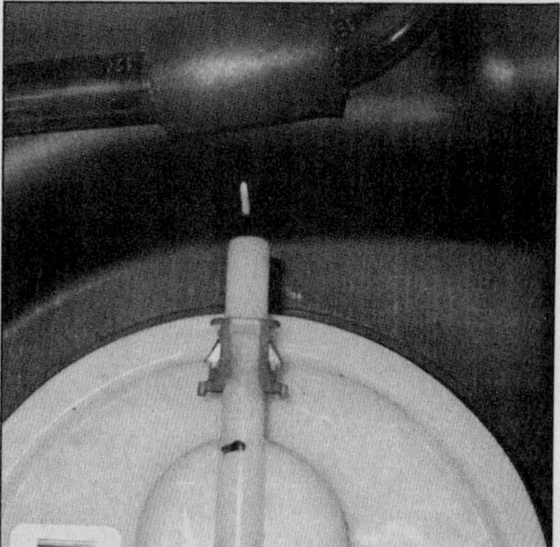

7.4 To ensure that the fuel pump module will be correctly realigned during installation, scribe a mark on the tank right below the fuel outlet pipe

7.5a To remove the fuel pump module on early models, unscrew the locknut with a pair of large water pump pliers

7.5b On later models, loosen the metal lock ring by tapping it counterclockwise with a hammer and brass drift (don't use a steel drift - it can cause sparks)

7.6 Carefully remove the fuel pump module from the fuel tank; be careful not to bend or damage the float level arm

## 8 Fuel level sending unit - removal and installation

### Removal

*Refer to illustrations 8.2, 8.3, 8.4, 8.5 and 8.6*

1 Remove the fuel pump module (see Section 7).

2 Depress the retaining tab **(see illustration)** and detach the electrical connector from the underside of the fuel pump module. **Note:** *The fuel pump module harness on top of the flange is NOT serviceable or removable.*

3 Remove the wedge lock from the electrical connector **(see illustration)**.

4 Using a special terminal remover tool or a suitable similar tool, remove the terminals

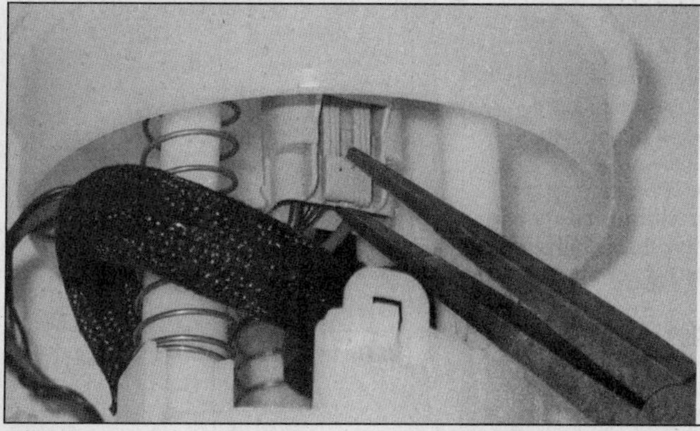

8.2 Depress the retaining tab and detach the electrical connector from the underside of the fuel pump module

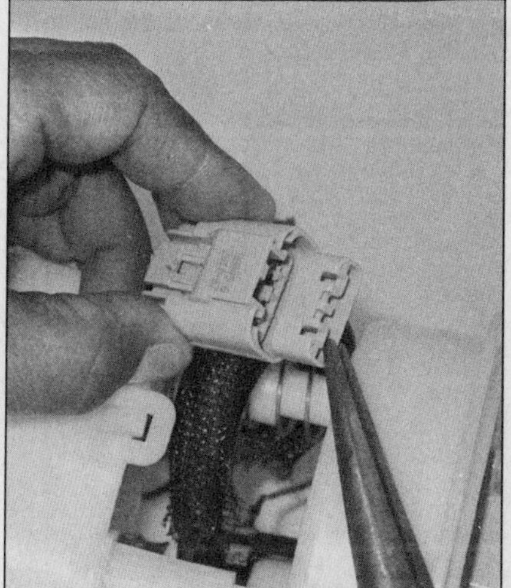

8.3 Remove the wedge lock from the electrical connector

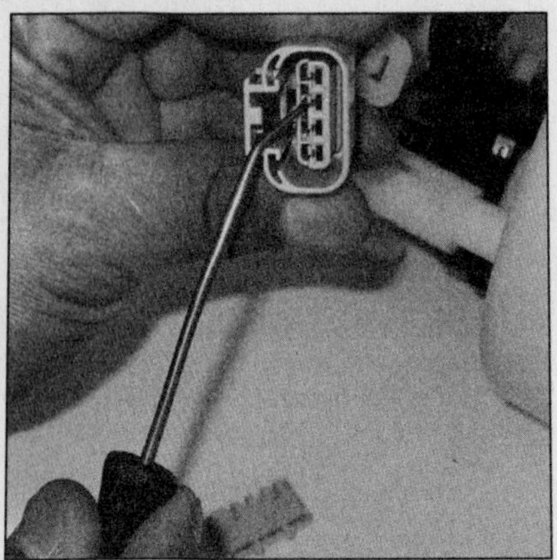

**8.4 Using a special terminal remover tool or a suitable similar tool, remove the terminals from the fuel level sending unit connector**

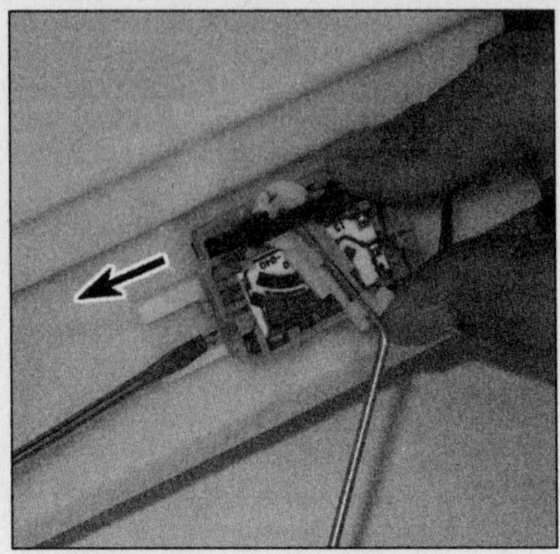

**8.5 Depress this locking tab and slide the fuel level sending unit off the fuel pump module**

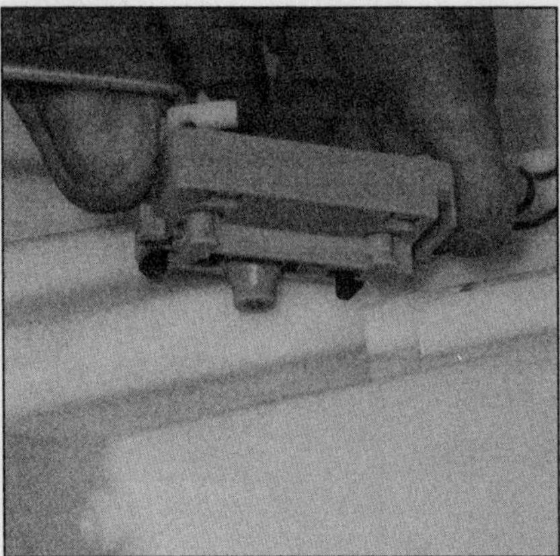

**8.6 Remove the fuel level sending unit from the fuel pump module**

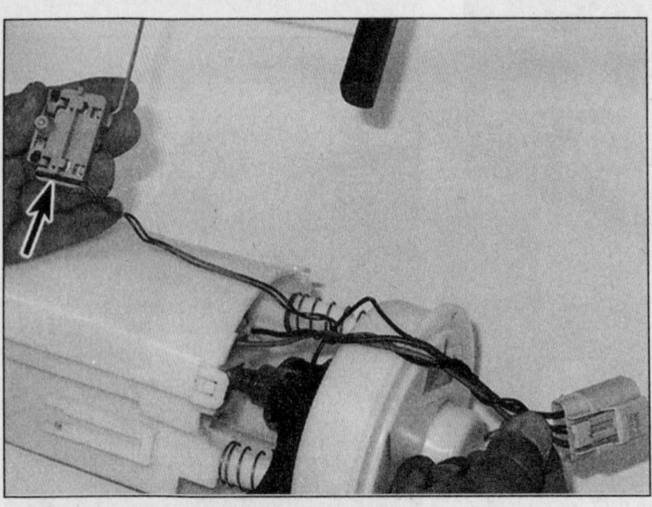

**8.7 Install the leads in the groove in the back of the fuel level sending unit**

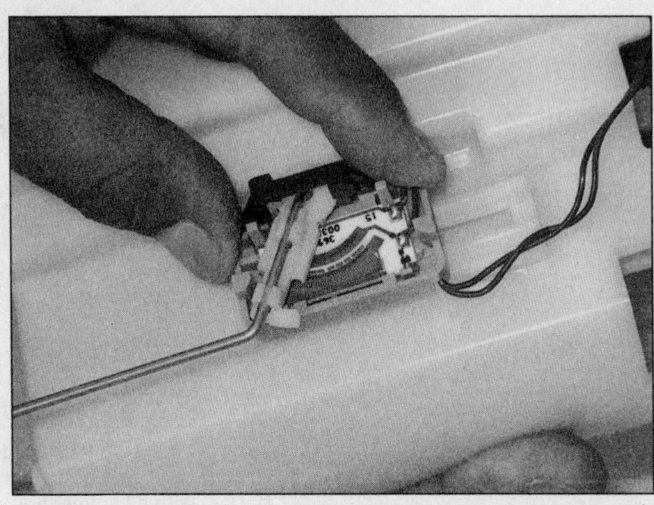

**8.8 Slide the fuel level sending unit up the channel until it snaps into place; make sure that the tab at the bottom of the sending unit locks into place**

from the fuel level sending unit connector **(see illustration)**.

5 Depress the tab and slide the fuel level sending unit toward the bottom of the fuel pump module **(see illustration)**.

6 Slide the fuel level sending unit out of the channel in the fuel pump module **(see illustration)**.

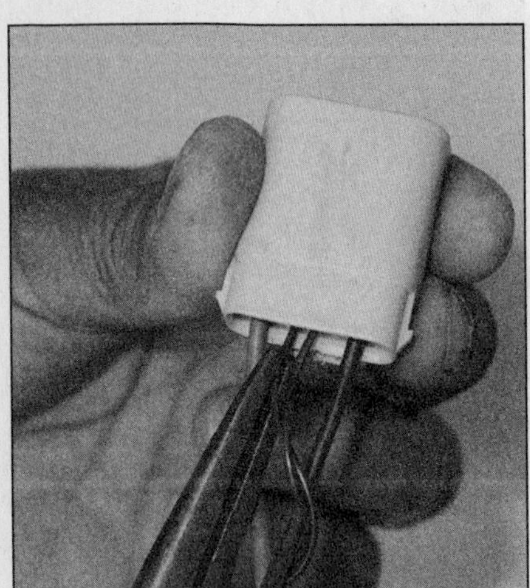

**8.9 Push the sending unit wires up through the connector until they lock into place**

## Installation

*Refer to illustrations 8.7, 8.8. 8.9, 8.10 and 8.11*

7 Install the electrical leads in the groove in the back of the fuel level sending unit **(see illustration)**.

8 Slide the fuel level sending unit up the channel until it snaps into place **(see illustration)**. Make sure that the tab at the bottom of the sending unit locks into place.

9 Push the sending unit wires up through the connector **(see illustration)** until they lock into place. Make sure that the signal and ground wires are installed in the correct position.

10 Install the locking wedge in the connector **(see illustration)**.

11 Push the electrical connector back up into the underside of the fuel pump module **(see illustration)**.

12 Install the fuel pump module (see Section 7).

**8.10 Install the locking wedge in the connector**

## 9 Air filter housing - removal and installation

*Refer to illustrations 9.1, 9.2a, 9.2b, 9.4a and 9.4b*

1 Loosen the clamp **(see illustration)** that secures the air intake duct to the air filter housing cover, then detach the duct from the air cleaner assembly.

2 Release the two air filter housing cover retaining clips and remove the cover **(see illustrations)**.

3 Remove the air filter element (see Chapter 1).

4 To detach the air filter housing assembly, simply pull it straight up and disengage the positioning pins from their grommets **(see illustration)**. The duct between the air filter housing and the hole in the inner fender directs outside air into the air filter housing. This duct **(see illustration)** comes off with the housing.

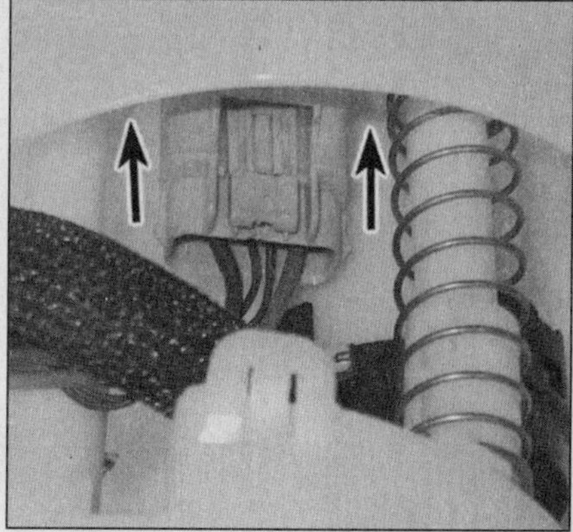

**8.11 Push the electrical connector back up into the underside of the fuel pump module**

5 Inspect the rubber mounting grommets **(see illustration)** for the air filter housing.

6 Installation is the reverse of removal.

**9.1 Loosen this hose clamp and detach the air intake duct from the air filter housing cover**

**9.2a To detach the air filter housing cover, release the two spring clips . . .**

**9.2b . . . and remove the cover**

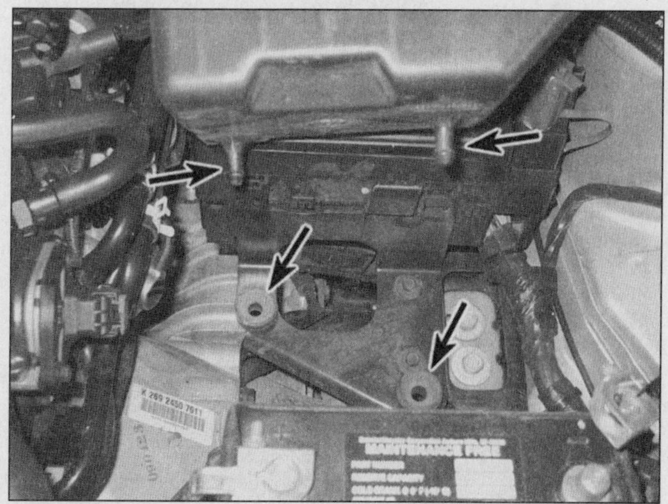

**9.4a To detach the air filter housing, simply pull it straight up and disengage the positioning pins from their grommets**

**9.4b The air intake duct is attached to the air filter housing; when removing the housing, wiggle the air intake duct free from the hole in the inner fender - don't try to detach the duct from the housing**

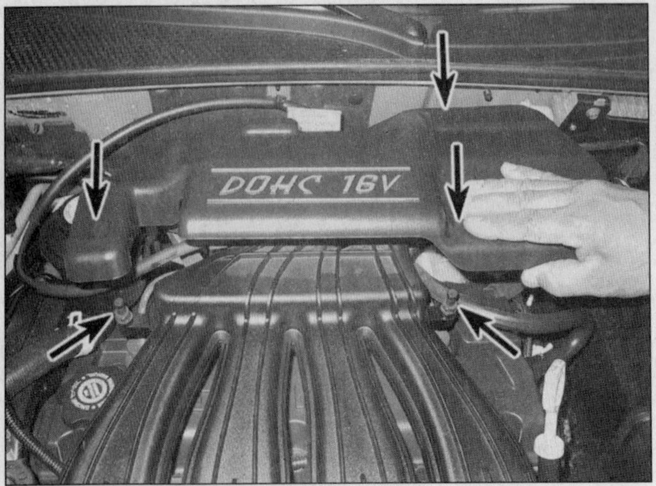


10.1 The throttle body/air intake plenum cover is attached to the plenum by three rubber grommets pushed down onto three positioning pins (rear positioning pin not visible in this photo); to remove the cover, simply pull it straight up

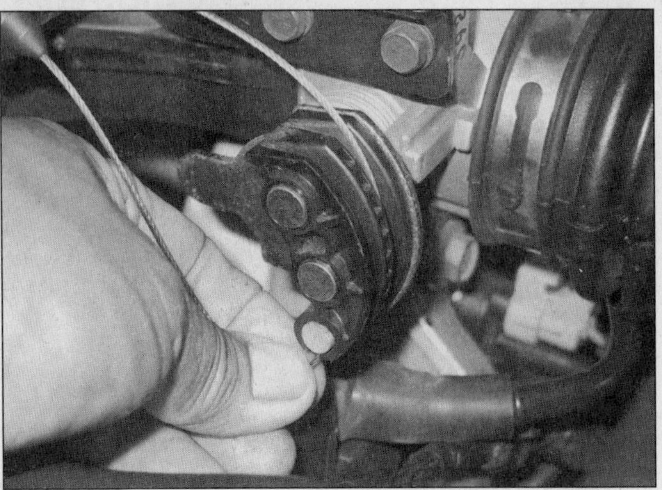

10.2 Pull the accelerator cable forward to put some slack in it, then disengage the cable end plug from its slot in the throttle cam

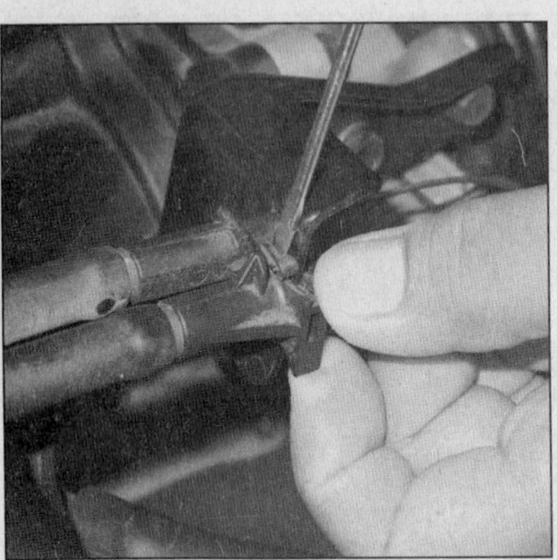

10.3 To disengage the cable retaining tab from its hole in the cable bracket, pry it away from the bracket with a small screwdriver

10.4 Pry open the cable clamp with a small screwdriver

10.5 Reach behind the accelerator pedal, pop the cable retainer (arrow) from the slot in the top of the pedal, then disengage the accelerator cable from the pedal

10.6 To remove the horseshoe-shaped clip that retains the cable grommet at the hole in the firewall, slide the clip straight up

## 10 Accelerator cable - removal and installation

*Refer to illustrations 10.1, 10.2, 10.3, 10.4, 10.5 and 10.6*

1 Remove the throttle body/air intake plenum cover **(see illustration)**.

2 Rotate the throttle lever to the wide-open position and then disengage the accelerator cable from the slot in the throttle lever cam **(see illustration)**.

3 Pry the retaining tab away from the cable bracket with a small screwdriver **(see illustration)** and slide the cable out of the cable bracket.

4 Using a small screwdriver, pop open the cable clamp **(see illustration)** and disengage the cable from the clamp. Note the routing of the cable before proceeding.

5 Inside the vehicle, under the dash, reach behind the accelerator pedal, push the retainer toward the rear of the vehicle **(see illustration)** and disengage the accelerator cable from the slot in the top of the accelerator pedal assembly.

6 Remove the horseshoe-shaped clip that retains the cable grommet to its hole in the firewall **(see illustration)**, pop the cable grommet out of the hole then push the cable through the hole.

7 Installation is the reverse of removal.

## 11 Sequential Fuel Injection (SFI) system - general information

The Sequential Fuel Injection (SFI) system consists of three sub-systems: air intake, electronic control and fuel delivery. The SFI system uses a Powertrain Control Module (PCM) and various information sensors to calculate the correct air/fuel ratio under all operating conditions. The SFI system and the emission control systems are closely linked. For more information on the emission control systems, refer to Chapter 6.

**12.7 Use a stethoscope to listen for the clicking sound that indicates that each injector is working correctly; the clicking sound should rise and fall with changes in engine speed**

**12.9 Using an ohmmeter, measure the resistance across the terminals of each injector with an ohmmeter (intake manifold removed for clarity)**

## Air intake system

The air intake system consists of the air filter housing, the air intake duct, the throttle body, the idle control system and the intake manifold. All models are equipped with a two-piece intake manifold (see Chapter 2A for the removal and installation procedures for the intake manifold).

The throttle body is a single-barrel, side-draft design. A Throttle Position (TP) sensor is attached to the throttle shaft to monitor changes in the throttle opening.

When the engine is idling, the air/fuel ratio is controlled by the idle air control system, which regulates the amount of airflow bypassing the throttle plate. The idle air control system consists of the PCM, the Idle Air Control (IAC) valve and various sensors such as the Engine Coolant Temperature (ECT) sensor, the Throttle Position (TP) sensor and the Manifold Absolute Pressure (MAP) sensor. The IAC valve is controlled by the PCM in accordance with the running conditions of the engine (air conditioning on, power steering demand, cold or warm temperature, etc.).

## Electronic control system

For information on the electronic control system, the Powertrain Control Module (PCM) and sensors, refer to Chapter 6.

## Fuel delivery system

The fuel delivery system consists of the fuel filter/fuel pump/fuel pressure regulator assembly, the fuel supply line connecting the fuel pump to the fuel rail, the fuel pulsation damper, the fuel rail and the fuel injectors.

The electric fuel pump is located inside the fuel tank. Fuel is drawn through a filter into the pump, flows through the fuel line and then to the fuel rail, from which it's sprayed by the injectors into the intake ports. The fuel pressure regulator, which is an integral part of the fuel pump module inside the tank, maintains a constant fuel pressure to the fuel rail and injectors. The fuel pulsation damper, which is located at the connection between the metal fuel supply line and the engine compartment fuel supply hose at the firewall, dampens the pressure pulses from the fuel pump.

Each injector consists of a solenoid coil, a pintle valve and the housing. When current is applied to the solenoid by the PCM, the pintle valve raises off its seat and the pressurized fuel inside the housing squirts out the nozzle. The amount of fuel injected is determined by the length of time that the pintle valve is open, which is determined by the length of time during which current is supplied to the solenoid. Because the injector on-time determines the air-fuel mixture ratio, injector timing must be very precise.

## 12 Fuel injection system - check

*Refer to illustrations 12.7 and 12.9*

**Warning:** *Gasoline is extremely flammable, so take extra precautions when you work on any part of the fuel system. See the* **Warning** *in Section 2.*

1 Inspect all system electrical connectors, especially the ground connections. Loose connectors and poor grounds are a common cause of many engine control system problems.

2 Verify that the battery is fully charged. The Powertrain Control Module (PCM) and sensors don't operate correctly without adequate supply voltage.

3 Inspect the air filter element (see Chapter 1). A dirty or partially blocked filter reduces performance and economy.

4 Check fuel pump operation (see Section 3). If the fuel pump fuse is blown, replace it and note whether it blows again. If it does, look for a short in the wiring harness to the fuel pump (see wiring diagrams in Chapter 12).

5 Inspect all vacuum hoses connected to the intake manifold for damage, deterioration and leakage.

6 Remove the air intake duct from the throttle body and look for dirt, carbon, varnish, or other residue inside the throttle body bore, particularly around the throttle plate. If it's dirty, refer to Chapter 6 and troubleshoot the PCV system for the cause of the excessive residue

7 With the engine running, place an automotive stethoscope against each injector **(see illustration)** and listen for a clicking sound, which indicates that the injector is operating. If you don't have a stethoscope, you can place the tip of a long screwdriver against the injector and listen through the handle.

8 Remove the intake manifold (see Chapter 2A).

9 With the engine off and the fuel injector electrical connectors disconnected, measure the resistance of each injector with an ohmmeter **(see illustration)**. Refer to the Specifications at the beginning of this Chapter for the correct resistance.

10 Refer to Chapter 6 for other system checks.

## 13 Throttle body - inspection, removal and installation

**Warning:** *Gasoline is extremely flammable, so take extra precautions when you work on any part of the fuel system. See the* **Warning** *in Section 2.*

### Inspection

*Refer to illustrations 13.3a and 13.3b*

1 Remove the throttle body/air intake plenum cover **(see illustration 10.1)**.

2 Verify that the throttle linkage operates smoothly. If it doesn't, examine the routing of the accelerator cable.

3 Remove the air intake duct from the throttle body and inspect the area around and

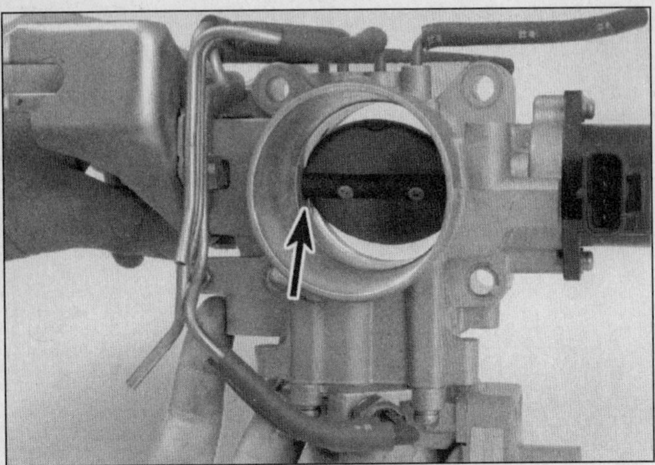

13.3a The area inside the throttle body behind the throttle plate (arrow) suffers from sludge build-up because of vapors vented into the throttle body by the PCV hose from the crankcase (throttle body removed for clarity)

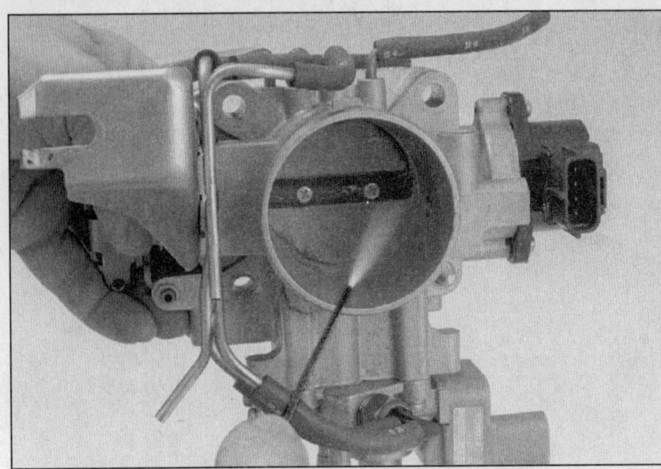

13.3b With the engine off, use aerosol carburetor cleaner (make sure it's approved for use with catalytic converters and oxygen sensors), a toothbrush and a rag to clean the throttle body; be sure to open the throttle plate and clean behind it

13.6 To remove the air intake duct, loosen the hose clamps at each end

13.7a Disconnect the electrical connector from the Intake Air Temperature sensor . . .

behind the throttle plate for carbon and residue build-up. If it's dirty, clean it with aerosol carburetor cleaner and a tooth brush. Make sure that the can specifically states that it is safe with oxygen sensor systems and catalytic converters **(see illustrations)**. **Caution:** *Do not clean the Throttle Position (TP) sensor or the Idle Air Control (IAC) valve with solvent.*

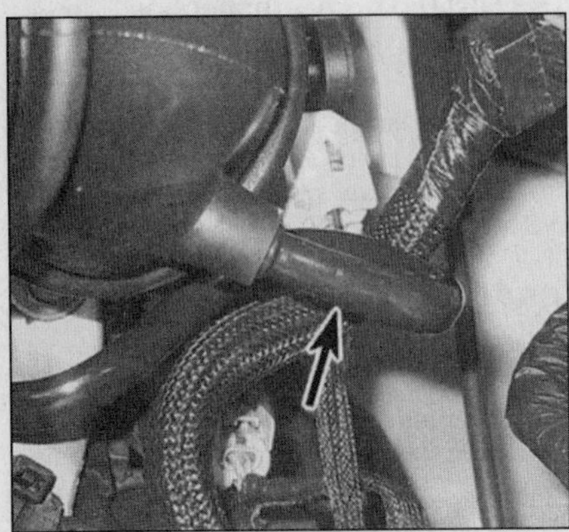

13.7b . . . and disconnect the make-up air hose from the air intake duct

## Removal and installation

*Refer to illustrations 13.6, 13.7a, 13.7b, 13.9, 13.10, 13.13, 13.14 and 13.15*

**Warning:** *Wait until the engine is completely cool before beginning this procedure.*

4 Disconnect the cable from the negative terminal of the battery (see Chapter 5).

5 Remove the throttle body/air intake plenum cover **(see illustration 10.1)**.

6 Loosen the hose clamps at the throttle body and at the air cleaner housing **(see illustration)**.

7 Disconnect the electrical connector from the Intake Air Temperature sensor, then disconnect the make-up air hose from the air intake duct **(see illustrations)**. Remove the intake duct.

8 Disconnect the accelerator cable from the throttle lever and from the cable bracket (see Section 10).

9 Disconnect the cruise control cable, if equipped, from the throttle lever and from the cable bracket. The cruise control cable is attached to the throttle lever the same way as the accelerator cable and can be removed from the cable bracket and from the cable clamp after the accelerator cable has been removed **(see illustration)**.

10 Disconnect the EVAP purge hose **(see illustration)** from the throttle body.

11 Disconnect the Idle Air Control (IAC) motor electrical connector **(see illustration 13.10)**.

12 Disconnect the Throttle Position (TP) sensor electrical connector **(see illustration 13.10)**.

13 Remove the two cable bracket bolts **(see illustration)** and then remove the cable bracket from the throttle body.

14 Unscrew the mounting bolts **(see illustration)** and remove the throttle body.

15 Remove the throttle body gasket **(see illustration)**. Replace it if it isn't in perfect condition.

16 Installation is the reverse of removal. Be sure to tighten the throttle body bolts to the torque listed in this Chapter's Specifications.

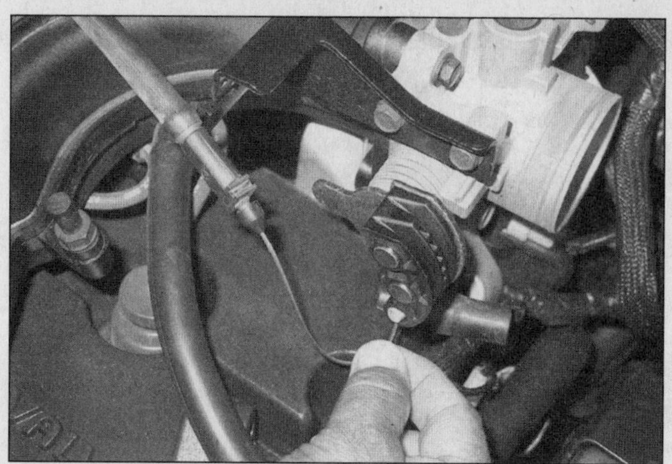

13.9 After disconnecting the accelerator cable from the throttle cam, disconnect the cruise control cable (if equipped) by disengaging the plug on the end of the cable from its slot in the cam

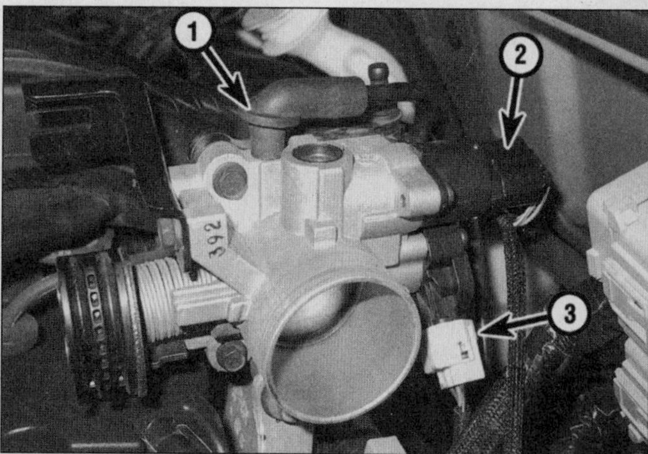


13.10 Disconnect the EVAP purge hose (1), the Idle Air Control (IAC) motor electrical connector (2) and the Throttle Position (TP) sensor electrical connector (3)

## 14 Fuel pressure regulator - removal and installation

The fuel pressure regulator is an integral component of the fuel pump module. It cannot be serviced separately. If the pressure regulator must be replaced, you will have to replace the fuel pump module (see Section 7).

## 15 Fuel rail and injectors - removal and installation

*Refer to illustrations 15.7, 15.8a, 15.8b, 15.9 and 15.11*

**Warning 1:** *Gasoline is extremely flammable, so take extra precautions when you work on any part of the fuel system. See the* **Warning** *in Section 2.*

**Warning 2:** *Wait until the engine is completely cool before beginning this procedure.*

1 Relieve system fuel pressure (see Section 2).

13.13 Remove the bolts and detach the cable bracket from the throttle body

13.14 Unscrew the mounting bolts and remove the throttle body

2 Disconnect the cable from the negative terminal of the battery (see Chapter 5).

3 Drain the engine coolant (see Chapter 1).

4 Remove the throttle body/air intake plenum cover **(see illustration 10.1)**.

5 Remove the upper intake manifold (see Chapter 2A).

6 Remove the upper radiator hose.

7 Disconnect the fuel supply line from the fuel rail **(see illustration)**.

13.15 Remove the throttle body gasket

15.7 To disconnect the fuel supply hose from the fuel rail, squeeze the two tabs on the quick-connect fitting together and pull up on the fitting

**15.8a To disconnect each fuel injector electrical connector, push up on the lock . . .**

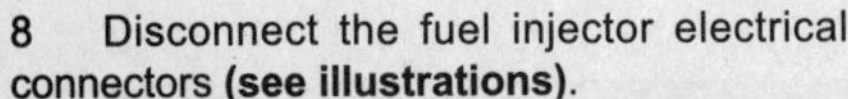

**15.8b . . . then squeeze the tab (on the same side of the connector as the lock) and pull up**

**15.9 To detach the fuel rail, remove these two bolts**

8 Disconnect the fuel injector electrical connectors **(see illustrations)**.

9 Remove the fuel rail bolts **(see illustration)**.

10 *Carefully* pull up on the fuel rail to disengage the injectors from their respective bores in the intake manifold, then remove the fuel rail and injectors. The injectors might initially stick in their bores, but they'll pull free when sufficient force is applied.

11 Remove the injector retaining clips and detach the injectors from the fuel rail **(see illustration)**. Again, the injectors might initially stick to their bores, but if you pull and wiggle them, they will come out.

12 Remove the O-rings from each injector **(see illustration 15.11)**. Discard these pieces and replace them with new O-rings and a new grommet.

13 Installation is the reverse of removal. Be sure to tighten the fuel rail retaining bolts to the torque listed in this Chapter's Specifications.

14 Refill and bleed the cooling system (see Chapter 1).

15 When you're done, start the engine and check for leaks at the fuel supply hose fitting at the fuel rail and at each injector.

## 16 Exhaust system servicing - general information

*Refer to illustration 16.1*

**Warning:** *Inspection and repair of exhaust system components should be done only after the system components have cooled completely.*

1 The exhaust system consists of the exhaust manifolds, the catalytic converters, the muffler, the tailpipe and all connecting pipes, brackets, hangers and clamps. The exhaust system is attached to the body with mounting brackets and rubber hangers **(see illustration)**. If any of these parts are damaged or deteriorated, excessive noise and vibration will be transmitted to the body.

2 Conducting regular inspections of the exhaust system will keep it safe and quiet. Look for any damaged or bent parts, open seams, holes, loose connections, excessive corrosion or other defects which could allow exhaust fumes to enter the vehicle. Pay particular attention to rubber exhaust hangers. Because they're subjected to constant exhaust heat, they dry out, break down, develop cracks and then tear apart, allowing the exhaust system to hang unsupported. Sometimes an unsupported exhaust system "clunks" when the vehicle is driven over bumps and dips in the road; sometimes the exhaust touches the axle or other metal parts, which produces an annoying vibration at certain speeds.

3 If the exhaust system components are extremely corroded or rusted together, they will probably have to be cut from the exhaust system. The convenient way to accomplish this is to have a muffler repair shop remove the corroded sections with a cutting torch. If, however, you want to save money by doing it yourself and you don't have an oxy/acetylene welding outfit with a cutting torch, simply cut off the old components with a hack-saw. If you have compressed air, special pneumatic cutting chisels can also be used. If you do decide to tackle the job at home, be sure to wear eye protection to protect your eyes from metal chips and work gloves to protect your hands.

4 Here are some simple guidelines to apply when repairing the exhaust system:

a) *Work from the back to the front when removing exhaust system components.*

b) *Apply penetrating oil to the exhaust system component fasteners to make them easier to remove.*

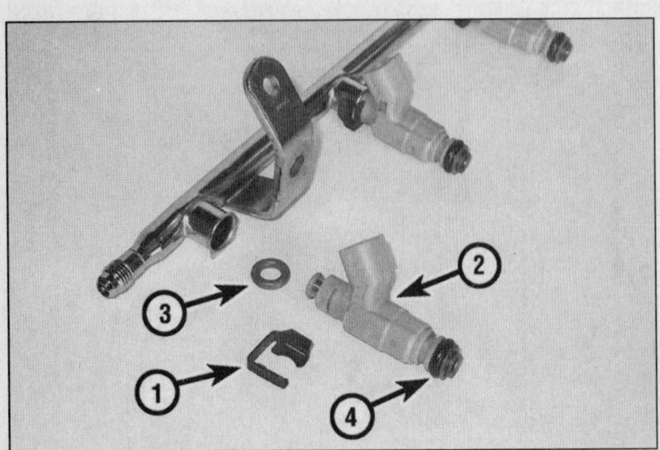


**15.11 To disassemble the fuel rail assembly, pull off each retaining clip (1), pull out the injector (2) and remove the O-rings (3 and 4)**

**16.1 A typical rubber exhaust hanger; inspect all rubber hangers regularly, and anytime you have to raise the vehicle to service any under-vehicle component**

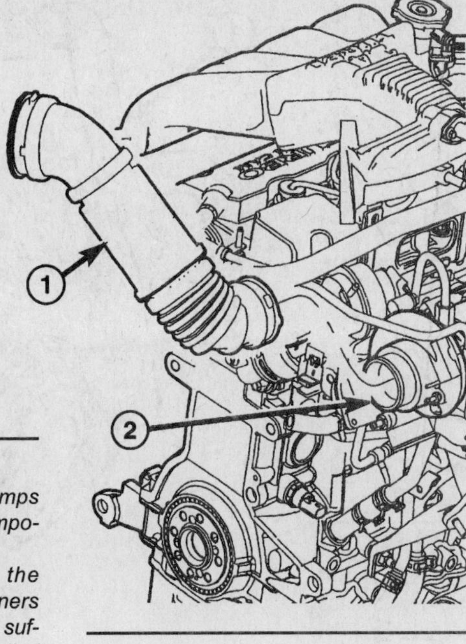


**18.4 Turbocharger clean air intake duct assembly details**

1 *Clean air intake duct*
2 *Turbocharger*

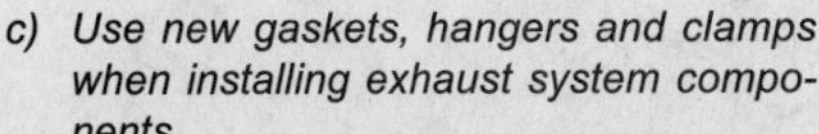

c) *Use new gaskets, hangers and clamps when installing exhaust system components.*

d) *Apply anti-seize compound to the threads of all exhaust system fasteners during reassembly. Be sure to allow sufficient clearance between newly installed parts and all points on the underbody to avoid overheating the floor pan and possibly damaging the interior carpet and insulation. Pay particularly close attention to the catalytic converter and its heat shield.* **Warning:** *The catalytic converter operates at very high temperatures and takes a long time to cool. Wait until it's completely cool before attempting to remove the converter. Failure to do so could result in serious burns.*

## 17 Turbocharger - general information and inspection

### General information

1 A turbocharger pressurizes the air entering the engine. Pressurizing the incoming air increases its density, which means more fuel can be injected into the cylinders, which produces more horsepower and even compensates somewhat for high-altitude driving by mitigating the effects of thinner (less dense) air at higher altitudes.

2 The turbocharger consists of a housing with a pair of turbines inside. The turbines are on opposite ends of the same shaft, but each turbine is isolated inside its own separate enclosure. One turbine, which is located in the exhaust system just below the exhaust manifold, is driven by hot exhaust gases on their way to the exhaust system. When the exhaust turbine spins, it turns the shaft, which spins the other turbine, known as the "impeller," on the other end of the shaft. The impeller, which is located in the intake system, compresses the air entering the engine.

3 When the air is compressed it heats up, so it is routed through a heat exchanger, known as the "charge air cooler," to remove the heat. Cooler air is denser, which promotes combustion efficiency, increases power and reduces emissions.

4 The amount of "boost" (intake manifold pressure) is regulated by a "wastegate" which prevents over-boosting at higher engine speeds. The wastegate is operated by a spring-loaded actuator assembly which controls the maximum boost level by allowing a certain amount of exhaust gas to bypass the turbine in accordance with the intake manifold pressure.

5 The turbocharger is cooled by engine coolant, which is delivered to the turbo by a supply line from the engine block. A coolant return line connects the turbo to heater tubes.

### Inspection

6 Though it's a relatively simple device, the turbocharger is a precision component. Special tools are needed to disassemble and overhaul a turbocharger, so servicing should be left to a dealer service department. However, you can inspect some things yourself, such as a cracked turbo mounting flange, a worn out or overheated turbine/compressor shaft bearing or a defective wastegate.

7 A turbocharger has its own distinctive sound, so a change in the quality or the quantity of noise can be a sign of potential problems. Before assuming that a funny sound is caused by a defective turbocharger, inspect the exhaust manifold for cracks and loose connections. For example, a high-pitched or whistling sound might indicate an intake air or exhaust gas leak. Inspect the turbocharger mounting flange at the exhaust manifold and make sure that the hose clamp that attaches the air intake duct to the turbocharger is tight.

8 If an unusual sound is coming from the turbocharger, allow the engine to cool completely, then remove the intake duct between the air cleaner housing and the turbocharger. Reach inside the housing and turn the compressor wheel to make sure it spins freely. If it doesn't, it's possible the turbo lubricating oil has sludged or coked up from overheating. Push in on the turbine wheel and check for binding. The turbine should rotate freely with no binding or rubbing on the housing. If it does, the turbine or compressor shaft bearing is worn out. **Warning:** *Inspect the turbocharger with the engine off and cool to the touch. Touching or reaching inside a hot and/or operating turbocharger can cause serious injury.*

9 The turbocharger is lubricated by engine oil that has been pressurized, cooled and filtered. Oil is delivered to the turbocharger by a supply line that is tapped into a lubrication passage in the engine block. Oil travels to the turbocharger's bearing housing, where it lubricates the shaft and bearings. A return line at the bottom of the bearing housing routes the engine oil back to the crankcase. Because the turbine and compressor wheels spin at speeds up to 140,000 rpm, severe damage can result from the interruption or contamination of the oil supply to the turbocharger bearings. Burned oil on the turbine housing is a sign of a blocked return line. **Caution:** *Whenever a major engine bearing such as a main, connecting rod or camshaft bearing is replaced, flush the turbocharger oil passages with clean oil.*

## 18 Turbocharger - removal and installation

**Warning:** *Wait until the engine is completely cool before beginning this procedure.*
**Caution:** *The turbocharger is a precision component which has been assembled and balanced to very fine tolerances. Do not disassemble it or try to repair it. Turbochargers should only be overhauled or repaired by authorized turbocharger repair facilities. An incorrectly assembled turbocharger could result in damage to the turbocharger and/or the engine.*

### Removal

*Refer to illustrations 18.4, 18.7, 18.8, 18.10, 18.12, 18.13 and 18.20*

1 Disconnect the cable from the negative terminal of the battery (see Chapter 5).

2 Drain the cooling system (see Chapter 1).

3 Remove the air filter housing (see Section 9).

4 Loosen the hose clamp and disconnect the clean air intake duct from the turbocharger **(see illustration)**.

5 Disconnect the accelerator cable from the throttle lever at the throttle body **(see illustration 10.2)** and disconnect the cruise control cable, if equipped, from the throttle lever **(see illustration 13.9)**.

6 Disconnect the electrical connectors from the Intake Air Temperature (IAT) sensor, the Manifold Absolute Pressure (MAP) sensor, the Idle Air Control (IAC) motor, the Throttle Position (TP) sensor and the upstream oxygen sensor (see Chapter 6).

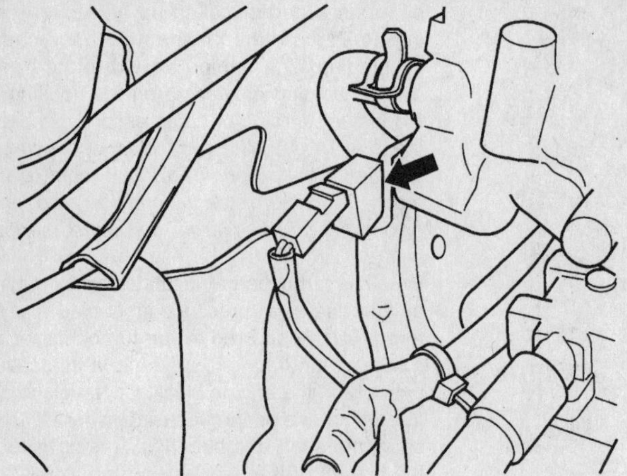

18.7 Disconnect the electrical connector from the ignition coil capacitor

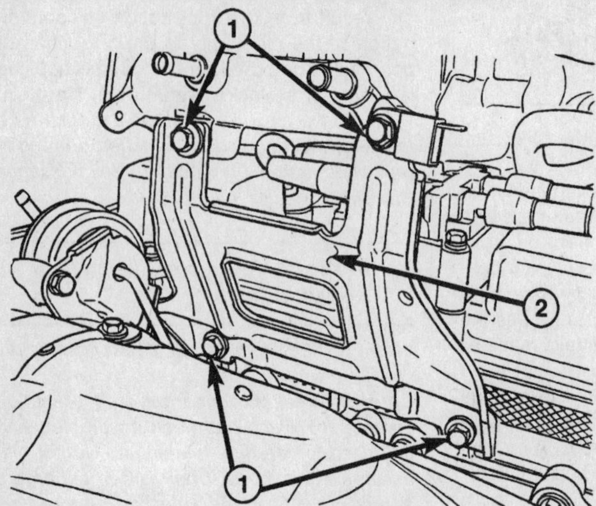


18.10 Remove these four bolts (1) and remove the upper intake manifold support bracket (2)

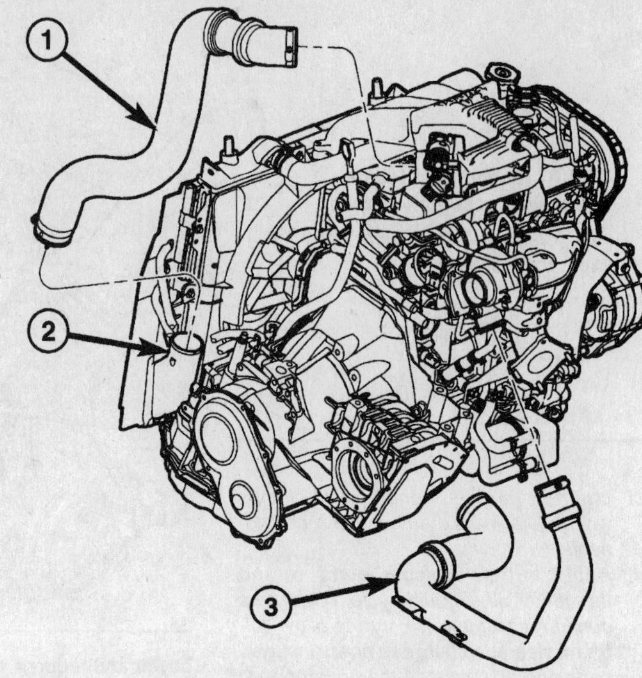


18.8 Air intake duct details

1. *Charge air cooler-to-throttle body air intake duct*
2. *Charge air cooler*
3. *Turbocharger-to-charge air cooler air intake duct*

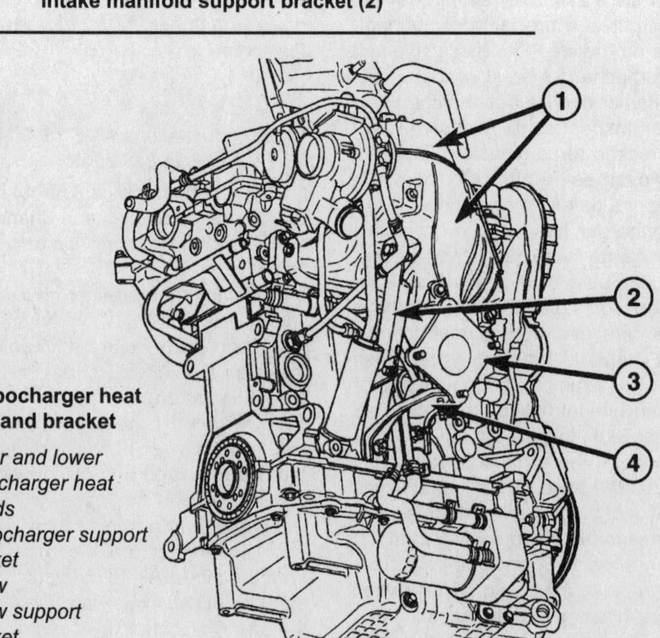


18.12 Turbocharger heat shields and bracket

1. *Upper and lower turbocharger heat shields*
2. *Turbocharger support bracket*
3. *Elbow*
4. *Elbow support bracket*

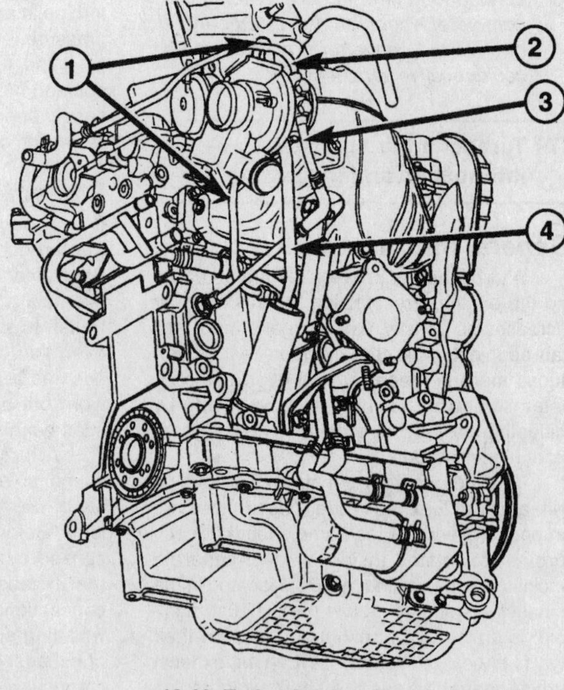


18.13 Turbocharger oil and coolant lines

1. *Oil supply line*
2. *Coolant return line*
3. *Coolant supply line*
4. *Oil return line*

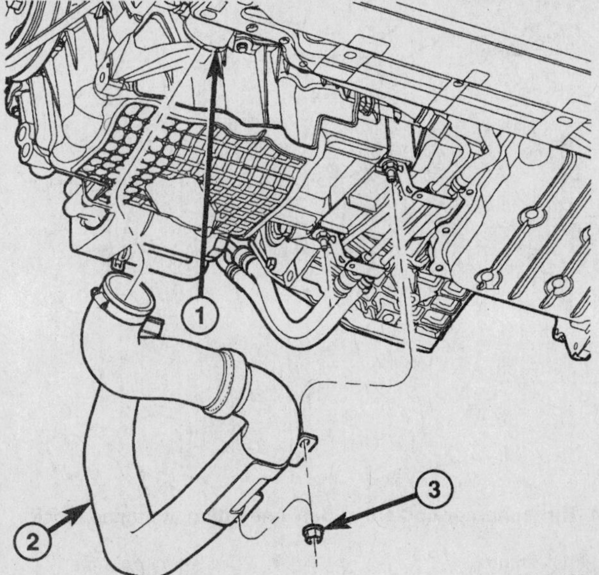


**18.20 Turbocharger-to-charge air cooler duct**

1 *Charge air cooler*
2 *Turbocharger-to-charge air cooler intake duct*
3 *Duct retaining nut*

**18.32 Exhaust manifold bolt tightening sequence (turbocharged models)**

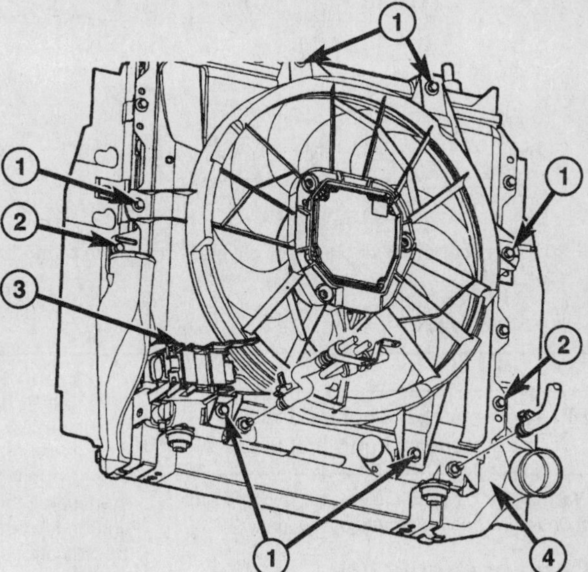


**19.8 Charge air cooler assembly details**

1 *Radiator fan and shroud fasteners*
2 *Charge air cooler fasteners*
3 *Radiator fan electrical connector*
4 *Charge air cooler*

7 Disconnect the electrical connector from the ignition coil capacitor **(see illustration)**.

8 Disconnect the air intake duct at the throttle body **(see illustration)**.

9 Clearly label and disconnect the vacuum hoses from the throttle body and from the intake manifold.

10 Remove the upper intake manifold support bracket **(see illustration)**.

11 Remove the upper part of the air intake manifold (see Chapter 2A). **Caution:** *Cover the intake passages in the lower half of the intake manifold to prevent dirt and debris from entering the engine.*

12 Remove the upper turbocharger heat shield **(see illustration)**.

13 Disconnect the oil supply line from the turbocharger **(see illustration)**.

14 Disconnect the coolant return line **(see illustration 18.13)**.

15 Clearly label and then disconnect the vacuum hoses from the turbocharger assembly.

16 Raise the vehicle and place it securely on jackstands.

17 Disconnect the muffler ground strap, then remove the muffler.

18 Disconnect the electrical connector from the downstream oxygen sensor (see Chapter 6).

19 Remove the nuts that attach the catalytic converter to the exhaust manifold flange, then remove the catalytic converter and the intermediate pipe as a single assembly (see Chapter 6).

20 Remove the turbocharger-to-charge air cooler duct **(see illustration)**.

21 Remove the turbocharger elbow support bracket and the turbocharger support bracket **(see illustration 18.12)**.

22 Remove the oil return line **(see illustration 18.13)**.

23 Remove the turbocharger coolant supply line **(see illustration 18.13)**.

24 Remove the lower turbocharger heat shield **(see illustration 18.12)**.

25 Remove the turbocharger elbow **(see illustration 18.12)**.

26 Remove the four lower exhaust manifold fasteners.

27 Lower the vehicle.

28 Remove the six upper exhaust manifold fasteners.

29 Remove the turbocharger/exhaust manifold assembly from above, between the engine and the firewall.

30 Remove and discard the old exhaust manifold gasket.

## Installation

*Refer to illustration 18.32*

**Note:** *When replacing the Turbocharger, the oil return tube should be cleaned and replacement of the oil pressure feed line is recommended.*

31 Install a new gasket.

32 Place the turbocharger/exhaust manifold assembly in position, install the fasteners and then, starting at the center and working your way out toward the ends of the manifold in the indicated sequence **(see illustration)**, gradually and evenly tighten the fasteners to the torque listed in this Chapter's Specifications.

33 The remainder of installation is the reverse of removal.

34 Refill and bleed the cooling system (see Chapter 1).

## 19 Charge air cooler (turbocharged models) - removal and installation

*Refer to illustration 19.8*

**Warning:** *Wait until the engine is completely cool before beginning this procedure.*

1 Drain the cooling system (see Chapter 1).

2 Remove the air filter housing (see Section 9).

3 Remove the battery, the battery tray and the battery tray support bracket (see Chapter 5).

4 Remove the grille (see Chapter 11).

5 Remove the upper radiator crossmember and the center support bracket (see *Radiator - removal and installation* in Chapter 3).

6 Remove the front bumper (see Chapter 11).

7 Loosen the hose clamps for both ducts at the charge air cooler, then disconnect the ducts **(see illustrations 18.8 and 18.20)**.

8 Remove the radiator fan and shroud assembly (see Chapter 3), then remove the charge air cooler fasteners **(see illustration)**.

9 Remove the radiator (see Chapter 3).

10 Remove the charge air cooler.

11 Installation is the reverse of removal.

12 Refill and bleed the cooling system (see Chapter 1).

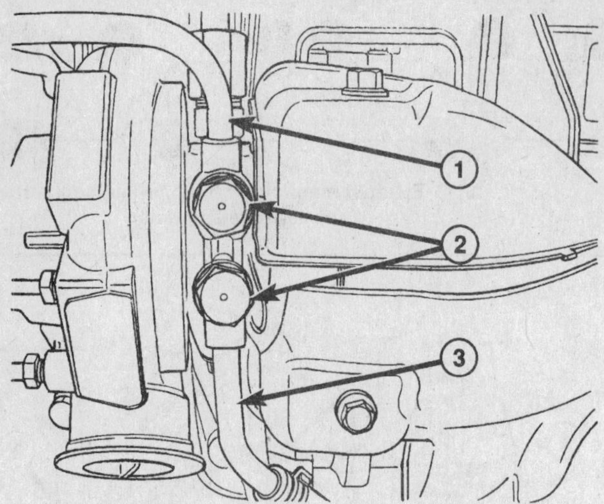


20.3 Turbocharger coolant supply and return line banjo bolts

1 Coolant return line
2 Banjo bolts
3 Coolant supply line

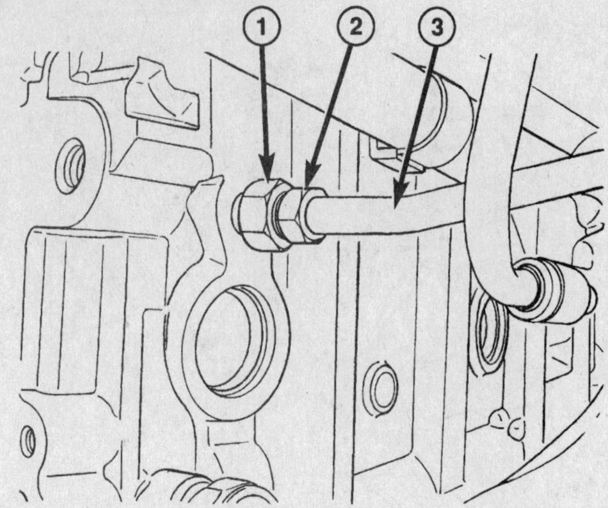


20.4 Turbocharger coolant supply line fitting at engine block

1 Brass fitting
2 Flared fitting
3 Coolant supply line

## 20 Turbocharger coolant and oil lines - removal and installation

**Warning:** *Wait until the engine is completely cool before beginning this procedure.*

### Coolant supply line

*Refer to illustrations 20.3 and 20.4*

1 Raise the vehicle and place it securely on jackstands.

2 Drain the cooling system (see Chapter 1).

3 Remove the banjo bolt from the coolant supply line at the turbocharger **(see illustration)**. Discard the old sealing washers.

4 Unscrew the coolant supply line flared fitting from the brass fitting at the engine block **(see illustration)**.

5 Remove the coolant supply line.

6 If you removed the brass fitting from the block, apply thread sealant to the threads, then install the brass fitting into the block and tighten it to the torque listed in this Chapter's Specifications.

7 Place the coolant supply line in position. Using new washers on the banjo bolt, hand-start - but don't tighten - the banjo bolt to secure the line.

8 Screw the flared fitting at the other end of the coolant supply line onto the brass fitting at the engine block.

9 Tighten the banjo bolt to the torque listed in this Chapter's Specifications. Tighten the flared fitting securely.

10 Installation is otherwise the reverse of removal. Refill and bleed the cooling system (see Chapter 1).

### Coolant return line

*Refer to illustrations 20.13 and 20.15*

11 Drain the cooling system (see Chapter 1).

12 Remove the air filter housing (see Section 9).

13 Disconnect the Intake Air Temperature (IAT) sensor and the Throttle Inlet Pressure (TIP) hose from the charge air cooler duct **(see illustration)**.

14 Loosen the air intake duct clamp at the throttle body **(see illustration 18.8)**, then disconnect the charge air cooler duct from the

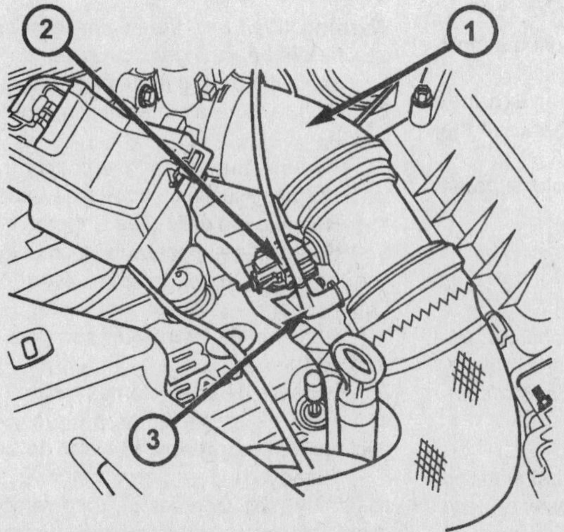


20.13 Intake Air Temperature (IAT) sensor (turbocharged models)

1 Charge air cooler-to-throttle body duct
2 Intake Air Temperature (IAT) sensor
3 Throttle Inlet Pressure (TIP) hose

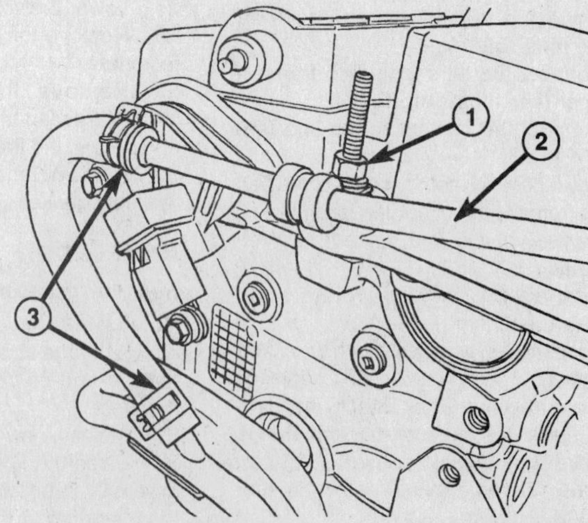


20.15 Turbocharger coolant return line bracket

1 Nut
2 Coolant return line
3 Hose clamps

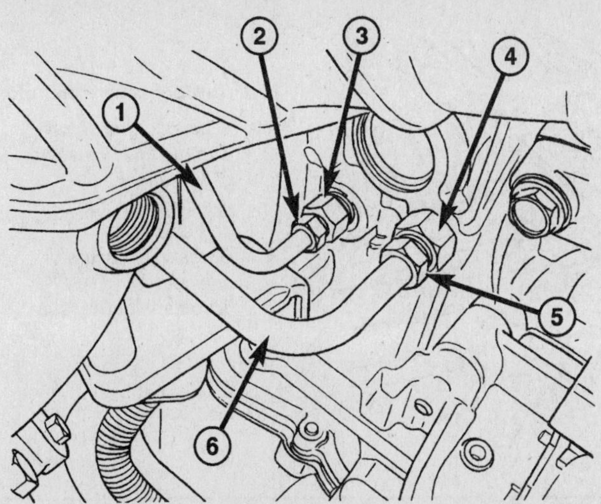


20.23 Turbocharger oil supply line and oil cooler coolant line fittings

1 Oil supply line
2 Flared fitting
3 Brass fitting
4 Brass fitting
5 Flared fitting
6 Oil cooler coolant line

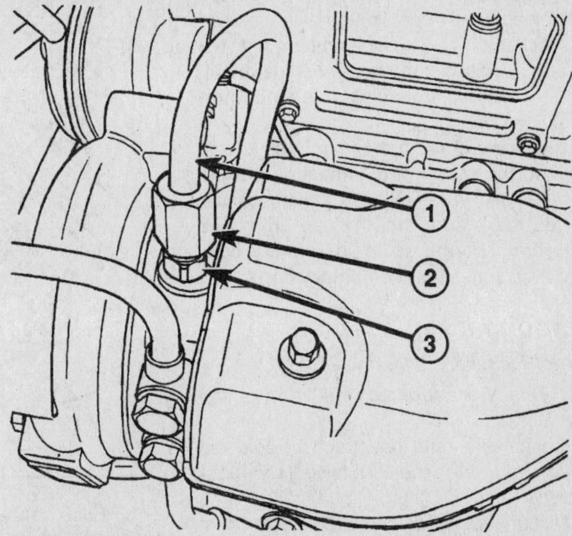


20.25 Turbocharger oil supply line fitting at turbocharger

1 Oil supply line
2 Flared fitting
3 Brass fitting

throttle body and place the duct out of the way.

15 Remove the nut that attaches the coolant return line bracket to the cylinder head cover stud **(see illustration)**.

16 Remove the hose clamp from the coolant return line at the heater tube **(see illustration 20.15)**.

17 Remove the banjo bolt from the coolant return line at the turbocharger **(see illustration 20.3)**. Discard the old sealing washers.

18 Remove the coolant return line.

19 Place the coolant return line in position. Using new washers on the banjo bolt, hand-start - but don't tighten - the banjo bolt to secure the line. Connect the hose to the heater tube and install the hose clamp. Tighten the banjo bolt to the torque listed in this Chapter's Specifications.

20 Installation is otherwise the reverse of removal. Refill and bleed the cooling system (see Chapter 1).

## Oil supply line

*Refer to illustrations 20.23 and 20.25*

21 Raise the vehicle and place it securely on jackstands.

22 Remove the elbow support bracket **(see illustration 18.12)**.

23 Unscrew the oil supply line flared fitting from the brass fitting at the engine block **(see illustration)**.

24 Lower the vehicle.

25 Unscrew the oil supply line flared fitting from the brass fitting at the turbocharger **(see illustration)**.

26 Remove the oil supply line.

27 If you removed the brass fitting from the block, apply thread sealant to the threads, install the fitting into the block and tighten it to the torque listed in this Chapter's Specifications.

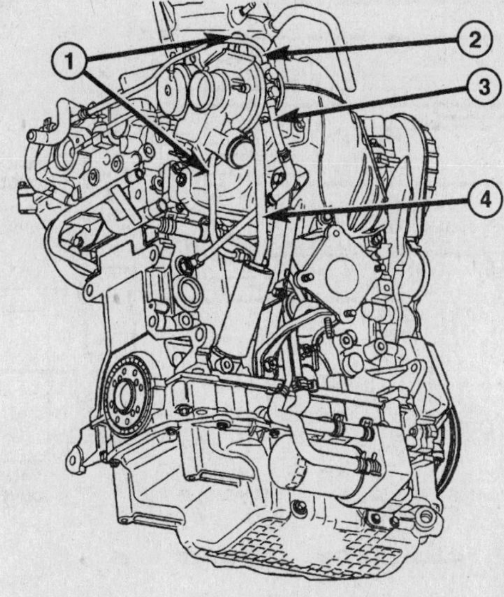


20.37 Turbocharger coolant and oil lines and hoses

1 Oil supply line
2 Coolant return line
3 Coolant supply line
4 Oil return line

28 Place the oil supply line in position. Screw the flared fitting at the end of the oil supply line onto the brass fitting at the turbocharger.

29 Raise the vehicle and place it securely on jackstands.

30 Screw the flared fitting at the other end of the oil supply line onto the brass fitting at the engine block.

31 Tighten the flared fitting securely.

32 Install the elbow support bracket **(see illustration 18.12)**.

33 Lower the vehicle.

## Oil return line

*Refer to illustration 20.37*

34 Raise the vehicle and place it securely on jackstands.

35 Remove the two fasteners that attach the oil return line to the turbocharger.

36 Remove the hose clamp from the oil return line.

37 Disconnect the oil return line from the crankcase **(see illustration)**.

38 Clean the gasket surfaces.

39 Install a new gasket.

40 Connect the oil return line to the crankcase to the turbocharger.

# 21 Turbocharger solenoids and vacuum hoses - general information and component replacement

## General information

*Refer to illustrations 21.1 and 21.2*

1 Turbocharged models are equipped with three PCM-controlled solenoids: the wastegate actuator solenoid, the surge valve actua-

tor solenoid and the Throttle Inlet Pressure (TIP) solenoid. All three solenoids are located on a bracket above the right strut tower at the right rear corner of the engine compartment, near the cruise control actuator **(see illustration)**.

2 Diagnosis of the turbocharger solenoids is beyond the scope of this manual. But the accompanying vacuum hose schematic will help you make sure that the vacuum hoses for the turbocharger solenoids are correctly routed and connected **(see illustration)**.

## Component replacement

*Refer to illustrations 21.3 and 21.6*

**Note:** *This procedure applies to all of the solenoids.*

3 Remove the nuts that attach the solenoid mounting bracket to the strut tower **(see illustration)**.

4 Disconnect the electrical connector from the solenoid.

5 Clearly label and disconnect the vacuum hoses from the solenoid.

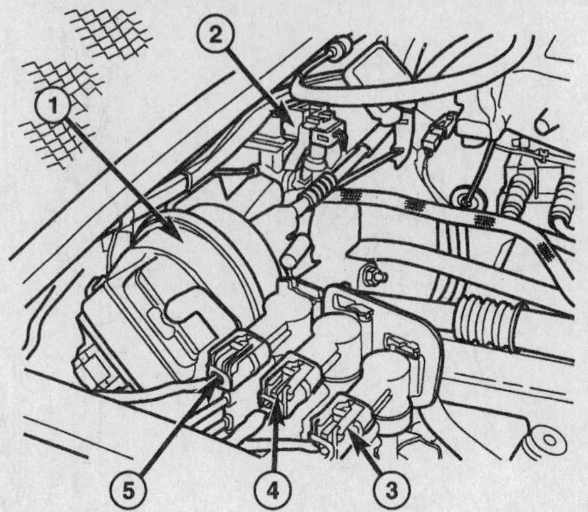


**21.1 Turbocharger solenoids**

1 *Cruise control servo*
2 *Throttle Inlet Pressure (TIP) sensor*
3 *Wastegate actuator solenoid*
4 *Surge valve actuator solenoid*
5 *Throttle Inlet Pressure (TIP) solenoid*

6 Push on the solenoid lock tab **(see illustration)** and disengage the solenoid from the bracket.

7 When installing a solenoid, slide it onto the bracket until the locking tab clicks into place.

8 Installation is otherwise the reverse of removal.

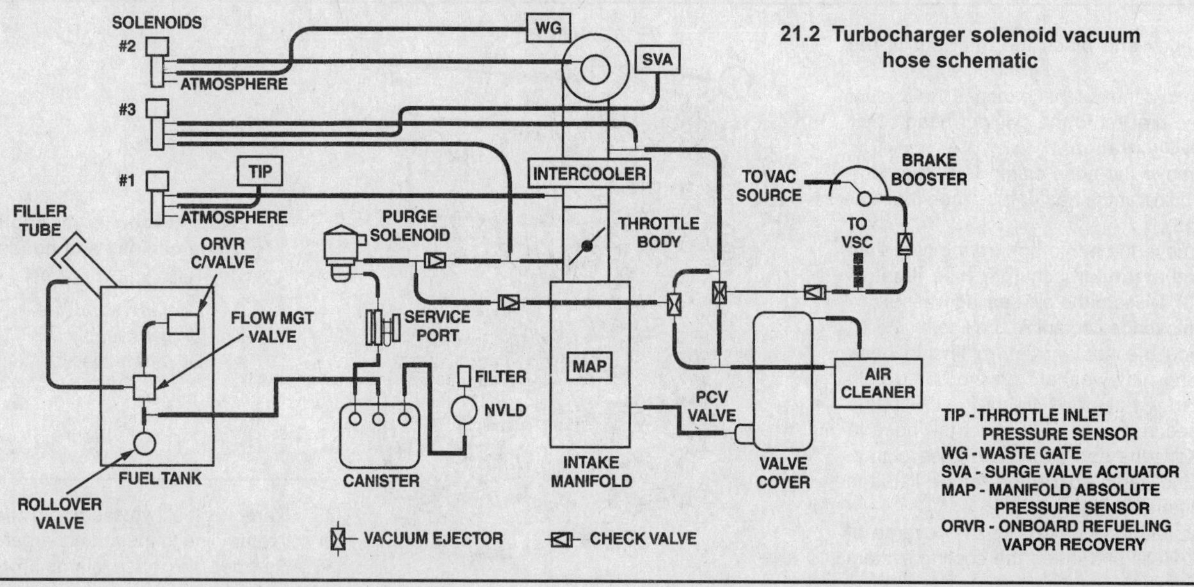


**21.2 Turbocharger solenoid vacuum hose schematic**

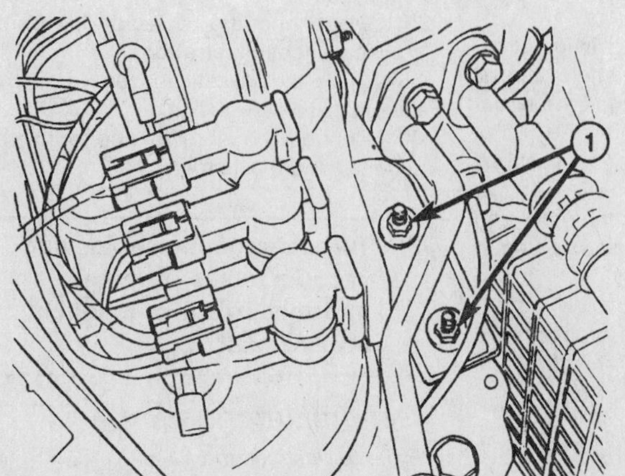


**21.3 Remove the nuts (1) that attach the solenoid mounting bracket to the strut tower**

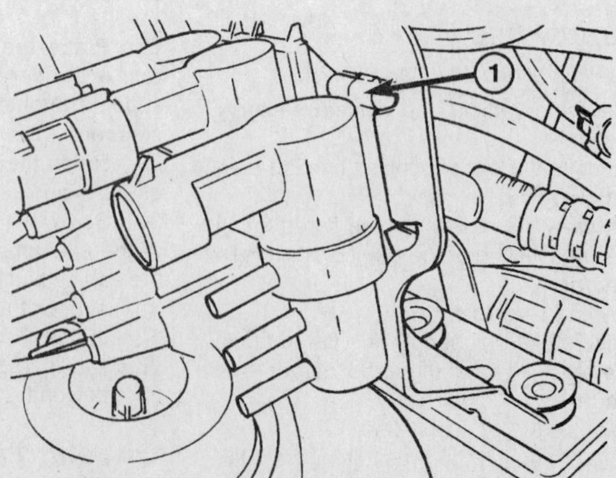


**21.6 Push on the solenoid lock tab (1) to disengage the solenoid from the bracket**

# Chapter 5
# Engine electrical systems

## Contents



## Specifications

### Ignition coil

| | |
|---|---|
| Primary resistance | |
| 2001, 2002 and 2008 and later | 0.51 to 0.61 ohms |
| 2003 through 2007 | 0.45 to 0.65 ohms |
| Secondary resistance | |
| 2001, 2002 and 2008 and later | 11.5 to 13.5 K-ohms |
| 2003 through 2007 | 11.5 to 14.5 K-ohms |

### Charging system

| | |
|---|---|
| Charging voltage | 14.7 to 15.3 volts |

## 1 General information, precautions and battery disconnection

The engine electrical systems include all ignition, charging and starting components. Because of their engine-related functions, these components are discussed separately from body electrical devices such as the lights, the instruments, etc. (which are included in Chapter 12).

### Precautions

Always observe the following precautions when working on the electrical system:

a) *Be extremely careful when servicing engine electrical components. They are easily damaged if checked, connected or handled improperly.*

b) *Never leave the ignition switched on for long periods of time when the engine is not running.*

c) *Never disconnect the battery cables while the engine is running.*

d) *Maintain correct polarity when connecting battery cables from another vehicle during jump starting - see the "Booster battery (jump) starting" section at the front of this manual.*

e) *Always disconnect the negative battery cable from the battery before working on the electrical system, but read the following battery disconnection procedure first.*

It's also a good idea to review the safety-related information regarding the engine electrical systems located in the *"Safety first!"* section at the front of this manual, before beginning any operation included in this Chapter.

### Battery disconnection

Several systems on the vehicle require battery power to be available at all times, either to ensure their continued operation (such as the radio, alarm system, power door locks, windows, etc.) or to maintain control unit memories (such as that in the engine management system's Powertrain Control Module [PCM]) which would be lost if the battery were to be disconnected. Therefore, whenever the battery is to be disconnected, first note the following to ensure that there are no unforeseen consequences of this action:

a) *The engine management system's PCM will lose the information stored in its memory when the battery is disconnected. This includes idling and operating values, any fault codes detected and system monitors required for emissions testing. Whenever the battery is disconnected, the computer may require a certain period of time to "re-learn" the operating values.*

b) *On any vehicle with power door locks, it is a wise precaution to remove the key from the ignition and to keep it with you, so that it does not get locked inside if the power door locks should engage accidentally when the battery is reconnected!*

Devices known as "memory-savers" can be used to avoid some of the above problems. Precise details vary according to the device used. Typically, it is plugged into the cigarette lighter and is connected by its own wires to a spare battery; the vehicle's own battery is then disconnected from the electrical system, leaving the "memory-saver" to pass sufficient current to maintain audio unit presets and PCM memory values, and also to run permanently live circuits such as the clock and radio memory, all the while isolating the battery in the event of a short-circuit occurring while work is carried out.

**Warning 1:** *Some of these devices allow a considerable amount of current to pass, which can mean that many of the vehicle's systems are still operational when the main battery is disconnected. If a "memory-saver" is used, ensure that the circuit concerned is actually "dead" before carrying out any work on it!*

**Warning 2:** *If work is to be performed around any of the airbag system components, the battery must be disconnected and no "memory-saver" device may be used. If a memory-saver device is used, power will be supplied to the airbag and personal injury may result if the airbag is accidentally deployed.*

The battery on all vehicles is located in the front left corner of the engine compartment. To disconnect the battery for service procedures requiring power to be cut from the vehicle, remove the cover from the air filter housing (see Chapter 1, Section 22), then loosen the negative cable clamp nut and detach the negative cable from the negative battery post (see Section 3). Isolate the cable end to prevent it from accidentally coming into contact with the battery post.

## 2 Battery - emergency jump starting

Refer to the *Booster battery (jump) starting* procedure at the front of this manual.

**3.1a Use a battery hydrometer to draw electrolyte from the battery cell - this hydrometer is equipped with a thermometer to make temperature corrections**

## 3 Battery - check, removal and installation

**Warning:** *Hydrogen gas is produced by the battery, so keep open flames and lighted cigarettes away from it at all times. Always wear eye protection when working around a battery. Rinse off spilled electrolyte immediately with large amounts of water.*

### Check

*Refer to illustrations 3.1a, 3.1b and 3.1c*

1 A battery cannot be accurately tested until it is at or near a fully charged state. Disconnect the negative battery cable from the battery and perform the following tests:

a) **Battery state of charge test** - *Visually inspect the indicator eye (if equipped) on the top of the battery. If the indicator eye is dark in color, charge the battery as described in Chapter 1. If the battery is equipped with removable caps, check the battery electrolyte. The electrolyte level should be above the upper edge of the plates. If the level is low, add distilled water. DO NOT OVERFILL. The excess electrolyte may spill over during periods of heavy charging. Test the specific gravity of the electrolyte using a hydrometer* **(see illustration)**. *Remove the caps and extract a sample of the electrolyte and observe the float inside the barrel of the hydrometer. Follow the instructions from the tool manufacturer and determine the specific gravity of the electrolyte for each cell. A fully charged battery will indicate approximately 1.270 (green zone) at 68-degrees F (20-degrees C). If the specific gravity of the electrolyte is low (red zone), charge the battery as described in Chapter 1.*

b) **Open circuit voltage test** - *Using a digital voltmeter, perform an open circuit voltage test* **(see illustration)**. *Connect the negative probe of the voltmeter to the negative battery post and the positive probe to the positive battery post. The battery voltage should be greater than 12.5 volts. If the battery is less than the specified voltage, charge the battery before proceeding to the next test. Do not proceed with the battery load test until the battery is fully charged.*

c) **Battery load test** - *An accurate check of the battery condition can only be performed with a load tester (available at most auto parts stores). This test evaluates the ability of the battery to operate the starter and other accessories during periods of heavy amperage draw (load). Install a special battery load testing tool onto the battery terminals* **(see illustration)**. *Load test the battery according to the tool manufacturer's instructions. This tool utilizes a carbon pile to increase the load demand (amperage draw) on the battery. Maintain the load on the battery for 15 seconds and observe*

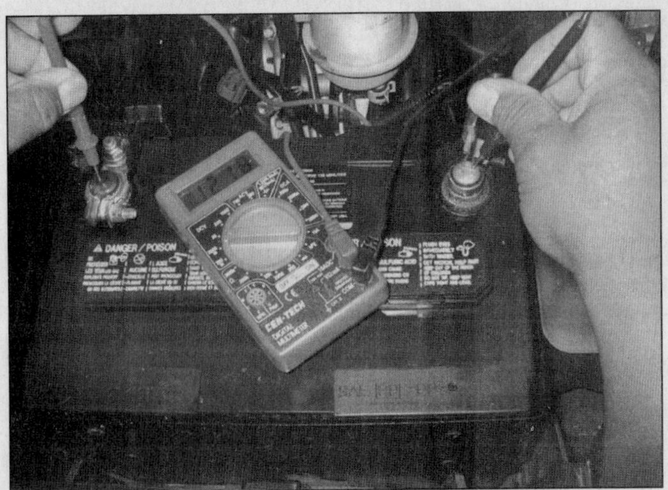

**3.1b To test the open circuit voltage of the battery, connect the black probe of the voltmeter to the negative terminal and the red probe to the positive terminal of the battery - a fully charged battery should indicate approximately 12.5 volts depending on the outside air temperature**

**3.1c Some battery load testers are equipped with an ammeter which enables the battery load to be precisely dialed in, as shown - less expensive testers have a load switch and a voltmeter only**

*that the battery voltage does not drop below 9.6 volts. If the battery condition is weak or defective, the tool will indicate this condition immediately.* **Note:** *Cold temperatures will cause the minimum voltage requirements to drop slightly. Follow the chart given in the tool manufacturer's instructions to compensate for cold climates. Minimum load voltage for freezing temperatures (32 degrees F/0-degrees C) should be approximately 9.1 volts.*

d) **Battery drain test** - *This test will indicate whether there's a constant drain on the vehicle's electrical system that can cause the battery to discharge. Make sure all accessories are turned Off. If the vehicle has an underhood light, verify it's working properly, then disconnect it. Connect one lead of a digital ammeter to the disconnected negative battery cable clamp and the other lead to the negative battery post. A drain of approximately 100 milliamps or less is considered normal (due to the Powertrain Control Module, digital clocks, digital radios and other components which normally cause a key-off battery drain). An excessive drain (approximately 500 milliamps or more) will cause the battery to discharge. The problem circuit or component can be located by removing the fuses, one at a time, until the excessive drain stops and normal drain is indicated on the meter.*

## Replacement

*Refer to illustrations 3.6, 3.8a, 3.8b and 3.8c*

**Caution:** *Always disconnect the negative cable first and hook it up last or the battery may be shorted by the tool being used to loosen the cable clamps.*

2 Remove the air filter housing cover (see *"Air filter housing - removal and installation"* in Chapter 4).

3 Loosen the cable clamp nut and remove the negative battery cable from the negative battery post. Isolate the cable end to prevent it from accidentally coming into contact with the battery post.

4 Loosen the cable clamp nut and remove the positive battery cable from the positive battery post.

5 Remove the air filter housing (see Chapter 4).

6 Remove the battery hold-down clamp bolt **(see illustration)**.

7 Lift out the battery. Be careful - it's heavy. **Note:** *Battery straps and handlers are available at most auto parts stores for a reasonable price. They make it easier to remove and carry the battery.*

8 While the battery is out, remove the battery tray **(see illustrations)** and then inspect the support bracket underneath **(see illustration)** for corrosion. If corrosion is present, remove it and clean the deposits with a mixture of baking soda and water to prevent fur-

**3.6 To detach the battery from the battery tray, remove this hold-down clamp bolt**

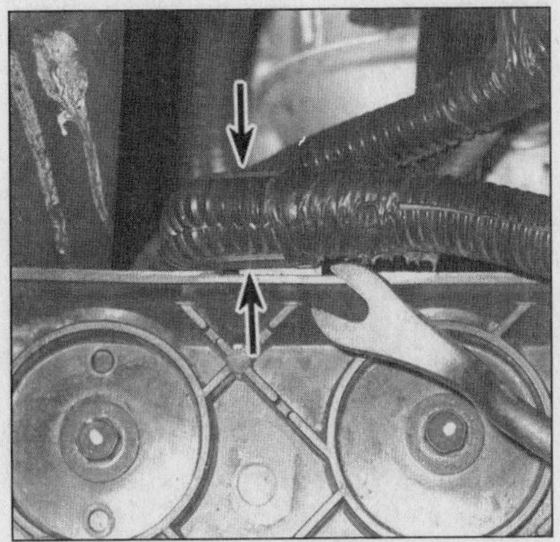

**3.8a To remove the battery tray, pry loose the pop-fastener that attaches the plastic cable guide for the positive battery cable to the tray . . .**

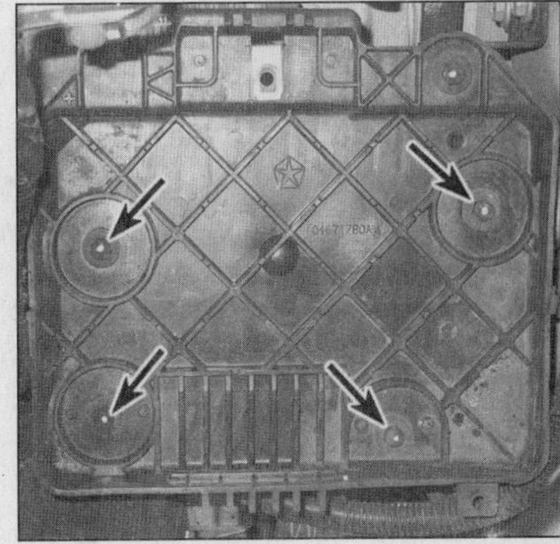

**3.8b . . . and then remove these bolts**

3.8c To remove the battery tray support bracket, remove these two bolts and the two bolts (not visible in this photo) on the front side of the bracket

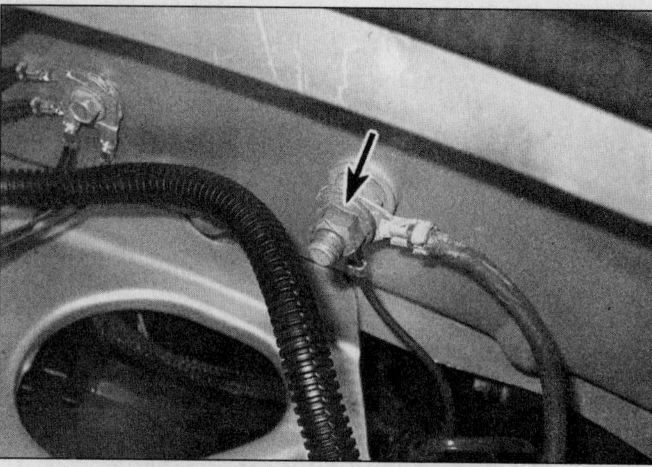

4.4 One of the two battery ground cables is bolted to the left side of the engine compartment, near the battery

ther corrosion. Flush the area with plenty of clean water and dry thoroughly.

9 If you are replacing the battery, make sure you replace it with a battery with the identical dimensions, amperage rating, cold cranking rating, etc.

10 Installation is the reverse of removal. Be sure to tighten the hold-down clamp bolt securely, but don't overtighten it, or you will crack the plastic tray.

## 4 Battery cables - replacement

### *All cables*

1 Periodically inspect the entire length of each battery cable for damage, cracked or burned insulation and corrosion. Poor battery cable connections can cause starting problems and decreased engine performance.

2 Check the cable-to-terminal connections at the ends of the cables for cracks, loose wire strands and corrosion. The presence of white, fluffy deposits under the insulation at the cable terminal connection is a sign that the cable is corroded and should be replaced. Check the terminals for distortion, missing mounting bolts and corrosion.

3 When removing the cables, always disconnect the negative cable from the negative battery post first and hook it up last, or the battery could be accidentally shorted by the tool used to loosen the cable clamps. Even if you're only replacing the positive cable, be sure to disconnect the negative cable first (see Chapter 1 for further information regarding battery cable maintenance).

### *Negative battery cables*

*Refer to illustrations 4.4 and 4.5*

**Note:** *There are two negative battery cables.*

4 The smaller negative battery cable is grounded to the left side of the engine compartment, near the battery **(see illustration)**.

5 The other negative battery cable is grounded to the transaxle **(see illustration)**. Before removing either cable, note the routing to ensure correct installation.

### *Positive battery cable*

*Refer to illustrations 4.8 and 4.10*

6 Remove the battery (see Section 3) and then remove the battery tray **(see illustrations 3.8a and 3.8b)**.

7 Remove the Power Distribution Center (PDC) cover (see Chapter 12).

8 Remove the two 10 mm nuts **(see illustration)** which connect the positive battery cable to the PDC.

9 Raise the vehicle and place it securely on jackstands.

10 Remove the nut on the starter solenoid terminal **(see illustration)**, then disconnect the positive battery cable from the starter solenoid.

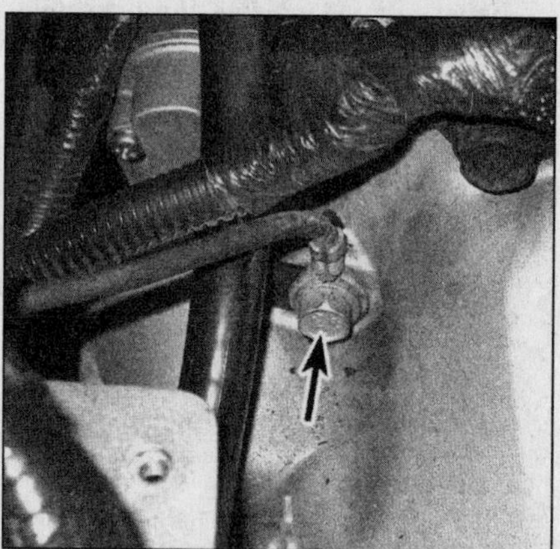

4.5 The other battery ground cable is bolted to the transaxle

### *All cables*

11 If you are replacing a battery cable, take it with you when buying a new cable. It is vitally important that you replace battery cables with identical parts. Battery cables have easily identifiable characteristics: Positive cables are usually red and larger in cross-section; ground cables are usually black and smaller in cross-section.

4.8 Remove the two 10 mm nuts which connect the positive battery cable to the PDC

4.10 Remove the nut on the starter solenoid terminal and then disconnect the positive battery cable from the starter solenoid

**6.2 To use a calibrated ignition tester, simply connect it to the spark plug wire boot, clip the tester to a convenient ground and then, with the fuel system pressure relieved and the fuel system disabled, crank the engine; if there's enough power to fire the plug, sparks will be visible between the electrode tip and the tester body**

**7.2a Ignition coil terminal guide (non-turbo model shown, turbo models similar)**

1 *Primary terminal No. 2 (to ignition coil No. 2 driver)*
2 *Battery voltage terminal (from Auto Shutdown Relay)*
3 *Primary terminal No. 1 (to ignition coil No. 1 driver)*

12 Clean the threads of the starter solenoid terminal or ground connection with a wire brush to remove rust and corrosion. Apply a light coat of battery terminal corrosion inhibitor or petroleum jelly to the threads to prevent future corrosion.

13 After attaching the lower end of the new cable(s), install the battery (see Section 3).

14 Before connecting the new cable(s) to the battery, make sure that the cable reaches the battery post without having to be stretched.

15 Installation is otherwise the reverse of removal.

## 5 Ignition system - general information and precautions

1 All models are equipped with a distributorless ignition system, which is referred to as a Direct Ignition System (DIS). As the name implies, there is no distributor. The DIS system includes the Powertrain Control Module (PCM), the Camshaft Position (CMP) sensor, the Crankshaft Position (CKP) sensor, the knock sensor, the ignition coil pack, the spark plug wires and the spark plugs. For more information on the spark plug wires and the spark plugs, refer to Chapter 1. For more information on the CMP sensor, the CKP sensor, the knock sensor and the PCM, refer to Chapter 6.

2 The coil pack, which consists of two ignition coils in one unit, is mounted on top of the valve cover. The Auto Shutdown Relay (ASD) controls battery voltage to the coil. A pair of drivers inside the PCM control the ground circuit for each coil. The ignition system is a waste spark design. Each time the PCM fires an ignition coil (each time a driver opens the ground circuit of a coil), the coil fires *two* spark plugs. One of these plugs is at the cylinder under compression, in which the piston is about to begin its power stroke. The other plug is at the cylinder in which the piston is on its exhaust stroke. The rear coil fires cylinder numbers 1 and 4; the front coil fires cylinder numbers 2 and 3. So, for example, when the ignition coil for the No. 1 cylinder fires the No. 1 spark plug, it also fires the spark plug for the No. 4 cylinder, which is also at Top Dead Center (TDC), but which is on its *exhaust* stroke, not its power stroke. Hence the spark is wasted.

3 When working on the ignition system, take the following precautions:

a) *Do not keep the ignition switch on for more than 10 seconds if the engine will not start.*
b) *Always connect a tachometer in accordance with the manufacturer's instructions. Some tachometers may be incompatible with this ignition system. Consult an auto parts counterperson before buying a tachometer for use with this vehicle.*
c) *Never allow the ignition coil terminals to touch ground. Grounding the coil could result in damage to the igniter and/or the ignition coil.*
d) *Do not disconnect the battery when the engine is running.*

## 6 Ignition system - check

*Refer to illustration 6.2*

**Warning:** *Because of the high voltage generated by the ignition system, extreme care should be taken whenever an operation is performed involving ignition components. This not only includes the igniter, coil and spark plug wires, but related components such as plug connectors, tachometer and other test equipment as well.*

1 If the engine turns over but won't start, disconnect the spark plug wire from the number one spark plug and attach it to a calibrated ignition tester, which is available at most auto parts stores.

2 Connect the clip on the tester to a bolt or metal bracket on the engine **(see illustration)**.

3 Relieve the fuel system pressure (see Chapter 4). Keep the fuel system disabled while testing the ignition system.

4 Crank the engine and watch the end of the tester to see if bright blue, well-defined sparks occur.

5 If sparks occur, sufficient voltage is reaching the two companion spark plugs (Nos. 1 and 4) to fire them.

6 If there is no spark, or only an intermittent spark, verify that there is battery voltage to the ignition coils (see wiring diagrams at the end of Chapter 12).

7 If there is battery voltage to the coils, inspect the plug wires (see Chapter 1).

8 If the spark plug wires are okay, remove and then check the spark plugs for fouling (see Chapter 1). If necessary, install new plugs.

9 If the spark plugs are good, check the coil resistance (see Section 7).

10 If the ignition system checks out, the CMP sensor, the CKP sensor or the PCM might be defective (see Chapter 6).

## 7 Ignition coil pack - check and replacement

### Check

*Refer to illustrations 7.2a, 7.2b and 7.3*

**Note:** *The following checks should be made with the engine cold. If the engine is hot, the resistance will be greater.*

1 Remove the ignition coil pack (see below).

2 Check the primary resistance of the ignition coil. With the ignition key turned to OFF,

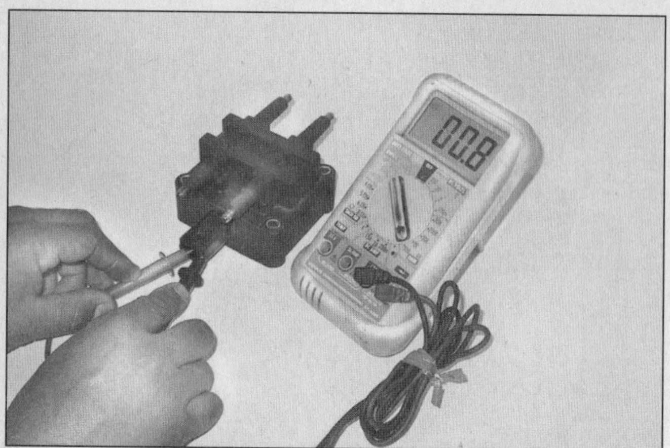

7.2b To check the primary resistance of the ignition coil, measure the resistance between the battery voltage center terminal and each primary terminal with an ohmmeter (non-turbo model shown, turbo models similar)

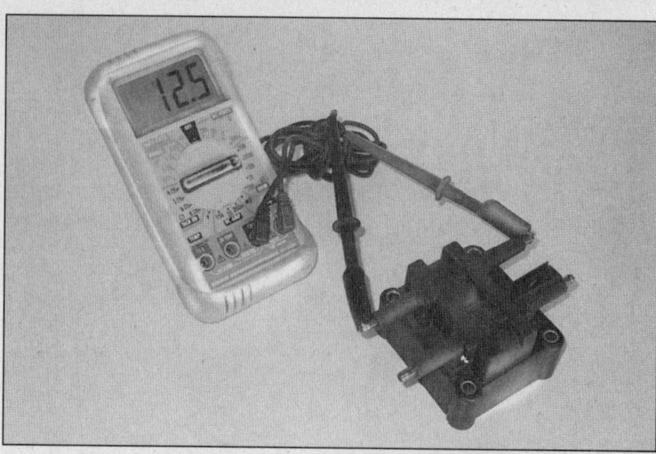

7.3 To check the secondary resistance of the ignition coil, remove the spark plug wires and then measure the resistance between each pair of high-tension terminals with an ohmmeter (non-turbo model shown, turbo models similar)

disconnect the electrical connector from each coil. Connect an ohmmeter across the coil primary terminals **(see illustrations)** and compare your measurement to the resistance listed in this Chapter's Specifications. If the primary resistance is incorrect, replace the coil.

3 Check the secondary resistance of each ignition coil. With the ignition key turned to OFF, label and detach the spark plug wires from each coil. Connect an ohmmeter across the two secondary terminals of each coil **(see illustration)**, then compare your measurement to the resistance listed in this Chapter's Specifications. If the secondary resistance is incorrect, replace the coil.

## Replacement

### Non-turbo models

*Refer to illustration 7.7*

4 Disconnect the cable from the negative terminal of the battery (see Section 1).

5 Remove the upper intake manifold (see Chapter 2A).

6 Label and disconnect the spark plug wires from the ignition coil (see Chapter 1). Pay close attention to the routing of the spark plug wires to ensure that they're correctly routed when reinstalled.

7 Disconnect the ignition coil electrical connector **(see illustration)**.

8 Remove the ignition coil mounting bolts **(see illustration 7.7)** and remove the coil pack from the valve cover.

9 Installation is the reverse of removal.

### Turbo models

*Refer to illustrations 7.11, 7.13, 7.16, 7.17a and 7.17b*

10 Disconnect the cable from the negative terminal of the battery (see Section 1).

11 Remove the throttle control shield **(see illustration)**.

12 Disconnect the accelerator cable and, if equipped, the cruise control cable from the throttle lever (see Chapter 4).

13 Remove the accelerator cable bracket **(see illustration)**.

14 Disconnect the spark plug wires from the ignition coil pack (see Chapter 1).

15 Disconnect the electrical connector from the ignition coil pack.

16 Remove the ignition coil mounting bolts. You'll have to twist the coil to remove two of the bolts **(see illustration)** before you can remove the coil itself.

17 To remove the coil pack, pull it up and out on the throttle body side of the air intake plenum **(see illustrations)**.

18 Installation is the reverse of removal.

## 8 Charging system - general information and precautions

The charging system includes the alternator, an internal voltage regulator, a charge indicator, the battery and the wiring between all the components. The charging system supplies electrical power for the ignition system, the lights, the radio, etc. The alternator is driven by a drivebelt at the front of the engine.

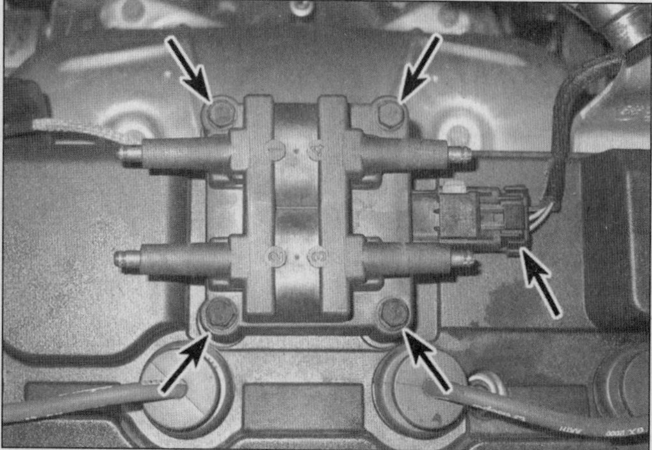

7.7 Disconnect the electrical connector from the coil pack; to detach the ignition coil pack from the valve cover, remove the coil pack mounting bolts (non-turbo models)

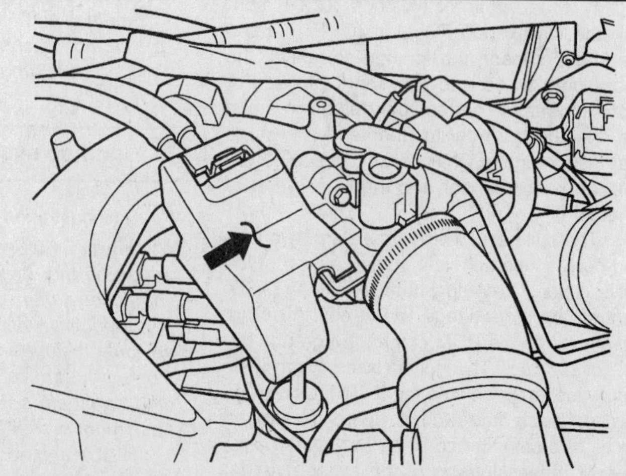

7.11 On turbo models, remove the throttle control shield

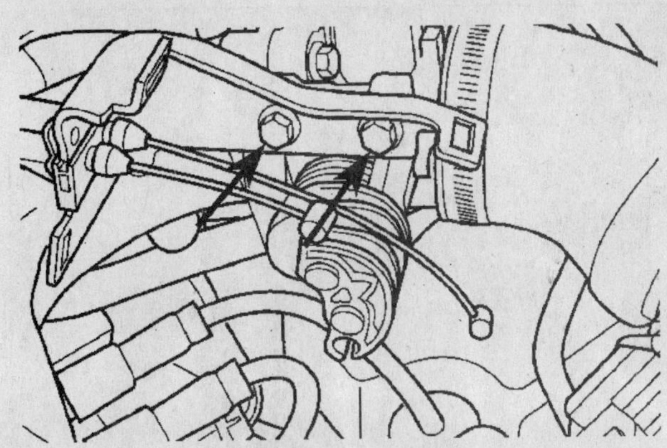

**7.13 To detach the accelerator cable bracket, remove these two bolts**

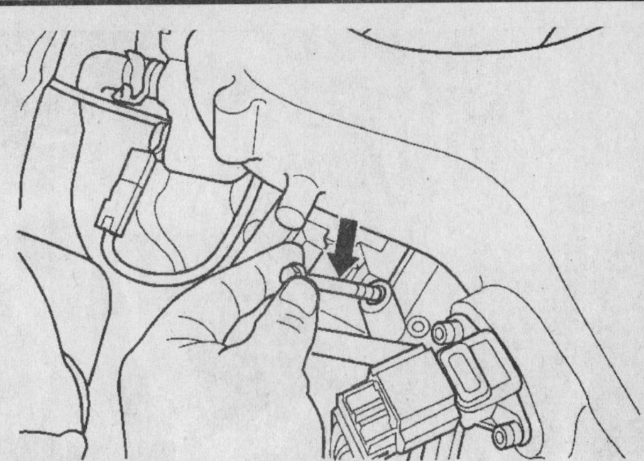

**7.16 There are four ignition coil pack mounting bolts; to remove two of them, you'll have to twist the coil like this (and you have to remove the bolts now, before you can remove the coil itself)**

The purpose of the voltage regulator is to limit the alternator's voltage to a preset value. This prevents power surges, circuit overloads, etc., during peak voltage output.

The charging system doesn't ordinarily require periodic maintenance. However, the drivebelt, battery and wires and connections should be inspected at the intervals outlined in Chapter 1.

The dashboard warning light should come on when the ignition key is turned to START, then should go off immediately. If it remains on, there is a malfunction in the charging system.

Be very careful when making electrical circuit connections to a vehicle equipped with an alternator and note the following:

a) *When reconnecting wires to the alternator from the battery, be sure to note the polarity.*
b) *Before using arc welding equipment to repair any part of the vehicle, disconnect the wires from the alternator and the battery terminals.*
c) *Never start the engine with a battery charger connected.*
d) *Always disconnect both battery leads before using a battery charger.*
e) *The alternator is driven by an engine drivebelt which could cause serious injury if your hand, hair or clothes become entangled in it with the engine running.*
f) *Because the alternator is connected directly to the battery, it could arc or cause a fire if overloaded or shorted out.*

## 9 Charging system - check

*Refer to illustration 9.2*

1 If a malfunction occurs in the charging circuit, do not immediately assume that the alternator is causing the problem. First, check the following items:

a) *Make sure the battery cable clamps, where they connect to the battery, are clean and tight.*
b) *Test the condition of the battery (see Section 3). If it does not pass all the tests, replace it with a new battery.*
c) *Check the external alternator wiring and connections.*
d) *Check the drivebelt condition and tension (see Chapter 1).*
e) *Check the alternator mounting bolts for tightness.*
f) *Run the engine and check the alternator for abnormal noise.*
g) *Check the charge light on the dash. It should illuminate when the ignition key is turned ON (engine not running). If it does not, check the circuit from the alternator to the charge light on the dash.*
h) *Check all the fuses that are in series with the charging system circuit. The location of these fuses may vary from year and model but the designations are generally the same. Refer to the wiring schematics at the end of Chapter 12 for additional information.*

2 With the ignition key off, check the battery voltage with no accessories operating **(see illustration)**. It should be approximately 12.5 volts. It may be slightly higher if the engine has been operating within the last hour.

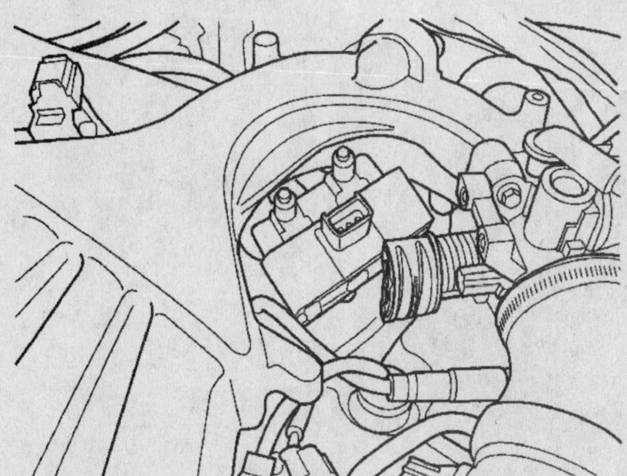

**7.17a To remove the ignition coil pack from a turbo model, turn it so that the electrical connector side is facing up . . .**

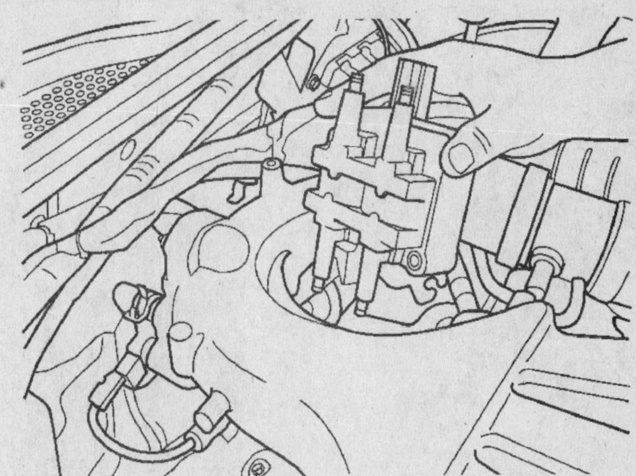

**7.17b . . . then pull it out between the air intake plenum and the throttle body**

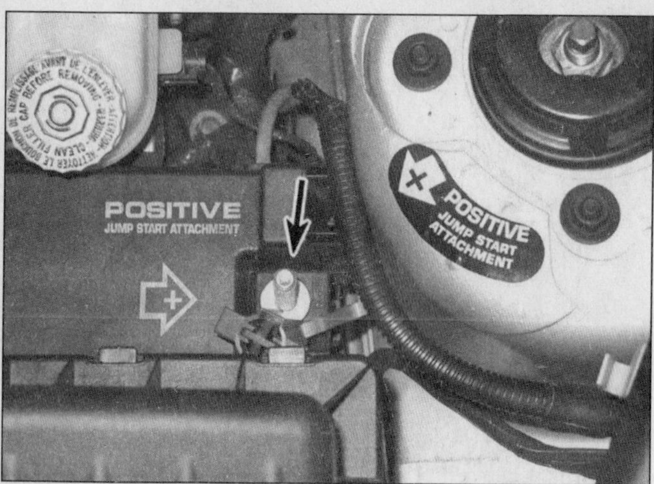


**9.2 Connect a voltmeter to the remote positive terminal (arrow) and a good ground and check the battery voltage with the engine Off and again with the engine running**

**10.2 Loosen the alternator pivot bolt nut (upper arrow) and the adjustment bolt (right arrow)**

3 Start the engine and check the battery voltage again. It should now be greater than the voltage recorded in Step 2, but not more than 14.5 volts. Turn on all the vehicle accessories (air conditioning, rear window defogger, blower motor, etc.) and increase the engine speed to 2,000 rpm - the voltage should not drop below the voltage recorded in Step 2.

4 If the indicated voltage is greater than the specified charging voltage, the voltage regulator is malfunctioning; replace the powertrain Control Module (PCM). **Note:** *The voltage regulator is an integral part of the PCM and cannot be replaced separately.*

5 If the indicated voltage reading is less than the specified charging voltage, the alternator is probably defective. Have the charging system checked at a dealer service department or other properly equipped repair facility. **Note:** *Many auto parts stores will bench test an alternator off the vehicle. Refer to your local auto parts store regarding their policy; many will perform this service free of charge.*

## 10 Alternator - removal and installation

*Refer to illustrations 10.2, 10.4, 10.5, 10.6, 10.8, 10.11, 10.12a, 10.12b and 10.14*

1 Disconnect the cable from the negative terminal of the battery (see Section 1).

2 Loosen the alternator adjustment bolt and pivot bolt nut **(see illustration)**.

3 Loosen the right front wheel lug nuts, then raise the vehicle and support it securely on jackstands. Remove the right front wheel.

4 Remove the support bracket **(see illustration)**.

5 Remove the accessory drivebelt splash shield **(see illustration)**.

6 Loosen the alternator lower pivot bolt **(see illustration)**.

7 Remove the alternator drivebelt.

8 Disconnect the electrical connectors from the alternator **(see illustration)**.

9 Remove the driveaxle (see Chapter 8).

10 Remove the alternator lower pivot bolt **(see illustration 10.6)** and swing the alternator out of the way (DO NOT remove the upper adjustment bolt and pivot bolt yet).

**10.4 To remove the support bracket, remove these fasteners**

11 Remove the alternator mounting bracket **(see illustration)**.

**10.5 To remove the accessory drivebelt splash shield, remove these fasteners**

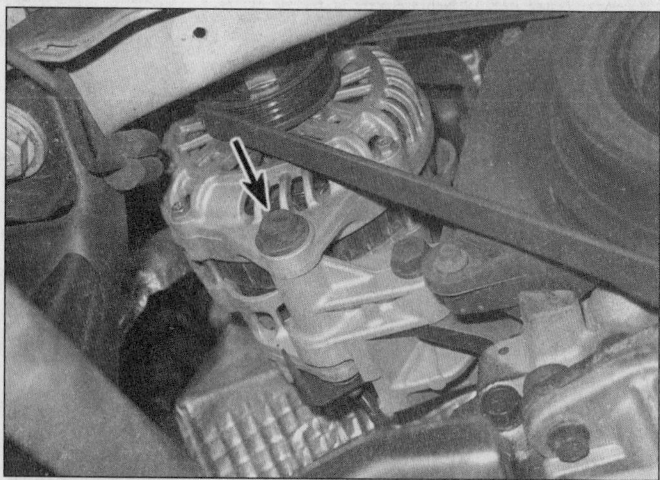

**10.6 Loosen the alternator lower pivot bolt then remove the alternator drivebelt**

10.8 Disconnect the electrical connectors from the alternator

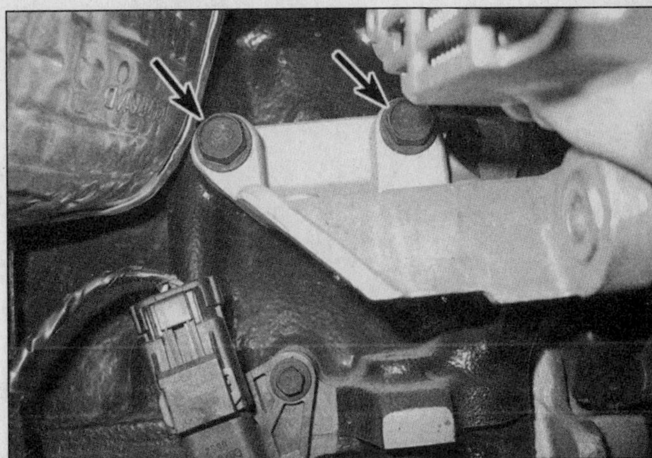

10.11 Remove the alternator lower mounting bracket bolts and remove the bracket

10.12a Remove the two bolts that attach the power steering oil cooler to the crossmember (bolts on top of crossmember, not visible in this photo) . . .

10.12b . . . then carefully set the oil cooler aside to provide clearance for removing the alternator

12 Remove the power steering oil cooler bolts and set the oil cooler aside to provide enough clearance to remove the alternator **(see illustrations)**.

13 Remove the alternator adjustment bolt, the pivot bolt nut and the pivot bolt **(see illustration 10.2)**.

10.14 Remove the alternator out the bottom

14 Remove the alternator out the bottom **(see illustration)**.

15 Installation is the reverse of removal. Be sure to tighten the alternator bolts securely. Tighten the driveaxle/hub nut to the torque listed in the Chapter 8 Specifications (be sure to install a new cotter pin). Tighten the wheel lug nuts to the torque listed in the Chapter 1 Specifications.

## 11 Starting system - general information and precautions

The starting system consists of the battery, the ignition switch, the starter relay, the starter motor, the starter solenoid and the electrical circuit connecting the components. The solenoid is mounted directly on the starter motor. The starting system on models with a manual transaxle also includes a clutch interlock/upstop switch, which is located at the top of the clutch pedal (see Chapter 8). The starting system on models with an automatic transaxle includes a Park/Neutral switch, which is located on the transaxle (see Chapter 7B).

The starter/solenoid motor assembly is installed on the front of the engine block, next to the transaxle bellhousing.

When the ignition key is turned to the START position, the starter solenoid is actuated through the starter control circuit. The starter solenoid then connects the battery to the starter. The battery supplies the electrical energy to the starter motor, which does the actual work of cranking the engine.

The starter motor on a vehicle equipped with a manual transaxle can be operated only when the clutch pedal is depressed; the starter on a vehicle equipped with an automatic transaxle can be operated only when the transaxle selector lever is in Park or Neutral.

Always observe the following precautions when working on the starting system:

a) *Excessive cranking of the starter motor can overheat it and cause serious damage. Never operate the starter motor for more than 15 seconds at a time without pausing to allow it to cool for at least two minutes.*

**12.3 To use an inductive ammeter, simply hold the ammeter over the positive or negative cable (whichever is easier in terms of clearance)**

**13.3 To remove the engine structural collar, remove these five bolts**

*b) The starter is connected directly to the battery and could arc or cause a fire if mishandled, overloaded or short circuited.*

*c) Always detach the cable from the negative terminal of the battery before working on the starting system.*

## 12 Starter motor and circuit - check

*Refer to illustration 12.3*

1 If a malfunction occurs in the starting circuit, do not immediately assume that the starter is causing the problem. First, check the following items:

*a) Make sure the battery cable clamps, where they connect to the battery, are clean and tight.*

*b) Check the condition of the battery cables (see Section 4). Replace any defective battery cables with new parts.*

*c) Test the condition of the battery (see Section 3). If it does not pass all the tests, replace it with a new battery.*

*d) Check the starter solenoid wiring and connections. Refer to the wiring diagrams at the end of Chapter 12.*

*e) Check the starter mounting bolts for tightness.*

*f) Check the ignition switch circuit for correct operation (see Chapter 12).*

*g) Check the operation of the Park/Neutral Position switch (automatic transaxle) or clutch start switch (manual transaxle). Make sure the shift lever is in PARK or NEUTRAL (automatic transaxle) or the clutch pedal is depressed (manual transaxle). Refer to Chapter 7 for the Park/Neutral Position switch check and adjustment procedure. Refer to Chapter 12 wiring diagrams, if necessary, when performing circuit checks. These systems must operate correctly to provide battery voltage to the ignition solenoid.*

*h) Check the operation of the starter relay. The starter relay is located in the fuse/relay box inside the engine compartment. Refer to Chapter 12 for the testing procedure.*

2 If the starter does not actuate when the ignition switch is turned to the start position, check for battery voltage to the solenoid. This will determine if the solenoid is receiving the correct voltage signal from the ignition switch. Connect a test light or voltmeter to the starter solenoid positive terminal and while an assistant turns the ignition switch to the start position. If voltage is not available, refer to the wiring diagrams in Chapter 12 and check all the fuses and relays in series with the starting system. If voltage is available but the starter motor does not operate, remove the starter (see Section 13) and bench test it (see Step 4).

3 If the starter turns over slowly, check the starter cranking voltage and the current draw from the battery. This test must be performed with the starter assembly on the engine. Crank the engine over (for 10 seconds or less) and observe the battery voltage. It should not drop below 8.0 volts on manual transaxle models or 8.5 volts on automatic transaxle models. Also, observe the current draw using an ammeter **(see illustration)**. It should not exceed 400 amps or drop below 250 amps. **Caution:** *The battery cables may be excessively heated because of the large amount of amperage being drawn from the battery. Discontinue the testing until the starting system has cooled down.* If the starter motor cranking amp values are not within the correct range, replace it with a new unit. There are several conditions that may affect the starter cranking potential. The battery must be in good condition and the battery cold-cranking rating must not be under-rated for the particular application. Be sure to check the battery specifications carefully. The battery terminals and cables must be clean and not corroded. Also, in cases of extreme cold temperatures, make sure the battery and/or engine block is warmed before performing the tests.

**13.4 Disconnect the starter motor wires from these terminals**

4 If the starter is receiving voltage but does not activate, remove and check the starter/solenoid assembly on the bench. Most likely the solenoid is defective. In some rare cases, the engine may be seized so be sure to try and rotate the crankshaft pulley (see Chapter 2A) before proceeding. With the starter/solenoid assembly mounted in a vise on the bench, connect one jumper cable from the negative battery terminal to the body of the starter. Connect the other jumper cable from the positive battery terminal to the B+ terminal on the starter. Connect a starter switch and apply battery voltage to the solenoid S terminal (for 10 seconds or less) and see if the solenoid plunger, shift lever and overrunning clutch extends and rotates the pinion drive. If the pinion drive extends but does not rotate, the solenoid is operating but the starter motor is defective. If there is no movement but the solenoid clicks, the solenoid and/or the starter motor is defective. If the solenoid plunger extends and rotates the pinion drive, the starter/solenoid assembly is working properly.

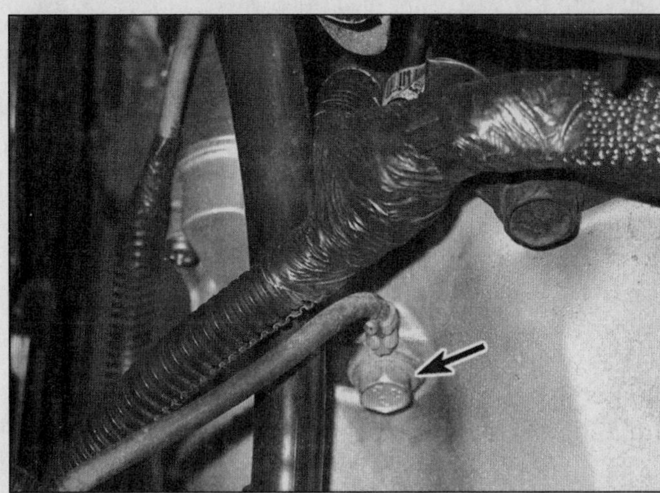

**13.5a To detach the starter motor assembly, remove this bolt from the bellhousing side (don't forget to reattach the ground wire when installing the starter) . . .**

**13.5b . . . then remove this bolt from the starter side**

## 13 Starter motor - removal and installation

*Refer to illustrations 13.3, 13.4, 13.5a and 13.5b*

1 Detach the cable from the negative terminal of the battery (see Section 1).

2 Raise the front of the vehicle and place it securely on jackstands.

3 Remove the engine structural collar **(see illustration)**.

4 Disconnect the electrical connectors from the starter/solenoid assembly **(see illustration)**.

5 Remove the starter motor mounting bolts **(see illustrations)**.

6 Lower the starter motor assembly from the engine compartment.

7 Installation is the reverse of removal. Be sure to tighten the starter mounting bolts and the structural collar bolts securely.

# Notes

# Chapter 6
# Emissions and engine control systems

## Contents



## Specifications

### Torque specifications

**Note:** *One foot-pound (ft-lb) of torque is equivalent to 12 inch-pounds (in-lbs) of torque. Torque values below approximately 15 foot-pounds are expressed in inch-pounds, because most foot-pound torque wrenches are not accurate at these smaller values.*

| | Ft-lbs (unless otherwise noted) | Nm |
|---|---|---|
| Camshaft Position (CMP) sensor | | |
| CMP sensor retaining bolts | 115 in-lbs | 13 |
| CMP sensor target magnet retaining screw | 32 in-lbs | 3.5 |
| Crankshaft Position (CKP) sensor retaining bolt | 80 in-lbs | 9 |
| Exhaust Gas Recirculation (EGR) valve | | |
| EGR tube fasteners | 97 in-lbs | 11 |
| EGR valve mounting bolts | 16 | 22 |
| Knock sensor | 84 in-lbs | 9.5 |

## 1 General information

*Refer to illustration 1.6*

To prevent pollution of the atmosphere from incompletely burned and evaporating gases, and to maintain good driveability and fuel economy, a number of emission control systems are incorporated. They include the:

*On-Board Diagnostic II (OBD-II) system*
*Multi-Port Electronic Fuel Injection (MPI) system*
*Exhaust Gas Recirculation (EGR) system*
*Evaporative Emissions Control (EVAP) system*
*Positive Crankcase Ventilation (PCV) system*
*Catalytic converter*

The Sections in this Chapter include general descriptions, checking procedures within the scope of the home mechanic and component replacement procedures (when possible) for each of the systems listed above.

Before assuming that an emissions control system is malfunctioning, check the fuel and ignition systems carefully. The diagnosis of some emission control devices requires specialized tools, equipment and training. If checking and servicing become too difficult or if a procedure is beyond your ability, consult a dealer service department or other repair shop. Remember, the most frequent cause of emissions problems is simply a loose or broken wire or vacuum hose, so always check the hose and wiring connections first.

This doesn't mean, however, that emissions control systems are particularly difficult to maintain and repair. You can quickly and easily perform many checks and do most of the regular maintenance at home with common tune-up and hand tools. **Note:** *Because of a Federally mandated warranty which covers the emissions control system components, check with your dealer about warranty coverage before working on any emissions-related systems. Once the warranty has expired, you may wish to perform some of the component checks and/or replacement procedures in this Chapter to save money.*

Pay close attention to any special precautions outlined in this Chapter. It should be noted that the illustrations of the various systems may not exactly match the system installed on your vehicle because of changes made by the manufacturer during production or from year-to-year.

A Vehicle Emissions Control Information (VECI) label is attached to the underside of the hood **(see illustration)**. Part of this label, the Vacuum Hose Routing Diagram, provides

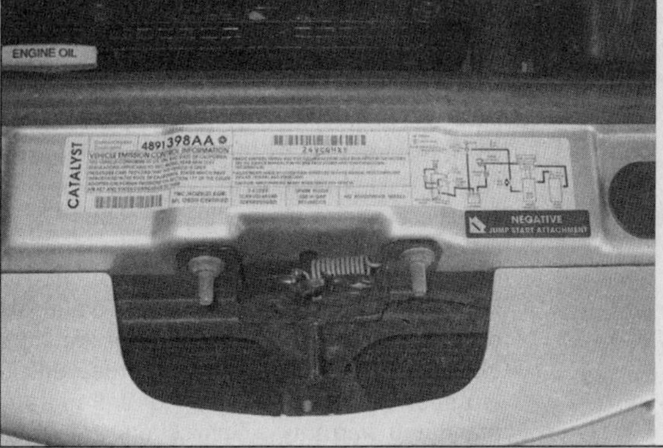


**1.6 The Vehicle Emission Control Information (VECI) label contains such essential information as the types of emission control systems installed on the engine and the spark plug type and gap; the vacuum hose routing diagram indicates important emission-control devices and components, and it shows how they're connected together by vacuum hoses**

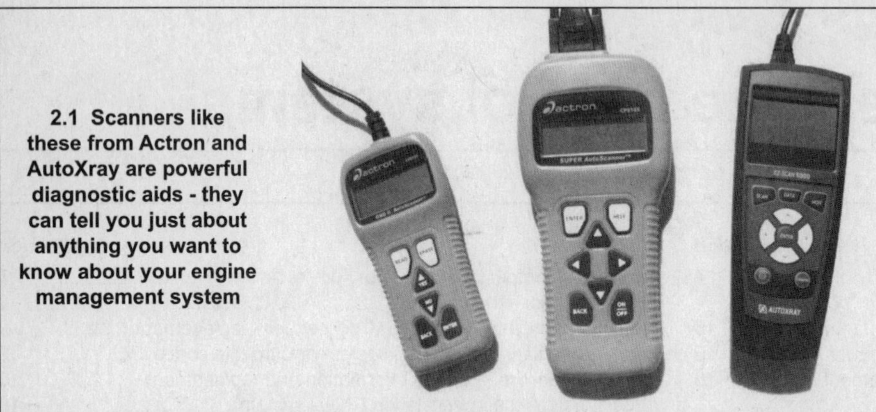

**2.1 Scanners like these from Actron and AutoXray are powerful diagnostic aids - they can tell you just about anything you want to know about your engine management system**

a vacuum hose schematic with emissions components identified. When servicing the engine or emissions systems, the VECI label and the vacuum hose routing diagram in your particular vehicle should always be checked for up-to-date information.

## 2 On-Board Diagnostic (OBD) system and trouble codes

### Scan tool information

*Refer to illustrations 2.1 and 2.2*

1 Hand-held scanners are the most powerful and versatile tools for analyzing engine management systems used on later model vehicles **(see illustration)**. Early model scanners handle codes and some diagnostics for many systems. Each brand scan tool must be examined carefully to match the year, make and model of the vehicle you are working on. Often, interchangeable cartridges are available to access the particular manufacturer (Ford, GM, Chrysler, Toyota etc.). Some manufacturers will specify by continent (Asia, Europe, USA, etc.). **Note:** *An aftermarket generic scanner should work with any model covered by this manual. However, some early OBD-II models, although technically classified as OBD-II compliant by the manufacturer and by the federal government, might not be fully compliant with all SAE standards for OBD-II. Some generic scanners are unable to extract all the codes from these early OBD-II models. Before purchasing a generic scan tool, contact the manufacturer of the scanner you're planning to buy and verify that it will work properly with the OBD-II system you want to scan. If necessary, of course, you can always have the codes extracted by a dealer service department or an independent repair shop with a professional scan tool.*

**2.2 Trouble code readers like the Actron OBD-II diagnostic tester simplify the task of extracting the trouble codes**

2 With the arrival of the Federally mandated emission control system (OBD-II), a specially designed scanner has been developed. Several tool manufacturers have released OBD-II scan tools for the home mechanic **(see illustration)**. Ask the parts salesman at a local auto parts store for additional information concerning dates and costs.

### OBD system general description

3 All models are equipped with the second generation on-board diagnostic (OBD-II) system. This system consists of an on-board computer known as the Powertrain Control Module (PCM), and information sensors, which monitor various functions of the engine and send data to the PCM. This system incorporates a series of diagnostic monitors that detect and identify fuel injection and emissions control systems faults and store the information in the computer memory. This updated system also tests sensors and output actuators, diagnoses drive cycles, freezes data and clears codes.

4 This powerful diagnostic computer must be accessed using an OBD-II scan tool and the 16 pin Data Link Connector (DLC) located under the driver's dash area. The PCM is the "brain" of the electronically controlled fuel and emissions system. It receives data from a number of sensors and other electronic components (switches, relays, etc.). Based on the information it receives, the PCM generates output signals to control various relays, solenoids (i.e. fuel injectors) and other actuators. The PCM is specifically calibrated to optimize the emissions, fuel economy and driveability of the vehicle.

5 It isn't a good idea to attempt diagnosis or replacement of the PCM or emission control components at home while the vehicle is under warranty. Because of a Federally mandated warranty which covers the emissions system components and because any owner-induced damage to the PCM, the sensors and/or the control devices may void this warranty, take the vehicle to a dealer service department if the PCM or a system component malfunctions.

### Information sensors

6 The PCM receives inputs from various information sensors and switches and uses the information it receives to control the operation of the engine in an appropriate and optimal manner. The following list provides a brief description of the function and location of each of the important information sensors.

7 **Camshaft Position (CMP) sensor -** The CMP sensor is one of two sensors that the PCM uses for cylinder identification and fuel injection synchronization (the CKP sensor is the other). The CMP sensor is located on the left end of the cylinder head.

8 **Crankshaft Position (CKP) sensor -** The CKP sensor, which provides information on crankshaft position and engine speed to the PCM, is also used (along with the CMP sensor) by the PCM to determine which spark plug to fire and which cylinder to inject with fuel. The CKP sensor is located on the rear side of the engine block, above the oil filter.

9 **Engine Coolant Temperature (ECT) sensor -** The ECT sensor monitors engine coolant temperature and sends the PCM a voltage signal that affects PCM control of the fuel mixture, ignition timing and EGR operation. The ECT sensor is located on the thermostat housing, which is located at the right front corner of the cylinder head, at the base of the coolant filler neck.

10 **Intake Air Temperature (IAT) sensor** - The IAT sensor is used by the PCM to calculate air density, one of the variables it must determine in order to calculate injector pulse width and adjust ignition timing. The IAT sensor is located on the air intake duct.

11 **Knock sensor** - The knock sensors monitor engine "knock" (pre-ignition or detonation) and signals the PCM when knock occurs, so that the PCM can retard ignition timing accordingly. The knock sensor is located on the front side of the engine block, below the intake manifold.

12 **Manifold Absolute Pressure (MAP) sensor** - The MAP sensor measures the intake manifold vacuum that draws the air/fuel mixture into the combustion chambers. The PCM uses this information to help it calculate injector pulse width and spark advance. The MAP sensor is located on the rear of the upper intake manifold.

13 **Oxygen sensors -** The oxygen sensors generate a voltage signal that varies in accordance with the difference between the oxygen content of the exhaust and the oxygen in the surrounding air. There are two oxygen sensors: an upstream, or pre-converter, oxygen sensor, and a downstream, or post-converter, oxygen sensor. The PCM uses the data from the upstream sensor to calculate the injector pulse width. The downstream oxygen sensor monitors the content of the exhaust gases as they

exit the downstream catalytic converter. This information is used by the PCM to predict catalyst deterioration and/or failure. The upstream sensor is located on top of the exhaust manifold, just ahead of the exhaust manifold flange. The downstream sensor is located on the left side of the catalytic converter.

14 **Power steering pressure switch** - The power steering pressure switch signals the PCM to increase the flow of air through the Idle Air Control (IAC) motor to prevent engine stalling when power steering pump pressure is excessive during, for example, parking maneuvers. The power steering pressure switch is located on the backside of the power steering gear assembly.

15 **Throttle Position (TP) Sensor** - The TP sensor, which is located on the throttle body, produces a variable voltage signal in proportion to the opening angle of the throttle valve. This signal, which is monitored by the PCM, enables the PCM to calculate throttle position.

16 **Vehicle Speed Sensor (VSS)** - The VSS provides information to the PCM to indicate vehicle speed. The PCM uses this information to adjust the idle air control motor to maintain MAP values within an acceptable range during deceleration and to maintain an acceptable engine speed when the engine is idling. The VSS is also used to operate the speedometer, as an input for the cruise control system and, on Canadian vehicles, the Daytime Running Lights. The VSS is located above the inner CV joint for the right driveaxle on models with a manual transaxle; on models with an automatic, its located on the rear of the transaxle.

## Output actuators

17 Based on the information it receives from the information sensors described above, the PCM adjusts fuel injector pulse width, idle speed, ignition spark advance, ignition coil dwell and EVAP canister purge operation. It does so by controlling the output actuators. The following list provides a brief description of the function and location of each of the important output actuators.

18 **Auto Shutdown (ASD) relay** - When energized by the PCM, the ASD relay provides battery voltage to the fuel injectors, the ignition coil, the alternator field and the oxygen sensor heaters. The ASD relay is located inside the Power Distribution Center (PDC) in the engine compartment.

19 **Exhaust Gas Recirculation (EGR) transducer** - The EGR transducer is an integral part of the EGR valve, which is located at the left end of the intake manifold, right behind the cylinder head. The EGR transducer consists of a PCM-controlled solenoid and a backpressure transducer. When the PCM energizes the solenoid, no vacuum reaches the transducer; when the PCM de-energizes the solenoid, vacuum flows to the transducer. When exhaust backpressure reaches a specified threshold, it closes a bleed valve inside the transducer. When the bleed valve is closed by backpressure and the solenoid is de-energized by the PCM, vacuum flows through the transducer to operate the EGR valve. When exhaust backpressure has not fully closed the bleed valve and the PCM has de-energized the solenoid, a partial vacuum flows to the EGR valve, which reduces the amount of exhaust gases allowed to enter the engine.

20 **Fuel injectors** - The PCM opens the fuel injectors sequentially (in firing order sequence). The PCM also controls the "pulse width," the interval of time during which each injector is open. The pulse width of an injector (measured in milliseconds) determines the amount of fuel delivered. For more information on the fuel delivery system and the fuel injectors, including injector replacement, refer to Chapter 4.

21 **Fuel pump relay** - When energized by the PCM, the fuel pump relay connects battery voltage to the fuel pump. The fuel pump relay provides battery voltage to the fuel pump. The fuel pump relay is located inside the Power Distribution Center (PDC) in the engine compartment.

22 **Ignition coils** - The ignition coils are triggered by the PCM. The ignition coils are mounted on the valve cover. Refer to Chapter 5 for more information on the ignition coils.

23 **Idle air control (IAC) motor** - The IAC motor, which is mounted on the throttle body, allows a certain amount of air to bypass the throttle plate when the throttle valve is closed or at idle position. It is controlled by the PCM.

24 **Proportional purge solenoid** - When the engine is cold or still warming up, no captive fuel vapors are allowed to escape from the EVAP canister. After the engine is warmed up, the PCM energizes the proportional purge solenoid, which regulates the flow of these vapors from the canister to the intake manifold. The rate of the flow of vapors is regulated by the proportional purge solenoid in accordance with the current level, which is controlled by the PCM. The proportional purge solenoid is located at the lower left rear corner of the engine compartment, to the left of the power steering pressure switch.

## Obtaining OBD-II system trouble codes

*Refer to illustration 2.26*

25 The PCM will illuminate the CHECK ENGINE light (also called the Malfunction Indicator Light) on the dash if it recognizes a component fault for two consecutive drive cycles. It will continue to set the light until the PCM does not detect any malfunction for three or more consecutive drive cycles.

26 The diagnostic codes for the OBD-II system can be extracted from the PCM by plugging a generic OBD-II scan tool **(see illustrations 2.1 and 2.2)** into the PCM's data link connector **(see illustration)**, which is located under the left side of the dash.

27 Plug the scan tool into the 16-pin data link connector (DLC), then follow the instructions included with the scan tool to extract all the diagnostic codes.

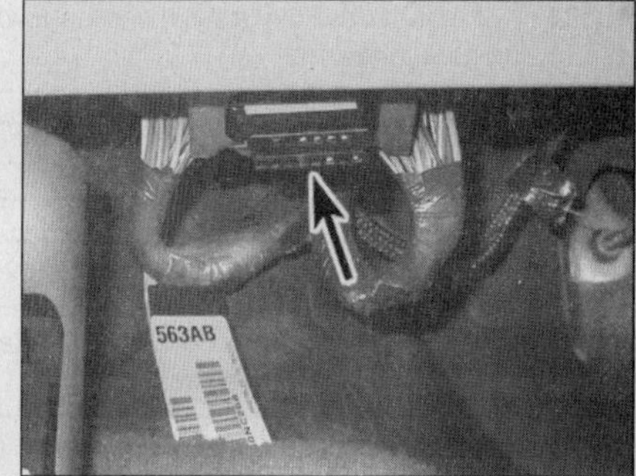

**2.26 The 16-pin Data Link Connector (DLC) is located under the left side of the dash**

## Diagnostic Trouble Codes

| Code | Probable cause |
|---|---|
| P0016 | Crankshaft / Camshaft timing misalignment |
| P0030 | Pre-converter oxygen sensor heater relay malfunction |
| P0031 | O2 sensor 1/1 heater circuit low |
| P0032 | O2 sensor 1/1 heater circuit high |
| P0033 | Surge valve solenoid circuit |
| P0036 | Post-converter oxygen sensor heater relay malfunction |
| P0037 | O2 sensor 1/2 heater circuit low |
| P0038 | O2 sensor 1/2 heater circuit high |
| P0068 | Manifold pressure/throttle position correlation |
| P0071 | Ambient air temperature sensor performance |
| P0072 | Ambient air temperature sensor circuit low |
| P0073 | Ambient air temperature sensor circuit high |
| P0106 | Manifold absolute pressure sensor input voltage out of range |
| P0107 | Manifold absolute pressure sensor input below acceptable minimum voltage |
| P0108 | Manifold absolute pressure sensor input above acceptable maximum voltage |

## Diagnostic Trouble Codes (continued)

| Code | Probable cause |
|---|---|
| P0111 | Intake air temperature sensor rationality |
| P0112 | Intake air temperature sensor input below minimum acceptable range |
| P0113 | Intake air temperature sensor input above maximum acceptable range |
| P0116 | Engine coolant temperature sensor range or performance problem |
| P0117 | Engine coolant temperature sensor input below minimum acceptable voltage |
| P0118 | Engine coolant temperature sensor input above maximum acceptable voltage |
| P0121 | Throttle position sensor signal does not correlate to manifold absolute pressure signal |
| P0122 | Throttle position sensor input below acceptable voltage range |
| P0123 | Throttle position sensor input above acceptable voltage range |
| P0125 | Time it takes to enter closed-loop fuel control is excessive |
| P0128 | Thermostat rationality |
| P0129 | Barometric pressure out-of-range low |
| P0130 | Pre-converter oxygen sensor heater relay circuit malfunction |
| P0131 | Pre-converter oxygen sensor input voltage below normal operating range |
| P0132 | Pre-converter oxygen sensor input voltage above normal operating range |
| P0133 | Pre-converter oxygen sensor response slower than minimum required switching frequency |
| P0134 | Neither rich nor lean condition is detected from pre-converter oxygen sensor input |
| P0135 | Pre-converter oxygen sensor heater or circuit fault |
| P0136 | Post-converter oxygen sensor heater relay circuit malfunction |
| P0137 | O2 sensor 1/2 circuit low |
| P0137 | Post-converter oxygen sensor input voltage below normal operating range. |
| P0138 | Post-converter oxygen sensor input voltage above normal operating range. |
| P0139 | Post-converter oxygen sensor response not as expected. |
| P0140 | Neither rich nor lean condition is detected from post-converter input |
| P0141 | Post-converter oxygen sensor heater or circuit fault |
| P0171 | Fuel injection system too lean |
| P0172 | Fuel injection system too rich |
| P0201 | Open or shorted condition detected in control circuit for injector No. 1 |

| Code | Probable cause |
|---|---|
| P0202 | Open or shorted condition detected in control circuit for injector No. 2 |
| P0203 | Open or shorted condition detected in control circuit for injector No. 3 |
| P0204 | Open or shorted condition detected in control circuit for injector No. 4 |
| P0234 | Overboost performance |
| P0243 | Wastegate solenoid circuit |
| P0300 | Multiple cylinder misfire detected |
| P0301 | Cylinder No. 1 misfire detected |
| P0302 | Cylinder No. 2 misfire detected |
| P0303 | Cylinder No. 3 misfire detected |
| P0304 | Cylinder No. 4 misfire detected |
| P0315 | No crank sensor learned |
| P0320 | No reference signal from crankshaft position sensor detected during cranking |
| P0325 | Knock sensor signal above or below minimum acceptable threshold voltage |
| P0335 | Crankshaft position sensor circuit |
| P0339 | Crankshaft position sensor intermittent |
| P0340 | No camshaft position sensor signal at PCM |
| P0344 | Camshaft position sensor intermittent |
| P0350 | Ignition coil draws too much current |
| P0351 | Ignition coil No. 1 peak primary circuit current not achieved with maximum dwell time |
| P0352 | Ignition coil No. 2 peak primary circuit current not achieved with maximum dwell time |
| P0401 | EGR system failure: required change in air/fuel ratio not detected |
| P0403 | Open or shorted condition detected in EGR solenoid control circuit |
| P0404 | EGR position sensor signal doesn't correlate to EGR duty cycle |
| P0405 | EGR position sensor input below acceptable voltage range |
| P0406 | EGR position sensor input above acceptable voltage range |
| P0420 | Catalyst system efficiency below threshold |
| P0440 | General evap system failure |
| P0441 | Insufficient or excessive purge flow detected in EVAP system |
| P0442 | Medium leak detected in EVAP system |
| P0443 | Open or shorted condition detected in EVAP purge control solenoid circuit |

| Code | Probable cause |
|---|---|
| P0452 | NVLD pressure switch stuck closed |
| P0453 | NVLD pressure switch stuck open |
| P0455 | Large leak detected in EVAP system |
| P0456 | Small leak detected in EVAP system |
| P0457 | Evap system - loose fuel cap |
| P0460 | No movement of fuel level sending unit detected |
| P0461 | Fuel level sensor 1 performance |
| P0462 | Fuel level sensor 1 circuit low |
| P0462 | Fuel level sending unit input voltage below acceptable voltage |
| P0463 | Fuel level sending unit input voltage above acceptable voltage |
| P0480 | Cooling fan 1 control circuit |
| P0481 | Cooling fan 2 control circuit |
| P0498 | NVLD canister vent valve solenoid circuit low |
| P0499 | NVLD canister vent valve solenoid circuit high |
| P0500 | No vehicle speed sensor signal detected |
| P0501 | Vehicle speed sensor #1 performance (manual trans) |
| P0501 | Vehicle speed sensor #1 performance (auto trans) |
| P0505 | Idle air control valve or circuit fault |
| P0506 | Idle speed low performance |
| P0507 | Idle speed high performance |
| P0508 | Idle air control valve sense circuit low |
| P0509 | Idle air control valve sense circuit high |
| P050A | Cold start idle air control system performance |
| P050B | Cold start ignition timing performance |
| P050D | Cold start rough idle |
| P0513 | Invalid skim key |
| P0522 | Oil pressure sending unit input below acceptable voltage |
| P0523 | Oil pressure sending unit input above acceptable voltage |
| P0551 | Incorrect power steering switch input detected |
| P0562 | Battery voltage low |
| P0563 | Battery voltage high |
| P0600 | No communication between detected between co-processors in control module |
| P0601 | Internal control module fault condition detected |
| P0604 | Transmission control module RAM self-test fault detected |
| P0605 | Transmission control module ROM self-test fault detected |
| P0615 | Open or short condition detected in starter relay circuit |
| P0622 | Open or short condition detected in alternator field control circuit |
| P0622 | Generator field control circuit |
| P0627 | Fuel pump control circuit |
| P0633 | Skim key not programmed in pcm |
| P063a | Generator voltage sense circuit |
| P0645 | Open or short condition detected in air conditioning clutch relay control circuit |
| P0685 | Auto shutdown relay control circuit |
| P0688 | Auto shutdown relay sense circuit low |
| P0691 | Cooling fan 1 control circuit low |
| P0692 | Cooling fan 1 control circuit high |
| P0693 | Cooling fan 2 control circuit low |
| P0694 | Cooling fan 2 control circuit high |
| P0700 | Transaxle control system malfunction |
| P0703 | Incorrect voltage input condition detected in brake switch circuit |
| P0711 | Transaxle fluid temperature sensor or circuit malfunction or failure |
| P0712 | Transaxle fluid temperature sensor input below acceptable voltage |
| P0713 | Transaxle fluid temperature sensor input above acceptable voltage |
| P0720 | Relationship between output shaft speed sensor and vehicle speed out of range |
| P0740 | Failure of torque converter clutch lock-up system |
| P0743 | Open or shorted condition detected in torque converter clutch solenoid control circuit |
| P0748 | Open or shorted condition detected in governor pressure solenoid or transaxle relay circuit |
| P0751 | Overdrive override switch input in a prolonged depressed state |
| P0753 | Open or shorted condition detected in overdrive solenoid control or transaxle relay circuit |
| P0756 | Shift solenoid B (2-3 shift) malfunction |
| P0783 | Overdrive solenoid unable to engage gear change from third gear to overdrive gear |
| P0801 | Open or short condition detected in transaxle reverse gear lock-out solenoid control circuit |
| P0833 | Clutch released switch circuit |
| P0850 | Park/Neutral switch performance |

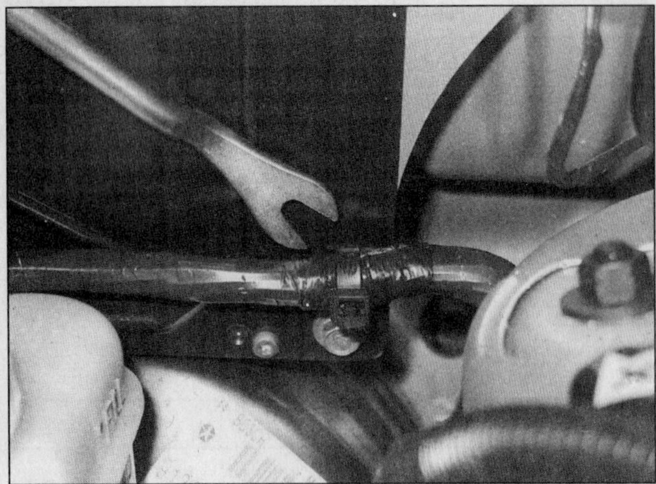

3.2a To detach the PCM from the firewall, pry loose this wiring harness clip . . .

3.2b . . . then remove these three mounting bolts

## 3 Powertrain Control Module (PCM) - replacement

*Refer to illustrations 3.2a, 3.2b and 3.3*

**Caution:** *To avoid electrostatic discharge damage to the PCM, handle the PCM only by its case. Do not touch the electrical terminals during removal and installation. If available, ground yourself to the vehicle with an anti-static ground strap, available at computer supply stores.*

1 Disconnect the cable from the negative terminal of the battery (see Chapter 5).

2 Detach the wiring harness clip from the PCM, remove the PCM retaining bolts **(see illustrations)** and move the PCM away from the firewall to provide easier access to the electrical connectors. **Caution:** *Avoid any static electricity damage to the computer by grounding yourself to the body before touching the PCM and using a special anti-static pad to store the PCM on once it is removed.*

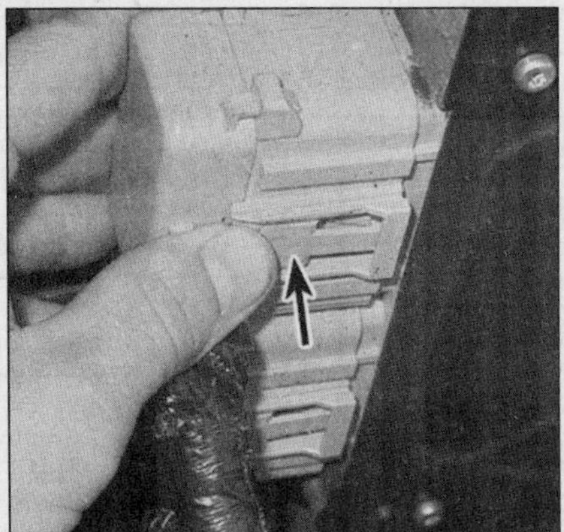

3.3 Release the locking tabs on the sides of the electrical connectors, unplug the connectors and remove the PCM

3 Disconnect the electrical connectors from the PCM **(see illustration)**.

4 Installation is the reverse of removal.

## 4 Camshaft Position (CMP) sensor - replacement

*Refer to illustrations 4.2, 4.4 and 4.5*

1 Disconnect the cable from the negative terminal of the battery (see Chapter 5).

2 Disconnect the CMP sensor electrical connector **(see illustration)**.

3 Remove the CMP sensor retaining bolts and remove the CMP sensor.

4 Remove the screw that attaches the target magnet to the camshaft **(see illustration)** and then remove the target magnet.

5 When installing the target magnet, make sure that the locating dowels on the back of the magnet are aligned with the locating holes in the end of the camshaft **(see illustration)**. Tighten the target magnet retaining screw to the torque listed in this Chapter's Specifications.

6 Installation is otherwise the reverse of removal. Tighten the CMP sensor retaining bolts to the torque listed in this Chapter's Specifications.

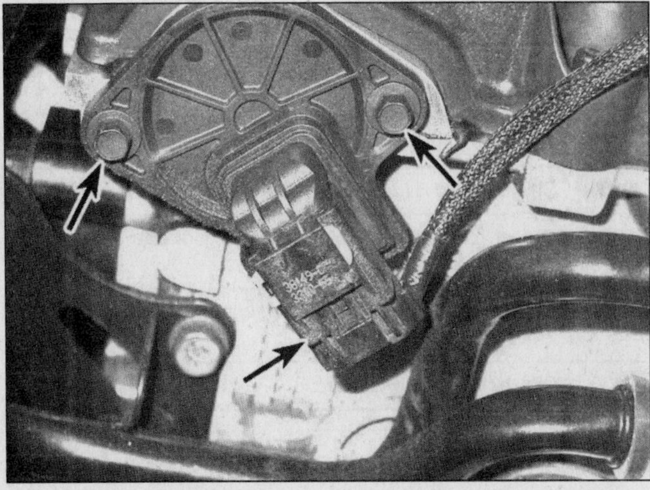

4.2 Disconnect the electrical connector from the Camshaft Position (CMP) sensor, remove the sensor retaining bolts and remove the sensor

4.4 To detach the CMP sensor target magnet from the end of the camshaft, remove this screw

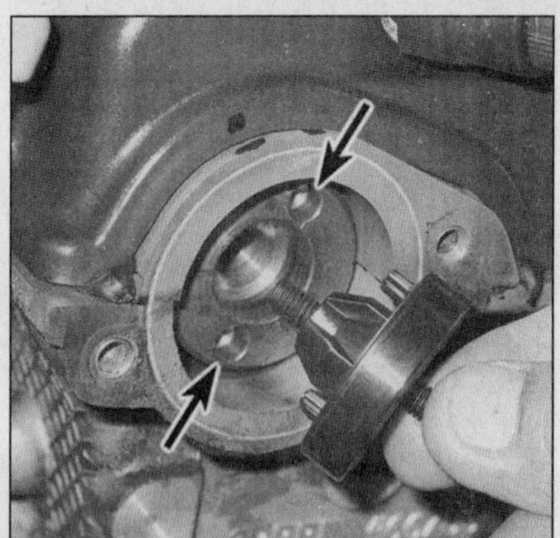

4.5 When installing the CMP sensor target magnet, make sure that the locating dowels on the back of the magnet are aligned with the locating holes in the end of the camshaft

## 5 Crankshaft Position (CKP) sensor - replacement

*Refer to illustration 5.3*

1 Disconnect the cable from the negative terminal of the battery (see Chapter 5).

2 Raise the front of the vehicle and place it securely on jackstands. Locate the sensor - it's on the front side of the engine block, below the starter motor.

3 Disconnect the CKP sensor electrical connector **(see illustration)**.

4 Remove the CKP sensor retaining bolt.

5 Installation is the reverse of removal. Be sure to tighten the CKP sensor retaining bolt to the torque listed in this Chapter's Specifications.

## 6 Engine Coolant Temperature (ECT) sensor - replacement

*Refer to illustrations 6.3 and 6.5*

**Warning:** *Wait until the engine has cooled completely before beginning this procedure.*

**Caution:** *Handle the Engine Coolant Temperature (ECT) sensor with care. Damage to the ECT sensor will affect the operation of the entire fuel injection system.*

1 Disconnect the cable from the negative terminal of the battery (see Chapter 5).

2 Drain the engine coolant (see Chapter 1).

3 Locate the sensor - it's threaded into the right front corner of the cylinder head, at the base of the coolant filler neck. Disconnect the electrical connector from the ECT sensor **(see illustration)**.

4 To remove the ECT sensor, unscrew it with a deep socket.

5 Before installing the new ECT sensor, wrap the threads of the sensor with Teflon tape to prevent coolant leakage **(see illustration)**. Installation is otherwise the reverse of removal. Be sure to tighten the ECT sensor securely. Refill and bleed the cooling system (see Chapter 1).

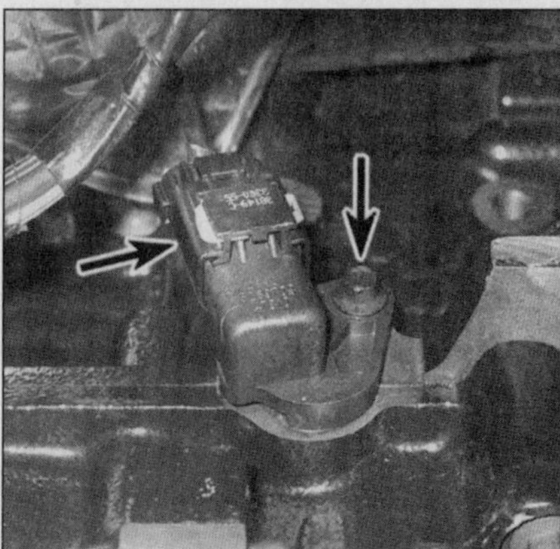

5.3 To remove the Crankshaft Position (CKP) sensor, unplug the electrical connector and remove the retaining bolt

## 7 Intake Air Temperature (IAT) sensor - replacement

*Refer to illustrations 7.2 and 7.3*

1 Disconnect the cable from the negative terminal of the battery (see Chapter 5).

2 The IAT sensor is located in the duct between the air filter housing and the throttle body. Disconnect the electrical connector from the IAT sensor **(see illustration)**.

3 Remove the IAT sensor by pulling it out of the air intake duct **(see illustration)**.

4 Installation is the reverse of removal.

## 8 Knock sensor - replacement

*Refer to illustration 8.4*

**Warning:** *Wait for the engine to cool completely before performing this procedure.*

1 Disconnect the cable from the negative terminal of the battery (see Chapter 5).

2 The knock sensor is threaded into the front side of the cylinder block, near the starter. Remove the battery for access (see Chapter 5).

3 Detach the fuel injector harness electri-

7.2 To unplug the electrical connector from the Intake Air Temperature (IAT) sensor, push the red tab (1) away from the IAT sensor (toward the harness), then squeeze the locking tab (2) and pull off the connector

6.3 To unplug the electrical connector from the Engine Coolant Temperature (ECT) sensor, push the red tab (1) away from the ECT sensor (toward the harness) then squeeze the locking tab (2) and pull off the connector

6.5 Wrap the threads of the ECT sensor with Teflon tape to prevent coolant leakage

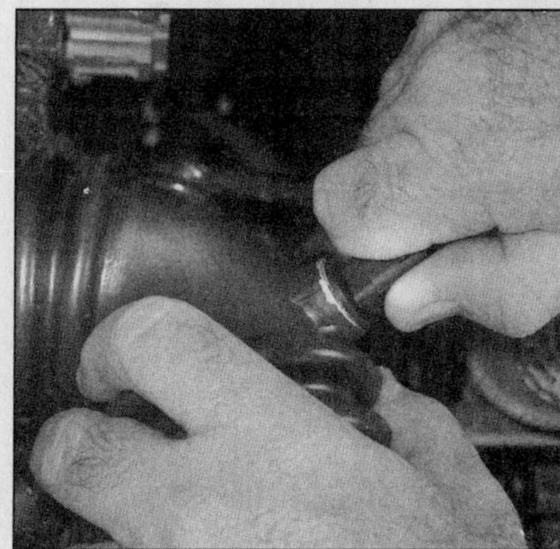

7.3 To remove the IAT sensor, firmly grasp the air intake duct with one hand and pull firmly on the sensor to work it loose from the duct; there is no insulating grommet, so be careful not to damage the duct

**8.4 To unplug the electrical connector from the knock sensor, push the red tab (1) away from the sensor (toward the harness), then squeeze the locking tab (2) and pull off the connector**

cal connector from its bracket (it's not necessary to unplug the connector).

4 Disconnect the electrical connector from the knock sensor **(see illustration)**.

5 Unscrew the knock sensor with a deep socket.

6 Installation is the reverse of removal. Be sure to tighten the knock sensor to the torque listed in this Chapter's Specifications.

## 9 Manifold Absolute Pressure (MAP) sensor - replacement

*Refer to illustration 9.2*

1 Disconnect the cable from the negative terminal of the battery (see Chapter 5).

2 Locate the MAP sensor - it's mounted to the rear of the upper intake manifold, near the coolant reservoir. Disconnect the MAF sensor electrical connector **(see illustration)**.

3 Remove the MAF sensor retaining screws and remove the sensor.

4 Installation is the reverse of removal.

## 10 Oxygen sensors - general information and replacement

### General information

1 Use special care when servicing an oxygen sensor or air/fuel ratio sensor:

a) *Oxygen sensors and air/fuel ratio sensors have a permanently attached pigtail and electrical connector which cannot be removed from the sensor. Damage or removal of the pigtail or electrical connector will ruin the sensor. Do not attempt to repair the oxygen sensor lead. If the lead is damaged, the sensor will need to be replaced.*

b) *Grease, dirt and other contaminants should be kept away from the electrical connector and the louvered end of the sensor.*

c) *Do not use cleaning solvents of any kind on an oxygen sensor or air/fuel ratio sensor.*

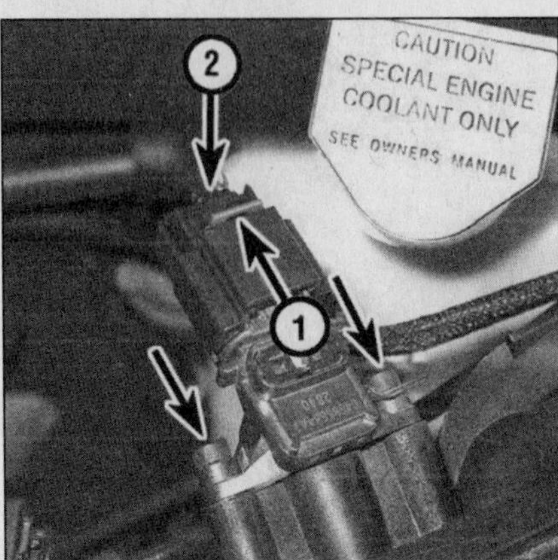


**9.2 To unplug the electrical connector from the Manifold Absolute Pressure (MAP) sensor, push the red tab (1) away from the sensor (toward the harness), then squeeze the locking tab (2) and pull off the connector; to detach the MAP sensor from the intake manifold plenum, remove the two retaining screws**

d) *Do not drop or roughly handle an oxygen sensor or air/fuel ratio sensor.*

e) *Be sure to install the silicone boot in the correct position to prevent the boot from melting and to allow the sensor to operate properly.*

### Replacement

**Note:** *Because it is installed in the exhaust manifold or catalytic converter, both of which contract when cool, an oxygen sensor might be very difficult to loosen when the engine is cold. Rather than risk damage to the sensor, start and run the engine for a minute or two, then shut it off. Be careful not to burn yourself during the following procedure.*

2 Disconnect the cable from the negative terminal of the battery (see Chapter 5).

3 Raise the vehicle and place it securely on jackstands.

#### Upstream oxygen sensor

*Refer to illustrations 10.5 and 10.6*

4 The upstream oxygen sensor is located

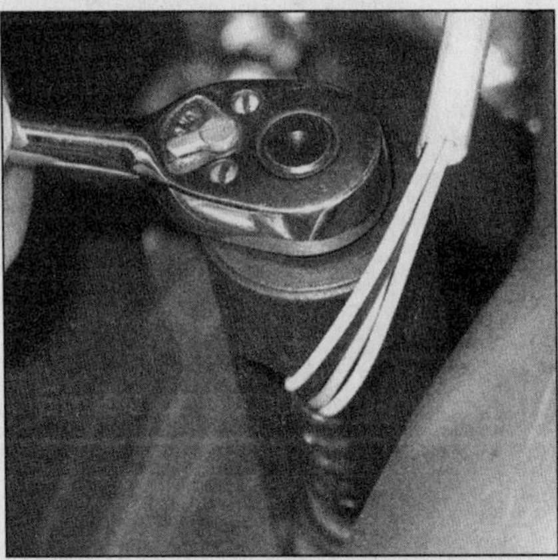

**10.6 Use a special oxygen sensor socket to unscrew the upstream oxygen sensor**

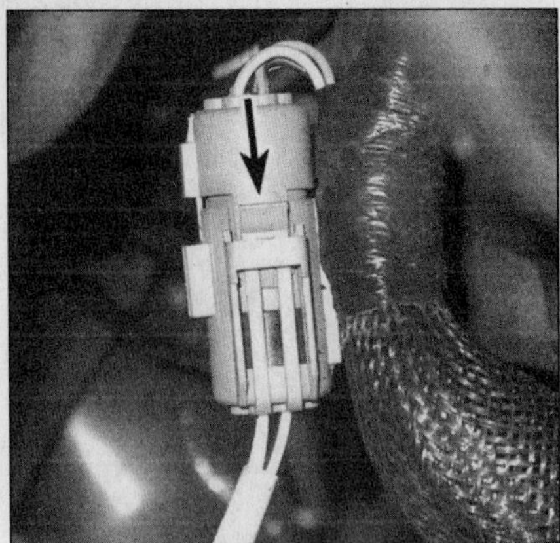

**10.5 The electrical connector for the upstream oxygen sensor is located to the left of the sensor; to unplug the connector, squeeze this locking tab and then pull the connector halves apart**

on top of the exhaust manifold, just above the flange.

5 Trace the electrical lead from the sensor to the electrical connector **(see illustration)** and disconnect it.

6 Using a special oxygen sensor socket, unscrew the sensor **(see illustration)**.

7 After removing the old upstream oxygen sensor, clean the threads of the sensor bore in the exhaust manifold.

8 If you're going to install the old sensor, apply anti-seize compound to the threads of the sensor to facilitate future removal. If you're going to install a new oxygen sensor, it's not necessary to apply anti-seize compound to the threads. The threads on new sensors already have anti-seize compound on them.

9 Install the upstream oxygen sensor and tighten it securely.

10 Installation is otherwise the reverse of removal.

#### Downstream oxygen sensor

*Refer to illustrations 10.12 and 10.13*

11 The downstream oxygen sensor is located on the left side of the catalytic converter.

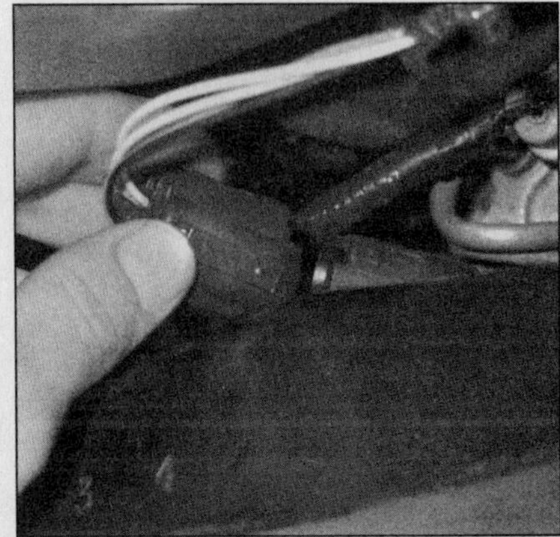

**10.12 The electrical connector for the downstream oxygen sensor is located above the left end of this crossmember**

10.13 To remove the downstream oxygen sensor, unscrew it with a suitable wrench (it's not necessary to use a special oxygen sensor socket, since you have plenty of room to turn a wrench)

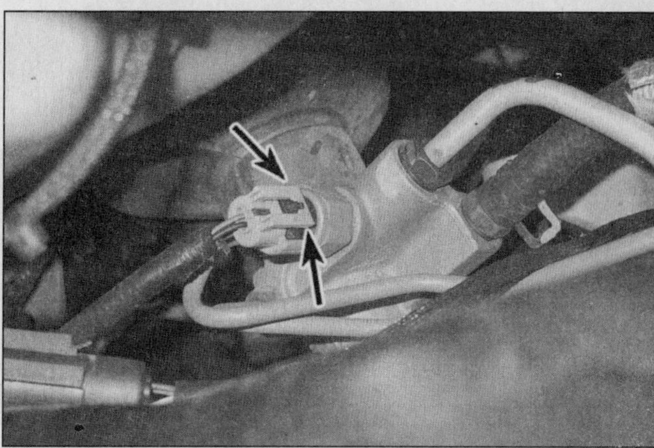

11.3 You'll find the power steering pressure switch on the backside of the power steering gear assembly; to unplug the electrical connector, pry up on the locking tab to release it, then pull off the connector

11.4 Use a deep socket to unscrew the power steering pressure switch

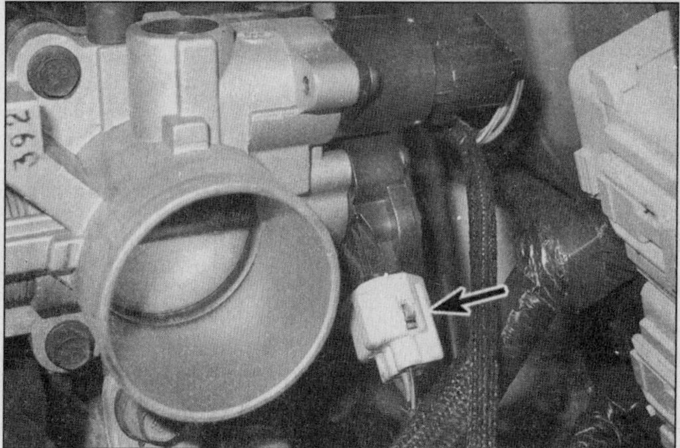

12.3 To unplug the electrical connector from the Throttle Position (TP) sensor, squeeze the single locking tab on top of the connector (the side of the connector facing toward the firewall, not visible in this photo), then pull off the connector

12 Trace the electrical lead from the sensor to the electrical connector and disconnect it **(see illustration)**.

13 Unscrew and remove the downstream oxygen sensor **(see illustration)**.

14 After removing the old downstream oxygen sensor, clean the threads of the sensor bore in the catalytic converter.

12.4 To detach the TP sensor from the throttle body, remove these two screws (throttle body assembly removed for clarity)

15 If you're going to install the old sensor, apply anti-seize compound to the threads of the sensor to facilitate future removal.

16 If you're going to install a new oxygen sensor, it's not necessary to apply anti-seize compound to the threads. The threads on new sensors already have anti-seize compound on them.

17 Install the upstream oxygen sensor and tighten it securely.

18 Installation is otherwise the reverse of removal.

## 11 Power steering fluid pressure switch - replacement

*Refer to illustrations 11.3 and 11.4*

1 Disconnect the cable from the negative terminal of the battery (see Chapter 5).

2 Raise the vehicle and place it securely on jackstands.

3 Disconnect the electrical connector from the power steering fluid pressure switch **(see illustration)**.

4 Using a deep socket and an extension **(see illustration)**, unscrew and remove the power steering fluid pressure switch.

5 Seal the threads of the new switch with Teflon tape.

6 Installation is the reverse of removal. Be sure to tighten the switch securely.

## 12 Throttle Position (TP) sensor - replacement

*Refer to illustrations 12.3, 12.4, 12.5, 12.7 and 12.8*

1 Disconnect the cable from the negative terminal of the battery (see Chapter 5).

2 Remove the air intake duct (see Chapter 4).

3 Disconnect the electrical connector from the TP sensor **(see illustration)**.

4 Remove the two TP sensor mounting screws **(see illustration)** and remove the TP sensor.

12.5 **Remove and discard the old TP sensor O-ring**

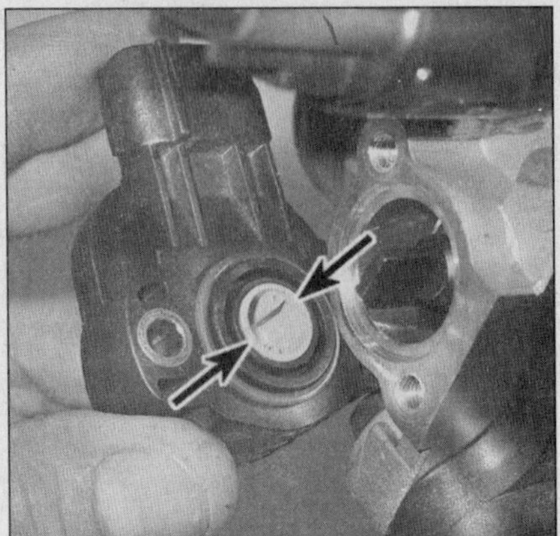

12.7 **When installing the TP sensor, make sure that the blade on the end of the throttle shaft fits between the two tabs inside the hole in the backside of the TP sensor**

12.8 **Install the TP sensor a few degrees to the left of its actual installed position then rotate it clockwise until the retaining screw holes in the sensor are aligned with the screw holes in the throttle body; you should feel some resistance as you line up the holes, but if the TP sensor is difficult to turn, take it off and reinstall it with the throttle shaft blade touching the opposite sides of the tabs**

5 Remove and discard the old TP sensor O-ring **(see illustration)**.

6 Before installing the TP sensor, install a new O-ring.

7 When installing the TP sensor, make sure that the blade on the end of the throttle shaft fits into the hole in the backside of the TP sensor **(see illustration)**. There are two tabs inside the hole. Each side of the blade should be touching one of the tabs.

8 Install the TP sensor a few degrees to the left of the mounting holes **(see illustration)** and then rotate it clockwise until the holes in the TP sensor and the holes in the throttle body are aligned. The TP sensor should offer a little resistance when rotated into position. But if it's difficult to rotate, you've got the throttle shaft blade on the wrong sides of the tabs. Reinstall the TP sensor with the throttle shaft blade on the *opposite* sides of the sensor tabs.

9 When the TP sensor holes are lined up, install the TP sensor screws and tighten them securely.

10 Installation is otherwise the reverse of removal.

## 13 Vehicle Speed Sensor (VSS) - replacement

1 Disconnect the cable from the negative terminal of the battery (see Chapter 5).

### *Models with a manual transaxle*

*Refer to illustration 13.3*

2 Raise the vehicle and place it securely on jackstands.

3 Unplug the VSS electrical connector **(see illustration)**.

4 Remove the VSS retaining bolt and then remove the VSS from the transaxle.

5 Remove the VSS drive gear from the VSS.

6 Remove and discard the old O-ring.

7 Install a new O-ring on the VSS.

8 Install the drive gear, then install the VSS.

9 Install the VSS retaining bolt and tighten it securely.

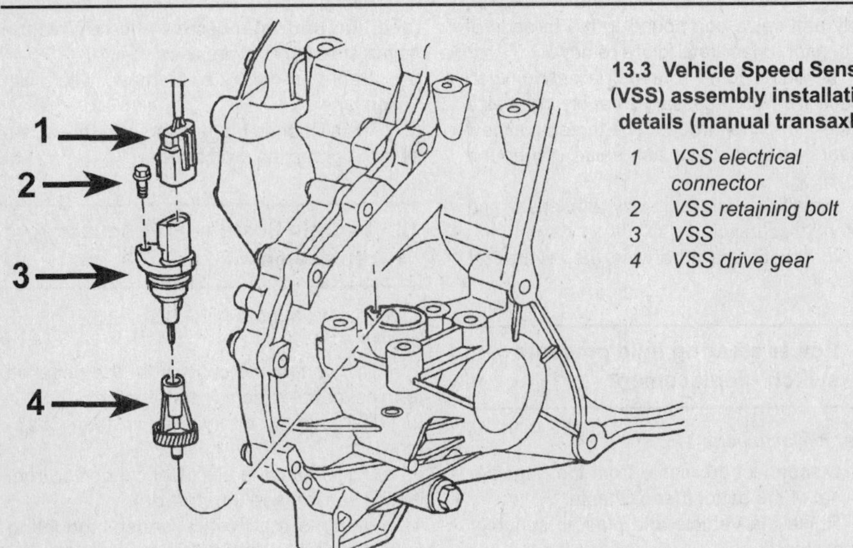


**13.3 Vehicle Speed Sensor (VSS) assembly installation details (manual transaxle)**

1 *VSS electrical connector*
2 *VSS retaining bolt*
3 *VSS*
4 *VSS drive gear*

10 Installation is otherwise the reverse of removal.

### *Models with an automatic transaxle*

11 Remove the air filter housing (see Chapter 4).

12 Remove the battery (see Chapter 5).

13 Remove the battery tray and the battery tray bracket (see "Battery - removal and installation" in Chapter 5).

#### Input shaft VSS

*Refer to illustrations 13.14 and 13.16*

14 Disconnect the input shaft VSS electrical connector **(see illustration)**.

15 Unscrew the input shaft VSS from the transaxle.

13.14 **To unplug the electrical connector from the input shaft VSS, pry open the locking tang on the underside of the connector (not visible in this photo), then pull off the connector; to remove the VSS, simply unscrew it**

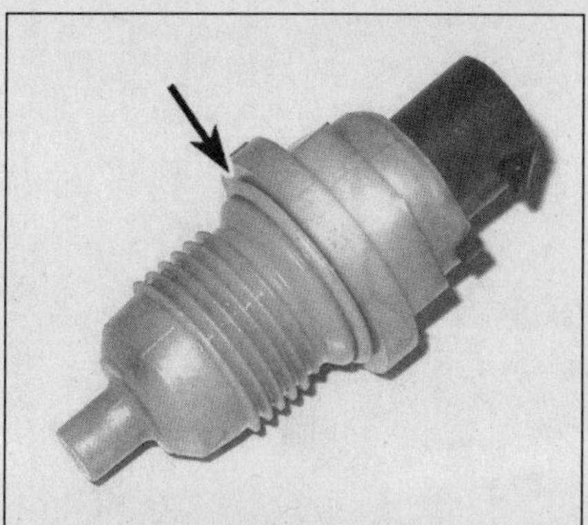

13.16 Remove and discard the old O-ring from the VSS

14.3 To detach the IAC motor from the throttle body, remove these two mounting screws

16 Remove and discard the old O-ring **(see illustration)**.
17 Install a new O-ring on the VSS.
18 Install the VSS and tighten it securely.

### Output shaft VSS

*Refer to illustration 13.19*

19 Unplug the output shaft VSS electrical connector **(see illustration)**.

13.19 To unplug the electrical connector from the output shaft VSS, pry open the locking tang on the underside of the connector (not visible in this photo), then pull off the connector; to remove the VSS, simply unscrew it

20 Unscrew the output shaft VSS from the transaxle.
21 Remove and discard the old O-ring **(see illustration 13.16)**.
22 Install a new O-ring on the VSS.
23 Install the VSS then tighten it securely.

## 14 Idle Air Control (IAC) motor - replacement

*Refer to illustrations 14.2, 14.3, 14.4 and 14.6*

1 Disconnect the cable from the negative terminal of the battery (see Chapter 5).
2 The Idle Air Control motor is located on the throttle body. Disconnect the IAC motor electrical connector **(see illustration)**.
3 Remove the IAC motor mounting screws **(see illustration)** and detach the IAC motor from the throttle body.
4 Remove and discard the old O-ring from the IAC motor **(see illustration)**.
5 Install a new O-ring on the IAC motor.
6 If you're going to install a new IAC motor, measure the length of the IAC motor pintle valve (the plunger) before installing the IAC motor **(see illustration)**. The pintle valve should not exceed one inch (25 mm) in length. If it does, carefully push the pintle in while wiggling it until it protrudes less than one inch.
7 Install the IAC motor and tighten the mounting screws securely.
8 Installation is otherwise the reverse of removal. **Note:** *The idle speed may "hunt" (vary in rpm) for a short period of time until the PCM determines the proper pintle position to stabilize the idle.*

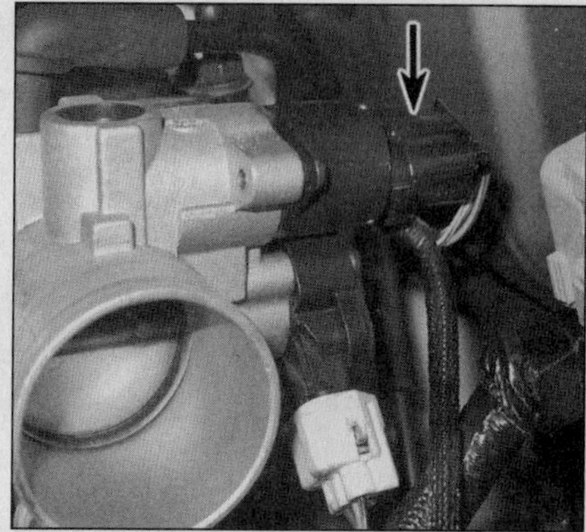

14.2 To unplug the electrical connector from the IAC motor, depress the locking tang on the bottom of the connector (not visible in this photo)

## 15 Catalytic converter - general information, check and replacement

**Note:** *Because of the Federally mandated extended warranty which covers emissions-related components such as the catalytic converter, check with a dealer service department before replacing the converter at your own expense.*

### General information

1 The catalytic converter is an emission control device installed in the exhaust system

14.4 Remove and discard the old O-ring from the IAC motor

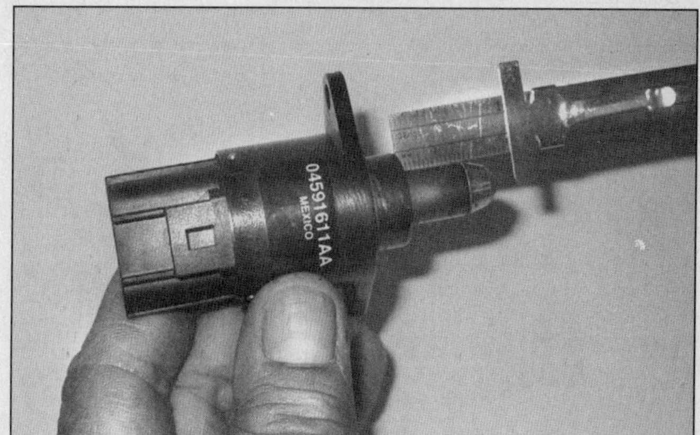


14.6 If you're installing a *new* IAC motor, measure the length of the pintle valve before installing the motor; the pintle valve should not exceed one inch (25 mm) in length

15.8a To remove the catalytic converter, loosen this clamp bolt behind the converter . . .

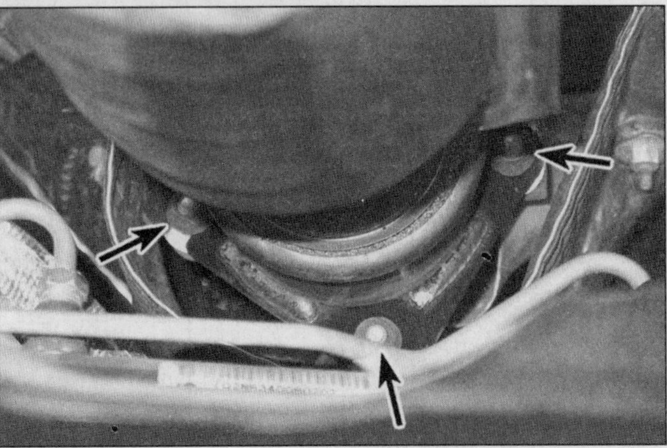

15.8b . . . then remove these four nuts from the exhaust manifold studs (upper nut not visible in this photo)

that reduces pollutants from the exhaust gas stream. There are two types of converters: The oxidation catalyst reduces the levels of hydrocarbon (HC) and carbon monoxide (CO) by adding oxygen to the exhaust stream. The reduction catalyst lowers the levels of oxides of nitrogen (NOx) by removing oxygen from the exhaust gases. These two types of catalysts are combined into a three-way catalyst that reduces all three pollutants.

## Check

2 The equipment for testing a catalytic converter is expensive. If you suspect that the converter on your vehicle is malfunctioning, take it to a dealer or authorized emissions inspection facility for diagnosis and repair.

3 Whenever the vehicle is raised for servicing underbody components, inspect the converter for leaks, corrosion, dents and other damage. Inspect the welds/flange bolts that attach the front and rear ends of the converter to the exhaust system. If damage is discovered, the converter should be replaced.

4 Although catalytic converters don't break too often, they can become plugged. The easiest way to check for a restricted converter is to use a vacuum gauge to diagnose the effect of a blocked exhaust on intake vacuum.

a) *Connect a vacuum gauge to an intake manifold vacuum source (see Chapter 2B).*
b) *Warm the engine to operating temperature, place the transaxle in Park (automatic) or Neutral (manual) and apply the parking brake.*
c) *Note and record the vacuum reading at idle.*
d) *Quickly open the throttle to near full throttle and release it. Note and record the vacuum reading.*
e) *Perform the test three more times, recording the reading after each test.*
f) *If the reading after the fourth test is more than one in-Hg lower than the reading recorded at idle, the exhaust system may be restricted (the catalytic converter could be plugged or an exhaust pipe or muffler could be restricted).*

## Replacement

*Refer to illustrations 15.8a and 15.8b*

5 Raise the vehicle and place it securely on jackstands.

6 Remove the downstream oxygen sensor (see Section 10).

7 Be sure to spray the nuts on the exhaust flange studs with penetrant before removing them from the catalytic converter.

8 Loosen the clamp behind the catalytic converter and remove the nuts that attach the catalyst to the exhaust manifold **(see illustrations)**. Separate the catalytic converter from the exhaust system.

9 Before installing the converter, coat the threads of the exhaust manifold studs and the clamp bolt with anti-seize compound. Be sure to tighten the fasteners securely.

10 Installation is otherwise the reverse of removal.

# 16 Evaporative emissions control (EVAP) system - general information and component replacement

## General description

*Refer to illustration 16.1*

1 The fuel evaporative emissions control (EVAP) system **(see illustration)** absorbs fuel vapors (unburned hydrocarbons) and, during engine operation, releases them into the intake manifold from which they're drawn into the intake ports where they mix with the incoming air-fuel mixture. The charcoal canister is mounted at the right front corner of the fuel tank.

2 When the engine is not operating, fuel

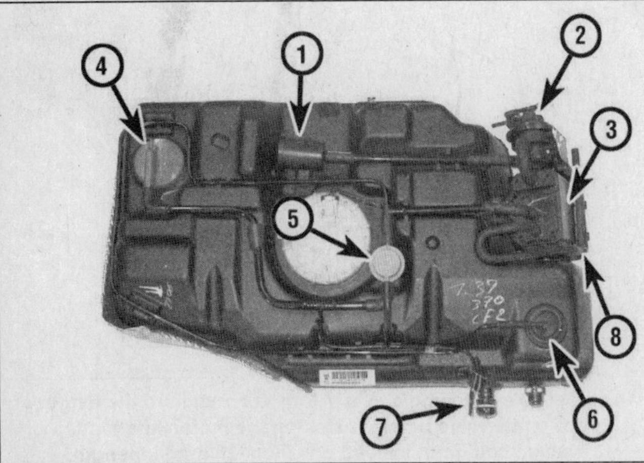



**16.1 Fuel evaporative emissions control (EVAP) system:**

1 *Leak Detection Pump (LDP) air filter*
2 *Leak Detection Pump (LDP)*
3 *EVAP canister*
4 *Control valve*
5 *Flow management valve*
6 *Rollover valve*
7 *Fuel filler neck breather hose*
8 *EVAP canister-to-proportional purge solenoid hose (solenoid in engine compartment)*

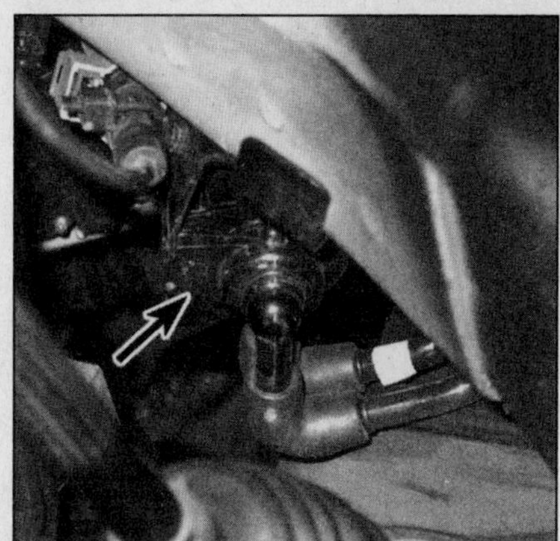

**16.6 The proportional purge solenoid is located in the lower right rear corner of the engine compartment; before detaching the EVAP hoses, label one of them to ensure correct reassembly**

vapors migrate through a system of hoses from the fuel tank and intake manifold to the EVAP canister, where they are stored until the next time the vehicle is operated. Vapors are routed through the control valve and then through the flow management valve on their way to the EVAP canister. The flow management valve also serves as a liquid separator to prevent fuel from contaminating the EVAP canister. The flow management valve is replaceable, but the control valve is not. If the control valve malfunctions, the fuel tank must be replaced. A rollover valve, which is located in the top of the fuel tank, prevents the flow of fuel through the vapor hoses if the vehicle rolls over. The rollover valve is also not serviceable. If it malfunctions, replace the fuel tank.

3 The Powertrain Control Module (PCM) purges the EVAP canister through the proportional purge solenoid. The solenoid regulates the rate of flow of vapors from the canister to the throttle body. The solenoid is not energized during cold starts and during warm-up. After the engine has been started and warmed up to its normal operating temperature, the PCM energizes the solenoid, which controls the rate of flow in proportion to the current level, which is controlled by the PCM.

4 The EVAP system is equipped with a Leak Detection Pump (LDP), which is mounted in front of the fuel tank, near the EVAP canister. The LDP, which is controlled by the PCM, tests for, and can detect, leaks in the system. When a leak is detected, the PCM stores a diagnostic trouble code (see Section 2). The LDP is equipped with a filter, which is located on top of the fuel tank.

## Replacement

**Warning:** *Gasoline is extremely flammable, so take extra precautions when you work on any part of the fuel system. Don't smoke or allow open flames or bare light bulbs near the work area, and don't work in a garage where a gas-type appliance (such as a water heater or a clothes dryer) is present. Since gasoline is carcinogenic, wear latex gloves when there's a possibility of being exposed to fuel, and, if you spill any fuel on your skin, rinse it off immediately with soap and water. Mop up any spills immediately and do not store fuel-soaked rags where they could ignite. The fuel system is under constant pressure, so, if any fuel lines are to be disconnected, the fuel pressure in the system must be relieved first (see Chapter 4). When you perform any kind of work on the fuel system, wear safety glasses and have a Class B type fire extinguisher on hand.*

### Proportional purge solenoid

*Refer to illustrations 16.6 and 16.7*

5 Raise the vehicle and place it securely on jackstands.

6 The proportional purge solenoid **(see illustration)** is located in the lower right rear corner of the engine compartment.

7 Disconnect the solenoid electrical connector **(see illustration)**. The solenoid connector is locked into place by a red tab on top of the connector. To release the locking tab, push it toward the front of the vehicle, then depress the locking tang in the center of the top side of the connector and pull off the connector.

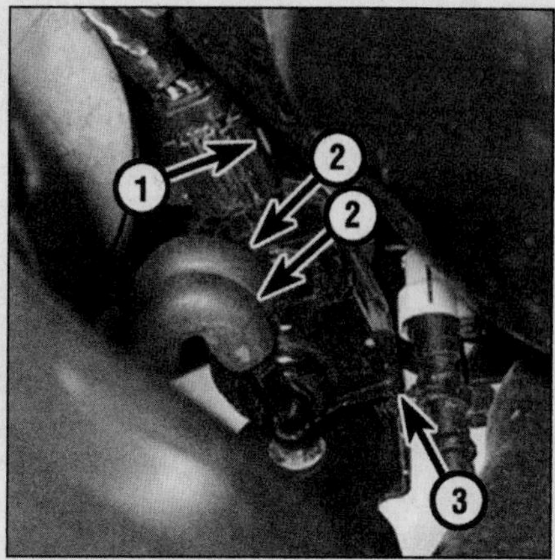


**16.7 To remove the proportional purge solenoid, disconnect the electrical connector (1), detach the two EVAP hoses (2), then push the solenoid toward the steering shaft to disengage it from the mounting bracket (3)**

8 Clearly label the EVAP hoses to ensure correct reassembly, then detach the two EVAP hoses from the solenoid.

9 To detach the solenoid from its mounting bracket, slide it off, in the direction of the steering shaft.

10 Installation is the reverse of removal.

### Leak Detection Pump (LDP)

#### 2001 through 2008

*Refer to illustrations 16.12 and 16.13*

11 Remove the fuel tank (see Chapter 4).

12 Clearly label and disconnect the EVAP hoses from the Leak Detection Pump (LDP) **(see illustration)**.

13 Disconnect the electrical connector from the LDP **(see illustration)**.

14 Remove the three LDP mounting bolts and remove the LDP.

15 Installation is the reverse of removal.

**16.12 Clearly label and disconnect the EVAP hoses from the leak detection pump**

**16.13 Unplug the electrical connector from the leak detection pump and remove the three pump mounting bolts to detach it from its mounting bracket**

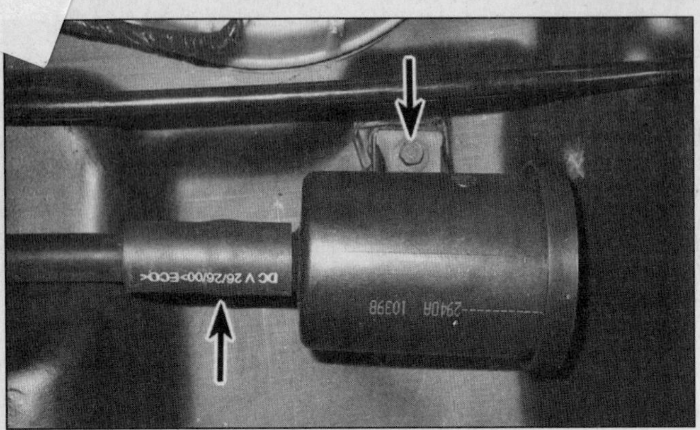


16.17 To replace the leak detection pump filter, disconnect the EVAP hose and remove the retaining bolt

16.26 Clearly label the hoses on top of the EVAP canister before disconnecting them

### Leak Detection Pump (LDP) filter

*Refer to illustration 16.17*

16 Remove the fuel tank (see Chapter 4).
17 Locate the Leak Detection Pump (LDP) filter **(see illustration)** on top of the fuel tank.
18 Disconnect the EVAP hose from the LDP filter.
19 Remove the LDP filter retaining bolt and remove the filter.
20 Installation is the reverse of removal.

### Natural Vacuum Leak Detector (NVLD) - 2009 models

21 Raise the vehicle and support it securely on jackstands.
22 Disconnect the electrical connector from the NVLD.
23 Remove the bolt attaching the NLVD bracket to the canister bracket, then remove the purge hoses from the NLVD and remove the NVLD
24 Installation is the reverse of removal

### EVAP canister

*Refer to illustrations 16.26, 16.27 and 16.28*

25 Remove the fuel tank (see Chapter 4).
26 Clearly label the hoses on top of the EVAP canister **(see illustration)**, then disconnect them from the canister.
27 The upper part of the EVAP canister is secured to its mounting bracket by a push pin **(see illustration)**. To detach the upper end of the canister from the bracket, simply pull out the push pin.
28 The lower part of the EVAP canister is secured to its mounting bracket by spring clips **(see illustration)**. To disengage it from the clips, simply push down on the front clip and push the straight up and to the rear.
29 Installation is the reverse of removal.

## 17 Exhaust Gas Recirculation (EGR) system - general information and component replacement

### General information

1 The Exhaust Gas Recirculation (EGR) system reduces oxides of nitrogen (NOx) and helps to prevent detonation, both of which are produced by high combustion temperatures. The EGR system does this by recirculating a small amount of spent exhaust gases from the exhaust system back into the intake manifold, which dilutes the intake charge and lowers combustion temperatures. The EGR system consists of an EGR valve, a control assembly/transducer and a metal tube connecting the exhaust manifold to the EGR valve. The EGR valve is a vacuum-operated diaphragm that opens in response to a vacuum signal from the intake manifold. The amount that it opens varies in accordance with the strength of the vacuum signal, which is regulated by a control assembly/transducer. When the PCM energizes a solenoid in the control assembly, a transducer allows vacuum to reach the EGR valve.

### Component replacement

*Refer to illustration 17.3, 17.4, 17.5, 17.6, 17.8 and 17.9*

**Warning:** *Make sure that the engine is cool before starting this procedure.*

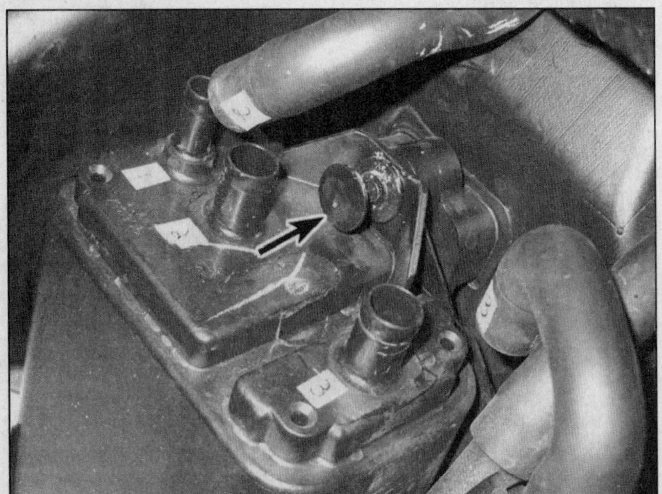

16.27 Pull out the push pin to disconnect the upper end of the EVAP canister from its mounting bracket

16.28 The lower end of the EVAP canister is secured to the mounting bracket by spring clips; to disengage the canister from the clips, simply push down on the front clip and push the canister straight up and to the rear

**17.3 To detach the Power Distribution Center (PDC) from the air filter housing bracket, disengage these clips and pull it straight up**

**17.4 To disconnect the EGR tube from the intake manifold, remove these bolts**

**17.5 To disconnect the EGR transducer bracket, unclip it here with a small screwdriver (lower arrow); to unlock the EGR transducer solenoid electrical connector, push the red tab (upper arrow) away from the solenoid and pull off the connector**

**17.6 Disconnect the vacuum hoses from the EGR valve control assembly (upper arrow) and from the transducer part of the control valve (lower arrow)**

2 Remove the air filter housing and the air intake duct (see Chapter 4).

3 Detach the Power Distribution Center (PDC) from the air filter housing bracket **(see illustration)** and then carefully push it out of the way.

4 Remove the bolts that attach the EGR tube to the intake manifold **(see illustration)**.

5 Unclip the EGR transducer bracket **(see illustration)**.

6 Disconnect the vacuum supply hose from the EGR valve control assembly and disconnect the backpressure hose from the transducer part of the control valve **(see illustration)**.

7 Disconnect the electrical connector from the transducer **(see illustration 17.5)**.

8 Disconnect the vacuum line from the EGR valve **(see illustration)**.

9 Remove the bolts that attach the EGR tube to the EGR valve **(see illustration)**.

**17.8 Disconnect the vacuum hose from the EGR valve**

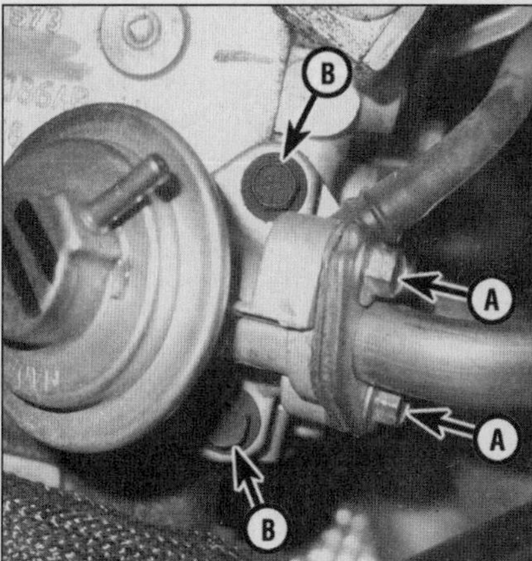


**17.9 To detach the EGR tube from the EGR valve, remove bolts (A); to detach the EGR valve from the cylinder head, remove bolts (B)**

Remove the EGR tube. Don't lose the O-ring at the intake manifold end of the EGR tube. Inspect the O-ring. If it's damaged or worn, replace it.

10 Remove the two EGR valve mounting bolts **(see illustration 17.9)** and remove the EGR valve and transducer assembly.

11 Remove the old EGR valve gasket and discard it.

12 Installation is the reverse of removal. Be sure to use a new gasket and tighten the EGR valve bolts and the EGR tube bolts to the torque listed in this Chapter's Specifications.

## 18 Positive Crankcase Ventilation (PCV) system

*Refer to illustration 18.2*

1 The Positive Crankcase Ventilation (PCV) system reduces hydrocarbon emissions by scavenging crankcase vapors. It does this by circulating fresh air from the air cleaner through the crankcase, where it mixes with blow-by gases, before being drawn through a PCV valve into the intake manifold.

2 The PCV system consists of the PCV valve and two hoses, one of which connects the air cleaner to the crankcase and the other (containing the PCV valve) which connects the crankcase to the throttle body **(see illustration)**.

3 To maintain idle quality, the PCV valve restricts the flow when the intake manifold vacuum is high. If abnormal operating conditions (such as piston ring problems) arise, the system is designed to allow excessive amounts of blow-by gases to flow back through the crankcase vent tube into the air cleaner to be consumed by normal combustion.

4 Checking and replacement of the PCV valve is covered in Chapter 1.

**18.2 The Positive Crankcase Ventilation (PCV) system consists of a hose between the crankcase and the air filter housing (not shown), this hose connecting the valve cover to the intake manifold and the PCV valve itself, which is screwed into the valve cover**

# Chapter 7 Part A
# Manual transaxle

## Contents



## Specifications

### General

| | |
|---|---|
| Lubricant type and capacity | See Chapter 1 |

### Torque specifications

| | Ft-lbs | Nm |
|---|---|---|
| Transaxle-to-engine bolts | | |
| G288 (Turbocharged models) | 80 | 108 |
| T-350 | 70 | 95 |
| Drain plug | See Chapter 1 | |

## 1 General information

The vehicles covered in this manual are equipped with either a 5-speed manual, or a 4-speed automatic transaxle. Information on the manual transaxles are included in this Part of Chapter 7. Service procedures for the automatic transaxles are contained in Chapter 7, Part B.

The manual transaxle is a compact, two-piece, lightweight aluminum alloy housing containing both the transmission and differential assemblies. Two different manual transaxle models are available, either the T350 for non-turbo vehicles or the G288 designed for the 2.4L turbocharged models.

Because of the complexity, unavailability of replacement parts and special tools necessary, internal repair procedures for the manual transaxle are beyond the scope of this manual. The bulk of information in this Chapter is devoted to removal and installation procedures.

## 2 Shift cables - replacement, installation and adjustment

**Warning:** *These vehicles are equipped with airbags. Always disable the airbag system before working in the vicinity of any airbag system components to avoid the possibility of accidental deployment of the airbag(s), which could cause personal injury (see Chapter 12).*

**Note:** *The selector cable and crossover cable are available as an assembly and must be replaced together.*

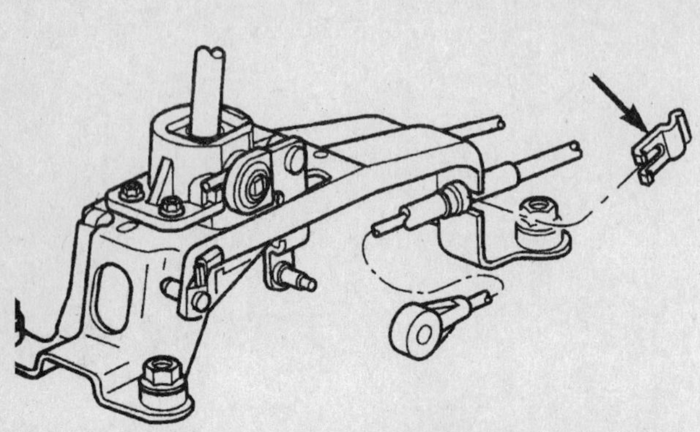

2.3 The cables are secured to the shift lever bracket by clips

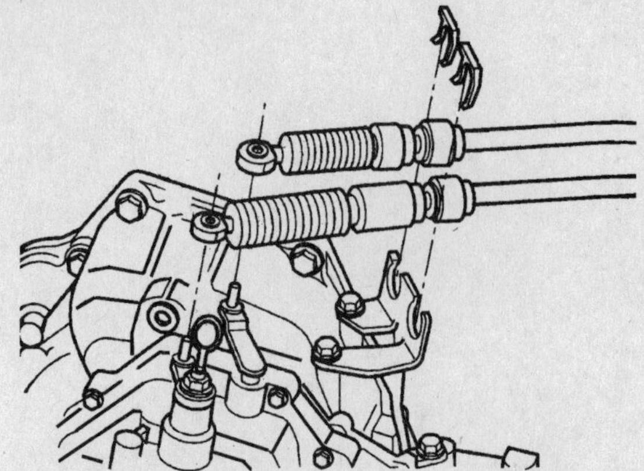

2.9 Remove the retaining clip using a pair of pliers

## Removal

*Refer to illustrations 2.3 and 2.9*

1 Remove the gearshift knob and lever boot (see Section 3).

2 Remove the center console (see Chapter 11).

3 Remove the clip securing the selector cable to the shift lever bracket and slide the cable off of the lever **(see illustration)**.

4 Remove the clip securing the crossover cable to the shift lever bracket and slide the cable off of the lever.

5 Remove the grommet plate-to-floor-pan fasteners.

6 Remove the air filter housing assembly (see Chapter 4).

7 Remove the battery and battery tray (see Chapter 5).

8 Use two flat blade screwdrivers and carefully pry the crossover and selector cables from the shifter levers at the transaxle.

9 Remove both cable retaining clips and remove the cables from the bracket **(see illustration)**.

10 Raise the vehicle and place it securely on jackstands.

11 Working under the vehicle, remove the catalytic converter heat shield.

12 Remove the last bolt and cable grommet from the floor pan and pull the cable assembly out from under vehicle.

13 Installation is the reverse of removal, noting the following points:

*a) Install new cable retaining clips.*

*b) Adjust the crossover cable (see Step 14).*

*c) Use a rubber mallet and strike the knob to engage it to the lever.*

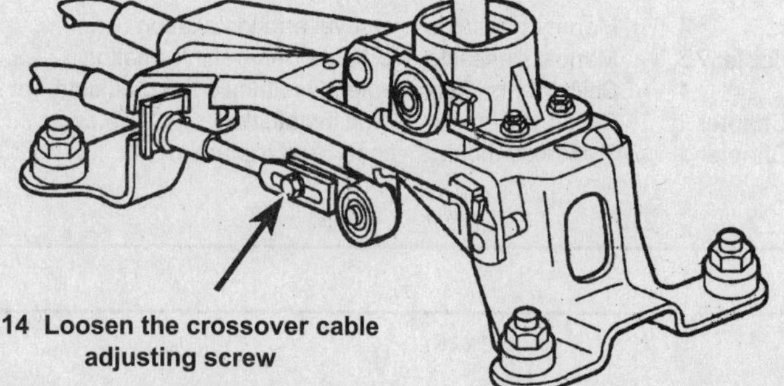

2.14 Loosen the crossover cable adjusting screw

## Adjustment

*Refer to illustration 2.14*

14 Loosen the crossover cable adjustment screw at the shifter **(see illustration)**.

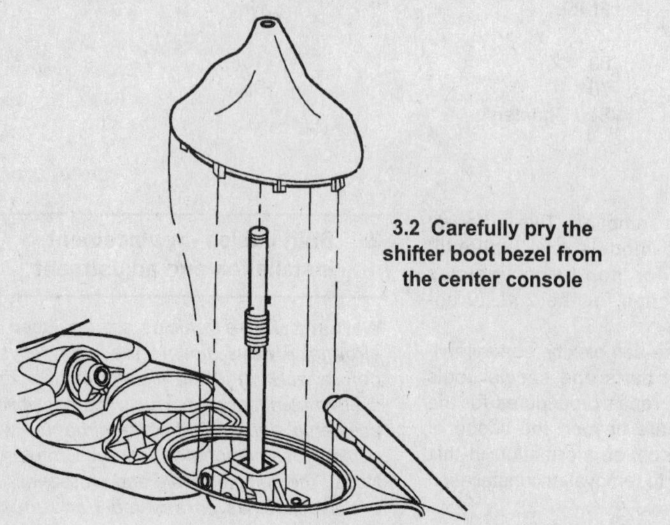

3.2 Carefully pry the shifter boot bezel from the center console

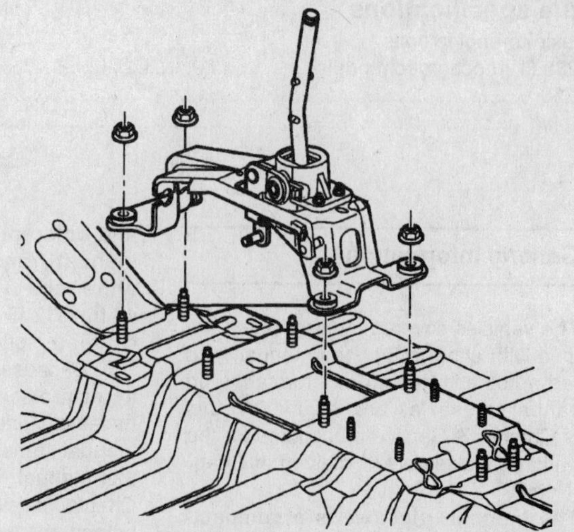

3.5 Remove the four shift lever mounting nuts

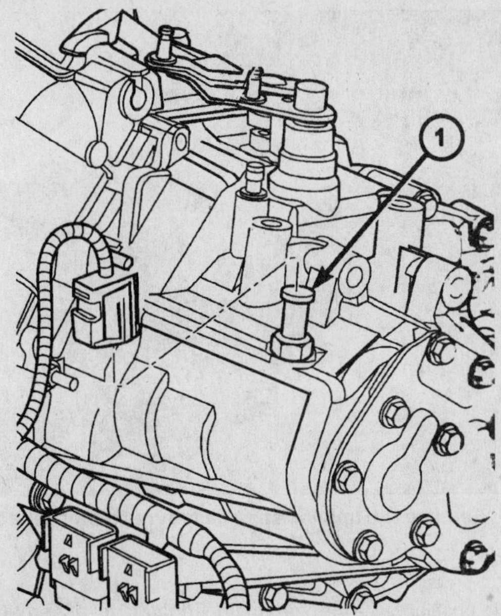


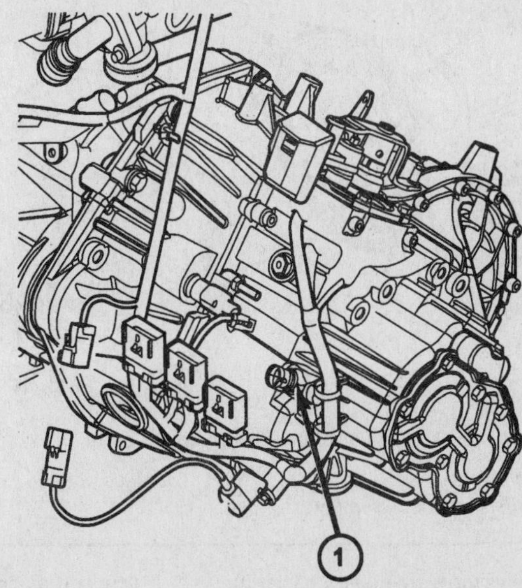


4.1a Back-up light switch location (1) (non-turbocharged models)

4.1b Back-up light switch location (1) (turbocharged models)

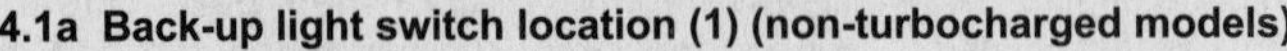

15 Allow the shift lever and crossover lever to relax in the neutral position.
16 Tighten the adjustment screw taking care not to let the shift lever move off-center.
17 Verify proper shifting pattern.

## 3 Shift lever - removal and installation

*Refer to illustrations 3.2 and 3.5*

1 Using moderate force, pull up on the gearshift knob and remove it from the lever.
2 Remove the shifter lever boot from the center console **(see illustration).**
3 Remove the center console (see Chapter 11).
4 Disconnect the crossover and selector cables from the shifter assembly.
5 Unbolt the shift lever bracket bolts and remove the shift lever **(see illustration).**
6 Installation is the reverse of removal. Carefully tap on the knob with a rubber mallet to seat it.

## 4 Back-up light switch - replacement

*Refer to illustrations 4.1a and 4.1b*

1 The back-up light switch is located on top of the transaxle **(see illustrations)**.

### Replacement

2 Disconnect the electrical connector from the back-up light switch.
3 Unscrew the switch from the case.
4 Wrap the threads of the new switch with Teflon tape, or equivalent.
5 Screw in the new switch and tighten it securely.
6 Connect the electrical connector.
7 Check the operation of the back-up lights.

## 5 Transaxle mounts - check and replacement

1 Insert a large screwdriver or prybar between the mount and the transaxle and pry up.
2 The transaxle should not move excessively away from the mount. If it does, replace the mount.
3 To replace a mount, support the transaxle with a jack, remove the nuts and bolts and remove the mount. It may be necessary to raise or lower the transaxle slightly to provide enough clearance to remove the mount.
4 Installation is the reverse of removal.

## 6 Manual transaxle - removal and installation

### Removal

*Refer to illustrations 6.18 and 6.20*

1 Open the hood and place protective covers on the front fenders and cowl. Special fender covers are available, but an old bedspread or blankets will also work.
2 Remove the battery (see Chapter 5). **Caution:** *Always disconnect the negative cable first and hook it up last or the battery may be shorted by the tool being used to loosen the cable clamps.*
3 Remove the air filter housing assembly (see Chapter 4).
4 On turbocharged models, remove the underhood fuse/relay box from the mounting bracket.
5 Disconnect the shift cables from the transaxle (see Section 2).
6 Disconnect the harness connectors from the vehicle speed sensor and back-up light switch.
7 On turbocharged models, remove the power steering reservoir (see Chapter 10).
8 Disconnect master cylinder hydraulic line from the quick connect fitting (see Chapter 8).
9 Remove the transaxle-to-engine upper bolts.
10 Loosen the driveaxle/hub nuts (see Chapter 8) and front wheel lug nuts. Raise the vehicle and place it securely on jackstands. Remove both front wheels. **Note:** *Depending on the type of wheels installed on the vehicle and the thickness of the socket you are using, you may have to loosen the driveaxle/hub nuts after the wheels have been removed.*
11 Support the engine from above with a hoist, or place a floor jack under the oil pan. Place a wood block on the jack head to spread the load on the oil pan.
12 Drain the transaxle lubricant (see Chapter 1).
13 Remove the driveaxles (see Chapter 8).
14 On turbocharged models, remove the intercooler connector pipe-to-engine oil pan bolts (see Chapter 4) and the oil pan-to-bellhousing bolt (see Chapter 2).
15 On non-turbocharged models remove the bolts securing the power steering hose to the structural collar and the right and left lateral bending braces.

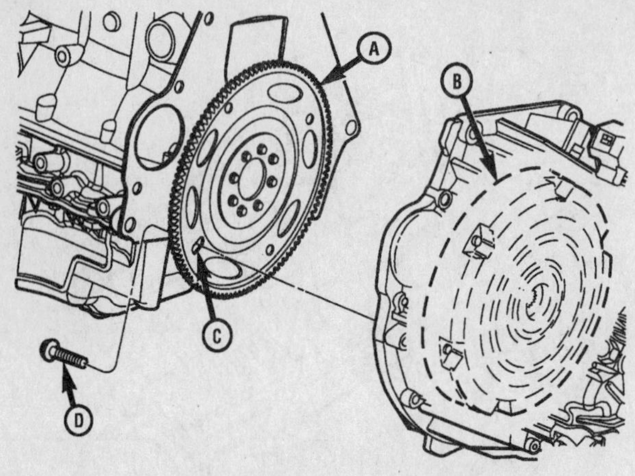


**6.18 Modular clutch-to-driveplate bolts**

a) *Driveplate*
b) *Modular clutch assembly*
c) *Tolerance hole*
d) *Bolt*

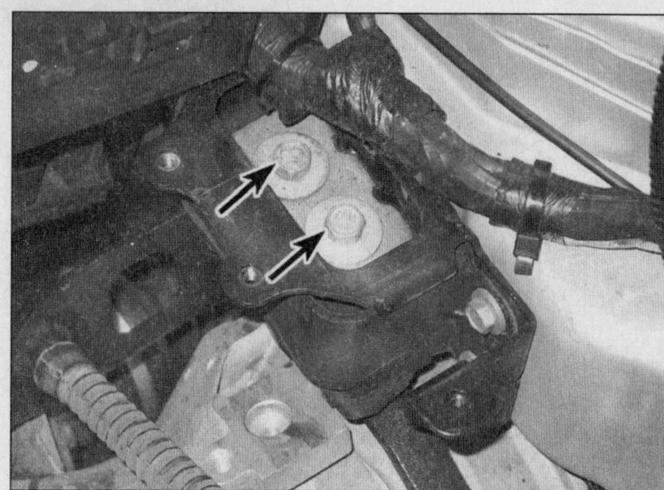

**6.20 Remove the upper transaxle mount-to-bracket bolts**

16 Remove the starter (see Chapter 5).
17 Remove the lower inspection cover.
18 On non-turbocharged models, if the modular clutch assembly is to be reinstalled, match-mark the clutch assembly to the driveplate at the slotted tolerance hole, and remove the four modular clutch assembly-to-driveplate bolts **(see illustration)**. To gain access to each bolt, rotate the engine from the drivebelt end of the engine using the crankshaft damper/pulley bolt. Remove all four bolts and discard them. Use a screwdriver placed in the ring gear of the driveplate to keep the crankshaft from turning during removal of the bolts.
19 Support the transaxle with a transmission jack, if available, or use a floor jack. Secure the transaxle to the jack using straps or chains so it doesn't fall off during removal.
20 Remove the upper transaxle mount-to-bracket bolts **(see illustration).**
21 On turbocharged models, remove the transaxle upper mount bracket.
22 Remove the lower transaxle clutch housing-to-engine bolts. Make sure all clutch housing-to-engine bolts are removed.
23 Make a final check that all wires, hoses and brackets have been disconnected from the transaxle, then with the engine properly supported, carefully lower the transaxle and remove it from under the vehicle. Make sure you keep the transaxle level as you maneuver it out or the modular clutch assembly may fall out. **Note:** *If necessary have someone help with the removal procedure.*

### Installation

24 With the transaxle secured to the hoist/floor jack as on removal, raise it into position, and then carefully slide it onto the engine.
25 Once the transaxle is successfully mated to the engine, insert as many of the mounting bolts as possible, and tighten them progressively, to draw the transaxle fully onto the locating dowels.
26 On turbo-charged models, install the transaxle upper mount bracket.
27 Install the remaining transaxle-to-engine bolts, and tighten all of them to the specified torque.
28 Install the driveplate-to-clutch module bolts.
29 Once the transaxle mount has been reinstalled, the engine hoist or supporting jack can be removed.
30 The remainder of installation is a reversal of removal, noting the following points:

a) *Install the structural collar and bending braces as described in Chapter 2A.*
b) *Install the starter motor as described in Chapter 5.*
c) *Install the driveaxles as described in Chapter 8.*
d) *Fill the transaxle with the specified lubricant (see Chapter 1).*
e) *Road test the vehicle and check for proper transaxle operation and check for fluid leaks.*

## 7 Manual transaxle overhaul - general information

1 Overhauling a manual transaxle unit is a difficult and involved job for the home mechanic. In addition to assembling and reassembling many small parts, clearances must be precisely measured and, if necessary, changed by selecting shims and spacers. Internal transaxle components are also often difficult to obtain and in many instances, extremely expensive. Because of this, if the transaxle develops a fault or becomes noisy, the best course of action is to have the unit overhauled by a transmission specialist or to obtain an exchange reconditioned unit.
2 Nevertheless, it is not impossible for the more experienced mechanic to overhaul the transaxle if the special tools are available and the job is carried out in a deliberate step-by-step manner, to ensure that nothing is overlooked.
3 The tools necessary for an overhaul include internal and external snap-ring pliers, bearing pullers, a slide hammer, a set of pin punches, a dial test indicator and possibly a hydraulic press. In addition, a large, sturdy workbench and a vise will be required.
4 During dismantling of the transaxle, make careful notes of how each component is fitted to make reassembly easier and accurate.
5 Before disassembling the transaxle, it will help if you have some idea of where the problem lies. Certain problems can be closely related to specific areas in the transaxle which can make component examination and replacement easier. Refer to the *Troubleshooting* section in this manual for more information.

# Chapter 7 Part B
# Automatic transaxle

## Contents



## Specifications

### General

| | |
|---|---|
| Lubricant type and capacity | See Chapter 1 |

### Torque specifications

| | Ft-lbs | Nm |
|---|---|---|
| Torque converter-to-driveplate bolts | 55 | 74 |
| Transaxle-to-engine bolts | | |
| 2001 through 2005 models | 80 | 108 |
| 2006 and later models | 70 | 95 |
| Right (rear) lateral bending brace | 60 | 81 |
| Structural collar | See Chapter 2A | |
| Left (front) lateral bending brace | See Chapter 2A | |

## 1 General information

All information on the automatic transaxle is included in this Part of Chapter 7. Information for the manual transaxle can be found in Part A of this Chapter.

The automatic transaxle and the differential are housed in a compact, lightweight, two-piece aluminum alloy housing. Operation of the transaxle is controlled electronically by the Transmission Control Module (TCM) which is the "brain" of the transaxle. The TCM monitors engine and transaxle operating parameters through numerous sensors and then generates output signals to various relays and solenoids to regulate hydraulic pressures, optimize driveability, provide efficient torque management and maintain maximum fuel economy. The TCM is part of the On-Board Diagnostic system OBD-II. For more information see Chapter 6.

Because of the complexity of the automatic transaxles and the specialized equipment necessary to perform most service operations, this Chapter contains only those procedures related to general diagnosis, adjustment and removal and installation procedures.

If the transaxle requires major repair work, it should be left to a dealer service department or an automotive or transmission repair shop. Once properly diagnosed you can, however, remove and install the transaxle yourself and save the expense, even if the repair work is done by a transmission shop.

## 2 Diagnosis - general

1 Automatic transaxle malfunctions may be caused by five general conditions:

- *a) Poor engine performance*
- *b) Improper adjustments*
- *c) Hydraulic malfunctions*
- *d) Mechanical malfunctions*
- *e) Malfunctions in the computer or its signal network*

2 Diagnosis of these problems should always begin with a check of the easily repaired items: fluid level and condition (see Chapter 1), shift cable adjustment and shift lever installation. Next, perform a road test to determine if the problem has been corrected or if more diagnosis is necessary. If the problem persists after the preliminary tests and corrections are completed, additional diagnosis should be performed by a dealer service department or other qualified transmission repair shop. Refer to the *Troubleshooting* section at the front of this manual for information on symptoms of transaxle problems.

### Preliminary checks

3 Drive the vehicle to warm the transaxle to normal operating temperature.

4 Check the fluid level as described in Chapter 1:

- *a) If the fluid level is unusually low, add enough fluid to bring the level within the designated area of the dipstick, then check for external leaks (see following).*

**3.3 Using a large screwdriver or prybar, carefully pry the oil seal out of the transaxle (if you can't remove the oil seal with a screwdriver or prybar, you may need to obtain a special seal removal tool - available at most auto parts stores - to do the job)**

**3.5 Using a seal installer, large section of pipe or a large deep socket as a drift, drive the new seal squarely into the bore and make sure that it's completely seated; lubricate the lip of the new seal with multi-purpose grease**

b) *If the fluid level is abnormally high, drain off the excess, then check the drained fluid for contamination by coolant. The presence of engine coolant in the automatic transmission fluid indicates that a failure has occurred in the internal radiator oil cooler walls that separate the coolant from the transmission fluid (see Chapter 3).*

c) *If the fluid is foaming, drain it and refill the transaxle, then check for coolant in the fluid, or a high fluid level.*

5 Check the engine idle speed. **Note:** *If the engine is malfunctioning, do not proceed with the preliminary checks until it has been repaired and runs normally.*

6 Check and adjust the shift cable, if necessary (see Section 4).

7 If hard shifting is experienced, inspect the shift cable under the center console and at the manual lever on the transaxle (see Section 4).

## *Fluid leak diagnosis*

8 Most fluid leaks are easy to locate visually. Repair usually consists of replacing a seal or gasket. If a leak is difficult to find, the following procedure may help.

9 Identify the fluid. Make sure it's transmission fluid and not engine oil or brake fluid (automatic transmission fluid is a deep red color).

10 Try to pinpoint the source of the leak. Drive the vehicle several miles, then park it over a large sheet of cardboard. After a minute or two, you should be able to locate the leak by determining the source of the fluid dripping onto the cardboard.

11 Make a careful visual inspection of the suspected component and the area immediately around it. Pay particular attention to gasket mating surfaces. A mirror is often helpful for finding leaks in areas that are hard to see.

12 If the leak still cannot be found, clean the suspected area thoroughly with a degreaser or solvent, then dry it thoroughly.

13 Drive the vehicle for several miles at normal operating temperature and varying speeds. After driving the vehicle, visually inspect the suspected component again.

14 Once the leak has been located, the cause must be determined before it can be properly repaired. If a gasket is replaced but the sealing flange is bent, the new gasket will not stop the leak. The bent flange must be straightened.

15 Before attempting to repair a leak, check to make sure that the following conditions are corrected or they may cause another leak. **Note:** *Some of the following conditions cannot be fixed without highly specialized tools and expertise. Such problems must be referred to a qualified transmission shop or a dealer service department.*

### Gasket leaks

16 Check the pan periodically. Make sure the bolts are tight, no bolts are missing, the gasket is in good condition and the pan is flat (dents in the pan may indicate damage to the valve body inside).

17 If the pan gasket is leaking, the fluid level or the fluid pressure may be too high, the vent may be plugged, the pan bolts may be too tight, the pan sealing flange may be warped, the sealing surface of the transaxle housing may be damaged, the gasket may be damaged or the transaxle casting may be cracked or porous. If sealant instead of gasket material has been used to form a seal between the pan and the transaxle housing, it may be the wrong type of sealant.

### Seal leaks

18 If a transaxle seal is leaking, the fluid level may be too high, the vent may be plugged, the seal bore may be damaged, the seal itself may be damaged or improperly installed, the surface of the shaft protruding through the seal may be damaged or a loose bearing may be causing excessive shaft movement.

19 Make sure the dipstick tube seal is in good condition and the tube is properly seated. Periodically check the area around the sensors for leakage. If transmission fluid is evident, check the seals for damage.

### Case leaks

20 If the case itself appears to be leaking, the casting is porous and will have to be repaired or replaced.

21 Make sure the oil cooler hose fittings are tight and in good condition.

### Fluid comes out vent pipe or fill tube

22 If this condition occurs the possible causes are: the transaxle is overfilled; there is coolant in the fluid; the dipstick is incorrect; the vent is plugged or the drain-back holes are plugged.

## 3 Driveaxle oil seals - replacement

*Refer to illustration 3.3 and 3.5*

1 The driveaxle oil seals are located on the sides of the transaxle, where the inner ends of the driveaxles are splined into the differential side gears. If you suspect that a driveaxle oil seal is leaking, raise the vehicle and support it securely on jackstands. If the seal is leaking, you'll see lubricant on the side of the transaxle, below the seal.

2 Remove the driveaxle (see Chapter 8).

3 Using a screwdriver or prybar, carefully pry the oil seal out of the transaxle bore **(see illustration)**. **Note:** *Driveaxle oil seals on the right side of the transaxle may require a slide hammer equipped with a hook-type tool for removal.*

4 If the oil seal cannot be removed with a screwdriver or prybar, a special oil seal removal tool (available at auto parts stores)

4.5 Use two flat blade screwdrivers and carefully pry the selector cable from the select lever

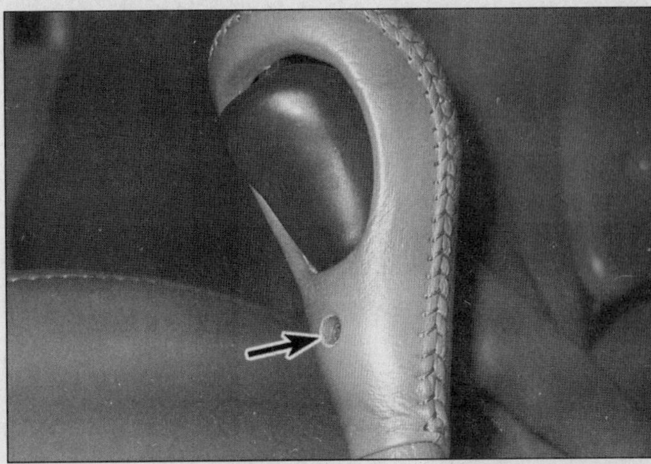

4.7 To remove the handle from the shift lever, loosen the set screw and pull the handle straight up

will be required.

5 Using a seal installer, install the new oil seal. Drive it into the bore squarely until it bottoms **(see illustration)**.

6 Install the driveaxle (see Chapter 8).

## 4 Shift cable - removal, installation and adjustment

**Warning:** *These vehicles are equipped with airbags. Always disconnect the negative battery cable and wait two minutes before working in the vicinity of any airbag system components to avoid the possibility of accidental deployment of the airbag(s), which could cause personal injury (see Chapter 12).*

### Removal

*Refer to illustration 4.5, 4.7, 4.9, 4.10 and 4.11*

1 In the event of hard shifting, disconnect the cable at the transaxle and operate the shifter from the driver's seat. If the shift lever moves smoothly through all positions with the cable disconnected, then the cable should be adjusted as described at the end of this Section. To remove and install the shift cable, perform the following.

2 Raise the hood and place a blanket over the left (driver's) fender to protect it.

3 Remove the air filter housing (see Chapter 4).

4 Remove the battery and battery tray (see Chapter 5).

5 Disconnect the shift cable from the shift lever **(see illustration)**.

6 Disconnect the shift cable from the bracket.

7 Working inside the vehicle remove the shift knob set screw and remove the knob from the shifter **(see illustration).**

8 Remove the center console (see Chapter 11).

9 Remove gearshift indicator lamp from the shift trim bezel **(see illustration).**

10 Remove the shift trim bezel screws and the bezel **(see illustration)**.

11 Use a flat-blade screwdriver and carefully pry the shift cable end from the shift lever pin **(see illustration)**.

12 Carefully pull the cable conduit end out from the shift mechanism. Pull up and remove the cable.

13 Remove the grommet plate-to-floorpan fasteners.

4.9 Remove the gearshift indicator lamp from the shift trim bezel

14 Raise the vehicle and support it securely on jackstands.

15 Remove the catalytic converter heat shield.

16 Remove the last remaining grommet plate fastener and remove the cable from the vehicle.

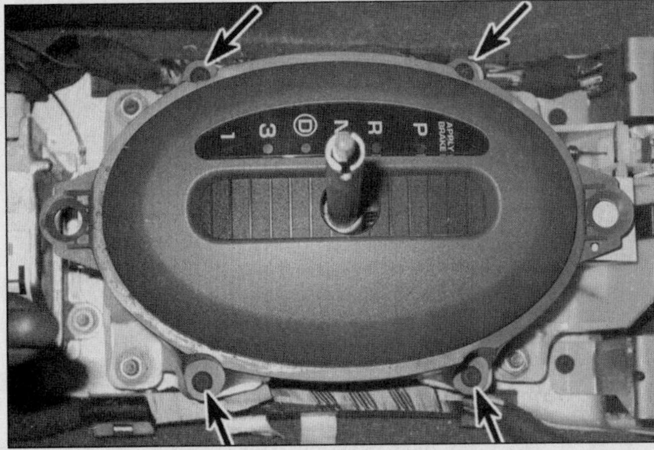


4.10 Remove all four of the shift lever bezel mounting screws

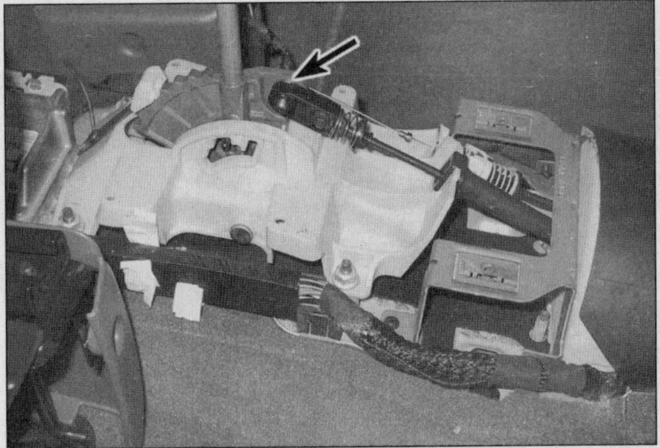

4.11 Carefully pry the shift cable end from the shift lever end

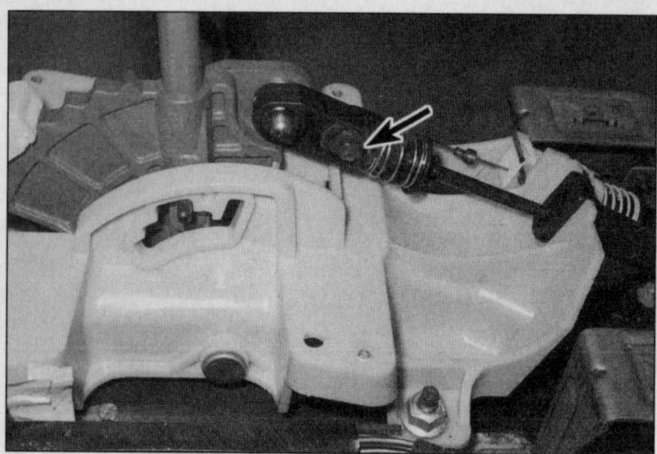
4.29 Gearshift cable adjustment screw

5.5 To detach the interlock cable, pry the cable up from the shifter base

### Installation

17 Working under the hood, install the shift cable into the bracket.

18 Connect the shift cable onto the shift lever post. Make sure it snaps into place.

19 Verify the shift lever is in the park position.

20 Raise the vehicle and support it securely on jackstands.

21 Route the shifter cable through to the floor pan and up to the shifter.

22 Install the grommet plate-to-floorpan fasteners and lower the vehicle.

23 Connect the shift cable to the shift lever pin.

24 The remainder of installation is the reverse of removal.

25 Adjust the shift cable as described in the following steps.

### Adjustment

*Refer to illustration 4.29*

26 Working inside the vehicle remove the shift knob set screw and remove knob from shifter.

27 Remove the center console (see Chapter 11).

28 Place the shift lever in the Park position.

29 Loosen the gearshift cable adjustment screw at the shifter cable **(see illustration)**.

30 Make sure the shift lever at the transaxle is in the Park position. The park sprag must be engaged when adjusting the cable. Rock the vehicle back and forth to ensure that the Park sprag is fully engaged.

31 Tighten the shift cable adjustment screw.

32 Install the center console (see Chapter 11).

33 Check the shift lever for proper operation. It should operate smoothly without binding. The engine should start only in the Park or Neutral positions.

34 Shift the transaxle into all gear positions to make sure the cable is functioning properly. Readjust if necessary.

## 5 Shift interlock cable - removal, installation and adjustment

### Removal

*Refer to illustrations 5.5, 5.8, 5.10 and 5.11*

1 The interlock cable slides into the housing behind the lock cylinder and attaches to the shift lever base. The floor-shift interlock system is adjusted by a nut at the shift lever assembly. If the system must be adjusted (but not replaced), adjust it as described in Steps 22 through 25.

2 Disconnect the cable from the negative battery terminal (see Chapter 5).

3 Remove the shift lever handle (see Section 4).

4 Remove the console bezel (see Chapter 11).

5 Detach the interlock cable from the shift lever base **(see illustration)**.

6 Remove the driver's side knee bolster and reinforcement (see Chapter 11).

7 Remove the steering column covers (see Chapter 11).

8 Disconnect the Brake/Transmission Shift Interlock solenoid from the interlock cable connector **(see illustration)**.

9 Turn the ignition key to the Run position.

10 Slide the cable end plug out of its groove in the interlock lever **(see illustration)**.

11 Turn the ignition key to Off or On/Run position. At the ignition key lock cylinder, squeeze the lock tab on the interlock cable and pull the cable out of the lock cylinder housing **(see illustration)**.

12 Disconnect the interlock cable from the retaining clips and remove the cable.

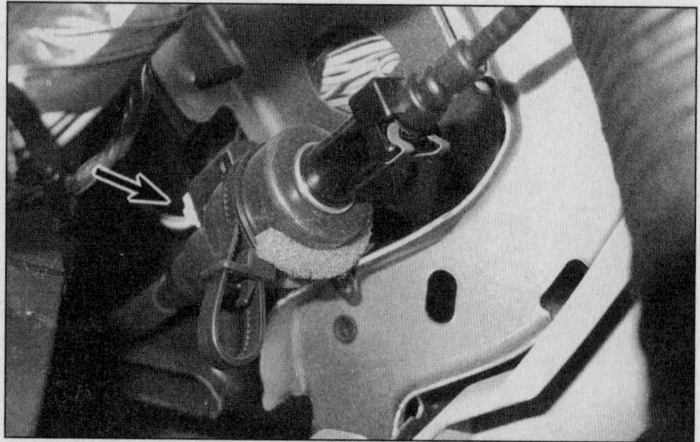
5.8 Disconnect the brake/transaxle shift interlock solenoid connector from the interlock cable

5.10 Slide the interlock cable end from the lever

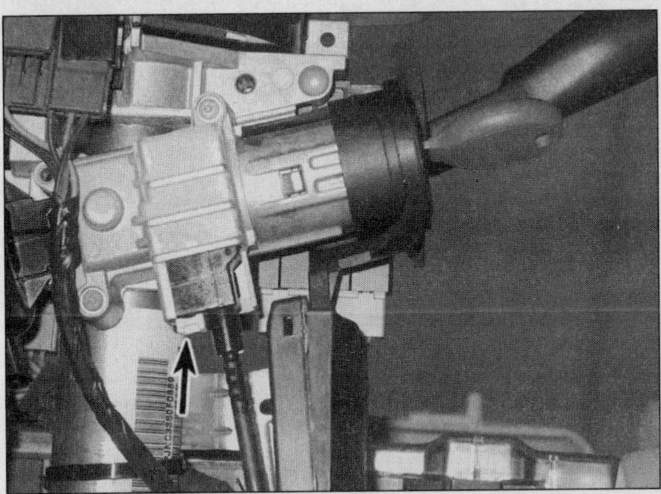

5.11 Squeeze the tab on the forward end of the interlock cable, then pull the cable housing straight out of the lock cylinder

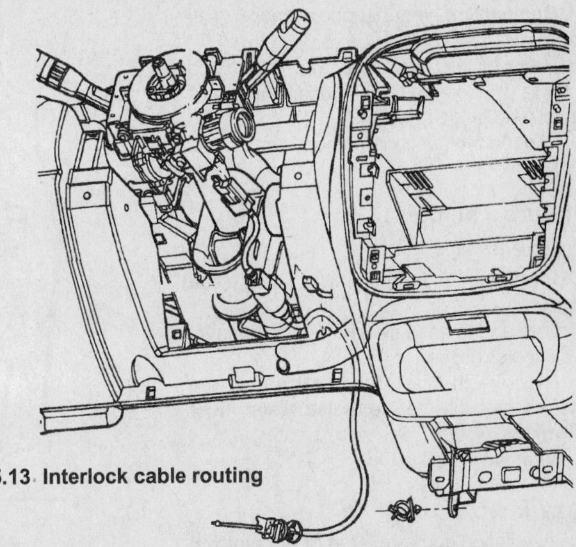

5.13 Interlock cable routing

## Installation

*Refer to illustration 5.13*

13 Route the interlock cable through the instrument panel, below the steering column and down to the shift lever assembly **(see illustration).**

14 Make sure the ignition switch is in the Off or On/Run position.

15 Insert the forward end of the interlock cable into the lock cylinder housing and push it in until it snaps into place.

16 Turn the ignition key to the Off/Lock position.

17 Connect the Brake/Transmission Shift Interlock solenoid to the interlock cable connector.

18 Insert the cable end plug into its groove in the interlock lever. Make sure the plug is properly seated in the groove.

19 Reattach the cable to the shift lever base. The cable housing is fully seated when it snaps into place.

20 Adjust the interlock cable (see Step 22).

21 The remainder of installation is the reverse of removal.

## Adjustment

22 Remove the ignition key from the lock cylinder with the switch in the Lock position.

23 When the adjustment clip on the interlock cable is disengaged, the cable automatically indexes itself to the correct position. Pry up on the adjuster lock and allow the cable to index itself. Snap the clip back into place. **Note:** *If you're installing a new cable, the cable will come with an adjustment pin; once the pin is removed, the cable will self-adjust. After that, snap the adjustment clip into place (and don't reinstall the pin).*

24 With the ignition key in the Off (locked) position, the shift lever should be locked in the Park position. If it isn't, inspect the system for binding and repeat the adjustment procedure.

25 Without starting the engine, place the ignition switch in the Run position. Move the shift lever to the Reverse position. You should be unable to remove the ignition key from the lock cylinder. If you can remove the key at this point, inspect the system for binding and repeat the adjustment procedure.

## 6 Transmission Control Module (TCM) - removal and installation

*Refer to illustration 6.5*

**Caution:** *The TCM is an Electro-Static Discharge (ESD) sensitive electronic device, meaning a static electricity discharge from your body could possibly damage electrical components. Be sure to properly ground yourself and the TCM before handling it. Avoid touching the electrical terminals of the TCM.*

**Note:** *On 2004 and later vehicles, transmission control is through the Powertrain Control Module. There is not a separate Transmission Control Module. For information on the Powertrain Control Module, refer to Chapter 6.*

**Note:** *Do not interchange TCMs from different year vehicles. After replacing a TCM take the vehicle to your local dealer service department or other qualified transmission shop to have the TCM calibrated for your vehicle.*

1 Disconnect the cable from the negative battery terminal (see Chapter 5).

2 Loosen the left-front wheel lug nuts, then raise the vehicle and support it securely on jackstands.

3 Remove the left front wheel.

4 Remove the fenderwell splash shield.

5 Detach the electrical connector from the TCM **(see illustration)**.

6 Remove the TCM bracket mounting screws and withdraw the TCM from the vehicle.

7 Installation is the reverse of removal.

## 7 External transaxle oil cooler - removal and installation

**Caution:** *When the hoses are separated from the cooler fittings they will most likely become damaged. It is recommended that the cooler hoses be replaced whenever they are disconnected to prevent possible leakage.*

## Removal

### Turbo models

*Refer to illustration 7.3*

1 Remove the grille and upper radiator crossmember (see Chapter 3).

6.5 Unscrew the bolt securing the connecter to the module

2 Remove the center support bracket (see Chapter 3).

3 Remove the fasteners that attach the transaxle oil cooler to the air conditioning condenser **(see illustration).**

4 Loosen the hose clamps and disconnect the oil cooler hoses, then remove the cooler.

### Non-turbo models

*Refer to illustration 7.7*

5 Remove the front bumper cover (see Chapter 11).

6 Loosen the hose clamps and disconnect the oil cooler hoses.

7 Remove the fasteners that attach the transaxle oil cooler to the radiator **(see illustration).**

8 Remove the oil cooler.

## Installation

9 Installation is the reverse of the removal Steps with the following additions:

- a) *Replace the clamps and hoses with new ones.*
- b) *Add the specified type of transaxle fluid, as necessary (see Chapter 1).*
- c) *Road test the vehicle to check for proper transaxle operation and check for leakage.*

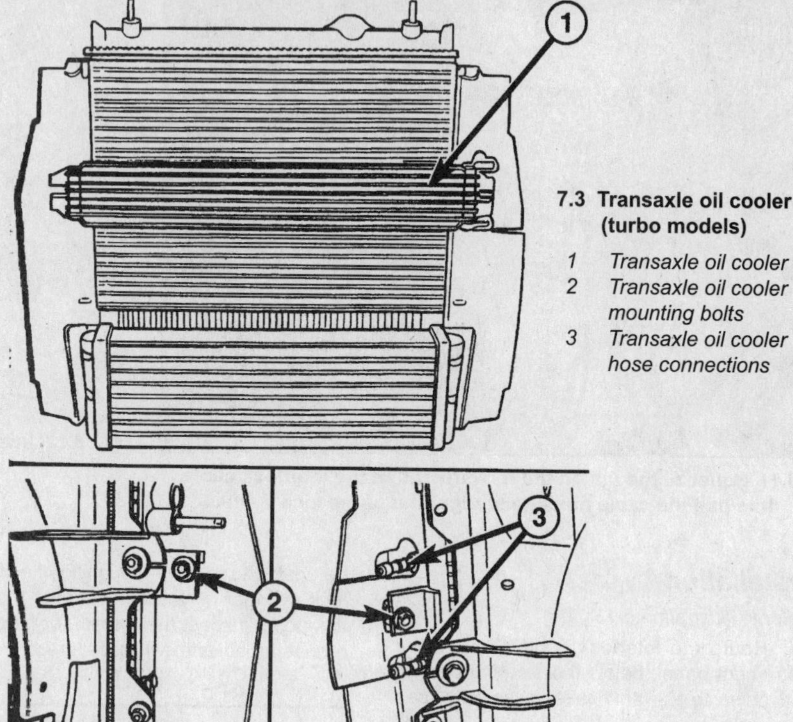


**7.3 Transaxle oil cooler (turbo models)**

1 *Transaxle oil cooler*
2 *Transaxle oil cooler mounting bolts*
3 *Transaxle oil cooler hose connections*

## 8 Automatic transaxle - removal and installation

## Removal

*Refer to illustrations 8.10, 8.15 and 8.17*

1 Remove the battery (see Chapter 5). **Caution:** *Always disconnect the negative cable first and hook it up last or the battery may be shorted by the tool being used to loosen the cable clamps.* Loosen the front wheel lug nuts and the driveaxle/hub nut (see Chapter 8). **Note:** *Depending on the type of wheels installed on the vehicle and the thickness of the socket you are using, you may have to loosen the driveaxle/hub nuts after the wheels have been removed.*

2 Remove the air filter/housing and air intake duct assembly (see Chapter 4).

3 Remove the upper starter-to-transaxle bellhousing bolt.

4 Remove the transaxle dipstick and tube.

5 Clearly label, then unplug, all electrical connectors.

6 Disconnect the shift cable from the manual lever and bracket (see Section 4).

7 Raise the vehicle and support it securely on jackstands. Remove the wheels.

8 Drain the transaxle fluid (see Chapter 1).

9 Remove both driveaxles (see Chapter 8).

10 Remove the bolts securing the power steering hose to the structural collar **(see illustration).**

11 Remove the left lateral bending brace and structural collar.

12 Remove the starter motor (see Chapter 5).

13 Support the engine from above with a hoist or place a jack and a block of wood

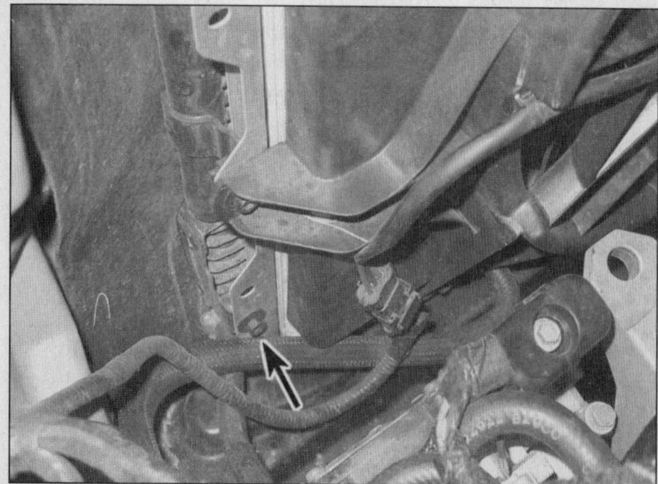

**7.7 Remove the fastners from each side of the transaxle oil cooler (left-side down)**

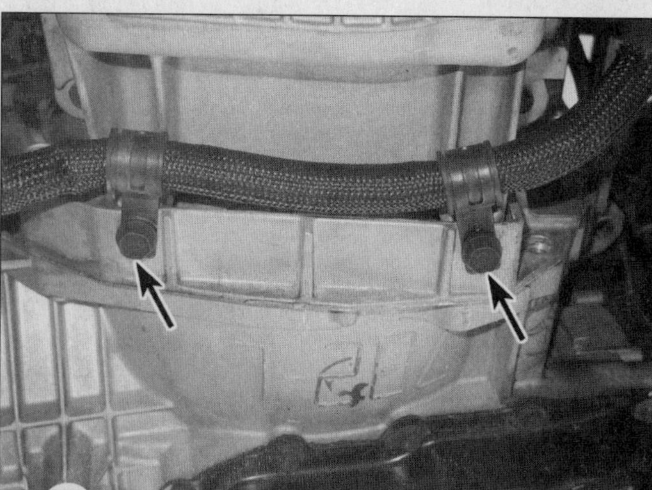

**8.10 Remove the bolts securing the power steering hose to the structural collar**

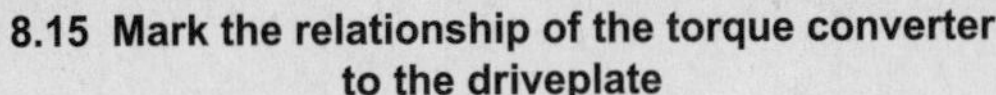

8.15 Mark the relationship of the torque converter to the driveplate

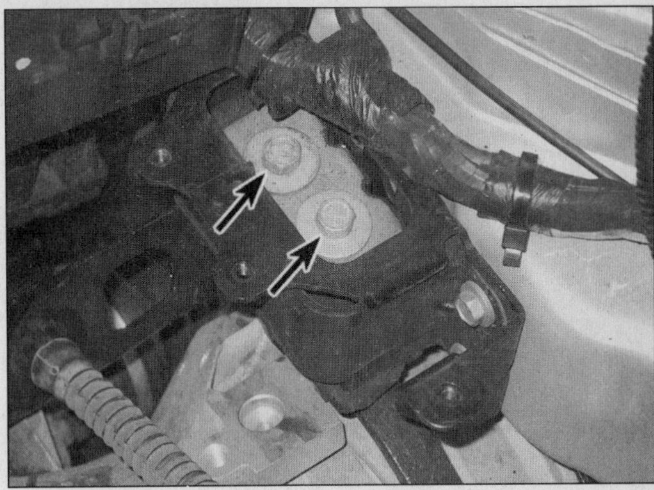

8.17 Remove the transaxle upper mount-to-bracket bolts

under the oil pan to spread the load.

14 Remove the torque converter cover.

15 Mark the relationship of the torque converter to the driveplate so they can be installed in the same position **(see illustration)**.

16 Remove the torque converter-to-driveplate bolts. Turn the crankshaft 120-degrees at a time for access to each bolt. After all three bolts are removed, push the torque converter into the bellhousing so it doesn't stay with the engine when the transaxle is removed.

17 Support the transaxle with a transmission jack, if available, or use a floor jack. Secure the transaxle to the jack using straps or chains so it doesn't fall off during removal.

18 Remove the transaxle upper mount-to-bracket bolts **(see illustration).** Remove the upper transaxle-to-engine bolts.

19 Make a final check that all wires and hoses have been disconnected from the transaxle, then move the transaxle jack toward the side of the vehicle until the transaxle is clear of the engine locating dowels. Make sure you keep the transaxle level as you do this.

### *Installation*

20 Installation of the transaxle is a reversal of the removal procedure, but note the following points:

*a) As the torque converter is reinstalled, ensure that the drive tangs at the center of the torque converter hub engage with the recesses in the automatic transaxle fluid pump inner gear. This can be confirmed by turning the torque converter while pushing it towards the transaxle. If it isn't fully engaged, it will clunk into place.*

*b) When installing the transaxle, make sure the matchmarks you made on the torque converter and driveplate line up.*

*c) Install all of the driveplate-to-torque converter bolts before tightening any of them.*

*d) Tighten the driveplate-to-torque converter bolts to the torque listed in this Chapter's Specifications.*

*e) Tighten the transaxle mounting bolts to the torque listed in this Chapter's Specifications.*

*f) Tighten the driveaxle/hub nuts to the torque value listed in the Chapter 8 Specifications.*

*g) Tighten the wheel lug nuts to the torque listed in the Chapter 1 Specifications.*

*h) Fill the transaxle with the correct type and amount of automatic transmission fluid as described in Chapter 1.*

*h) On completion, adjust the shift cable (see Section 4).*

## 9 Automatic transaxle overhaul - general information

In the event of a problem occurring, it will be necessary to establish whether the fault is electrical, mechanical or hydraulic in nature, before repair work can be contemplated. Diagnosis requires detailed knowledge of the transaxle's operation and construction, as well as access to specialized test equipment, and so is deemed to be beyond the scope of this manual. It is therefore essential that problems with the automatic transaxle are referred to a dealer service department or other qualified repair facility for assessment.

**Note**: *A faulty transaxle should not be removed before the vehicle has been diagnosed by a knowledgeable technician equipped with the proper tools, as troubleshooting must be performed with the transaxle installed in the vehicle.*

# Notes

# Chapter 8
# Clutch and driveaxles

## Contents



## Specifications

### Torque specifications

**Note:** *One foot-pound (ft-lb) of torque is equivalent to 12 inch-pounds (in-lbs) of torque. Torque values below approximately 15 foot-pounds are expressed in inch-pounds, because most foot-pound torque wrenches are not accurate at these smaller values.*

| Torque specifications | **Ft-lbs** (unless otherwise indicated) | **Nm** |
|---|---|---|
| Clutch pressure plate-to-flywheel bolts (turbo models) | 20 | 27 |
| Modular clutch-to-driveplate bolts | 65 | 88 |
| Driveaxle/hub nut | 180 | 244 |
| Release cylinder-to-transaxle bolts (turbocharged models) | 74 in-lbs | 8 |
| Wheel lug nuts | See Chapter 1 | |

## 1 General information

The information in this Chapter deals with the components from the rear of the engine to the front wheels, except for the transaxle, which is dealt with in Chapter 7A and 7B. For the purposes of this Chapter, these components are grouped into two categories: Clutch and driveaxles. Separate Sections within this Chapter offer general descriptions and checking procedures for both groups.

Since nearly all the procedures covered in this Chapter involve working under the vehicle, make sure it's securely supported on sturdy jackstands or a hoist where the vehicle can be easily raised and lowered.

## 2 Clutch - description and check

1 All vehicles with a manual transaxle use a single dry plate, diaphragm spring type clutch. The clutch disc has a splined hub which allows it to slide along the splines of the transaxle input shaft. The clutch and pressure plate are held in contact by spring pressure exerted by the diaphragm in the pressure plate. All models use a modular clutch assembly that includes a clutch assembly where the clutch pressure plate and friction disc are an integral unit. 2.0L and 2.4L models (except turbo) incorporate a self-adjusting design. Turbo models incorporate a modular design with a Dual-Mass Flywheel that may be serviced if necessary.

2 The clutch release system is operated by hydraulic pressure. The system consists of the clutch pedal, a master cylinder, the hydraulic line, a release-cylinder which actuates the clutch release lever and the clutch release (or throw-out) bearing.

3 When pressure is applied to the clutch pedal to release the clutch, hydraulic pressure is exerted against the outer end of the release lever, which pivots, moving the release bearing. The bearing pushes against the fingers of the diaphragm spring of the pressure plate assembly, which in turn releases the clutch plate.

4 Terminology can be a problem regarding the clutch components because common names have in some cases changed from that used by the manufacturer. For example, the driven plate is also called the clutch plate or disc, The pressure plate assembly is sometimes referred to as the clutch cover, the clutch release bearing is sometimes called a throw-out bearing, and so on.

5 Other than replacing components that have obvious damage, some preliminary checks should be performed to diagnose a clutch system failure:

a) *The first check should be of the fluid level in the clutch master cylinder. If the fluid level is low, add fluid as necessary and inspect the hydraulic clutch system for leaks. If the master cylinder reservoir has run dry, bleed the system as described in Section 6 and re-test the clutch operation.*
b) *To check clutch spin down time, run the engine at normal idle speed with the transaxle in Neutral (clutch pedal up - engaged). Disengage the clutch (pedal down), wait several seconds and shift the transaxle into Reverse. No grinding noise should be heard. A grinding noise would most likely indicate a problem in the pressure plate or the clutch disc.*
c) *To check for complete clutch release, run the engine (with the parking brake applied to prevent movement) and hold the clutch pedal approximately 1/2-inch from the floor. Shift the transaxle between 1st gear and Reverse several times. If the shift is not smooth, component failure is indicated.*
d) *Visually inspect the clutch pedal bushings at the top of the clutch pedal to make sure there is no sticking or excessive wear.*

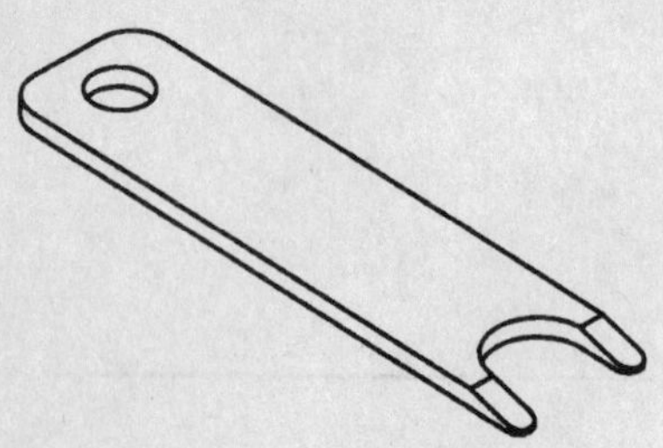

3.7 Tool for separating the quick-connect fitting on the clutch hydraulic line

## 3 Clutch master and release cylinders - removal and installation

### *Master cylinder*

#### Removal

*Refer to illustration 3.7*

1 Disconnect the cable from the negative battery terminal (see Chapter 5).

2 Working inside the vehicle, remove the knee bolster (see Chapter 11), remove the clip that secures the master cylinder pushrod to the clutch pedal and slide the pushrod off the clutch pedal pin.

3 Remove the clip securing the brake pedal to the brake booster push rod, and remove the brake booster mounting nuts (see Chapter 9).

4 Move the brake booster forward and out of the way to gain access to the master cylinder.

5 On 2001 through 2004 models, remove the clutch fluid reservoir.

6 Raise the vehicle and support it securely on jackstands.

#### 2001 through 2004 models

7 Working under the vehicle, separate the hydraulic line using the special tool **(see illustration).**

8 Lower the vehicle.

9 Working in the engine compartment, remove the clutch master cylinder mounting nuts.

10 Using care not to damage the hydraulic line, work the master cylinder and line from the engine compartment.

#### 2005 and later models

11 Working under the vehicle, use a small screwdriver to disconnect the snap-ring retainers from the hydraulic line at the release cylinder. Remove the hydraulic line from the clutch release cylinder. Be sure to place a pan under the vehicle to catch residual fluid.

12 Lower the vehicle.

13 Working in the engine compartment, remove the clutch master cylinder mounting nuts. **Note:** *It will be necessary to remove the PDC (Power Distribution Center) bracket (early models) or the TIPM (Totally Integrated Power Module) bracket to access the clutch master cylinder.*

14 Using care not to damage the hydraulic line, remove the clutch master cylinder from the engine compartment.

#### Installation

15 Place the master cylinder pushrod through the firewall and carefully route the hydraulic line into position and install the fasteners finger tight.

16 Working inside the vehicle, connect the master cylinder pushrod to the clutch pedal pin and install a new clip.

17 Connect the clutch fluid reservoir supply line to the clutch master cylinder and connect the release cylinder. Verify proper connection by hearing an audible click (2001 through 2004 models) or by installing the snap ring retainers onto the line connector and locking the assembly into the notches (2005 and later models).

18 The remainder of installation is the reverse of removal. Tighten the mounting fasteners securely.

19 Wash off any spilled brake fluid with water. **Caution:** *Don't allow brake fluid to come into contact with paint, as it will damage the finish.*

### *Release cylinder*

20 Disconnect the cable from the negative battery terminal (see Chapter 5).

21 Raise the vehicle and support it securely on jackstands.

#### Non-turbocharged models

*Refer to illustration 3.24*

22 On 2002 and earlier models disconnect the hydraulic quick-disconnect fitting from the release cylinder **(see illustration 3.7).**

23 On 2003 and 2004 models remove the clip securing the hydraulic hose to the release cylinder. Using a punch, drive out the roll pin and disconnect the hose from the release cylinder. **Note:** *2005 and later models do not use a roll pin; the hydraulic hose can be disconnected after removing the snap ring retainers with a screwdriver.* Have rags handy as some fluid will be lost as the line is removed. **Caution:** *Don't allow brake fluid to come into contact with paint as it will damage the finish.*

24 Remove the bolts securing the release cylinder to the transaxle. On 2002 and earlier models, remove the lateral bending brace and release cylinder mounting bolts **(see illustration).**

25 Installation is the reverse of the removal Steps with the following additions:

a) *Install the release cylinder and, if applicable, the lateral bending brace mounting bolts and tighten them securely.*

b) *Connect the hydraulic line and check the hydraulic fluid level in the reservoir, adding fluid if necessary, until the level is correct.*

#### Turbocharged models

**Note:** *Turbo models utilize a release bearing that is integral to the release cylinder (see Section 6).*

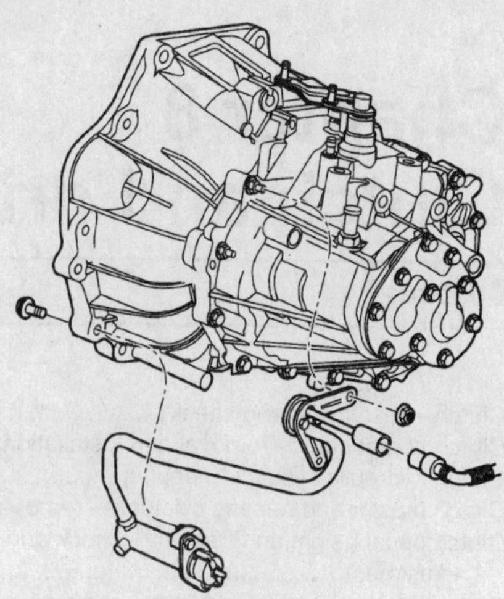

3.24 Clutch release cylinder mounting details (non-turbo models)

## 4 Clutch hydraulic system - bleeding

**Note:** *Although clutch hydraulic system components are pre-filled at the factory, the clutch hydraulic system may require bleeding after servicing. Follow the preliminary bleeding procedure (see Step 1), and if this does not produce a proper operating clutch pedal, bleed the system.*

1 Make sure the clutch fluid reservoir is full. Actuate the clutch pedal between 60 to 100 times and check the operation of the clutch pedal. If the pedal remains spongy or the clutch does not engage properly, perform the release cylinder bleeding procedure.

### *2004 and earlier models*

#### Non-turbocharged models

2 Verify the clutch fluid reservoir is properly filled (see Chapter 1).

3 Raise the vehicle and support it securely on jackstands.

4 Remove the release cylinder bolts, separate it from the transaxle (see Section 5) but do not disconnect the hydraulic line from the release cylinder.

5 Allow the release cylinder to hang down so that it's the lowest point in the system. **Caution:** *Do not actuate the clutch pedal or master cylinder while the release cylinder is detached.*

6 Depress the release cylinder pushrod until it bottoms then releases, forcing air out the top of the clutch fluid reservoir. Repeat this several times.

7 Continue bleeding until all the air has been eliminated from the hydraulic system.

8 Install the clutch release cylinder (see Section 3).

9 Actuate the clutch pedal 30 times and check the operation of the clutch pedal. If the pedal remains spongy or the clutch does not engage properly, perform Steps 2 through 6.

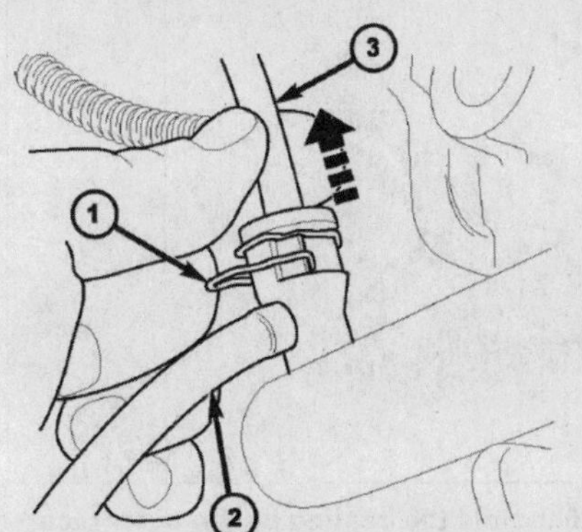


**4.14 Hydraulic circuit bleeder port details (2.4L non-turbocharged model shown - others similar)**

1 *Tube clamp ring*
2 *Hose connected to bleeder port*
3 *Hydraulic line*

10 If after several attempts the clutch hydraulic system is still not properly bled, replace the clutch master and release cylinders.

## Turbocharged models

**Caution:** *Do not allow hydraulic fluid to contaminate the clutch bellhousing or any clutch components. Contamination may severely reduce clutch operation.*

**Note:** *The following procedure is best performed by a qualified repair facility or a dealership service department, as special tools are necessary.*

11 The manufacturer recommends a reverse fluid injection method for bleeding the clutch hydraulic system on turbocharged models. The kind of equipment used for reverse bleeding is commercially available. The bleed screw is located just inside the transaxle bellhousing, covered by an access cap on the side of the housing **(see illustration 6.8)**. Follow the tool manufacturer's instructions for this type of bleeding procedure.

## *2005 and later models*

*Refer to illustration 4.14*

12 Verify the clutch fluid reservoir is properly filled but leave the cap off (see Chapter 1).

13 Raise the vehicle and support it securely on jackstands.

14 Remove the small protective cover from the bleeder port and install a clear hose **(see illustration)**. Guide the hose to a small container to catch the fluid during bleeding.

15 Release the hydraulic tube clamp ring that is closest to the bleeder port **(see illustration 4.14),** then pull the hydraulic tube outward until it stops against the other tube clamp ring; this opens the hydraulic circuit allowing air and fluid to come out.

16 Fill the master cylinder while air and fluid continue to flow from the bleeder port. When no air is present in the escaping fluid, bleeding is complete. Push the hydraulic tube back into position and re-set the tube clamp ring. Pull outward on the hydraulic tube to confirm that it is properly seated. **Caution:** *Do not allow the master cylinder to run dry while draining fluid from the bleeder port. If this occurs, the master cylinder will have to be removed and held vertically (with the pushrod facing downward) for 10 seconds, then reinstalled.*

17 Remove drain tube and replace bleeder port protective cover. Ensure the level in the master cylinder is correct, then replace the cap.

18 Make sure the clutch fluid reservoir is full. Actuate the clutch pedal between 60 to 100 times and check the operation of the clutch pedal. Start the engine and confirm proper clutch operation. If the pedal remains spongy or the clutch does not engage properly, on non-turbocharged models, perform Steps 4 through 8. On turbocharged models, remove the master cylinder and hold it vertically (with the pushrod facing downward) for 10 seconds, then reinstall it.

19 Confirm proper clutch operation and repeat the bleeding procedure if necessary.

## 5 Clutch components - removal and installation

**Warning:** *Dust produced by clutch wear and deposited on clutch components is hazardous to your health. DO NOT blow it out with compressed air and DO NOT inhale it. DO NOT use gasoline or petroleum-based solvents to remove the dust. Brake system cleaner should be used to flush the dust into a drain pan. After the clutch components are wiped clean with a rag, dispose of the contaminated rags and cleaner in a labeled, covered container.*

**Note:** *If the clutch pressure plate or flywheel on non-turbocharged models requires replacement, the modular clutch assembly must be replaced as a set. Separate components are not available.*

## *Removal*

**Note:** *Access to the clutch components is normally accomplished by removing the transaxle, leaving the engine in the vehicle. If, of course, the engine is being removed for major overhaul, then the opportunity should always be taken to check the clutch for wear and replace worn components as necessary. However, the relatively low cost of the clutch components compared to the time and labor involved in gaining access to them warrants their replacement any time the engine or transaxle is removed, unless they are new or in near-perfect condition. The following procedures assume that the engine will stay in place.*

1 Remove the transaxle from the vehicle (see Chapter 7A). Support the engine while the transaxle is out. Preferably, an engine hoist should be used to support it from above. However, if a jack is used underneath the engine, make sure a piece of wood is used between the jack and oil pan to spread the load.

2 Remove the modular clutch assembly from the transaxle input shaft. **Caution:** *Do not touch the clutch disc facing with your oily or dirty hands as the clutch surface will become contaminated.* **Note:** *On turbo-charged models the clutch pressure plate can be unbolted from the flywheel, allowing the clutch disc to be removed.*

**5.7 Clutch disc-to-flywheel alignment**

A *Clutch disc*
B *Flywheel*
C *Alignment at equal distance*

## *Installation*

### Non-turbocharged models

3 Install the clutch release bearing and lever (see Section 7).

4 Install the modular clutch assembly onto the transaxle input shaft.

5 Install the transaxle (see Chapter 7A). **Note:** *Be sure to install new bolts when attaching a modular clutch to the driveplate.* Tighten the modular clutch-to-driveplate bolts to the torque listed in this Chapter's Specifications.

### Turbocharged models

*Refer to illustration 5.7*

6 Before installation, carefully wipe the flywheel and pressure plate machined surfaces clean with brake system cleaner. It's important that no oil or grease is on these surfaces or the lining of the clutch disc. Handle these parts only with clean hands.

7 Position the clutch disc against the flywheel and center it **(see illustration)**. Make sure it's installed properly (most replacement clutch plates will be marked "flywheel side" or something similar). While holding the disc in place, install the pressure plate against the flywheel using the locating dowels.

8 Install the pressure plate-to-flywheel bolts and tighten them to the torque listed in this Chapter's Specifications, in a criss-cross pattern.

9 Using moly-base grease, lubricate the face of the release bearing where it contacts the fingers of the pressure plate diaphragm spring. Lightly lubricate the splines of the transaxle input shaft. **Caution:** *Don't use too much grease.*

10 Install the clutch release bearing, if removed (see Section 6).

11 Install the transaxle (see Chapter 7A) and all components removed previously, tightening all fasteners to the proper torque specifications.

6.4 Hold the release bearing in place, disengage the clip and pull the release lever from the pivot stud. Then slide the release lever up to disengage it from the release bearing

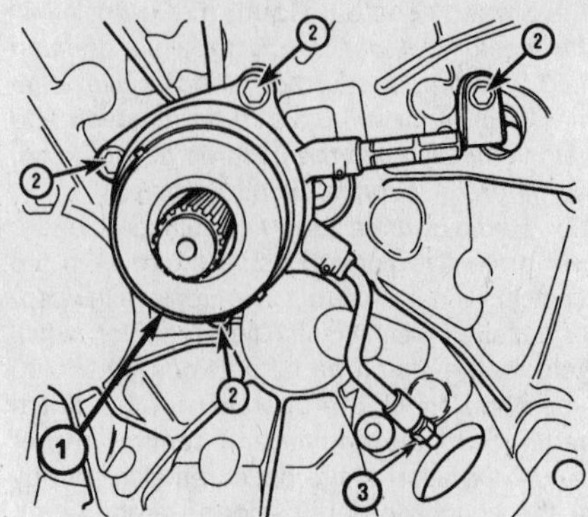


6.8 Clutch release cylinder - 2.4L Turbocharged models

1 *Slave cylinder*
2 *Slave cylinder-to-transaxle mounting bolts*
3 *Bleeder screw*

6.9 Hold the bearing by the outer race and rotate the inner race while applying pressure - if the bearing doesn't turn smoothly or if it's noisy, it must be replaced (it's a good idea to replace the bearing even if it checks out good)

## 6 Clutch release bearing and lever - removal, inspection and installation

**Warning:** *Dust produced by clutch wear and deposited on clutch components is hazardous to your health. DO NOT blow it out with compressed air and DO NOT inhale it. DO NOT use gasoline or petroleum-based solvents to remove the dust. Brake system cleaner should be used to flush it into a drain pan. After the clutch components are wiped clean with a rag, dispose of the contaminated rags and cleaner in a labeled, covered container.*
**Caution:** *Don't allow brake fluid to come into contact with paint as it will damage the finish.*

### Removal

#### Non-turbocharged models

*Refer to illustration 6.4*

**Note:** *Because of the difficulty involved in removing the transaxle for release bearing replacement, we recommend routinely replacing the release bearing when the clutch components are replaced.*

1 Disconnect the cable from the negative terminal of the battery (see Chapter 5).
2 Remove the transaxle (see Chapter 7A).
3 **Caution:** *Do not use a screwdriver or prybar to disengage the lever as the spring clip will be damaged.* Move the lever and bearing so the lever is at right angles to the input shaft. Secure the spring clip in place with a screwdriver or needle-nose pliers.
4 Hold the release bearing in place and pull the release the lever from the pivot stud and remove it **(see illustration).**
5 Slide the release bearing off the input shaft.

#### Turbocharged models

*Refer to illustration 6.8*

6 Disconnect the hydraulic quick-connect fitting from the release cylinder (see Section 3, Step 8).
7 Remove the transaxle (see Chapter 7A).
8 Remove the bolts securing the release cylinder to the transaxle and slide the release cylinder assembly off the transaxle input shaft **(see illustration)**.

### Inspection

*Refer to illustration 6.9*

9 Hold the bearing by the outer race and rotate the inner race while applying pressure **(see illustration)**. If the bearing doesn't turn smoothly or if it's noisy, replace the bearing assembly with a new one. Wipe the bearing with a clean rag and inspect it for damage, wear and cracks. Don't immerse the bearing in solvent - it's sealed for life and to do so would ruin it. Also check the release lever and fork for cracks and bends.
10 Check the release lever for wear or damage especially in the area where the lever contacts the release bearing. Also be sure to clean any dirt off the pivot ball stud and stud pocket in the release fork.

### Installation

#### Non-turbocharged models

*Refer to illustrations 6.11a, 6.11b and 6.11c*

11 Lubricate the release lever ends, the inner diameter of the release bearing and the input shaft **(see illustrations)**.
12 Install the release bearing onto the input shaft. Install the release lever fingers onto the release bearing and onto the pivot ball. Snap the lever into place on the pivot ball. Make sure it is properly seated and that the spring clip is inserted through the release lever slot.
13 Install the transaxle (see Chapter 7A).

#### Turbocharged models

14 Installation is the reverse of the removal

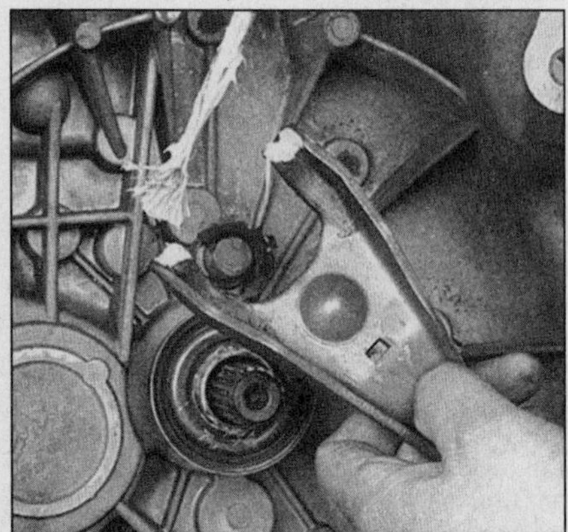

6.11a Using high-temperature grease, lubricate the release lever ends . . .

6.11b . . . the inner groove of the release bearing . . .

6.11c . . . and the sleeve around the input shaft

Steps with the following additions:

a) *Install the release cylinder mounting bolts and tighten them in 3 steps to the torque listed in this Chapter's Specifications.*
b) *Install the transaxle (see Chapter 7A).*
c) *Connect the hydraulic line and check the brake fluid level in the reservoir, adding fluid if necessary, until the level is correct.*

## 7 Clutch start switch - check and replacement

### Check

1 Verify that the engine will not start when the clutch pedal is released.

2 Verify that the engine will start when the clutch pedal is depressed all the way.

3 If the engine won't start with the pedal depressed, or starts with the pedal released, unplug the electrical connector to the switch (located near the top of the clutch pedal) and check continuity between the connector terminals with the clutch pedal depressed.

4 If there's continuity between the terminals with the pedal depressed, the switch is okay; if there's no continuity between the terminals with the pedal depressed, replace the switch. If there's continuity between the terminals when the clutch pedal is released, replace the switch.

### Replacement

*Refer to illustration 7.9*

5 Remove the knee bolster from the instrument panel (see Chapter 11).

6 Unplug the switch electrical connector, if you haven't already done so.

7 Depress the wing tabs on the switch and push the switch out of the mounting bracket.

8 Remove the clip securing the clutch master cylinder pushrod to the pedal pin.

9 Remove the switch and wires out of the slot in the bracket **(see illustration).**

10 Installation is the reverse of removal.

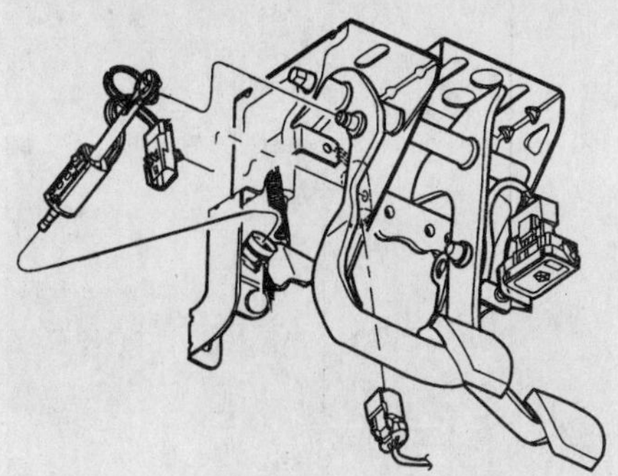

**7.9 Clutch start switch installation details**

### Adjustment

*Refer to illustration 7.11*

11 Loosen the adjustment screw on the clutch master cylinder pushrod **(see illustration).**

12 Carefully lift the pedal upward and connect the pushrod to the pedal pin.

13 Tighten the pushrod adjustment screw.

14 Verify the switch operates properly.

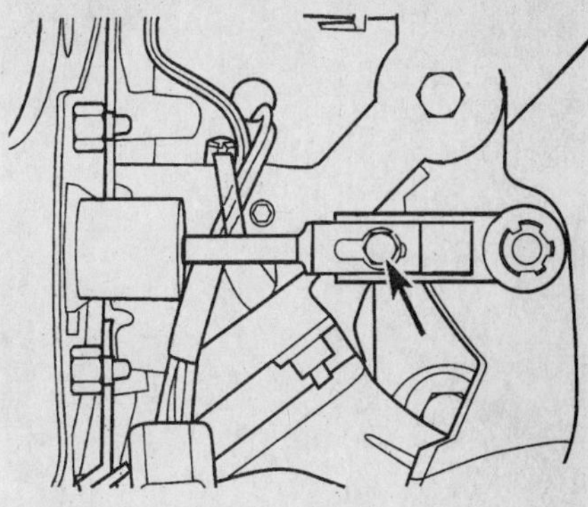

**7.11 Clutch master cylinder pushrod adjustment screw**

## 8 Driveaxles - general information and inspection

1 Power is transmitted from the transaxle to the wheels through a pair of driveaxles. The inner end of each driveaxle is splined to the differential side gears. The driveaxles can be pulled out to replace the oil seals (see Chapter 7A). The outer ends of the driveaxles are splined to the front hubs and locked in place by a large nut.

2 Each driveaxle assembly consists of an inner and outer constant velocity (CV) joint connected together by a driveaxle shaft. The inner ends of the driveaxles are equipped with a tripot joint on all models. The design is capable of both angular and axial motion. In other words, the inner CV joints are free to slide in-and-out as the driveaxle moves up-and-down with the wheel. These joints can be disassembled and cleaned in the event of a boot failure, but if any parts are damaged, the entire driveaxle assembly must be replaced as a unit.

3 The outer CV joint on all models is a ball-and-socket design, are capable of angular - but not axial - movement. These joints can be cleaned and repacked if an outer boot is torn, but if any parts are damaged, the entire driveaxle assembly must be replaced as a unit.

4 The boots should be inspected periodically for damage and leaking lubricant. Torn CV joint boots must be replaced immediately or the joints can be damaged. Boot replacement involves removal of the driveaxle (see Sections 9 and 10). **Note:** *Some auto parts stores carry "split" type replacement boots, which can be installed without removing the driveaxle from the vehicle. This is a convenient alternative; however, the driveaxle should be removed and the CV joint disassembled and cleaned to ensure the joint is free from contaminants such as moisture and dirt which will accelerate CV joint wear.* The most common symptom of worn or damaged CV joints, besides lubricant leaks, is a clicking noise in turns, a clunk when accelerating after coasting and vibration at highway speeds. To check for wear in the CV joints and driveaxle shafts, grasp each axle (one at a time) and rotate it in both directions while holding the CV joint housings, feeling for play indicating worn splines or sloppy CV joints. Also check the axleshafts for cracks, dents and distortion.

## 9 Driveaxle - removal and installation

### Removal

*Refer to illustrations 9.2a, 9.2b, 9.3, 9.7, 9.8, 9.10a and 9.10b*

1 Loosen the front wheel lug nuts, raise the vehicle and support it securely on jackstands. Remove the wheel.

2 Remove the hub nut cotter pin and discard it **(see illustration)**. Discard the old cotter pin - you'll need a new one for reassembly. Remove the driveaxle hub nut lock and spring washer **(see illustration)**.

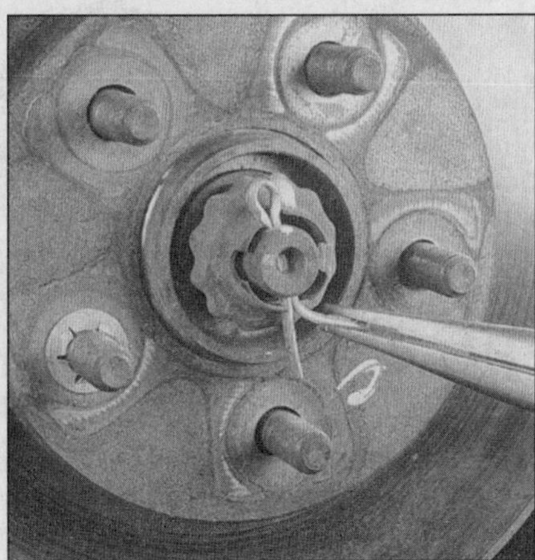

**9.2a Remove the hub nut cotter pin . . .**

**9.2b . . . then remove the lock and spring washer**

**9.3 To prevent the hub from turning while you're loosening the driveaxle hub nut, wedge a prybar between two of the wheel studs**

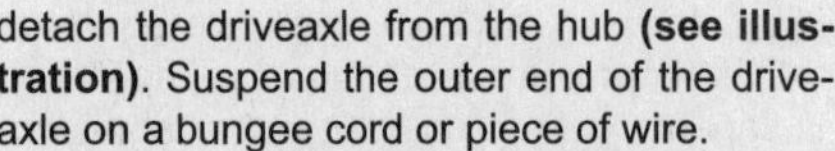

**9.7 To loosen the driveaxle from the hub splines, tap the end of the driveaxle with a soft-faced hammer**

**9.8 Angle the steering knuckle as required and pull the driveaxle from the wheel hub**

3 Loosen the driveaxle/hub nut with a large socket and breaker bar **(see illustration)**. If equipped with anti-lock brakes, disconnect the front wheel speed sensor and move the harness out of the way.

4 It's not absolutely necessary that you drain the transaxle lubricant prior to removing a driveaxle, but if the mileage on the odometer indicates that the transaxle is nearing the lubricant-change interval prescribed in Chapter 1, now is a good time to do it.

5 Separate the tie-rod end from the steering knuckle (see Chapter 10).

6 Remove the bolt and nut securing the balljoint to the steering knuckle then pry the lower control arm down to separate the components (see Chapter 10).

7 To loosen the driveaxle from the hub splines, tap the end of the driveaxle with a soft-faced hammer **(see illustration).** If the driveaxle is stuck in the hub splines and won't move, it may be necessary to push it from the hub with a puller.

8 Pull out on the steering knuckle and detach the driveaxle from the hub **(see illustration)**. Suspend the outer end of the driveaxle on a bungee cord or piece of wire.

9 Before you remove the driveaxle, look for lubricant leakage in the area around the differential seal. If there's evidence of a leak, you'll want to replace the seal after removing the driveaxle (see Chapter 7 Part A).

10 To remove a non-turbo, right (passenger's side) driveaxle, position the prybar against the inner joint and carefully pry the joint off the transaxle side gear and retaining clip **(see illustration).** On turbo models tap the inner joint off the intermediate shaft using a brass punch **(see illustration)**. Do not use the driveaxle to pull the on the inner joint. Doing so might damage the inner joint components. Pry straight out on the driveaxle to avoid damage to the transaxle oil seal. Remove the driveaxle assembly, being careful not to over extend the inner joint or damage the axleshaft boots.

11` To remove the left (driver's side) driveaxle, position a prybar against the inner joint and carefully pry the joint off the transaxle side gear and retaining clip. Do not use the driveaxle to pull on the inner tripot joint. Doing so might damage the inner joint components. Pull straight out on the driveaxle to avoid damage to the transaxle oil seal. Remove the driveaxle assembly, being careful not to over extend the inner joint or damage the axleshaft boots.

12 Should it become necessary to move the vehicle while the driveaxle is out, place a large bolt with two large washers (one on each side of the hub) through the hub and tighten the nut securely.

13 If you noted evidence of a leaking driveaxle seal, refer to Chapter 7B for the seal replacement procedure.

## Installation

14 Installation is the reverse of removal, but with the following additional points:

*a) Apply an even bead of multi-purpose grease around the splines of the inner joint.*

**9.10a Using a large prybar, pry the inner CV joint out sharply to disengage it from the differential gears inside the transaxle**

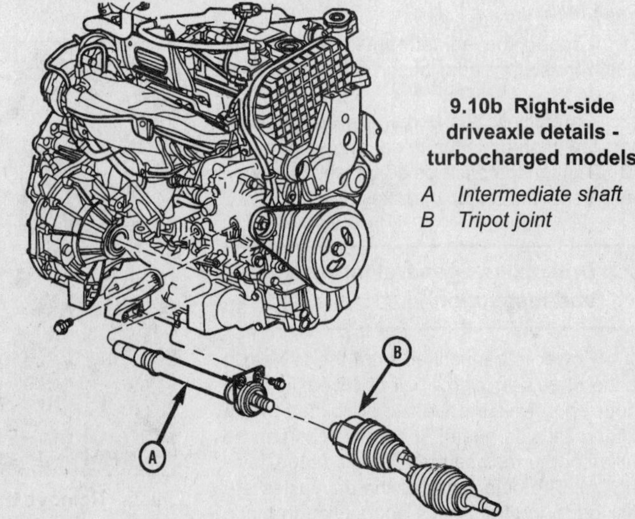


**9.10b Right-side driveaxle details - turbocharged models**

*A Intermediate shaft*
*B Tripot joint*

**10.4 Remove the boot from the inner CV joint and slide the tripod from the joint housing**

**10.5 Remove the snap-ring with a pair of snap-ring pliers**

**10.6 Mark the relationship of the tripod bearing assembly to the axleshaft**

*b) When installing the driveaxle, hold the driveaxle straight out, push it in sharply to seat the driveaxle snap-ring into the groove in the transaxle side gear. To make sure the snap-ring is properly seated in the gear groove, attempt to pull the driveaxle out of the transaxle by hand. If the snap-ring is properly seated the inner joint will not move out.*

*c) Clean all foreign matter from the driveaxle outer CV joint threads. Install the spring washer and the nut. Tighten the hub nut to the torque listed in this Chapter's specifications. Install the nut lock and a NEW cotter pin. Bend the ends over completely.*

*d) Install the wheel and lug nuts, then lower the vehicle. Tighten the lug nuts to the torque listed in the Chapter 1 Specifications.*

*e) Add transaxle lubricant as necessary (see Chapter 1).*

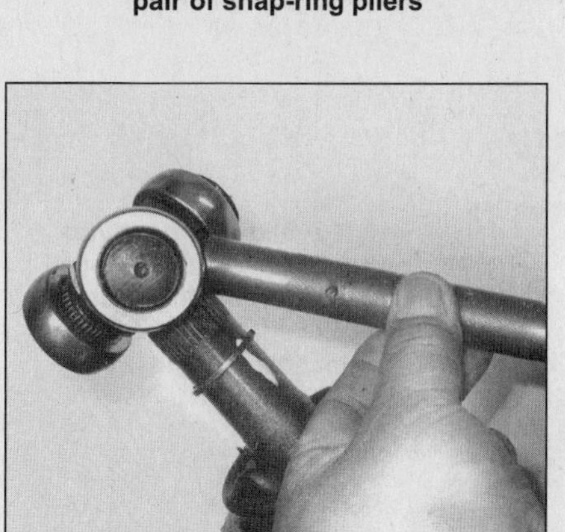

**10.7 Drive the tripod joint off the axleshaft with a brass punch and hammer; be careful not to damage the bearing surfaces or the splines on the shaft**

**10.10a Wrap the axleshaft splines with electrical tape to prevent damaging the boot as it's slid onto the shaft**

## 10 Driveaxle boot replacement and CV joint inspection

**Note:** *If the CV joints or boots must be replaced, explore all options before beginning the job. Complete, rebuilt driveaxles may be available on an exchange basis, eliminating much time and work. Whichever route you choose to take, check on the cost and availability of parts before disassembling the vehicle.*

**Note:** *The inner and outer boots on the vehicles covered in this manual are constructed from different materials: The inner boots are made from either high-temperature application silicone material or Hytrel thermoplastic; the outer boot is made of Hytrel thermoplastic. Make sure you obtain a boot made of the correct material for the CV joint boot you're replacing.*

### *Inner CV joint*

1 Remove the driveaxle (see Section 9).

2 Mount the driveaxle in a vise with wood-lined jaws (to prevent damage to the axleshaft). Check the CV joints for excessive play in the radial direction, which indicates worn parts. Check for smooth operation throughout the full range of motion for each CV joint. If a boot is torn, the recommended procedure is to disassemble the joint, clean the components and inspect for damage due to loss of lubrication and possible contamination by foreign matter. If the CV joint is in good condition, lubricate it with CV joint grease and install a new boot.

### Disassembly

*Refer to illustrations 10.4, 10.5, 10.6, 10.7*

3 Cut the boot clamps with side-cutters, then remove and discard them.

4 Using a screwdriver, carefully pry up on the edge of the CV boot, pull it off the CV joint housing and slide it down the axleshaft, exposing the tripod spider assembly. To separate the axleshaft and spider assembly from the inner tripod joint housing, simply pull them straight out **(see illustration)**. **Note:** *When removing the spider assembly, hold the rollers in place on the spider trunnion to protect the rollers and the needle bearings from falling free.*

5 Remove the spider assembly snap-ring with a pair of snap-ring pliers **(see illustration)**.

6 Mark the tripod to the axleshaft to ensure that they are reassembled properly **(see illustration)**.

7 Use a hammer and a brass drift to drive the spider assembly from the axleshaft **(see illustration)**.

8 Slide the boot off the shaft.

### Inspection

9 Thoroughly clean all components with solvent until the old CV joint grease is completely removed. Inspect the bearing surfaces of the inner tripods and housings for cracks, pitting, scoring and other signs of wear. If any part of the inner CV joint is worn, you must replace the entire driveaxle assembly (inner tripod joint, axleshaft and outer CV joint). The only components that can be purchased separately are the boots themselves and the boot clamps.

### Reassembly

*Refer to illustrations 10.10a, 10.10b, 10.10c, 10.10.d, 10.11a, 10.11b, 10.12a, 10.12b, 10.13, 10.15a, 10.15b,10.15c and 10.15d*

10 Wrap the splines on the inner end of the axleshaft with electrical or duct tape to protect the boots from the sharp edges of the splines and slide the clamps and boot onto

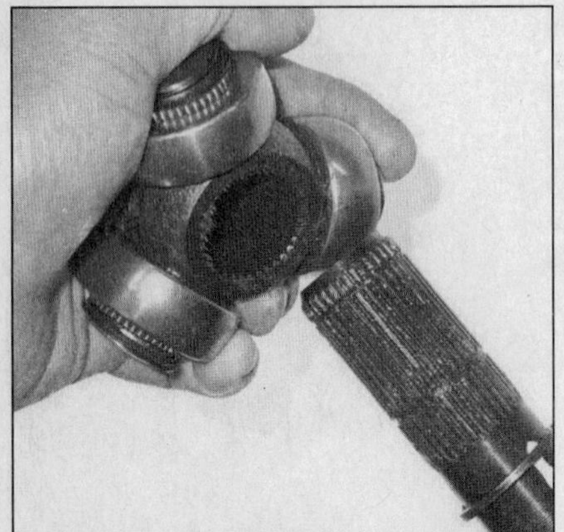

10.10b Install the tripod spider on the axleshaft (make sure your match mark is facing out)

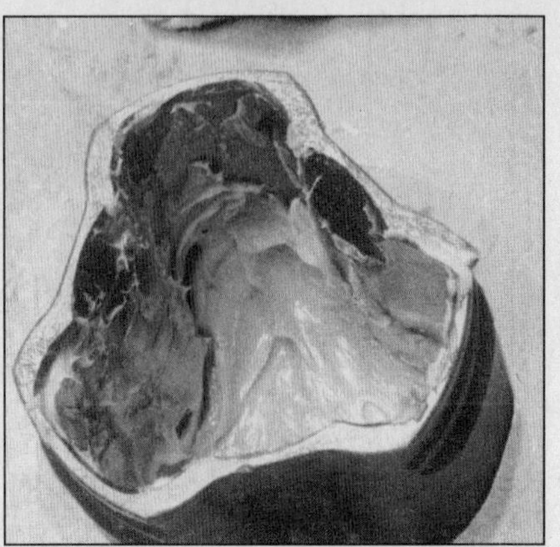

10.10c Place grease at the bottom of the CV joint housing

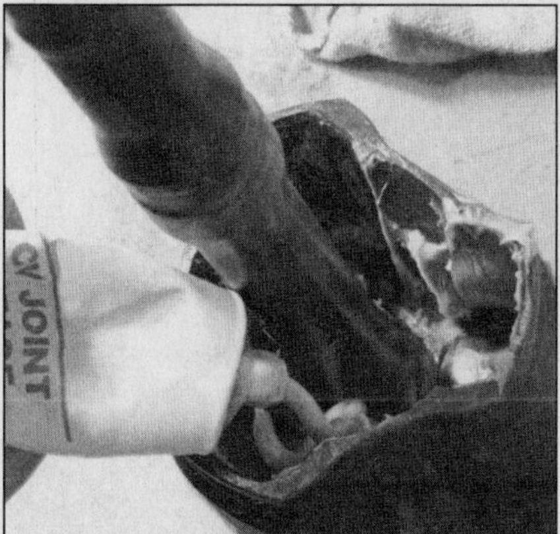


10.10d Install the boot and clamps onto the axleshaft, then insert the tripod into the housing, followed by the rest of the grease

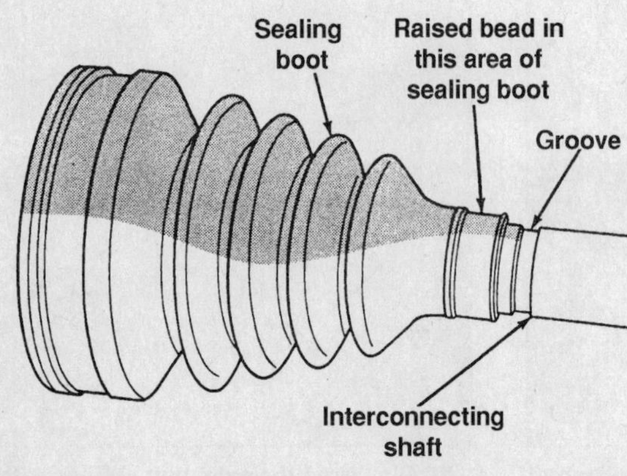


10.11a Slide the boot into place, making sure the small end seats in the flat spot on the axleshaft between the locating shoulders

10.11b Make sure that the thinnest groove on the axleshaft is the only one showing

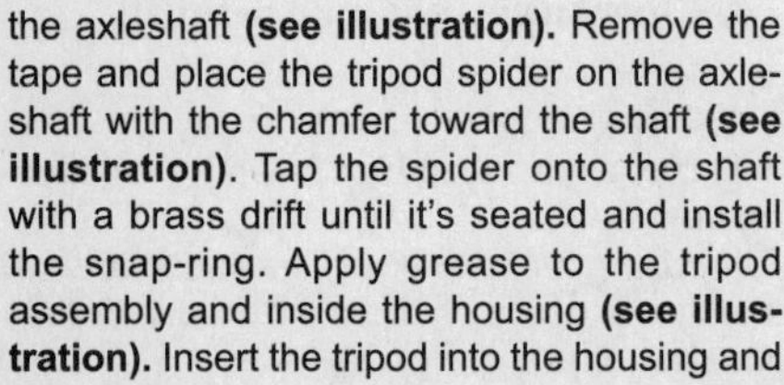

the axleshaft **(see illustration).** Remove the tape and place the tripod spider on the axleshaft with the chamfer toward the shaft **(see illustration)**. Tap the spider onto the shaft with a brass drift until it's seated and install the snap-ring. Apply grease to the tripod assembly and inside the housing **(see illustration).** Insert the tripod into the housing and pack the remainder of the grease around the tripod **(see illustration).**

11 Slide the boot into place; making sure the raised bead on the inside of the seal boot is positioned in the groove on the interconnecting shaft **(see illustration).** If the driveaxle has multiple locating grooves on the shaft, position the boot so only one of the grooves (the thinnest) is exposed **(see illustration)**. Position the sealing boot into the groove on the tripod housing retaining groove.

12 Adjust the length of the CV joint **(see illustrations)**.

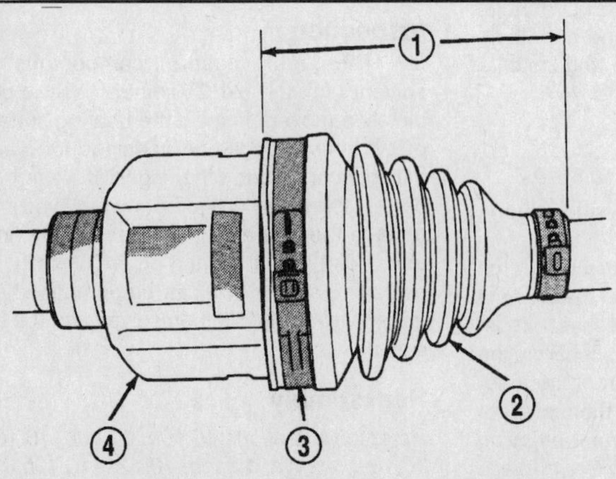


**10.12a CV joint adjustment details - Hytrel boot**

*1 107 mm*
*2 Boot*
*3 Clamp*
*4 Inner CV joint*

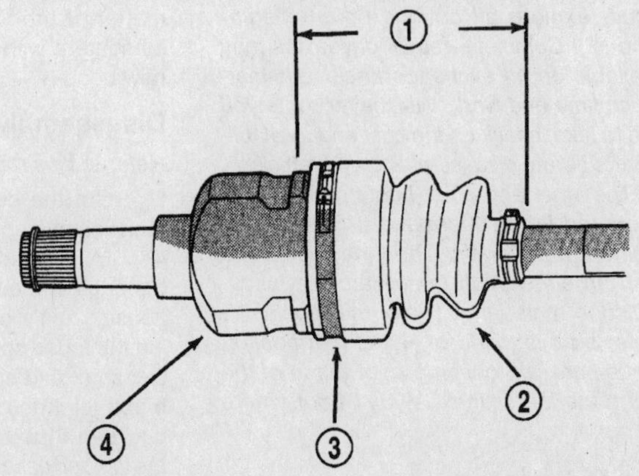


**10.12b CV joint adjustment details - silicone boot**

*1 105 mm*
*2 Boot*
*3 Clamp*
*4 Inner CV joint*

13 Equalize the pressure inside the boot by inserting a small, dull, flat screwdriver tip between the boot and the CV joint housing **(see illustration)**. Then remove the screwdriver tip.

14 Make sure each end of the boot is seated properly, and the boot is not distorted.

15 Two types of clamps are used on the inner CV joint. If a crimp-type clamp is used, clamp the new boot clamps onto the boot with a special crimping tool (available at most automotive parts stores). Place the crimping tool over the bridge of each new boot clamp, then tighten the nut on the crimping tool until the jaws are closed **(see illustrations)**. If a low profile latching type clamp is used, place the prongs of the clamping tool (available at most automotive parts stores) in the holes of the clamp and squeeze the tool together until the top band latches behind the tabs of the lower band **(see illustrations)**.

16 The driveaxle is now ready for installation (see Section 11).

## *Outer CV joint*

### Disassembly

*Refer to illustrations 10.21a and 10.21b*

17 Remove the driveaxle (see Section 9).

18 Mount the driveaxle in a vise with wood-lined jaws (to prevent damage to the axleshaft). Check the CV joints for excessive play in the radial direction, which indicates worn parts. Check for smooth operation throughout the full range of motion for each CV joint. If a boot is torn, the recommended procedure is to disassemble the joint, clean the components and inspect for damage due to loss of lubrication and possible contamination by foreign matter. If the CV joint is in good condition, lubricate it with CV joint grease and install a new boot.

19 Cut the boot clamps with side-cutters, then remove and discard them.

20 Slide the boot away from the outer CV joint, and clean the CV joint and the interconnecting parts.

21 Strike the edge of the CV joint housing

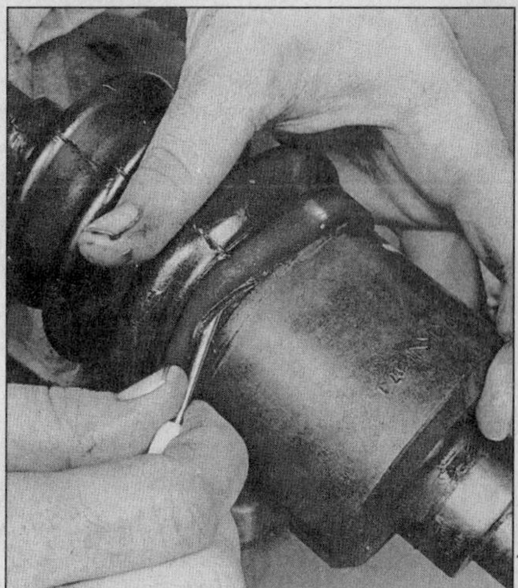

**10.13 Equalize the pressure inside the boot by inserting a small, dull screwdriver between the boot and the CV joint housing**

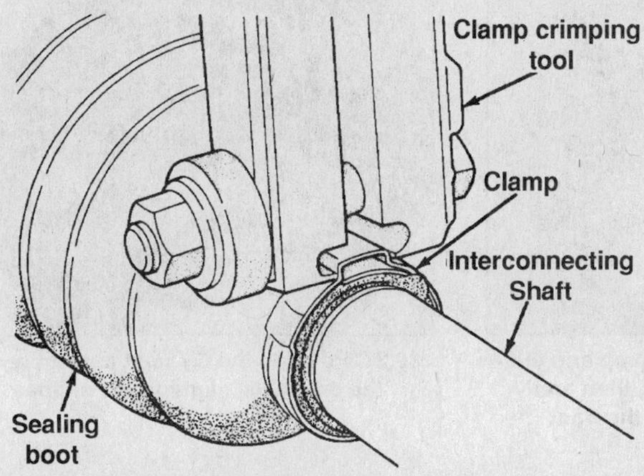


**10.15a Clamp the new boot clamps onto the boot with a crimping tool such as this one (available at most auto parts stores). Place the crimping tool over the bridge of each new boot clamp . . .**

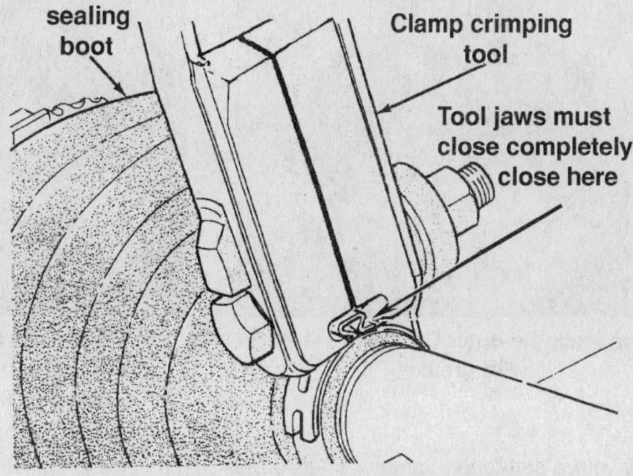


**10.15b . . . then tighten the nut on the crimping tool until the jaws are closed**

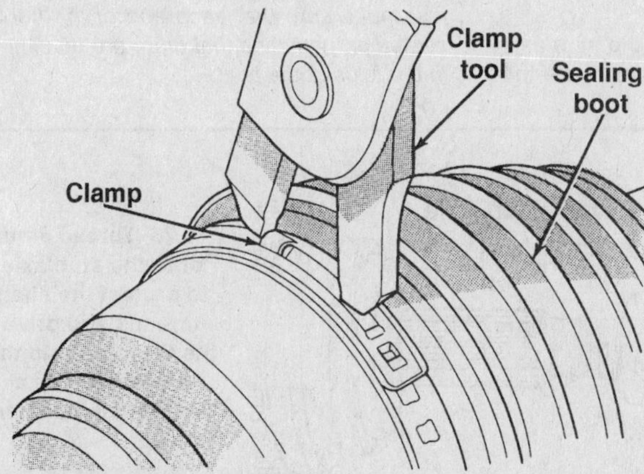


**10.15c For the low profile latching type boot clamp, place the prongs of the clamping tool in the holes of the clamp . . .**

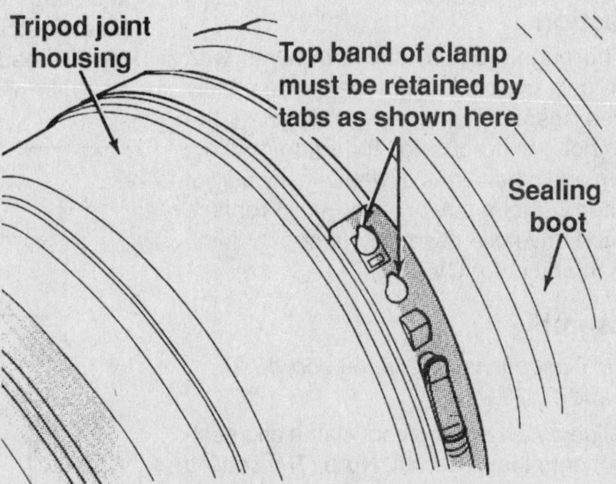


**10.15d . . .and squeeze the tool together until the top band latches behind the tabs of the lower band**

10.21a Strike the edge of the CV joint housing sharply with a soft-faced hammer to dislodge the CV joint from the shaft

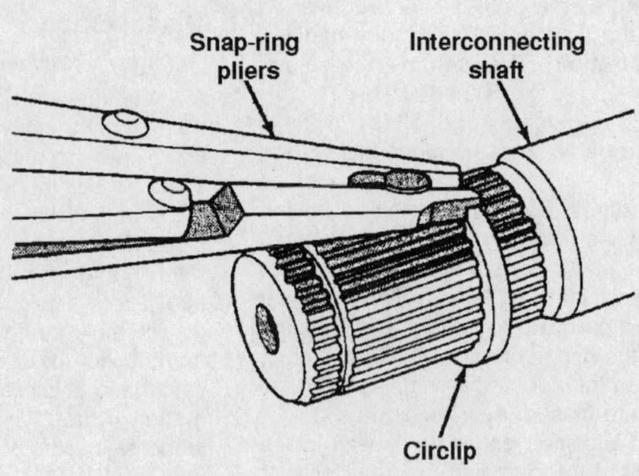


10.21b Using a pair of snap-ring pliers remove the circlip from the axleshaft

10.26a Pack the outer CV joint assembly with grease

10.26b Install the small clamp and the new boot on the driveaxle, then apply grease to the inside of the boot

10.27 Position the CV joint assembly on the driveaxle, aligning the splines

sharply with a soft-faced hammer to dislodge the outer CV joint housing from the axleshaft **(see illustration)**. Remove the circlip from the shaft **(see illustration).**

22 Slide the outer CV joint and the sealing boot off the axleshaft.

## Inspection

23 Thoroughly clean all components with solvent until the old CV grease is completely removed. Inspect the bearing surfaces of the inner tripods and housings for cracks, pitting, scoring, and other signs of wear. If any part of the outer CV joint is worn, you must replace the entire driveaxle assembly (inner CV joint, axleshaft and outer CV joint).

## Reassembly

*Refer to illustrations 10.26a, 10.26b, 10.27, 10.28 and 10.36*

24 Slide a new sealing boot clamp and sealing boot onto the axleshaft. **Note:** *The sealing boot must be positioned on the shaft so the raised bead on the inside of the boot is in the groove on the shaft.*

25 Replace the circlip onto the axleshaft.

26 Place half the grease provided in the sealing boot kit into the outer CV joint assembly housing. Put the remaining grease into the sealing boot **(see illustrations).**

27 Align the splines on the axleshaft with the splines on the outer CV joint assembly and start the outer CV joint onto the axleshaft **(see illustration).**

28 Thread a nut loosely onto the stub axle and use a soft-faced hammer to strike the nut (the nut is installed to protect the threads) **(see illustration)**.

29 Drive the CV joint onto the axleshaft until the CV joint is seated to the axleshaft.

30 Install the outer CV joint sealing boot to the axleshaft (see Steps 11 through 16). **Note:** *The length of the outer joint isn't adjustable; just make sure that each end of the boot is seated properly and that there are no dimples in the folds of the boot.*

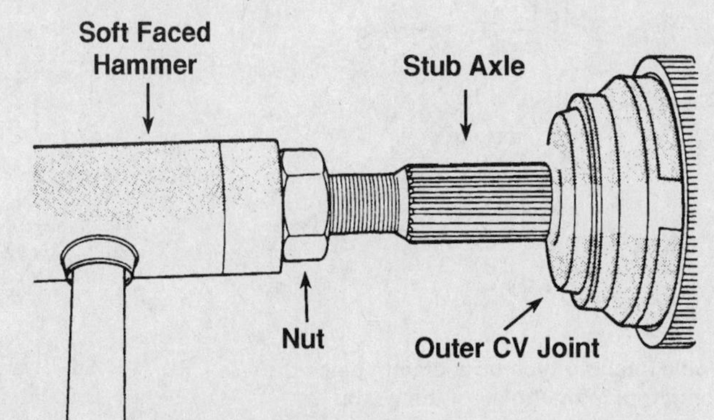


10.28 Thread a nut onto the stub axle to protect the shaft threads and drive the CV joint onto the axleshaft with a soft-faced hammer

# Chapter 9 Brakes

## Contents



## Specifications

### General

| | |
|---|---|
| Brake fluid type | See Chapter 1 |

### Disc brakes

| | |
|---|---|
| Minimum pad lining thickness | See Chapter 1 |
| Disc minimum thickness | Cast into disc |
| Disc runout limit (front or rear) | 0.005 inch (0.13 mm) |
| Parallelism (thickness variation) | |
| Front | 0.0004 inch (0.010 mm) |
| Rear | 0.0005 inch (0.013 mm) |

### Drum brakes

| | |
|---|---|
| Shoe lining minimum thickness | See Chapter 1 |
| Maximum drum diameter | Cast into drum |

### Torque specifications

**Note:** *One foot-pound (ft-lb) of torque is equivalent to 12 inch-pounds (in-lbs) of torque. Torque values below approximately 15 foot-pounds are expressed in inch-pounds, because most foot-pound torque wrenches are not accurate at these smaller values.*

| | **Ft-lbs** (unless otherwise indicated) | **Nm** |
|---|---|---|
| ABS wheel speed sensor bolt | 105 in-lbs | 12 |
| Caliper guide pin/lock pin (mounting) bolts | | |
| Front | 26 | 35 |
| Rear | 16 | 22 |
| Caliper mounting bracket bolts | | |
| Front | 77 | 104 |
| Rear | 70 | 95 |
| Brake hose banjo bolt | 18 | 24 |
| Master cylinder-to-brake booster nuts | 156 in-lbs | 18 |
| Power brake booster mounting nuts | 25 | 34 |

2.2 The ABS hydraulic unit (located below the master cylinder)

2.9a Front wheel speed sensor mounting bolt

2.9b Rear wheel speed sensor mounting bolt

## 1 General information

The vehicles covered by this manual are equipped with a hydraulically operated brake system. The front brakes are disc type and the rear brakes are either drum or disc type. Both the front and rear disc brakes automatically compensate for disc and pad wear. As the pads wear down, the pistons gradually protrude farther from the calipers, but don't retract as far, automatically compensating for the thinner pads. Rear drum brakes have automatic adjusters which compensate for wear of the brake shoes.

### Hydraulic system

The hydraulic system consists of two separate circuits that are diagonally split (one circuit operates the left front and right rear brakes, while the other circuit operates the right front and left rear brakes). The master cylinder has separate reservoirs for the two circuits, and, in the event of a leak or failure in one hydraulic circuit, the other circuit will remain operative.

### Power brake booster

The power brake booster, which is mounted on the firewall, utilizes engine manifold vacuum and atmospheric pressure to provide assistance to the hydraulically operated brakes.

### Parking brake

The parking brake operates the rear brakes only, through cable actuation. It's activated by a lever mounted in the center console. The parking brake on rear disc brake models uses brake shoes and small brake drums integral with the rear brake discs.

### Service

After completing any operation involving disassembly of any part of the brake system, always test drive the vehicle to check for proper braking performance before resuming normal driving. When testing the brakes, perform the tests on a clean, dry, flat surface. Conditions other than these can lead to inaccurate test results.

Test the brakes at various speeds with both light and heavy pedal pressure. The vehicle should stop evenly without pulling to one side or the other. Avoid locking the brakes, because this slides the tires and diminishes braking efficiency and control of the vehicle.

Tires, vehicle load and wheel alignment are factors which also affect braking performance.

## 2 Anti-lock Brake System (ABS) - general information and speed sensor removal and installation

### General information

*Refer to illustration 2.2*

1 The anti-lock brake system is designed to maintain vehicle steerability, directional stability and optimum deceleration under severe braking conditions on most road surfaces. It does so by monitoring the rotational speed of each wheel and controlling the brake line pressure to each wheel during braking. This prevents the wheels from locking up.

2 The ABS system has three main components - the wheel speed sensors, the electronic control unit (ECU) and the hydraulic unit **(see illustration)**. Four wheel speed sensors - one at each wheel - send a variable voltage signal to the control unit, which monitors these signals, compares them to its program and determines whether a wheel is about to lock up. When a wheel is about to lock up, the control unit signals the hydraulic unit to reduce hydraulic pressure (or not increase it further) at that wheel's brake caliper. Pressure modulation is handled by electrically-operated solenoid valves.

3 If a problem develops within the system, an "ABS" warning light will glow on the dashboard. Sometimes, a visual inspection of the ABS system can help you locate the problem. Carefully inspect the ABS wiring harness. Pay particularly close attention to the harness and connections near each wheel. Look for signs of chafing and other damage caused by incorrectly routed wires. If a wheel sensor harness is damaged, the sensor must be replaced. **Warning:** *Do NOT try to repair an ABS wiring harness. The ABS system is sensitive to even the smallest changes in resistance. Repairing the harness could alter resistance values and cause the system to malfunction. If the ABS wiring harness is damaged in any way, it must be replaced.* **Caution:** *Make sure the ignition is turned off before unplugging or reattaching any electrical connections.*

### Diagnosis and repair

4 If a dashboard warning light comes on and stays on while the vehicle is in operation, the ABS system requires attention. Although a special scan tool is necessary to properly diagnose the system, you can perform a few preliminary checks before taking the vehicle to a dealer service department.

- a) *Check the brake fluid level in the reservoir.*
- b) *Verify that the computer electrical connectors are securely connected.*
- c) *Check the electrical connectors at the hydraulic control unit.*
- d) *Check the fuses.*
- e) *Follow the wiring harness to each wheel and verify that all connections are secure and that the wiring is undamaged.*

5 If the above preliminary checks do not rectify the problem, the vehicle should be diagnosed by a dealer service department or other qualified repair shop. Due to the complex nature of this system, all actual repair work must be done by a qualified automotive technician.

### Wheel speed sensor - removal and installation

*Refer to illustrations 2.9a and 2.9b*

6 Loosen the wheel lug nuts, raise the vehicle and support it securely on jackstands. Remove the wheel.

7 Make sure the ignition key is turned to the Off position.

**3.4 Always wash the brakes with brake system cleaner before working on them**

**3.5 Push the piston back into the caliper bore with a large C-clamp**

8 Trace the wiring back from the sensor, detaching all brackets and clips while noting its correct routing, then disconnect the electrical connector.

9 Remove the mounting bolt and carefully pull the sensor out from the knuckle or brake backing plate **(see illustrations)**.

10 Installation is the reverse of the removal procedure. Tighten the mounting bolt to the torque listed in this Chapter's Specifications.

11 Install the wheel and lug nuts, tightening them securely. Lower the vehicle and tighten the lug nuts to the torque listed in the Chapter 1 Specifications.

## 3 Disc brake pads - replacement

**Warning:** *Disc brake pads must be replaced on both front or rear wheels at the same time - never replace the pads on only one wheel. Also, the dust created by the brake system is harmful to your health. Never blow it out with compressed air and don't inhale any of it. An approved filtering mask should be worn when working on the brakes. Do not, under any circumstances, use petroleum-based solvents to clean brake parts. Use brake system cleaner only!*

**Caution:** *Don't depress the brake pedal with the caliper removed.*

**Note:** *Some 2003 and later vehicles are equipped with an optional performance brake system. Calipers for the performance brake system can be identified by the "Turbo" mark on each caliper. When ordering replacement pads or parts, be sure to specify the correct brake system.*

1 Remove the cap from the brake fluid reservoir. Remove about two-thirds of the fluid from the reservoir, then reinstall the cap. **Warning:** *Brake fluid is poisonous - never siphon it by mouth. Use a suction gun or old poultry baster. If a baster is used, never again use it for the preparation of food.* **Caution:** *Brake fluid will damage paint. If any fluid is spilled, wash it off immediately with plenty of clean, cold water.*

2 Loosen the wheel lug nuts, raise the end of the vehicle you're working on and support it securely on jackstands. Block the wheels that remain on the ground.

3 Remove the wheels. Work on one brake assembly at a time, using the assembled brake for reference if necessary.

### Front

*Refer to illustrations 3.4, 3.5 and 3.6a through 3.6k*

4 Position a drain pan under the brake assembly and clean the caliper and surrounding area with brake system cleaner **(see illustration)**.

5 Push the piston back into its bore using a C-clamp **(see illustration)**. As the piston is depressed to the bottom of the caliper bore, the fluid level in the master cylinder will rise as the brake fluid is displaced. Make sure it doesn't overflow. If necessary, siphon off some more of the fluid.

6 To replace the brake pads, follow the accompanying photos, beginning with **illustration 3.6a**. Be sure to stay in order and read the caption under each illustration.

7 While the pads are removed, inspect the

**3.6a To remove the front brake caliper, remove the two guide pin bolts**

**3.6b Hang the caliper from the coil spring with a piece of wire - don't let it hang by the hose**

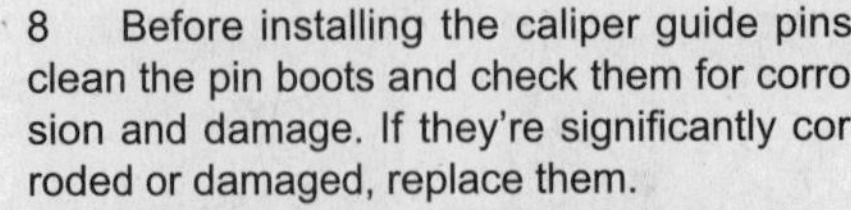

caliper for brake fluid leaks and ruptures of the piston dust boot. Replace the caliper if necessary (see Section 4). Also inspect the brake disc carefully (see Section 5). If machining is necessary, follow the information in that Section to remove the disc. Inspect the brake hoses for damage and replace if necessary (see Section 10).

8 Before installing the caliper guide pins, clean the pin boots and check them for corrosion and damage. If they're significantly corroded or damaged, replace them.

9 Tighten the guide pins to the torque listed in this Chapter's Specifications.

10 Repeat the procedure on the opposite wheel, then install the wheels and lug nuts, lower the vehicle and tighten the lug nuts to the torque listed in the Chapter 1 Specifications.

11 Add the specified type of brake fluid to the reservoir until it's full (see Chapter 1).

12 Pump the brake pedal a few times to bring the pads into contact with the disc. Check the level of the brake fluid, adding some if necessary.

**3.6c Remove the inner pad and shim(s)**

**3.6d Remove the outer pad and shim(s)**

**3.6e Remove the anti-rattle clips, paying close attention to how they're installed in the mounting bracket**

**3.6f Lubricate the guide pins with multi-purpose grease before installing it**

**3.6g Install the anti-rattle clips in the torque plate - make sure both are fully seated**

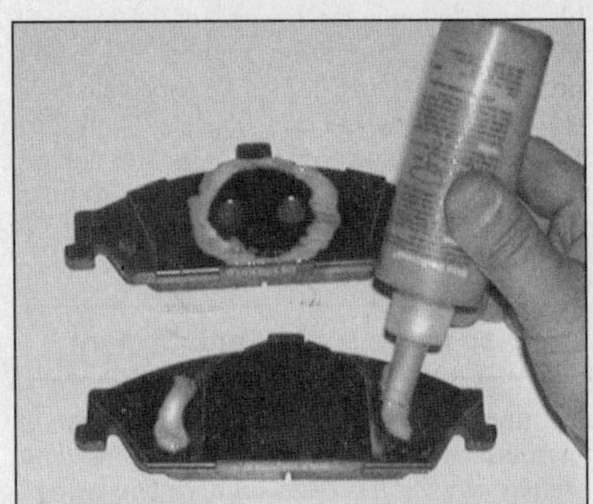

**3.6h Anti-squeal compound (available at auto parts stores) can be applied to the back of the brake pads - follow the label instructions**

**3.6i Install the inner pad (make sure the wear indicator is at the top)**

**3.6j . . . and the outer pad into the mounting bracket - make sure both pads are fully seated . . .**

**3.6k . . . then place the caliper down into position, install the guide pins and tighten them to the torque listed in this Chapter's Specifications**

13 Check the operation of the brakes carefully before placing the vehicle into normal service. Try to avoid heavy brake application until the brakes have been applied lightly several times to seat the pads.

## Rear

*Refer to illustrations 3.14a through 3.14k*

14 To replace the brake pads, follow the accompanying photos, beginning with **illustration 3.14a**. Be sure to stay in order and read the caption under each illustration.

15 While the pads are removed, inspect the caliper for brake fluid leaks and ruptures of the piston dust boot. Replace the caliper if necessary (see Section 4). Also inspect the brake disc carefully (see Section 5). If machin-

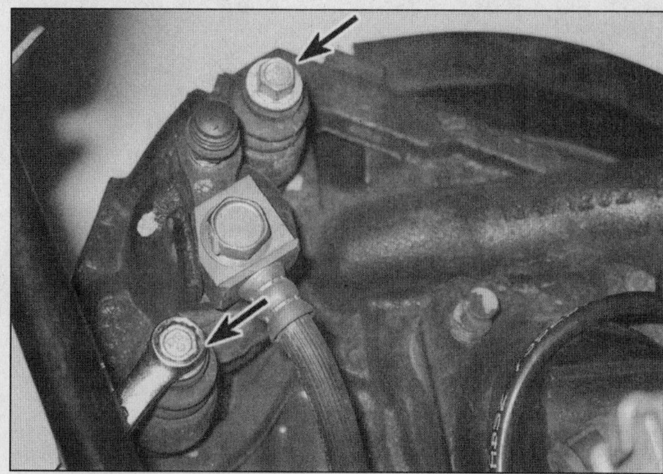

**3.14a To remove the rear brake caliper, remove the two guide pin bolts**

**3.14b Push the piston back into the caliper bore with a large C-clamp**

**3.14c Remove the caliper**

**3.14d To disengage the outer pad, pry up on the retaining spring at either end of the pad and remove the pad**

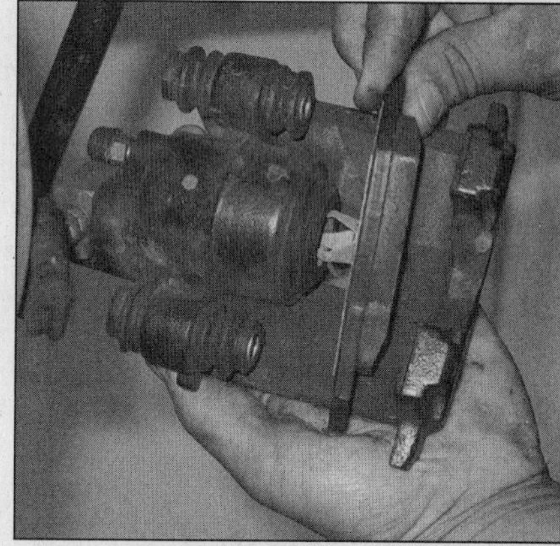

**3.14e To remove the inner pad from the caliper, pull on the pad to disengage the retaining clips from the bore of the piston**

**3.14f Hang the caliper from the coil spring with a piece of wire - don't let it hang by the hose**

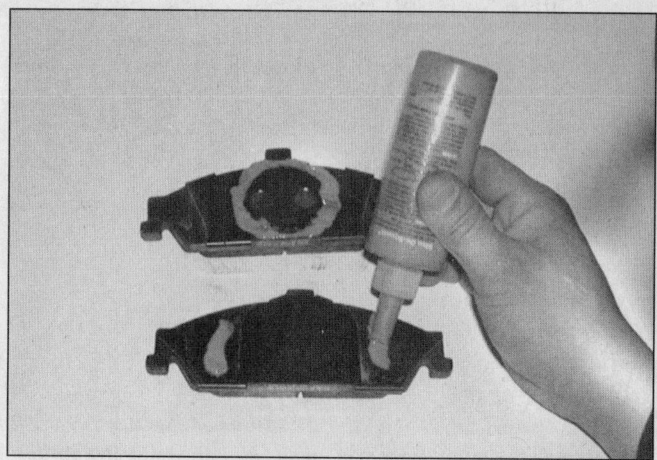

**3.14g Anti-squeal compound (available at auto parts stores - follow the label instructions) can be applied to the back of the brake pads**

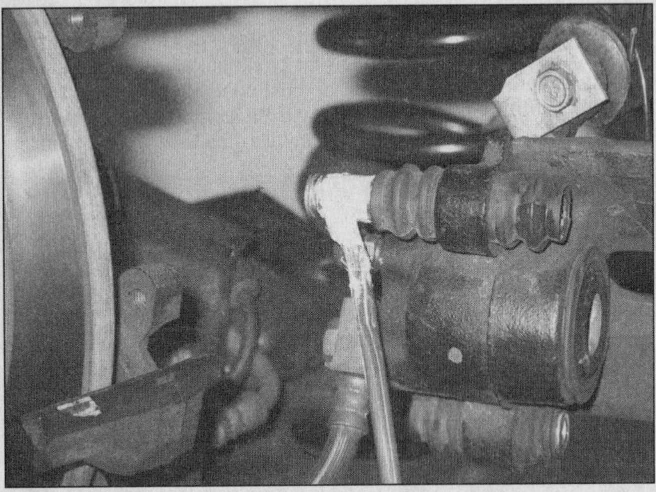

**3.14h Lubricate the guide pin bushings with high-temperature grease before installing them**

**3.14i Install the inner brake pad - make sure the retaining spring is fully seated into the piston bore**

ing is necessary, follow the information in that Section to remove the disc. Inspect the brake hoses for damage and replace if necessary (see Section 10).

16 Before installing the caliper guide pins, clean the pin boots and check them for corrosion and damage. If they're significantly corroded or damaged, replace them. Be sure to tighten them to the torque listed in this Chapter's Specifications

17 Repeat the procedure on the opposite wheel, then install the wheels and lug nuts, lower the vehicle and tighten the lug nuts to the torque listed in the Chapter 1 Specifications.

18 Add the specified type of brake fluid to the reservoir until it's full (see Chapter 1).

19 Pump the brake pedal a few times to bring the pads into contact with the disc. Check the level of the brake fluid, adding some if necessary.

20 Check the operation of the brakes carefully before placing the vehicle into normal service. Try to avoid heavy brake application until the brakes have been applied lightly several times to seat the pads.

## 4 Disc brake caliper - removal and installation

**Warning:** *Dust created by the brake system is harmful to your health. Never blow it out with compressed air and don't inhale any of it. An approved filtering mask should be worn when working on the brakes. Do not, under any circumstances, use petroleum-based solvents to clean brake parts. Use brake system cleaner only.*

**Note:** *If replacement is indicated (usually because of fluid leakage), it is recommended that the calipers be replaced, not overhauled. New and factory rebuilt units are available on an exchange basis. Always replace the calipers in pairs - never replace just one of them.*

**Note:** *Some 2003 vehicles are equipped with an optional performance brake system. Calipers for the performance brake system can be identified by the "Turbo" mark on each caliper. When ordering replacement pads or parts, be sure to specify the correct brake system.*

### Removal

*Refer to illustration 4.2*

1 Loosen the wheel lug nuts, raise the vehicle and support it securely on jackstands. Remove the wheel.

2 Remove the banjo bolt and disconnect the brake hose from the caliper **(see illustration)**. Plug the brake hose to keep contaminants out of the brake system and to prevent losing any more brake fluid than is necessary. Discard the sealing washers - new ones should be used during installation. **Note:** *If the caliper is being removed for access to another component, don't disconnect the hose.*

3 Remove the caliper guide pin bolts **(see illustration 3.6a [front] or 3.14a [rear])**.

**3.14j Install the outer brake pad - make sure the retaining spring is properly engaged with the caliper body**

**3.14k First place the lower end of the caliper and brake pads over the disc (be sure that the caliper's bottom is seated properly into the mounting bracket) then rotate the top of the caliper into position**

**4.2 To disconnect the brake hose from the caliper, remove the banjo bolt**

**5.3 The brake pads on this vehicle were obviously neglected - they wore down completely and cut deep grooves into the disc (wear this severe means the disc must be replaced)**

**5.4a Use a dial indicator to measure disc runout - if the reading exceeds the maximum allowable runout limit, the disc will have to be machined or replaced**

## Installation

4 Install the caliper by reversing the removal procedure. Remember to replace the sealing washers at the brake hose-to-caliper connection. Tighten the caliper guide pin bolts to the torque listed in this Chapter's Specifications.

5 Bleed the brake circuit according to the procedure in Section 11 (only if the brake hose was disconnected). Make sure there are no leaks from the hose connections. If you didn't disconnect the hose, be sure to pump the brake pedal several times to bring the pads into contact with the disc.

6 Test the brakes carefully before returning the vehicle to normal service.

## 5 Brake disc - inspection, removal and installation

**Note:** *This procedure applies to both front and rear brake discs.*

**Note:** *Some 2003 and later vehicles are equipped with an optional performance brake system. Calipers for the performance brake system can be identified by the "Turbo" mark on each caliper. When ordering replacement pads or parts, be sure to specify the correct brake system.*

## Inspection

*Refer to illustrations 5.3, 5.4a, 5.4b, 5.5a and 5.5b*

1 Loosen the wheel lug nuts, raise the vehicle and support it securely on jackstands. Remove the wheel and reinstall the lug nuts to hold the disc in place (washers may be required). If the rear brake disc is being worked on, release the parking brake.

2 Remove the brake caliper and pads (see Section 3). Don't disconnect the brake hose from the caliper, or you'll have to bleed the brakes when everything is reassembled. After removing the caliper bolts, suspend the caliper out of the way with a piece of wire.

3 Visually inspect the disc surface for score marks and other damage. Light scratches and shallow grooves are normal after use and may not always be detrimental to brake operation, but deep scoring requires disc removal and refinishing by an automotive machine shop. Be sure to check both sides of the disc **(see illustration)**. If pulsating has been noticed during application of the brakes, suspect excessive disc runout.

4 To check disc runout, place a dial indicator at a point about 1/2-inch from the outer edge of the disc **(see illustration)**. Set the indicator to zero and turn the disc. The indicator reading should not exceed the specified allowable runout limit. If it does, the disc should be refinished by an automotive machine shop. **Note:** *The discs should be resurfaced regardless of the dial indicator reading, as this will impart a smooth finish and ensure a perfectly flat surface, eliminating any brake pedal pulsation or other undesirable symptoms related to questionable discs. At the very least, if you elect not to have the discs resurfaced, remove the glaze from the surface with emery cloth using a swirling motion* **(see illustration)**.

5 It's absolutely critical that the disc not be machined to a thickness under the specified minimum allowable thickness. The minimum thickness is cast into the inside of the disc **(see illustration)**. The disc thickness can be checked with a micrometer **(see illustration)**.

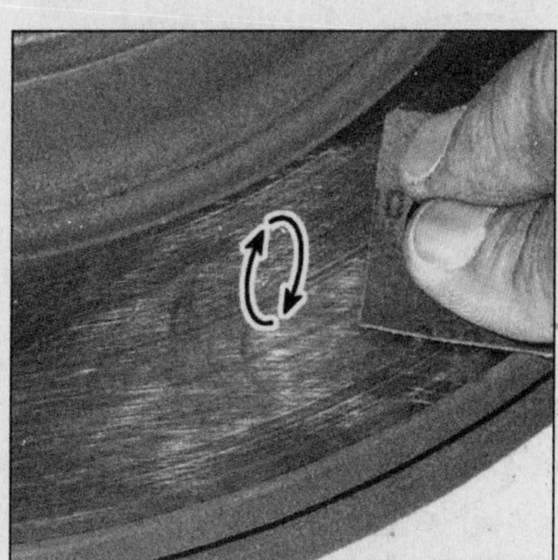

**5.4b Using a swirling motion, remove the glaze from the disc surface with sandpaper or emery cloth**

**5.5a The minimum wear dimension is cast into the back side of the disc (typical)**

**5.5b Use a micrometer to measure disc thickness**

5.6a Caliper mounting bracket (also known as the "torque plate") bolts (front shown, rear similar)

5.6b Using two bolts to force a stuck disc off the hub flange

## Removal

*Refer to illustrations 5.6a and 5.6b*

6 If you're removing a front disc, remove the caliper mounting bracket **(see illustration)**. Remove the lug nuts which were put on to hold the disc in place and remove the disc from the hub. Some models are equipped with threaded holes in the hub portion of the disc; if the disc sticks to the hub, screw in two bolts of the proper size and thread pitch and tighten them to force the disc off the hub **(see illustration)**.

## Installation

7 Place the disc in position over the wheel studs. Install the mounting bracket (if you're installing a front disc), tightening the bolts to the torque listed in this Chapter's Specifications.

8 Install the brake pads and caliper (see Section 3). Tighten the caliper guide pins to the torque listed in this Chapter's Specifications.

9 Install the wheel, lower the vehicle and tighten the lug nuts to the torque listed in the Chapter 1 Specifications.

10 Pump the brake pedal a few times to bring the brake pads into contact with the disc. Bleeding won't be necessary unless the brake hose was disconnected from the caliper. Check the operation of the brakes carefully before driving the vehicle.

# 6 Drum brake shoes - replacement

*Refer to illustrations 6.2, 6.4, 6.5, 6.6, 6.7, 6.8, 6.12 and 6.13*

**Warning:** *Drum brake shoes must be replaced on both wheels at the same time - never replace the shoes on only one wheel. Also, the dust created by the brake system is harmful to your health. Never blow it out with compressed air and don't inhale any of it. An approved filtering mask should be worn when working on the brakes. Do not, under any circumstances, use petroleum-based solvents to clean brake parts. Use brake system cleaner only!*

1 Loosen the rear wheel lug nuts, raise the rear end of the vehicle and support it securely on jackstands. Block the front wheels to keep the vehicle from rolling. Release the parking brake and remove the rear wheels.

2 Remove the brake drum. If the drum won't come off, the brake shoes must be retracted from their fully adjusted position. Insert a screwdriver through the adjuster hole in the brake backing plate and turn the adjuster wheel to retract the shoes **(see illustration)**.

3 Once the drum is removed, clean the brake assembly with brake system cleaner.

4 Using locking pliers, unhook the lever return spring from the adjuster lever and brake shoe **(see illustration)**.

5 Unhook and remove the upper return spring **(see illustration)**.

6 Unhook and remove the lower return spring **(see illustration)**.

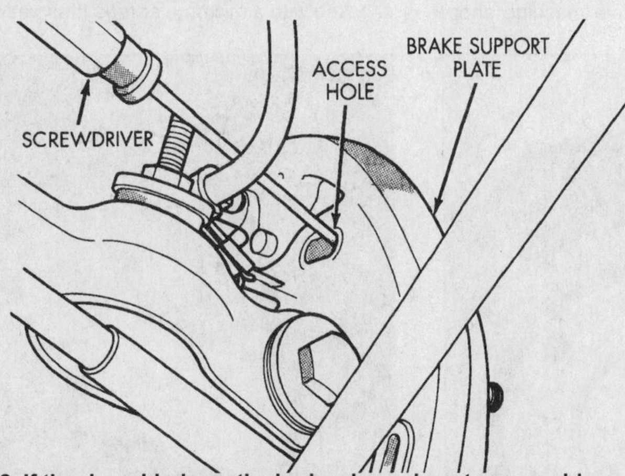

6.2 If the drum binds on the brake shoes, insert a screwdriver through the hole in the backing plate and turn the adjuster wheel to retract the shoes

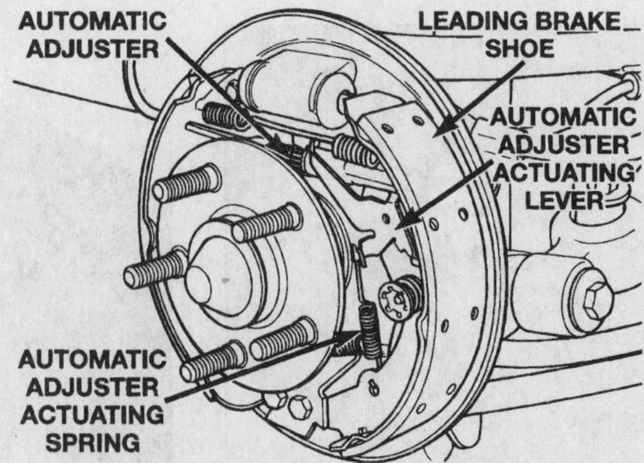

6.4 Remove the spring from the automatic adjuster lever, then detach the lever from the shoe

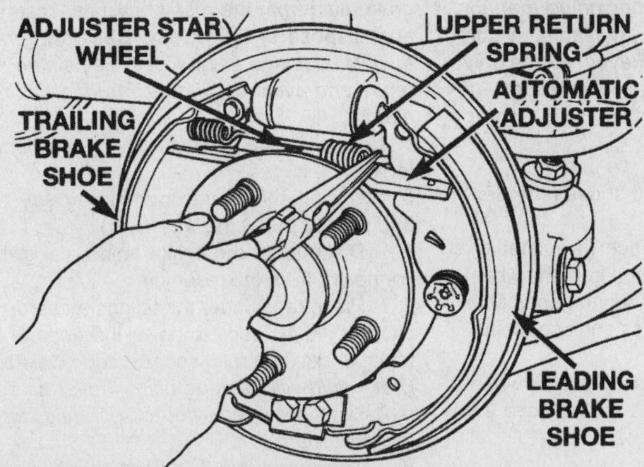

6.5 Unhook the upper return spring from the shoes

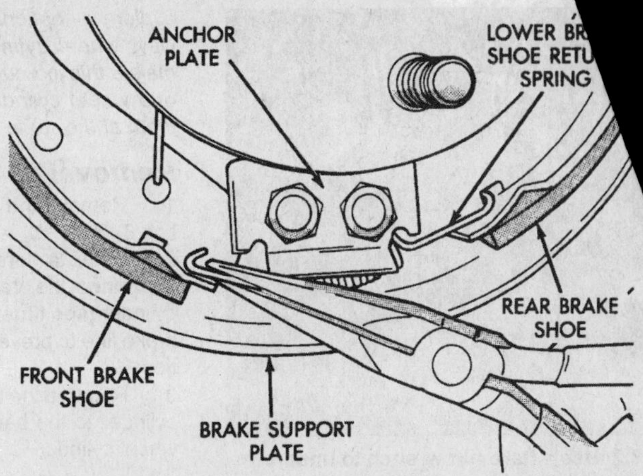

6.6 Detach the lower return spring from the shoes

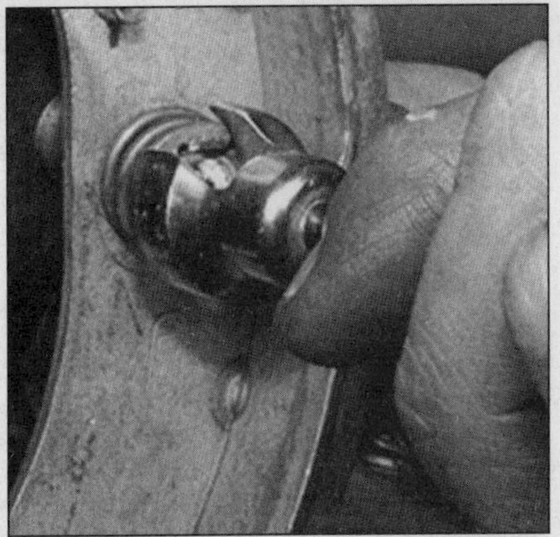
6.7 Remove the hold-down spring and retainer from the leading shoe

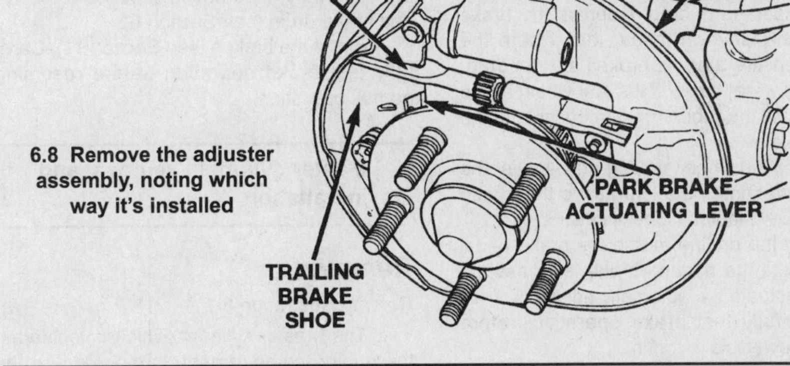

6.8 Remove the adjuster assembly, noting which way it's installed

7 Remove the hold-down spring and retainer from the leading shoe **(see illustration)**. Remove the leading shoe.

8 Remove the automatic adjuster assembly from between the brake shoes **(see illustration)**.

9 Pry the retainer on the parking brake lever open just far enough to remove it, then remove the hold-down spring and retainer and separate the trailing shoe from the parking brake lever. Don't lose the wave washer from the pin on the parking brake lever.

10 If necessary, disengage the parking brake lever from the cable.

11 Check all parts for wear and damage, paying special attention to metal-to-metal contact points. Replace worn or damaged parts. **Note:** *If the vehicle has high mileage, it's a good idea to replace all of the springs as well as any parts that have visible problems.*

12 Check the brake drum for score marks, cracks, deep scratches and hard spots, which will appear as small discolored areas. If the hard spots cannot be removed with emery cloth or if any of the other conditions are seen, the drum must be resurfaced by an automotive machine shop. **Note:** *Professionals recommend resurfacing the drum whenever a brake job is performed. Resurfacing will correct out-of-roundness in the drums as well as removing visible problems. If the drums are so worn that they can't be resurfaced without exceeding the maximum allowable diameter stamped into the drum* **(see illustration)**, *then new ones will be required. At the very least, if you don't have the drums resurfaced, remove the glazing from the surface with emery cloth or sandpaper using a swirling motion.*

13 Apply a small amount of high-temperature brake grease to the shoe contact areas of the backing plate **(see illustration)**, the moving parts of the adjuster assembly and where the adjuster contacts the brake shoes.

14 Install the wave washer and attach the parking brake lever to the new brake shoe. Place the retainer in the pin groove and secure it with pliers.

15 Reverse the removal steps to install the brake shoes. Expand the shoes with the adjuster screw, until the drum will just fit over them.

6.12 The maximum allowable diameter is stamped into the drum (typical)

6.13 Apply a small amount of high-temperature grease to the areas where the brake shoes contact the backing plate

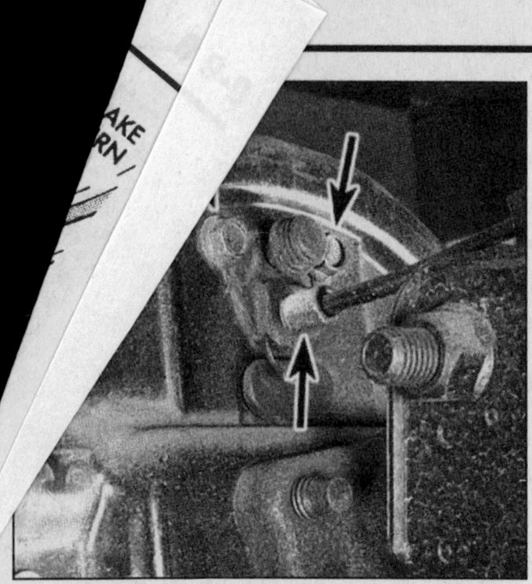

7.2 Use a flare-nut wrench to unscrew the brake line fitting at the wheel cylinder, then remove the wheel cylinder bolts

16 Now, working through the backing plate, turn the adjuster screw wheel until the shoes drag on the drum when the drum is turned. Finally, back off the adjuster screw wheel so the shoes don't drag. Depress the brake pedal firmly several times, then rotate the drum to ensure that the brakes are not dragging. If they are, back off the star wheel a little more. Install the rubber plug in the hole in the backing plate.

17 Install the wheel and lug nuts. Lower the vehicle and tighten the lug nuts to the torque listed in the Chapter 1 Specifications.

18 Start the engine, pump the brake pedal and operate the parking brake lever several times to actuate the automatic adjusters.

19 Carefully test brake operation before driving the vehicle in traffic.

## 7 Wheel cylinder - removal and installation

*Refer to illustration 7.2*

**Note:** *If replacement is warranted (usually because of fluid leakage or sticky operation) explore all options before beginning the job. New wheel cylinders are available, which makes this job quite easy. Never replace only one wheel cylinder. Always replace both of them at the same time.*

### Removal

1 Remove the rear brake shoes (see Section 6).

2 Using a flare-nut wrench (if available), disconnect the brake line fitting from the wheel cylinder **(see illustration)**. Plug the end of the brake line to prevent fluid loss and contamination.

3 Remove the two bolts securing the wheel cylinder to the backing plate and remove the wheel cylinder.

### Installation

4 Installation is the reverse of removal. Tighten the wheel cylinder mounting bolts to the torque listed in this Chapter's Specifications. Tighten the line fitting securely.

5 Install the brake shoes, wheel hub/bearing assembly, if removed (see Chapter 10) and brake drum (see Section 6).

6 Bleed the brakes (see Section 11). Carefully test brake operation before resuming normal operation.

## 8 Master cylinder - removal and installation

### Removal

*Refer to illustration 8.1*

1 The master cylinder, which is located in the engine compartment, is mounted on the power brake booster **(see illustration).**

2 Disconnect the cable from the negative battery terminal (see Chapter 5). Pump the brake pedal several times to deplete the vacuum reserve in the power brake booster (this will prevent contamination from being sucked into the booster).

3 Using a syringe or equivalent, siphon the brake fluid from the master cylinder reservoir and dispose of it properly. **Caution:** *Brake fluid will damage paint. Cover all painted surfaces and avoid spilling fluid during this procedure.*

4 Remove the air filter housing (see Chapter 4).

5 Unbolt the underhood fuse/relay box and place it out of the way.

6 Disconnect the brake fluid level switch connector from the reservoir.

7 Place rags under the fittings and prepare caps or plastic bags to cover the ends of the lines once they're disconnected. **Caution:** *Brake fluid will damage paint. Cover all body parts and be careful not to spill fluid during this procedure.*

8 Disconnect the fluid lines from the master cylinder with a flare-nut wrench. **Note:** *On 2005 and later models, disconnect the clutch master cylinder supply line from the brake master cylinder. Plug the port on the brake fluid reservoir.*

9 Remove the nuts attaching the master cylinder to the power booster and pull the master cylinder off the studs. Again, be careful not to spill the fluid as this is done.

### Installation

*Refer to illustration 8.11*

10 Bench bleed the master cylinder before installing it. Mount the master cylinder in a vise, with the jaws of the vise clamping on the mounting flange.

11 Attach a pair of master cylinder bleeder tubes to the outlet ports of the master cylinder **(see illustration)**.

12 Fill the reservoir with brake fluid of the recommended type (see Chapter 1).

13 Slowly push the pistons into the master cylinder (a large Phillips screwdriver can be used for this) - air will be expelled from the pressure chambers and into the reservoir. Because the tubes are submerged in fluid, air can't be drawn back into the master cylinder when you release the pistons.

**8.1 Master cylinder mounting details**

1 *Electrical connector for fluid level switch*
2 *Brake line fittings*
3 *Mounting nuts*

**8.11 The best way to bleed the master cylinder before installing it on the vehicle is with a pair of bleeder tubes that direct fluid into the reservoir during bleeding**

9.12 Remove the retaining clip from the pushrod clevis pin . . .

9.13 . . . then remove the four booster-to-firewall nuts

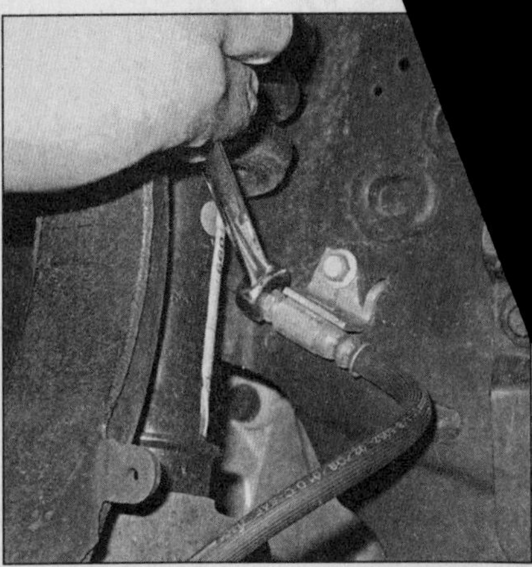

10.3 Loosening a brake line fitting from a front brake hose (typical)

14 Repeat the procedure until no more air bubbles are present.

15 Remove the bleed tubes, one at a time, and install plugs in the open ports to prevent fluid leakage and air from entering. Install the reservoir cap.

16 Install the master cylinder over the studs on the power brake booster and tighten the nuts only finger-tight at this time.

17 Thread the brake line fittings into the master cylinder. Since the master cylinder is still a bit loose, it can be moved slightly so the fittings thread in easily. Don't strip the threads as the fittings are tightened.

18 Tighten the mounting nuts to the torque listed in this Chapter's Specifications. Tighten the brake line fittings securely.

19 Fill the master cylinder reservoir with fluid, then bleed the master cylinder and the rest of the brake system (see Section 11). To bleed the master cylinder on the vehicle, have an assistant depress the brake pedal and hold it down. Loosen the fitting to allow air and fluid to escape. Tighten the fitting, then allow your assistant to return the pedal to its rest position. Repeat this procedure on the other fittings until the fluid is free of air bubbles. **Warning:** *If you do not have a firm brake pedal at the end of the bleeding procedure, or have any doubts as to the effectiveness of the brake system, DO NOT drive the vehicle. Have it towed to a dealer service department or other qualified repair shop for diagnosis.*

20 Reinstall any components that were removed for access to the master cylinder.

21 Re-check the brake fluid level, then check the operation of the brake system carefully before driving the vehicle in traffic.

## 9 Power brake booster - check, removal and installation

### Operating check

1 Depress the brake pedal several times with the engine off and make sure that there is no change in the pedal reserve distance.

2 Depress the pedal and start the engine. If the pedal goes down slightly, operation is normal.

### Airtightness check

3 Start the engine and turn it off after one or two minutes. Depress the brake pedal several times slowly. If the pedal goes down farther the first time but gradually rises after the second or third depression, the booster is airtight.

4 Depress the brake pedal while the engine is running, then stop the engine with the pedal depressed. If there is no change in the pedal reserve travel after holding the pedal for 30 seconds, the booster is airtight.

5 The power brake booster unit requires no special maintenance apart from periodic inspection of the vacuum hoses and the case. The booster is not serviceable. If a problem develops, it must be replaced with a new one.

### Removal

*Refer to illustrations 9.12 and 9.13*

6 Disconnect the cable from the negative battery terminal (see Chapter 5).

7 Remove the air filter housing (See Chapter 4).

8 Unbolt the underhood fuse/relay box and position it out of the way.

9 Disconnect the vacuum hoses from the power brake booster vacuum fitting.

10 Label and disconnect the vacuum hoses and electrical connector from the EGR valve transducer (see Chapter 6). Remove the EGR valve transducer.

11 Remove the master cylinder from the vehicle (see Section 8).

12 Working inside the vehicle under the dash, disconnect the power brake pushrod from the top of the brake pedal by prying off the retaining clip **(see illustration)**. For safety reasons, discard the old pushrod retaining clip and buy a new clip for reassembly.

13 Remove the nuts attaching the booster to the firewall **(see illustration).**

14 Working inside the engine compartment, carefully withdraw the power brake booster unit from the firewall and out of the engine compartment. On vehicles with anti-lock brakes or with turbocharged engines it will be necessary to remove the Integrated Power Module and bracket before removing the booster.

### Installation

15 To install the booster, place it into position on the firewall and tighten the retaining nuts to the torque listed in this Chapter's Specifications. Connect the pushrod to the brake pedal. **Warning:** *Use a new retainer clip. DO NOT reuse the old clip.*

16 Install the master cylinder and bleed the brake hydraulic system (see Sections 8 and 11).

17 The remaining installation steps are the reverse of removal.

18 Carefully test the operation of the brakes before placing the vehicle in normal operation.

## 10 Brake hoses and lines - inspection and replacement

### Inspection

1 Whenever the vehicle is raised and supported securely on jackstands, the rubber hoses which connect the steel brake lines with the front and rear brake assemblies should be inspected for cracks, chafing of the outer cover, leaks, blisters and other damage. These are important and vulnerable parts of the brake system and inspection should be thorough. A light and mirror will be helpful for a complete check. If a hose exhibits any of the above conditions, replace it immediately.

### Flexible hose replacement

*Refer to illustration 10.3*

2 Clean all dirt away from the hose fittings.

3 Using a flare-nut wrench, disconnect the metal brake line from the hose fitting **(see illustration)**. Be careful not to bend the frame bracket or line. If the threaded fitting is corroded, spray it with penetrating oil and allow it to soak in for about 10 minutes, then try again. If you try to break loose a fitting nut that's fro-

metal line, which will ...ced.

...ake hose from the bracket ...d to a bracket with a retain- ... have an integral bracket/fit- ...he brake hose from the bracket ...rom the vehicle as applicable. ...ly plug the metal line to prevent ...e leakage and contamination.

... you're removing a rear brake hose on ...m-brake model, use a flare-nut wrench ...osen the line fitting at the wheel cylinder ...d remove the hose.

6 On hoses that are attached to the caliper with a banjo bolt, unscrew the banjo bolt at the caliper and remove the hose, discarding the sealing washers on either side of the fitting.

7 Attach the new brake hose to the caliper or wheel cylinder as applicable. **Note:** *When connecting a brake hose to a caliper, always use new sealing washers.* Tighten the banjo bolt to the torque listed this Chapter's Specifications.

8 Insert the other end of the new hose through the bracket or loosely attach the fitting/bracket to the vehicle as applicable making sure the hose isn't kinked or twisted. Then fit the metal line to the hose (or hose fitting), tighten the hose bracket (if applicable) and tighten the brake tube fitting nut securely.

9 Carefully check to make sure the suspension or steering components don't make contact with the hose. Have an assistant push down on the vehicle while you watch to see whether the hose interferes with suspension operation. If you're replacing a front hose, have your assistant turn the steering wheel lock-to-lock while you make sure the hose doesn't interfere with the steering linkage or the steering knuckle.

10 After installation, check the master cylinder fluid level and add fluid as necessary. Bleed the brakes (see Section 11). Carefully test brake operation before resuming normal operation.

### Metal brake lines

11 When replacing brake lines, be sure to use the correct parts. Do not use copper tubing for any brake system components. Purchase steel brake lines from a dealer parts department or auto parts store.

12 Prefabricated brake line, with the tube ends already flared and fittings installed, is available at auto parts stores and dealer parts departments. If it is necessary to bend a line, use a tubing bender to prevent kinking the line.

13 When installing the new line make sure it's well supported in the brackets and has plenty of clearance between moving or hot components. Make sure you tighten the fittings securely.

14 After installation, check the master cylinder fluid level and add fluid as necessary. Bleed the brakes (see Section 11). Carefully test brake operation before resuming normal operation.

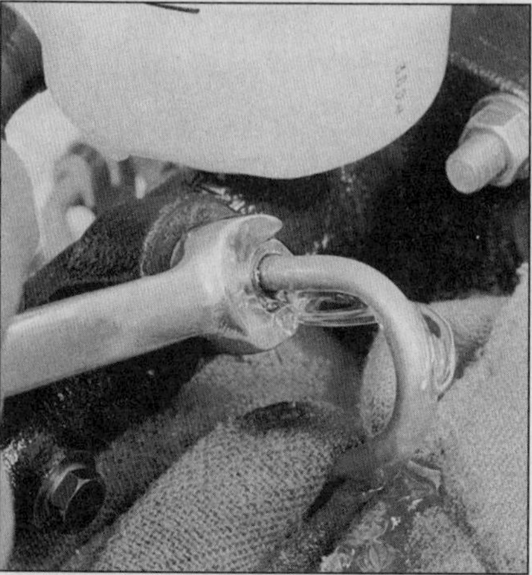

**11.7 Have an assistant depress the brake pedal and hold it down, then loosen the fitting nut, allowing air and brake fluid to escape; repeat this procedure on the other fitting(s) until the fluid is clear of air bubbles**

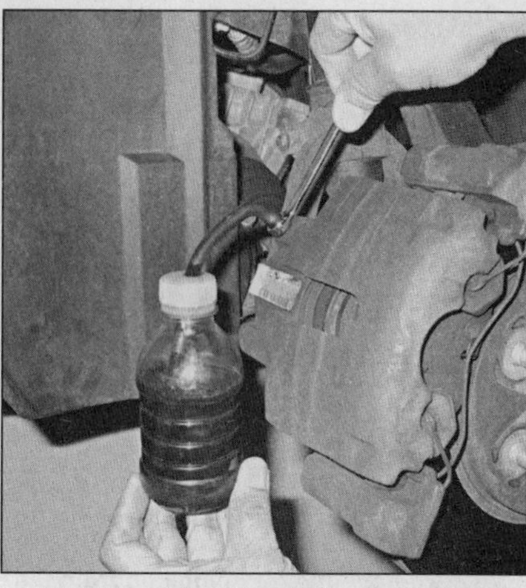

**11.9 When bleeding the brakes, a hose is connected to the bleed screw at the caliper or wheel cylinder and then submerged in clean brake fluid - air will be seen as bubbles exiting the tube (typical)**

## 11 Brake hydraulic system - bleeding

*Refer to illustrations 11.7 and 11.9*

**Warning 1:** *The following procedure is a manual bleeding procedure. This is the only bleeding procedure which can be performed at home without special tools. However, if air has found its way into the hydraulic control unit, the entire system must be bled manually, then with a DRB scan tool, then manually a second time. If the brake pedal feels "spongy" even after bleeding the brakes, or the ABS light on the instrument panel does not go off, or if you have any doubts whatsoever about the effectiveness of the brake system, have the vehicle towed to a dealer service department or other repair shop equipped with the necessary tools for bleeding the system.*

**Warning 2:** *Wear eye protection when bleeding the brake system. If the fluid comes in contact with your eyes, immediately rinse them with water and seek medical attention.*

**Note:** *Bleeding the hydraulic system is necessary to remove any air that manages to find its way into the system when it's been opened during removal and installation of a hydraulic component.*

1 It will be necessary to bleed the complete system if air has entered the system due to low fluid level, or if the brake lines have been disconnected at the master cylinder.

2 If a brake line was disconnected only at a wheel, then only that caliper or wheel cylinder must be bled.

3 If a brake line is disconnected at a fitting located between the master cylinder and any of the brakes, that part of the system served by the disconnected line must be bled. The following procedure describes bleeding the entire system, however.

4 Remove any residual vacuum from the brake power booster by applying the brake several times with the engine off.

5 Remove the cap from the master cylinder reservoir and fill the reservoir with brake fluid. Reinstall the cap. **Note:** *Check the fluid level often during the bleeding operation and add fluid as necessary to prevent the fluid level from falling low enough to allow air bubbles into the master cylinder.*

6 Have an assistant on hand, as well as a supply of new brake fluid, a clear container partially filled with clean brake fluid, a length of clear tubing to fit over the bleeder valve and a wrench to open and close the bleeder valve.

7 Begin the bleeding process by bleeding the master cylinder **(see illustration)**.

8 Moving to the first wheel in the bleeding sequence, loosen the bleeder valve slightly, then tighten it to a point where it is snug but can still be loosened quickly and easily. The bleeding sequence is as follows:

Left rear
Right front
Right rear
Left front

9 Place one end of the hose over the bleeder valve and submerge the other end in brake fluid in the container **(see illustration)**.

10 Have the assistant push the brake pedal slowly to the floor, then hold the pedal firmly depressed.

11 While the pedal is held depressed, open the bleeder valve just enough to allow a flow of fluid to leave the valve. Watch for air bubbles to exit the submerged end of the tube. When the fluid flow slows after a couple of seconds, close the valve and have your assistant release the pedal.

12 Repeat Steps 10 and 11 until no more air is seen leaving the tube, then tighten the bleeder valve and proceed to bleed the other calipers/wheel cylinders, in the proper sequence, using the same procedure. Be

sure to check the fluid in the master cylinder reservoir frequently.

13 Never use old brake fluid. It contains moisture which can boil, rendering the brakes inoperative.

14 Refill the master cylinder with fluid at the end of the operation.

15 Check the operation of the brakes. The pedal should feel solid when depressed, with no sponginess. If necessary, repeat the entire process. **Warning:** *If, after bleeding the system you do not have a firm brake pedal, or if the ABS light on the instrument panel does not go off, or if you have any doubts whatsoever about the effectiveness of the brake system, have it towed to a dealer service department or other repair shop to have the system bled.*

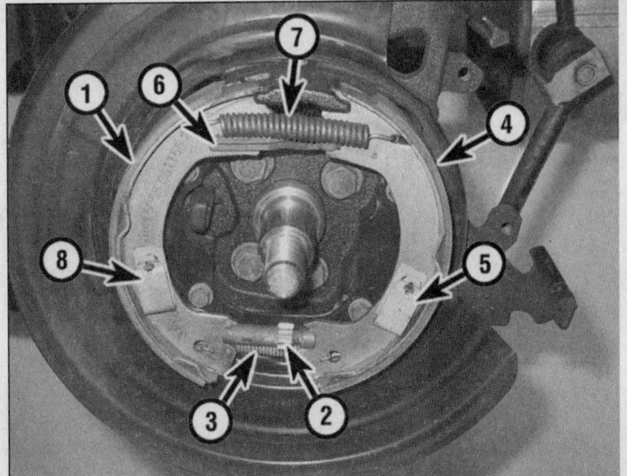


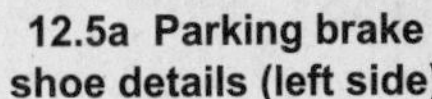

**12.5a Parking brake shoe details (left side)**

1 *Leading shoe*
2 *Adjuster screw assembly*
3 *Lower return spring*
4 *Trailing shoe*
5 *Hold-down clip*
6 *Adjuster lever*
7 *Upper return spring*
8 *Hold-down clip*

## 12 Parking brake shoes (models with rear disc brakes) - replacement

**Warning:** *Parking brake shoes must be replaced on both wheels at the same time - never replace the shoes on only one wheel. Also, the dust created by the brake system is harmful to your health. Never blow it out with compressed air and don't inhale any of it. An approved filtering mask should be worn when working on the brakes. Do not, under any circumstances, use petroleum-based solvents to clean brake parts. Use brake system cleaner only!*

### *Replacement*

*Refer to illustrations 12.5a through 12.5p and 12.8*

1 Loosen the rear wheel lug nuts, raise the rear of the vehicle and support it securely on jackstands. Block the front wheels and remove the rear wheels. Release the parking brake.

2 Remove the rear calipers (see Section 4). Support the caliper assemblies with a coat hanger or heavy wire and don't disconnect the brake line from the caliper.

3 Remove the rear discs (see Section 5). Remove the rear hub and bearing assemblies (see Chapter 10).

4 Clean the parking brake assembly with brake system cleaner.

5 Follow the accompanying sequence of photos to replace the parking brake shoes **(see illustrations)**. Be sure to stay in order and read the caption under each illustration.

6 Inspect the drum surface inside the disc for score marks, deep grooves, hard spots (which will appear as small, discolored areas) and cracks. If the disc/drum is worn, scored or out of round, it will have to be resurfaced by an automotive machine shop, or replaced.

7 Install the hub and bearing assemblies (see Chapter 10).

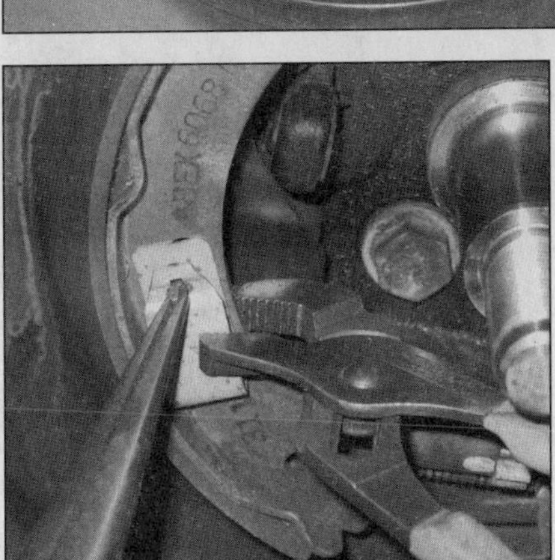

**12.5b Squeeze the hold-down clip on the leading shoe with pliers and turn the pin 90-degrees, then remove the clip**

**12.5c Pull the leading shoe back and remove the adjuster screw assembly (note how it's installed; it must be reinstalled the same way)**

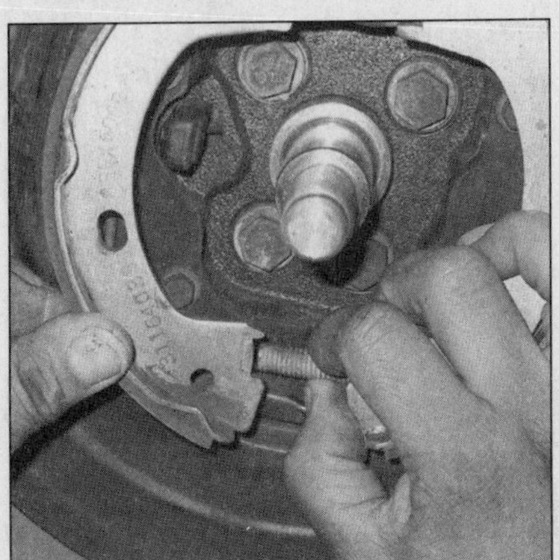

**12.5d Remove the lower return spring**

**12.5e Remove the hold-down clip from the trailing shoe**

**12.5f Unhook the upper return spring and remove the trailing shoe**

12.5g Remove the leading shoe

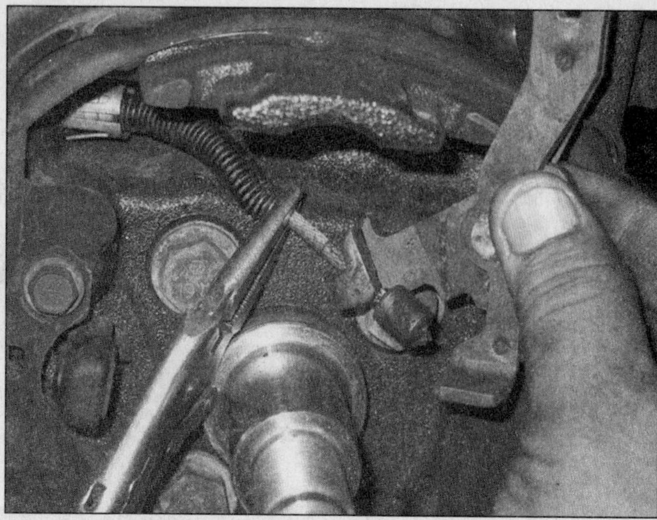

12.5h Detach the parking brake cable from the adjuster lever

12.5i Clean the backing plate, then apply a thin coat of high-temperature grease to the shoe contact points on the backing plate . . .

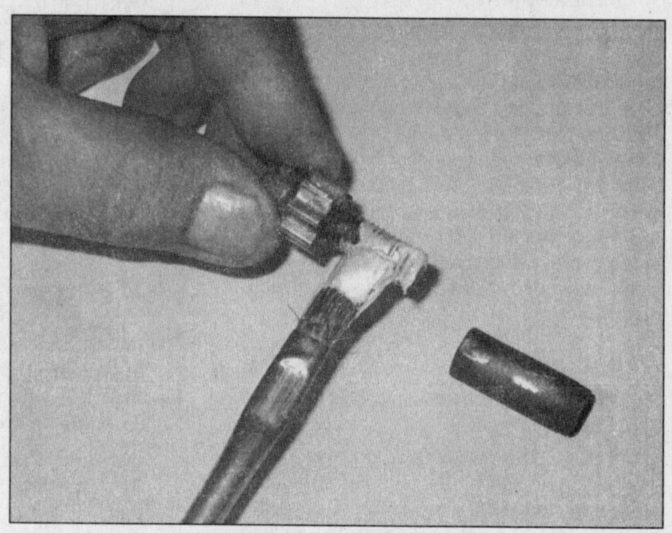

12.5j Clean and lubricate the friction surfaces of the adjuster screw assembly

12.5k Connect the adjuster lever to the cable, mount the leading shoe on the backing plate, making sure the notch in the shoe engages with the adjuster lever . . .

12.5l . . . and secure the shoe with the hold-down clip

12.5m Connect the upper return spring to the top of each shoe and install the trailing shoe. . .

12.5n . . . then secure the shoe with the hold-down clip

12.5o Install the lower return spring

12.5p Spread the shoes apart and install the adjuster screw assembly

8 Before installing the disc, rotate the star wheel on the adjuster until the distance across the friction surfaces of the parking brake shoes is 6-3/4 inches **(see illustration)**.

9 Install the disc/drum over the shoes. Using a screwdriver or brake adjusting tool, turn the star wheel on the parking brake shoe adjuster until the shoes slightly drag as the disc is turned, then back-off the adjuster until the shoes don't drag.

10 Install the caliper (see Section 4).

11 Repeat this sequence for the other parking brake shoes at the other rear wheel.

12 Adjust the parking brake (see Step 13).

## Adjustment

13 Place the parking brake lever in the released position.

14 Now, working through the backing plate, turn the adjuster screw wheel until the shoes drag on the drum when the disc is turned. Finally, back off the adjuster screw wheel so the shoes don't drag. Depress the brake pedal firmly several times, then rotate the drum to ensure that the brakes are not dragging. If they are, back off the star wheel a little more. Install the rubber plug in the hole in the backing plate.

15 Install the wheel and lug nuts. Lower the vehicle and tighten the lug nuts to the torque listed in the Chapter 1 Specifications.

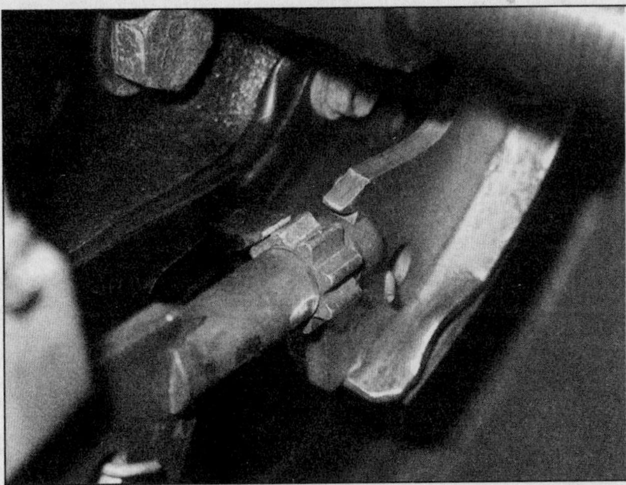

12.8 Turn the adjuster screw star wheel until the span across the shoes is 6-3/4 inches (tool is inserted through the backing plate to illustrate how the shoes can be adjusted with the disc in place)

## 13 Brake light switch - check, replacement and adjustment

### Check

*Refer to illustration 13.1*

1 The brake light switch is located on the brake pedal mounting bracket **(see illustration)**. The switch activates the brake lights at the rear of the vehicle when the pedal is depressed. To gain access to the switch, remove the under-dash panel and the heater/air conditioning duct.

2 If the brake lights are inoperative, check the fuse first (see Chapter 12).

3 If the fuse is good, check for voltage to the switch on the feed wire (refer to the wiring diagrams at the end of this manual for the proper color wire to check). If no voltage is present, repair the wire between the switch and the fuse box.

4 If voltage is present, depress the brake pedal and check for voltage at the output wire terminal (again, refer to the wiring diagrams). If no voltage is present, replace the switch.

5 If voltage is present, check for power on the brake light wires at the tail light housings (with the brake pedal depressed). If voltage is not present, repair the circuit between the switch and the brake lights.

6 If voltage is present, check for a bad ground; using a jumper wire connected to a good ground, probe the ground wire terminal at the tail light connector. If the brake lights go on, repair the ground circuit (follow the ground wire from the tail light housing).

**13.1 Brake light switch**

7 Keep in mind that the brake light bulbs *could* be burned out, but the likelihood of all the bulbs being burned out is very slim.

### Replacement and adjustment

**Note:** *Whenever the brake light switch is removed, it must be replaced with a new one.*

8 Depress and hold the brake pedal, then rotate the brake light switch about 30-degrees in a counterclockwise direction and remove it from the mounting bracket.

9 Unplug the electrical connector from the switch and remove it from the vehicle.

10 Grasp the switch plunger and pull it outward until it has ratcheted to it's fully extended position.

11 Depress the brake pedal as far as it will go, then install the switch in the bracket by aligning the index key on the switch with the slot at the top of the square hole in the mounting bracket. When the switch is fully installed in the bracket, rotate the switch clockwise about 30-degrees to lock the switch into the bracket.

12 **Note:** *The small lever on the side of the switch should be angled approximately 45-degrees. If it is parallel with the electrical connector portion of the switch, the switch has already been installed once, or someone has moved the lever. In any case, a new switch will be required.* Allow the brake pedal to slowly come to rest, then move the lever on the switch until it is parallel to the electrical connector.

13 Plug the electrical connector into the switch.

# Chapter 10
# Suspension and steering systems

## Contents



## Specifications

### General

| | |
|---|---|
| Power steering fluid type | See Chapter 1 |

### Torque specifications

**Note:** *One foot-pound (ft-lb) of torque is equivalent to 12 inch-pounds (in-lbs) of torque. Torque values below approximately 15 foot-pounds are expressed in inch-pounds, because most foot-pound torque wrenches are not accurate at these smaller values.*

| | **Ft-lbs** (unless otherwise indicated) | **Nm** |
|---|---|---|
| **Front suspension** | | |
| Strut | | |
| Upper mounting nuts | 25 | 34 |
| Strut-to-steering knuckle bolts/nuts | | |
| Step 1 | 40 | 54 |
| Step 2 | Tighten an additional 1/4-turn (90-degrees) | |
| Stabilizer bar | | |
| Clamp bolts | 21 | 28 |
| Link nuts | 21 | 28 |
| Lower control arm | | |
| Balljoint-to-steering knuckle pinch bolt/nut | 70 | 95 |
| Front pivot bolt/nut | 125 | 170 |
| Control arm-to-crossmember rear bolt | 185 | 250 |
| Crossmember mounting bolts | 113 | 153 |
| Driveaxle/hub nut | See Chapter 8 | |

## Torque specifications (continued)

**Note:** *One foot-pound (ft-lb) of torque is equivalent to 12 inch-pounds (in-lbs) of torque. Torque values below approximately 15 foot-pounds are expressed in inch-pounds, because most foot-pound torque wrenches are not accurate at these smaller values.*

| | **Ft-lbs** (unless otherwise indicated) | **Nm** |
|---|---|---|
| **Rear suspension** | | |
| Hub-to-spindle nut | 160 | 217 |
| Shock absorber upper mounting bolt | 73 | 99 |
| Shock absorber lower mounting bolt | | |
| 2001 models | 50 | 68 |
| 2002 and later models | 65 | 88 |
| Spindle retaining nuts | 70 | 95 |
| Stabilizer bar | | |
| Clamp bolts | 45 | 61 |
| Bar link-to-frame bolt | 48 | 65 |
| Bar-to-link nut | 48 | 65 |
| Trailing arm | | |
| Pivot bolt | | |
| 2001 models | 80 | 108 |
| 2002 and later models | 90 | 122 |
| Bracket-to-body bolts | 40 | 54 |
| Watts linkage | | |
| Bellcrank pivot bolt | | |
| 2001 models | 90 | 122 |
| 2002 and later models | 110 | 149 |
| Upper link-to-bellcrank | | |
| Step 1 | 120 in-lbs | 14 |
| Step 2 | Tighten an additional 1/2-turn (180-degrees) | |
| Lower link-to-bellcrank | | |
| Step 1 | 120 in-lbs | 14 |
| Step 2 | Tighten an additional 1/2-turn (180-degrees) | |
| Link-to-body bracket (upper or lower) | | |
| 2001 models | 60 | 81 |
| 2002 and later models | 68 | 92 |
| **Steering system** | | |
| Steering wheel bolt | 40 | 54 |
| Steering gear mounting bolts | 45 | 61 |
| Steering column mounting nuts | 156 in-lbs | 17.5 |
| Steering shaft U-joint pinch bolt | 21 | 28 |
| Power steering pump | | |
| Pump-to-bracket bolts | 21 | 28 |
| Bracket-to-engine bolts | 40 | 54 |
| Tie-rod end-to-steering knuckle nut | | |
| 2001 through 2003 models | 55 | 75 |
| 2004 and later models | 40 | 54 |

## 1 General information

*Refer to illustrations 1.1 and 1.2*

The front suspension is a MacPherson strut design. The upper end of each strut is attached to the vehicle's body strut support. The lower end of the strut is connected to the upper end of the steering knuckle. The steering knuckle is attached to a balljoint mounted on the outer end of the suspension control arm. A stabilizer bar connected to each control arm and mounted to the suspension crossmember reduces body roll during cornering **(see illustration)**.

The rear suspension consists of a torsion axle with shock absorbers and coil springs **(see illustration)**. A Watts linkage locates the axle laterally. A stabilizer bar is clamped to the axle beam and connected to the chassis by two links.

The power-assisted rack-and-pinion steering gear is attached to the front suspension crossmember. The steering gear actuates the tie-rods, which are attached to the steering knuckles. The steering column is designed to collapse in the event of an accident.

Frequently, when working on the suspension or steering system components, you may come across fasteners which seem impossible to loosen. These fasteners on the underside of the vehicle are continually subjected to water, road grime, mud, etc., and can become rusted or "frozen" in place, making them extremely difficult to remove. In order to unscrew these stubborn fasteners without damaging them (or other components), be sure to use lots of penetrating oil and allow it to soak in for a while. Using a wire brush to clean exposed threads will also ease removal of the nut or bolt and prevent damage to the threads. Sometimes a sharp blow with a hammer and punch will break the bond between a nut and bolt threads, but care must be taken to prevent the punch from slipping off the fastener and ruining the threads. Heating the stuck fastener and surrounding area with a torch sometimes helps too, but isn't recommended because of the obvious dangers associated with fire. Long breaker bars and extension, or "cheater," pipes will increase leverage, but never use an extension pipe on a ratchet - the ratcheting mechanism could be damaged. Sometimes tightening the nut or bolt first will help to break it loose. Fasteners that require drastic measures to remove should always be replaced with new ones.

Since most of the procedures dealt with in this Chapter involve jacking up the vehicle and working underneath it, a good pair of jackstands will be needed. A hydraulic floor jack is the preferred type of jack to lift the vehicle, and it can also be used to support certain components during various operations. **Warning:** *Never, under any cir-*

1.1 Front suspension and steering components

1 Strut/coil spring assembly
2 Steering knuckle
3 Control arm
4 Balljoint
5 Tie-rod end
6 Stabilizer bar link
7 Stabilizer bar bushing clamp
8 Stabilizer bar

1.2 Rear suspension components

1 Stabilizer bar link
2 Coil spring
3 Watts link (upper)
4 Watts link bellcrank
5 Stabilizer bar
6 Shock absorber
7 Stabilizer bar bushing clamp
8 Watts link (lower)
9 Rear axle assembly
10 Trailing arm pivot bolt

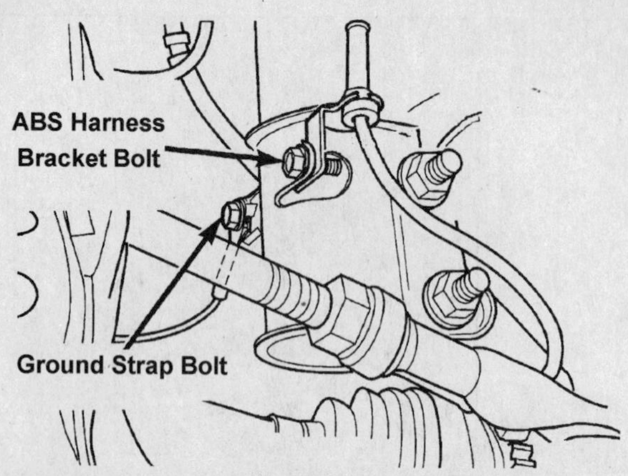


**2.4 Unscrew the bolt and detach the ground strap and, if equipped, the ABS wheel speed sensor harness from the strut**

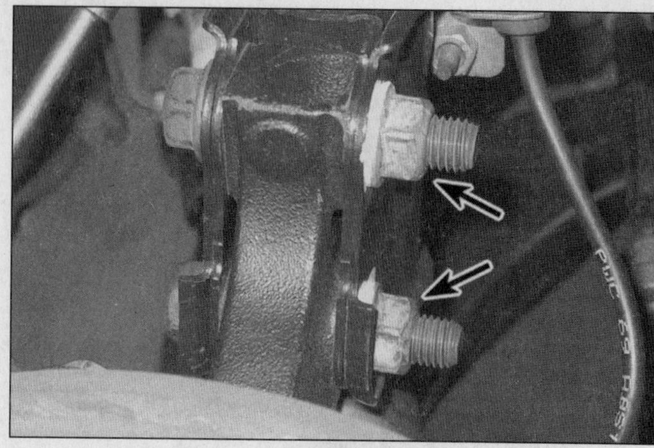

**2.5 Remove the strut-to-steering knuckle nuts and bolts**

*cumstances, rely on a jack to support the vehicle while working on it. Whenever any of the suspension or steering fasteners are loosened or removed they must be inspected and, if necessary, replaced with new ones of the same part number or of original equipment quality and design. Torque specifications must be followed for proper reassembly and component retention. Never attempt to heat or straighten any suspension or steering components. Instead, replace any bent or damaged part with a new one.*

## 2 Strut assembly (front) - removal, inspection and installation

*Refer to illustrations 2.4, 2.5 and 2.6*

**Warning:** *Always replace the struts and/or coil springs in pairs - never replace just one strut or one coil spring (this could cause dangerous handling peculiarities).*

### Removal

1 Loosen the front wheel lug nuts.

2 Raise the vehicle and support it securely on jackstands. Remove the front wheels.

3 **Note:** *If both strut assemblies are going to be removed, mark the assemblies Right and Left so they will be reinstalled on the correct side.* Mark the position of the strut to the steering knuckle. **Note:** *This is only necessary if special camber adjusting bolts have been installed in place of the regular strut-to-knuckle bolts.*

4 Remove the bolt and disconnect the ground strap from the strut. On ABS equipped models, also remove the bolt securing the speed sensor harness to the strut **(see illustration)**.

5 Remove the strut-to-steering knuckle nuts and bolts **(see illustration).**

6 Remove the upper mounting nuts **(see illustration)**, disengage the strut from the steering knuckle and detach it from the vehicle.

### Inspection

7 Inspect the strut body for leaking fluid, dents, damage and corrosion. Check the spring for nicks, chips or cracks in the spring coating (this could lead to premature spring failure due to corrosion). If the strut or coil spring is damaged, see Section 3.

### Installation

8 To install the strut, place it in position with the studs extending up through the strut tower. Install the nuts and tighten them to the torque listed in this Chapter's Specifications.

9 Attach the strut to the steering knuckle, then insert the strut-to-steering knuckle bolts. If equipped with special camber adjusting bolts, align the marks you made in Step 3. Hold the bolts and tighten the nuts to the torque listed in this Chapter's Specifications.

10 Attach the ground strap and, if equipped, the ABS sensor harness bracket to the strut and tighten the bolt(s) securely.

11 Install the wheel and lug nuts and lower the vehicle. Tighten the lug nuts to the torque listed in the Chapter 1 Specifications.

12 If special camber adjusting bolts have been installed sometime in the past, have the front end alignment checked and, if necessary, adjusted.

## 3 Strut/coil spring - replacement

**Note:** *You'll need a spring compressor for this procedure. Spring compressors are available on a daily rental basis at most auto parts stores or equipment yards.*

1 If the struts or coil springs exhibit the telltale signs of wear (leaking fluid, loss of damping capability, chipped, sagging or cracked coil springs) explore all options before beginning any work. The strut/coil spring assemblies are not serviceable and must be replaced if a problem develops. However, strut assemblies complete with springs may be available on an exchange basis, which eliminates much time and work. Whichever route you choose to take, check on the cost and availability of parts before disassembling your vehicle. **Warning:** *Disassembling a strut is potentially dangerous and utmost attention must be directed to the job, or serious injury may result. Use only a high-quality spring compressor and carefully follow the manufacturer's instructions furnished with the tool. After removing the coil spring from the strut assembly, set it aside in a safe, isolated area.*

**2.6 Remove these three strut upper mounting nuts - DO NOT remove the center nut!**

**3.3 Mount the strut clevis bracket portion of the strut assembly in a vise**

**3.4 Install the spring compressor in accordance with the tool manufacturer's instructions and compress the spring until all pressure is removed from the upper suspension support**

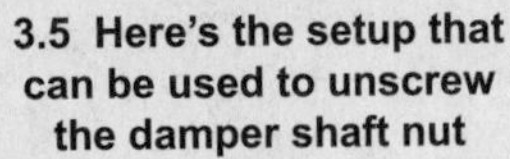

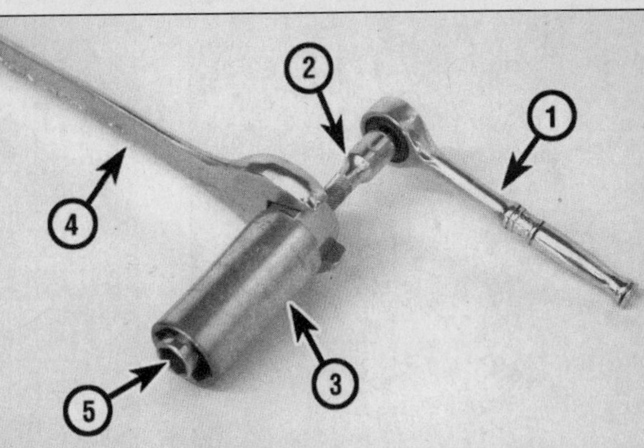


**3.5 Here's the setup that can be used to unscrew the damper shaft nut**

1 *1/4-inch drive ratchet*
2 *Extension*
3 *13/16-inch spark plug socket*
4 *Wrench to turn socket*
5 *10 mm socket (to hold damper shaft)*

## *Disassembly*

*Refer to illustrations 3.3, 3.4, 3.5, 3.6, 3.7a, 3.7b, 3.8 and 3.9*

2 Remove the strut and spring assembly (see Section 2).

3 Mount the strut clevis bracket portion of the strut assembly in a vise **(see illustration)**. **Caution:** *Do not clamp any other portion of the strut assembly in the vise as it will be damaged.* Line the vise jaws with wood or rags to prevent damage to the unit and don't tighten the vise excessively.

4 Following the tool manufacturer's instructions, install the spring compressor (which can be obtained at most auto parts stores or equipment yards on a daily rental basis) on the spring and compress it sufficiently to relieve all pressure from the upper spring seat **(see illustration)**. This can be verified by wiggling the spring.

5 While holding the damper shaft from turning, loosen the shaft nut with a socket. A special tool is available to do this, but a substitute can be made from a 13/16-inch spark plug socket (with a hex surface at the top), a ratchet, a 1/4-inch drive extension inserted through the hole in the spark plug socket, and a 10 mm socket attached to the extension **(see illustration)**.

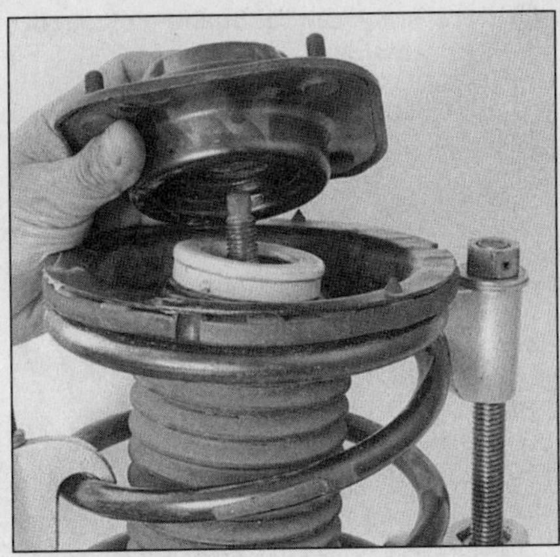

**3.6 Remove the damper shaft nut and suspension support**

**3.7a Remove the upper spring seat . . .**

6 Remove the nut and suspension support **(see illustration)**. Inspect the bearing in the suspension support for smooth operation. If it doesn't turn smoothly, replace the suspension support. Check the rubber portion of the suspension support for cracking and general deterioration. If there is any separation of the rubber, replace it.

7 Remove the upper spring seat and dust boot from the damper shaft **(see illustrations)**. Check the spring seat for cracking and hardness; replace it if necessary.

8 Slide the rubber bumper off the damper shaft **(see illustration).**

9 Carefully lift the compressed spring from the assembly **(see illustration)** and set it in a safe place. **Warning:** *When removing the compressed spring, lift it off very carefully and set it in a safe place. Keep the ends of the spring away from your body.* **Note:** *Mark the spring so it can be reinstalled on the same side of the vehicle from which it was removed.*

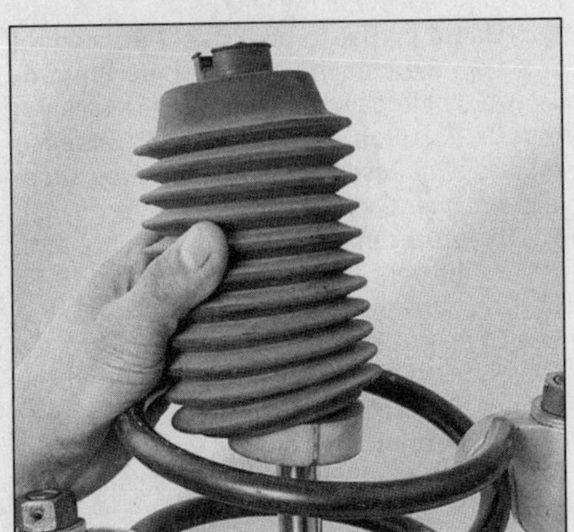

**3.7b . . . and the dust boot from the damper shaft**

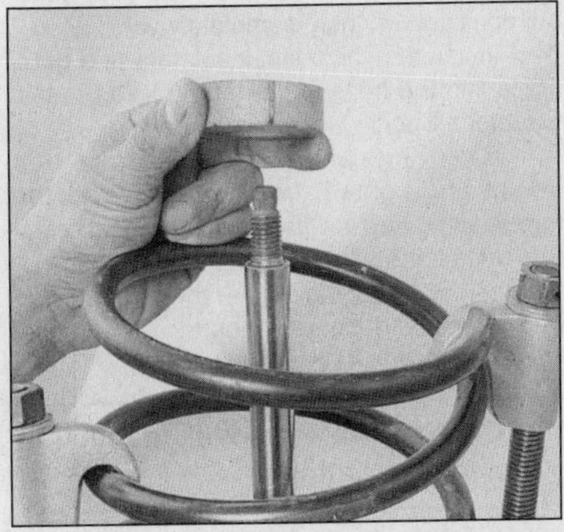

**3.8 Remove the rubber bumper from the damper shaft**

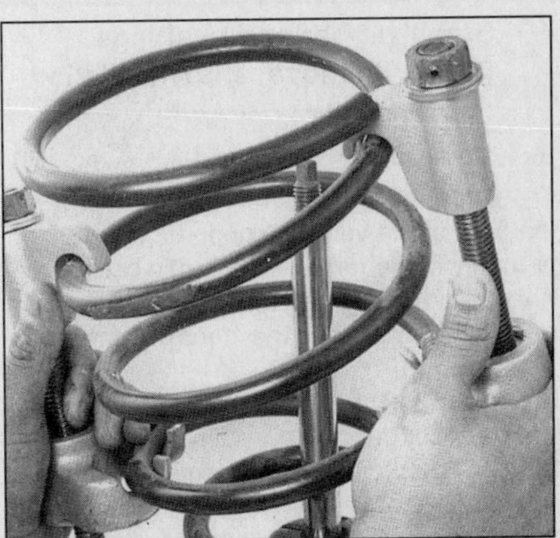

**3.9 Carefully lift the compressed spring from the assembly and set it in a safe place - keep the ends of the spring pointed away from your body**

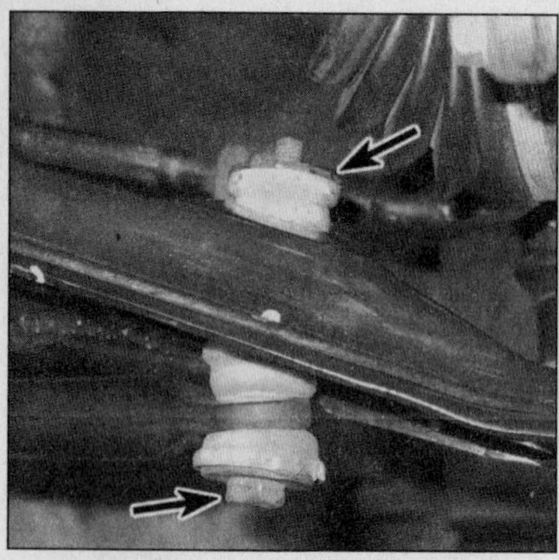
4.2 Hold the nut (upper arrow) with a wrench, unscrew the link bolt (lower arrow) and detach the link from the control arm (note the order of the insulators as you remove the bolt) - repeat on the other side

4.3 Each stabilizer bar bushing clamp is retained by two bolts

5.2 Remove the nut from this pinch bolt, then remove the bolt

5.4 Pry the control arm down to separate the balljoint from the steering knuckle

5.6 To detach the control arm from the crossmember, remove the pivot bolt (upper arrow) and nut (center arrow) - lower arrow indicates the vertical rear mounting bolt

## Reassembly

10 Extend the damper rod to its full length and install the rubber bumper.

11 Position the coil spring with the smaller coils going on first and carefully place the coil onto the damper shaft.

12 Install the rubber bumper onto the damper shaft and push it all the way down until it bottoms out.

13 Install the upper spring seat and dust boot onto the damper shaft.

14 Install the suspension support and align the support notch with the clevis bracket on the strut support. Install the suspension support to the damper shaft.

15 Install the nut and tighten it to the torque listed in this Chapter's Specifications.

16 Loosen the coil spring compressor(s) until the top coil is properly seated against the upper spring seat and suspension support. Relieve all tension from the spring compressor(s) and remove them from the coil spring.

17 Install the strut/spring assembly (see Section 2).

# 4 Stabilizer bar and bushings (front) - removal and installation

*Refer to illustrations 4.2 and 4.3*

1 Loosen the front wheel lug nuts, raise the front of the vehicle, support it securely on jackstands and remove the front wheels.

2 Remove the stabilizer bar link bolts, nuts and insulators from the control arms **(see illustration)**.

3 Support the stabilizer bar and remove the stabilizer bar clamp bolts and clamps from the front suspension crossmember **(see illustration)**. Remove the stabilizer bar from the vehicle.

4 Check the bar for damage, corrosion and signs of twisting.

5 Check the clamps, bushings and retainers for distortion, damage and wear. Replace the inner bushings by prying them open at the split and removing them. Install the new bushings with the split facing toward the front of the vehicle.

6 Attach the bar to the crossmember so the slits are facing forward and the cutouts in the stabilizer bar bushings are aligned with the raised bead on the crossmember. Install the clamps, aligning the raised bead on the clamp with the bushing cutouts and install the bolts, but don't tighten them completely yet.

7 Install the link bolts, insulators and nuts, tightening the bolts to the torque listed in this Chapter's Specifications.

8 Raise the control arms to normal ride height and tighten the clamp bolts to the torque listed in this Chapter's Specifications.

9 Install the wheels and lower the vehicle. Tighten the wheel lug nuts to the torque listed in the Chapter 1 Specifications.

# 5 Control arm - removal, inspection and installation

## Removal

*Refer to illustrations 5.2, 5.4 and 5.6*

1 Loosen the wheel lug nuts, raise the front of the vehicle, support it securely on jackstands and remove the wheel.

2 Remove the balljoint pinch bolt and nut **(see illustration)**.

3 Disconnect the stabilizer bar links from the control arms (see Section 4) and rotate the bar down, out of the way.

4 Use a prybar to disconnect the control arm from the steering knuckle **(see illustration)**. Pull the balljoint stud from the steering knuckle. **Caution:** *Do not move the steering knuckle/strut assembly out or you may separate the inner CV joint.*

5 If you're removing the right control arm, remove the pencil strut **(see illustration 19.7)**, then remove the engine lower torque strut (see Chapter 2A, Section 18).

6 Remove the bolt and nut securing the front of the control arm to the crossmember **(see illustration)**. **Note:** *Turn the bolt, not the nut (the nut is equipped with an anti-rotation tang).*

7 Remove the bolt that attaches the rear of the control arm to the crossmember **(see illustration 5.6)**.

8 Remove the control arm.

### Inspection

9 Make sure the control arm is straight. If it's bent, replace it. Do not attempt to straighten a bent control arm.

10 Inspect the bushings. If the rear bushing is cracked or shows signs of wear, it can be replaced at an automotive machine shop. If the front pivot bushing is cracked or worn out, replace the control arm.

### Installation

11 Installation is the reverse of removal, noting the following points:

a) *Don't tighten the pivot bolt and rear mounting bolt until the outer end of the control arm is raised with a floor jack to simulate normal ride height.*
b) *Tighten the control arm's front bolt first, then the rear bolt.*
c) *Install and align the engine lower torque strut following the procedure in Chapter 2A.*
d) *Be sure to tighten all other fasteners to the torque listed in this Chapter's Specifications.*

12 Install the wheel and lug nuts, lower the vehicle and tighten the lug nuts to the torque listed in the Chapter 1 Specifications.

## 6 Balljoints - check and replacement

*Refer to illustration 6.2*

1 The suspension balljoints are designed to operate without freeplay.

2 With the weight of the vehicle resting on its wheels, try to wiggle the snapped-off grease fitting in the center of the balljoint, using only your fingers **(see illustration)**. If there is any movement, the balljoint is worn and must be replaced with a new one. Remove the control arm (see Section 5) and take it to an automotive machine shop to have the old balljoint pressed out and a new one pressed in.

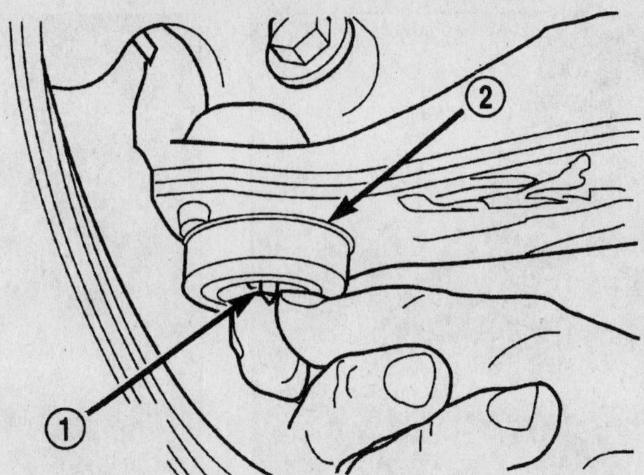


**6.2 If you can feel any play when wiggling the snapped-off grease fitting (1), the balljoint (2) is worn out and should be replaced**

## 7 Steering knuckle and hub - removal and inspection

### Removal

1 With the vehicle weight resting on the front suspension, remove the hub cap, cotter pin, nut lock and spring washer. Loosen, but do not remove, the driveaxle/hub nut and wheel lug nuts.

2 Loosen the wheel lug nuts. Raise the front of the vehicle, support it securely on jackstands and remove the wheel.

3 Remove the brake caliper and brake pads, then remove the caliper mounting bracket from the steering knuckle (see Chapter 9). Hang the caliper out of the way in the wheel well with a piece of wire.

4 Disconnect the tie-rod end from the steering knuckle (see Section 18).

5 Loosen (but don't remove) the strut-to-steering knuckle bolts (see Section 2). Also detach the ground strap bracket and, if equipped, the ABS sensor harness bracket from the strut.

6 Detach the control arm balljoint from the steering knuckle (see Section 5).

7 With the knuckle and hub assembly in the straight-ahead position, grasp it securely and pull it directly out and off the driveaxle splines. **Caution:** *Be careful not to pull the driveaxle out or you may pull the inner CV joint apart.* It may be necessary to tap on the axle end with a soft-face hammer to dislodge the driveaxle from the hub. Secure the end of the driveaxle with a piece of wire; don't let it hang by the inner CV joint.

8 Remove the strut-to-steering knuckle nuts and bolts. Remove the steering knuckle and hub assembly.

### Installation

9 Prior to installation, clean the CV joint boot and the hub grease seal with solvent (don't get any solvent on the CV joint boot). Lubricate the entire circumference of the CV joint wear sleeve and seal contact surface with multi-purpose grease. Also lubricate the splines at the end of the driveaxle with the same grease.

10 Carefully place the knuckle and hub assembly in position. Align the splines of the axle and the hub and slide the hub into place.

11 Install the strut-to-knuckle bolts and nuts, followed by the balljoint pinch bolt and nut. Tighten the steering strut-to-knuckle nuts to the torque listed in this Chapter's Specifications. **Caution:** *Hold the bolt stationary and tighten the nut.* Also tighten the balljoint pinch bolt nut to the torque listed in this Chapter's Specifications.

12 Reattach the tie-rod end to the steering knuckle and tighten the nut to the torque listed in this Chapter's Specifications (see Section 18).

13 Install the brake disc, caliper mounting bracket, pads and caliper (see Chapter 9).

14 Reattach the ground strap and, if equipped, the ABS sensor harness bracket(s) to the strut.

15 Install the washer and driveaxle/hub nut. Tighten the nut securely, but don't try to tighten it completely yet.

16 Install the wheels and lug nuts. Lower the vehicle and tighten the lug nuts to the torque listed in the Chapter 1 Specifications.

17 Tighten the driveaxle/hub nut to the torque listed in the Chapter 8 Specifications. Install the spring washer, nut lock and a new cotter pin.

18 If special camber adjusting bolts have been installed sometime in the past, have the front end alignment checked and, if necessary, adjusted.

## 8 Hub and bearing assembly (front) - replacement

Due to the special tools and expertise required to press the hub and bearing from the steering knuckle, this job should be left to a professional mechanic. However, the steering knuckle and hub may be removed and the assembly taken to an automotive machine shop or other qualified repair facility equipped with the necessary tools. See Section 7 for the steering knuckle and hub removal procedure.

## 9 Shock absorber (rear) - removal, inspection and installation

*Refer to illustrations 9.3 and 9.4*

**Warning:** *Always replace the shock absorbers in pairs - never replace just one of them.*

1 Loosen the rear wheel lug nuts. Chock the front wheels to keep the vehicle from rolling, then raise the rear of the vehicle and support it securely on jackstands placed underneath the rear jacking points not under the rear axle beam; see *Jacking and towing* at the front of this manual if necessary). Remove the rear wheels.

2 Support the rear axle with a floor jack near the shock absorber to be removed. **Warning:** *The jack must remain in this position until the shock absorber is reinstalled.*

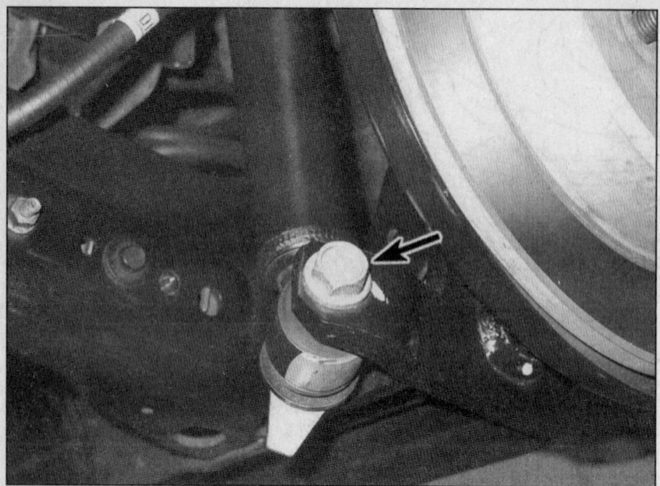
9.3 Rear shock absorber lower mounting bolt

9.4 Rear shock absorber upper mounting bolt/nut

3 Remove the shock absorber lower mounting bolt/nut **(see illustration)**.
4 Remove the shock absorber upper mounting nut and bolt and remove the shock absorber **(see illustration)**.
5 To install the shock absorber, reverse the removal procedure.
6 Tighten the upper mounting bolt nut to the torque listed in this Chapter's Specifications.
7 Raise the rear axle with the jack to simulate normal ride height, then tighten the lower mounting bolt/nut to the torque listed in this Chapter's Specifications.
8 Repeat the procedure to replace the other rear shock absorber.
9 Install the wheels and lug nuts and lower the vehicle. Tighten the lug nuts to the torque listed in the Chapter 1 Specifications.

## 10 Stabilizer bar and bushings (rear) - removal and installation

*Refer to illustrations 10.2 and 10.3*

1 Loosen the rear wheel lug nuts. Raise the rear of the vehicle and place it securely on jackstands. Block the front wheels to prevent the vehicle from rolling. Remove the rear wheels.
2 Detach the stabilizer bar links from the bar **(see illustration)**.
3 Unbolt the stabilizer bar bushing clamps from the rear axle beam **(see illustration)**.
4 The stabilizer bar can now be removed from the vehicle. To remove the bushing clamps, bend the tab at the top of the clamp and detach the clamp halves.
5 Check the bushings for wear, hardness, distortion, cracking and other signs of deterioration, replacing them if necessary. Also check the link bushings for these signs.
6 Using a wire brush, clean the areas of the bar where the bushings ride.
7 Installation is the reverse of the removal procedure. Install the new bushings with the split facing toward the front of the vehicle. If necessary, use a light coat of vegetable oil to ease bushing and clamp installation (don't use petroleum-based products or brake fluid, as these will damage the rubber).
8 Installation is the reverse of removal.

## 11 Watts linkage - removal and installation

*Refer to illustrations 11.2a, 11.2b and 11.3*

1 Raise the rear of the vehicle and support it securely on jackstands. Block the front wheels to prevent the vehicle from rolling.
2 Remove the bolts securing the Watts links to the chassis **(see illustrations)**.
3 Remove the nut from the bellcrank pivot bolt, then slide the bolt out and detach the bellcrank/Watts link assembly from the rear axle beam **(see illustration)**.
4 If necessary to detach a Watts link from the bellcrank, remove the nut from the ballstud and use a two-jaw puller to push the ballstud from the bellcrank. **Note:** *If you're removing the upper (right) Watts link, you'll have to remove the protector from the ballstud before removing the nut. Be sure to reinstall this protector during installation.*
5 When installing the bellcrank, be sure the words "BACK UP" are positioned properly (facing the rear of the vehicle, with the words right-side-up).

10.2 Stabilizer bar link attaching bolts

10.3 Stabilizer bar bracket bolts

6 Installation is the reverse of the removal procedure. Before tightening the fasteners to the torque listed in this Chapter's Specifications, raise the rear axle with a floor jack to simulate normal ride height.

## 12 Coil springs (rear) - removal and installation

*Refer to illustration 12.8*

**Warning:** *Always replace the coil springs in pairs - never replace just one of them.*

1 Loosen the wheel lug nuts. Chock the front wheels to prevent the vehicle from rolling, then raise the rear of the vehicle and support it securely on jackstands placed under the rear jacking points (not under the rear axle). Remove the wheels.

2 Remove the nut and pivot bolt securing the Watts linkage bellcrank to the rear axle **(see illustration 11.3)**.

3 Unbolt the rear stabilizer bar bushing clamps from the rear axle (see Section 10).

4 Support the center of the rear axle with a floor jack. **Note:** *If you have access to two floor jacks, it is preferable to support each side of the axle beam with a floor jack.* Raise the jack(s) slightly to take the spring pressure off the shock absorber lower mounts.

5 Remove the shock absorber lower mounting bolts **(see illustration 9.3)**.

6 Slowly lower the floor jack(s) until the coil springs are fully extended.

7 Remove the coil springs and the upper and lower insulators. Check the spring for cracks and chips, replacing the springs as a set if any defects are found. Also check the insulators for damage and deterioration, replacing them as necessary.

**11.2a Left-side Watts link-to-chassis bolt**

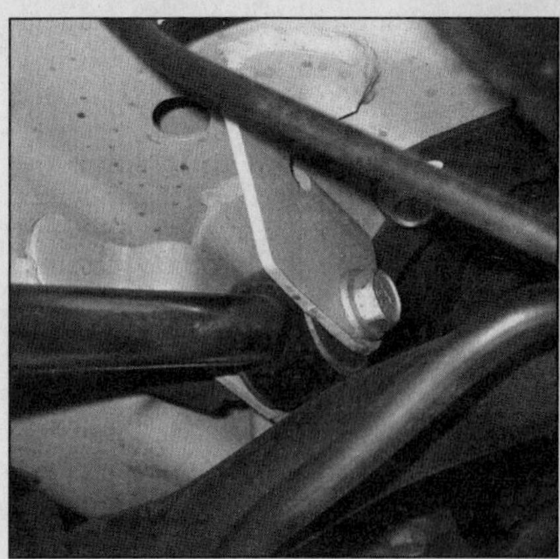

**11.2b Right-side Watts link-to-chassis bolt**

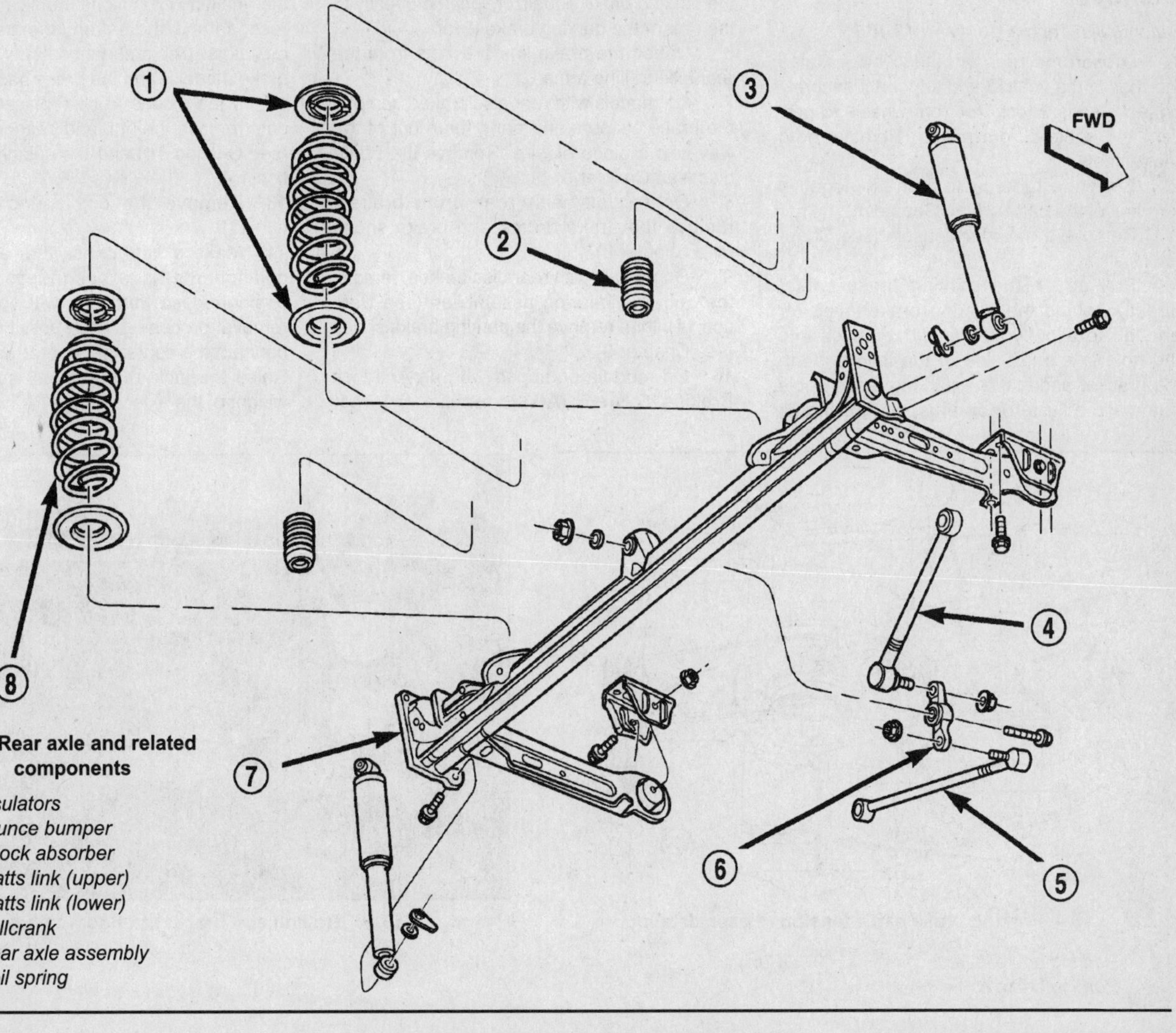

**11.3 Rear axle and related components**

1 *Insulators*
2 *Jounce bumper*
3 *Shock absorber*
4 *Watts link (upper)*
5 *Watts link (lower)*
6 *Bellcrank*
7 *Rear axle assembly*
8 *Coil spring*

8 Installation is the reverse of the removal procedure, but make sure the coil springs are positioned properly against their upper mounts **(see illustration)**. **Note:** *The springs don't have a "top" or a "bottom;" just make sure the pigtail of the right-side spring points towards the front of the vehicle, and the pigtail of the left-side coil spring points towards the rear of the vehicle.*

9 Before tightening any of the suspension fasteners to the torque values listed in this Chapter's Specifications, raise the rear axle to normal ride height with the floor jack(s).

10 Install the wheel and lug nuts. Lower the vehicle and tighten the lug nuts to the torque listed in the Chapter 1 Specifications.

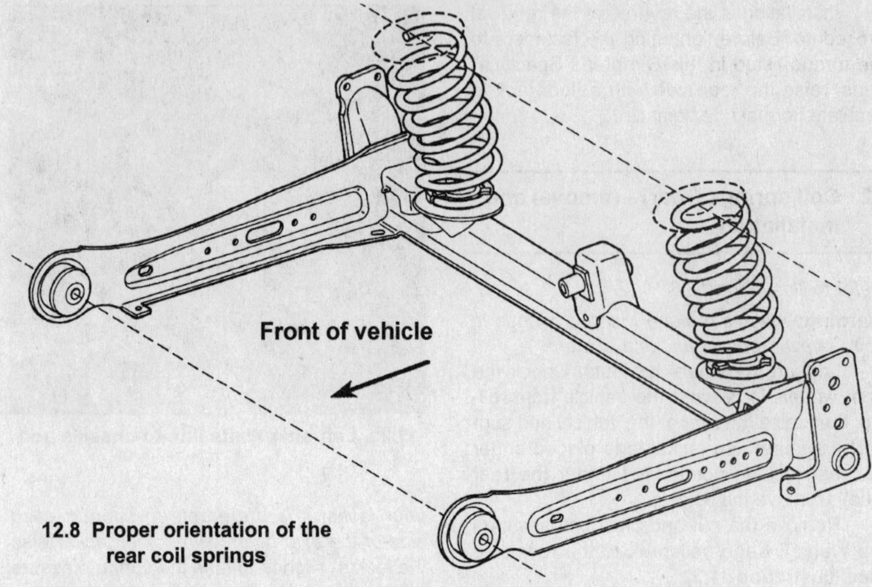


**12.8 Proper orientation of the rear coil springs**

## 13 Rear axle assembly - removal and installation

**Warning:** *These models are equipped with airbags. Always the airbag system before working in the vicinity of any airbag system component to avoid the possibility of accidental deployment of the airbag, which could cause personal injury (see Chapter 12).*

### *Removal*

*Refer to illustrations 13.4 and 13.16*

1 Loosen the rear wheel lug nuts. Raise the rear of the vehicle and support it securely on jackstands. Block the front wheels to prevent the vehicle from rolling. Remove both rear wheels.

2 Disconnect the cable from the negative terminal of the battery (see Chapter 5).

3 Remove the center console (see Chapter 11).

4 Pull up on the parking brake cable, directly behind the parking brake lever, far enough to allow you to insert a punch into the hole in the left side of the lever mounting bracket and into the parking brake cable automatic adjuster **(see illustration)**. Slowly release tension on the cable and check to make sure that all tension has been relieved.

5 Detach the parking brake cables from the parking brake equalizer, located directly to the rear of the parking brake lever.

6 Unbolt the brake line brackets from the rear axle trailing arms.

7 On models with rear disc brakes, remove the brake calipers and hang them out of the way with a piece of wire. Remove the brake disc (see Chapter 9).

8 On models with rear drum brakes, remove the brake drums and brake shoes (see Chapter 9).

9 On models with rear disc brakes, remove the hub and bearing assemblies (see Section 14), then remove the parking brake shoes (see Chapter 9).

10 On models equipped with an Anti-lock Braking System (ABS), remove the rear wheel speed sensors and detach the sensor harnesses from the rear axle.

11 Detach the parking brake cables from the retaining clips along the axle trailing arms. Also detach them from the parking brake actuators (disc brake models) or levers (drum brake models) and the brake backing plates.

12 If the axle is to be replaced with a new one, remove the hub and bearing assemblies (see Section 14) and the spindles (see Section 15).

13 Remove the coil springs (see Section 12).

14 Make a final check that all necessary components have been disconnected and positioned so that they will not hinder the removal procedure, then position a floor jack beneath the center of the rear axle assembly. Raise the jack until it is just supporting the weight of the axle.

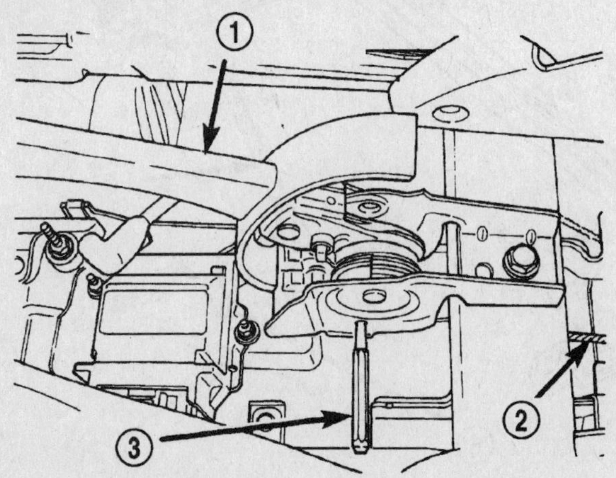


**13.4 Parking brake cable tension release details**

1 *Parking brake lever*
2 *Parking brake cable*
3 *Punch*

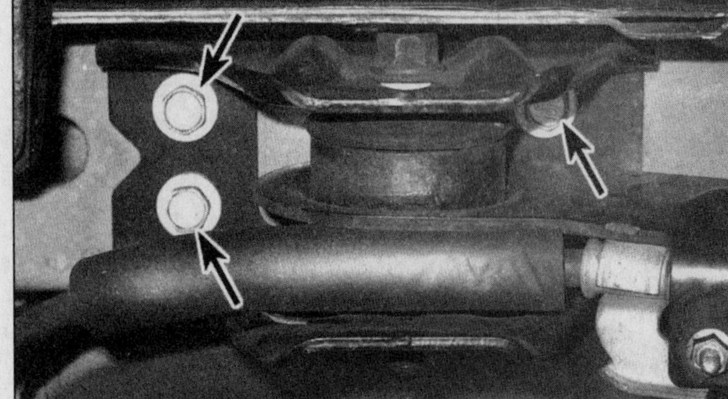

**13.16 Trailing arm bracket-to-floorpan bolts**

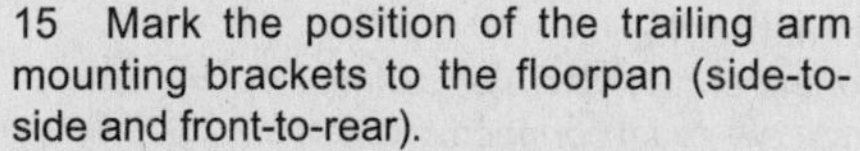

**14.3 Using a hammer and chisel, tap the grease cap off the hub**

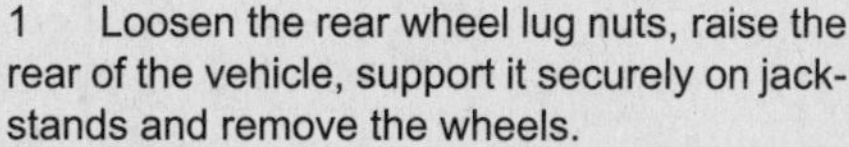

**14.4 Unscrew the wheel bearing locknut . . .**

**14.5 . . . and remove the hub and bearing assembly from the spindle**

15 Mark the position of the trailing arm mounting brackets to the floorpan (side-to-side and front-to-rear).

16 Unbolt the trailing arm brackets from the floorpan **(see illustration)**, then lower the jack and remove the axle assembly out from under the vehicle.

17 Inspect the axle pivot bushings for signs or damage or deterioration. If replacement is necessary, take the axle to an automotive machine shop to have the old bushings removed and the new ones installed.

## Installation

18 Installation of the rear axle is the reverse of the removal procedure, with the following points:

- a) *If the brackets were removed from the trailing arm, be sure to reinstall them with the bolts inserted from the outside, pointing inward.*
- b) *Ensure that the brake lines, parking brake cables and wiring (as applicable) are correctly routed, and retained by all the necessary retaining clips.*
- c) *When installing the trailing arm mounting brackets to the floorpan, be sure to line up the marks made in Step 15.*
- d) *Don't tighten the rear axle pivot bolts (if they were removed) or the shock absorber lower mounting bolts until the weight of the vehicle is on its wheels (or until the rear suspension has been raised to simulate normal ride height). This will prevent the bushings from "winding-up," which could eventually damage them.*
- e) *Tighten all fasteners to the proper torque Specifications.*
- f) *Bleed the brake system (see Chapter 9).*

## 14 Hub and bearing assembly (rear) - removal and installation

*Refer to illustrations 14.3, 14.4 and 14.5*

**Warning:** *The manufacturer recommends replacing the hub nut with a new one whenever it is removed.*

1 Loosen the rear wheel lug nuts, raise the rear of the vehicle, support it securely on jackstands and remove the wheels.

2 Remove the brake drum or disc (see Chapter 9).

3 Remove the grease cap **(see illustration)**.

4 Remove the wheel bearing locknut **(see illustration)**.

5 Remove the hub and bearing assembly from the spindle **(see illustration)**.

6 Before installing the hub and bearing assembly, clean the spindle and apply a coat of wheel bearing grease to the area on the spindle where the bearing rides.

7 Installation is the reverse of removal. Install a ***new*** hub nut and tighten it to the torque listed in this Chapter's Specifications. On models with rear disc brakes, tighten the caliper mounting bolts to the torque listed in the Chapter 9 Specifications.

8 Install the wheel and lug nuts. Lower the vehicle and tighten the lug nuts to the torque listed in the Chapter 1 Specifications.

## 15 Spindle (rear) - removal and installation

**Warning:** *The manufacturer recommends replacing the hub nut with a new one whenever it is removed.*

1 Loosen the wheel bolts. Chock the front wheels, then raise the rear of the vehicle and support it securely on jackstands. Remove the rear wheel.

2 Remove the hub and bearing assembly (see Section 14). On models with disc brakes, be sure to hang the caliper with a piece of wire - don't let it hang by the brake hose.

3 Inspect the spindle surface for signs of damage such as scoring, and replace if necessary. Do not attempt to straighten the spindle. Also check the threads; if they are damaged in any way, replace the spindle. Don't attempt to clean up the threads with a thread file or a die.

4 If the vehicle is equipped with an Anti-lock Braking System (ABS), remove the rear wheel speed sensor (see Chapter 9).

5 If the vehicle is equipped with rear drum brakes, unscrew the brake line fitting from the wheel cylinder. Use a flare-nut wrench, if available, to prevent rounding-off the fitting.

6 Remove the spindle mounting bolts. Remove the spindle along with the disc splash shield or, on models with rear drum brakes, the brake backing plate/brake shoe assembly.

7 Installation is the reverse of removal, with the following points:

- a) *Make sure the spindle mating surfaces and the mounting bolt holes on the axle are clean.*
- b) *Install a new seal on the spindle.*
- c) *Tighten the mounting bolts to the torque listed in this Chapter's Specifications.*
- d) *On models with rear drum brakes, tighten the brake line fitting securely.*
- e) *Install a* **new** *hub nut and tighten it to the torque listed in this Chapter's Specifications.*
- f) *On models with rear disc brakes, tighten the caliper bolts to the torque listed in the Chapter 9 Specifications.*
- g) *On models with rear drum brakes, bleed the brake system (see Chapter 9).*

## 16 Steering wheel - removal and installation

### Removal

*Refer to illustrations 16.3, 16.5 and 16.8*

**Warning:** *These models have airbags. Always disable the airbag system before working in the vicinity of any airbag system components to avoid the possibility of accidental deployment of the airbag, which could cause personal injury (see Chapter 12).*

**Warning:** *Do not use a memory saving device to preserve the ECM's memory when working on or near airbag system components.*

1 Park the vehicle with the wheels pointing straight ahead. Disconnect the cable from the negative terminal of the battery (see Chapter 5).

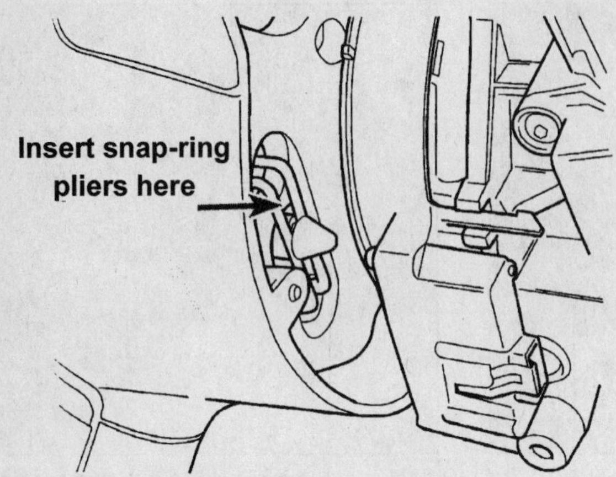


16.3 To disengage the airbag module retaining pins from the clips, spread the clips apart with angled snap-ring pliers

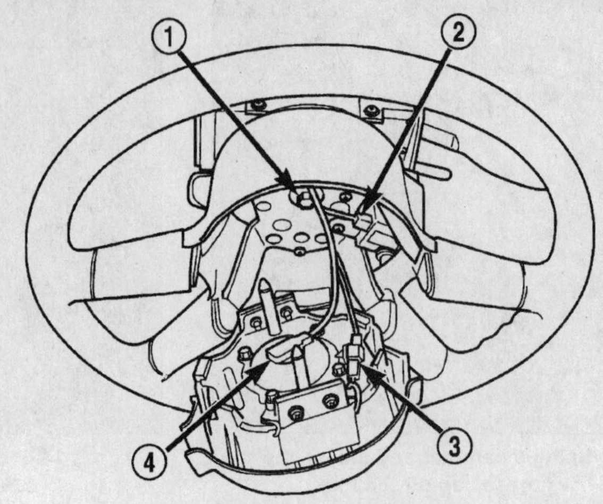


16.5 Airbag module and steering wheel details

1 *Steering wheel bolt*
2 *Cruise control switch electrical connector*
3 *Horn switch electrical connector*
4 *Airbag module electrical connector*

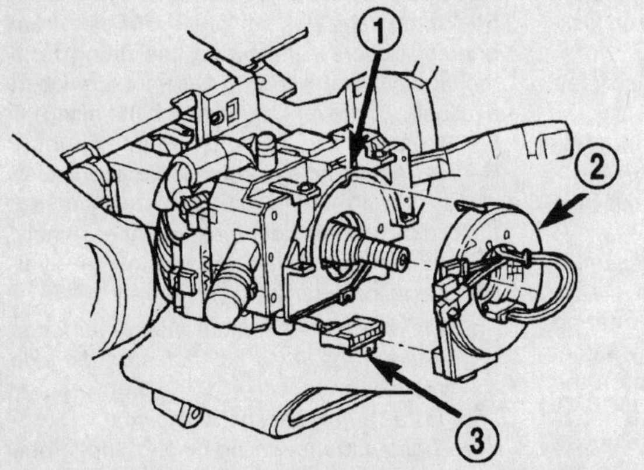


16.8 Clockspring mounting details

1 *Steering column*
2 *Clockspring*
3 *Clockspring electrical connector*

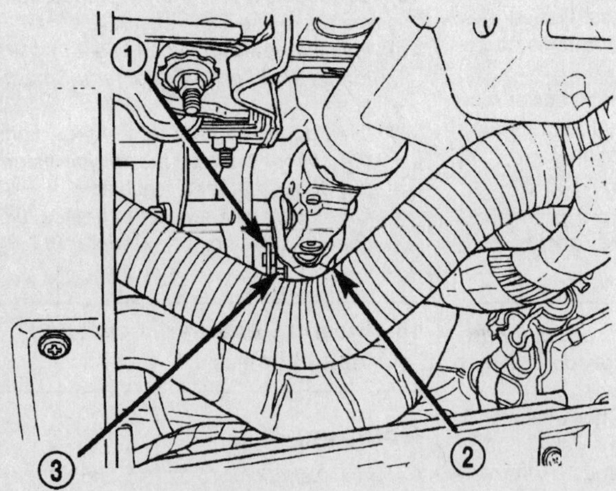


17.8 Steering shaft universal joint details

1 *Retainer pin*
2 *Pinch bolt*
3 *Nut*

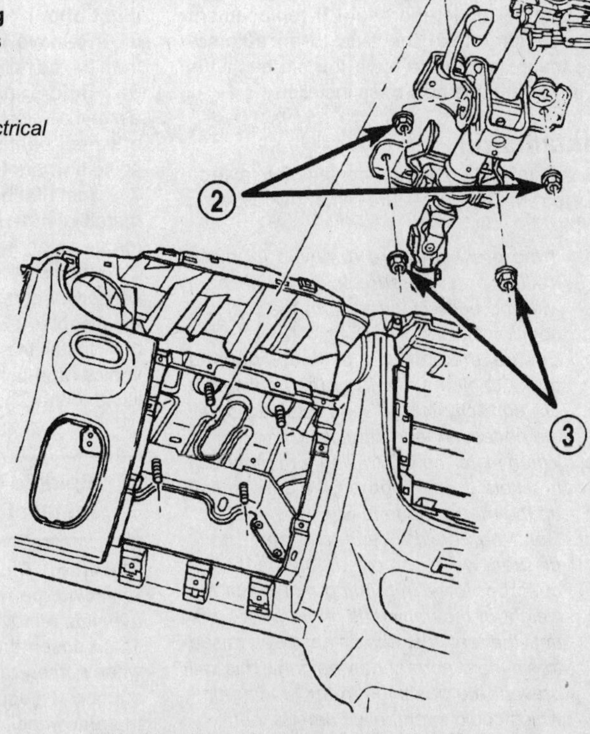


17.9 Steering column mounting details

1 *Steering column*
2 *Upper mounting nuts*
3 *Lower mounting nuts*

2 Remove the steering column covers (see Chapter 11).

## 2001 through 2005 models

3 Turn the steering wheel 1/2-turn (180-degrees) clockwise. **Note:** *The steering shaft must be in this position when the steering wheel is installed.* Working from the back side of the steering wheel, use a pair of 90-degree snap-ring pliers to spread apart the spring clips that retain the airbag module (there's one at the top and one at the bottom) **(see illustration)**. Pull out on the airbag module while doing this to disengage the retaining pins from the spring clips.

## 2006 and later models

4 From the rear of the steering wheel, locate

the three airbag retaining hook access holes in the steering wheel back cover. Using a small flat blade screwdriver, insert the tip into any one of the access holes. Gently pull on the driver airbag trim cover while twisting the screwdriver either way enough to release the loop from the hook. Repeat at the other two holes.

5 Disconnect the electrical connector from the airbag module **(see illustration)**. Also unplug the horn and cruise control electrical connectors. Set the module aside in a safe, isolated area, with the airbag side of the module facing UP. **Warning:** *When carrying the airbag module, keep the driver's (trim) side of it away from your body and, when you set it down, make sure the driver's side is facing up.*

6 Remove the steering wheel retaining bolt and mark the position of the steering wheel to the shaft, if marks don't already exist or don't line up.

7 Now reinstall the bolt until about 1/2-inch of threads are showing between the bolt head and the steering wheel. Install a steering wheel puller; the puller screw must be contacting the steering wheel bolt. Tighten the puller screw until the wheel is freed from the shaft. **Caution:** *Don't hammer on the shaft or steering wheel in an attempt to remove the wheel.* **Warning:** *Don't allow the steering shaft to turn with the steering wheel removed. If the shaft turns, the airbag clockspring will become uncentered, which may cause the wire inside to break when the vehicle is returned to service.*

8 If it's necessary to remove the clockspring from the steering column, unclip the latches, disconnect the electrical connector and remove the clockspring **(see illustration)**. Turn the clockspring rotor 1/2-turn counterclockwise, then insert a straightened-out paper clip through the hole at the 10 o'clock position (this will lock the clockspring in the centered position). Now bend the paperclip to prevent it from falling out.

### Installation

9 If it was removed, reinstall the clockspring:

a) *Remove the paper clip from the clockspring, then turn the clockspring rotor 1/2-turn (180-degrees) clockwise.*
b) *Install the clockspring on the steering column, making sure the latch hooks engage properly. Make sure the electrical connector is plugged in completely.*
c) *If a new clockspring is being installed, it will already be in the centered position and secured with a grenade pin; because of this, you'll have to turn the front wheels to the straight-ahead position before installing it. Be sure to remove the pin.*

10 If you aren't sure if the clockspring is centered or not (if you didn't lock it in the centered position as described in Step 8 and it has since turned), turn the hub in either direction until it stops (don't apply too much force). Now, rotate the hub in the other direction, counting the number of turns it takes to reach the opposite stop. Divide that number by two, then turn the hub back that many turns, approximately, until a paper clip can be inserted through the hole in the 10 o'clock position. Now remove the pin and turn the clockspring rotor 1/2-turn clockwise. Install the clockspring, making sure the locking tabs engage securely. Install the steering column covers.

11 Install the wheel on the steering shaft, aligning the marks.

12 Install the steering wheel bolt and tighten it to the torque listed in this Chapter's Specifications.

13 Reconnect the electrical connectors, then position the airbag module on the steering wheel and push it in until the retaining pins on the module engage with the spring clips.

**18.2 If the tie-rod end stud spins when loosening the nut, hold the stud with a wrench or socket**

**18.3a Hold the tie-rod with a pair of pliers while loosening the jam nut**

## 17 Steering column - removal and installation

*Refer to illustrations 17.8 and 17.9*

**Warning:** *These models are equipped with airbags. Always disable the airbag system before working in the vicinity of any airbag system component to avoid the possibility of accidental deployment of the airbag(s), which could cause personal injury* (see Chapter 12). **Warning:** *Do not use a memory saving device to preserve the ECM's memory when working on or near airbag system components.*

### Removal

1 Park the vehicle with the wheels in the straight-ahead position. Disconnect the cable from the negative terminal of the battery and wait a minimum of two minutes before proceeding (see Chapter 5).

2 Remove the steering wheel (see Section 16).

3 Remove the lower instrument panel trim (under the steering column) (see Chapter 11).

4 Remove the steering column covers (see Chapter 11).

5 Remove the airbag system clockspring (see Section 16).

6 Remove the multi-function switch (see Chapter 12).

7 On models with an automatic transmission, detach the shift interlock cable from the key lock cylinder housing (see Chapter 7B).

8 Mark the relationship of the steering shaft lower universal joint to the steering gear input shaft, then remove the retainer pin and unscrew the pinch bolt (don't try to unscrew the nut - it's caged to the joint **(see illustration)**. Separate the universal joint from the steering gear input shaft.

9 Remove the steering column mounting nuts **(see illustration)**, then guide the column out from the instrument panel.

### Installation

10 Guide the column into position, connecting the U-joint with the steering gear input shaft.

11 Install the mounting nuts and tighten them to the torque listed in this Chapter's Specifications.

12 Install the bolt through the U-joint and tighten it to the torque listed in this Chapter's Specifications. Install the retaining pin.

13 The remainder of installation is the reverse of the removal procedure. When installing the steering wheel, be sure the airbag clockspring is centered (see Section 16), and tighten the steering wheel bolt to the torque listed in this Chapter's Specifications.

## 18 Tie-rod ends - removal and installation

### Removal

*Refer to illustrations 18.2, 18.3a, 18.3b and 18.4*

1 Loosen the wheel lug nuts. Apply the parking brake, raise the front of the vehicle and support it securely on jackstands. Remove the front wheel.

2 Loosen the nut on the tie-rod end stud. If the stud turns, hold it with a wrench **(see illustration)**.

3 Hold the tie-rod with a pair of locking pliers or wrench and loosen the jam nut enough to mark the position of the tie-rod end in relation to the threads **(see illustrations)**.

18.3b Back off the jam nut and mark the exposed threads

18.4 Use a two-jaw puller to push the tie-rod end stud out of the steering knuckle

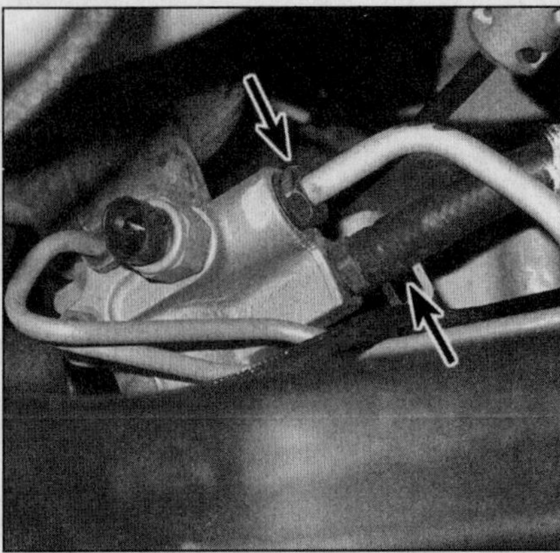

19.6a Detach the power steering fluid pressure (upper arrow) and return (lower arrow) lines from the steering gear

4 Disconnect the tie-rod from the steering knuckle arm with a puller **(see illustration)**. Remove the nut and detach the tie-rod end. Note how the heat shield is installed.

5 Unscrew the tie-rod end from the tie-rod.

### Installation

6 Thread the tie-rod end on to the marked position and insert the tie-rod stud into the steering knuckle arm. Make sure the heat shield is positioned properly. Tighten the jam nut securely.

7 Install the nut on the stud and tighten it to the torque listed in this Chapter's Specifications.

8 Install the wheel and lug nuts. Lower the vehicle and tighten the lug nuts to the torque listed in the Chapter 1 Specifications.

9 Have the alignment checked and, if necessary, adjusted.

## 19 Steering gear - removal and installation

*Refer to Illustrations 19.6a, 19.6b, 19.7, 19.10, 19.13, 19.14, 19.15 and 19.16*

**Warning:** *These models are equipped with airbags. Always disable the airbag system before working in the vicinity of any airbag system component to avoid the possibility of accidental deployment of the airbag(s), which could cause personal injury (see Chapter 12). Make sure the steering shaft is not turned while the steering gear is removed or you could damage the airbag system. To prevent the shaft from turning, turn the ignition key to the lock position before beginning work or run the seat belt through the steering wheel and clip the seat belt into place. Due to the possible damage to the airbag system, we recommend only experienced mechanics attempt this procedure.*

**Note:** *These models are designed and assembled using **"net build"** front suspension alignment settings. The front suspension alignment settings are determined as the vehicle is being built by accurately locating the front suspension crossmember to the master gauge holes located in the underbody of the vehicle. Therefore whenever the front crossmember is removed from the vehicle's body it must be reinstalled in the **exact** same location on the body to maintain correct front end alignment.*

1 Disconnect the negative battery cable and wait at least two minutes before proceeding (see Chapter 5).

2 Detach the steering column lower universal joint from the steering gear input shaft (see Section 17).

3 Loosen the wheel lug nuts, raise the front of the vehicle and support it securely on jackstands. Remove the front wheels.

4 Detach the tie-rod ends from the steering knuckles (see Section 18).

5 Unplug the electrical connector from the power steering fluid pressure switch.

6 Place a drain pan under the steering gear. Detach the power steering fluid pressure and return lines from the steering gear **(see illustration)**, then unbolt the cooler from the suspension crossmember **(see illustration)**. Free the lines from any clips on the crossmember. Plug the lines and fittings to prevent excessive fluid loss and system contamination.

7 Working at the right front corner of the suspension crossmember, unscrew the nuts and remove the pencil strut **(see illustration)**.

8 Remove the drivebelt splash shield.

9 Remove the lower torque strut-to-crossmember bolt **(see illustration 19.7)**.

10 At each mounting point of the crossmember, scribe or paint a line around the mounts, side-to-side and front-to-rear **(see illustration)**. This is to preserve front-end alignment when the crossmember is reinstalled.

11 Using a transmission jack, support the center of the crossmember. Transmission

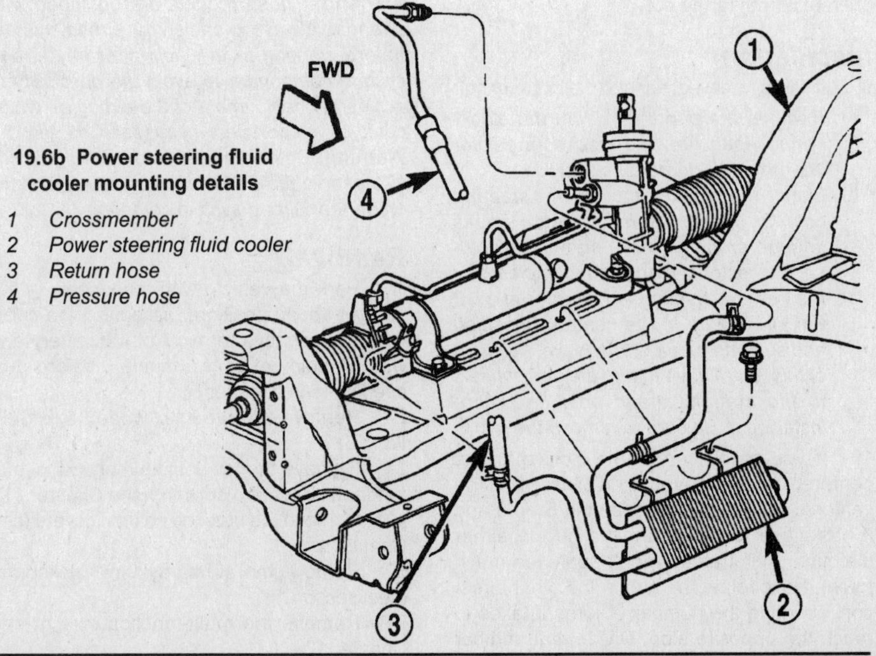


19.6b Power steering fluid cooler mounting details

1 Crossmember
2 Power steering fluid cooler
3 Return hose
4 Pressure hose

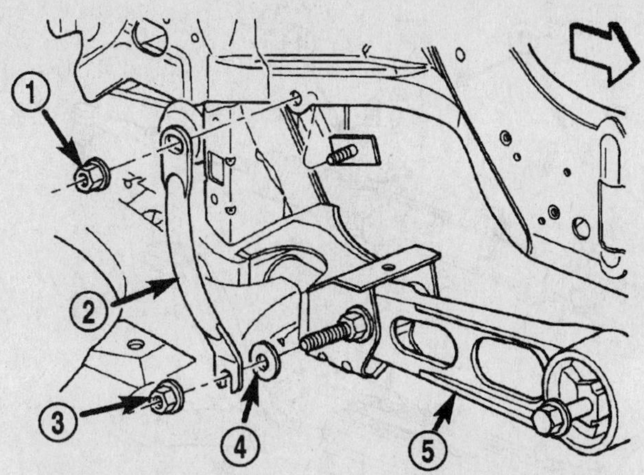


19.7 Pencil strut and lower torque strut details

1 *Nut*
2 *Pencil strut*
3 *Nut*
4 *Washer*
5 *Lower torque strut*

19.10 To preserve the front-end alignment, mark the relationship of each corner of the crossmember to the underbody

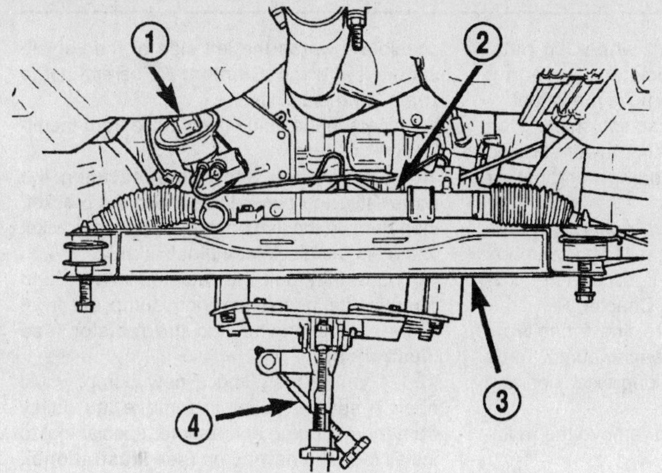


19.13 Power steering gear mounting details (crossmember lowered)

1 *Steering shaft coupling*
2 *Steering gear*
3 *Crossmember*
4 *Transmission jack*

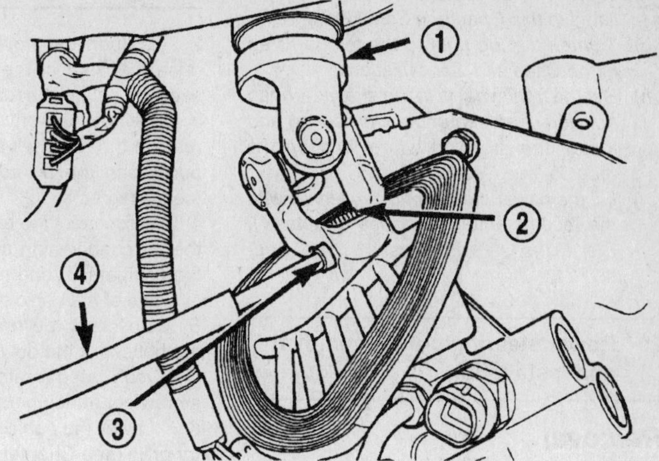


19.14 Steering shaft roll pin removal details

1 *Steering shaft coupling*
2 *Steering gear input shaft*
3 *Roll pin*
4 *Punch*

jacks are available at most equipment rental yards and even some auto parts stores. If you don't have access to a transmission jack, at the very least use a good-quality floor jack.

12 Remove the six crossmember-to-body bolts. **Note:** *Don't completely unscrew the two control arm rear bushing bolts; just unscrew them enough to free them from the holes in the body.*

13 Lower the crossmember far enough for access to the steering gear mounts and coupling **(see illustration)**. **Caution:** *Make sure the crossmember is supported at all times - don't let it hang by the control arms.*

14 Using a hammer and punch, drive out the roll pin retaining the steering shaft coupling to the steering gear input shaft **(see illustration)**.

15 Remove the input shaft cover seal from the steering gear. You may need to carefully pry the cover from the tabs on the steering gear **(see illustration)**.

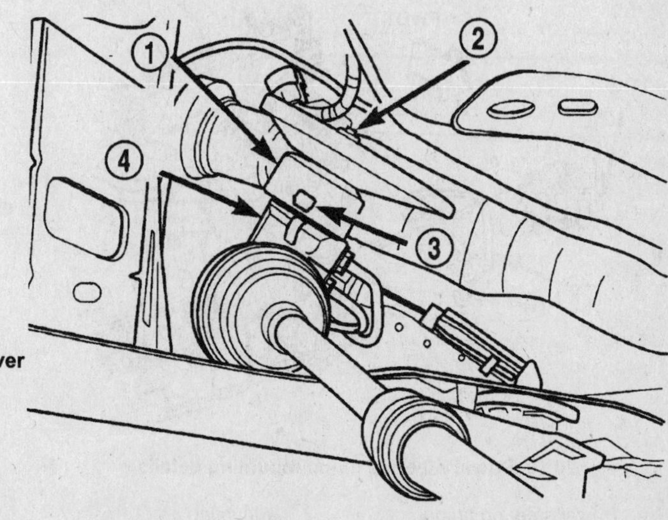


19.15 Input shaft cover seal details

1 *Seal*
2 *Input shaft*
3 *Tab*
4 *Steering gear*

16 Remove the mounting bolts and detach the steering gear from the crossmember **(see illustration)**.

### Installation

17 Installation is the reverse of removal, noting the following points:

a) *When connecting the steering gear input shaft to the steering shaft coupling, be sure to line up the flats on the shaft and in the coupling.*
b) *Make sure the steering gear rack is positioned in the center of its travel.*
c) *Lubricate the cover seal, where it contacts the coupling's plastic collar, with multi-purpose grease.*
d) *When installing the crossmember-to-body bolts, be sure to align the matchmarks.*
e) *Follow the procedure in Chapter 2A, Section 18, to install and align the lower torque strut.*
f) *Tighten all fasteners to the torque values listed in this Chapter's Specifications.*
g) *Tighten the lug nuts to the torque listed in the Chapter 1 Specifications.*
h) *Set the front wheels in the straight-ahead position, then center the clockspring and install the steering wheel and airbag module (see Section 16).*
i) *Fill the power steering fluid reservoir with the recommended fluid (see Chapter 1). Bleed the steering system (see Section 21).*

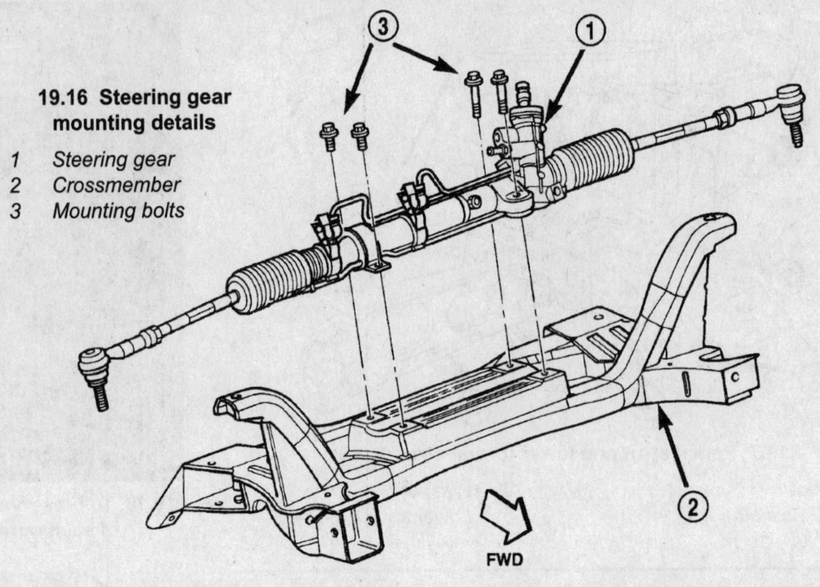


**19.16 Steering gear mounting details**

1 *Steering gear*
2 *Crossmember*
3 *Mounting bolts*

## 20 Power steering pump - removal and installation

### Removal

*Refer to illustrations 20.10, 20.11, 20.12a and 20.12b*

1 Using a suction gun, remove as much fluid from the power steering fluid reservoir as you can.

2 Loosen the right front wheel lug nuts, raise the front of the vehicle and support it securely on jackstands. Remove the wheel.

3 Remove the drivebelt splash shield, then remove the drivebelt from the power steering pump and the air conditioning compressor (see Chapter 1).

4 Disconnect the electrical connectors from the air conditioning compressor, then unbolt the compressor and move it towards the driver's side of the vehicle (see Chapter 3).

5 Unscrew the pressure line fitting from the bottom of the power steering pump. To do this, you'll need a ratchet, long extension and a crowfoot attachment.

6 Lower the vehicle and remove the radiator grille (see Chapter 11).

7 Remove the weatherstrip from the upper radiator crossmember, then remove the crossmember and brace (see Chapter 3).

8 Lift the radiator and fan assembly up and out of its mounts, then reposition it as far as possible towards the left side of the vehicle and tie it in place. **Caution:** *Be careful not to strain the radiator hoses.*

9 Detach the fluid supply hose from the fitting on the pump.

10 Remove the three bolts securing the power steering pump to its mounting bracket, then remove the two bolts securing the bracket to the engine block **(see illustration)**.

11 Carefully pull the radiator forward and remove the power steering pump out from between the engine and the radiator **(see illustration)**.

12 If you're installing a new pump, you'll need a special puller to remove the pulley from the old pump and another special tool to install it on the new pump **(see illustrations)**. These tools are available at most auto parts stores. When installing the pulley, press it onto the pump shaft until the hub of the pulley is flush with the end of the shaft.

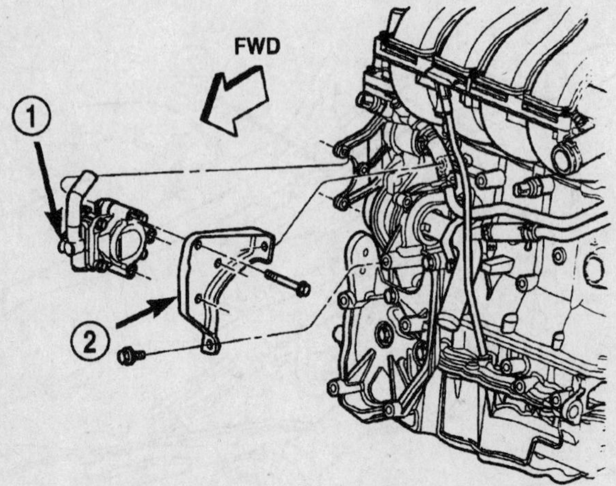


**20.10 Power steering pump mounting details**

1 *Power steering pump*
2 *Mounting bracket*

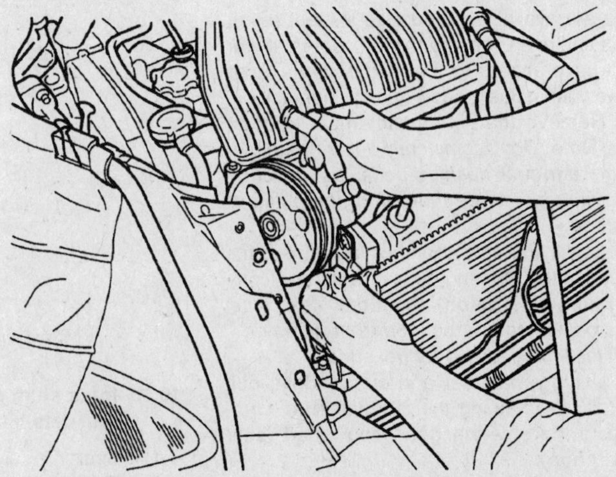

**20.11 Remove the power steering pump, being careful not to nick the radiator in the process**

### Installation

13 Installation is the reverse of removal, noting the following points:

- a) *Before installing the pump, check the condition of the O-ring on the pressure line fitting, replacing it if necessary.*
- b) *Tighten the pump mounting bracket bolts and the pump-to-mounting bracket bolts to the torque listed in this Chapter's Specifications.*
- c) *Refill the power steering fluid reservoir with the recommended fluid.*
- d) *Bleed the power steering system as described in the next Section.*

## 21 Power steering system - bleeding

1 Following any operation in which the power steering fluid lines have been disconnected, the power steering system must be bled to remove all air and obtain proper steering performance.

2 With the front wheels in the straight ahead position, check the power steering fluid level and, if low, add fluid until it reaches the Cold mark on the dipstick.

3 Start the engine and allow it to run at fast idle. Recheck the fluid level and add more if necessary to reach the Cold mark on the dipstick.

4 Bleed the system by turning the wheels from side to side, without hitting the stops. This will work the air out of the system. Keep the reservoir full of fluid as this is done.

5 When the air is worked out of the system, return the wheels to the straight ahead position and leave the vehicle running for several more minutes before shutting it off.

6 Road test the vehicle to be sure the steering system is functioning normally and noise free.

7 Recheck the fluid level to be sure it is up to the Hot mark on the dipstick while the engine is at normal operating temperature. Add fluid if necessary (see Chapter 1).

## 22 Wheel studs - replacement

*Refer to illustrations 22.3 and 22.4*

**Note:** *This procedure applies to both the front and rear wheel studs.*

1 Loosen the wheel lug nuts, raise the vehicle and support it securely on jackstands. Remove the wheel.

2 Remove the brake disc or drum (see Chapter 9).

3 Install a lug nut part way onto the stud being replaced. Push the stud out of the hub flange with a press tool **(see illustration).**

4 Insert the new stud into the hub flange from the back side and install some flat washers and a lug nut on the stud **(see illustration).**

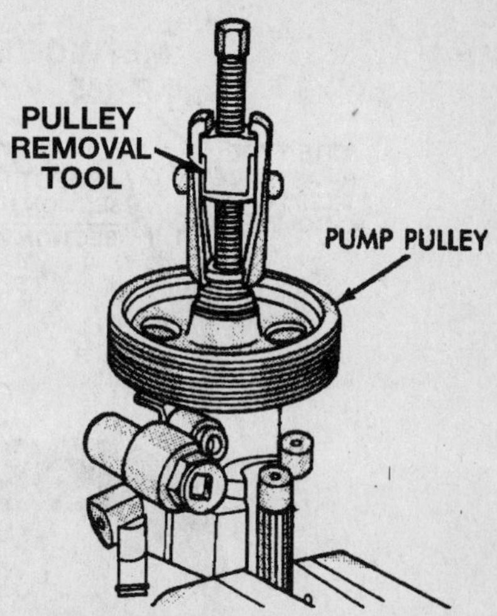


**20.12a If you're installing a new pump, you'll need a special puller to remove the pulley from the old pump . . .**

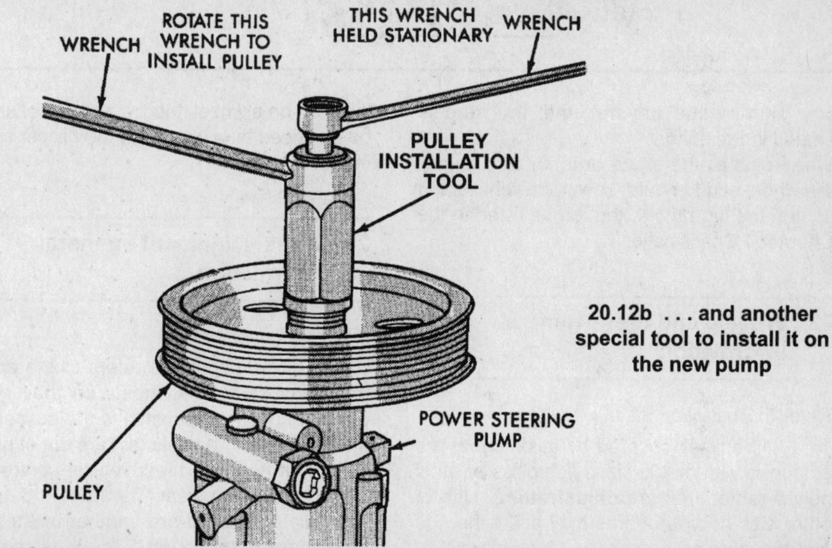


**20.12b . . . and another special tool to install it on the new pump**

**22.3 Use a press tool to push the stud out of the flange**

1 *Hub flange*
2 *Lug nut on stud*
3 *Press tool*

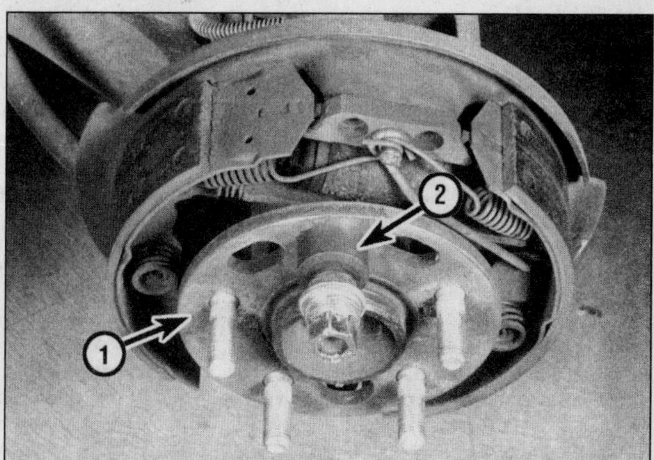


**22.4 Install a spacer and a lug nut on the stud, then tighten the nut to draw the stud into place**

1 *Hub flange*
2 *Spacer*

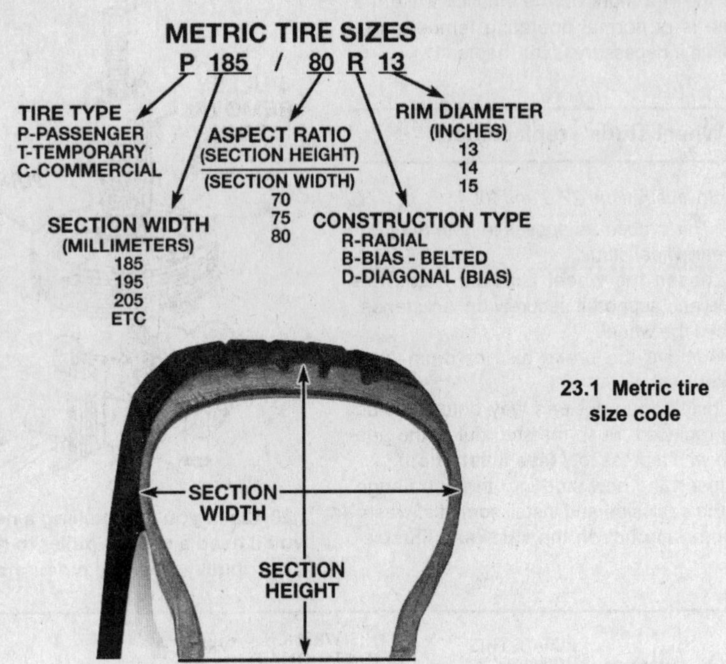


23.1 Metric tire size code

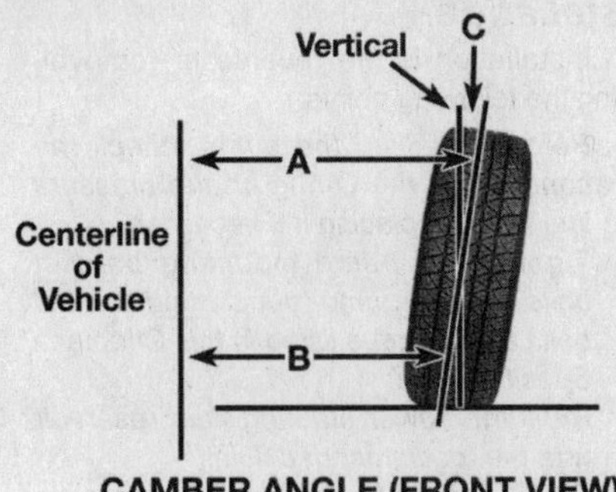


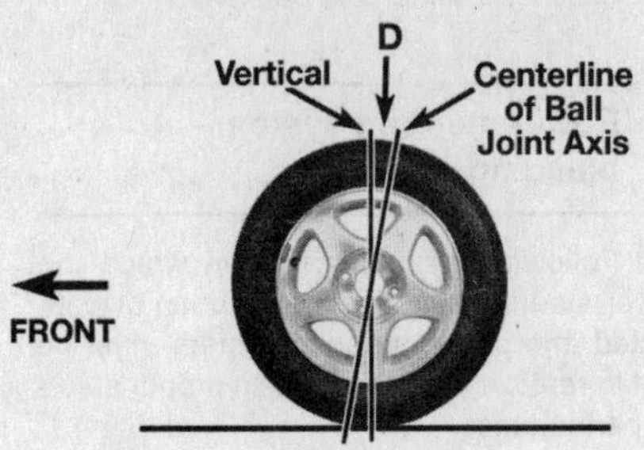


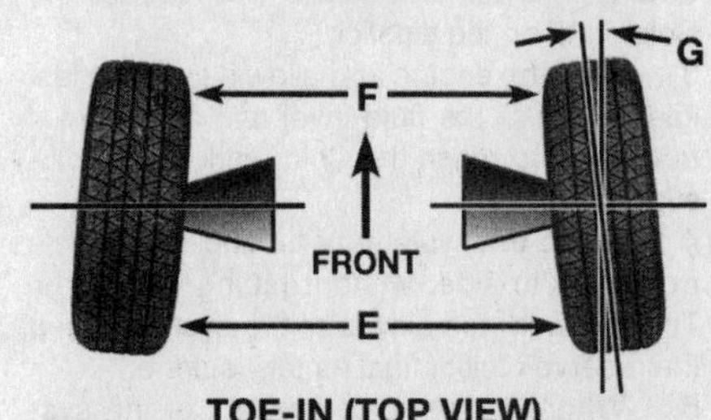


24.1 Camber, caster and toe-in angles

*A minus B = C (degrees camber)*
*D = degrees caster*
*E minus F = toe-in (measured in inches)*
*G = toe-in (expressed in degrees)*

5 Tighten the lug nut until the stud is seated in the flange.

6 Reinstall the brake drum or disc. Install the wheel and lug nuts. Lower the vehicle and tighten the lug nuts to the torque listed in the Chapter 1 Specifications.

## 23 Wheels and tires - general information

*Refer to illustration 23.1*

1 All vehicles covered by this manual are equipped with metric-sized fiberglass or steel belted radial tires **(see illustration)**. Use of other size or type of tires may affect the ride and handling of the vehicle. Don't mix different types of tires, such as radials and bias belted, on the same vehicle as handling may be seriously affected. It's recommended that tires be replaced in pairs on the same axle, but if only one tire is being replaced, be sure it's the same size, structure and tread design as the other.

2 Because tire pressure has a substantial effect on handling and wear, the pressure on all tires should be checked at least once a month or before any extended trips (see Chapter 1).

3 Wheels must be replaced if they are bent, dented, leak air, have elongated bolt holes, are heavily rusted, out of vertical symmetry or if the lug nuts won't stay tight. Wheel repairs that use welding or peening are not recommended.

4 Tire and wheel balance is important in the overall handling, braking and performance of the vehicle. Unbalanced wheels can adversely affect handling and ride characteristics as well as tire life. Whenever a tire is installed on a wheel, the tire and wheel should be balanced by a shop with the proper equipment.

## 24 Wheel alignment - general information

*Refer to illustration 24.1*

A wheel alignment refers to the adjustments made to the wheels so they are in proper angular relationship to the suspension and the ground. Wheels that are out of proper alignment not only affect vehicle control, but also increase tire wear. The front end angles normally measured are camber, caster and toe-in **(see illustration)**. Toe-in is the only routine adjustment made; camber is adjustable, but only after installing special strut-to-knuckle bolts. If the caster is not correct, check for bent components. There are no adjustments possible to the rear wheels.

Getting the proper wheel alignment is a very exacting process, one in which complicated and expensive machines are necessary to perform the job properly. Because of this, you should have a technician with the proper equipment perform these tasks. We will, however, use this space to give you a basic idea of what is involved with a wheel alignment so you can better understand the process and deal intelligently with the shop that does the work.

Toe-in is the turning in of the wheels. The purpose of a toe specification is to ensure parallel rolling of the wheels. In a vehicle with zero toe-in, the distance between the front edges of the wheels will be the same as the distance between the rear edges of the wheels. The actual amount of toe-in is normally only a fraction of an inch. Toe-in is controlled by the tie-rod end position on the tie-rod. Incorrect toe-in will cause the tires to wear improperly by making them scrub against the road surface.

Camber is the tilting of the wheels from vertical when viewed from one end of the vehicle. When the wheels tilt out at the top, the camber is said to be positive (+). When the wheels tilt in at the top the camber is negative (-). The amount of tilt is measured in degrees from vertical and this measurement is called the camber angle. This angle affects the amount of tire tread which contacts the road and compensates for changes in the suspension geometry when the vehicle is cornering or traveling over an undulating surface. On the front end it is adjusted using special camber adjusting bolts, which alter the relationship between the strut and the steering knuckle. At the rear end camber is not adjustable.

Caster is the tilting of the front steering axis from the vertical. A tilt toward the rear is positive caster and a tilt toward the front is negative caster.

# Chapter 11 Body

## Contents



## 1 General information

The models covered by this manual feature a "unibody" layout, using a floor pan with front and rear frame side rails which support the body components, front and rear suspension systems and other mechanical components. Certain components are particularly vulnerable to accident damage and can be unbolted and repaired or replaced. Among these parts are the body moldings, bumpers, front fenders, the hood and trunk lids and all glass. Only general body maintenance practices and body panel repair procedures within the scope of the do-it-yourselfer are included in this Chapter.

## 2 Body - maintenance

1 The condition of the vehicle's body is very important, because the resale value depends a great deal on it. It's much more difficult to repair a neglected or damaged body than it is to repair mechanical components. The hidden areas of the body, such as the wheel wells, the frame and the engine compartment, are equally important, although they don't require as frequent attention as the rest of the body.

2 Once a year, or every 12,000 miles, it's a good idea to have the underside of the body steam cleaned. All traces of dirt and oil will be removed and the area can then be inspected carefully for rust, damaged brake lines, frayed electrical wires, damaged cables and other problems.

3 At the same time, clean the engine and the engine compartment with a steam cleaner or water-soluble degreaser.

4 The wheel wells should be given close attention, since undercoating can peel away and stones and dirt thrown up by the tires can cause the paint to chip and flake, allowing rust to set in. If rust is found, clean down to the bare metal and apply an anti-rust paint.

5 The body should be washed about once a week. Wet the vehicle thoroughly to soften the dirt, then wash it down with a soft sponge and plenty of clean soapy water. If the surplus dirt is not washed off very carefully, it can wear down the paint.

6 Spots of tar or asphalt thrown up from the road should be removed with a cloth soaked in solvent.

7 Once every six months, wax the body and chrome trim. If a chrome cleaner is used to remove rust from any of the vehicle's plated parts, remember that the cleaner also removes part of the chrome, so use it sparingly.

## 3 Vinyl trim - maintenance

Don't clean vinyl trim with detergents, caustic soap or petroleum-based cleaners. Plain soap and water works just fine, with a soft brush to clean dirt that may be ingrained. Wash the vinyl as frequently as the rest of the vehicle. After cleaning, application of a high-quality rubber and vinyl protectant will help prevent oxidation and cracks. The protectant can also be applied to weatherstripping, vacuum lines and rubber hoses, which often fail as a result of chemical degradation, and to the tires.

## 4 Upholstery and carpets - maintenance

1 Every three months remove the floor mats and clean the interior of the vehicle (more frequently if necessary). Use a stiff whiskbroom to brush the carpeting and loosen dirt and dust, then vacuum the upholstery and carpets thoroughly, especially along seams and crevices.

2 Dirt and stains can be removed from carpeting with basic household or automotive carpet shampoos available in spray cans. Follow the directions and vacuum again, then use a stiff brush to bring back the "nap" of the carpet.

3 Most interiors have cloth or vinyl upholstery, either of which can be cleaned and maintained with a number of material-specific cleaners or shampoos available in auto supply stores. Follow the directions on the product for usage, and always spot-test any upholstery cleaner on an inconspicuous area (like the bottom edge of a back seat cushion) to ensure that it doesn't cause a color shift in the material.

4 After cleaning, vinyl upholstery should be treated with a protectant. **Note:** *Make sure the protectant container indicates the product can be used on seats - some products may make a seat too slippery.* **Caution:** *Do not use a protectant on vinyl-covered steering wheels.*

5 Leather upholstery requires special care.

It should be cleaned regularly with saddle soap or leather cleaner. Never use alcohol, gasoline, nail polish remover or thinner to clean leather upholstery.

6 After cleaning, regularly treat leather upholstery with a leather conditioner, rubbed in with a soft cotton cloth. Never use car wax on leather upholstery.

7 In areas where the interior of the vehicle is subject to bright sunlight, cover leather seating areas of the seats with a sheet if the vehicle is to be left out for any length of time.

## 5 Body repair

### *Minor damage*

#### Repair of scratches

1 If the scratch is superficial and does not penetrate to the metal of the body, repair is very simple. Lightly rub the scratched area with a fine rubbing compound to remove loose paint and built up wax. Rinse the area with clean water.

2 Apply touch-up paint to the scratch, using a small brush. Continue to apply thin layers of paint until the surface of the paint in the scratch is level with the surrounding paint. Allow the new paint at least two weeks to harden, then blend it into the surrounding paint by rubbing with a very fine rubbing compound. Finally, apply a coat of wax to the scratch area.

3 If the scratch has penetrated the paint and exposed the metal of the body, causing the metal to rust, and a different repair technique is required. Remove all loose rust from the bottom of the scratch with a pocket knife, then apply rust inhibiting paint to prevent the formation of rust in the future. Using a rubber or nylon applicator, coat the scratched area with glaze-type filler. If required, the filler can be mixed with thinner to provide a very thin paste, which is ideal for filling narrow scratches. Before the glaze filler in the scratch hardens, wrap a piece of smooth cotton cloth around the tip of a finger. Dip the cloth in thinner and then quickly wipe it along the surface of the scratch. This will ensure that the surface of the filler is slightly hollow. The scratch can now be painted over as described earlier in this Section.

#### Repair of dents

*See photo sequence*

4 When repairing dents, the first job is to pull the dent out until the affected area is as close as possible to its original shape. There is no point in trying to restore the original shape completely as the metal in the damaged area will have stretched on impact and cannot be restored to its original contours. It is better to bring the level of the dent up to a point which is about 1/8-inch below the level of the surrounding metal. In cases where the dent is very shallow, it is not worth trying to pull it out at all.

5 If the back side of the dent is accessible, it can be hammered out gently from behind using a soft-face hammer. While doing this, hold a block of wood firmly against the opposite side of the metal to absorb the hammer blows and prevent the metal from being stretched.

6 If the dent is in a section of the body which has double layers, or some other factor makes it inaccessible from behind, a different technique is required. Drill several small holes through the metal inside the damaged area, particularly in the deeper sections. Screw long, self tapping screws into the holes just enough for them to get a good grip in the metal. Now pulling on the protruding heads of the screws with locking pliers can pull out the dent.

7 The next stage of repair is the removal of paint from the damaged area and from an inch or so of the surrounding metal. This is easily done with a wire brush or sanding disk in a drill motor, although it can be done just as effectively by hand with sandpaper. To complete the preparation for filling, score the surface of the bare metal with a screwdriver or the tang of a file or drill small holes in the affected area. This will provide a good grip for the filler material. To complete the repair, see the subsection on *filling and painting*.

#### Repair of rust holes or gashes

8 Remove all paint from the affected area and from an inch or so of the surrounding metal using a sanding disk or wire brush mounted in a drill motor. If these are not available, a few sheets of sandpaper will do the job just as effectively.

9 With the paint removed, you will be able to determine the severity of the corrosion and decide whether to replace the whole panel, if possible, or repair the affected area. New body panels are not as expensive as most people think and it is often quicker to install a new panel than to repair large areas of rust.

10 Remove all trim pieces from the affected area except those which will act as a guide to the original shape of the damaged body, such as headlight shells, etc. Using metal snips or a hacksaw blade, remove all loose metal and any other metal that is badly affected by rust. Hammer the edges of the hole on the inside to create a slight depression for the filler material.

11 Wire brush the affected area to remove the powdery rust from the surface of the metal. If the back of the rusted area is accessible, treat it with rust inhibiting paint.

12 Before filling is done, block the hole in some way. This can be done with sheet metal riveted or screwed into place, or by stuffing the hole with wire mesh.

13 Once the hole is blocked off, the affected area can be filled and painted. See the following subsection on *filling and painting*.

#### Filling and painting

14 Many types of body fillers are available, but generally speaking, body repair kits which contain filler paste and a tube of resin hardener are best for this type of repair work. A wide, flexible plastic or nylon applicator will be necessary for imparting a smooth and contoured finish to the surface of the filler material. Mix up a small amount of filler on a clean piece of wood or cardboard (use the hardener sparingly). Follow the manufacturer's instructions on the package, otherwise the filler will set incorrectly.

15 Using the applicator, apply the filler paste to the prepared area. Draw the applicator across the surface of the filler to achieve the desired contour and to level the filler surface. As soon as a contour that approximates the original one is achieved, stop working the paste. If you continue, the paste will begin to stick to the applicator. Continue to add thin layers of paste at 20-minute intervals until the level of the filler is just above the surrounding metal.

16 Once the filler has hardened, the excess can be removed with a body file. From then on, progressively finer grades of sandpaper should be used, starting with a 180-grit paper and finishing with 600-grit wet-or-dry paper. Always wrap the sandpaper around a flat rubber or wooden block, otherwise the surface of the filler will not be completely flat. During the sanding of the filler surface, the wet-or-dry paper should be periodically rinsed in water. This will ensure that a very smooth finish is produced in the final stage.

17 At this point, the repair area should be surrounded by a ring of bare metal, which in turn should be encircled by the finely feathered edge of good paint. Rinse the repair area with clean water until all of the dust produced by the sanding operation is gone.

18 Spray the entire area with a light coat of primer. This will reveal any imperfections in the surface of the filler. Repair the imperfections with fresh filler paste or glaze filler and once more smooth the surface with sandpaper. Repeat this spray-and-repair procedure until you are satisfied that the surface of the filler and the feathered edge of the paint are perfect. Rinse the area with clean water and allow it to dry completely.

19 The repair area is now ready for painting. Spray painting must be carried out in a warm, dry, windless and dust free atmosphere. These conditions can be created if you have access to a large indoor work area, but if you are forced to work in the open, you will have to pick the day very carefully. If you are working indoors, dousing the floor in the work area with water will help settle the dust, which would otherwise be in the air. If the repair area is confined to one body panel, mask off the surrounding panels. This will help minimize the effects of a slight mismatch in paint color. Trim pieces such as chrome strips, door handles, etc., will also need to be masked off or removed. Use masking tape and several thickness of newspaper for the masking operations.

20 Before spraying, shake the paint can thoroughly, then spray a test area until the spray painting technique is mastered. Cover the repair area with a thick coat of primer. The thickness should be built up using sev-

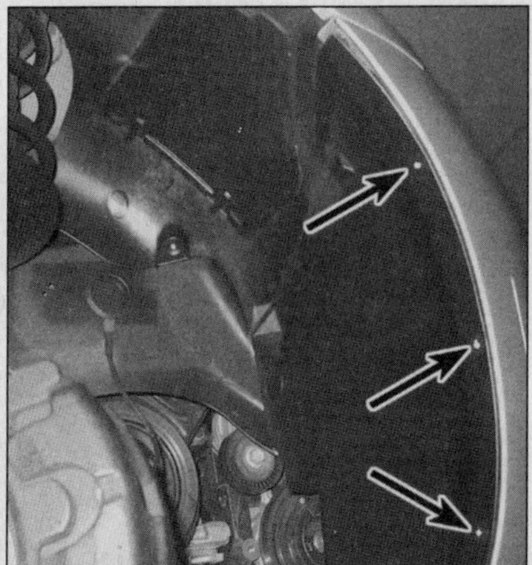
8.2a Remove the splash shield mounting fasteners along the front edge of the fender . . .

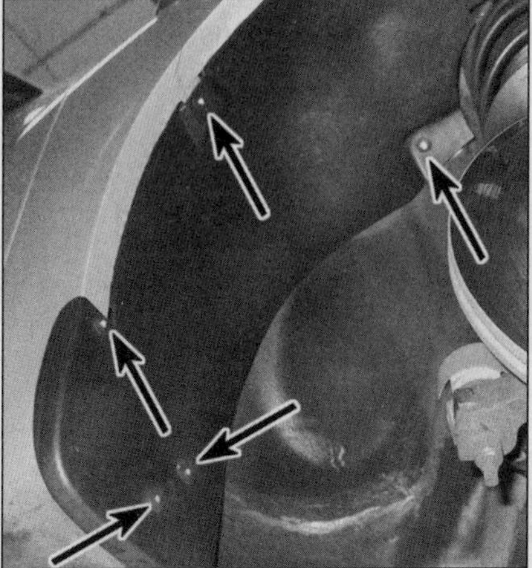
8.2b . . . then remove these screws from the rear of the splash shield (not all fasteners are in the exact same location on all models)

8.3a Remove the bolts along the top of the front fender

eral thin layers of primer rather than one thick one. Using 600-grit wet-or-dry sandpaper, rub down the surface of the primer until it is very smooth. While doing this, the work area should be thoroughly rinsed with water and the wet-or-dry sandpaper periodically rinsed as well. Allow the primer to dry before spraying additional coats.

21 Spray on the top coat, again building up the thickness by using several thin layers of paint. Begin spraying in the center of the repair area and then, using a circular motion, work out until the whole repair area and about two inches of the surrounding original paint is covered. Remove all masking material 10 to 15 minutes after spraying on the final coat of paint. Allow the new paint at least two weeks to harden, then use a very fine rubbing compound to blend the edges of the new paint into the existing paint. Finally, apply a coat of wax.

## Major damage

22 Major damage must be repaired by an auto body shop specifically equipped to perform unibody repairs. These shops have the specialized equipment required to do the job properly.

23 If the damage is extensive, the body must be checked for proper alignment or the vehicle's handling characteristics may be adversely affected and other components may wear at an accelerated rate.

24 Due to the fact that all of the major body components (hood, fenders, etc.) are separate and replaceable units, any seriously damaged components should be replaced rather than repaired. Sometimes the components can be found in a auto salvage or wrecking yard that specializes in used vehicle components, often at considerable savings over the cost of new parts.

## 6 Hinges and locks - maintenance

Once every 3000 miles, or every three months, the hinges and latch assemblies on the doors, hood and trunk should be given a few drops of light oil or lock lubricant. The door latch strikers should also be lubricated with a thin coat of grease to reduce wear and ensure free movement. Lubricate the door and trunk locks with spray-on graphite lubricant.

## 7 Windshield and fixed glass - replacement

Replacement of the windshield and fixed glass requires the use of special fast-setting adhesive/caulk materials and some specialized tools and techniques. These operations should be left to a dealer service department or a shop specializing in glass work.

## 8 Front fender - replacement

*Refer to illustrations 8.2a, 8.2b, 8.3a, 8.3b, 8.3c and 8.3d*

1 Remove the headlight housing (see Chapter 12). Remove the radiator grille (see Section 11).

2 Remove the screws and detach the fenderwell splash shield **(see illustrations)**.

3 Remove the fasteners and detach the fender **(see illustrations)**.

4 Installation is the reverse of removal.

8.3b Lower fender retaining bolt location

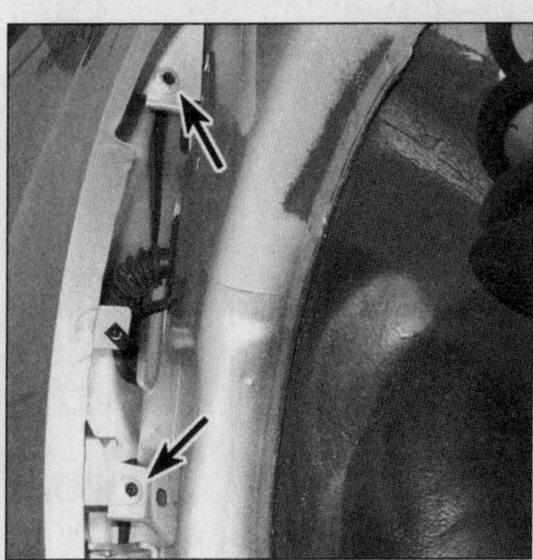
8.3c Front fender-to-body retaining bolts

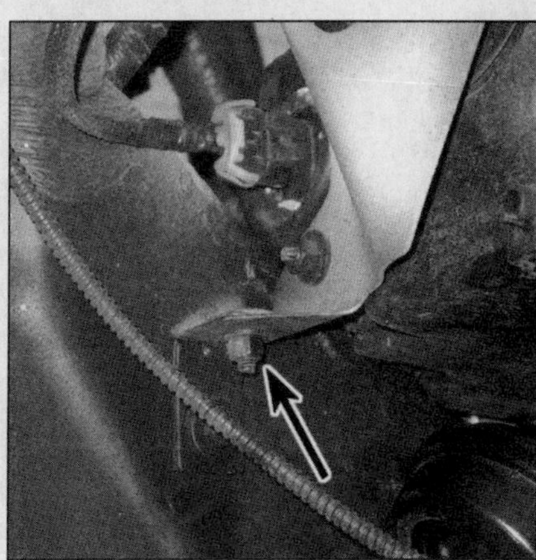
8.3d Remove the front fender retaining nut

**These photos illustrate a method of repairing simple dents. They are intended to supplement *Body repair - minor damage* in this Chapter and should not be used as the sole instructions for body repair on these vehicles.**

**1 If you can't access the backside of the body panel to hammer out the dent, pull it out with a slide-hammer-type dent puller. In the deepest portion of the dent or along the crease line, drill or punch hole(s) at least one inch apart . . .**

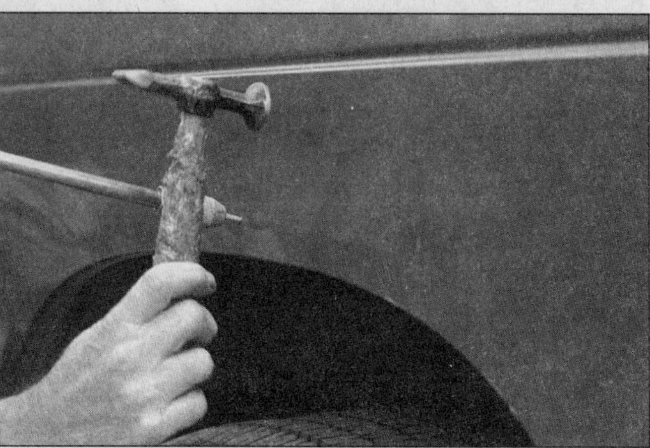

**2 . . . then screw the slide-hammer into the hole and operate it. Tap with a hammer near the edge of the dent to help 'pop' the metal back to its original shape. When you're finished, the dent area should be close to its original contour and about 1/8-inch below the surface of the surrounding metal**

**3 Using coarse-grit sandpaper, remove the paint down to the bare metal. Hand sanding works fine, but the disc sander shown here makes the job faster. Use finer (about 320-grit) sandpaper to feather-edge the paint at least one inch around the dent area**

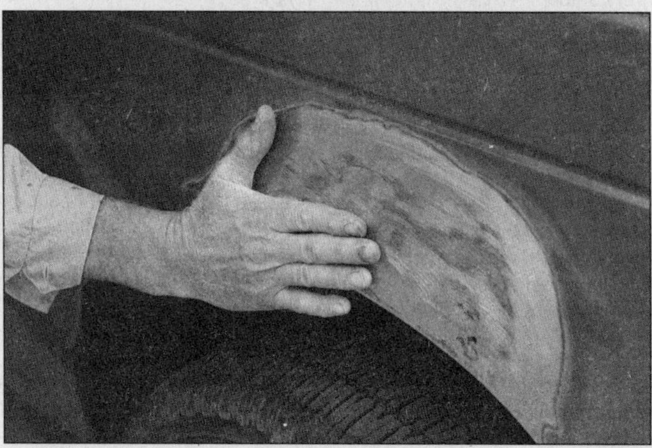

**4 When the paint is removed, touch will probably be more helpful than sight for telling if the metal is straight. Hammer down the high spots or raise the low spots as necessary. Clean the repair area with wax/silicone remover**

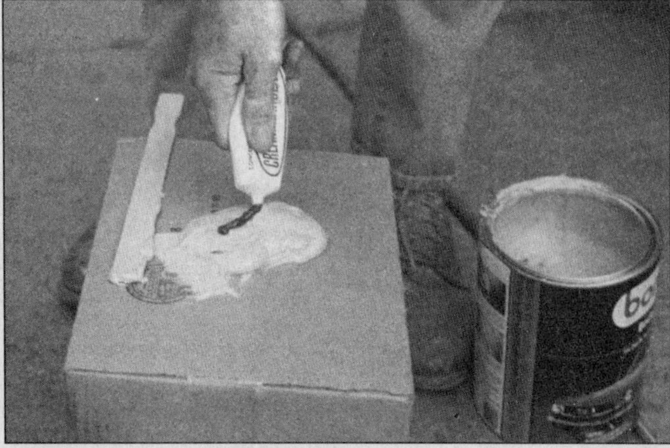

**5 Following label instructions, mix up a batch of plastic filler and hardener. The ratio of filler to hardener is critical, and, if you mix it incorrectly, it will either not cure properly or cure too quickly (you won't have time to file and sand it into shape)**

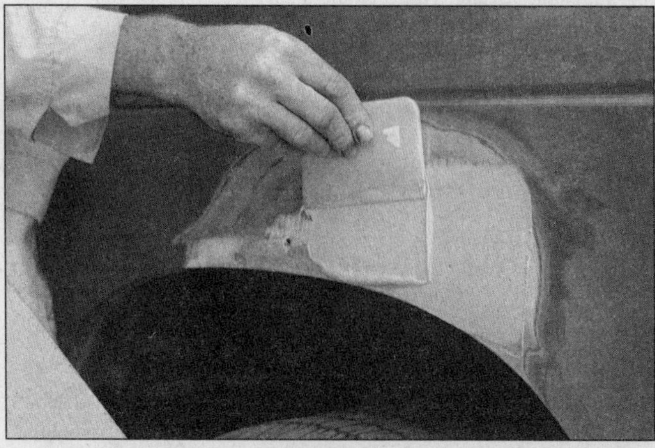

**6 Working quickly so the filler doesn't harden, use a plastic applicator to press the body filler firmly into the metal, assuring it bonds completely. Work the filler until it matches the original contour and is slightly above the surrounding metal**

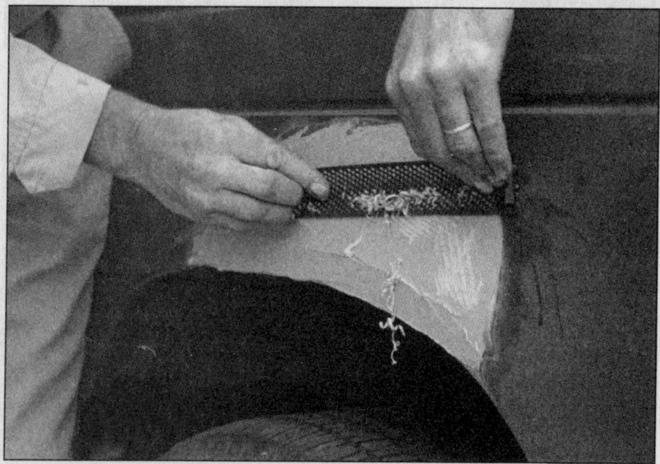

7 Let the filler harden until you can just dent it with your fingernail. Use a body file or Surform tool (shown here) to rough-shape the filler

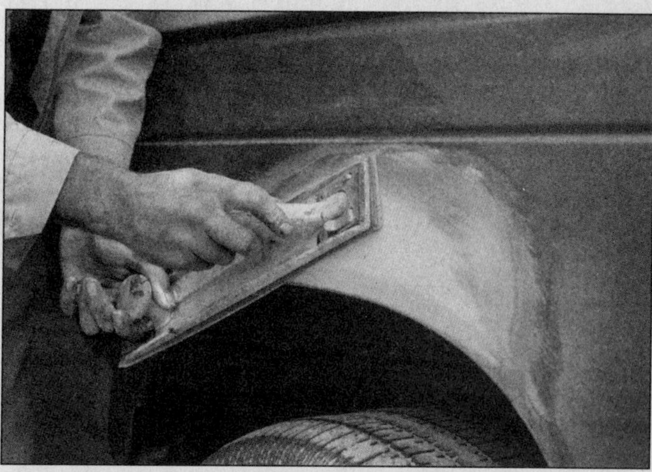

8 Use coarse-grit sandpaper and a sanding board or block to work the filler down until it's smooth and even. Work down to finer grits of sandpaper - always using a board or block - ending up with 360 or 400 grit

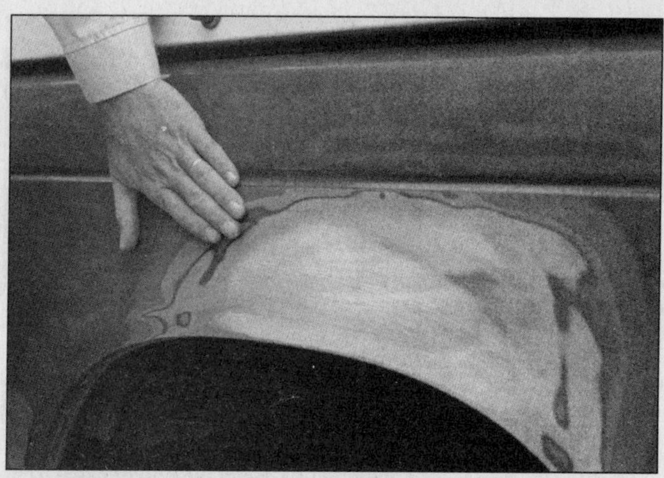

9 You shouldn't be able to feel any ridge at the transition from the filler to the bare metal or from the bare metal to the old paint. As soon as the repair is flat and uniform, remove the dust and mask off the adjacent panels or trim pieces

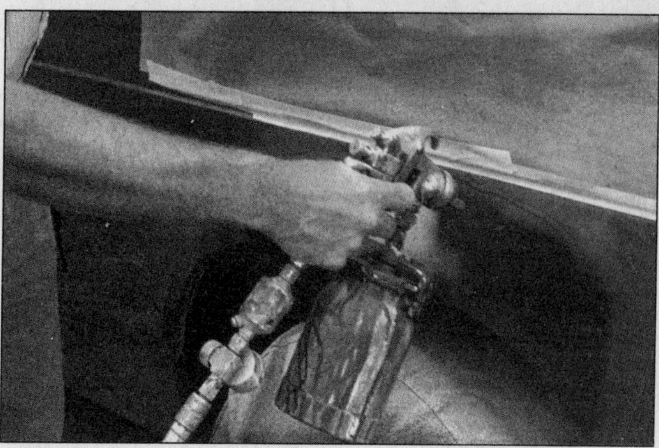

10 Apply several layers of primer to the area. Don't spray the primer on too heavy, so it sags or runs, and make sure each coat is dry before you spray on the next one. A professional-type spray gun is being used here, but aerosol spray primer is available inexpensively from auto parts stores

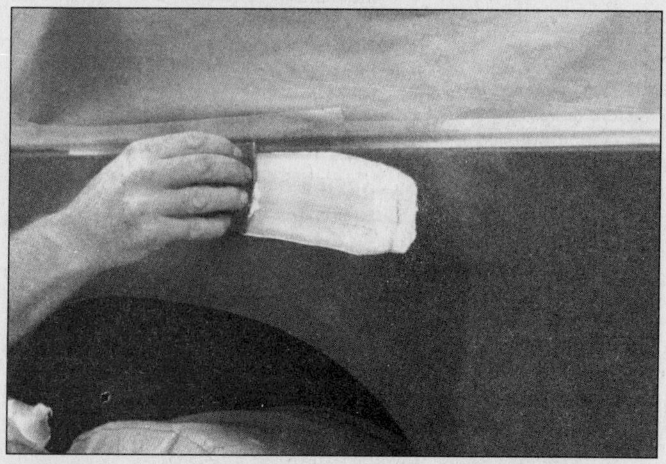

11 The primer will help reveal imperfections or scratches. Fill these with glazing compound. Follow the label instructions and sand it with 360 or 400-grit sandpaper until it's smooth. Repeat the glazing, sanding and respraying until the primer reveals a perfectly smooth surface

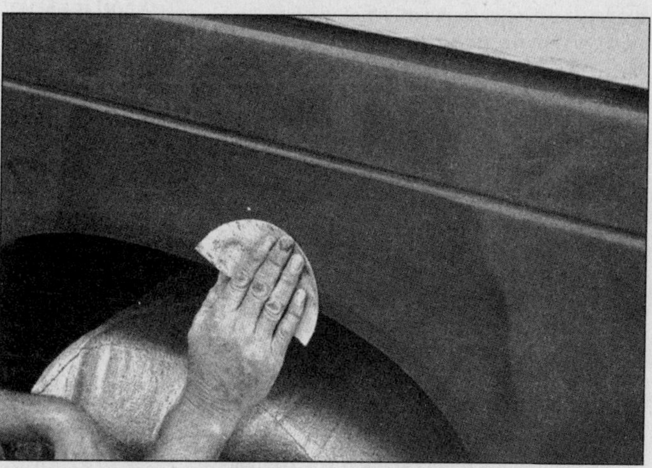

12 Finish sand the primer with very fine sandpaper (400 or 600-grit) to remove the primer overspray. Clean the area with water and allow it to dry. Use a tack rag to remove any dust, then apply the finish coat. Don't attempt to rub out or wax the repair area until the paint has dried completely (at least two weeks)

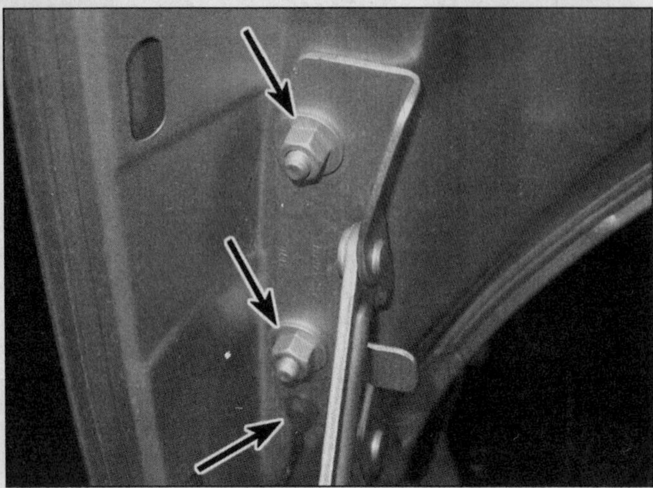
9.3 For a reference point at installation, outline the hinges on the hood with a felt tip marker or white paint before removing the ground wire bolt and retaining nuts

9.11 Screw the hood bumpers in or out to adjust the hood flush with the fenders

## 9 Hood - removal, installation and adjustment

**Note:** *The hood is heavy and somewhat awkward to remove and install - at least two people should perform this procedure.*

### Removal

*Refer to illustration 9.3*

1 Use blankets or pads to cover the cowl area of the body and both fenders. This will protect the body and paint as the hood is lifted off.

2 Open the hood and support it on the prop rod.

3 Mark the location of the hood hinge to aid alignment during installation (a permanent-type felt-tip marker will work for this) **(see illustration)**.

4 Disconnect the ground wire.

5 Have an assistant support one side of the hood while you support the other. Simultaneously remove the hinge-to-hood nuts.

6 Lift off the hood. **Note:** *A good place to store the hood is on the roof of the vehicle. Place blankets or pads on the roof first and lay the hood painted side down on the blankets.*

### Installation

7 Installation is the reverse of removal. Align the marks around the hinges (one side at a time) and then check for proper clearance. Readjust as necessary (see below).

### Adjustment

*Refer to illustration 9.11*

8 Slight fore-and-aft and side-to-side adjustment of the hood can be made by moving the hood in relation to the hinge plate after loosening the nuts. The hood must be aligned so there is a 5/32-inch gap (approximate) to the front fenders and flush with the top surface.

9 Trace a line around the entire hinge plate so you can judge the amount of movement.

10 Loosen the nuts and move the hood into correct alignment. Move it only a little at a time. Tighten the hinge nuts and carefully lower the hood to check the alignment.

11 Adjust the hood bumpers on the radiator support so the hood is flush with the fenders when closed **(see illustration)**.

12 The hood latch assembly can also be adjusted up-and-down and side-to-side after loosening the nuts. Make sure you place alignment marks around the hood latch assembly before loosening the mounting nuts.

13 The hood latch assembly, as well as the hinges, should be periodically lubricated with white lithium-base grease to prevent sticking and wear.

## 10 Hood latch and cable - removal and installation

**Warning:** *These models have airbags. Always disable the airbag system before working in the vicinity of any airbag system components to avoid the possibility of accidental deployment of the airbag, which could cause personal injury (see Chapter 12).*

### Latch

#### Removal

*Refer to illustration 10.3*

1 Open the hood and support it on the prop rod.

2 Scribe alignment marks around the hood latch assembly to aid alignment during installation (a permanent-type felt-tip marker or paint will also work for this).

3 Remove the bolts, detach the latch assembly from the radiator support, then disconnect the release cable from the hood latch assembly **(see illustration)**.

10.3 Slide the grommet straight out of the housing and detach the end of cable from the hood latch

#### Installation

4 Installation is the reverse of removal. Align the hood latch assembly with the marks on the radiator support and then tighten the nuts. Check hood latch operation. Readjust as necessary.

### Cable

#### Removal

5 Disconnect the release cable from the hood latch **(see illustration 10.3)**.

6 Detach the cable from the clips securing it to the radiator support.

7 Inside the vehicle remove the left front kick panel to gain access to the hood release handle bolts.

8 Remove the bolts securing the hood release handle/cable assembly to the cowl panel.

9 Under the dash, locate and disengage the push-in retainer and cable grommet from the firewall.

10 Connect a piece of heavy string or flexible wire to the engine compartment end of

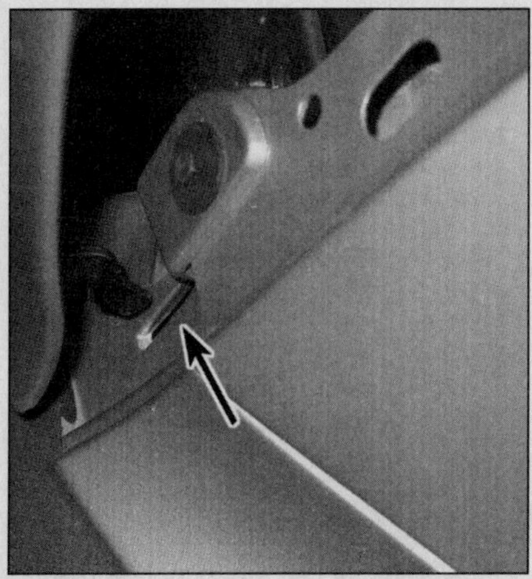

**11.3 After removing the bolts at the top, pull the grille locating tabs out of the body**

the cable, then from inside the vehicle, pull the cable with string or wire attached through the firewall into the vehicle. Disconnect the string or wire from the old cable.

### Installation

11 Connect the string or wire to the new cable and carefully pull it through the firewall into the engine compartment.

12 The remaining installation steps are the reverse of removal.

## 11 Radiator grille - removal and installation

*Refer to illustration 11.3*

1 Open the hood and support it on the prop rod.

2 Remove the four bolts at the top of the grille.

3 Pull the grille out and separate the locating tabs from the body **(see illustration)**.

4 Installation is the reverse of removal.

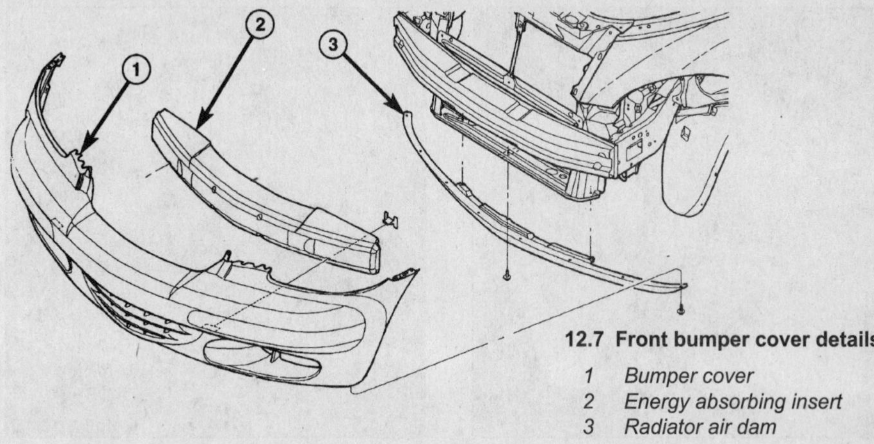


**12.7 Front bumper cover details**

1 *Bumper cover*
2 *Energy absorbing insert*
3 *Radiator air dam*

## 12 Bumpers - removal and installation

### *Front bumper*

*Refer to illustration 12.7*

1 Open the hood and support it on the prop rod.

2 Remove the radiator grille (see Section 11).

3 Remove the fasteners securing the front fender inner splash shields to the lower section of the bumper cover.

4 Pull the splash shields away from the fenderwell as necessary to remove the bolts securing the bumper cover to the front fender.

5 If equipped, disconnect the foglight wiring harness connectors.

6 Remove the fasteners securing the top edge of the bumper cover to the chassis.

7 Disengage the bumper cover from the front fenders and remove the bumper from the vehicle **(see illustration)**. **Note:** *If you are performing this job alone, place some blankets or other suitable padding on the ground below the bumper to protect the paint should the bumper fall during removal.*

8 If required, the bumper bar can be removed at this time.

9 Installation is the reverse of removal.

### *Rear bumper*

*Refer to illustrations 12.15 and 12.16*

10 Open the liftgate and remove the nuts retaining the bumper cover to the rear floor.

11 Raise the vehicle and support it securely on jackstands.

12 Disconnect the license plate light.

13 Remove the rear wheel housing covers.

14 Remove the fasteners or bolts securing the bumper cover.

15 Slide the bumper cover rearward to disengage it and remove it from the vehicle **(see illustration)**. **Note:** *If you are performing this job alone, place some blankets or other suitable padding on the ground below the bumper to protect the paint should the bumper cover fall during removal.*

16 If required, the bumper bar can be removed at this time, however, before removal use a felt tip pen to mark the position of the nuts on the bar to aid with installation **(see illustration)**.

17 Installation is the reverse of removal.

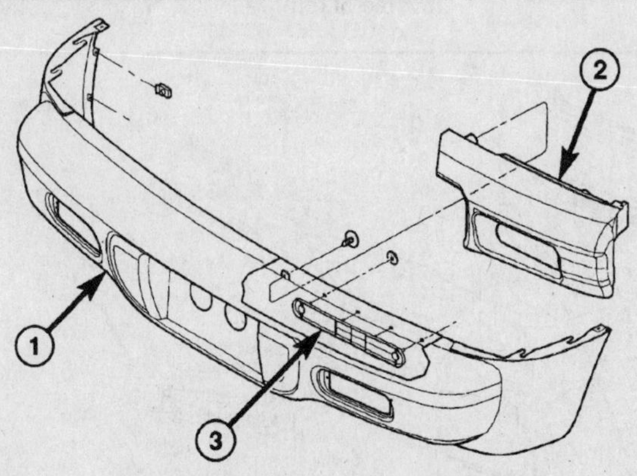


**12.15 Rear bumper cover details**

1 *Bumper cover*
2 *Energy absorbing foam insert*
3 *Bumper stud plate and nuts*

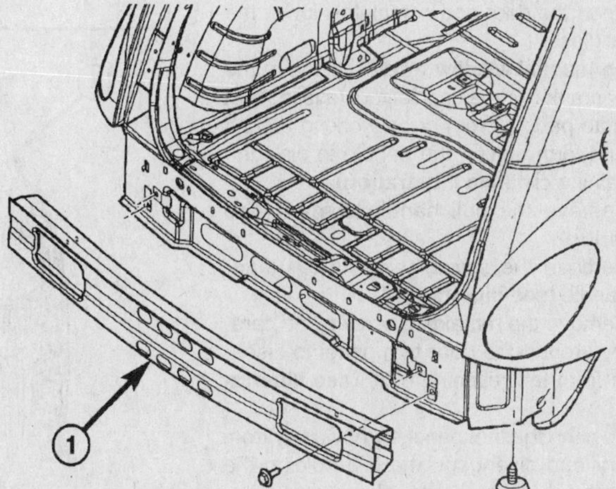


**12.16 Rear bumper bar (1) details**

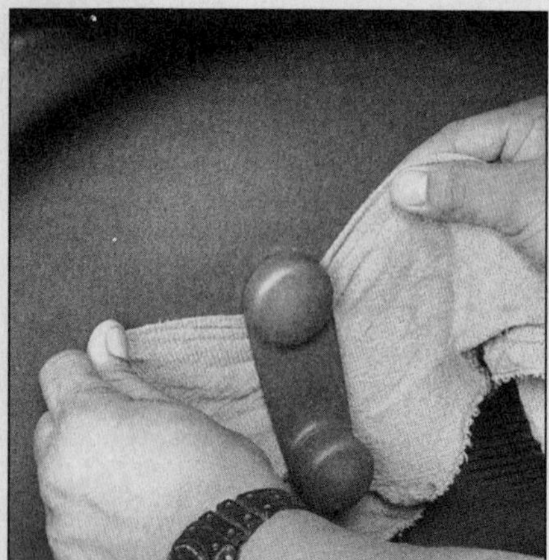

13.2 If you don't have a window crank removal tool (which is available at most auto parts stores and relatively inexpensive), place a shop cloth behind the window crank handle and work it back-and-forth to dislodge the retaining clip

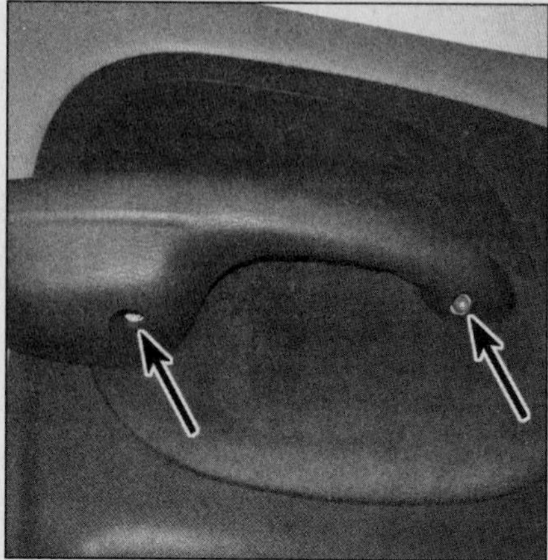

13.3 Remove the door pull handle screws

13.4 Remove the door handle screw

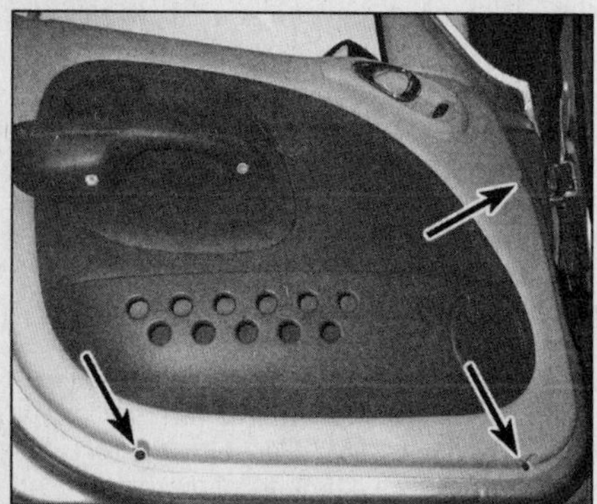

13.5a Remove the door trim panel screws

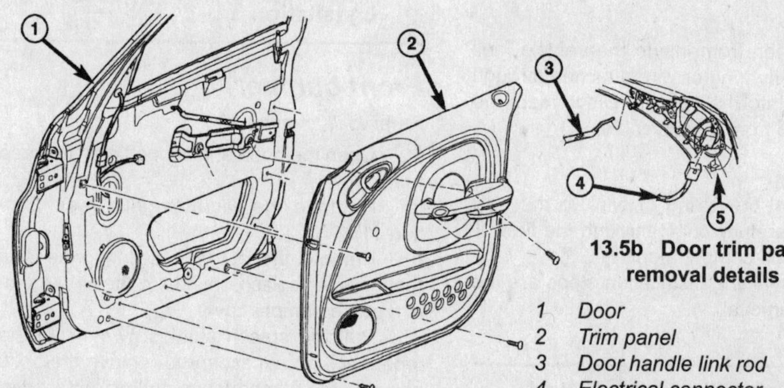


13.5b Door trim panel removal details

1 Door
2 Trim panel
3 Door handle link rod
4 Electrical connector
5 Inner door handle remote handle and power door lock bezel

## 13 Door trim panel - removal and installation

### Removal

*Refer to illustration 13.2, 13.3, 13.4, 13.5a, 13.5b and 13.8*

1 Open the door and completely lower the window glass.

2 On manual window models, remove the window crank using a special tool (available at most auto parts stores) or by working a cloth back-and-forth behind the handle to dislodge the retaining clip **(see illustration)**.

3 Remove the pull handle screws **(see illustration)**.

4 Remove the screw securing the inner door handle **(see illustration)**.

5 Remove the remaining screws and carefully pry around the door trim panel to disengage it from the retaining clips **(see illustrations)**.

6 Position the trim panel slightly away from the door and disengage the clip holding the door latch linkage to the door handle.

7 Disconnect the electrical connectors from the speaker, power door lock switch, the mirror switch and power window switch, then remove the trim panel. **Caution:** *Do not allow the trim panel to hang from the electrical wires.*

8 The inner door watershield can be removed if necessary by removing the armrest bracket and carefully peeling the watershield off, taking care not to damage it **(see illustration)**.

### Installation

9 Reconnect any electrical connectors and install the latch linkage into the door handle. Secure it with the retaining clip.

10 Press the trim panel into place and seat all clip fasteners, then install the retaining screws.

11 The remainder of installation is the reverse of removal.

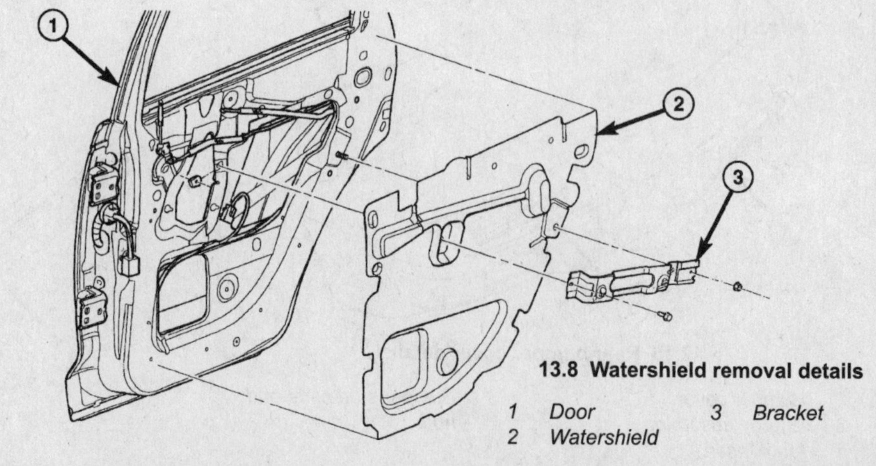


13.8 Watershield removal details

1 Door
2 Watershield
3 Bracket

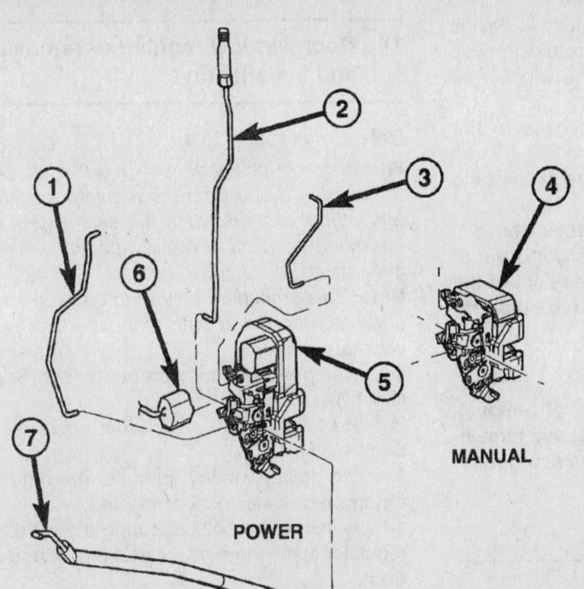


14.4 Front door latch assembly details

1 Outside handle-to-latch linkage
2 Door lock button and linkage
3 Key-to-latch linkage
4 Manual override lock latch
5 Power override lock latch
6 Latch lock connector
7 Remote handle-to-latch link rod

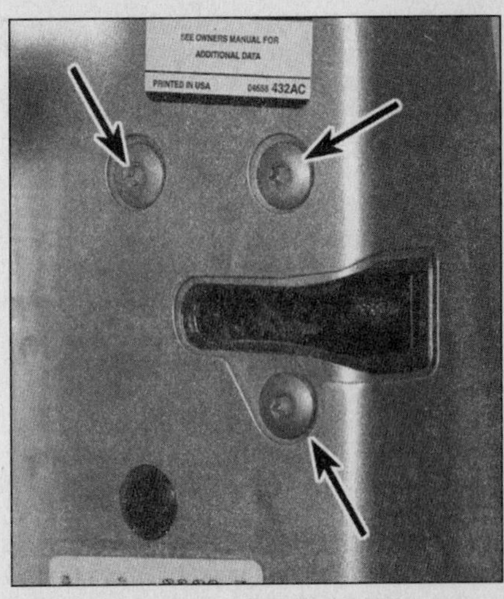

14.6 The door latch is retained by three screws

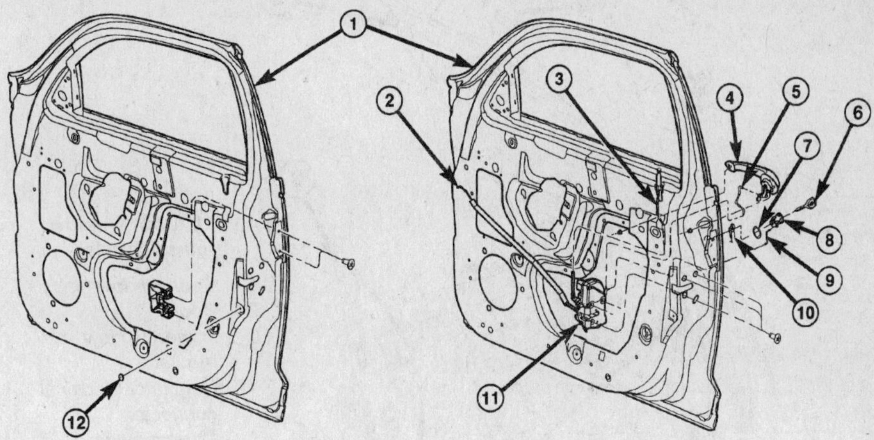


14.16 Outside door handle details

1 Front door
2 Handle-to-latch link rod
3 Door lock button and linkage
4 Outside handle
5 Outside handle-to-latch link
6 Key
7 Lock cylinder gasket
8 Lock cylinder
9 Lock cylinder-to-latch link rod
10 Central lock switch
11 Latch lock override switch
12 Door ajar switch actuating bumper

## 14 Door latch, outside handle and lock cylinder - removal and installation

## *Latch*

### Removal

*Refer to illustrations 14.4 and 14.6*

1 Remove the door trim panel (see Section 13). On vehicles equipped with electric windows, close the window before disconnecting the door trim panel electrical connectors.

2 On vehicles with manual windows, install the window crank (without the retaining clip) and roll up the window.

3 If you are removing a rear door latch, remove the window glass lower rear run channel.

4 Disconnect the lock cylinder, lock button and latch release operating rods from the door latch **(see illustration)**.

5 On vehicles equipped with central door locks, disconnect the electrical connector.

6 Remove the three mounting screws from the end of the door and remove the door latch **(see illustration)**.

### Installation

7 Place the latch in position, install the screws and tighten them securely.

8 Connect the operating rods to the latch and secure with retaining clips. **Caution:** *Do not close the door until the latch has been properly adjusted* (see below), *otherwise it may not reopen.*

### Adjustment

9 Insert a Torx-head wrench through the elongated hole in the end of the door near the latch.

10 Engage the wrench in the Torx head screw located inside the door latch linkage and loosen it a couple of turns.

11 Push the outside door handle all the way in and release it.

12 Tighten the socket head screw on the door latch linkage and check the door operation

## *Outside handle*

13 Remove the door trim panel (see Section 13). On vehicles equipped with electric windows, close the window before disconnecting the door trim panel electrical connectors.

14 On vehicles with manual windows, install the window crank (without the retaining clip) and roll up the window.

15 On vehicles so equipped, disconnect the central locking electrical connector.

16 Disconnect the operating rod, remove the mounting nuts and withdraw the handle from the door **(see illustration)**.

17 Installation is the reverse of removal.

## *Lock cylinder*

18 Remove the outside door handle (see Steps 13 through 16).

19 Detach the operating rod retaining clip and operating rod from the lock cylinder.

20 Disconnect the electrical connector (if equipped).

21 Using a screwdriver, pry off the lock cylinder retainer and withdraw it from the door or handle.

22 Installation is the reverse of removal.

## 15 Door window glass - removal and installation

### Removal

*Refer to illustration 15.10*

1 Remove the door trim panel (see Section 13).

2 Carefully remove the plastic water shield from the door.

3 Remove the inner belt weatherstrip from the window sill.

4 If you are removing the rear door glass, remove the window glass lower rear run channel.

5 On vehicles equipped with power windows, remove the switch from the door trim panel and connect it to the wiring harness. This will allow you to move the window as necessary.

6 On vehicles with manual windows, install the window crank (without the retaining clip). This will allow you to move the window as necessary.

7 Lower the window for access to the attaching bolts.

8 Loosen the bolts that secure the glass to the regulator lift plates.

9 Detach the glass from the regulator.

10 Lift the glass up while tilting it down at the front and maneuver the glass out of the opening in the top of the door **(see illustration)**.

### Installation

11 Installation is the reverse of removal. Make sure there is enough adhesive remaining on the water shield to seal properly; replace adhesive if necessary.

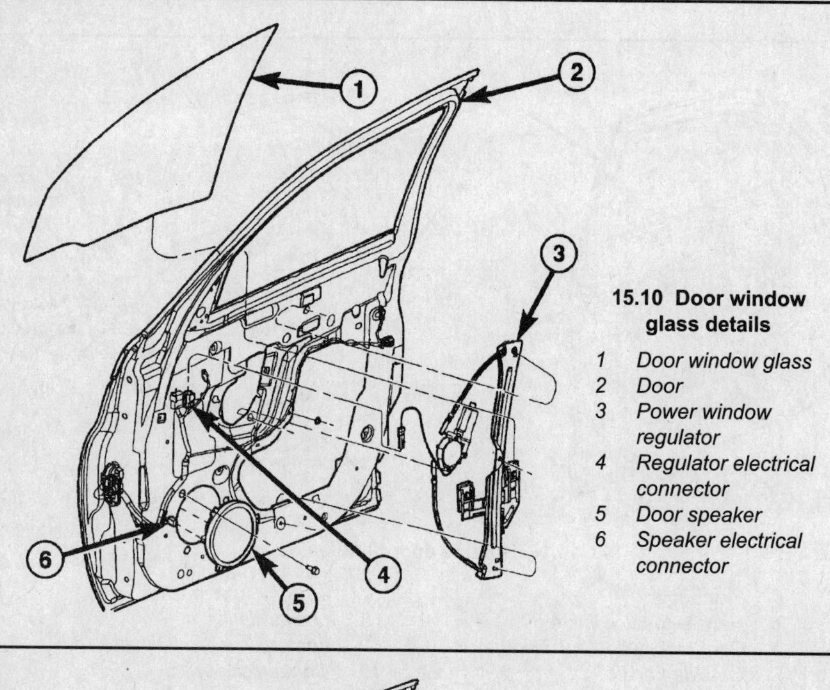


**15.10 Door window glass details**

1 *Door window glass*
2 *Door*
3 *Power window regulator*
4 *Regulator electrical connector*
5 *Door speaker*
6 *Speaker electrical connector*

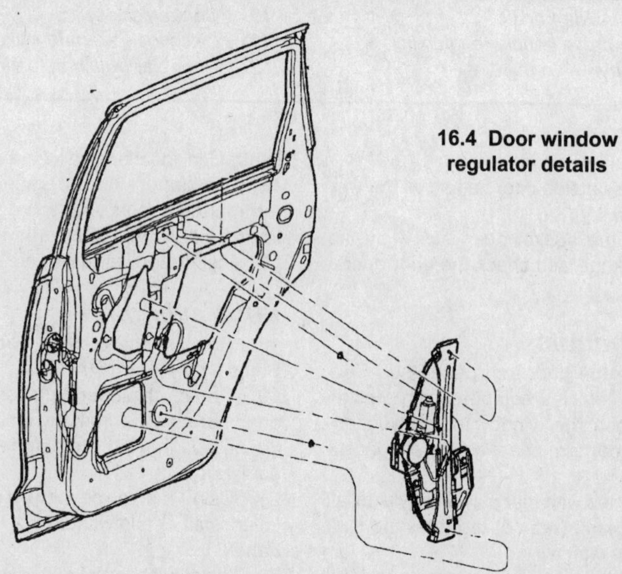

**16.4 Door window regulator details**

## 16 Door window regulator - removal and installation

*Refer to illustration 16.4*

**Warning:** *On power window models, do not remove the motor from the regulator assembly without first clamping the sector gear to the mounting plate or serious personal injury may result.*

**Note:** *This procedure applies to both the front and rear doors and both manual and power operated windows.*

1 Remove the door trim panel (see Section 13).

2 Remove the door window glass (see Section 15).

3 On power window models, disconnect window motor electrical connector.

4 Remove the bolts securing the window regulator to the inner door panel **(see illustration)**.

5 Slide the window regulator rearward, then rotate forward end of the lower roller channel through the access hole in the door and remove the regulator.

6 Installation is the reverse of removal.

## 17 Door - removal and installation

**Note:** *This procedure applies to both the front and rear doors.*

**Note:** *The door is heavy and somewhat awkward to remove and install - at least two people should perform this procedure.*

### Removal

*Refer to illustrations 17.2 and 17.4*

1 Open the door and disconnect the wiring harness connector at the door pillar.

2 Remove the bolts and detach the check strap from the door pillar **(see illustration)**. Detach the electrical connection.

3 Place a jack or jackstands under the door or have an assistant on hand to support

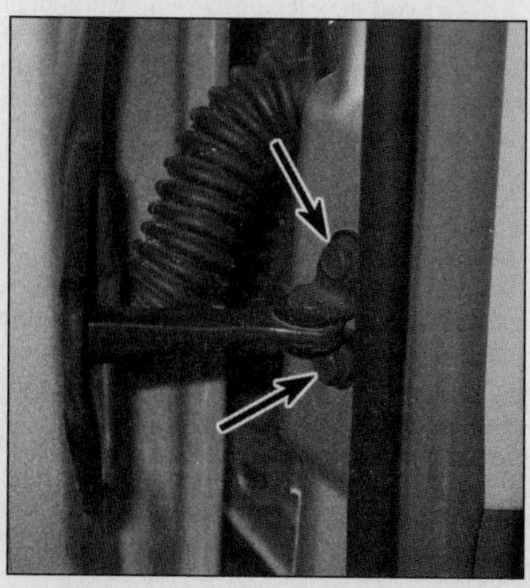

**17.2 Remove the bolts and detach the check strap**

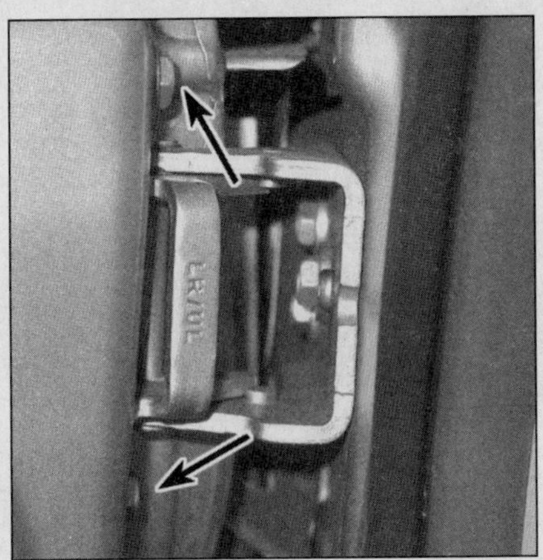

**17.4 After marking the hinge location, remove the two door retaining bolts**

**18.2a Remove the Torx head bolt from the lower . . .**

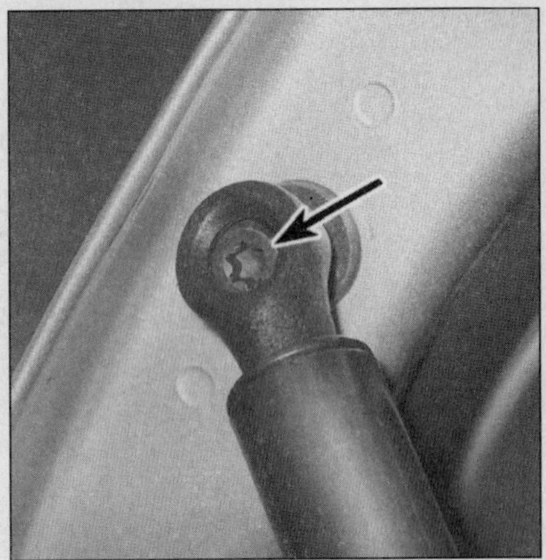

**18.2b . . . and the upper end of the support strut**

it when the hinge pins or bolts are removed. **Note:** *If you use a jack or jackstands, place a rag and a piece of wood between it and the door to protect the door's painted surfaces.*

4 Mark around the hinges, then remove the bolts and remove the door **(see illustration)**.

### Installation

5 Installation is the reverse of removal. Install the bolts and tighten them securely. Check door fit and adjust if necessary by loosening the hinge bolts. **Note:** *Place scribe marks around the hinges before loosening the bolts to maintain a reference point.*

## 18 Liftgate, outside handle, latch and lock cylinder - removal, installation and adjustment

### Liftgate

*Refer to illustrations 18.2a, 18.2b and 18.4*

**Note:** *The liftgate is heavy and somewhat awkward to remove and install - at least two people should perform this procedure.*

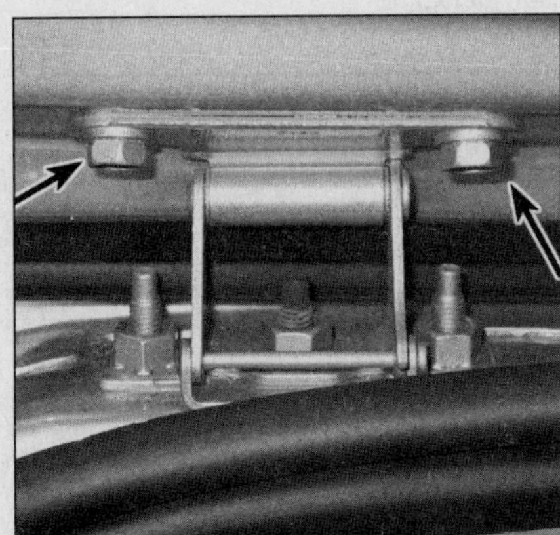

**18.4 Mark the hinge location and remove the liftgate bolts**

1 Disconnect the negative cable from the negative terminal of the battery (see Chapter 5).

2 Open the liftgate and support it securely. Remove the bolts and detach the liftgate struts **(see illustrations)**.

3 Disconnect the wire harness between the liftgate and the body.

4 Mark the relationship of the hinges to the liftgate, then unbolt them **(see illustration)**.

5 Installation is the reverse of removal.

### Adjustment

6 If the liftgate requires adjustment to close properly, there are four adjustments available. To move the liftgate forward, rearward or vertically in relation to the body, loosen the bolts that attach the hinges to the body and lightly tap the hinges with a small plastic hammer in the direction you want to move the liftgate, then tighten the bolts securely. **Note:** *To access the hinge-to-body bolts, the rear pillar trim panels must be removed and the rear portion of the headliner pulled down.* To adjust the liftgate to the left or right, or up or down, in relation to the body, loosen the hinge bolts on the liftgate, carefully move the liftgate the direction you want to go, then tighten the bolts securely. To adjust the liftgate striker, loosen the striker screws and carefully tap the striker with a small plastic hammer until the liftgate lock and the striker are engaging properly, then tighten the striker screws securely. The liftgate-to-body gap is adjusted by loosening the mounting bolts and moving the rubber stoppers in increments until the proper gap is achieved.

### Outside handle

*Refer to illustrations 18.7, 18.8 and 18.9*

7 Remove the liftgate trim panel **(see illustration)**.

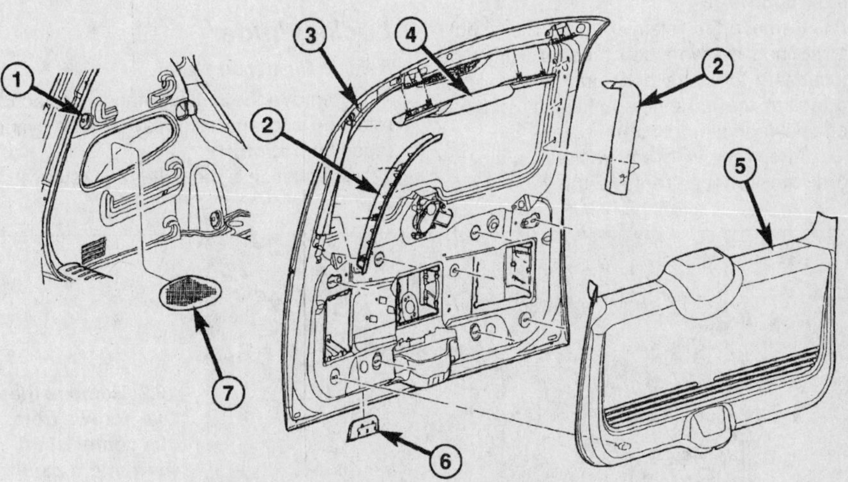


**18.7 Liftgate trim panel details**

| | | | | | |
|---|---|---|---|---|---|
| 1 | *Tiedown opening* | 4 | *Brake light cover* | 7 | *Storage compartment cover* |
| 2 | *Liftgate edge trim* | 5 | *Trim panel* | | |
| 3 | *Liftgate* | 6 | *Pull handle* | | |

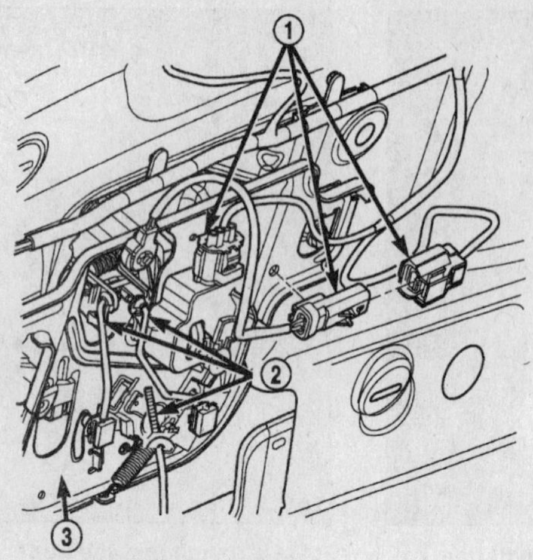


**18.8 Disconnect the linkage and connectors from the liftgate control assembly**

1 *Electrical connectors*
2 *Linkage*
3 *Outside handle control assembly*

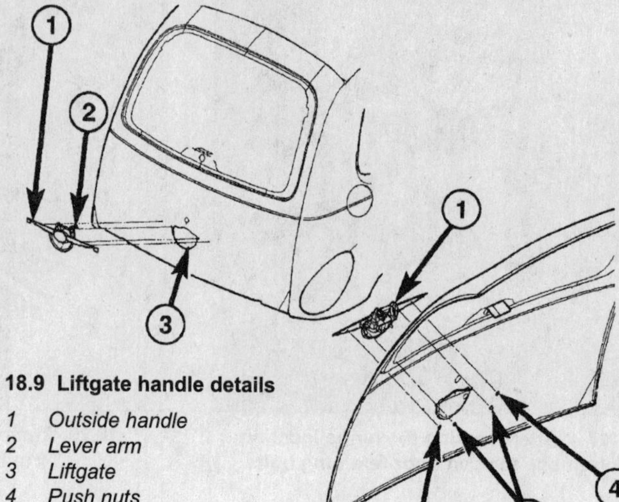


**18.9 Liftgate handle details**

1 *Outside handle*
2 *Lever arm*
3 *Liftgate*
4 *Push nuts*
5 *Nuts*

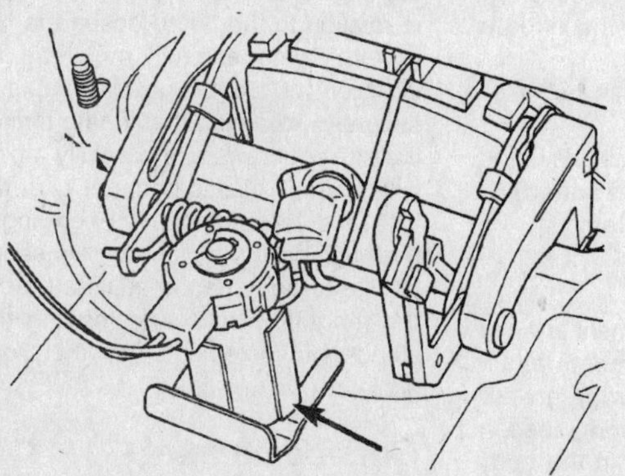
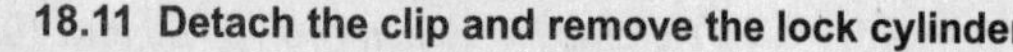

**18.11 Detach the clip and remove the lock cylinder**

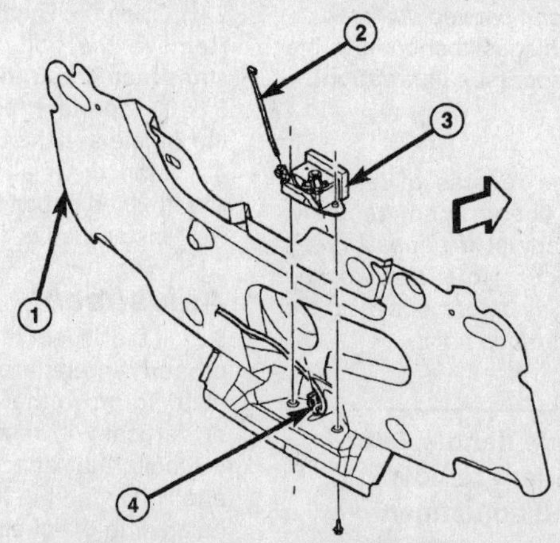


**18.13 Disconnect the linkage and connectors from the tailgate latch assembly**

1 *Liftgate inner panel*
2 *Latch link rod*
3 *Latch*
4 *Electrical connector*

8 Disconnect the linkage and electrical connectors from the control assembly **(see illustration)**.

9 Remove the retaining nuts. The handle is retained by two-sided tape so it may be necessary to use a heat gun or hair dryer to loosen the adhesive sufficiently to allow removal **(see illustration)**.

10 After removing any residual adhesive from the surface, remove the tape cover, press the new handle into place and install the retaining nuts.

## Lock cylinder

*Refer to illustration 18.11*

11 Remove the outside handle, detach the retaining clip and remove the lock cylinder **(see illustration)**.

12 Installation is the reverse of removal.

## Latch

*Refer to illustration 18.13*

13 Detach the link rod from the latch **(see illustration)**.

14 Remove the attaching screws and detach the latch assembly from the liftgate trim panel.

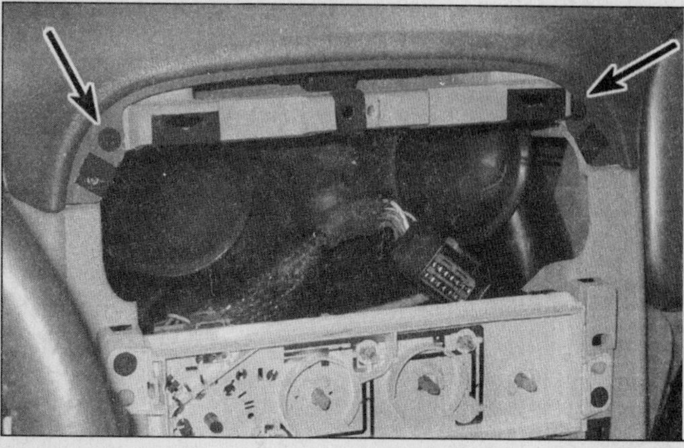

**19.2 Remove the two screws from the center of the instrument panel top cover**

## 19 Instrument panel top cover - removal and installation

**Warning:** *These models have airbags. Always disable the airbag system before working in the vicinity of any airbag system components to avoid the possibility of accidental deployment of the airbag, which could cause personal injury* (see Chapter 12).

**Caution:** *The cover can be easily scratched or bent, take care in removing the top cover to avoid damage.*

## Removal

*Refer to illustrations 19.2 and 19.3*

**Note:** *On later models, instrument panel top*

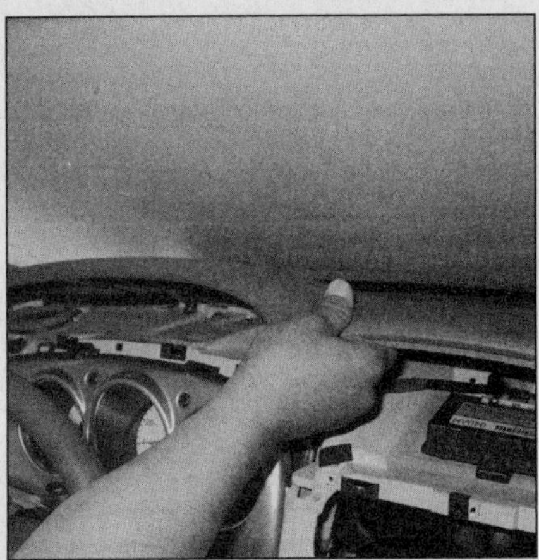

19.3 After removing the retaining screws, detach the instrument panel top cover and pull it rearward

*covers do not have screws in the instrument cluster area. They are secured only with clips.*

1 Disconnect the cable from the negative terminal of the battery (see Chapter 5). Carefully pry off the A-pillar trim pieces end caps (see Section 20).

2 Remove the dashboard center trim bezel for access (see Section 20) and remove the two screws retaining the cover **(see illustration)**.

3 Using a screwdriver with a taped tip to avoid damage, disengage the clips along the rear edge of the top cover starting from the right side and proceeding to the left. To avoid damage, do not pry on the top cover during removal **(see illustration)**.

4 Lift the rear edge and slide the top cover rearward to disengage the clips, then remove the top cover.

### Installation

5 Installation is the reverse of removal, but be sure to engage the top cover retaining tabs into their slots, then push the cover forward until they snap into place.

## 20 Dashboard trim panels - removal and installation

**Warning:** *These models have airbags. Always disable the airbag system before working in the vicinity of any airbag system components to avoid the possibility of accidental deployment of the airbag, which could cause personal injury* (see Chapter 12).

**Caution:** *The following trim covers can be easily scratched, take care in removing them to avoid damage.*

### A-pillar trim pieces

*Refer to illustration 20.1*

1 Use a screwdriver to carefully detach the left and right A-pillar trim pieces **(see illustration)**.

2 Installation is the reverse of removal.

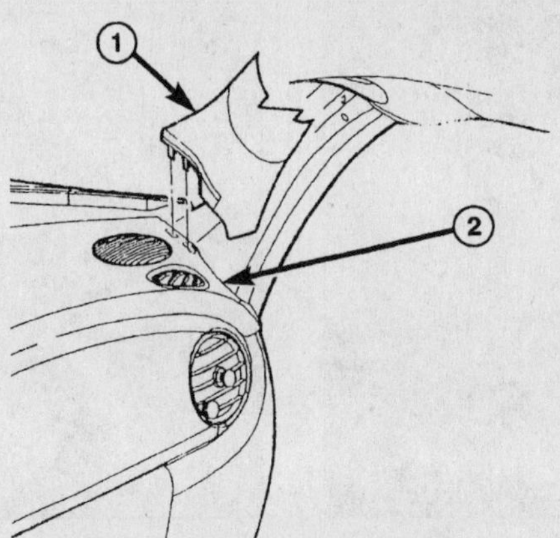


20.1 A-pillar trim piece details

1 *A-pillar trim piece*
2 *Instrument panel*

### Dashboard end covers

*Refer to illustrations 20.3 and 20.4*

3 On the left side end cover remove the mirror switch (see Chapter 12) and the knee bolster (see below), then remove the bolts and detach the cover **(see illustration)**.

4 On the right side end cover, remove the glove box (see Step 12), then remove the retaining screws and lower the cover from the dashboard **(see illustration)**.

5 Installation is the reverse of removal.

### Knee bolster

*Refer to illustration 20.6*

6 Grasp the knee bolster securely at the top, pull back sharply to detach it and rotate it out of the dashboard **(see illustration)**.

7 Installation is the reverse of removal.

### Center bezel

*Refer to illustration 20.10*

8 Pull off the heater/air conditioning unit control knobs.

9 Remove the power window switch (see Chapter 12).

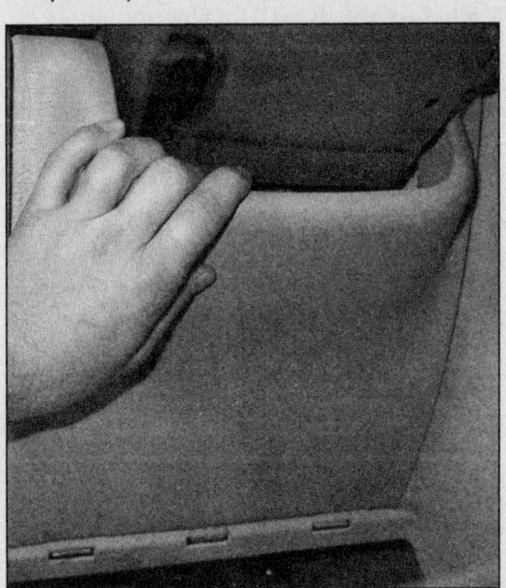

20.6 Grasp the knee bolster securely and pull out sharply to detach it

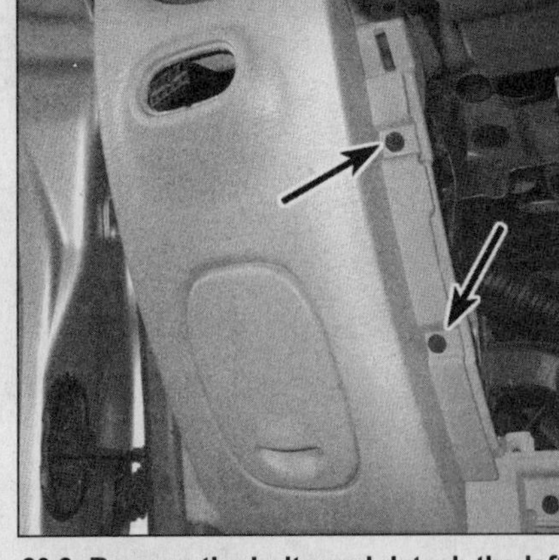

20.3 Remove the bolts and detach the left side dashboard end cover

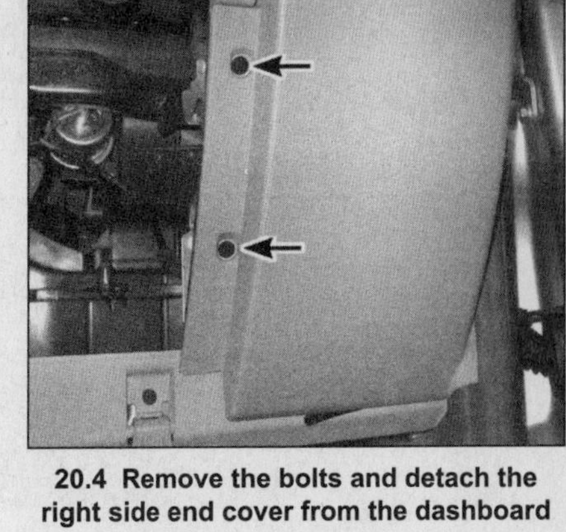

20.4 Remove the bolts and detach the right side end cover from the dashboard

10 Remove the retaining screw(s) and carefully pry around the edges to detach the bezel **(see illustration)**. **Note:** *On some models, the retaining screws are accessible through the vents.*

11 Installation is the reverse of removal.

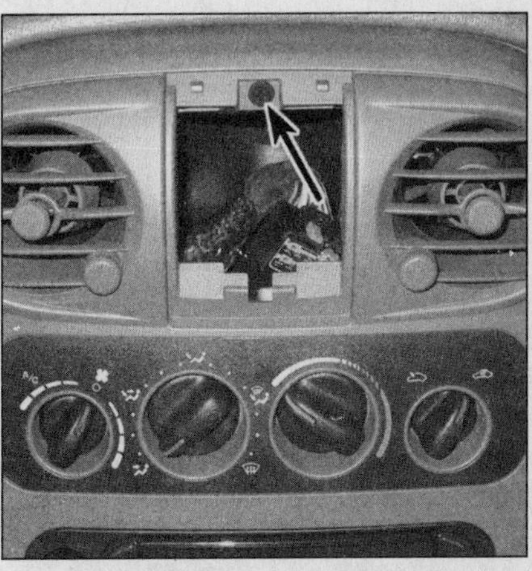

20.10 To remove the center bezel, remove the screw and pry the bezel out (later models have two screws, one inside each vent)

20.12 Lower the glove box until the hooks can be detached from the dashboard

21.4 Pull the instrument cluster bezel straight out to remove it

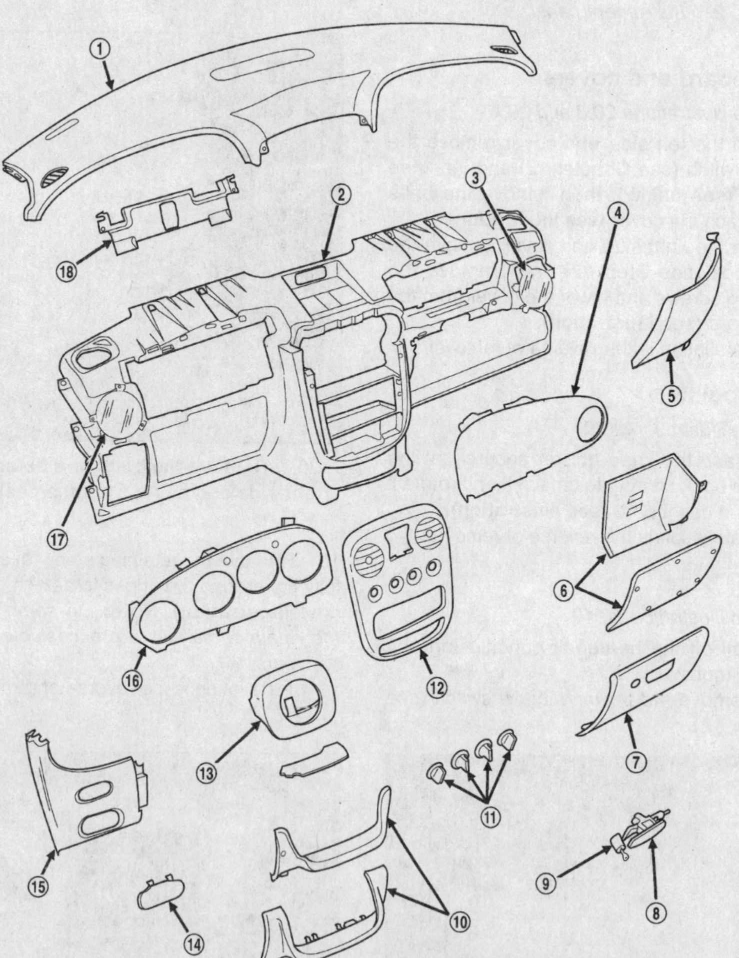

22.3 Instrument panel details

1 Top cover
2 Instrument panel
3 Heater/air conditioning outlet housing
4 Passenger airbag and airbag module
5 Dashboard end cover
6 Glove box
7 Glove box door
8 Glove box latch
9 Glove box lock cylinder
10 Knee bolster
11 Control knobs
12 Center bezel
13 Steering column covers
14 Fuse block cover
15 Dashboard end cover
16 Cluster bezel
17 Heater/air conditioning outlet housing
18 Instrument cluster support panel

### Glove box

*Refer to illustration 20.12*

12 Open the glove box, squeeze the sides in and lower the glove box door all the way down until the hooks at the base can be rotated out of the dashboard **(see illustration)**.

13 Installation is the reverse of removal.

## 21 Instrument cluster bezel - removal and installation

*Refer to illustration 21.4*

**Warning:** *These models have airbags. Always disable the airbag system before working in the vicinity of any airbag system components to avoid the possibility of accidental deployment of the airbag, which could cause personal injury (see Chapter 12).*

1 Disconnect the cable from the negative terminal of the battery (see Chapter 5).

2 Remove the instrument panel top cover (see Section 19).

3 Remove the left end cover, knee bolster and center bezel from the dashboard (see Section 20).

4 Grasp the sides of the instrument cluster bezel securely and pull it straight out to detach it from the dashboard **(see illustration)**.

5 Disconnect the turn signal bulbs and remove the bezel from the vehicle.

6 Installation is the reverse of removal.

## 22 Instrument panel - removal and installation

**Warning:** *These models have airbags. Always disable the airbag system before working in the vicinity of any airbag system components to avoid the possibility of accidental deployment of the airbag, which could cause personal injury (see Chapter 12).*

**Note:** *It is not necessary, but it is suggested to remove both front seats to allow additional working space and lessen the chance of damage to the seats during this procedure.*

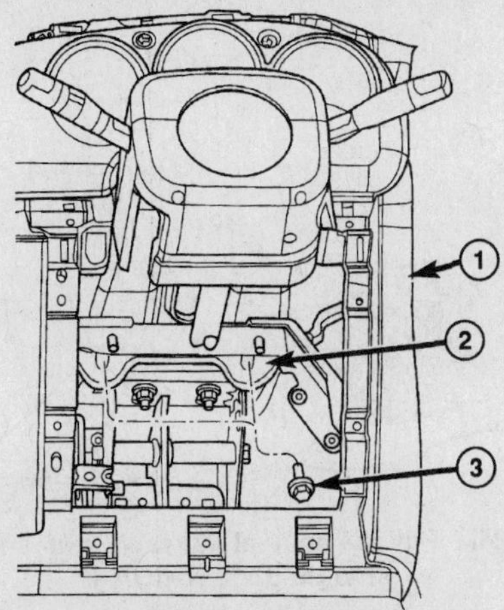


22.11 Remove the brake pedal support/ instrument panel support bolts

1 Instrument panel
2 Floor pan bracket
3 Bolts

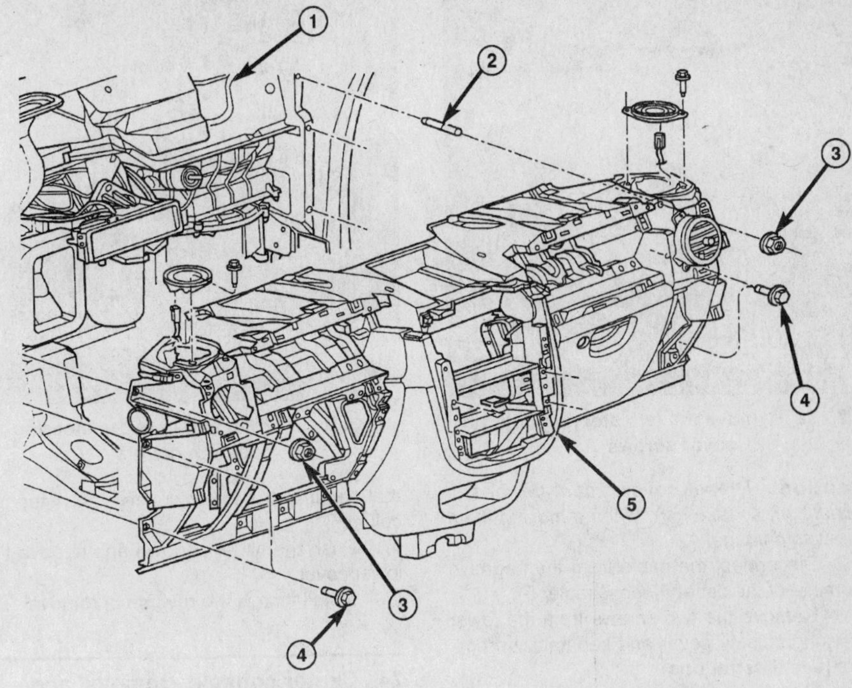


22.13 Remove the bolts and nut retaining the instrument panel

1 Windshield cowl
2 Instrument panel-to-cowl stud
3 Instrument panel-to-cowl nut
4 Instrument panel retaining bolts
5 Instrument panel

## Removal

*Refer to illustrations 22.3, 22.11, 22.13 and 22.14*

1 Disconnect the cable from the negative terminal of the battery (see Chapter 5).

2 Remove the instrument panel top cover (see Section 19).

3 Refer to Section 20 and remove the dashboard trim panels and glove box **(see illustration)**.

4 Remove the instrument cluster bezel (see Section 21).

5 Remove the steering column covers (see Section 23).

6 Remove the heater/air conditioning unit.

7 Remove the floor console (see Section 24).

8 Disconnect the electrical connectors for the ignition switch, turn signal switch and airbag clockspring.

9 Lock the steering wheel in the straight ahead position and remove the steering column pinch bolt at the base of the column (see Chapter 10).

10 Remove the four retaining nuts, pull the steering column assembly rearward and remove it from the vehicle.

11 Remove the brake pedal/instrument panel support bracket bolts **(see illustration)**.

12 Disconnect the instrument panel left side electrical connectors.

13 Remove the instrument panel-to-A pillar bolts/nuts **(see illustration)**.

14 Remove the bolts attaching the instrument panel fence line to the cowl **(see illustration)**.

15 Lift up the instrument panel, pull rearward and withdraw it from the vehicle.

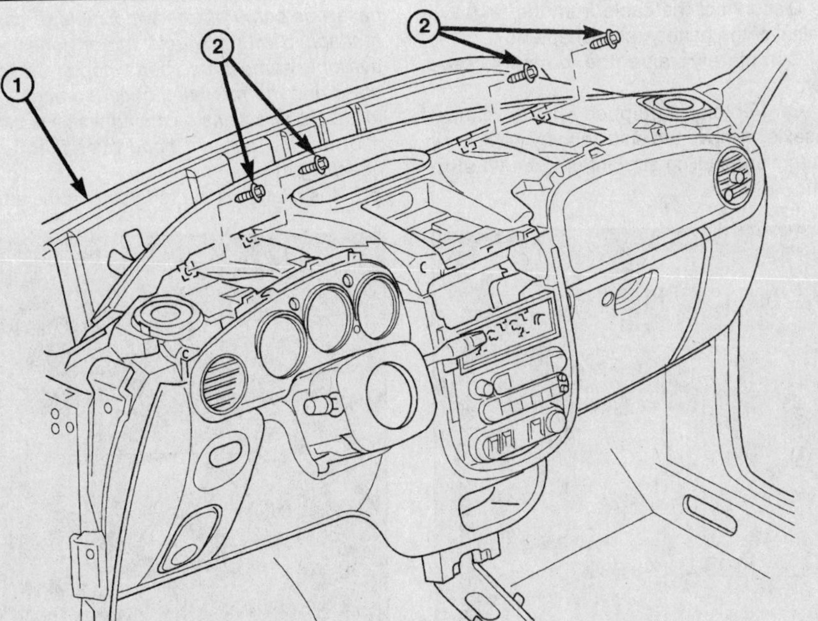


22.14 Remove the four bolts retaining the instrument panel fence line to the cowl

1 Windshield cowl
2 Instrument panel fence line-to-cowl bolts

## Installation

16 Installation is the reverse of removal.

## 23 Steering column covers - removal and installation

*Refer to illustrations 23.3a and 23.3b*

**Warning:** *These models have airbags. Always disable the airbag system before working in the vicinity of any airbag system components to avoid the possibility of accidental deployment of the airbag, which could cause personal injury (see Chapter 12).*

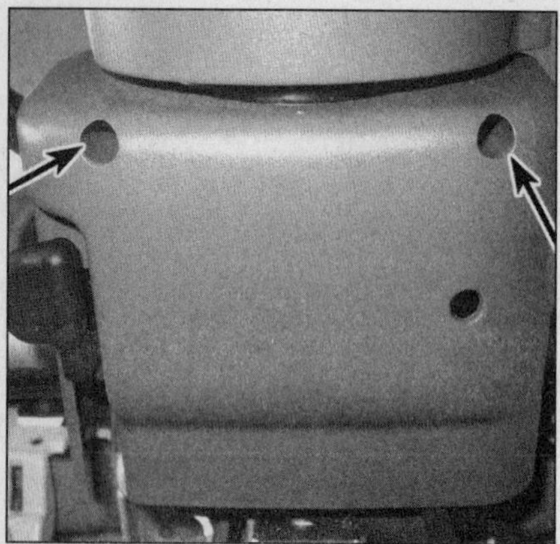

23.3a Remove the two steering column cover screws . . .

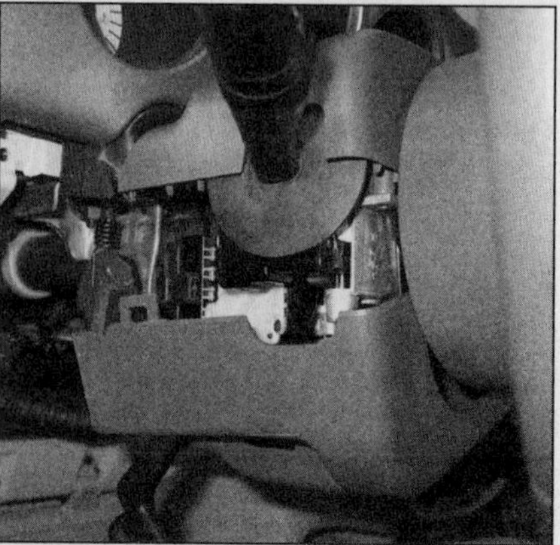

23.3b . . . then separate the steering column covers

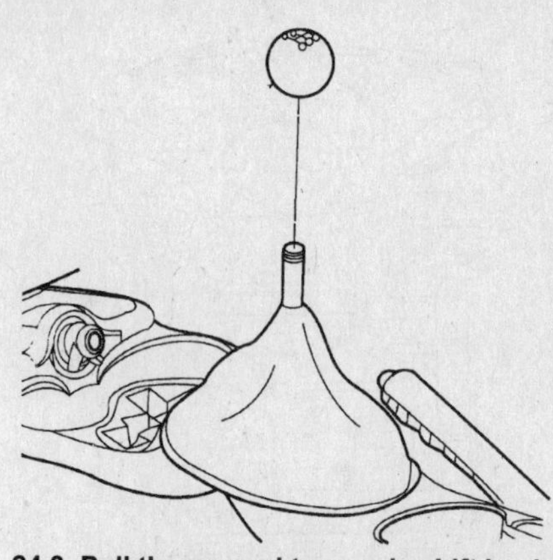

24.3 Pull the manual transaxle shift knob straight up to remove it

**Caution:** *These covers can be easily scratched, so take care when removing them to avoid damage.*

1 Disconnect the cable from the negative terminal of the battery (see Chapter 5).

2 Remove the two screws from the lower steering column cover and separate the covers **(see illustrations)**.

3 On later models, remove the third screw that secures the lower cover to the steering column.

4 Push the tilt lever down and remove the lower cover.

5 Installation is the reverse of removal.

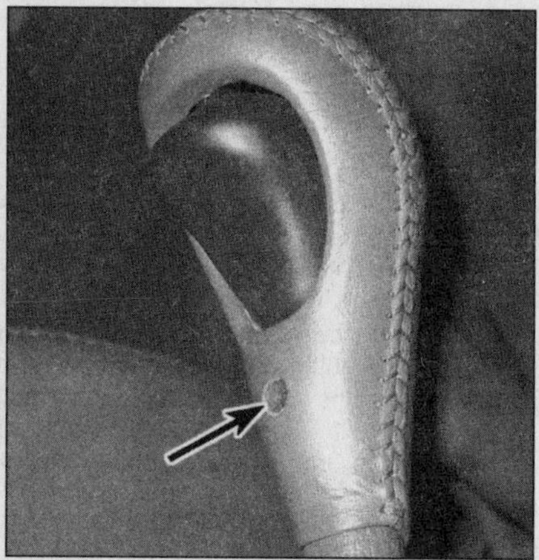

24.4 Remove the set screw and detach the automatic transaxle shift knob

## 24 Center console - removal and installation

*Refer to illustrations 24.3, 24.4, 24.5a and 24.5b*

**Warning:** *These models have airbags. Always disable the airbag system before working in the vicinity of any airbag system components to avoid the possibility of accidental deployment of the airbag, which could cause personal injury (see Chapter 12).*

**Caution:** *The center console can be easily scratched, so take care in removing the assembly to avoid damage.*

1 Disconnect the cable from the negative terminal of the battery (see Chapter 5).

2 Completely raise the parking brake lever.

3 On vehicles equipped with a manual transaxle, remove the shift knob by grasping it securely and pulling straight up **(see illustration)**.

4 On vehicles equipped with an automatic transaxle, remove the set screw and lift the knob off the shift lever **(see illustration)**.

5 Remove the securing screws and detach the console **(see illustrations)**.

6 Maneuver the floor console up and over the shift lever and parking brake handle and remove it from vehicle.

7 Installation is the reverse of removal.

## 25 Mirrors - removal and installation

### *Interior*

*Refer to illustration 25.1*

1 Use a Torx bit to loosen the screw, slide the mirror up and off its mounting base and, if equipped, disconnect the electrical connector **(see illustration)**. **Note:** *If the mounting base has come off the windshield, it can be reattached with a special mirror adhesive kit available at most auto parts stores. Clean the glass and the mounting base thoroughly and follow the directions on the adhesive package, allowing the base to bond overnight before attaching the mirror.*

2 Installation is the reverse of removal.

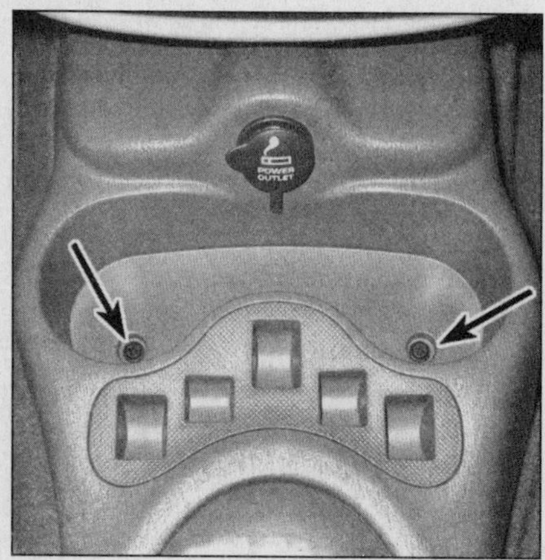



24.5a Remove the screws at the rear . . .

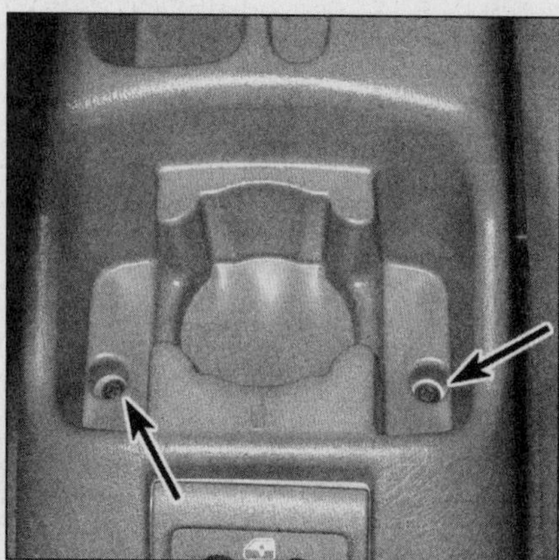

24.5b . . . and front of the console, then lift it out (early model shown; later models have four screws)

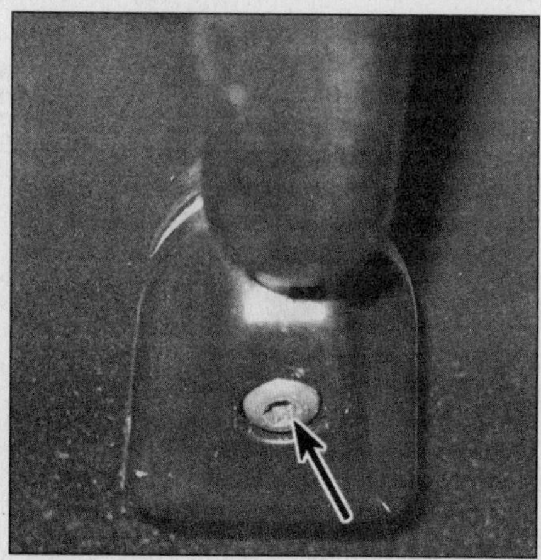

25.1 Loosen the set screw and slide the mirror up and off its base

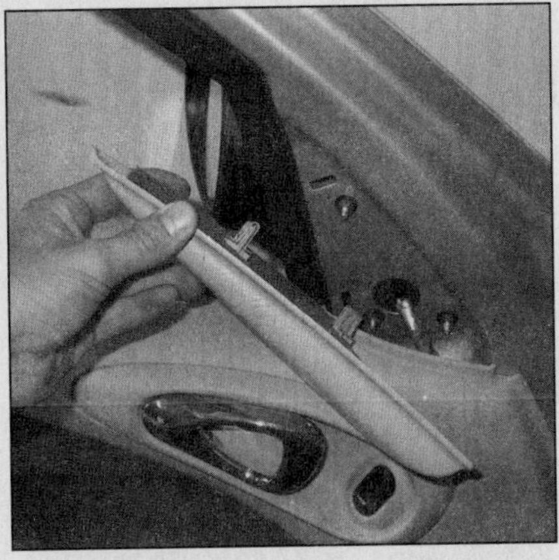
25.3 Remove the exterior mirror cover

25.5 Remove the exterior mirror mounting nuts

26.2a Remove the screws from the right side of the cowl grille screen

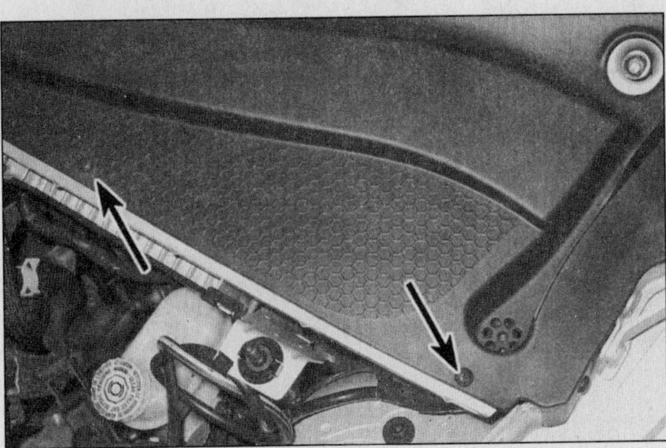
26.2b Locations of the left side cowl grille screen screws

27.1a Remove the rear mounting bolts from the seat first

## Exterior

*Refer to illustrations 25.3 and 25.5*

3 Detach the mirror cover by pulling it straight off **(see illustration)**.

4 On vehicles equipped with power mirrors, detach the mirror electrical connector. **Note:** *If the wiring harness can't be pulled up far enough, the door panel will have to be removed for access to the electrical connector.*

5 Remove the three nuts securing the mirror bezel and remove it from the door **(see illustration)**.

6 Installation is the reverse of removal.

## 26 Cowl grille screen - removal and installation

*Refer to illustration 26.2a and 26.2b*

1 Remove the wiper arms.

2 Remove the retaining screws on each cowl grille screen and lift them from the vehicle **(see illustrations)**.

3 Installation is the reverse of removal.

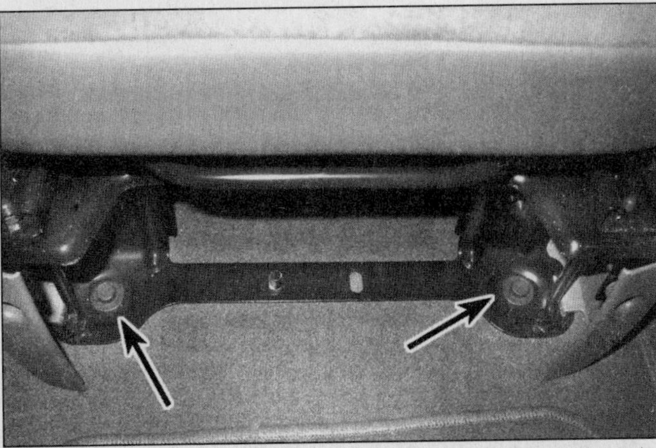
27.1b Move the front seat rearward for access to the front mounting bolts

## 27 Seats - removal and installation

**Warning:** *Some of the models covered by this manual are equipped with side-impact airbags located in the seat backs. Some are also equipped with seat belt pre-tensioners, which are pyrotechnic (explosive) devices which tighten the seat belts during an impact of sufficient force. Be sure to disarm the airbag system when working in the vicinity of any of the airbag system or seat belt pre-tensioner components (see Chapter 12).*

### Front

#### Removal

*Refer to illustrations 27.1a and 27.1b*

1 Move the seat fully forward and remove the seat track rear bolts **(see illustrations)**.

2 Move the seat fully rearward and remove the seat track front bolts.

3 If the vehicle is equipped with power seats, side impact airbags and/or seat belt pre-tensioners, disconnect the electrical connector(s) and lift the seat out of the vehicle.

### Installation

4 Place the seat in position, taking care not to lift it by the head rest, side shield, recliner handle or the adjuster bar.

5 Reconnect the electrical connector(s), install the retaining bolts and tighten them securely.

### *Rear*

*Refer to illustration 27.6*

6 Fold the seat back down and the seat forward, then disengage the seat hooks and lift the seat out of the vehicle **(see illustration)**.

7 Installation is the reverse of removal. Press down firmly over the seat retainers to ensure they are fully engaged in the floorpan.

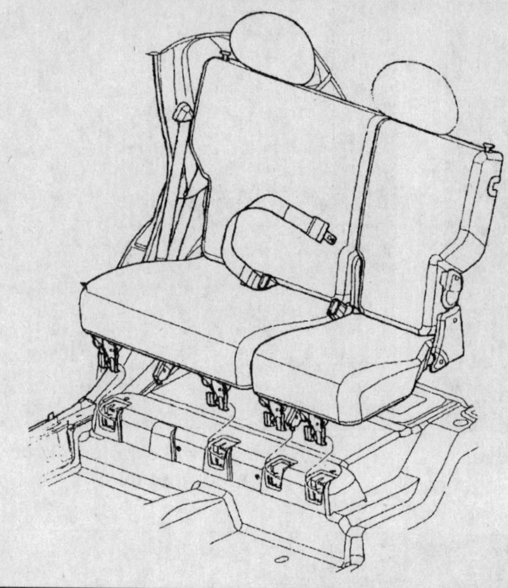

**27.6 Disengage the hooks and lift the rear seat out**

## 28 Convertible top - adjustment

1 Adjustment of the convertible top should be preformed if the top exhibits any of the following problems:

*Canopy wrinkles*
*Hard to pull the canopy down and latch*
*Header doesn't engage properly*

2 To make this adjustment, position the top in the closed and latched position.

3 Two adjustment screws are located inside the trunk, one per side. The right adjustment screw is located in the jack storage door opening. Remove the rubber plugs to access the screws.

4 Mark the position of the adjustment screws, then turn the hex screw counter clockwise to loosen the top, or clockwise to tighten it. **Note:** *The adjustment barrels should not be adjusted more than 0.10 in (2.5 mm).*

5 When the adjustment is complete, cycle the top to the stowed position, then raise it up and latch it in the closed position.

# Chapter 12
# Chassis electrical system

## Contents



### 1 General information

The electrical system is a 12-volt, negative ground type. Power for the lights and all electrical accessories is supplied by a lead/acid-type battery, which is charged by the alternator.

This Chapter covers repair and service procedures for the various electrical components not associated with the engine. Information on the battery, alternator, distributor and starter motor can be found in Chapter 5.

It should be noted that when portions of the electrical system are serviced, the cable should be disconnected from the negative battery terminal (see Chapter 5) to prevent electrical shorts and/or fires.

### 2 Electrical troubleshooting - general information

*Refer to illustrations 2.5a, 2.5b, 2.6 and 2.9*

A typical electrical circuit consists of an electrical component, any switches, relays, motors, fuses, fusible links or circuit breakers related to that component and the wiring and connectors that link the component to both the battery and the chassis. To help you pinpoint an electrical circuit problem, wiring diagrams are included at the end of this Chapter.

Before tackling any troublesome electrical circuit, first study the appropriate wiring diagrams to get a complete understanding of what makes up that individual circuit. Trouble spots, for instance, can often be narrowed down by noting if other components related to the circuit are operating properly. If several components or circuits fail at one time, chances are the problem is in a fuse or ground connection, because several circuits are often routed through the same fuse and ground connections.

Electrical problems usually stem from simple causes, such as loose or corroded connections, a blown fuse, a melted fusible link or a failed relay. Visually inspect the condition of all fuses, wires and connections in a problem circuit before troubleshooting the circuit.

If test equipment and instruments are going to be utilized, use the diagrams to plan ahead of time where you will make the necessary connections in order to accurately pinpoint the trouble spot.

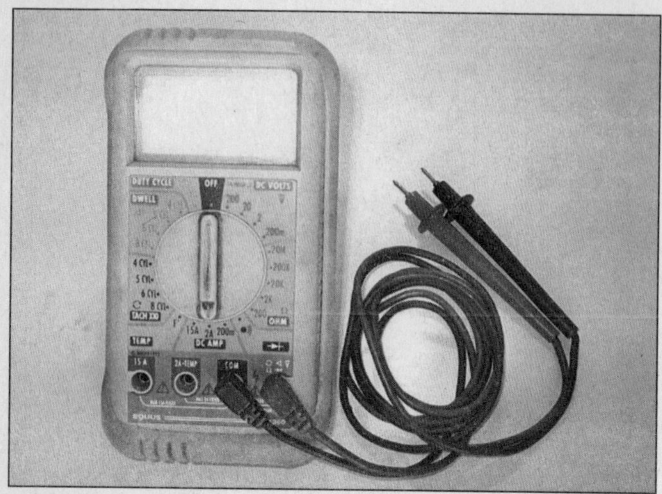

2.5a The most useful tool for electrical troubleshooting is a digital multimeter that can check volts, amps, and test continuity

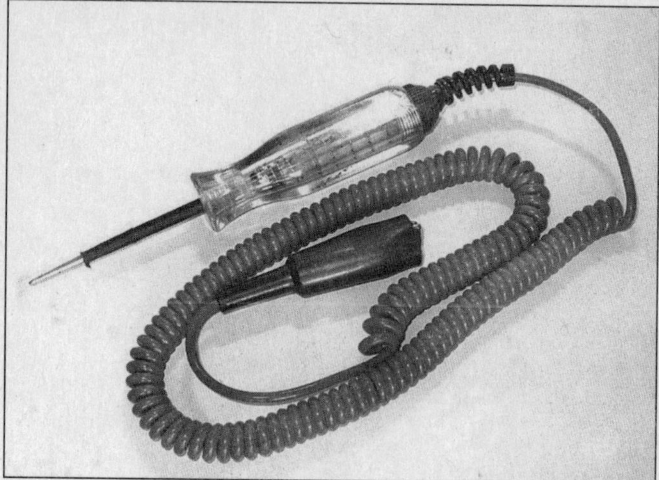

2.5b A simple test light is a very handy tool for testing voltage

The basic tools needed for electrical troubleshooting include a circuit tester or voltmeter (a 12-volt bulb with a set of test leads can also be used), a continuity tester, which includes a bulb, battery and set of test leads, and a jumper wire, preferably with a circuit breaker incorporated, which can be used to bypass electrical components **(see illustrations)**. Before attempting to locate a problem with test instruments, use the wiring diagram(s) to decide where to make the connections.

## Voltage checks

Voltage checks should be performed if a circuit is not functioning properly. Connect one lead of a circuit tester to either the negative battery terminal or a known good ground. Connect the other lead to a connector in the circuit being tested, preferably nearest to the battery or fuse **(see illustration)**. If the bulb of the tester lights, voltage is present, which means that the part of the circuit between the connector and the battery is problem free. Continue checking the rest of the circuit in the same fashion. When you reach a point at which no voltage is present, the problem lies between that point and the last test point with voltage. Most of the time the problem can be traced to a loose connection. **Note:** *Keep in mind that some circuits receive voltage only when the ignition key is in the Accessory or Run position.*

## Finding a short

One method of finding shorts in a live circuit is to remove the fuse and connect a test light in place of the fuse terminals (fabricate two jumper wires with small spade terminals, plug the jumper wires into the fuse box and connect the test light). There should be voltage present in the circuit. Move the suspected wiring harness from side-to-side while watching the test light. If the bulb goes off, there is a short to ground somewhere in that area, probably where the insulation has rubbed through.

## Ground check

Perform a ground test to check whether a component is properly grounded. Disconnect the battery and connect one lead of a continuity tester or multimeter (set to the ohms scale), to a known good ground. Connect the other lead to the wire or ground connection being tested. If the resistance is low (less than 5 ohms), the ground is good. If the bulb on a self-powered test light does not go on, the ground is not good.

## Continuity check

A continuity check is done to determine if there are any breaks in a circuit - if it is passing electricity properly. With the circuit off (no power in the circuit), a self-powered continuity tester or multimeter can be used to check the circuit. Connect the test leads to both ends of the circuit (or to the "power" end and a good ground), and if the test light comes on the circuit is passing current properly **(see illustration)**. If the resistance is low (less than 5 ohms), there is continuity; if the reading is 10,000 ohms or higher, there is a break somewhere in the circuit. The same procedure can be used to test a switch, by connecting the continuity tester to the switch terminals. With the switch turned On, the test light should come on (or low resistance should be indicated on a meter).

## Finding an open circuit

When diagnosing for possible open circuits, it is often difficult to locate them by sight because the connectors hide oxidation or terminal misalignment. Merely wiggling a connector on a sensor or in the wiring harness may correct the open circuit condition. Remember this when an open circuit is indicated when troubleshooting a circuit. Intermittent problems may also be caused by oxidized or loose connections.

Electrical troubleshooting is simple if you keep in mind that all electrical circuits are basically electricity running from the battery, through the wires, switches, relays, fuses and fusible links to each electrical component (light bulb, motor, etc.) and to ground, from which it is passed back to the battery. Any electrical problem is an interruption in the flow of electricity to and from the battery.

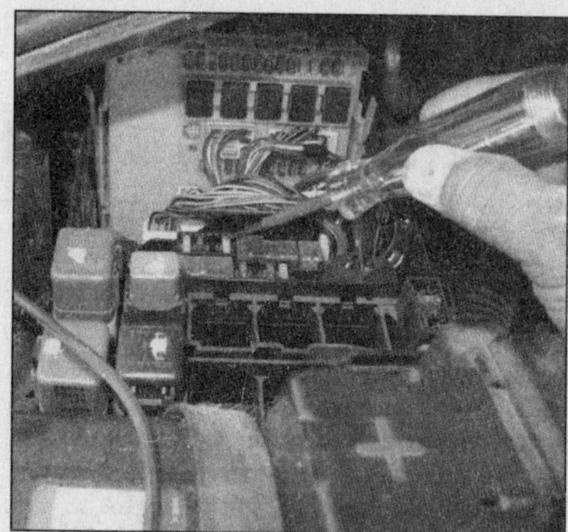

2.6 In use, a basic test light's lead is clipped to a known good ground, then the pointed probe can test connectors, wires or electrical sockets - if the bulb lights, the circuit being tested has battery voltage

## Connectors

Most electrical connections on these vehicles are made with multiwire plastic connectors. The mating halves of many connectors are secured with locking clips molded into the plastic connector shells. The mating halves of large connectors, such as some of those under the instrument panel, are held together by a bolt through the center of the connector.

To separate a connector with locking clips, use a small screwdriver to pry the clips apart carefully, then separate the connector halves. Pull only on the shell, never pull on the wiring harness as you may damage the individual wires and terminals inside the connectors. Look at the connector closely before trying to separate the halves. Often the

2.9 With a multimeter set to the ohms scale, resistance can be checked across two terminals - when checking for continuity, a low reading indicates continuity, a high reading or infinity indicates lack of continuity

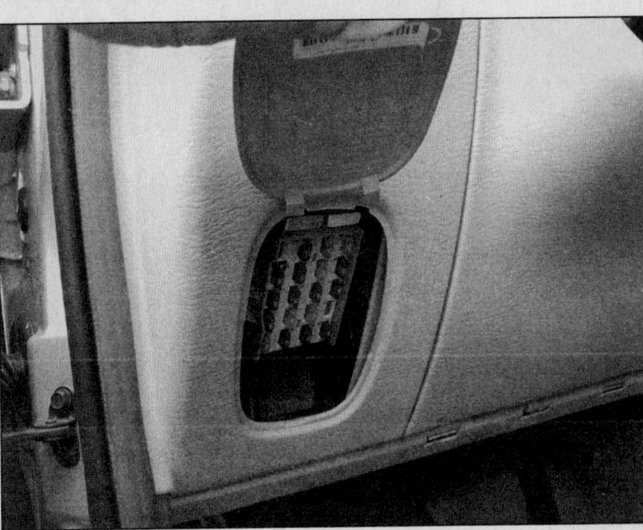

3.1a The interior fuse box is located under a cover on the left end of the instrument panel

locking clips are engaged in a way that is not immediately clear. Additionally, many connectors have more than one set of clips.

Each pair of connector terminals has a male half and a female half. When you look at the end view of a connector in a diagram, be sure to understand whether the view shows the harness side or the component side of the connector. Connector halves are mirror images of each other, and a terminal shown on the right side end-view of one half will be on the left side end view of the other half.

## 3 Fuses and fusible links - general information

### Fuses

*Refer to illustrations 3.1a, 3.1b and 3.3*

The electrical circuits of the vehicle are protected by a combination of fuses, circuit breakers and fusible links. Fuse blocks are located under the left end of instrument panel and in the engine compartment **(see illustrations)**.

Each of the fuses is designed to protect a specific circuit, and the various circuits are identified on the fuse panel cover.

Miniaturized fuses are employed in the fuse blocks. These compact fuses, with blade terminal design, allow fingertip removal and replacement. If an electrical component fails, always check the fuse first. The best way to check a fuse is with a test light. Check for power at the exposed terminal tips of each fuse. If power is present on one side of the fuse but not the other, the fuse is blown. A blown fuse can also be confirmed by visually inspecting it **(see illustration)**.

Be sure to replace blown fuses with the correct type. Fuses of different ratings are physically interchangeable, but only fuses of the proper rating should be used. Replacing a fuse with one of a higher or lower value than specified is not recommended. Each electrical circuit needs a specific amount of protection. The amperage value of each fuse is molded into the fuse body.

If the replacement fuse immediately fails, don't replace it again until the cause of the problem is isolated and corrected. In most cases, this will be a short circuit in the wiring caused by a broken or deteriorated wire.

### Fusible links

Some circuits are protected by fusible links. The links are used in circuits which are not ordinarily fused, or which carry high current.

Cartridge type fusible links are located in the engine compartment fusible link box and are similar to a large fuse. After disconnecting the negative battery cable, simply unplug and replace a fusible link of the same amperage.

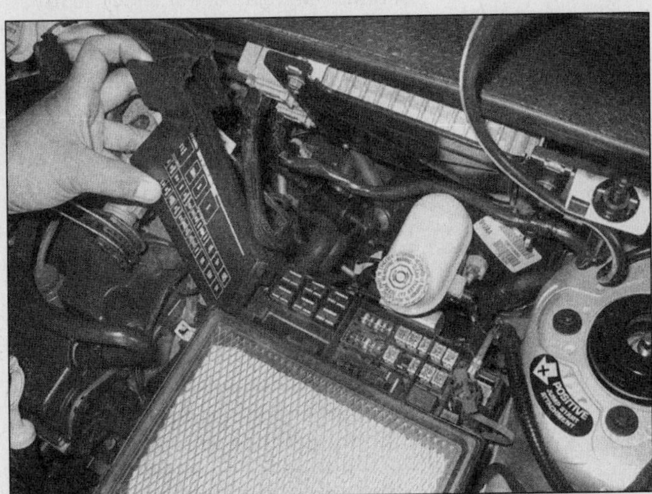

3.1b The main engine compartment fuse/relay box is located behind the air filter housing (remove the filter housing cover for access)

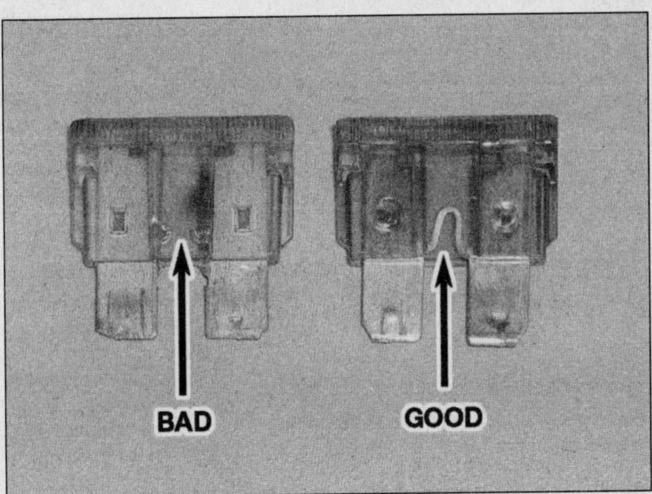


3.3 When a fuse blows, the element between the terminals melts

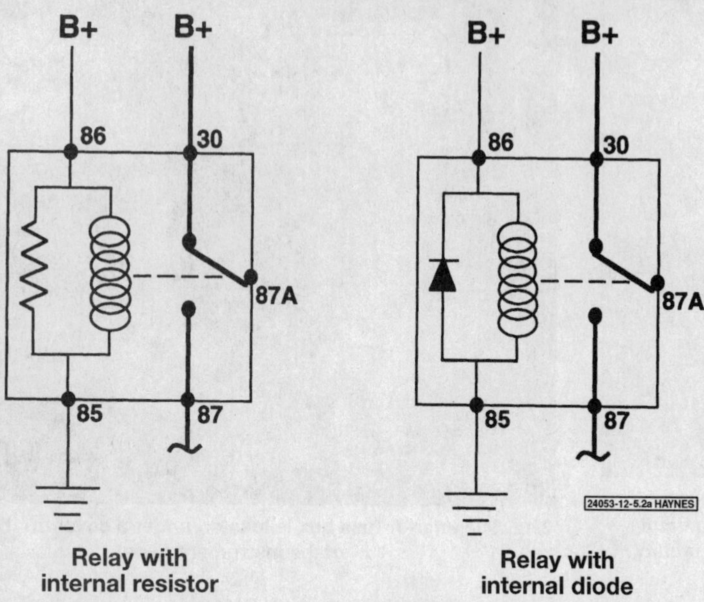


**5.2a Typical ISO relay designs, terminal numbering and circuit connections**

**5.2b Most relays are marked on the outside to easily identify the control circuits and the power circuits - four terminal type shown**

## 4 Circuit breakers - general information

Circuit breakers protect certain circuits, such as the power windows or heated seats. Depending on the vehicle's accessories, there may be one or two circuit breakers, located in the fuse/relay box in the engine compartment **(see illustration 3.1b)**.

Because the circuit breakers reset automatically, an electrical overload in a circuit-breaker-protected system will cause the circuit to fail momentarily, then come back on. If the circuit does not come back on, check it immediately.

For a basic check, pull the circuit breaker up out of its socket on the fuse panel, but just far enough to probe with a voltmeter. The breaker should still contact the sockets.

With the voltmeter negative lead on a good chassis ground, touch each end prong of the circuit breaker with the positive meter probe. There should be battery voltage at each end. If there is battery voltage only at one end, the circuit breaker must be replaced.

Some circuit breakers must be reset manually.

## 5 Relays - general information and testing

### General information

1 Several electrical accessories in the vehicle, such as the fuel injection system, horns, starter, and fog lamps use relays to transmit the electrical signal to the component. Relays use a low-current circuit (the control circuit) to open and close a high-current circuit (the power circuit). If the relay is defective, that component will not operate properly. Most relays are mounted in the engine compartment fuse/relay box, with some specialized relays located above the interior fuse box in the dash **(see illustrations 3.1a and 3.1b)**. If a faulty relay is suspected, it can be removed and tested using the procedure below or by an automotive technician. Defective relays must be replaced as a unit.

### Testing

*Refer to illustrations 5.2a and 5.2b*

2 Most of the relays used in these vehicles are of a type often called "ISO" relays, which refers to the International Standards Organization. The terminals of ISO relays are numbered to indicate their usual circuit connections and functions. There are two basic layouts of terminals on the relays used in the covered vehicles **(see illustrations)**.

3 Refer to the wiring diagram for the circuit to determine the proper connections for the relay you're testing. If you can't determine the correct connection from the wiring diagrams, however, you may be able to determine the test connections from the information that follows.

4 Two of the terminals are the relay control circuit and connect to the relay coil. The other relay terminals are the power circuit. When the relay is energized, the coil creates a magnetic field that closes the larger contacts of the power circuit to provide power to the circuit loads.

5 Terminals 85 and 86 are normally the control circuit. If the relay contains a diode, terminal 86 must be connected to battery positive (B+) voltage and terminal 85 to ground. If the relay contains a resistor, terminals 85 and 86 can be connected in either direction with respect to B+ and ground.

6 Terminal 30 is normally connected to the battery voltage (B+) source for the circuit loads. Terminal 87 is connected to the ground side of the circuit, either directly or through a load. If the relay has several alternate terminals for load or ground connections, they usually are numbered 87A, 87B, 87C, and so on.

7 Use an ohmmeter to check continuity through the relay control coil.

a) *Connect the meter according to the polarity shown in the illustration for one check; then reverse the ohmmeter leads and check continuity in the other direction.*
b) *If the relay contains a resistor, resistance will be indicated on the meter, and should be the same value with the ohmmeter in either direction.*
c) *If the relay contains a diode, resistance should be higher with the ohmmeter in the forward polarity direction than with the meter leads reversed.*
d) *If the ohmmeter shows infinite resistance in both directions, replace the relay.*

8 Remove the relay from the vehicle and use the ohmmeter to check for continuity between the relay power circuit terminals. There should be no continuity between terminal 30 and 87 with the relay de-energized.

9 Connect a fused jumper wire to terminal 86 and the positive battery terminal. Connect another jumper wire between terminal 85 and ground. When the connections are made, the relay should click.

10 With the jumper wires connected, check for continuity between the power circuit terminals. Now, there should be continuity between terminals 30 and 87.

11 If the relay fails any of the above tests, replace it.

## 6 Turn signal and hazard flasher - check and replacement

*Refer to illustration 6.4*

**Warning:** *The models covered by this manual are equipped with Supplemental Restraint*

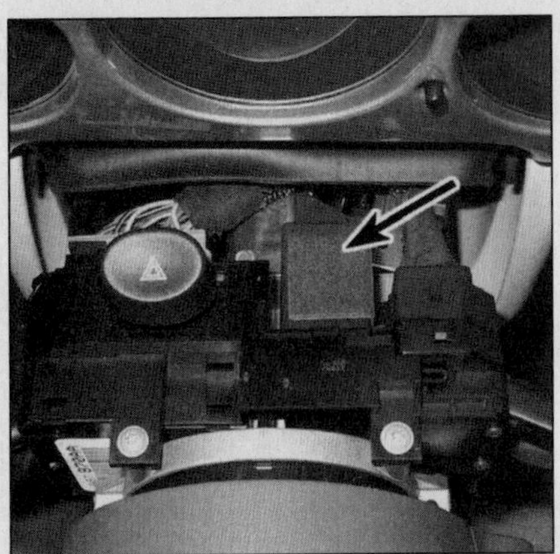

**6.4 The turn signal/hazard flasher unit is located on the steering column and plugged into the multi-function switch**

*Systems (SRS), more commonly known as airbags. Always disable the airbag system before working in the vicinity of any airbag system components to avoid the possibility of accidental deployment of the airbags, which could cause personal injury* (see Section 25).

**Note:** *On 2006 and later year models, instead of using a flasher, the turn signal and hazard warning are controlled by the multi function switch and various modules in the vehicle. If a problem exist, first check all the related fuses and bulbs then if necessary have the vehicle diagnosed by a service professional.*

1 The turn signal and hazard flasher is a single combination unit.

2 When the flasher unit is functioning properly, an audible click can be heard during its operation. If the turn signals fail on one side or the other and the flasher unit does not make its characteristic clicking sound, or if a bulb on one side of the vehicle flashes much faster than normal but the bulb at the other end of the vehicle (on the same side) doesn't light at all, a faulty turn signal bulb may be indicated.

3 If both turn signals fail to blink, the problem may be due to a blown fuse, a faulty flasher unit, a defective switch or a loose or open connection. If a quick check of the fuse box indicates that the turn signal fuse has blown, check the wiring for a short before installing a new fuse.

4 To replace the flasher, remove the steering column covers (see Chapter 11) then unplug the flasher from the back of the multi-function switch **(see illustration)**.

5 Make sure that the replacement unit is identical to the original. Compare the old one to the new one before installing it.

6 Installation is the reverse of removal.

## 7 Steering column switches - replacement

*Refer to illustration 7.5*

**Warning:** *The models covered by this manual are equipped with Supplemental Restraint Systems (SRS), more commonly known as airbags. Always disable the airbag system before working in the vicinity of any airbag system components to avoid the possibility of accidental deployment of the airbags, which could cause personal injury* (see Section 25).

1 The multi-function switch (steering column switches) is located on the steering column. It incorporates the turn signals, the hazard warning, the headlights, the headlight beam select (Hi/Lo), the headlight flasher, the instrument panel dimmer switch, the windshield wiper and windshield washer functions. There are two levers on the multi-function switch. The left side lever controls the signaling and the lighting while the right side controls the wipers and washer system.

2 Disconnect the cable from the negative terminal of the battery (see Chapter 5).

3 Remove the steering column covers (see Chapter 11).

4 Disconnect the electrical connectors from the backside of the switch.

5 Remove the multi-function switch retaining screws **(see illustration)**, then detach the switch from the column.

6 Insert the connectors into the new multi-function switch, pushing in until they are securely locked in place.

7 The remainder of installation is the reverse of removal.

## 8 Ignition switch and key lock cylinder - replacement

**Warning:** *The models covered by this manual are equipped with Supplemental Restraint Systems (SRS), more commonly known as airbags. Always disable the airbag system before working in the vicinity of any airbag system components to avoid the possibility of accidental deployment of the airbags, which could cause personal injury* (see Section 25).

### Ignition switch

*Refer to illustration 8.9*

1 Disconnect the cable from the negative terminal of the battery (see Chapter 5).

2 Remove the instrument cluster bezel (see Chapter 11).

3 Remove the center bezel (see Chapter 11).

4 Remove the lower knee bolster (see Chapter 11).

5 Remove the steering column covers (see Chapter 11).

6 Tilt the steering wheel lever down and slide the upper steering column cover off the steering column. Remove the screws securing the multi-function switch **(see illustration 7.5)** and re-position the switch.

7 Remove the key lock cylinder (see Steps 11 through 13).

8 Disconnect the electrical connector from the ignition switch.

9 Remove the Torx head screw securing the switch to the steering column **(see illustration)**. Depress the retaining tabs, then detach the switch from the steering column.

10 Place the switch in the RUN position, then reinstall the switch, lock cylinder and all other components by reversing the removal procedure.

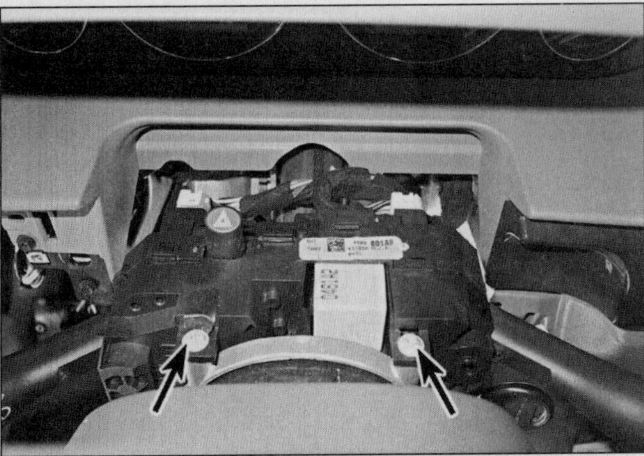

**7.5 Remove the mounting screws and detach the multi-function switch**

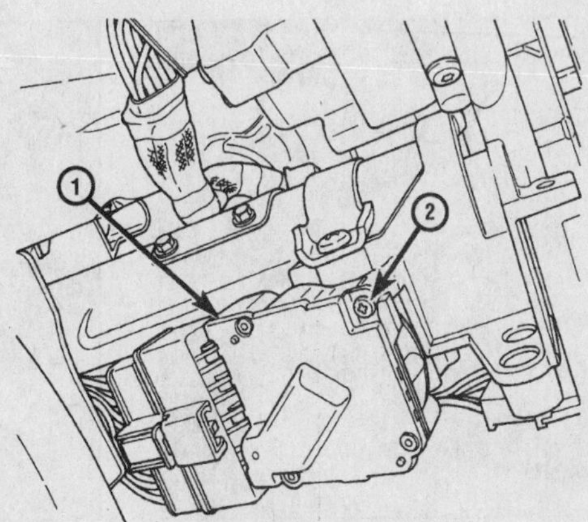


**8.9 Location of the ignition switch (1); it is secured by a single screw (2)**

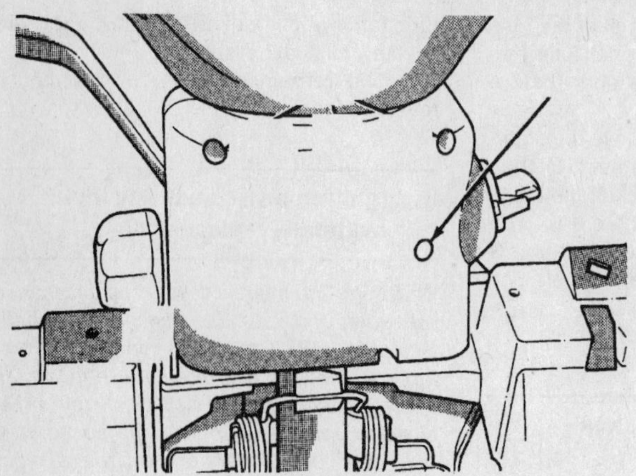

8.13 With the lock cylinder in the RUN position, locate the hole in the steering column cover, insert a small screwdriver and depress the retaining pin, then pull the lock cylinder straight out

8.22 Depress the key cylinder retaining tab and pull key cylinder out of the lock cylinder housing

## Lock cylinder

### 2005 and earlier models

#### Removal

*Refer to illustration 8.13*

11 Disconnect the cable from the negative terminal of the battery (see Chapter 5).

12 Insert the ignition key and turn the switch to the RUN position.

13 Insert a small screwdriver through the access hole in the lower steering column cover and depress the retaining tab, then withdraw the lock cylinder from the housing **(see illustration)**.

#### Installation

14 Make sure the slot in the ignition switch is in the RUN position and insert the lock cylinder into the housing until the retaining tab locates the housing. Check the key operation.

15 The remaining installation steps are the reverse of removal.

### 2006 and later models

*Refer to illustration 8.22*

16 Disconnect the cable from the negative terminal of the battery (see Chapter 5).

17 Remove steering column covers (see Chapter 11).

18 Remove the screws attaching the right multi-function switch to the mounting bracket. Slide the switch away from the clockspring far enough to disengage the slide tab on the bottom of the switch housing from the channel in the mounting bracket. Position the multi-function switch aside.

19 Position steering column to the full down position then turn the key to RUN.

20 Remove screw attaching the ignition key module to the lock cylinder.

21 Unhook the ignition key module retainer fingers from the lock cylinder and position the ignition key module back on the lock cylinder.

22 Insert a small screwdriver or an awl into the slot on the lock cylinder housing. Depress the key cylinder retaining tab and pull key cylinder out of the lock cylinder housing **(see illustration)**.

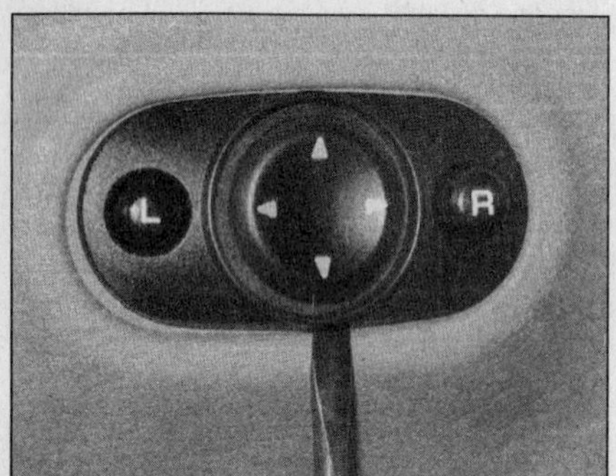


9.1 Use a small screwdriver to carefully pry the power mirror switch from the dashboard

## 9 Instrument panel switches - replacement

**Warning:** *The models covered by this manual are equipped with Supplemental Restraint Systems (SRS), more commonly known as airbags. Always disable the airbag system before working in the vicinity of any airbag system components to avoid the possibility of accidental deployment of the airbag(s), which could cause personal injury* (see Section 25).

### Power mirror control switch

*Refer to illustrations 9.1 and 9.2*

1 Carefully pry the switch assembly from the instrument panel **(see illustration)**.

2 Disconnect the electrical connector and remove the switch **(see illustration)**.

3 Installation is the reverse of the removal procedure.

9.2 Disengage the tabs and disconnect the power mirror switch electrical connector

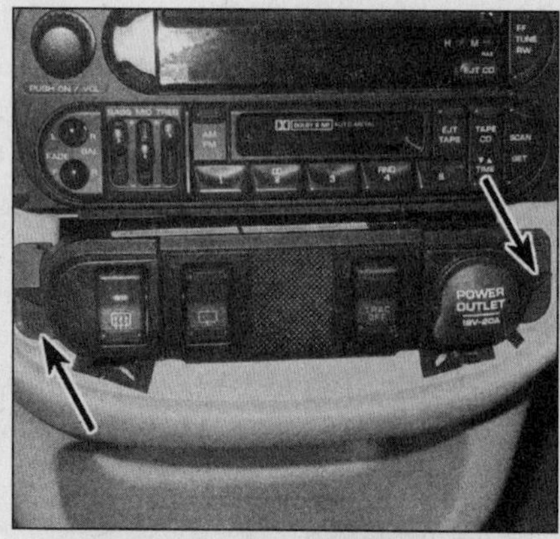


9.6 Remove the switch bezel retaining screws

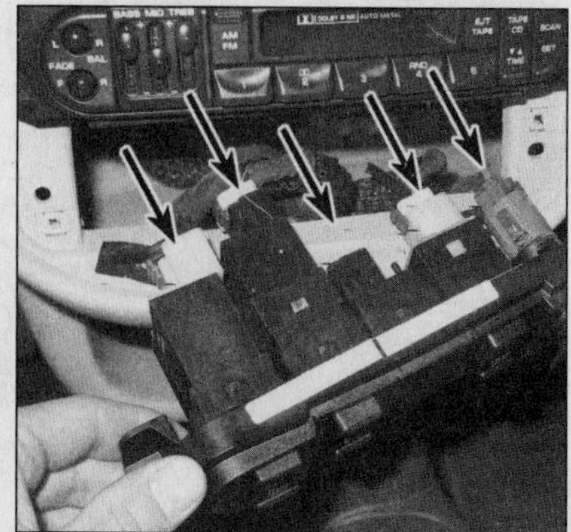

9.7 Pull the switch bezel out and disconnect the electrical connectors

9.10 Pry the front power window switch from the dashboard

9.11 Disconnect the front power window switch electrical connector

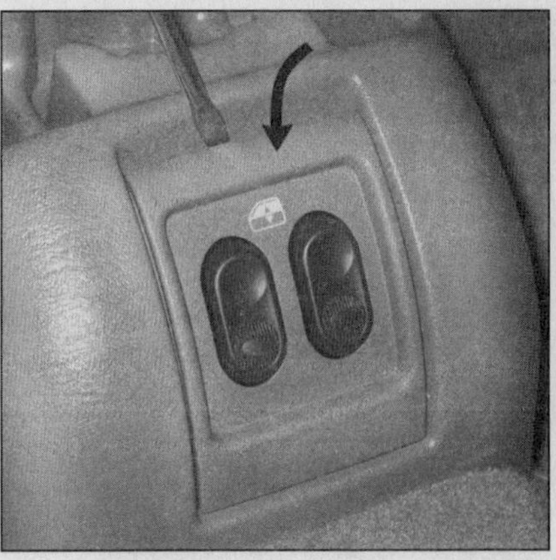

9.13 Detach the power window switch assembly from the center console using a flat bladed screwdriver

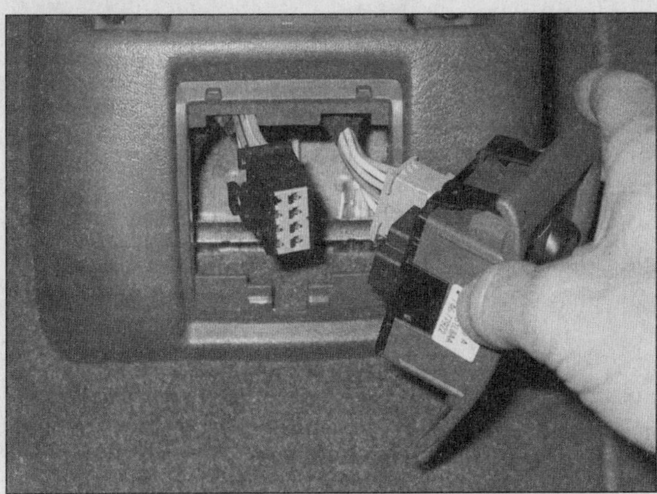

9.14 Pry out the power window switch and disconnect the electrical connectors

10.3 Remove the instrument cluster mounting screws

## Accessory bezel switches

*Refer to illustrations 9.6 and 9.7*

4 The rear window defogger, wiper/washer and traction control switches are located in the switch bezel in the dashboard. They can all be easily replaced once the switch bezel is removed.

5 Remove the center bezel (see Chapter 11).

6 Remove the screws and detach the switch bezel from the dashboard **(see illustration)**.

7 Disconnect the electrical connectors and remove the switch bezel housing **(see illustration)**.

8 To remove a switch from the bezel housing pull the retaining clips out and slide the switch out.

9 Installation is the reverse of the removal procedure.

## Power window control switches

### Front

*Refer to illustrations 9.10 and 9.11*

10 Carefully pry the switch assembly from the dashboard **(see illustration)**.

11 Disconnect the electrical connector and remove the switch **(see illustration)**.

12 Installation is the reverse of the removal procedure.

### Rear

*Refer to illustrations 9.13 and 9.14*

13 Carefully pry the switch assembly from the center console **(see illustration)**.

14 Disconnect the electrical connector and remove the switch **(see illustration)**.

15 Installation is the reverse of the removal procedure.

## 10 Instrument cluster - removal and installation

*Refer to illustration 10.3*

**Warning:** *The models covered by this manual are equipped with Supplemental Restraint Systems (SRS), more commonly known as airbags. Always disable the airbag system before working in the vicinity of any airbag system components to avoid the possibility of accidental deployment of the airbag(s), which could cause personal injury* (see Section 25).

1 Disconnect the cable from the negative terminal of the battery (see Chapter 5).

2 Remove the instrument cluster bezel (see Chapter 11).

3 Remove the cluster mounting screws and separate the instrument cluster from the instrument panel **(see illustration)**.

4 Disconnect any electrical connectors that would interfere with removal.

5 Installation is the reverse of removal.

## 11 Wiper motor - replacement

### Front

*Refer to illustrations 11.2, 11.4a, 11.4b, 11.4c and 11.5*

1 Remove the ignition key from the key lock cylinder.

2 Mark their positions, then remove the

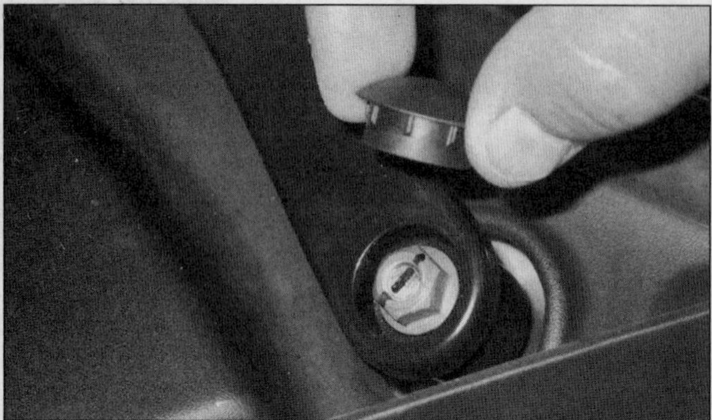

11.2 Draw or paint a line across the stud and wiper arm to mark its position so it can be reinstalled in the same relationship to the windshield

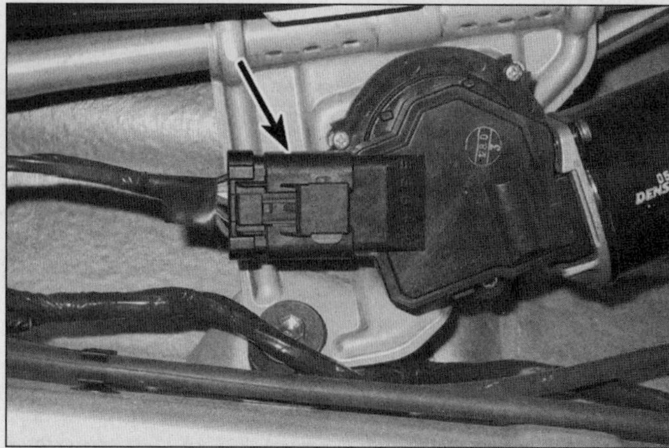

11.4a Disconnect the wiper motor electrical connector

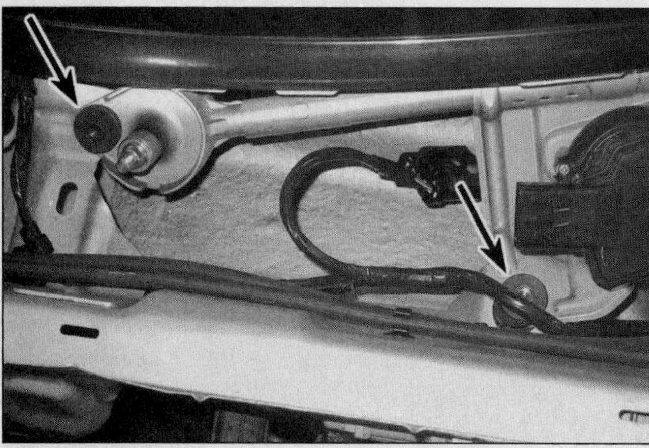

11.4b Remove the two right-side wiper module bolts

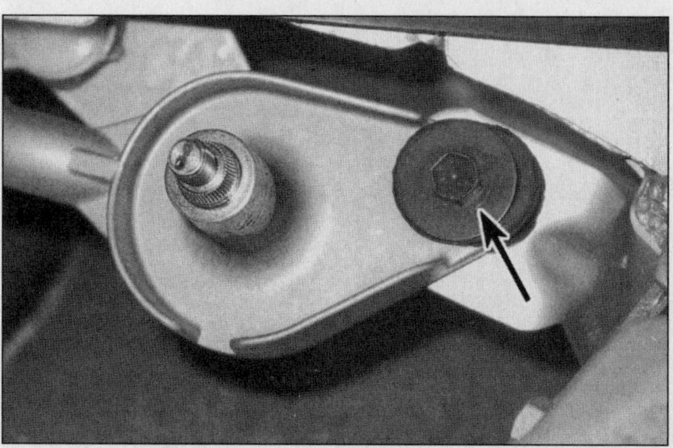

11.4c Remove the left-side wiper module bolt

wiper arms **(see illustration)**.

3 Remove the cowl grille screens (see Chapter 11).

4 Disconnect the wiper motor harness connector and remove the windshield wiper module assembly mounting bolts **(see illustrations)**.

5 Remove the crank arm nut and the wiper motor mounting bolts, then separate the motor from the assembly **(see illustration)**.

6 Installation is the reverse of removal. Before installing the wiper arms, turn the wiper motor on, then off, to make sure it is in the Park position.

## Rear

*Refer to illustrations 11.8 and 11.10*

7 Remove the ignition key from the key lock cylinder.

8 Mark the position of the wiper arm, then remove it **(see illustration)**. A battery terminal puller or similar tool might be required to detach the arm from the wiper shaft splines.

9 Remove the liftgate trim panel (see Chapter 11).

10 Disconnect the wiper motor harness connector, remove the mounting bolts and detach the rear wiper motor assembly **(see illustration)**.

11 Installation is the reverse of removal. Before installing the wiper arms, turn the wiper motor on, then off, to make sure it is in the Park position.

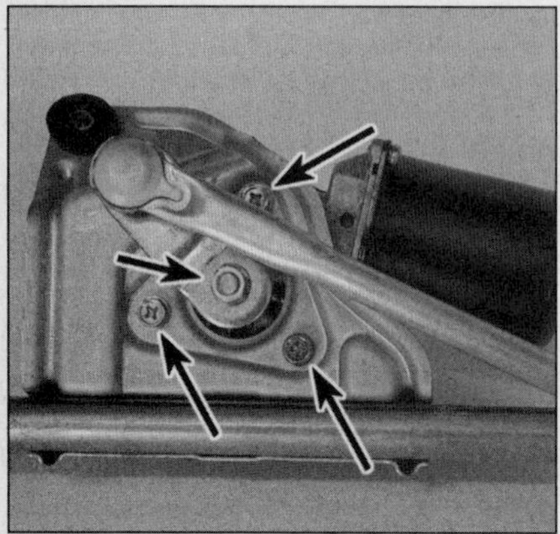

11.5 Remove the crank arm nut and wiper mounting bolts

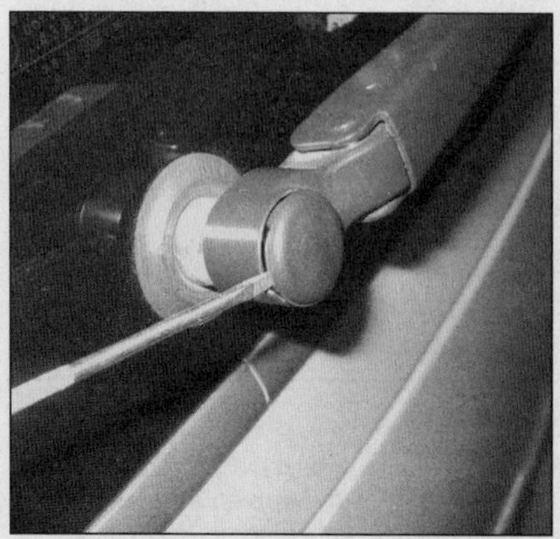

11.8 Pry out the cover for access to the rear wiper arm retaining nut

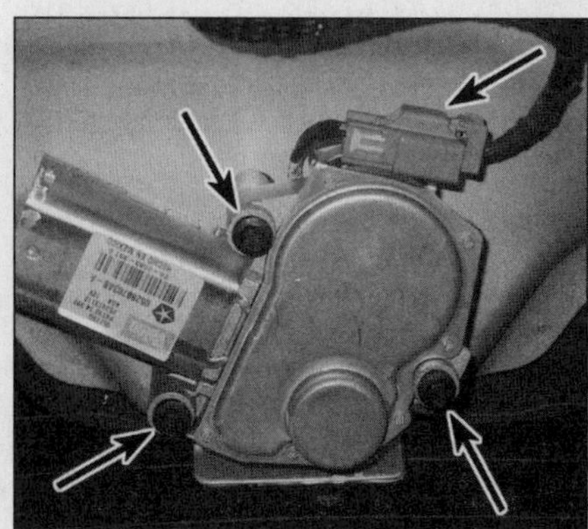

11.10 Disconnect the electrical connector, remove the bolts and detach the rear wiper motor

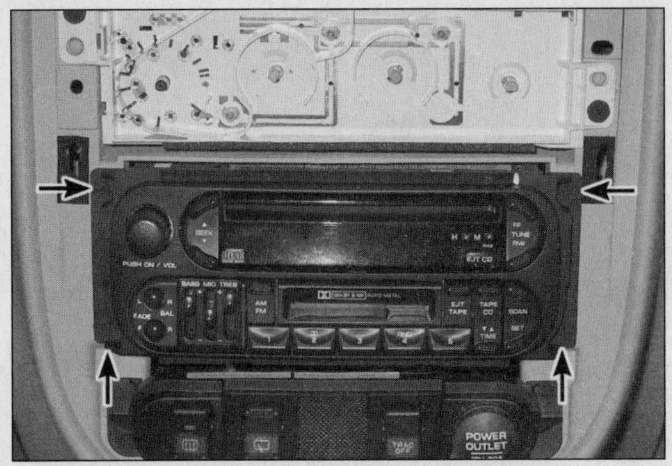


12.3a Location of the radio mounting screws

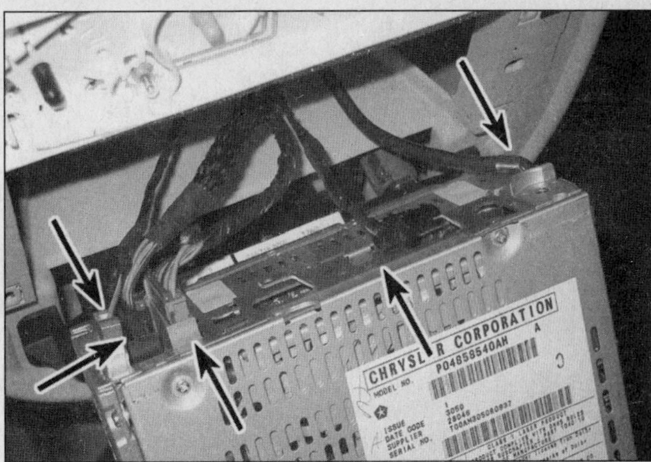


12.3b Pull the radio out and disconnect the electrical and antenna connectors

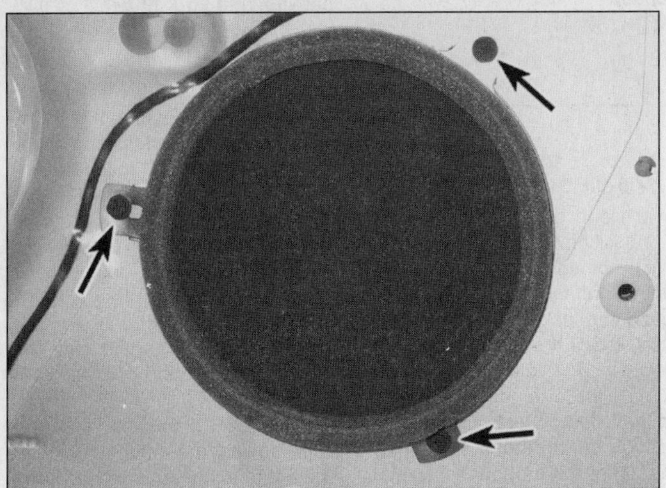

12.6a Remove the speaker screws . . .

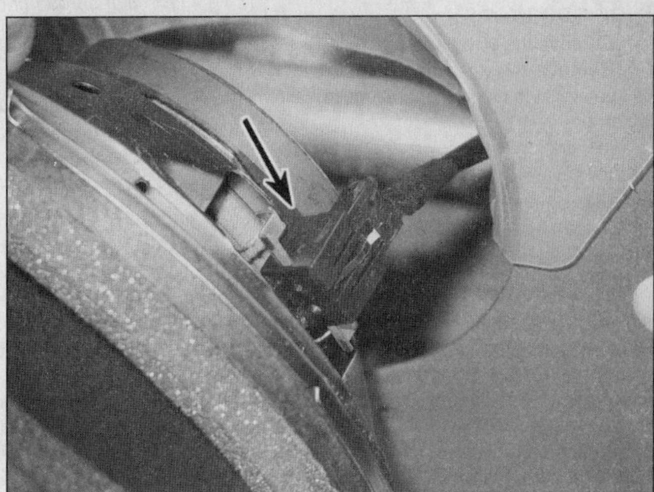

12.6b . . . then pull the speaker out and disconnect the electrical connector

## 12 Radio and speakers - removal and installation

**Warning:** *The models covered by this manual are equipped with Supplemental Restraint Systems (SRS), more commonly known as airbags. Always disable the airbag system before working in the vicinity of any airbag system components to avoid the possibility of accidental deployment of the airbag(s), which could cause personal injury* (see Section 25).

1 Disconnect the cable from the negative terminal of the battery (see Chapter 5).

### Radio

*Refer to illustration 12.3a and 12.3b*

2 Access the radio by removing the dashboard center bezel (see Chapter 11).

3 Remove the retaining screws and pull the radio outward to access the backside, then disconnect the electrical connectors and the antenna lead **(see illustration)**.

4 Installation is the reverse of removal.

### Door speakers

*Refer to illustrations 12.6a and 12.6b*

5 Remove the door trim panel (see Chapter 11).

6 Remove the speaker screws **(see illustration)**. Disconnect the electrical connector and the antenna lead and remove the speaker from the vehicle **(see illustration)**.

7 Installation is the reverse of removal.

### Dash speakers

*Refer to illustration 12.9*

8 Remove the instrument panel top cover (see Chapter 11).

9 Remove the speaker screws **(see illustration)**. Lift the speaker up and disconnect the electrical connector.

10 Installation is the reverse of removal.

12.9 Remove the dash speaker screws

13.1 Use a small wrench to unscrew the antenna mast

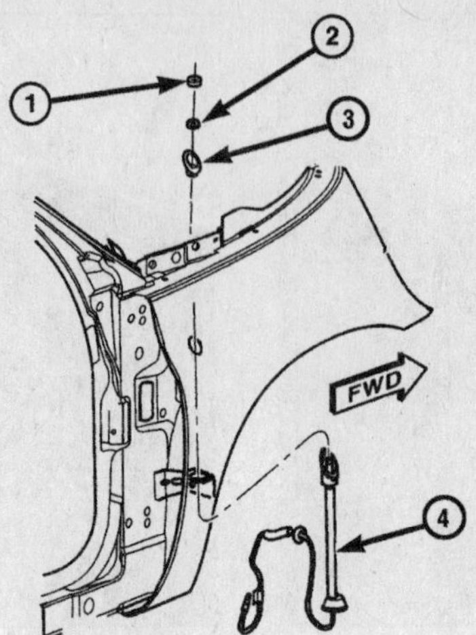


13.2 Antenna mounting details

1. *Nut shroud (if equipped)*
2. *Upper mounting nut*
3. *Antenna adapter*
4. *Antenna body*

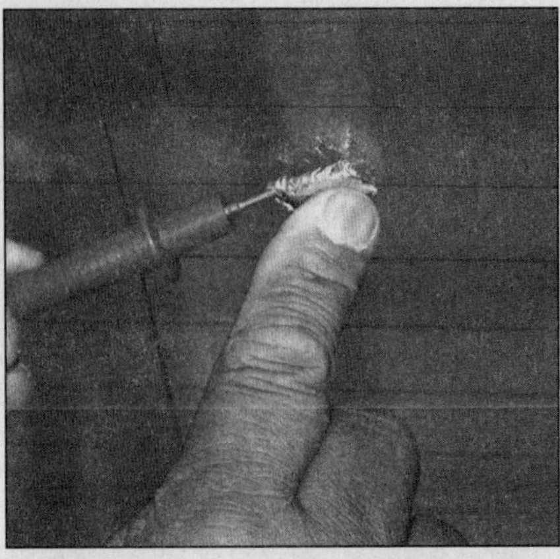

14.4 When measuring the voltage at the rear window defogger grid, wrap a piece of aluminum foil around the positive probe of the voltmeter and press the foil against the wire with your finger

### Rear speakers

11 Remove the trim panel.

12 Remove the speaker screws. Remove the speaker and disconnect the electrical connector.

13 Installation is the reverse of removal.

## 13 Antenna - replacement

*Refer to illustrations 13.1 and 3.2*

**Warning:** *The models covered by this manual are equipped with Supplemental Restraint Systems (SRS), more commonly known as airbags. Always disable the airbag system before working in the vicinity of any airbag system components to avoid the possibility of accidental deployment of the airbag(s), which could cause personal injury (see Section 25).*

1 Use a small open end wrench and unscrew the antenna mast from the body **(see illustration)**.

2 Unscrew the antenna upper mounting nut **(see illustration)**. Special sockets are available at most auto parts stores for this purpose, but a pair of needle-nose or snap-ring pliers will also work (but you'll have to be very careful not to let the pliers slip off the nut and scratch the paint).

3 Working inside the fender, detach the liner (see Chapter 11). Disconnect the antenna lead from the base of the antenna body.

4 Remove the mounting bolt securing the antenna body to the rear quarter panel.

5 Withdraw the antenna body from the rear quarter panel.

6 Installation is the reverse of removal.

## 14 Rear window defogger - check and repair

1 The rear window defogger consists of a number of horizontal elements baked onto the glass surface.

2 Small breaks in the element can be repaired without removing the rear window.

### Check

*Refer to illustrations 14.4, 14.5 and 14.7*

3 Turn the ignition switch and defogger system switches to the ON position. Using a voltmeter, place the positive probe against the defogger grid positive terminal and the negative probe against the ground terminal. If battery voltage is not indicated, check the fuse, defogger switch and related wiring. If voltage is indicated, but all or part of the defogger doesn't heat, proceed with the following tests.

4 When measuring voltage during these tests, wrap a piece of aluminum foil around the tip of the voltmeter positive probe and press the foil against the heating element with your finger **(see illustration)**. Place the negative probe on the defogger grid ground terminal.

5 Check the voltage at the center of each heating element **(see illustration)**. If the voltage is 5 or 6-volts, the element is okay (there is no break). If the voltage is 0-volts, the element is broken between the center of the element and the positive end. If the voltage is 10 to 12-volts the element is broken between the center of the element and ground. Check each heating element.

6 Connect the negative lead to a good body ground. The reading should stay the same. If it doesn't, the ground connection is bad.

7 To find the break, place the voltmeter negative probe against the defogger ground terminal. Place the voltmeter positive probe with the foil strip against the heating element at the positive terminal end and slide it toward the negative terminal end. The point at which the voltmeter deflects from several volts to

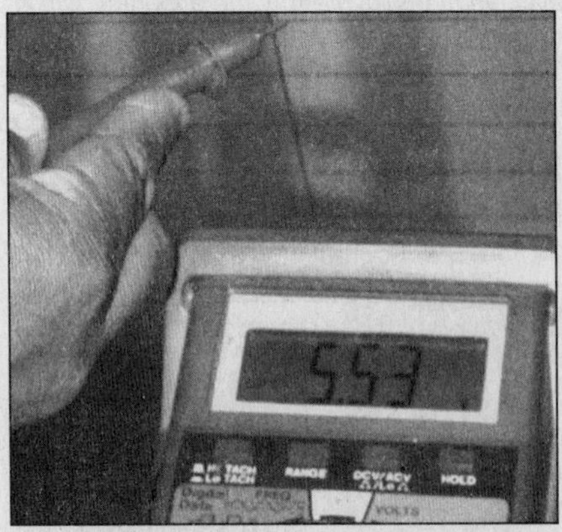


14.5 To determine if a heating element has broken, check the voltage at the center of each element - if the voltage is 5 or 6-volts, the element is unbroken - if the voltage is 10 or 12-volts, the element is broken between the center and the ground side - if there is no voltage, the element is broken between the center and the positive side

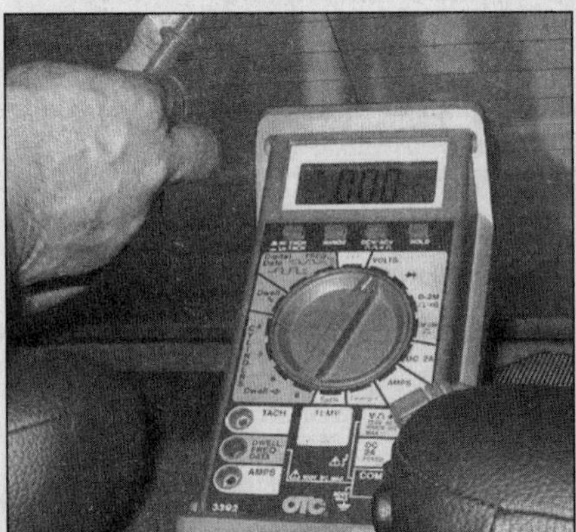


14.7 To find the break, place the voltmeter negative lead against the defogger ground terminal, place the voltmeter positive lead with the foil strip against the heating element at the positive terminal end and slide it toward the negative terminal end - the point at which the voltmeter reading changes abruptly is the point at which the element is broken

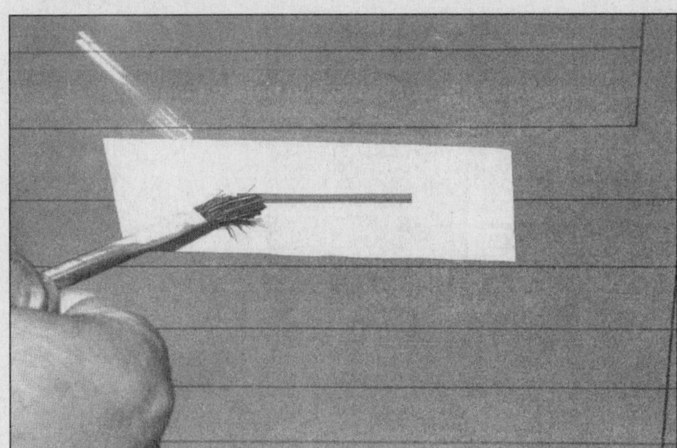

14.13 To use a defogger repair kit, apply masking tape to the inside of the window at the damaged area, then brush on the special conductive coating

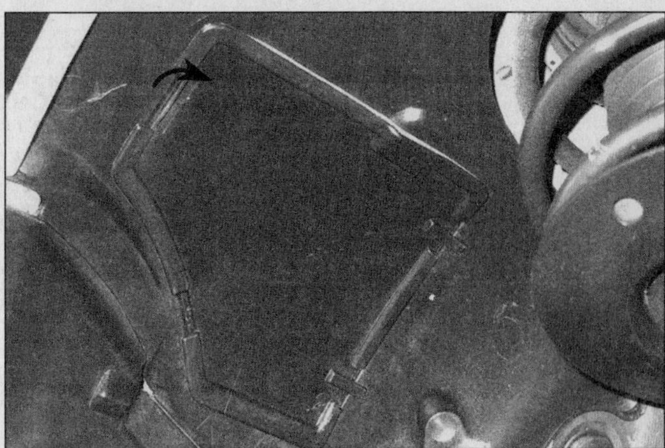

15.2 Detach the headlight access panel and rotate it out of the fenderwell

zero is the point at which the heating element is broken **(see illustration)**.

## Repair

*Refer to illustration 14.13*

8 Repair the break in the element using a repair kit specifically recommended for this purpose, available at most auto parts stores. Included in this kit is plastic conductive epoxy.

9 Prior to repairing a break, turn off the system and allow it to cool for a few minutes.

10 Lightly buff the element area with fine steel wool, then clean it thoroughly with rubbing alcohol.

11 Use masking tape to mask off the area being repaired.

12 Thoroughly mix the epoxy, following the instructions provided with the repair kit.

13 Apply the epoxy material to the slit in the masking tape, overlapping the undamaged area about 3/4-inch on either end **(see illustration)**.

14 Allow the repair to cure for 24 hours before removing the tape and using the system.

## 15 Headlight and park/turn signal bulbs - replacement

*Refer to illustrations 15.2, 15.3a and 15.3b*

**Warning:** *Halogen gas filled bulbs are under pressure and may shatter if the surface is scratched or the bulb is dropped. Wear eye protection and handle the bulbs carefully, grasping only the base whenever possible. Do not touch the surface of the bulb with your fingers because the oil from your skin could cause it to overheat and fail prematurely. If you do touch the bulb surface, clean it with rubbing alcohol.*

**Note:** *On these models the headlight high and low beam and park/turn signal bulbs are separate and mounted in the headlight housing.*

1 Loosen the front wheel lug nuts. Raise the vehicle and support it securely on jackstands.

2 Remove the wheel and detach the headlight access panel from the fenderwell splash shield **(see illustration)**.

3 Grasp the appropriate bulb holder, rotate it counterclockwise and remove the bulb holder from the headlight housing **(see illustrations)**.

4 The headlight bulbs are integral with the holder and replaced as a unit. Unplug the electrical connector and connect it to the new bulb. **Note:** *Don't touch the surface of the bulb with your fingers because the oil from your skin could cause it to overheat and fail prematurely. If you happen to touch the bulb surface, clean it with rubbing alcohol.*

5 On park/turn signals, grasp the bulb and pull it out of the holder. Using gloves or a clean shop towel, insert the new bulb into the holder.

6 Install the bulb and holder in the headlight housing and rotate it clockwise to lock it in place.

7 Install the headlight access panel, then install the wheel and lug nuts. Tighten the lug nuts to the torque listed in the Chapter 1 Specifications.

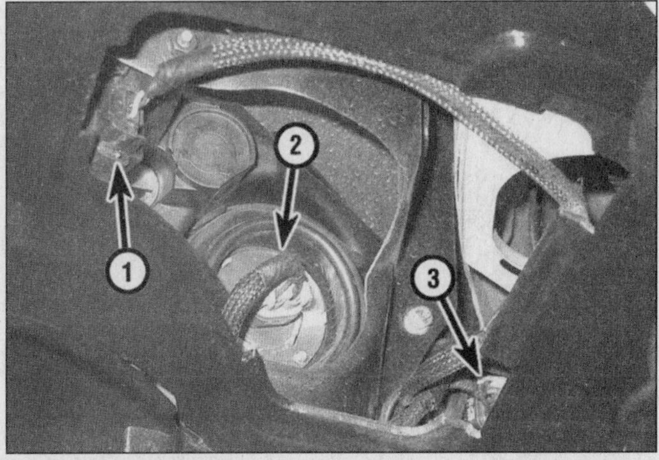


15.3a Headlight housing bulb locations (left headlight shown)

*1 Turn signal*
*2 Headlight low beam*
*3 Headlight high beam*

15.3b Remove the bulb holder by rotating it counterclockwise

16.1 The headlight adjusting screw location

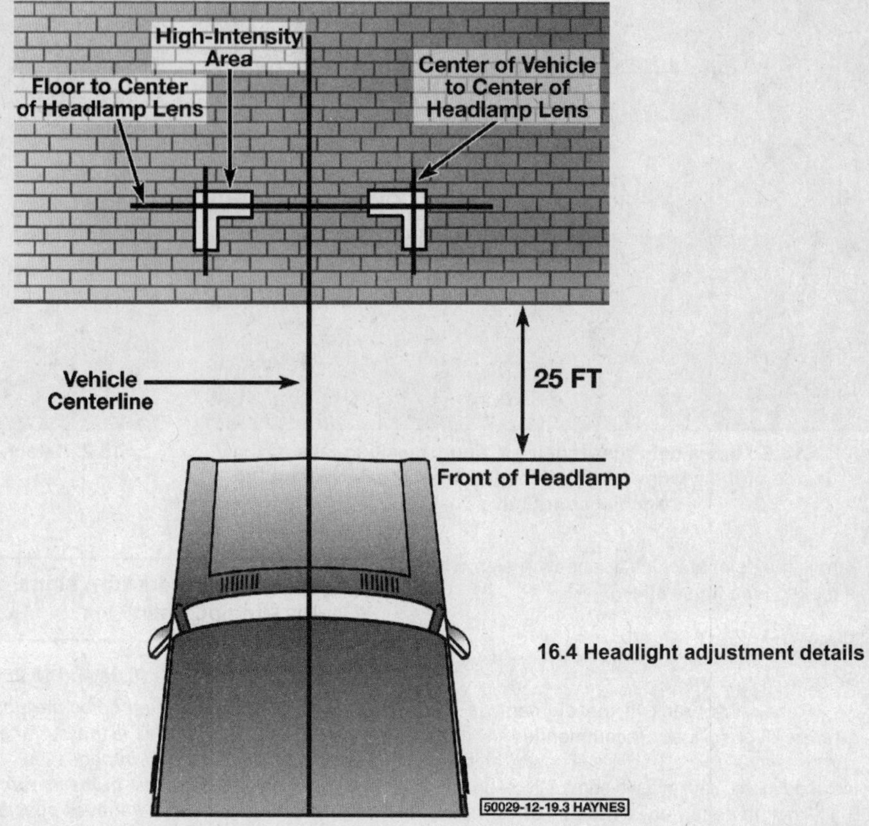


16.4 Headlight adjustment details

## 16 Headlights - adjustment

*Refer to illustrations 16.1 and 16.4*

**Note:** *The headlights must be aimed correctly. If adjusted incorrectly they could blind the driver of an oncoming vehicle and cause a serious accident or seriously reduce your ability to see the road. The headlights should be checked for proper aim every 12 months and any time a new headlight housing is installed or front end body work is performed. It should be emphasized that the following procedure is only an interim step, which will provide temporary adjustment until a properly equipped shop can adjust the headlights.*

1 These vehicles have a built-in horizontal adjustment screw located at the outer end of the headlight housing below the park/turn signal light for adjusting only the low and high beam simultaneously **(see illustration)**. Insert a Phillips screwdriver into the gear-drive mechanism and turn the screw to make adjustments.

2 Adjustment should be made with the vehicle on a level surface, with a full gas tank and a normal load in the vehicle.

3 There are several methods of adjusting the headlights. The simplest method requires masking tape, a blank wall and a level floor.

4 Position masking tape vertically on the wall in reference to the vehicle centerline and the centerlines of both headlight bulbs **(see illustration)**.

5 Position a horizontal tape line in reference to the centerline of all the headlights. **Note:** *It may be easier to position the tape on the wall with the vehicle parked only a few inches away.*

6 Adjustment should be made with the vehicle parked 25 feet (7.6 meters) from the wall, sitting level, the gas tank half-full and no unusually heavy load in the vehicle.

7 Position the high intensity zone so it is two inches below the horizontal line and two inches to the side of the headlight vertical line, away from oncoming traffic. Adjustment is made by turning the horizontal adjusting screw to move the beam left or right. The high beams on these aero type headlights are automatically adjusted along with the low beam.

8 Have the headlights adjusted by a dealer service department or service station at the earliest opportunity.

## 17 Headlight housing - replacement

*Refer to illustration 17.5*

**Warning:** *These vehicles are equipped with halogen gas-filled headlight bulbs, which are under pressure and may shatter if the surface is damaged or the bulb is dropped. Wear eye protection and handle the bulbs carefully, grasping only the base whenever possible. Do not touch the surface of the bulb with your fingers because the oil from your skin could cause it to overheat and fail prematurely. If you do touch the bulb surface, clean it with rubbing alcohol.*

1 Loosen the front wheel lug nuts. Raise the front of the vehicle and support it securely on jackstands.

2 Remove the front wheel and the fender well splash shield (see Chapter 11).

3 Remove the radiator grille (see Chapter 11).

4 Remove the three bumper cover-to-

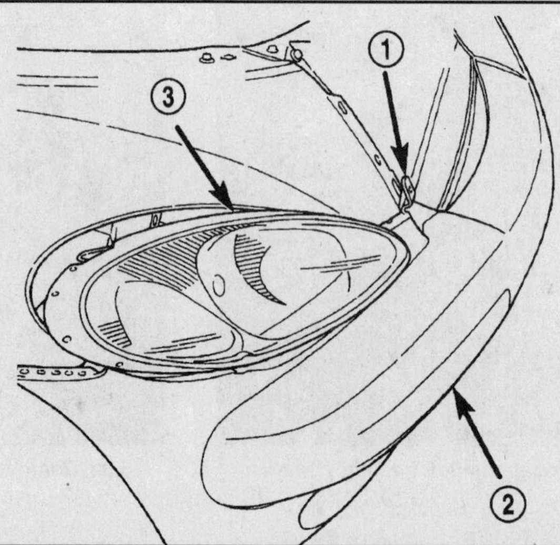


17.5 The headlight housing is retained by these three nuts

1 *Bumper cover fastener*
2 *Bumper cover*
3 *Headlight housing*

18.3 Disconnect the horn electrical connector(s) and remove the bracket bolt(s)

19.3 Unplug the fog light electrical connector from the bulb holder . . .

fender fasteners on the side you are working on. This will provide the space needed to allow the headlight housing to be removed. **Note:** *It may also be necessary to remove one or more bumper cover-to-radiator crossmember bolts.*

5 Working in the fenderwell, remove the retaining nuts **(see illustration)**, detach the headlight housing and withdraw it from the vehicle. Disconnect the headlight and park/turn signal bulb electrical connectors.

6 Installation is the reverse of removal. Be sure to check headlight adjustment (see Section 16).

## 18 Horn - replacement

*Refer to illustration 18.3*

1 Loosen the left front wheel lug nuts. Raise the vehicle, support it on jackstands and remove the left front wheel.

2 Remove the fenderwell splash shield (see Chapter 11).

3 To replace the horn(s), disconnect the electrical connector(s) and remove the bracket bolt(s) **(see illustration)**.

4 Installation is the reverse of removal.

## 19 Bulb replacement

**Note:** *Refer to Section 15 for the headlight and park/turn signal bulb replacement procedures.*

### Fog light

*Refer to illustrations 19.3 and 19.4*

1 Loosen the front wheel lug nuts, then raise the front of the vehicle and support it securely on jackstands. Remove the wheel.

2 Remove the fasteners securing the front of the fenderwell splash shield (see Chapter 11), then pull the splash shield back for access to the fog light.

3 Disconnect the bulb electrical connector **(see illustration)**.

4 Rotate the bulb holder counterclockwise and pull it out of the fog light housing **(see illustration)**.

5 The bulb and holder are replaced as a unit. **Caution:** *Do not touch the surface of the bulb with your fingers, because the oil from your skin could cause it to overheat and fail prematurely. If you do touch the bulb surface, clean it with rubbing alcohol.*

6 Installation is the reverse of removal.

19.4 . . . then rotate the bulb holder and pull it out of the fog light housing

### Tail light/brake light/rear turn signal light

*Refer to illustrations 19.7, 19.8 and 19.9*

7 Unscrew the Torx head screw securing the tail light housing to the quarter panel **(see illustration)**.

8 Withdraw the tail light housing from the quarter panel **(see illustration)**.

19.7 Remove the Torx head screw retaining the tail light housing

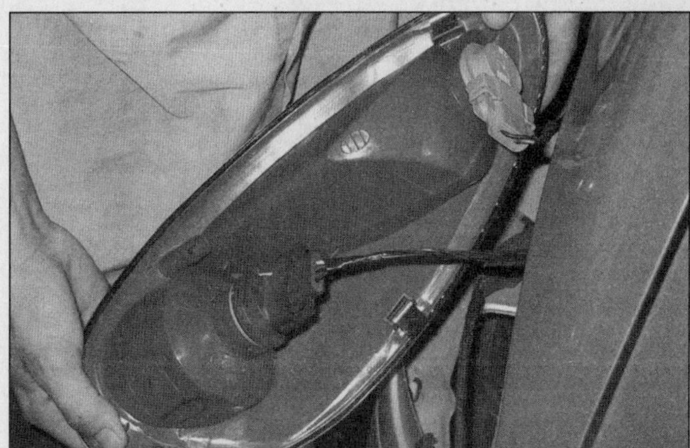

19.8 Lift the housing away from the body and turn it over for access to the bulb holders

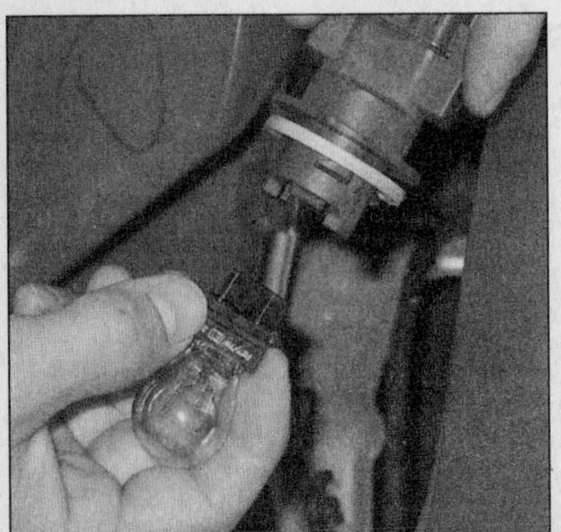

19.9 The tail light bulbs pull straight out of the holders

19. 11 Remove the license plate light housing screws

9 Replace a bulb by turning the bulb holder counterclockwise and withdraw the holder from the housing. Pull the bulb straight out of the holder **(see illustration)**.

10 Installation is the reverse of removal.

When installing the housing, engage the tab at the front of the housing with the slot in the body, then carefully swing the housing into its opening while pushing it forward.

## *License plate light*

*Refer to illustrations 19.11 and 19.12*

11 Unscrew and remove the Torx-head screws securing the light assembly **(see illustration)**.

12 Remove the light assembly from the bumper, rotate the bulb holder counterclockwise and withdraw it **(see illustration)**.

13 To replace a bulb, pull it straight out of the holder.

14 Installation is the reverse of removal.

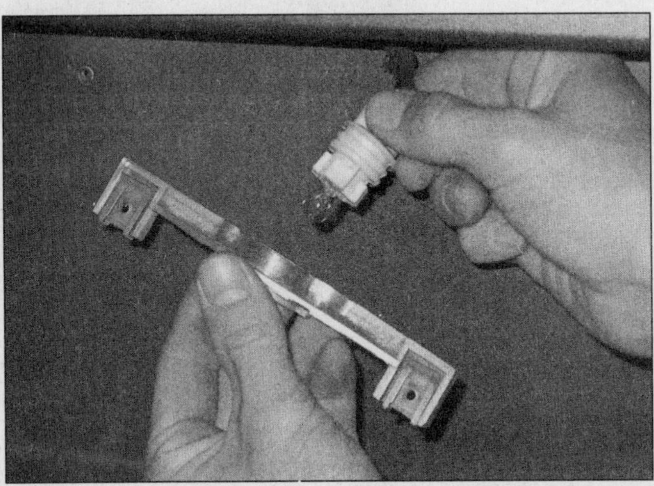

19.12 Remove the license plate bulb holder by turning it counterclockwise and pulling it out

19.15 Remove the back-up light housing screws

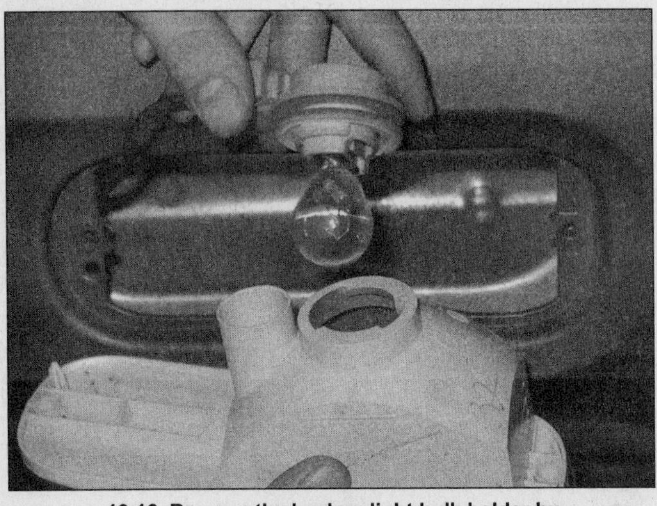

19.16 Remove the backup light bulb holder by turning it counterclockwise . . .

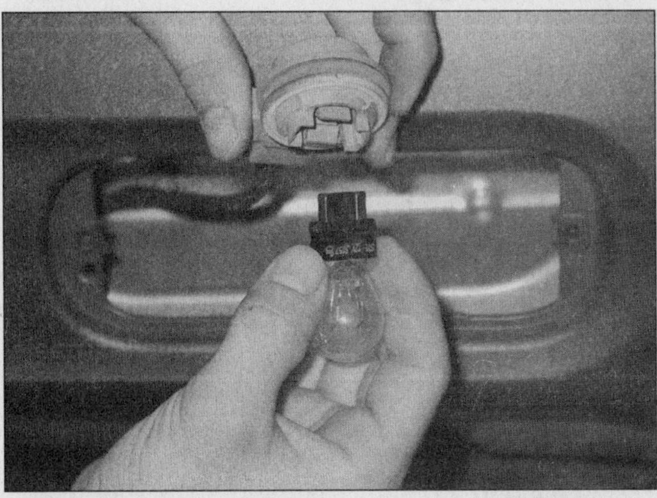

19.17 . . . then pull the bulb straight out of the holder

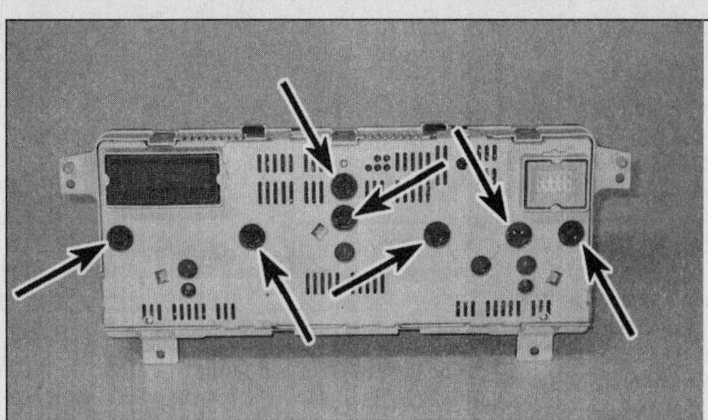
19.21 Instrument cluster bulbs

## *Back-up light*

*Refer to illustration 19.15, 19.16 and 19.17*

15 On 2005 and earlier models, remove the screws and detach the light housing from the bumper cover **(see illustration)**. On 2006 and later models, pry out on the outboard side of the lamp housing at the fascia gap.

16 Twist the bulb holder counterclockwise **(see illustration)**.

17 Pull the bulb straight out of holder **(see illustration)**. Installation is the reverse of removal.

## *High-mounted brake light*

18 Open the liftgate and pry off the brake light trim cover. Pull the tabs on either side of the lens outward, then detach the lens from the light housing.

19 The bulbs are removed by pulling them straight out of the housing. Installation is the reverse of removal.

## *Instrument cluster lights*

*Refer to illustration 19.21*

20 To gain access to the instrument cluster illumination bulbs, the instrument cluster will have to be removed (see Section 10). The bulbs can then be removed and replaced from the rear of the cluster.

21 Rotate the bulb holder counterclockwise to remove it **(see illustration)**.

22 Installation is the reverse of removal.

## *Courtesy/reading light*

*Refer to illustrations 19.24*

23 Use a small screwdriver to carefully pry the lens from the light housing.

24 Remove the bulb by carefully prying the ends of the bulb out of the spring clips at each end. **Warning:** *Don't pry on the glass - you'll break the bulb.*

25 Installation is the reverse of removal.

## *Dome light*

*Refer to illustration 19.27*

26 Pry the left side of the lens out of the dome light housing. Don't pry on the right side - you'll break the lens.

27 Remove the bulb by pulling it straight out of its holder (to the right) **(see illustration)**.

28 Installation is the reverse of removal.

## *Cargo light*

*Refer to illustration 19.29*

29 Remove the access door from the trim panel, then remove the jack bag. Pull down on the light housing to detach it from the trim panel **(see illustration)**; the lens will probably pop out of the trim panel.

30 Pull the light housing and wiring harness out through the trim panel opening. Pull the bulb straight out of the holder to remove it, then push the new bulb straight in.

31 Guide the bulb holder back into position, then push the entire bulb holder through the trim panel (from the back side). Now attach the lens to the holder, lining up the tangs on the lens with the slots in the holder.

32 Push the lens/bulb holder assembly into the trim panel until it snaps into place.

## 20 Electric side view mirrors - description

1 Most electric rear view mirrors use two motors to move the glass; one for up and down adjustments and one for left-right adjustments.

2 The control switch has a selector portion which sends voltage to the left or right side mirror. With the ignition ON but the engine OFF, roll down the windows and operate the mirror control switch through all functions (left-right and up-down) for both the left and right side mirrors.

3 Listen carefully for the sound of the electric motors running in the mirrors.

4 If the motors can be heard but the mirror glass doesn't move, there's a problem with the drive mechanism inside the mirror.

5 If the mirrors do not operate and no sound comes from the mirrors, check the fuse (see Chapter 1).

6 If the fuse is OK, remove the mirror control switch. Have the switch continuity checked by a dealership service department or other qualified automobile repair facility.

7 Test the ground connections. Refer to the wiring diagrams at the end of Chapter 12.

8 If the mirror still doesn't work, remove the mirror and check the wires at the mirror for voltage.

9 If there's no voltage in each switch position, check the circuit between the mirror and control switch for opens and shorts.

10 If there's voltage, remove the mirror and test it off the vehicle with jumper wires. Replace the mirror if it fails this test.

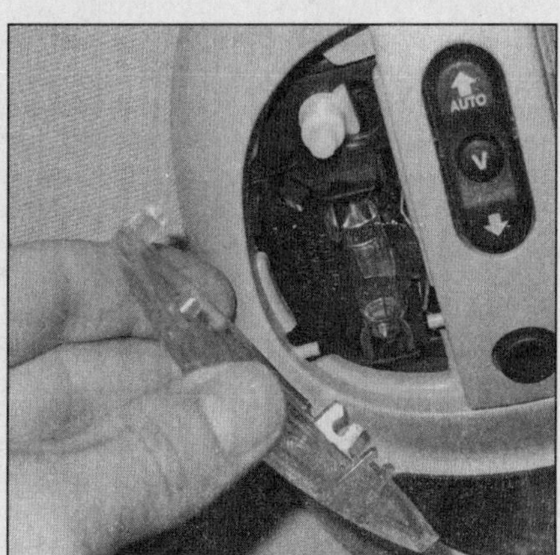

19.24 After detaching the lens, carefully pry the metal ends of the bulb from the spring clips

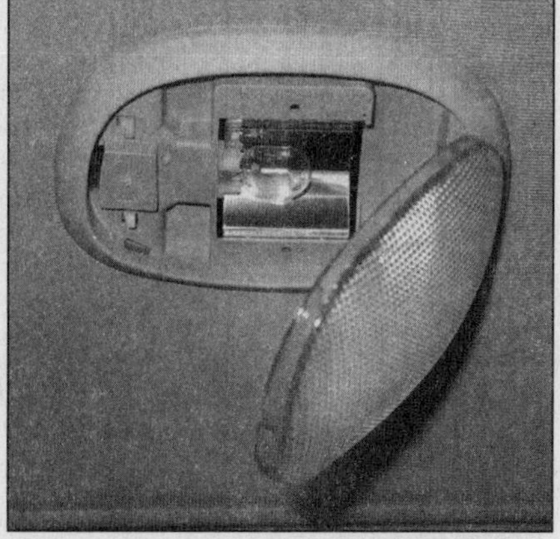
19.27 Detach the left side of the lens for access to the dome light bulb

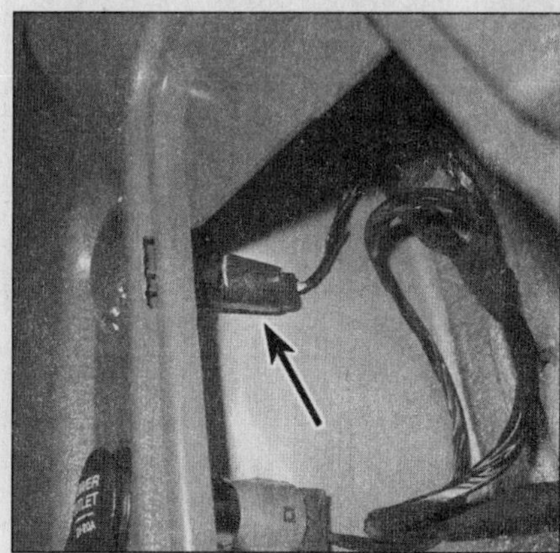
19.29 Grasp the cargo light housing and pull it downward to detach it from the trim panel

## 21 Cruise control system - description

*Refer to illustration 21.5*

1 The cruise control system maintains vehicle speed with an electronically controlled, vacuum operated servo located in the engine compartment, which is connected to the throttle body by a cable. The system consists of the PCM, vacuum servo, brake switch, control switches and vehicle speed sensor. Some features of the system require special testers and diagnostic procedures, which are beyond the scope of this manual. Listed below are some general procedures that may be used to locate common problems.

2 Check the fuses (see Section 3).

3 Have an assistant operate the brake pedal while you check the brake lights (voltage from the brake light switch deactivates the cruise control).

4 If the brake lights don't come on or stay on all the time, correct the problem and retest the cruise control.

5 Visually inspect the control cable between the cruise control servo and the throttle linkage for free movement **(see illustration)**. Replace it if necessary.

6 The cruise control system uses inputs from the Vehicle Speed Sensor (VSS). Refer to Chapter 6 for more information on the VSS.

7 Test drive the vehicle to determine if the cruise control is now working. If it isn't, take it to a dealer service department or an automotive electrical specialist for further diagnosis.

## 22 Power window system - description

1 The power window system operates electric motors, mounted in the doors, which lower and raise the windows. The system consists of the control switches, relays, the motors, regulators, glass mechanisms and associated wiring.

**21.5 Cruise control servo**

2 The power windows can be lowered and raised from the master control switches by the driver or by remote switches located at the individual windows. Each window has a separate motor that is reversible. The position of the control switch determines the polarity and therefore the direction of operation.

3 The circuit is protected by a fuse and a circuit breaker. Each motor is also equipped with an internal circuit breaker; this prevents one stuck window from disabling the whole system.

4 The power window system will only operate when the ignition switch is ON. In addition, many models have a window lockout switch at the master control switch that, when activated, disables the switches at the rear windows and, sometimes, the switch at the passenger's window also. Always check these items before troubleshooting a window problem.

5 These procedures are general in nature, so if you can't find the problem using them, take the vehicle to a dealer service department or other properly equipped repair facility.

6 If the power windows won't operate, always check the fuse and circuit breaker first.

7 If only the rear windows are inoperative, or if the windows only operate from the master control switch, check the rear window lockout switch for continuity in the unlocked position. Replace it if it doesn't have continuity.

8 Check the wiring between the switches and fuse panel for continuity. Repair the wiring, if necessary.

9 If only one window is inoperative from the master control switch, try the other control switch at the window. **Note:** *This doesn't apply to the driver's door window.*

10 If the same window works from one switch, but not the other, check the switch for continuity. Have the switch checked at a dealer service department or other qualified automobile repair facility.

11 If the switch tests OK, check for a short or open in the circuit between the affected switch and the window motor.

12 If one window is inoperative from both switches, remove the trim panel from the affected door and check for voltage at the switch and at the motor while the switch is operated.

13 If voltage is reaching the motor, disconnect the glass from the regulator (see Chapter 11). Move the window up and down by hand while checking for binding and damage. Also check for binding and damage to the regulator. If the regulator is not damaged and the window moves up and down smoothly, replace the motor. If there's binding or damage, lubricate, repair or replace parts, as necessary.

14 If voltage isn't reaching the motor, check the wiring in the circuit for continuity between the switches and motors. You'll need to consult the wiring diagram for the vehicle. If the circuit is equipped with a relay, check that the relay is grounded properly and receiving voltage.

15 Test the windows after you are done to confirm proper repairs.

## 23 Power door lock system - description

1 A power door lock system operates the door lock actuators mounted in each door. The system consists of the switches, actuators, a control unit and associated wiring. Diagnosis can usually be limited to simple checks of the wiring connections and actuators for minor faults that can be easily repaired.

2 Power door lock systems are operated by bi-directional solenoids located in the doors. The lock switches have two operating positions: Lock and Unlock. When activated, the switch sends a ground signal to the door lock control unit to lock or unlock the doors. Depending on which way the switch is activated, the control unit reverses polarity to the solenoids, allowing the two sides of the circuit to be used alternately as the feed (positive) and ground side.

3 Some vehicles may have an anti-theft system incorporated into the power locks. If you are unable to locate the trouble using the following general Steps, consult a dealer service department or other qualified repair shop.

4 Always check the circuit protection first. Some vehicles use a combination of circuit breakers and fuses.

5 Operate the door lock switches in both directions (Lock and Unlock) with the engine off. Listen for the click of the solenoids operating.

6 Test the switches for continuity. Remove the switches and have them checked by a dealer service department or other qualified automobile repair facility.

7 Check the wiring between the switches, control unit and solenoids for continuity. Repair the wiring if there's no continuity.

8 Check for a bad ground at the switches or the control unit.

9 If all but one lock solenoids operate, remove the trim panel from the affected door (see Chapter 11) and check for voltage at the solenoid while the lock switch is operated. One of the wires should have voltage in the Lock position; the other should have voltage in the Unlock position.

10 If the inoperative solenoid is receiving voltage, replace the solenoid.

11 If the inoperative solenoid isn't receiving voltage, check the relay for an open or short in the wire between the lock solenoid and the control unit. **Note:** *It's common for wires to break in the portion of the harness between the body and door (opening and closing the door fatigues and eventually breaks the wires).*

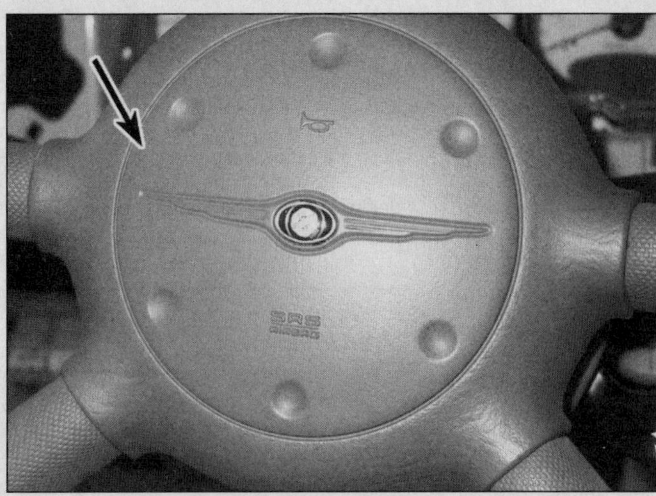


25.1a The driver's side airbag is located in the steering wheel horn pad

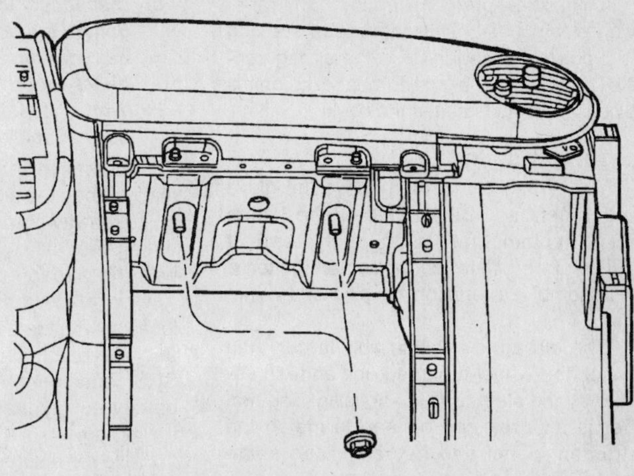

25.1b The passenger's airbag is located on the dashboard above the glove box

## 24 Daytime Running Lights (DRL) - general information

The Daytime Running Lights (DRL) system used on Canadian models illuminates the headlights whenever the engine is running. The only exception is with the engine running and the parking brake engaged. Once the parking brake is released, the lights will remain on as long as the ignition switch is on, even if the parking brake is later applied.

The DRL system supplies reduced power to the headlights so they won't be too bright for daytime use, while prolonging headlight life.

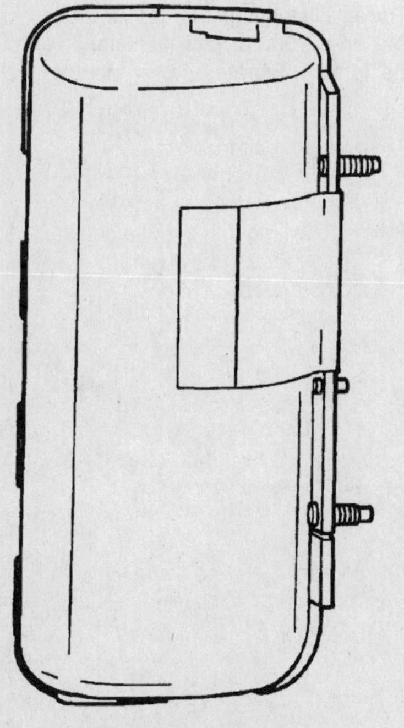

25.1c Seat airbag

## 25 Airbag system - general information and precautions

### General information

*Refer to illustrations 25.1a, 25.1b, 25.1c and 25.1d*

1 All models are equipped with a Supplemental Restraint System (SRS), more commonly known as an airbag. This system is designed to protect the driver, and the front seat passenger, from serious injury in the event of a head-on or frontal collision. It consists of a control module mounted in the center of the vehicle, under the floor console, an airbag module mounted on the steering wheel **(see illustration)**, the top surface of the passenger's side dash and, on some models, in the sides of the front seats **(see illustrations)**. The airbag control module is mounted under the center console **(see illustration)**.

Some later models are equipped with seatbelt pre-tensioners, also part of the airbag system. The pre-tensioners are pyrotechnic (explosive) devices designed to retract the seat belts in the event of a collision. On models equipped with pre-tensioners, do not remove the front seat belt retractor assemblies, and do not disconnect the electrical connectors leading to the assemblies. Problems with the pre-tensioners will turn on the SRS (airbag) warning light on the dash. If any pre-tensioner problems are suspected, take the vehicle to a dealer service department.

### Airbag module

#### Driver's side

2 The airbag inflator module contains a housing incorporating the cushion (airbag) and inflator unit, mounted in the center of the steering wheel. The inflator assembly is mounted on the back of the housing over a hole through which gas is expelled, inflating the bag almost instantaneously when an electrical signal is sent from the system. A clockspring assembly on the steering column under the steering wheel carries this signal to the module.

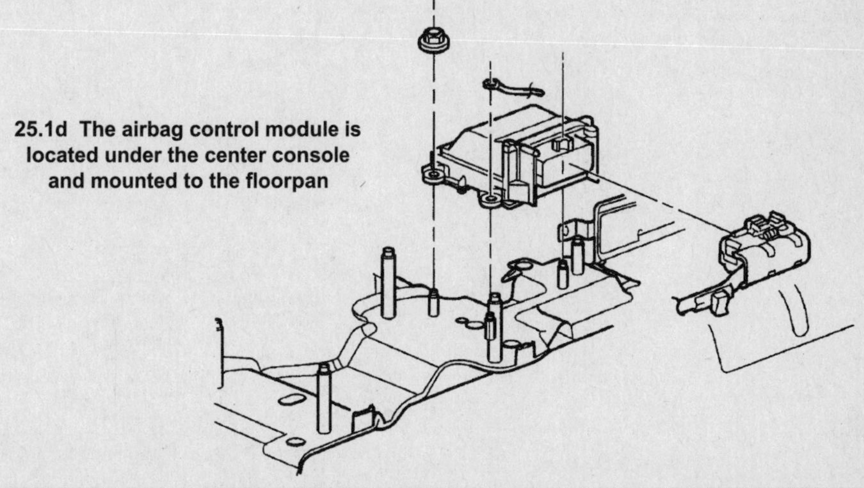

25.1d The airbag control module is located under the center console and mounted to the floorpan

3 This clockspring assembly can transmit an electrical signal regardless of steering wheel position. The igniter in the airbag converts the electrical signal to heat and ignites the powder, which inflates the bag.

### Passenger's side

4 The airbag is mounted above the glove compartment and designated by the letters SRS (Supplemental Restraint System). It consists of an inflator containing an igniter, a bag assembly, a reaction housing and a trim cover.

5 The airbag is considerably larger than the steering wheel-mounted unit and is supported by the steel reaction housing. The trim cover is textured and painted to match the instrument panel and has a molded seam which splits when the bag inflates.

## Control module

6 The control module supplies the current to the airbag system in the event of the collision, even if battery power is cut off. It checks this system every time the vehicle is started, causing the "SRS" light to go on then off, if the system is operating properly. If there is a fault in the system, the light will go on and stay on, flash, or the dash will make a beeping sound. If this happens, the vehicle should be taken to your dealer immediately for service.

## Disarming the system and other precautions

**Warning:** *Failure to follow these precautions could result in accidental deployment of the airbag and personal injury.*

7 Whenever working in the vicinity of the steering wheel, steering column or any of the other SRS system components, the system must be disarmed. To disarm the system:

a) *Point the wheels straight ahead and turn the key to the Lock position.*

b) *Disconnect the cable from the negative battery terminal. Isolate the cable terminal so it won't accidentally contact the battery post.*

c) *Wait at least two minutes for the back-up power supply to be depleted.*

8 Whenever handling an airbag module, always keep the airbag opening (the trim side) pointed away from your body. Never place the airbag module on a bench or other surface with the airbag opening facing the surface. Always place the airbag module in a safe location with the airbag opening facing up.

9 Never measure the resistance of any SRS component. An ohmmeter has a built-in battery supply that could accidentally deploy the airbag.

10 Never dispose of a live airbag module. Return it to a dealer service department or other qualified repair shop for safe deployment and disposal.

## Component removal and installation

### Driver's side airbag module and clockspring

11 Refer to Chapter 10, *Steering wheel - removal and installation*, for the driver's side airbag module and clockspring removal and installation procedures.

### Passenger's side airbag module

12 Disarm the airbag system as described previously in this Section.

13 Remove the glove box to gain access to the airbag, then unplug the electrical connector and remove the airbag module mounting fasteners **(see illustration 25.1b)**. Be sure to heed the precautions outlined previously in this Section.

14 Installation is the reverse of the removal procedure. Tighten the airbag module mounting fasteners securely.

### Seat airbag

15 This procedure will require removal and disassembly of the seat(s). Under normal circumstances there would never be a reason to remove a seat airbag. However, if it has been determined that there is a problem with the seat airbag module, the work should be left to a dealer service department or other qualified repair shop.

## 26 Wiring diagrams - general information

Since it isn't possible to include all wiring diagrams for every year covered by this manual, the following diagrams are those that are typical and most commonly needed.

Prior to troubleshooting any circuits, check the fuse and circuit breakers (if equipped) to make sure they're in good condition. Make sure the battery is properly charged and check the cable connections (see Chapter 1).

When checking a circuit, make sure that all connectors are clean, with no broken or loose terminals. When unplugging a connector, do not pull on the wires. Pull only on the connector housings.

2006 and later model vehicles use a Totally Integrated Power Module. This module receives inputs from various sensors and switches such as Back-up lamp, Turn and Headlamp just to name a few. The complexity of the system (and need to use scan tool diagnosis along with the accompanying diagnostic trouble code) makes diagnosis best left to service professionals. The following wiring diagrams can be used to perform basic checks and tests on vehicles with a Totally Integrated Power Module. Where you see "Power Distribution Center" you can assume that on a 2006 or later vehicle, it represents the Totally Integrated Power Module.

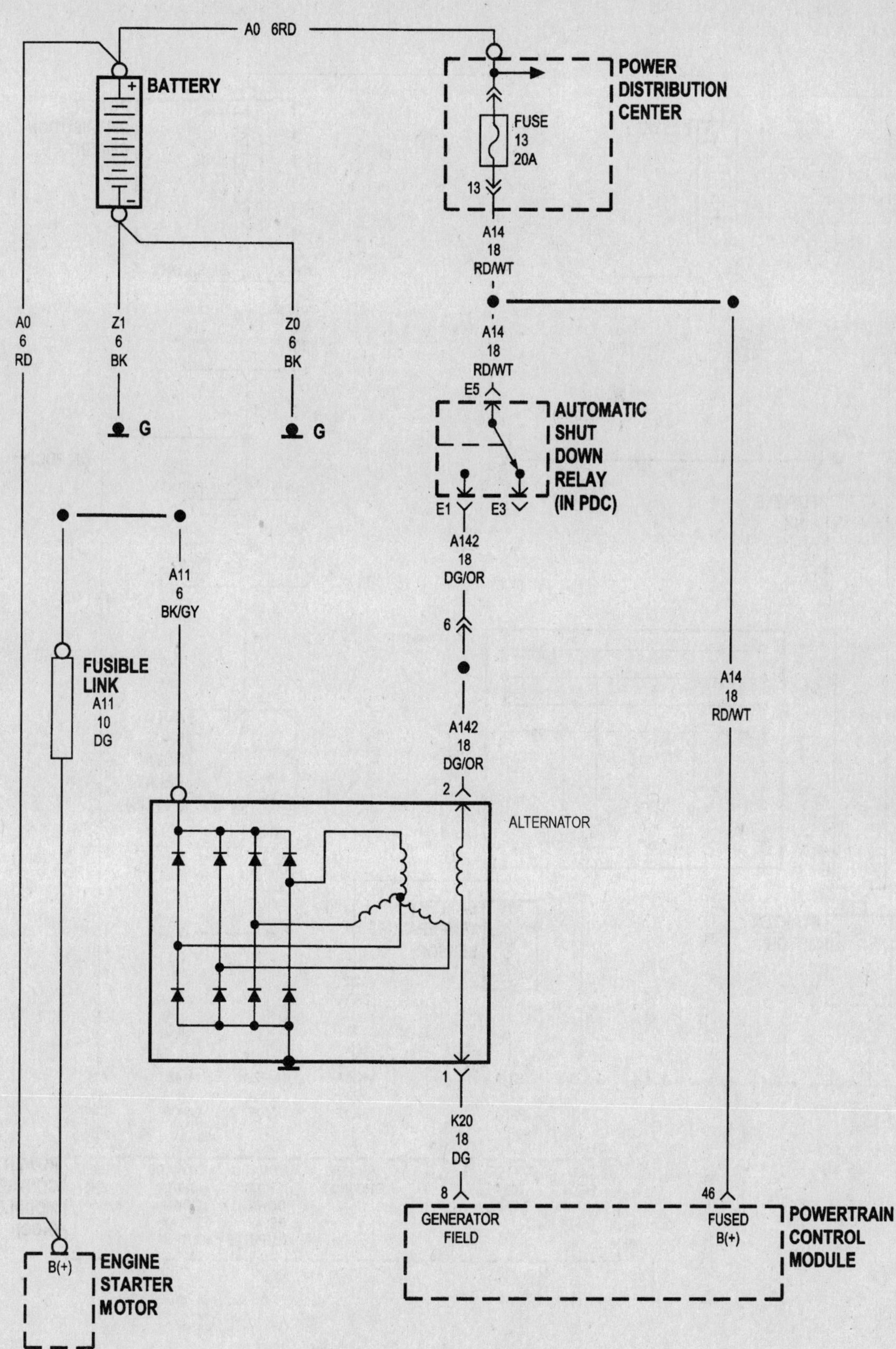


Charging system - 2001 and 2002 models

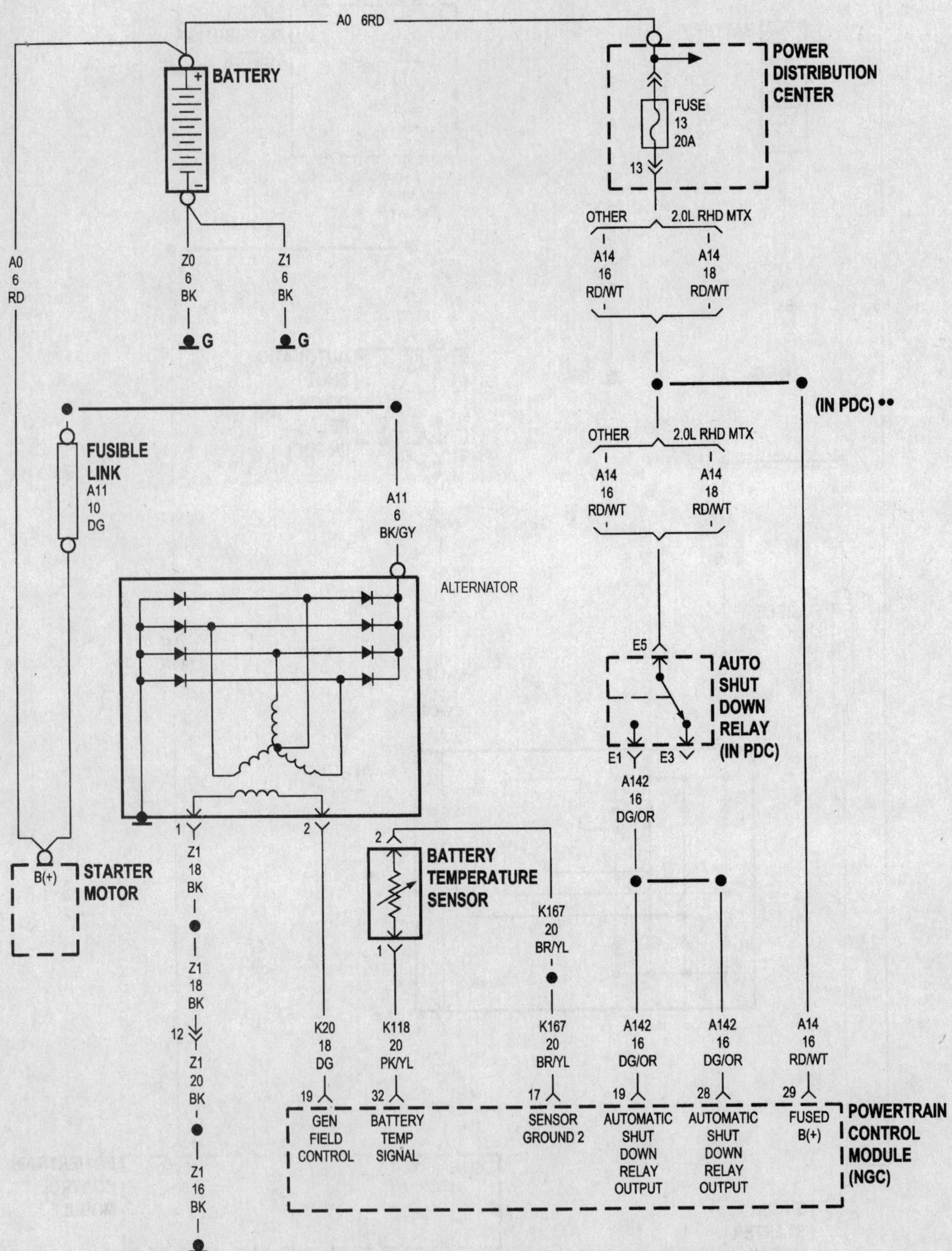


Charging system - 2003 and later non-turbocharged models

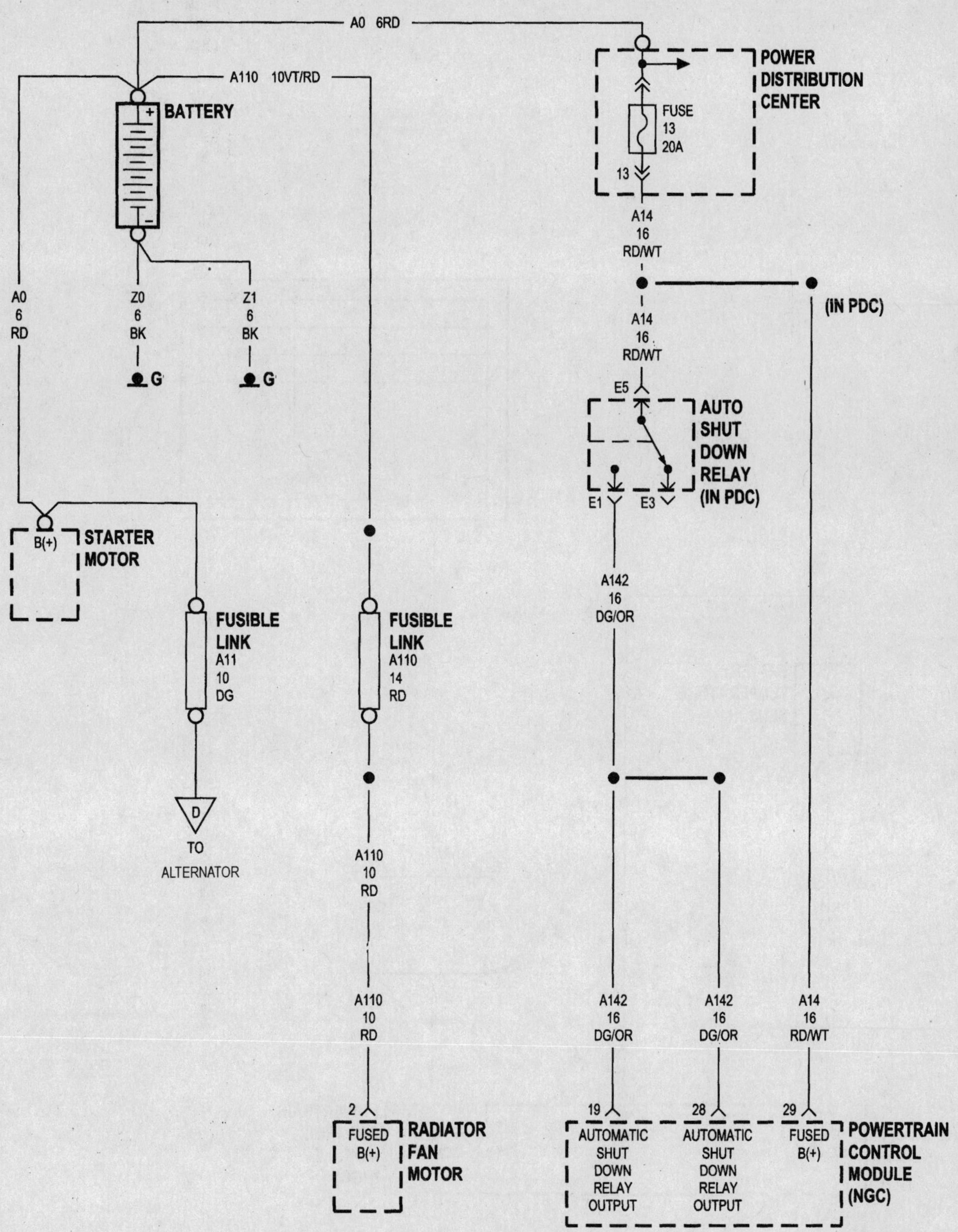


Charging system - 2003 and later turbocharged models (1 of 2)

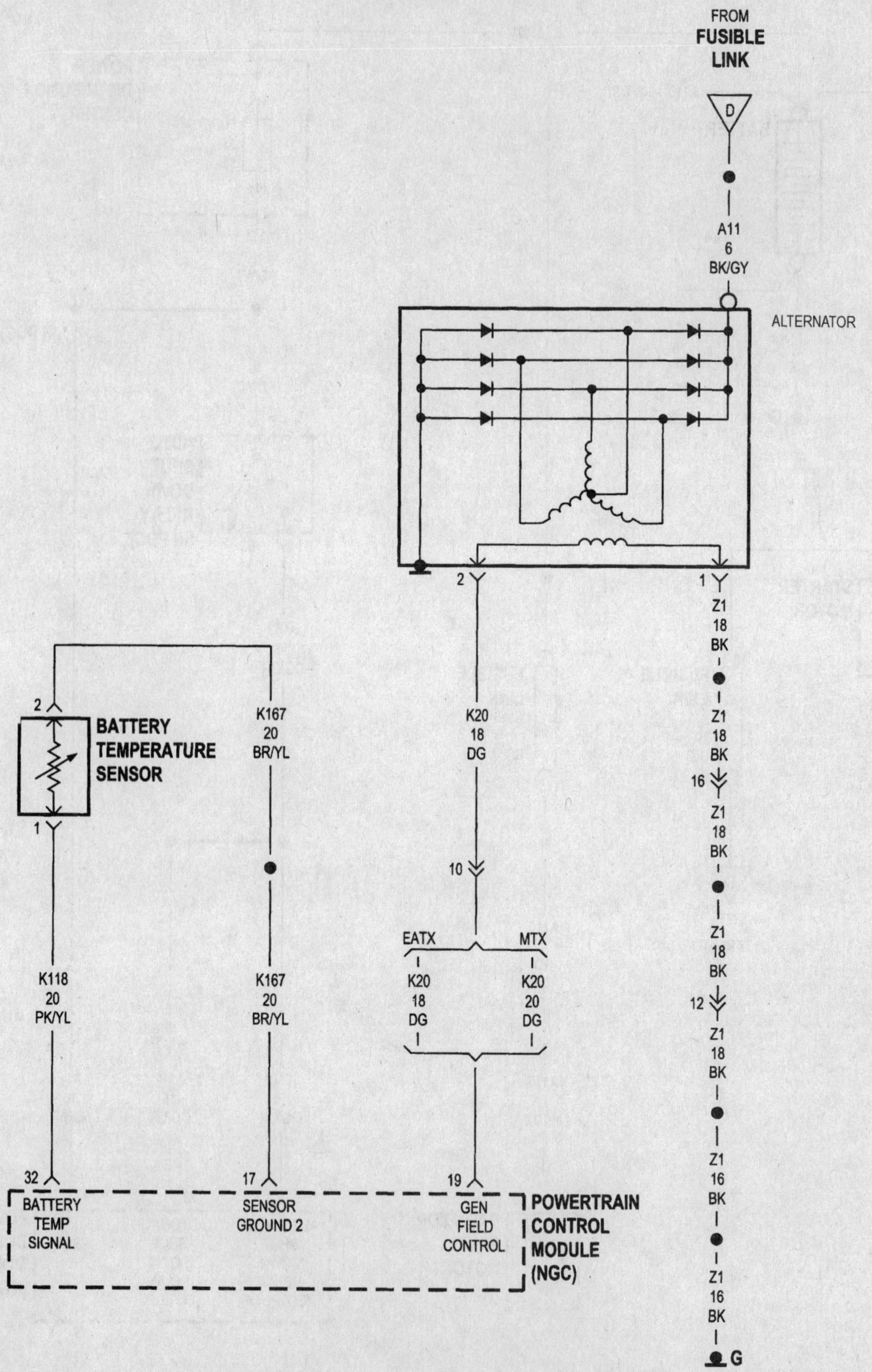


Charging system - 2003 turbocharged models (2 of 2)

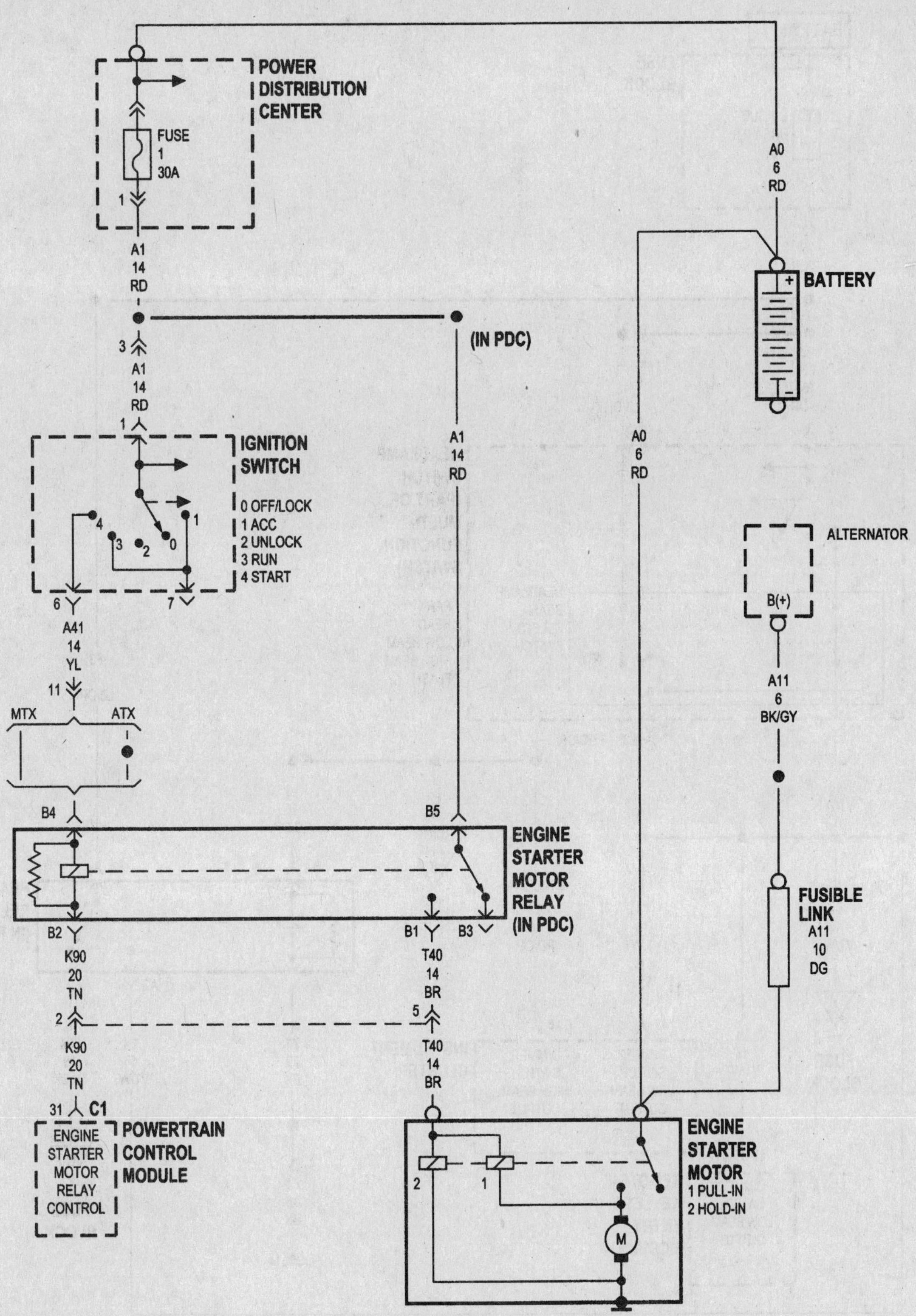


Starting system

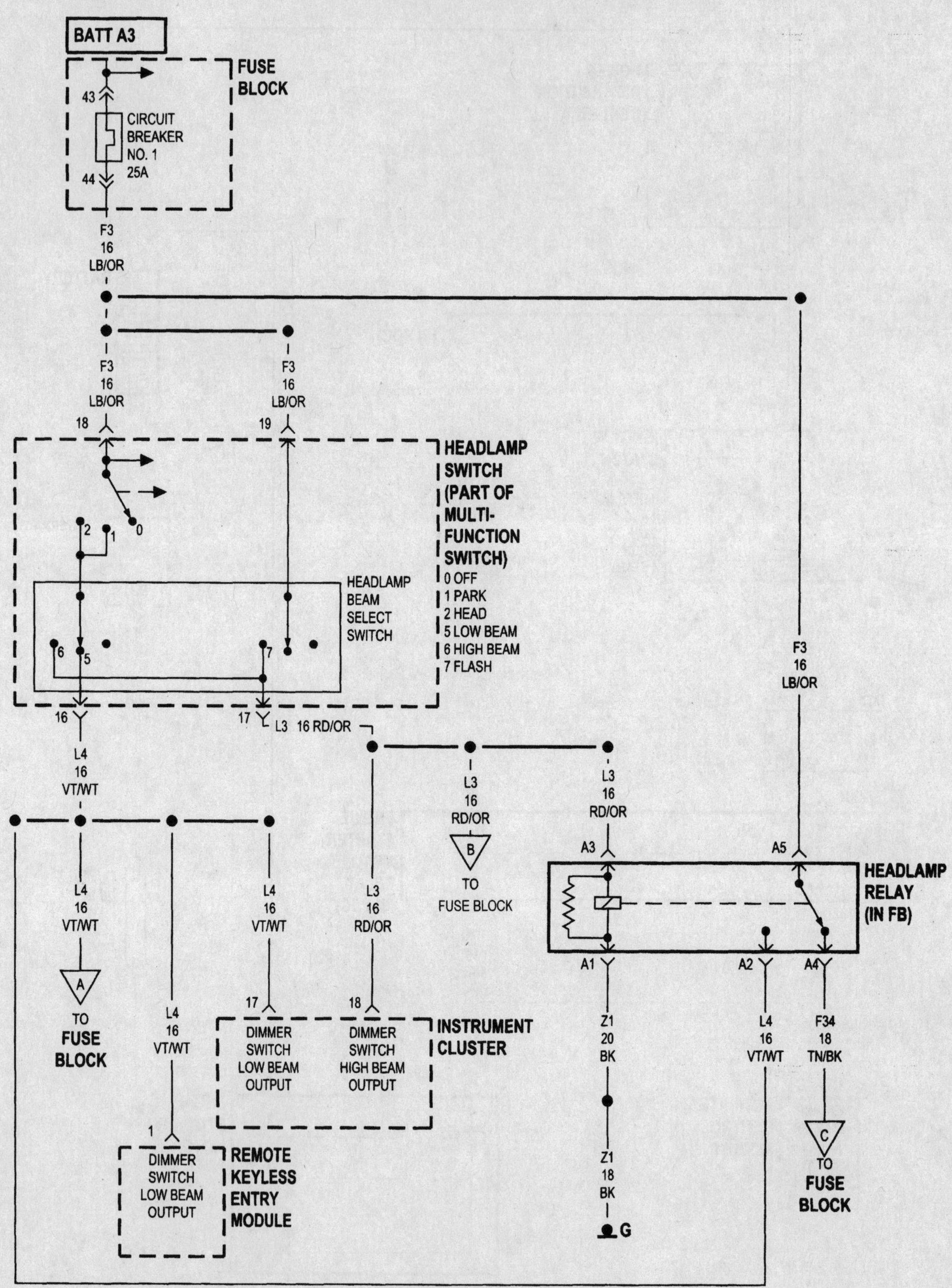


Exterior lights (headlights) (1 of 11)

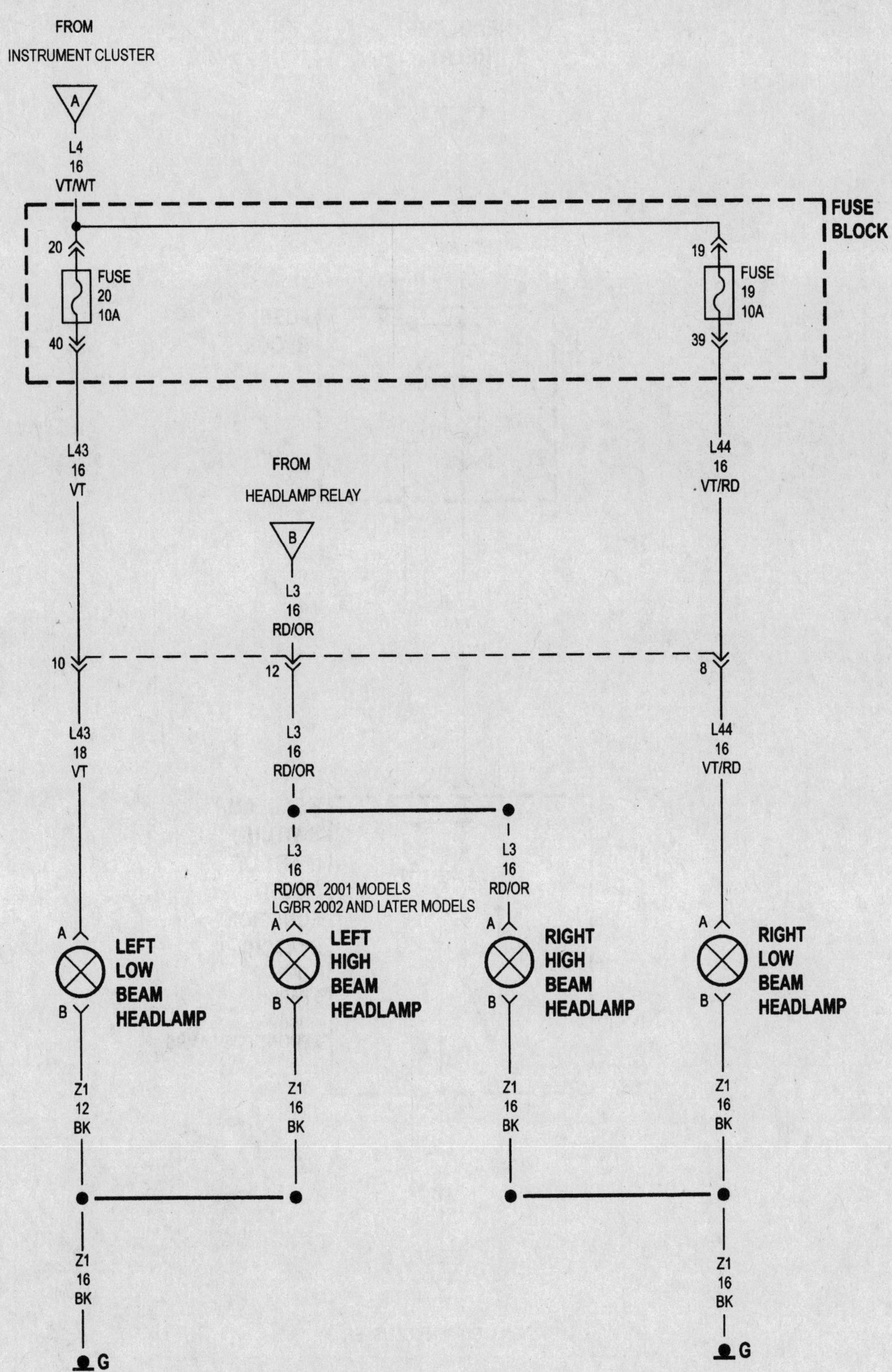


Exterior lights (headlights) (2 of 11)

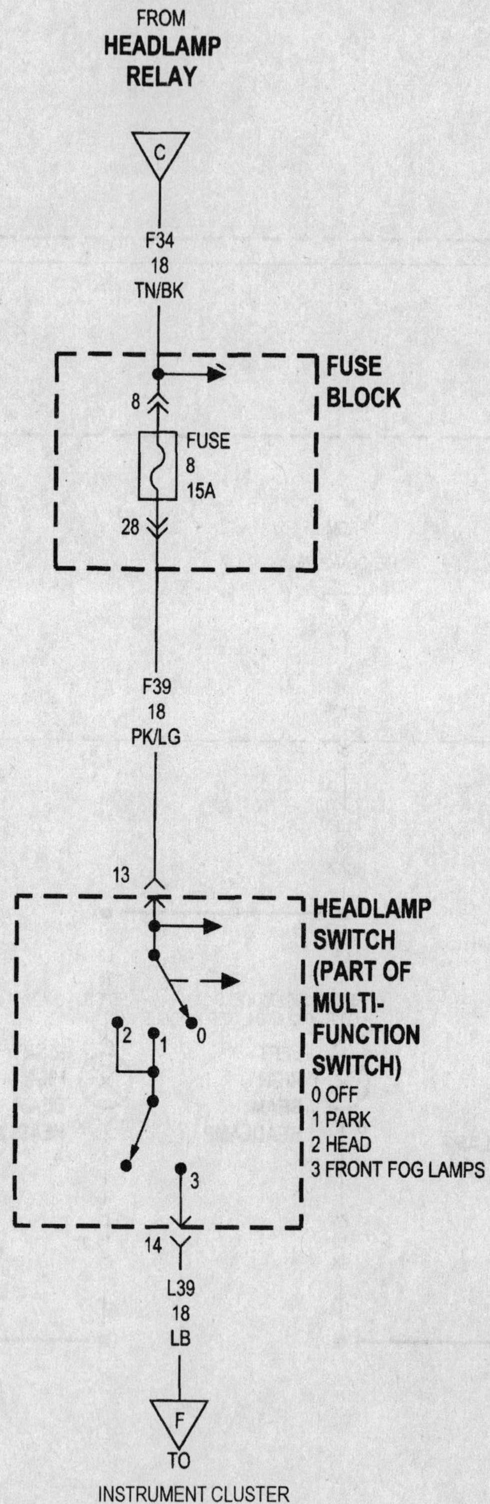


Exterior lights (front lights) (3 of 11)

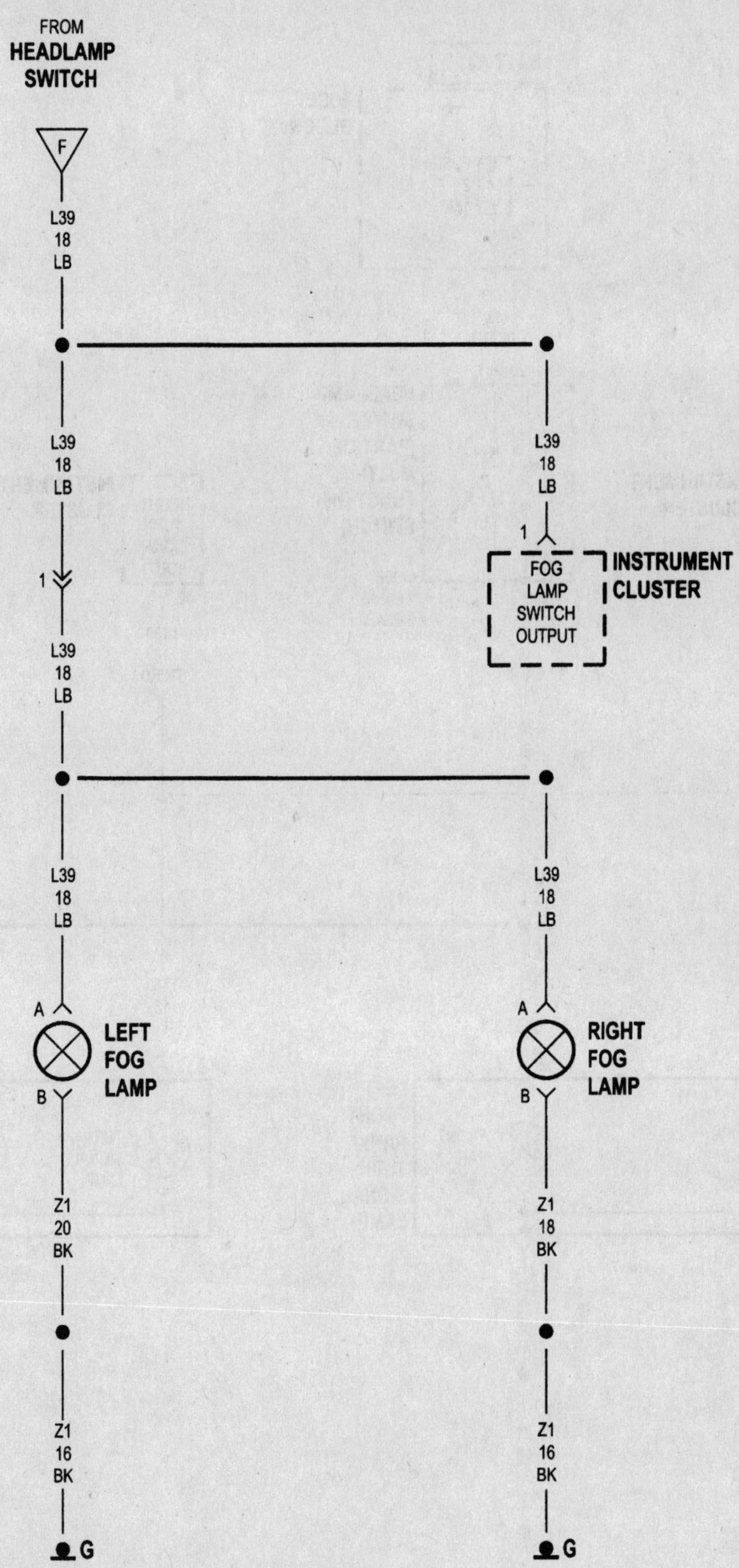


Exterior lights (front lights) (4 of 11)

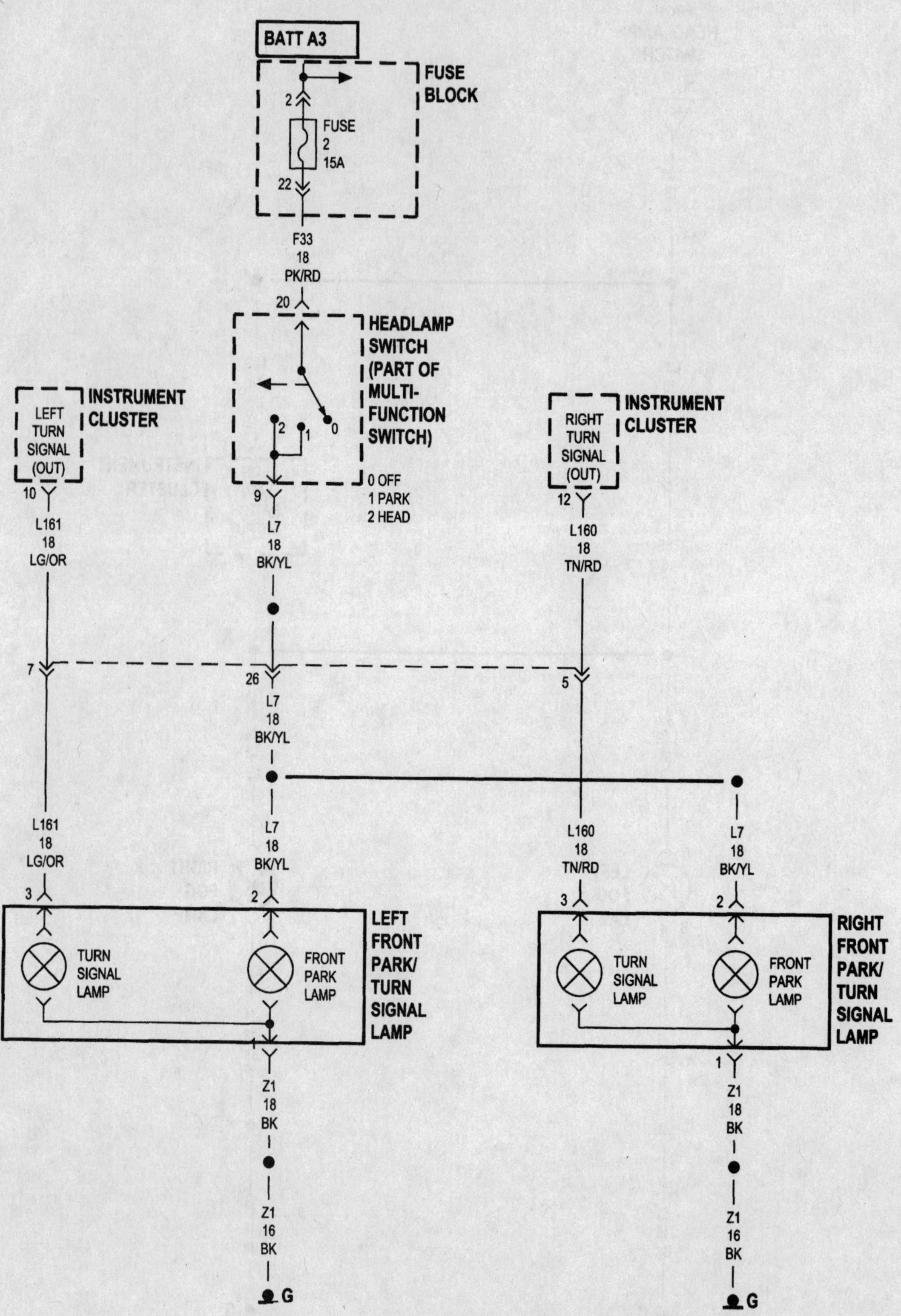


Exterior lights (front lights) (5 of 11)

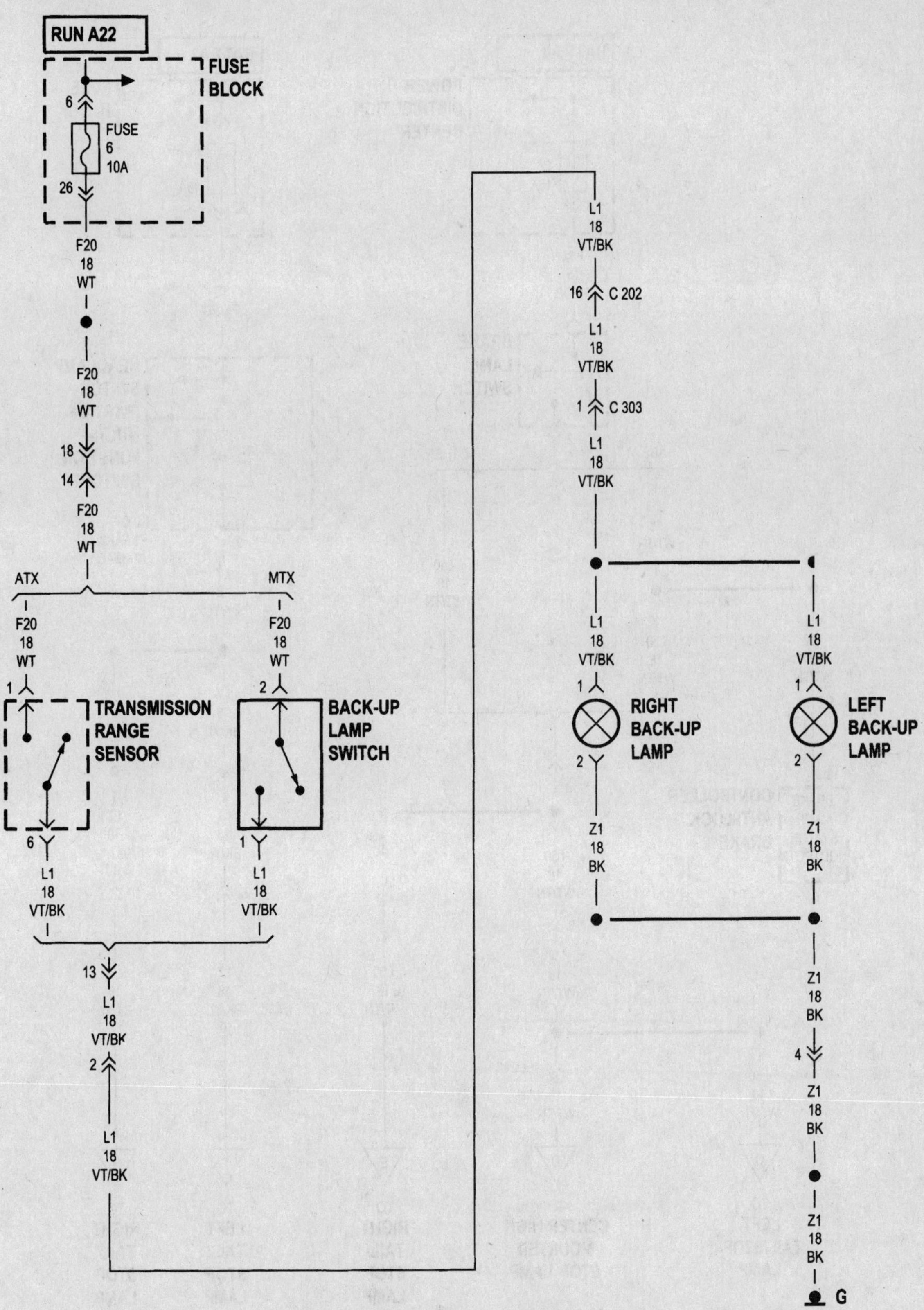


Exterior lights (rear lights) (6 of 11)

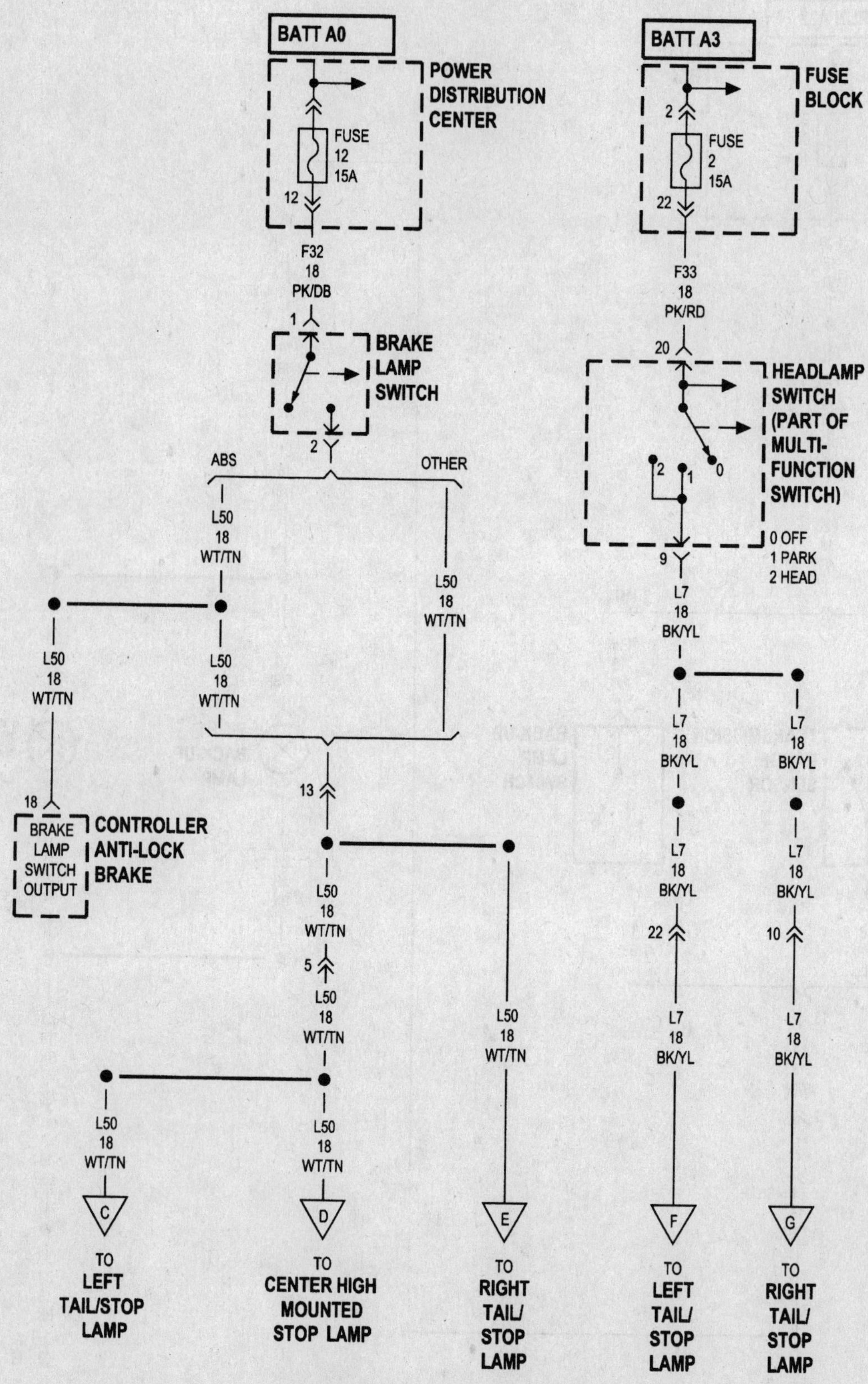


Exterior lights (rear lights) (7 of 11)

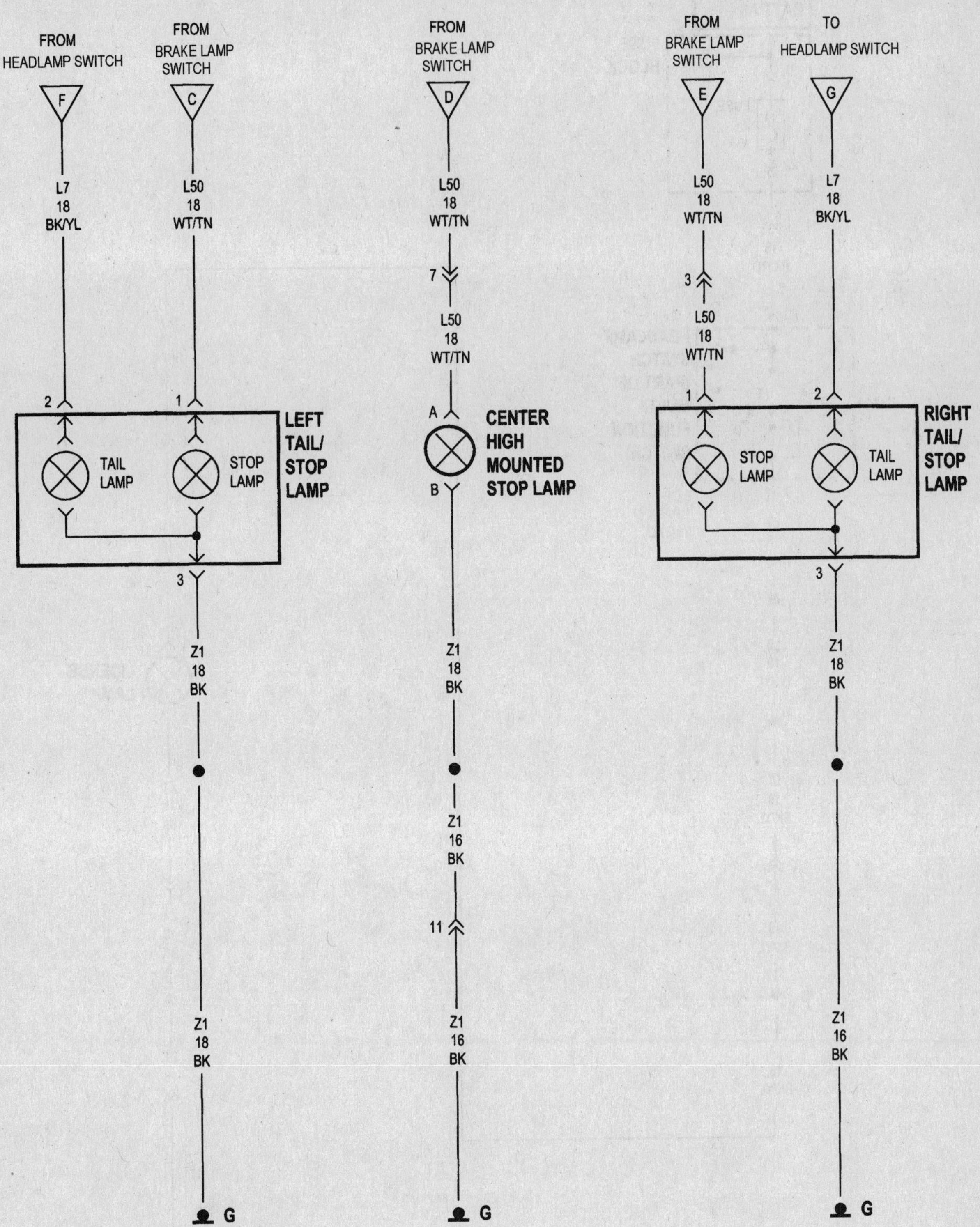


Exterior lights (rear lights) (8 of 11)

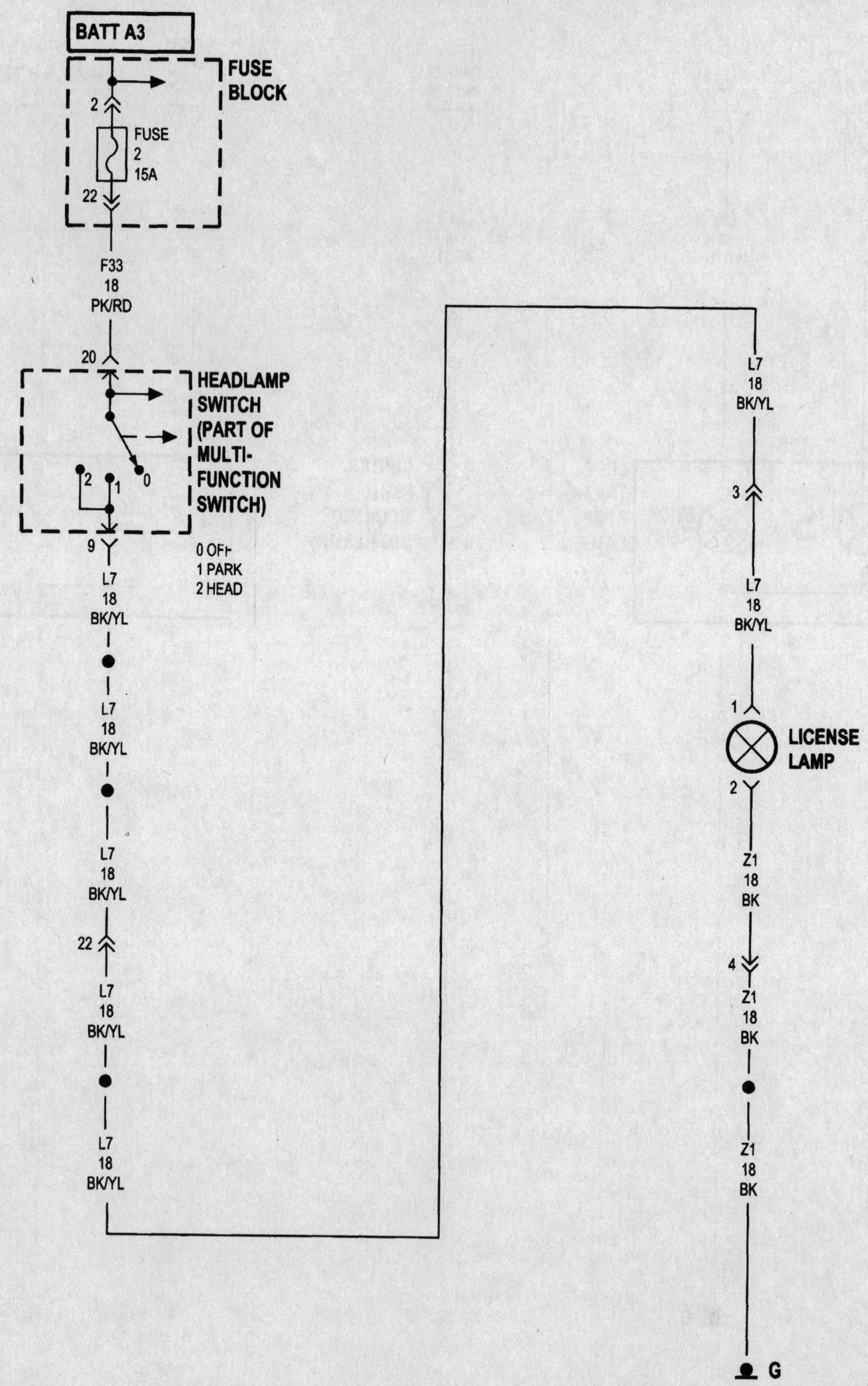


Exterior lights (rear lights) (9 of 11)

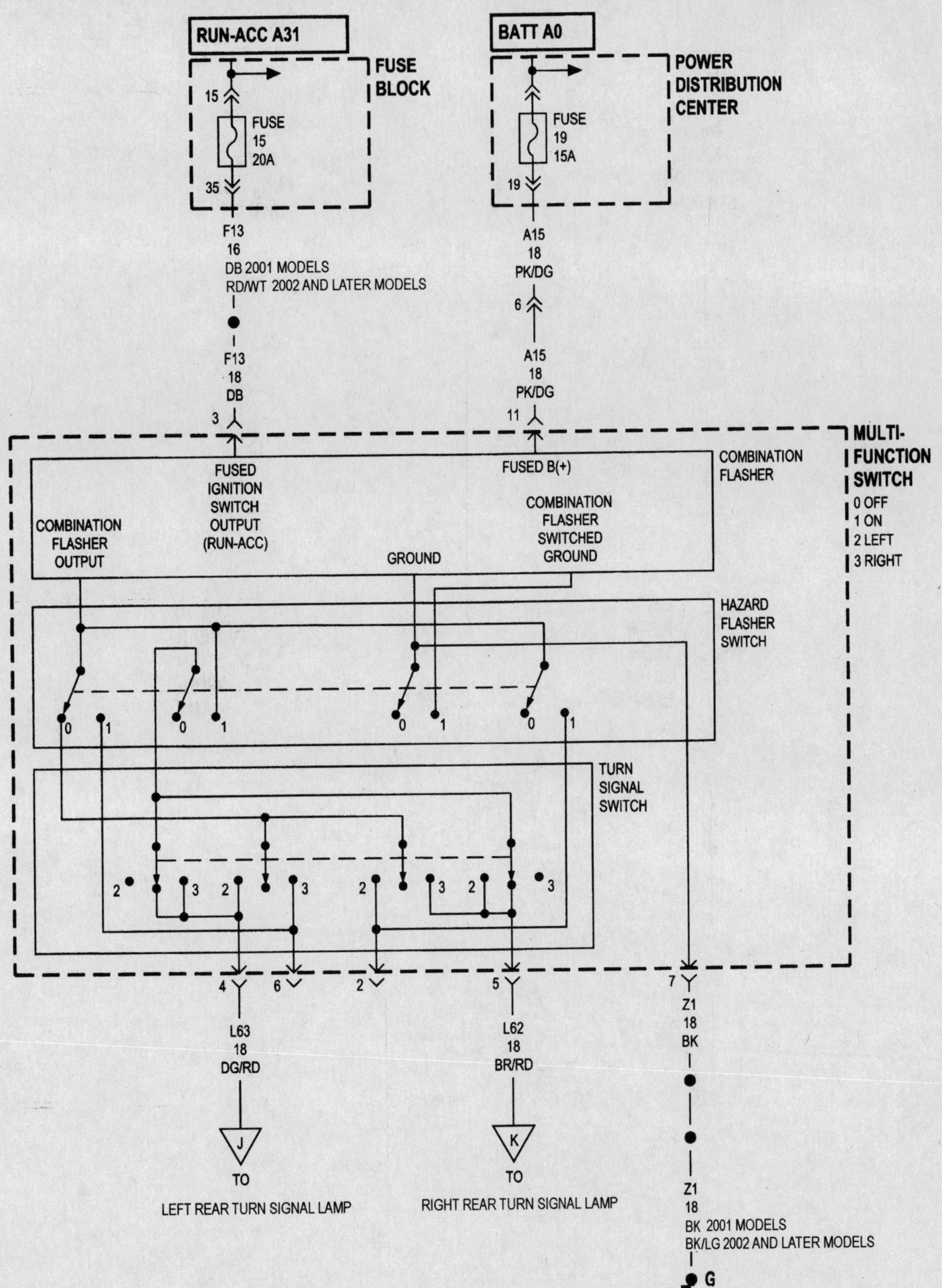


Exterior lights (rear lights) (10 of 11)

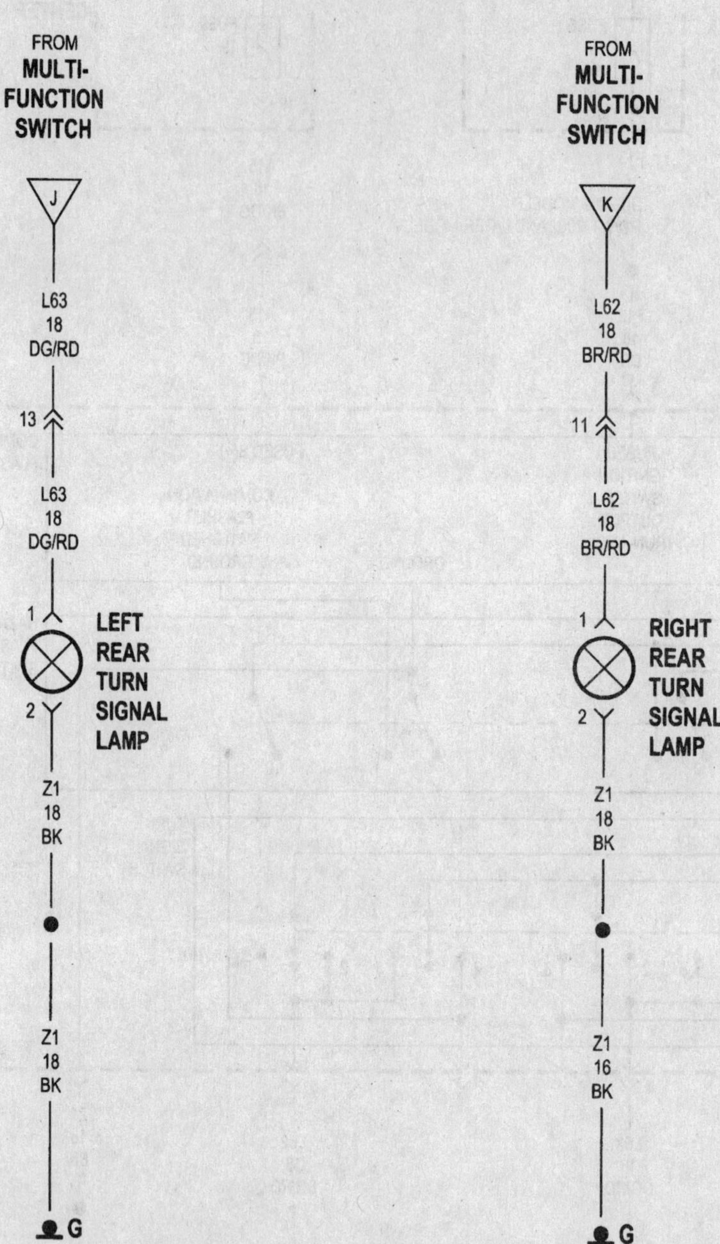


Exterior lights (rear lights) (11 of 11)

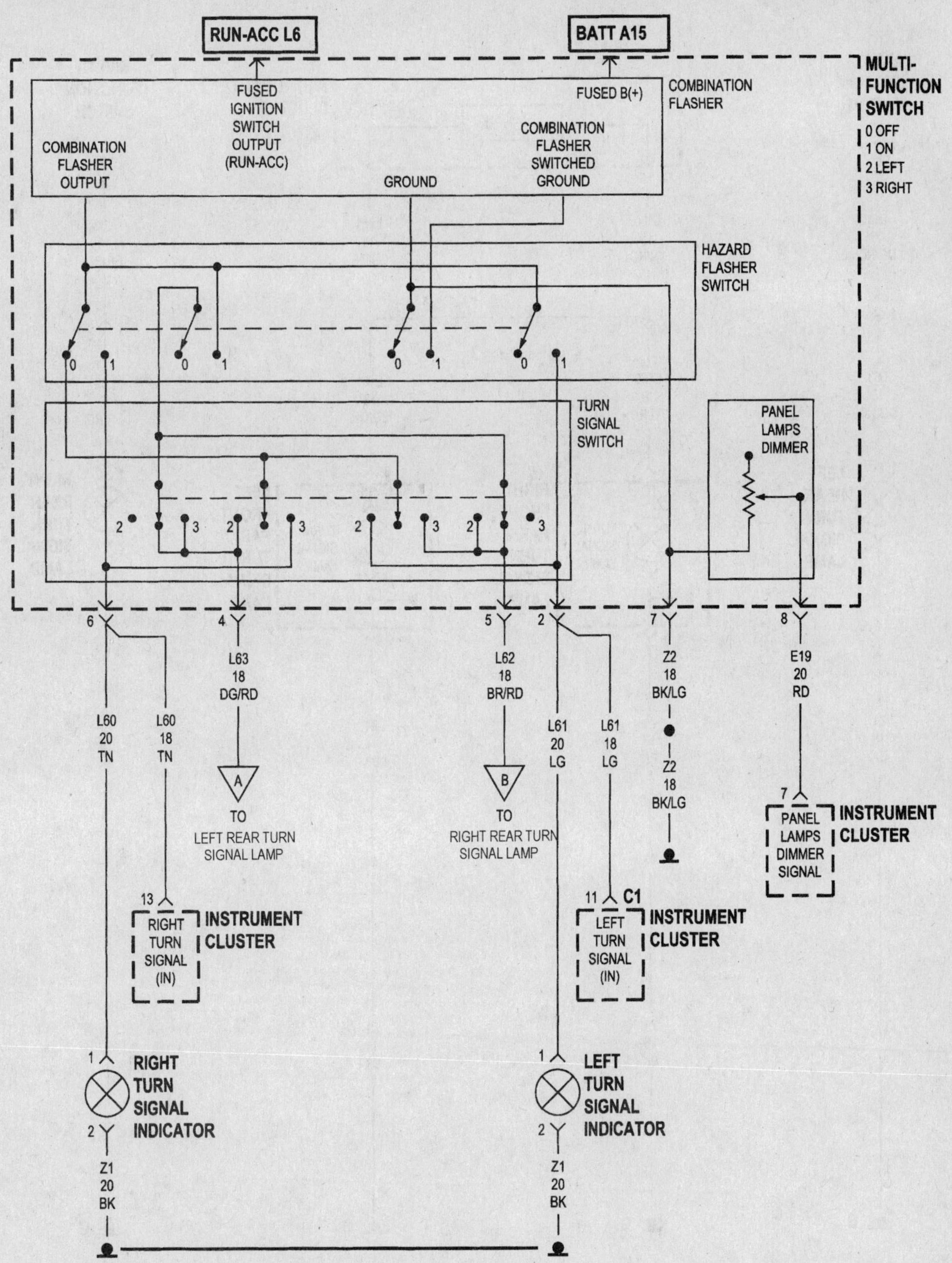


Turn signal system (1 of 2)

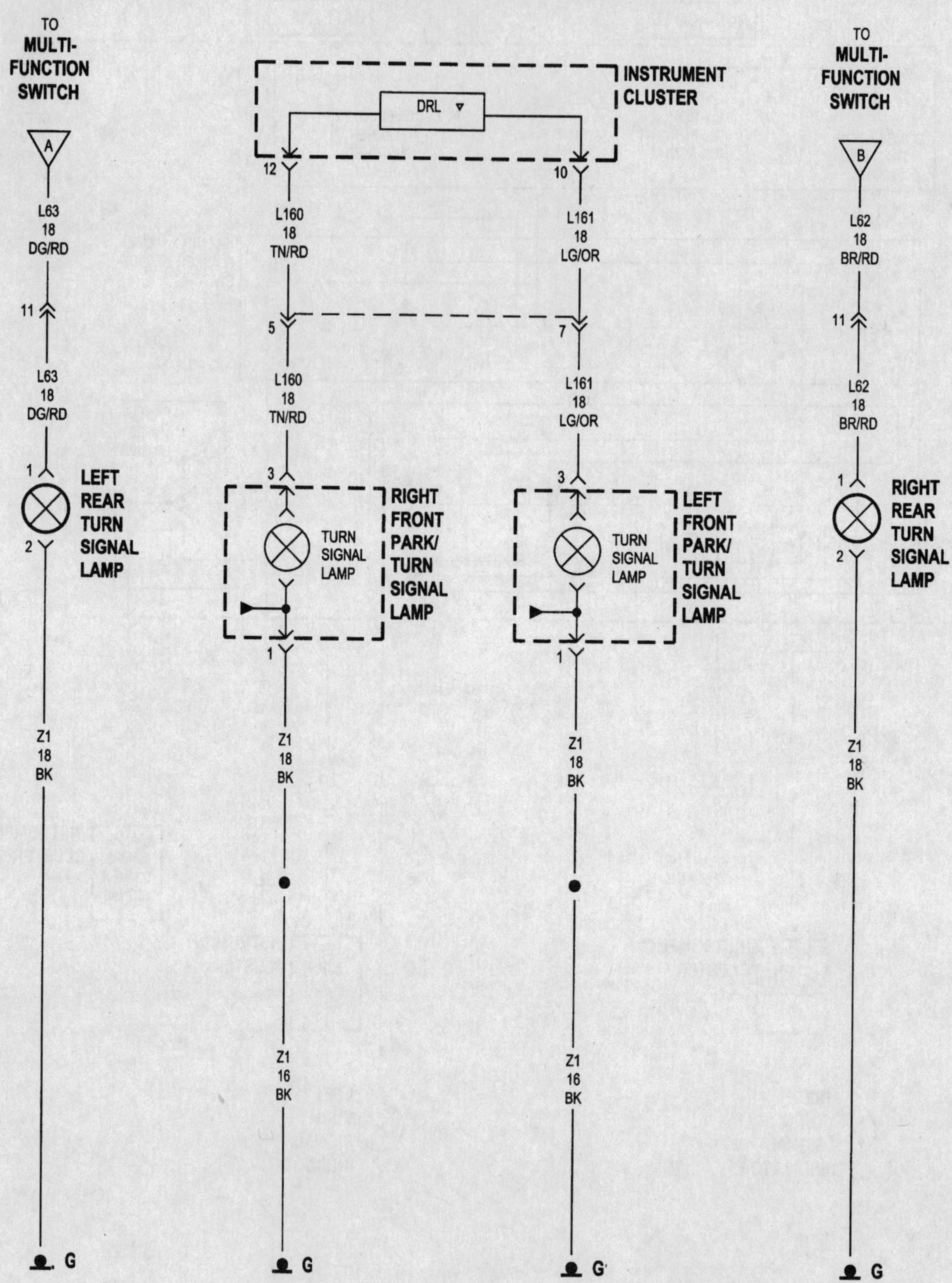


Turn signal system (2 of 2)

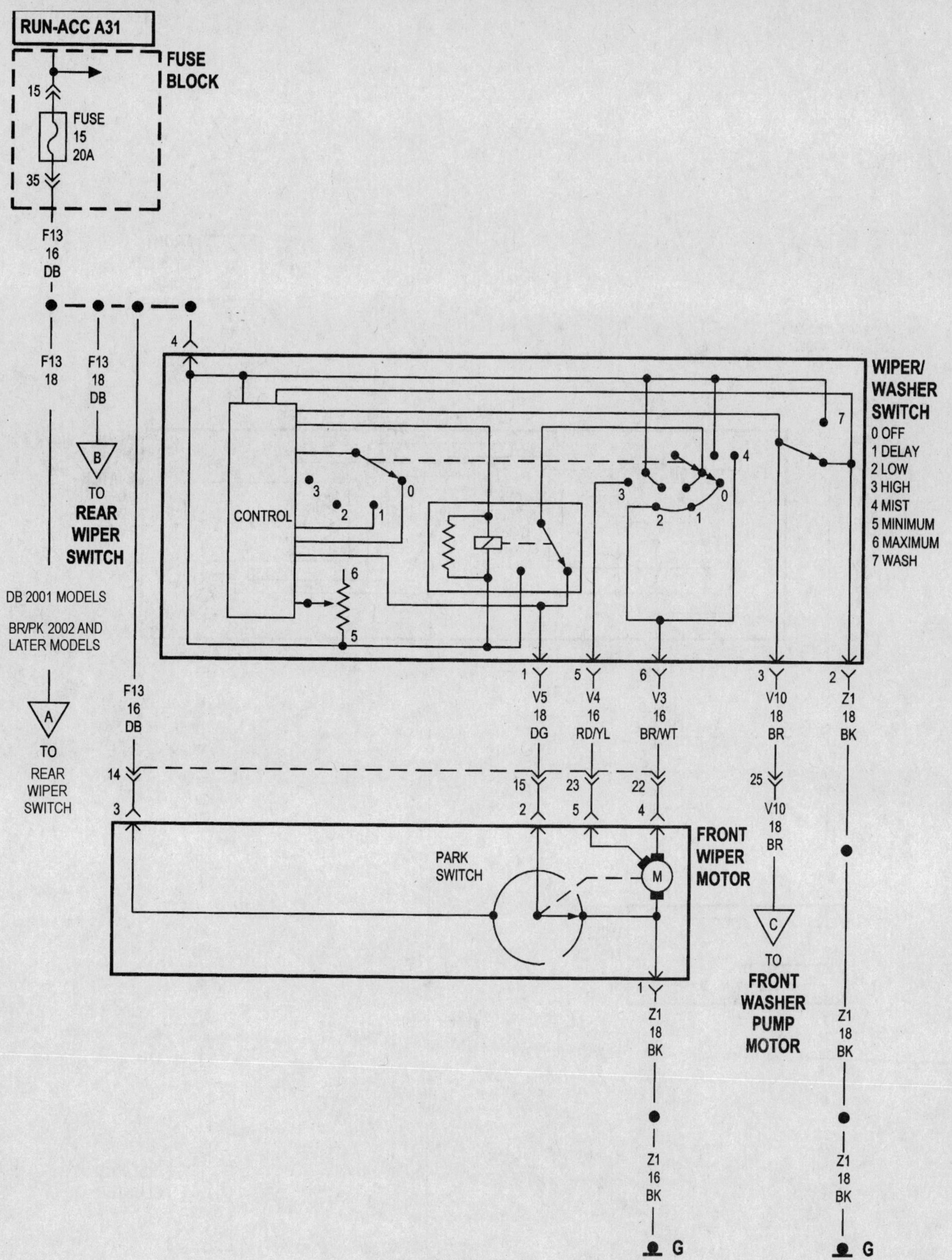


Windshield/rear window wiper system (1 of 2)

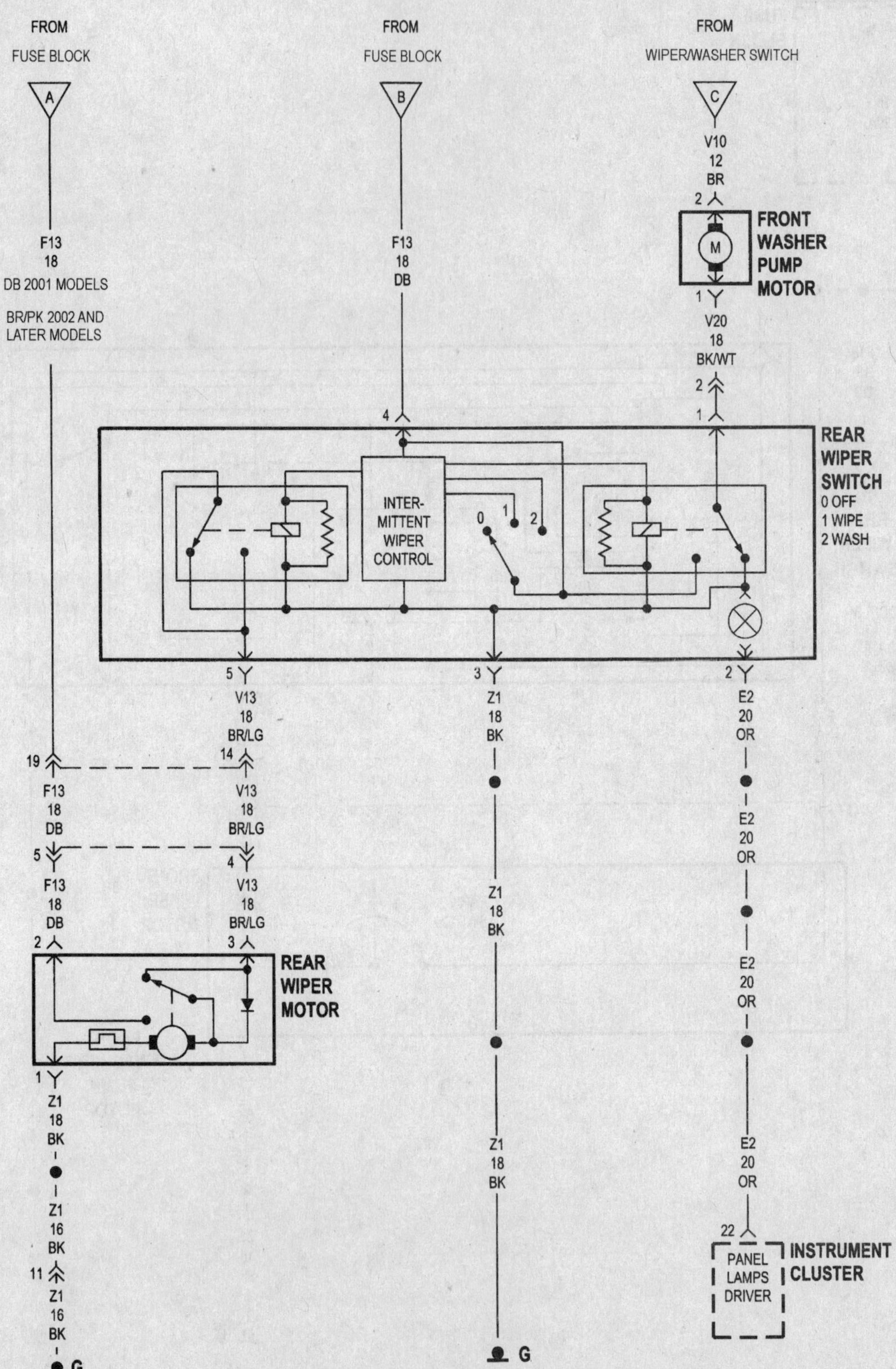


Windshield/rear window wiper system (2 of 2)

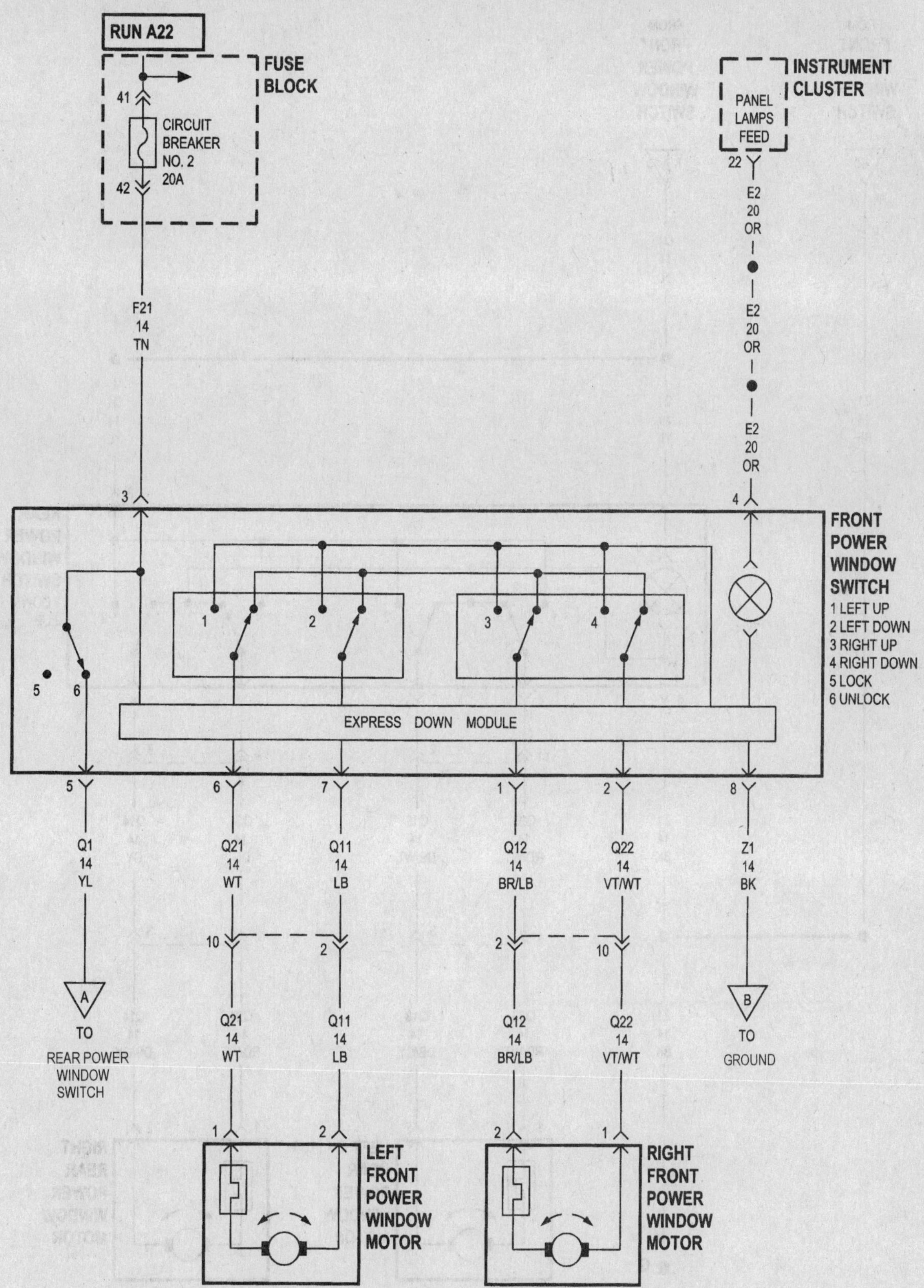


Power windows - 2001 models (1 of 2)

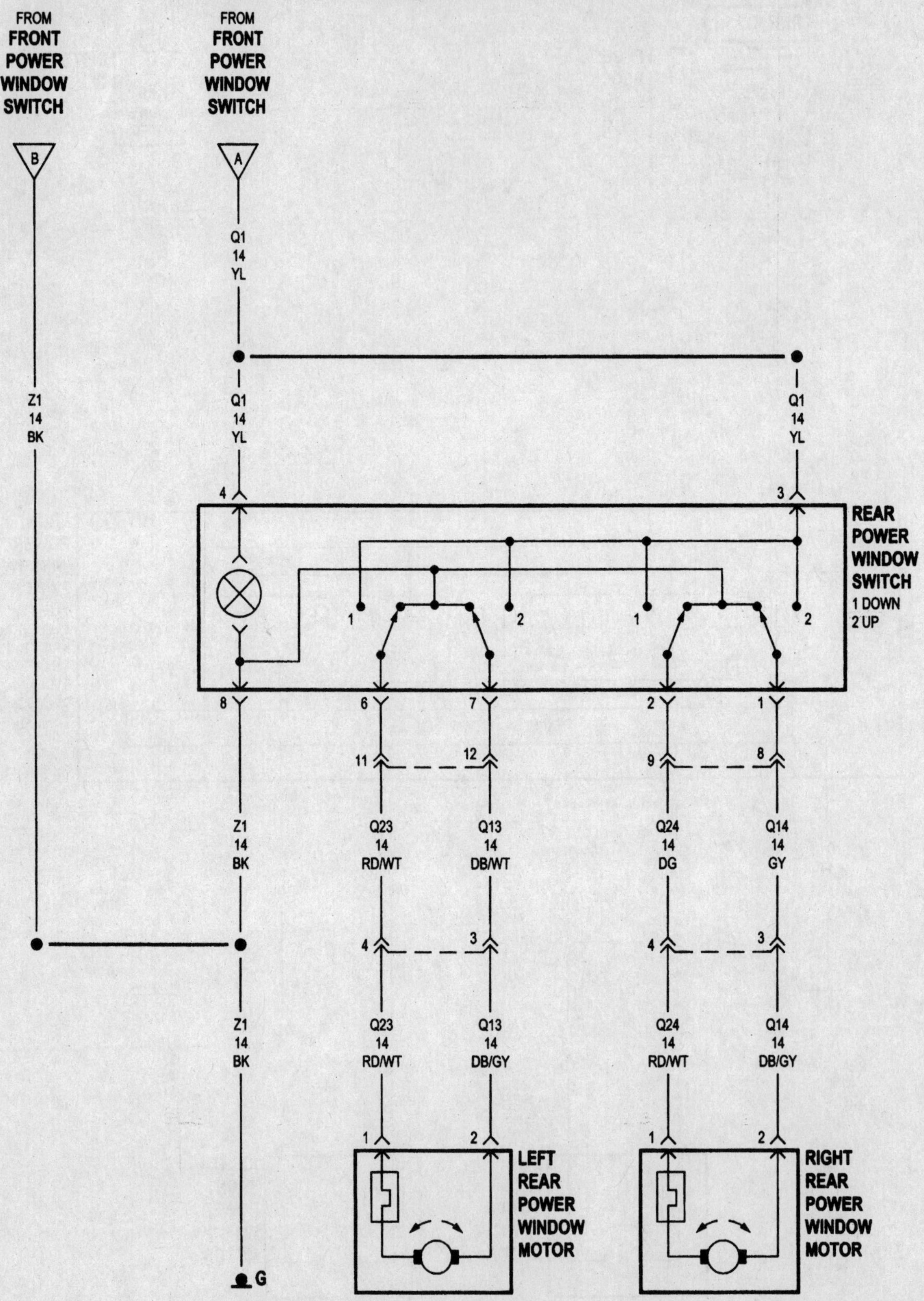


Power windows - 2001 models (2 of 2)

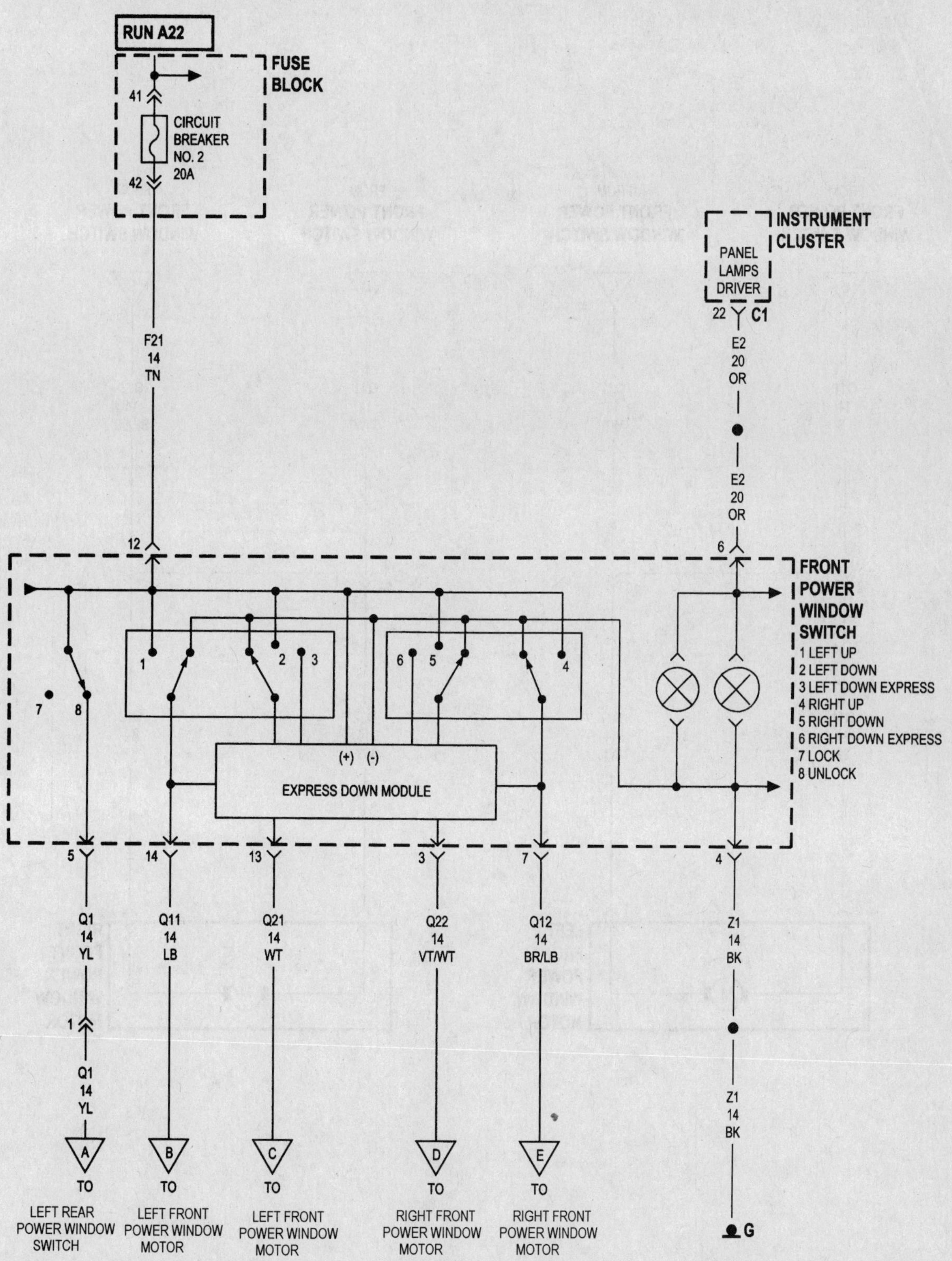


**Power windows (with Express Down Module) - 2002 and later models (1 of 5)**

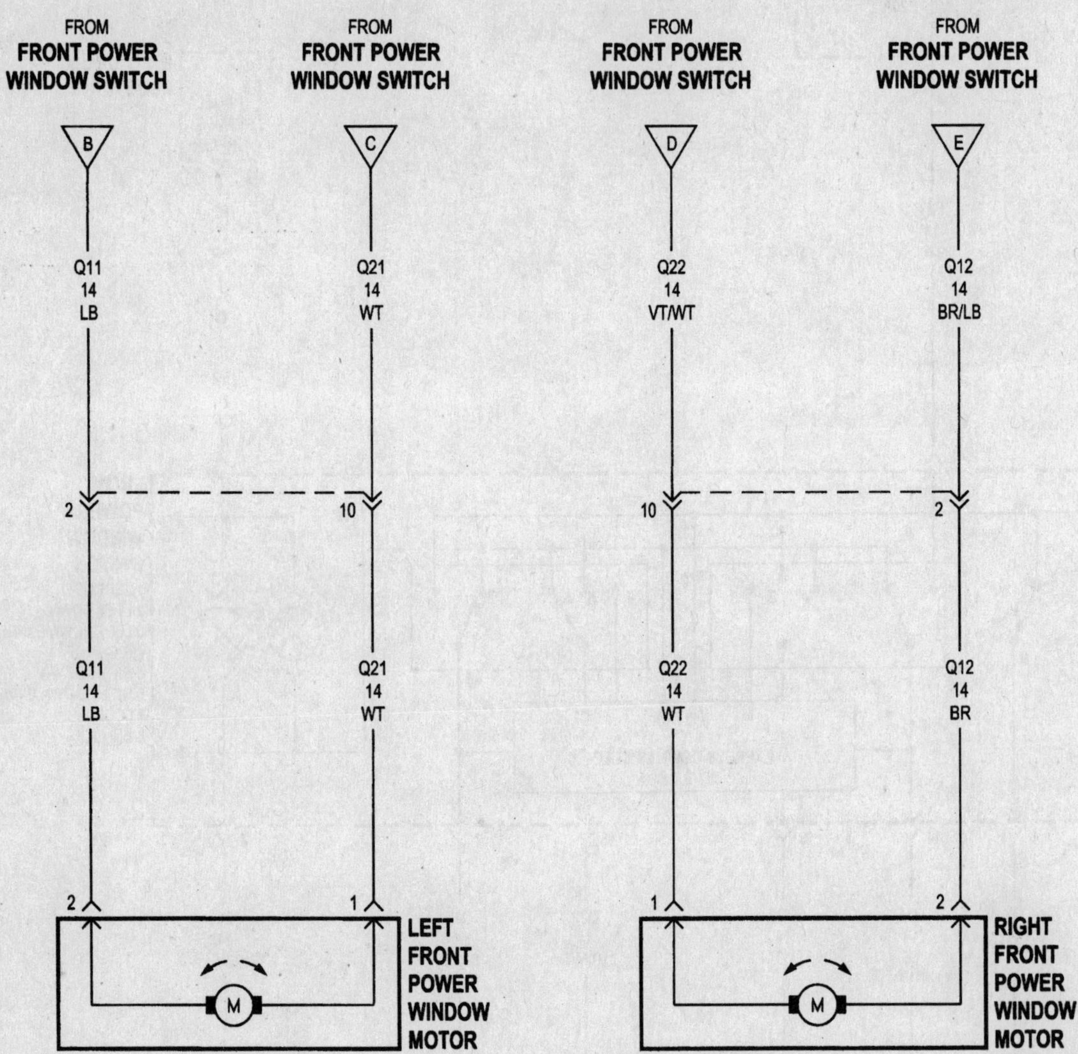


Power windows - 2002 and later models (2 of 5)

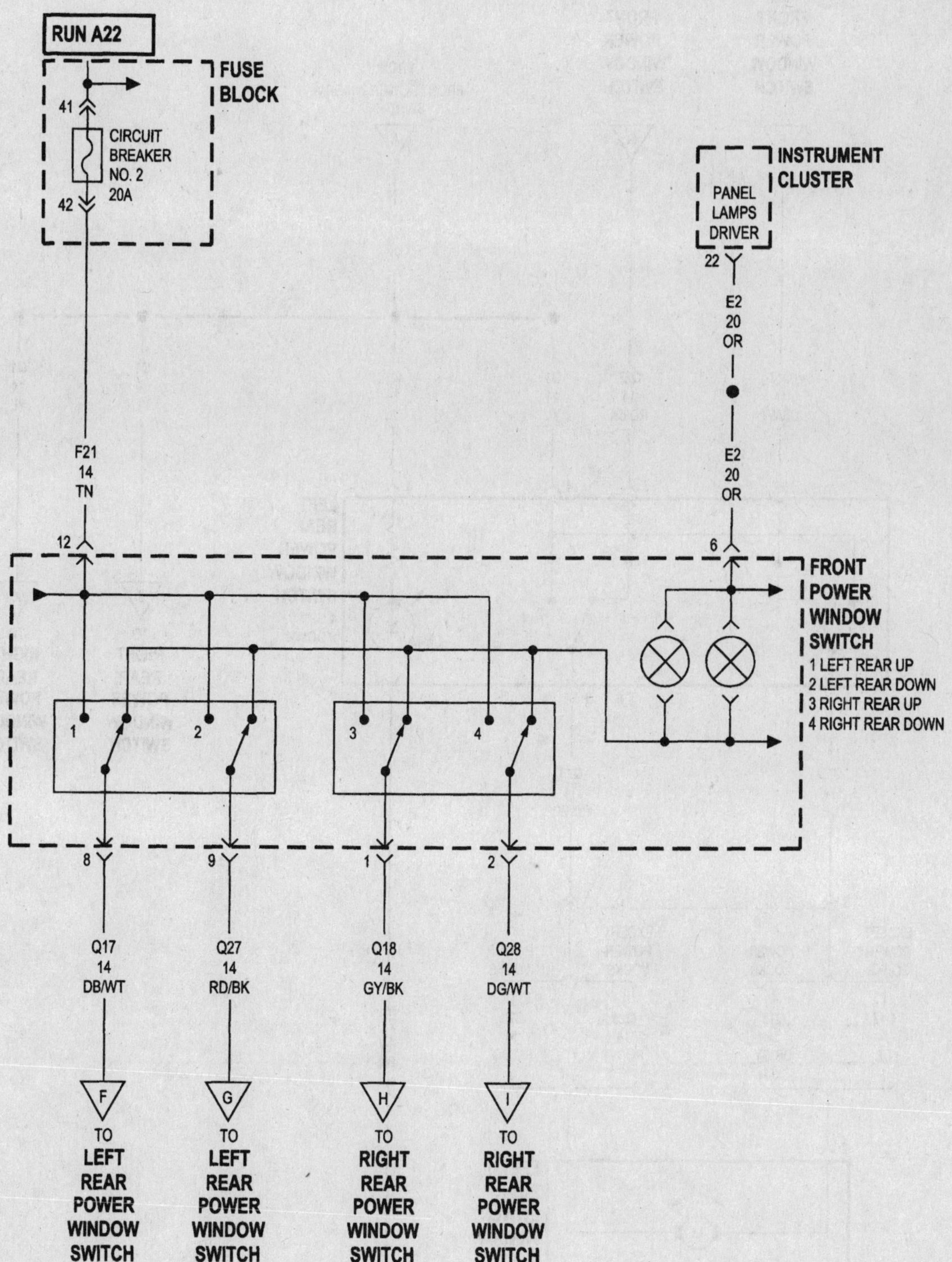


Power windows - 2002 and later models (3 of 5)

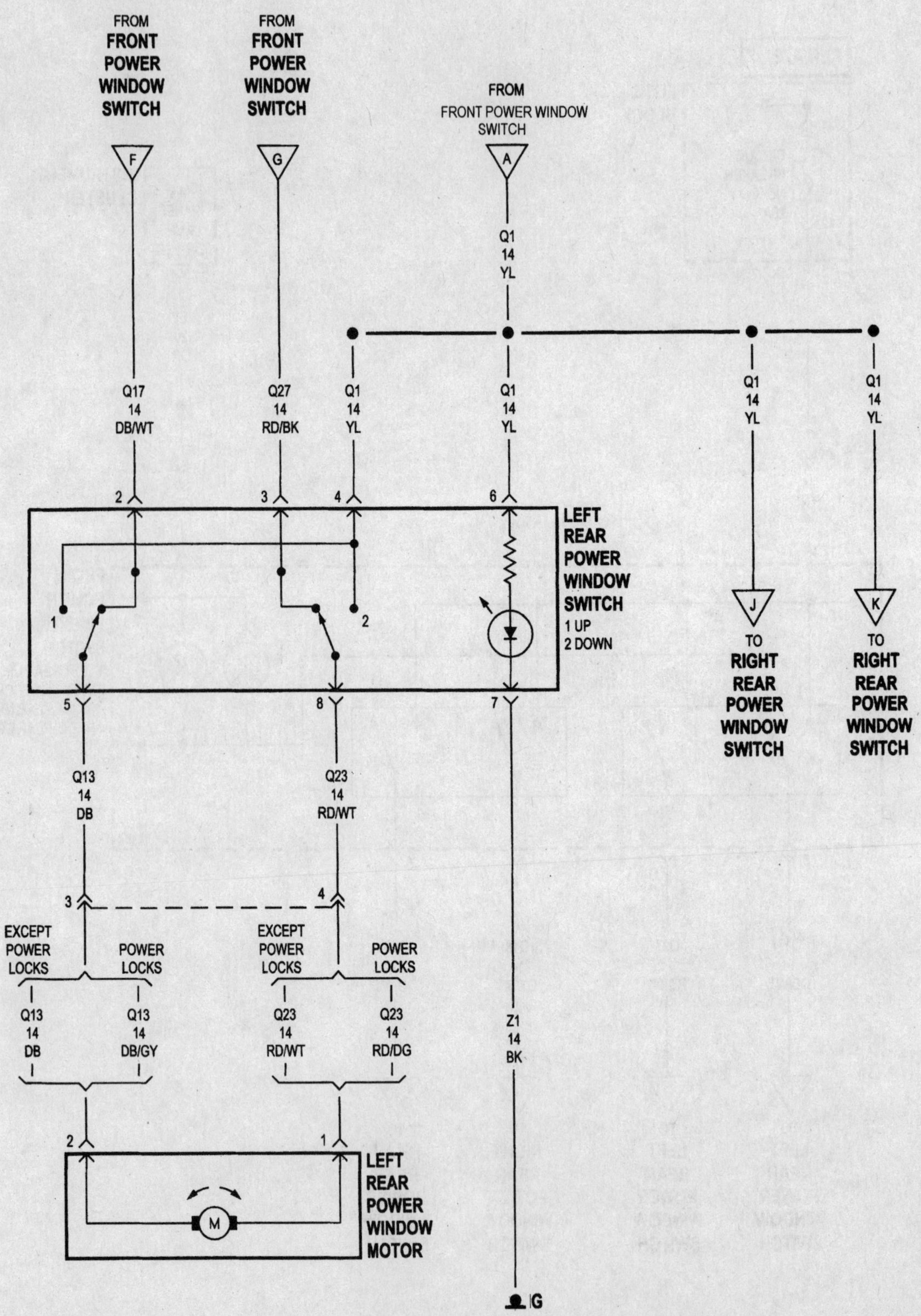


Power windows - 2002 and later models (4 of 5)

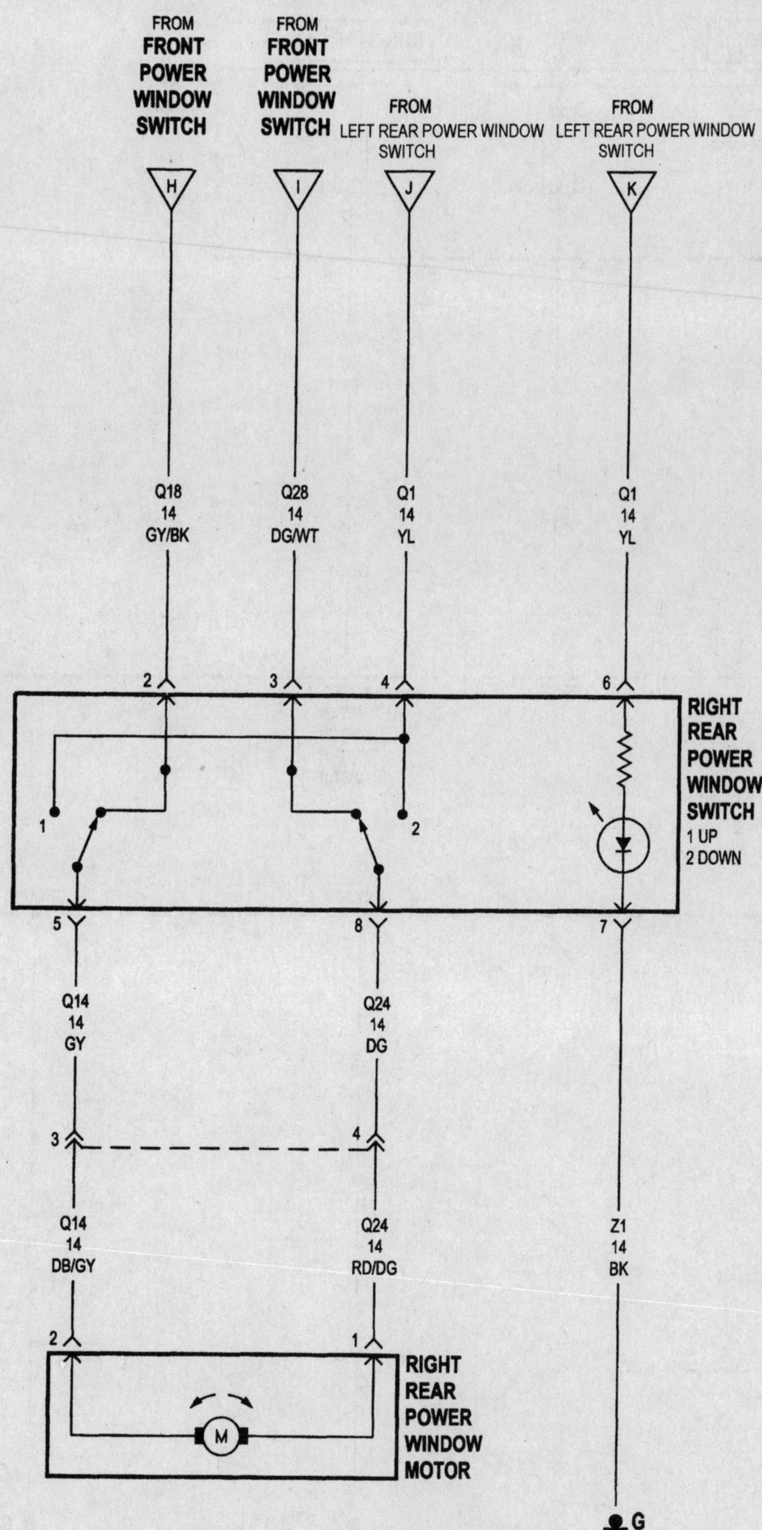


Power windows - 2002 and later models (5 of 5)

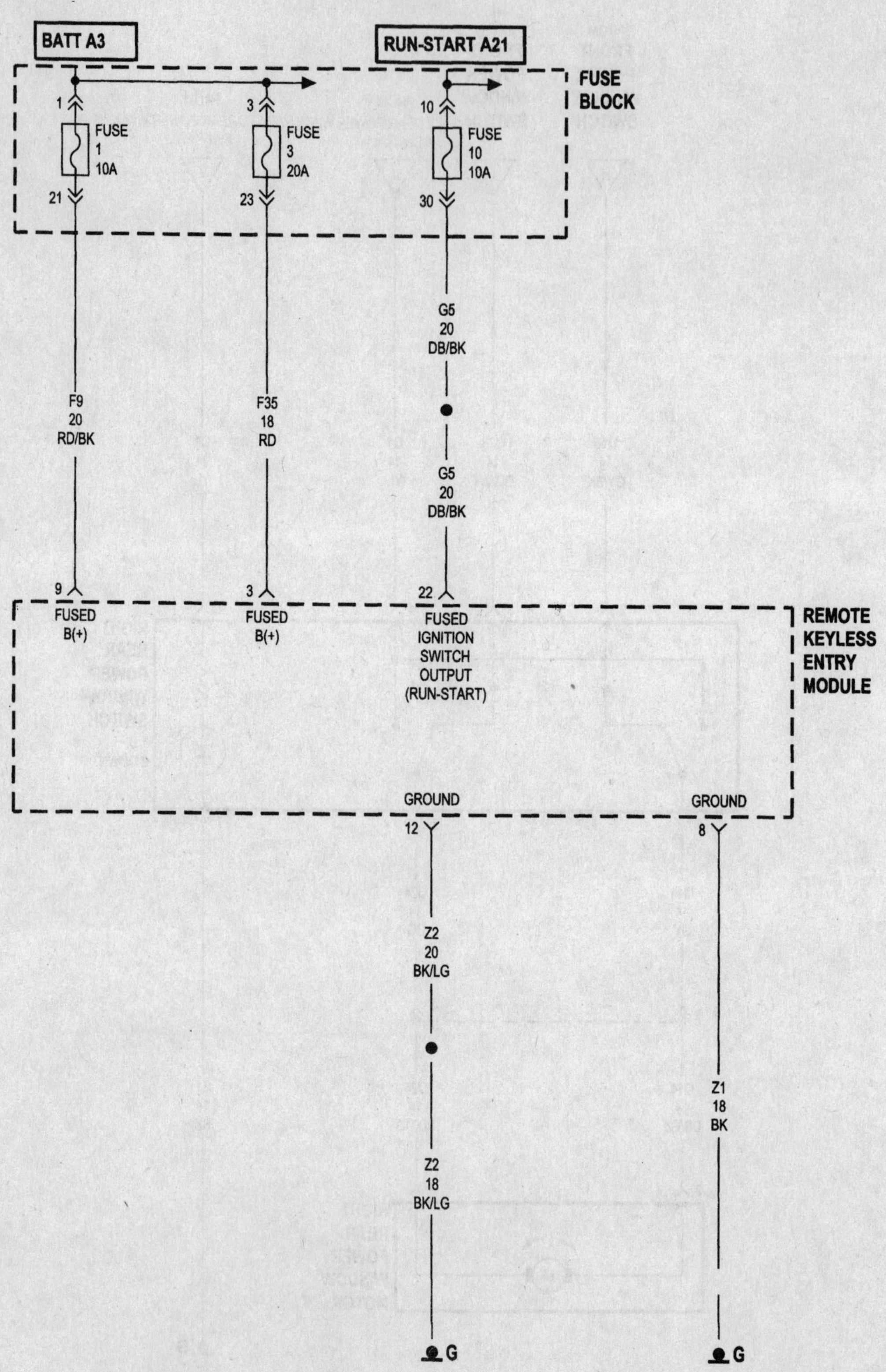


Power door locks (1 of 5)

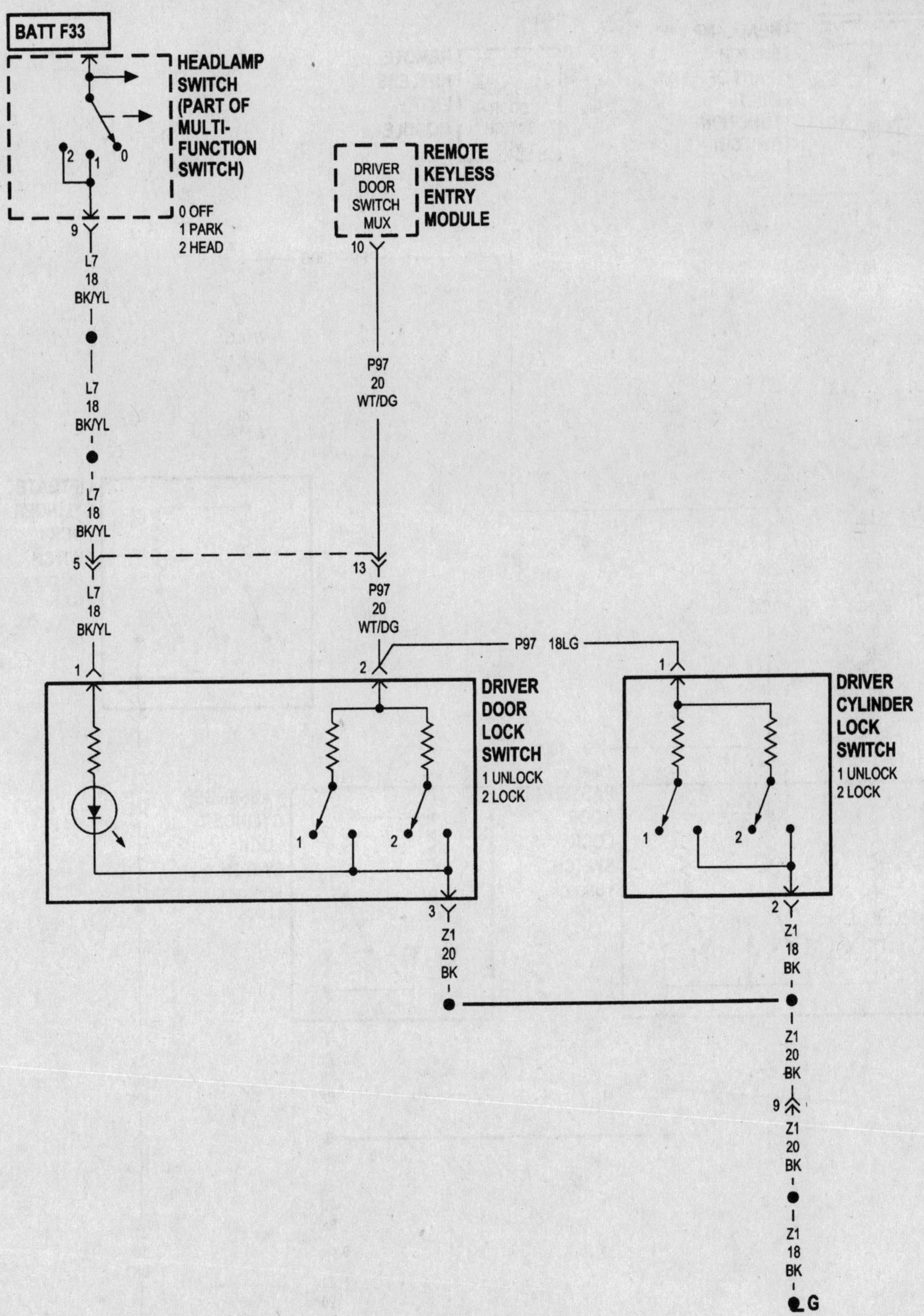


Power door locks (2 of 5)

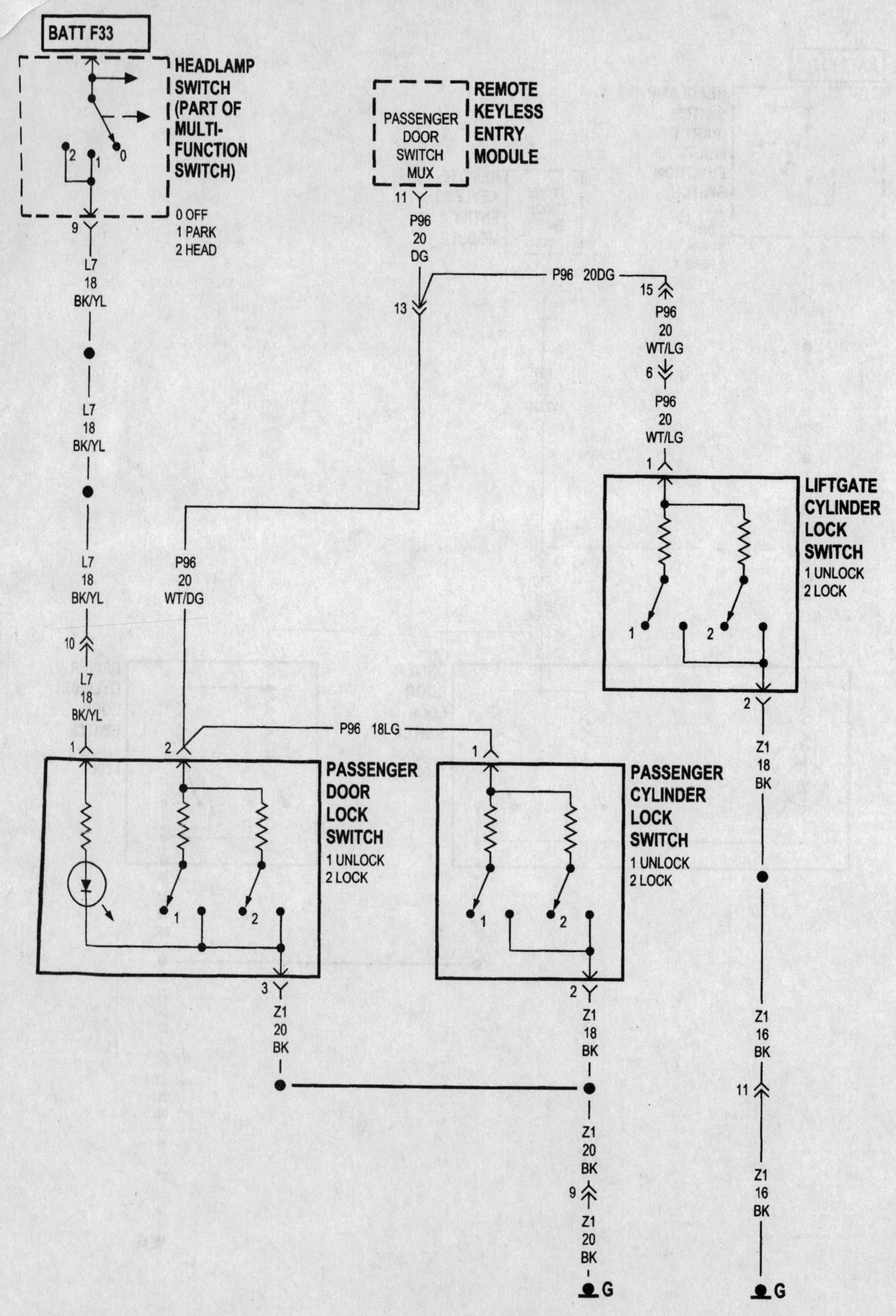


Power door locks (3 of 5)

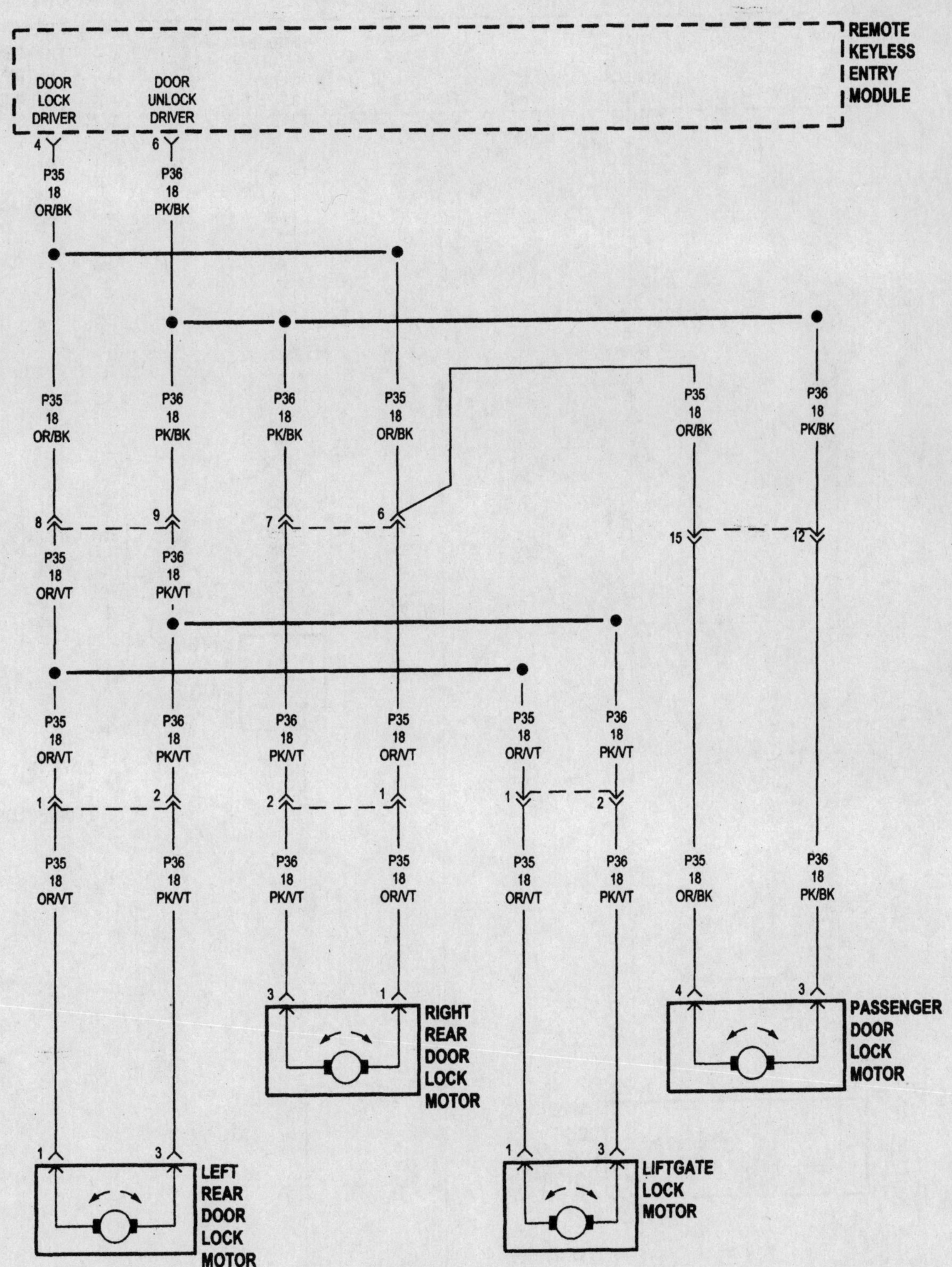


Power door locks (4 of 5)

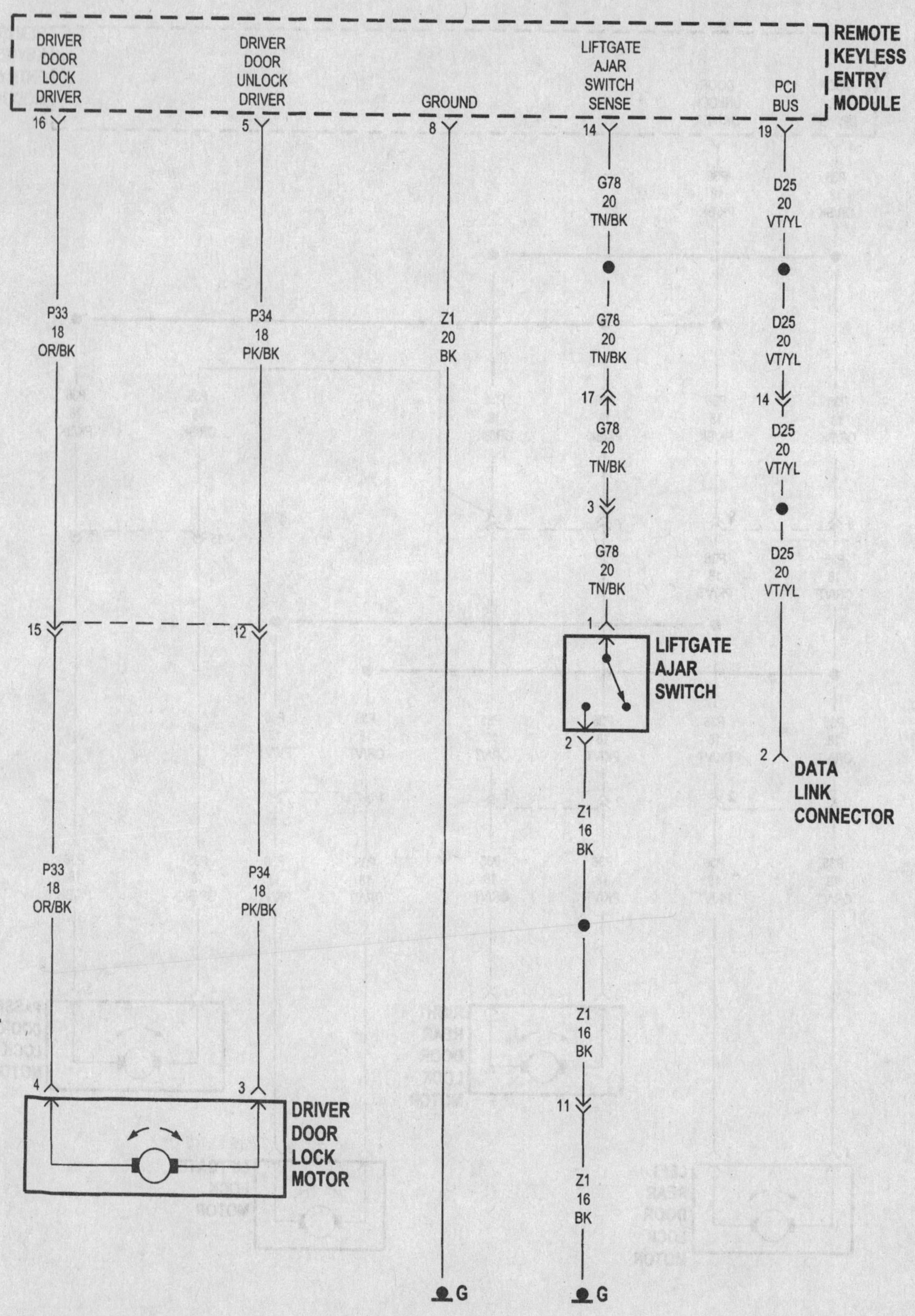


Power door locks (5 of 5)

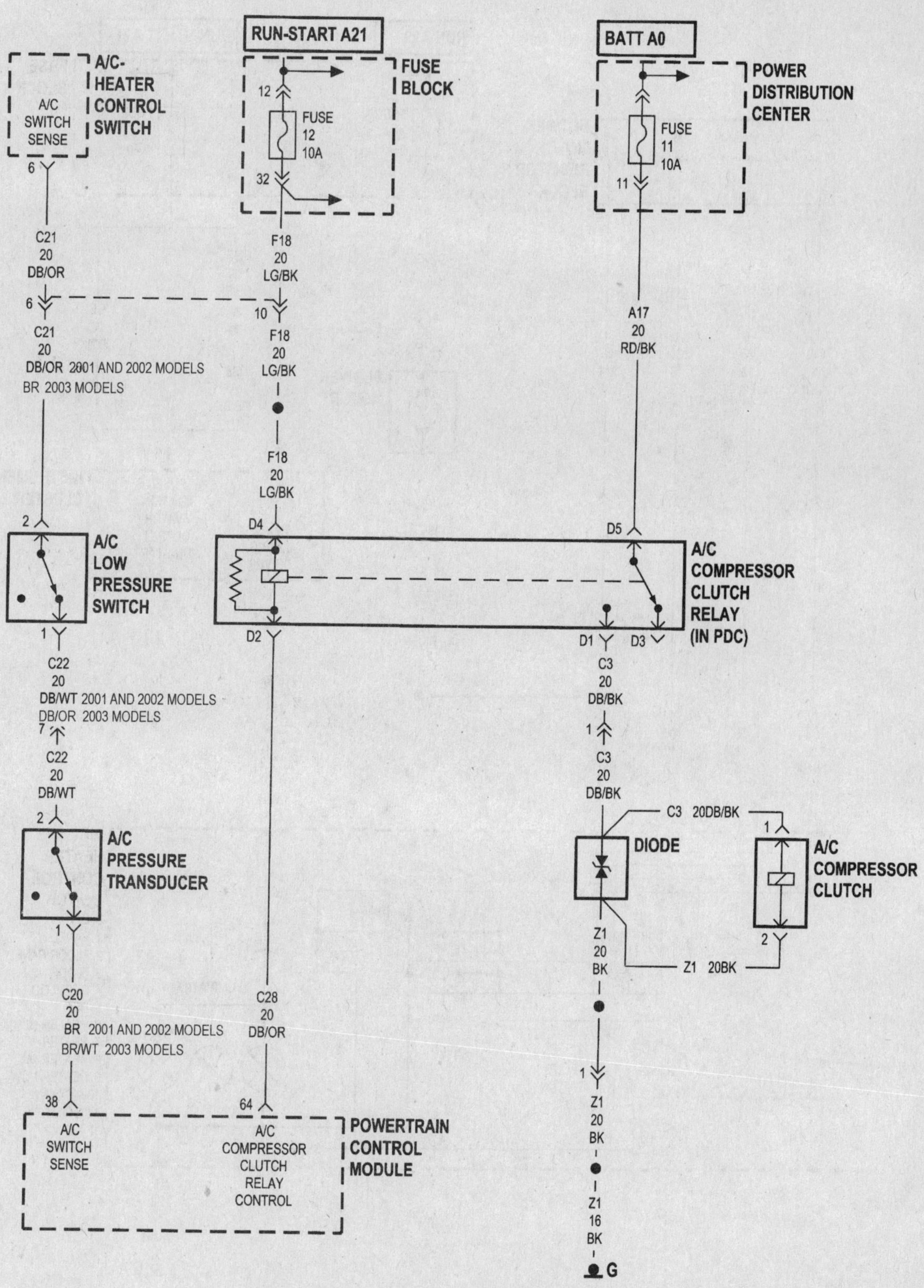


Air conditioning and heating system (1 of 2)

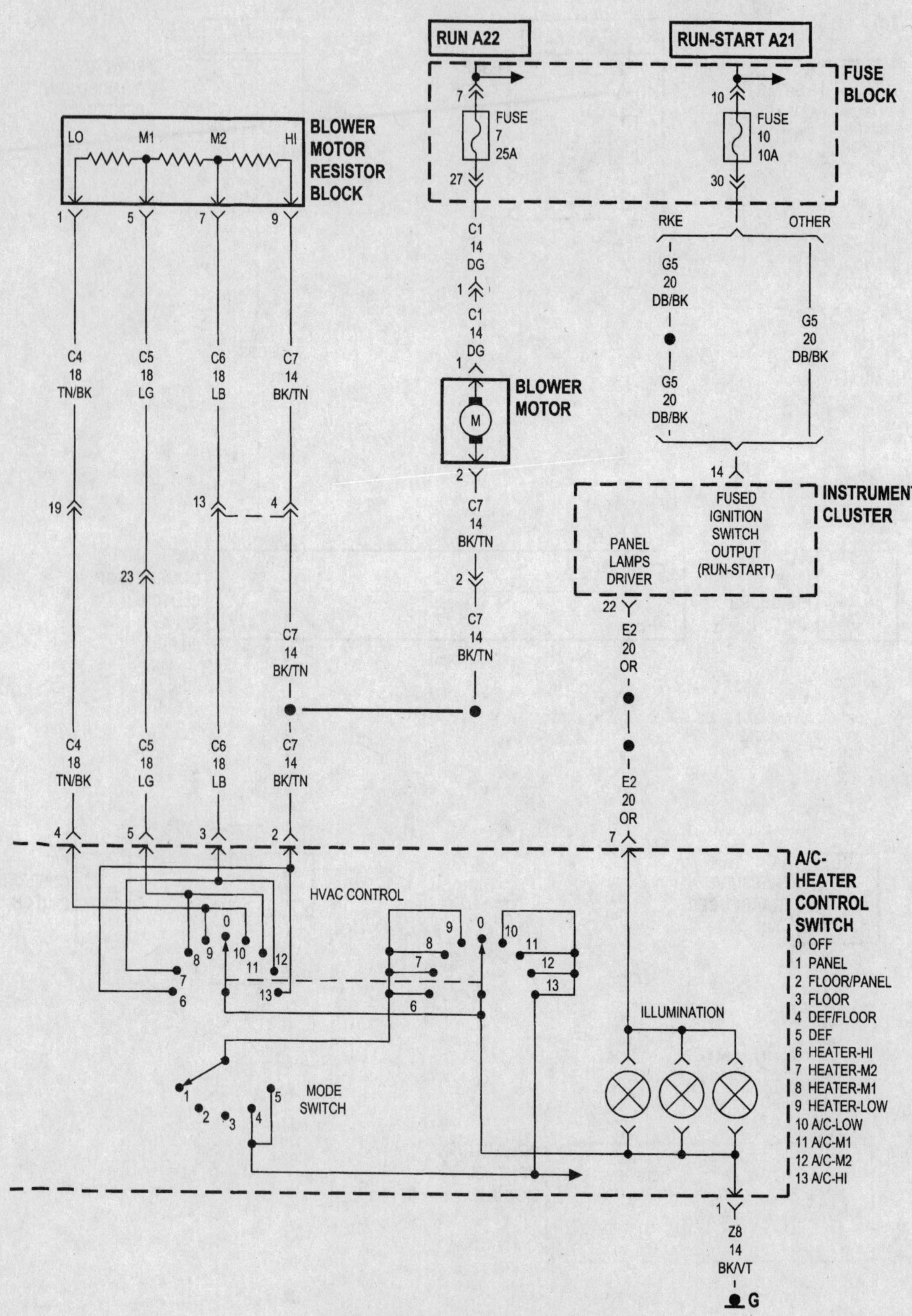


Air conditioning and heating system (2 of 2)

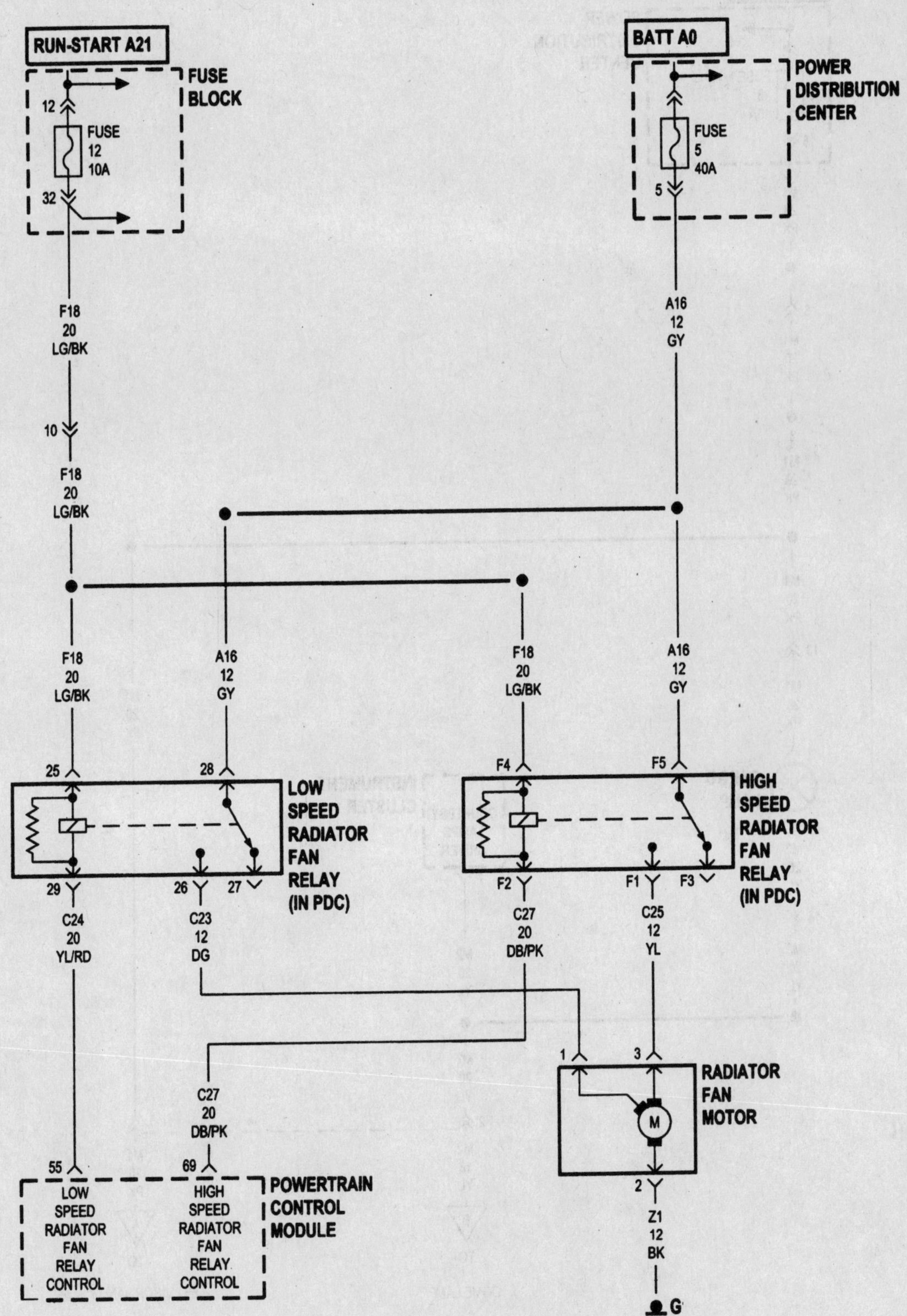


Engine cooling fan system (with hi-lo speed cooling fan relays)

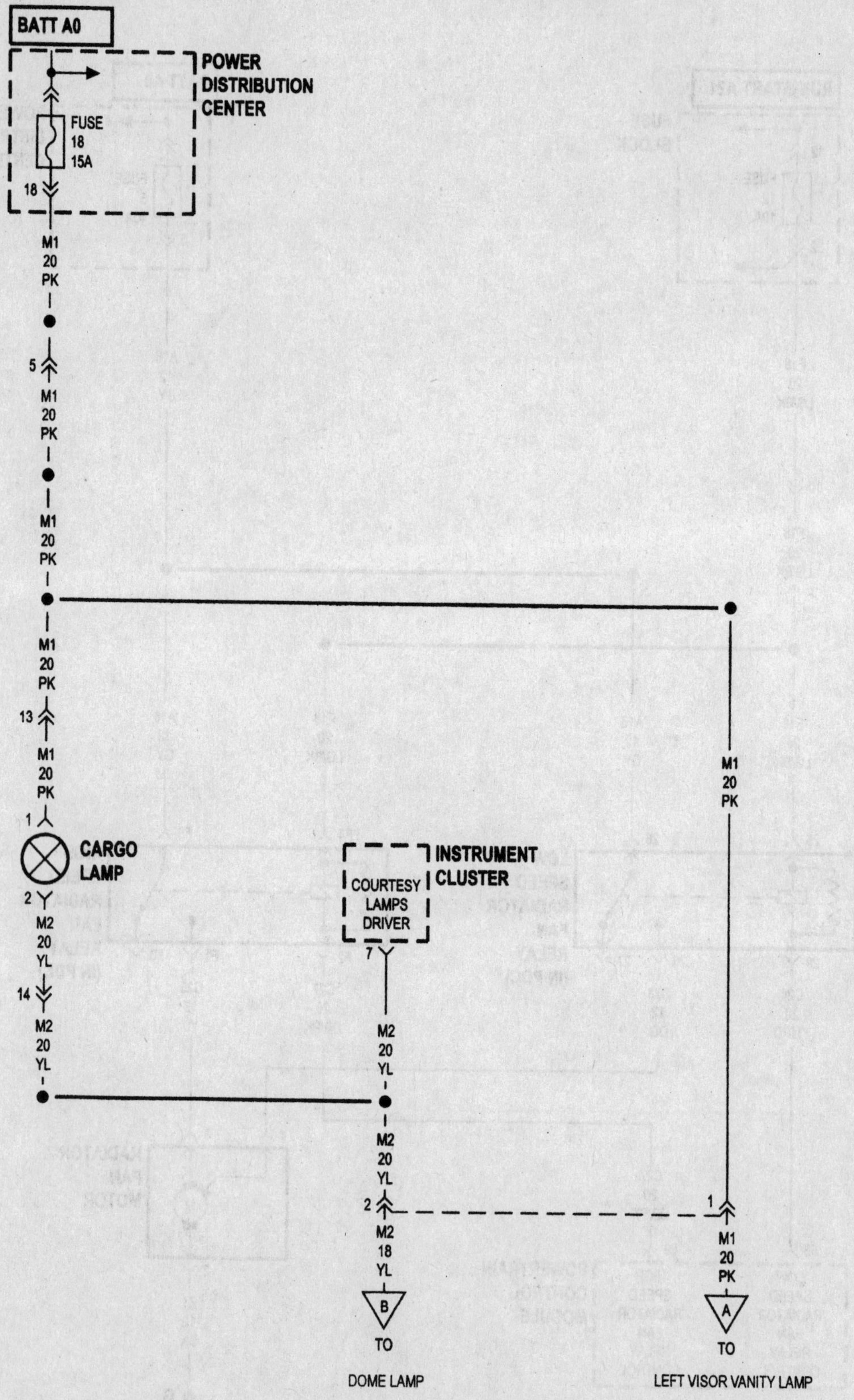

BATT A0
POWER DISTRIBUTION CENTER
FUSE 18 15A
18
M1 20 PK
5
M1 20 PK
M1 20 PK
M1 20 PK
13
M1 20 PK
1
CARGO LAMP
2
M2 20 YL
14
M2 20 YL
INSTRUMENT CLUSTER
COURTESY LAMPS DRIVER
7
M2 20 YL
M2 20 YL
2
M2 18 YL
B
TO
DOME LAMP
M1 20 PK
1
M1 20 PK
A
TO
LEFT VISOR VANITY LAMP

Interior lighting system - 2001 models (1 of 5)

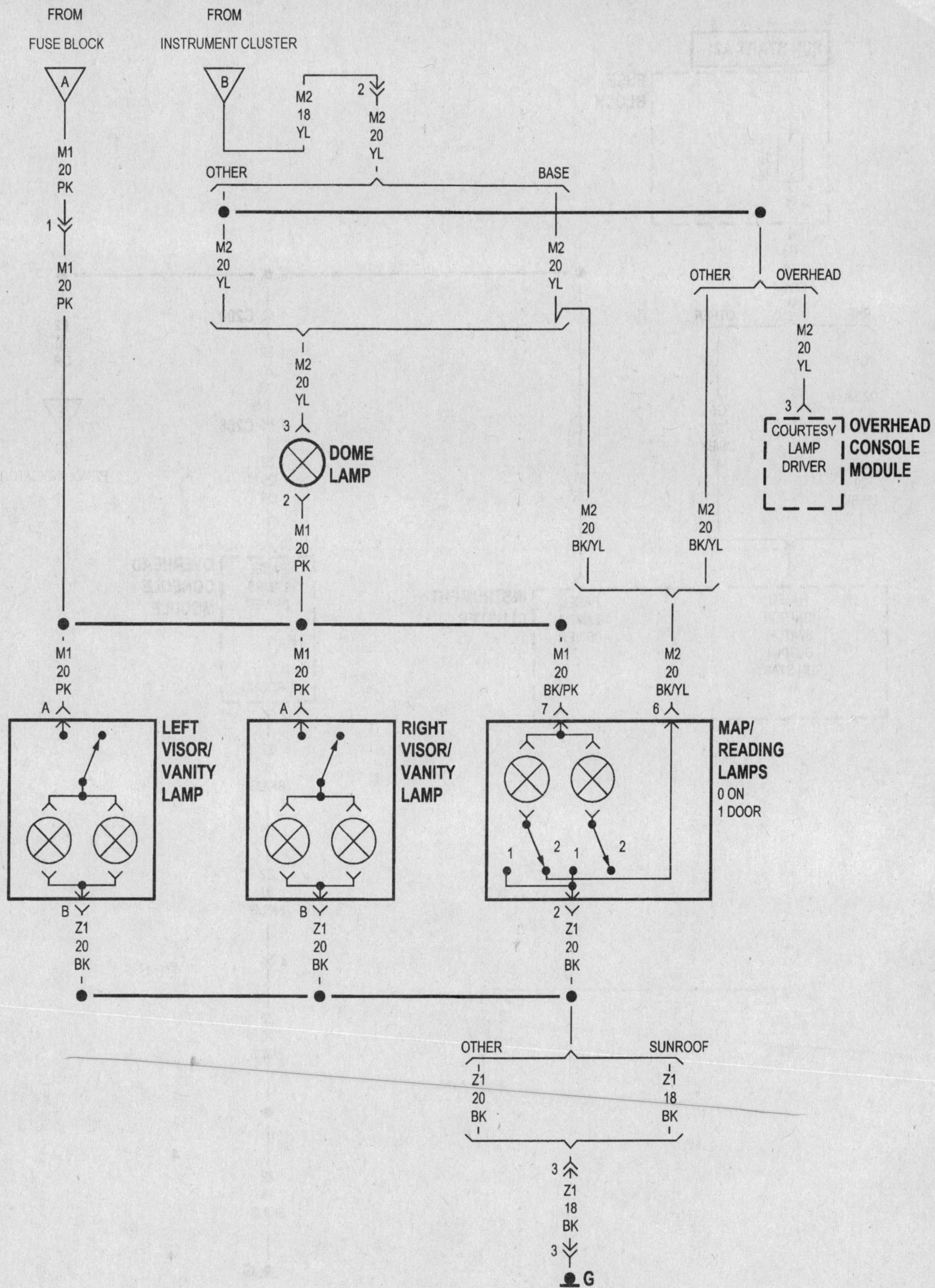


Interior lighting system - 2001 models (2 of 5)

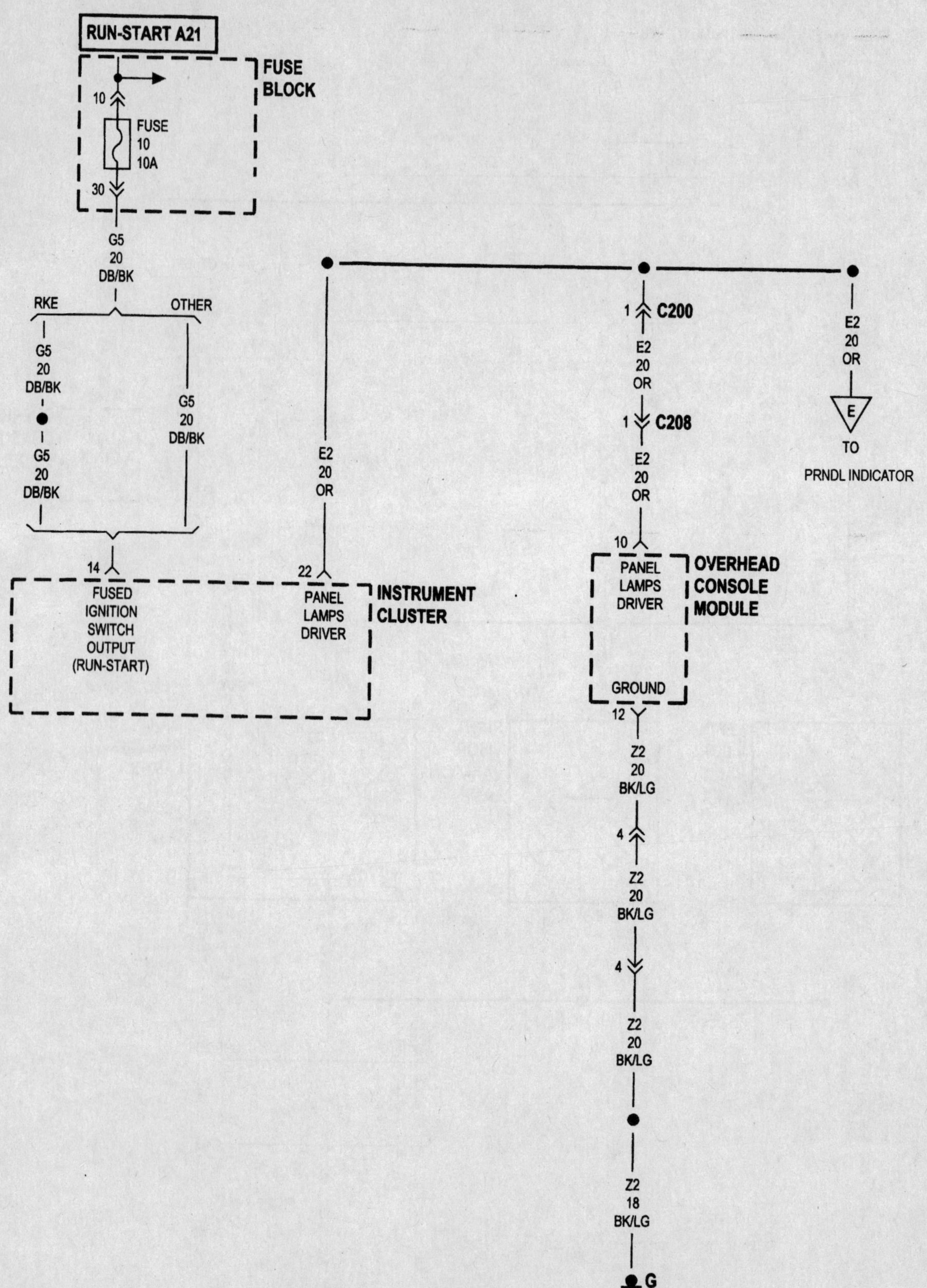


Interior lighting system - 2001 models (3 of 5)

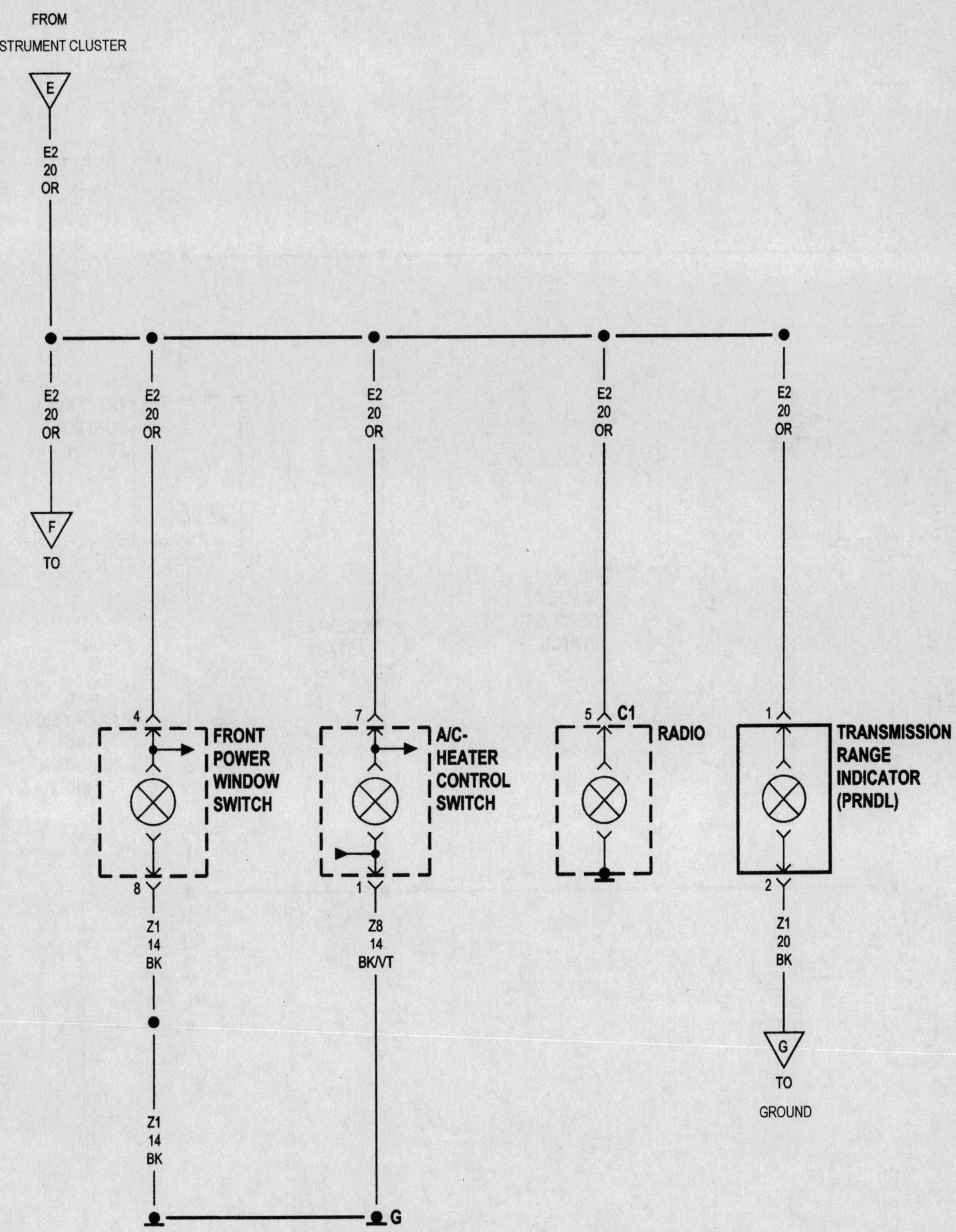


Interior lighting system - 2001 models (4 of 5)

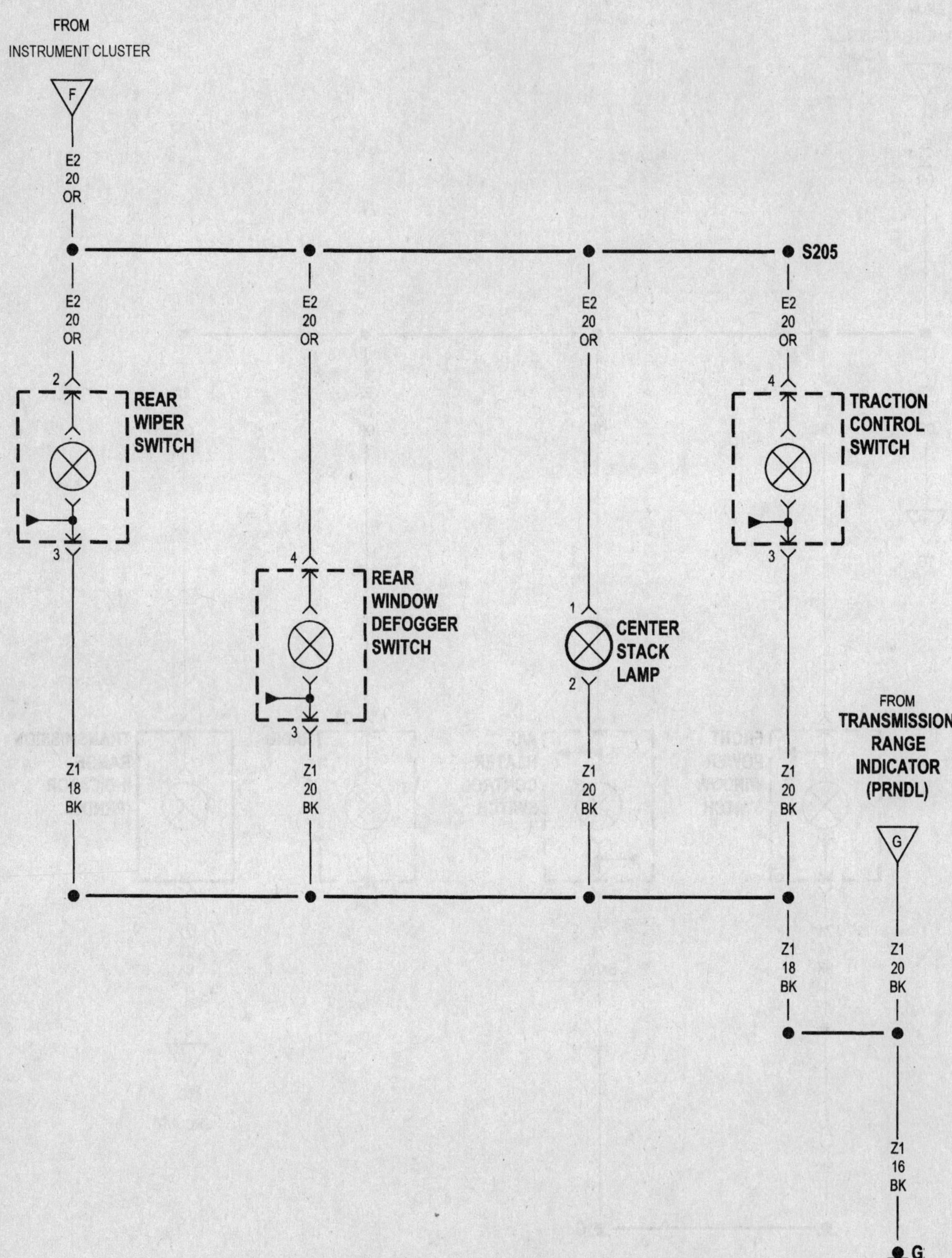


Interior lighting system - 2001 models (5 of 5)

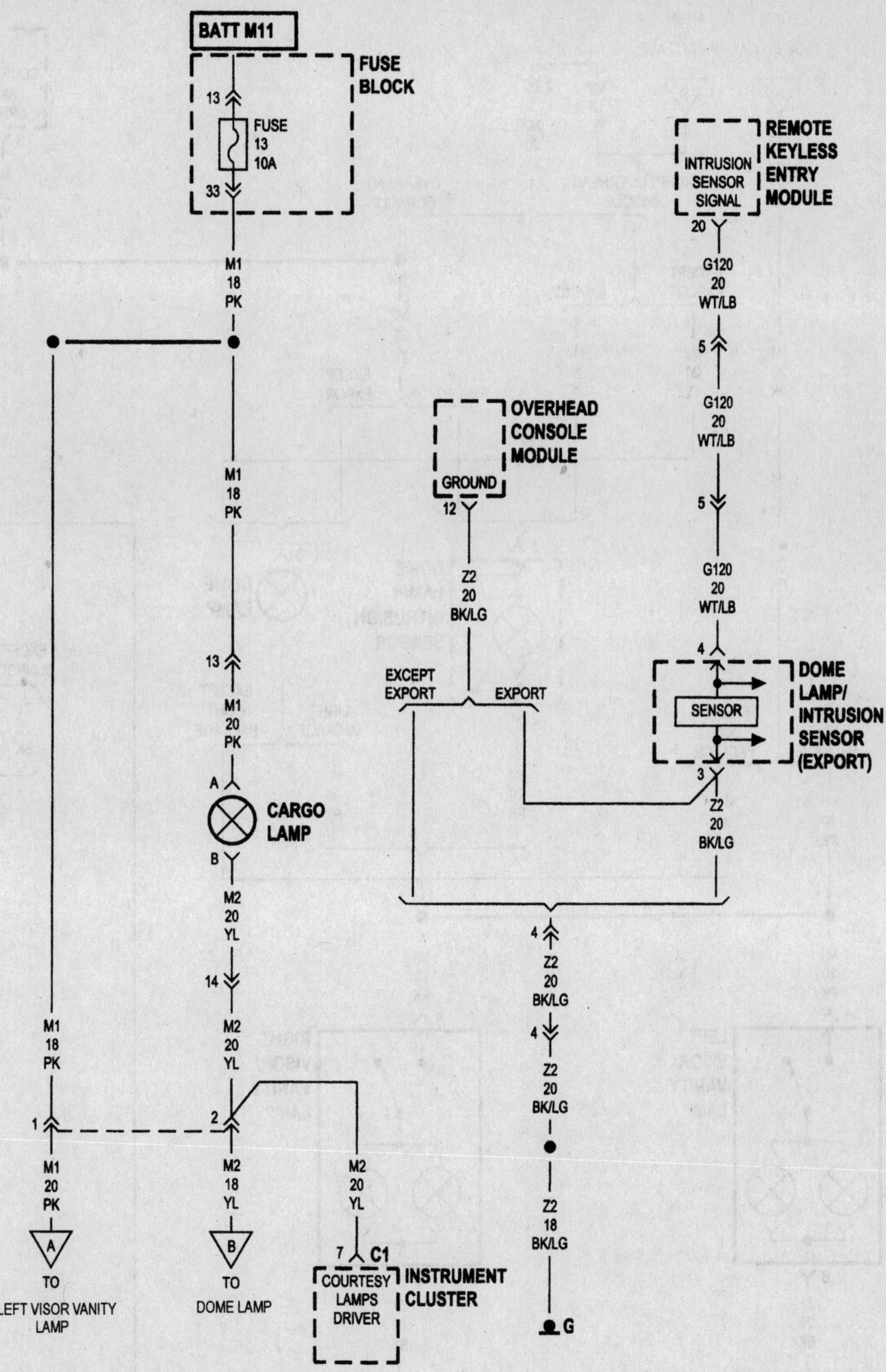


Interior lighting system - 2002 and later models (1 of 5)

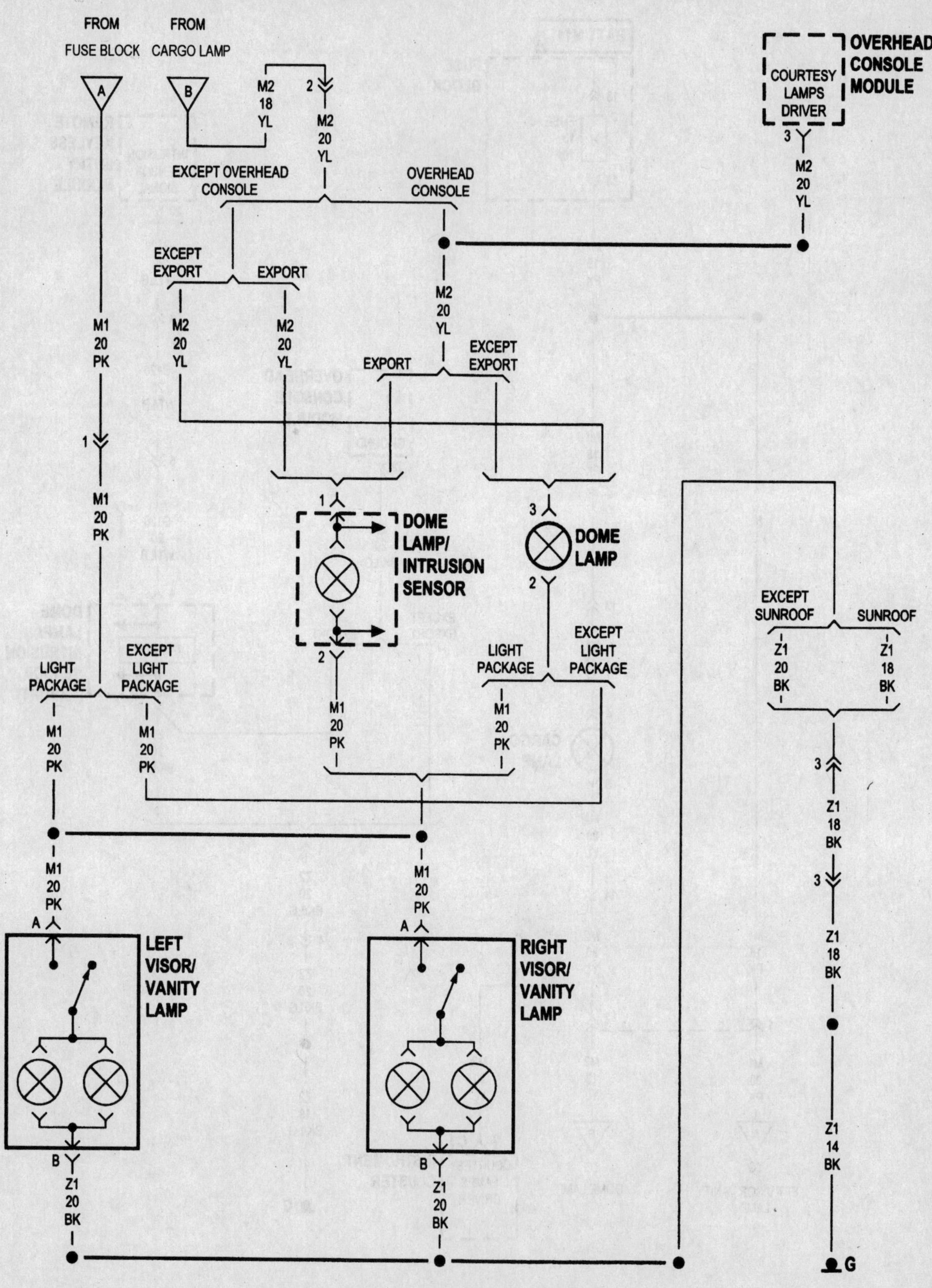


Interior lighting system - 2002 and later models (2 of 5)

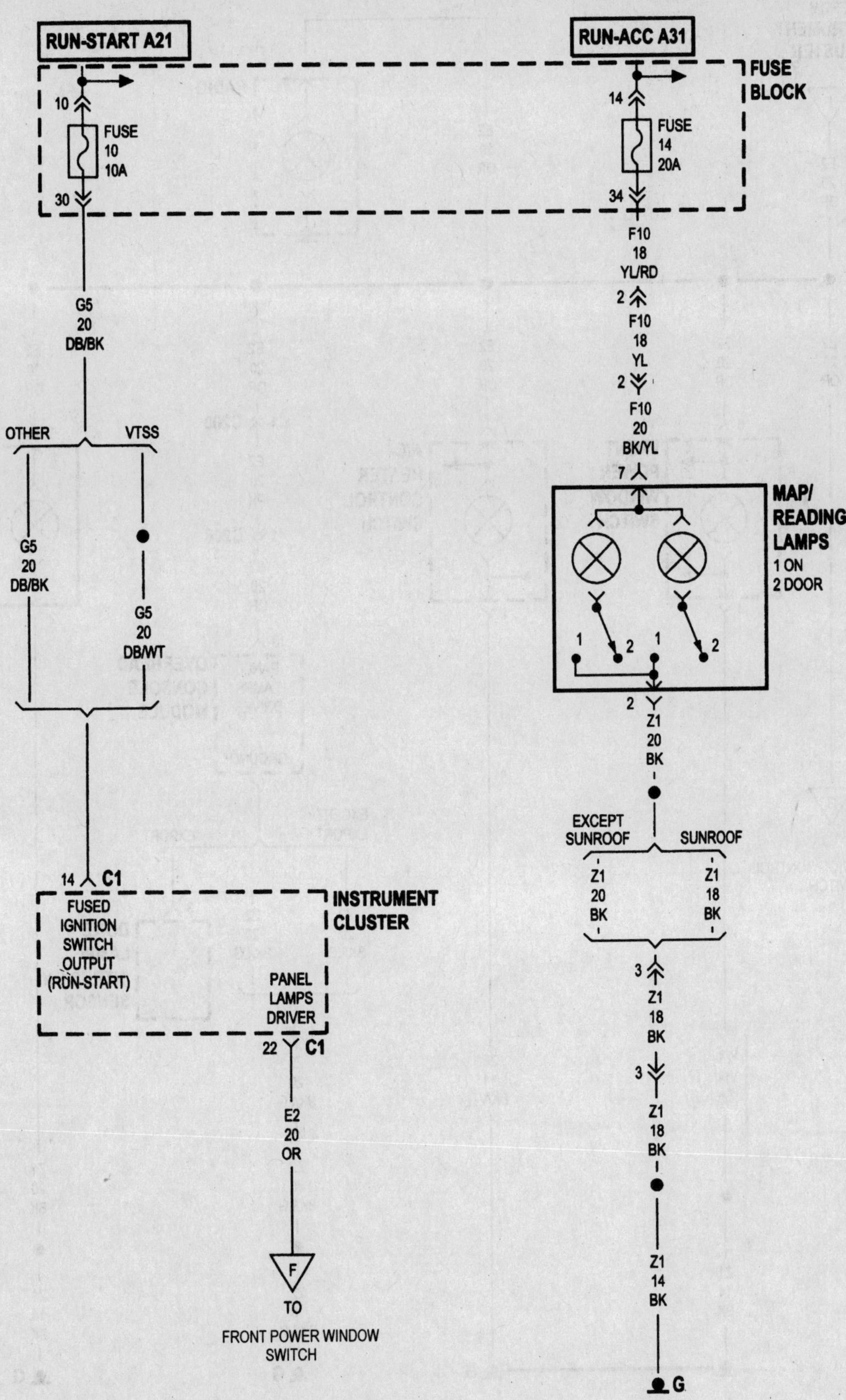


Interior lighting system - 2002 and later models (3 of 5)

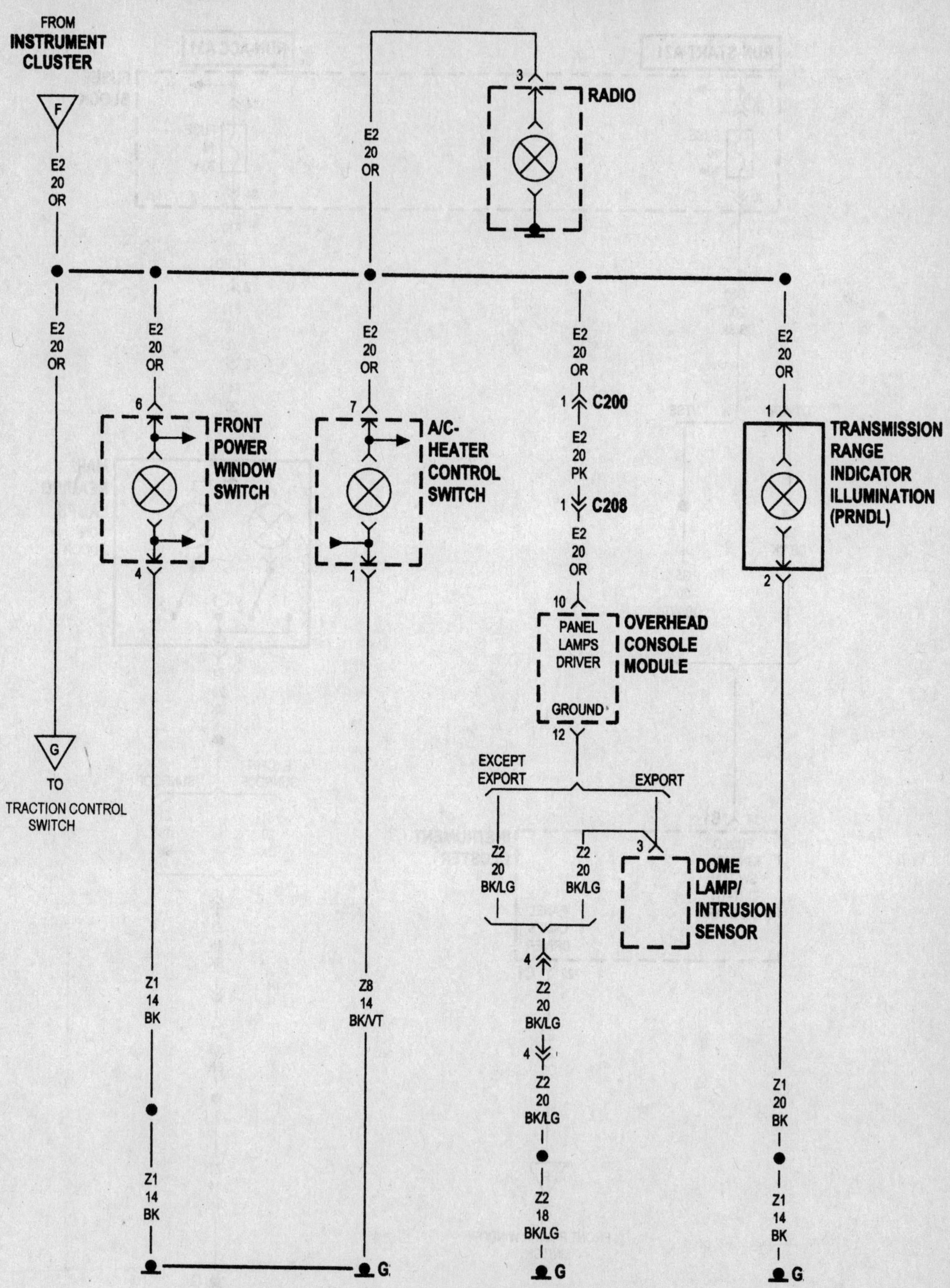


Interior lighting system - 2002 and later models (4 of 5)

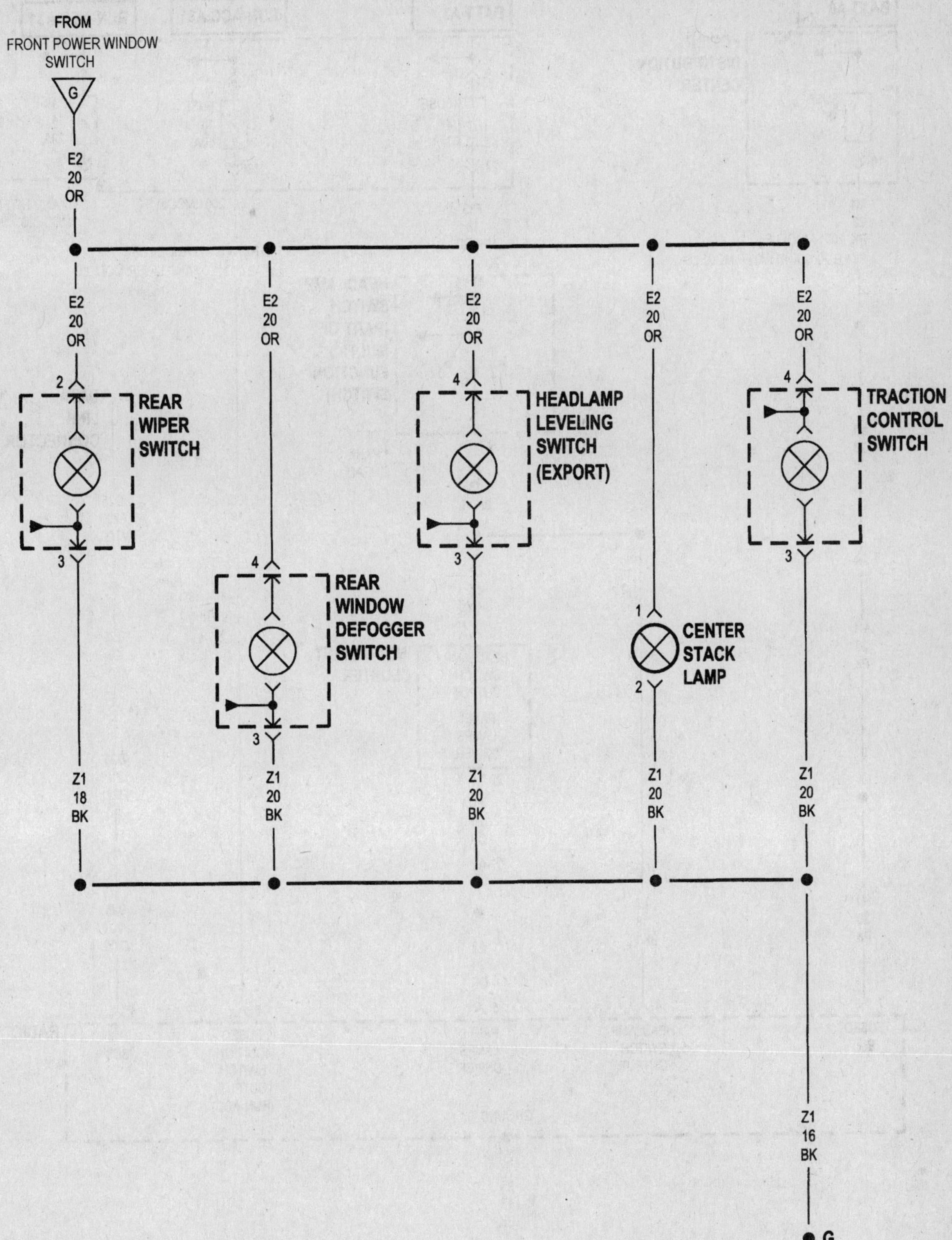


Interior lighting system - 2002 and later models (5 of 5)

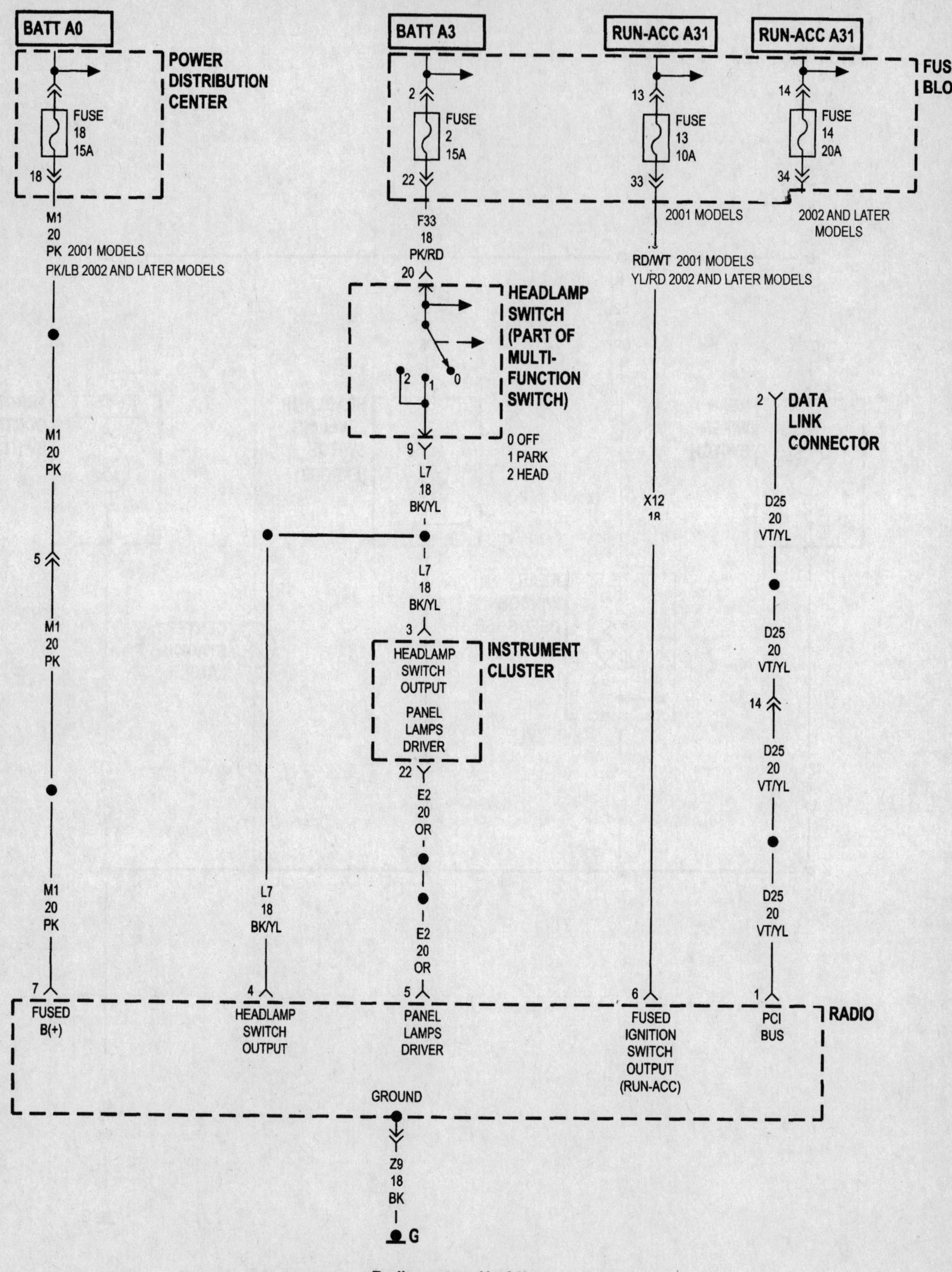


Radio system (1 of 3)

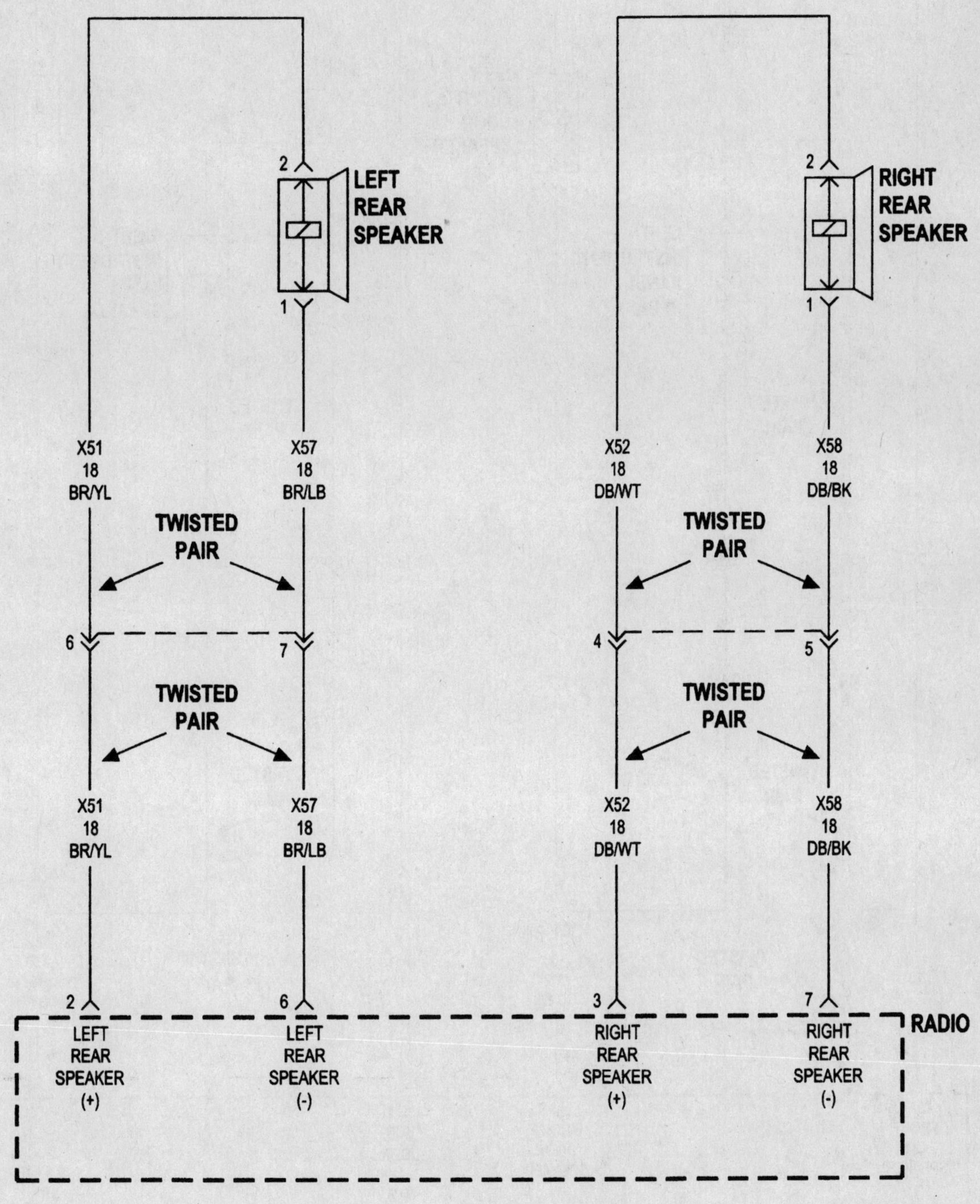


**Radio system (2 of 3)**

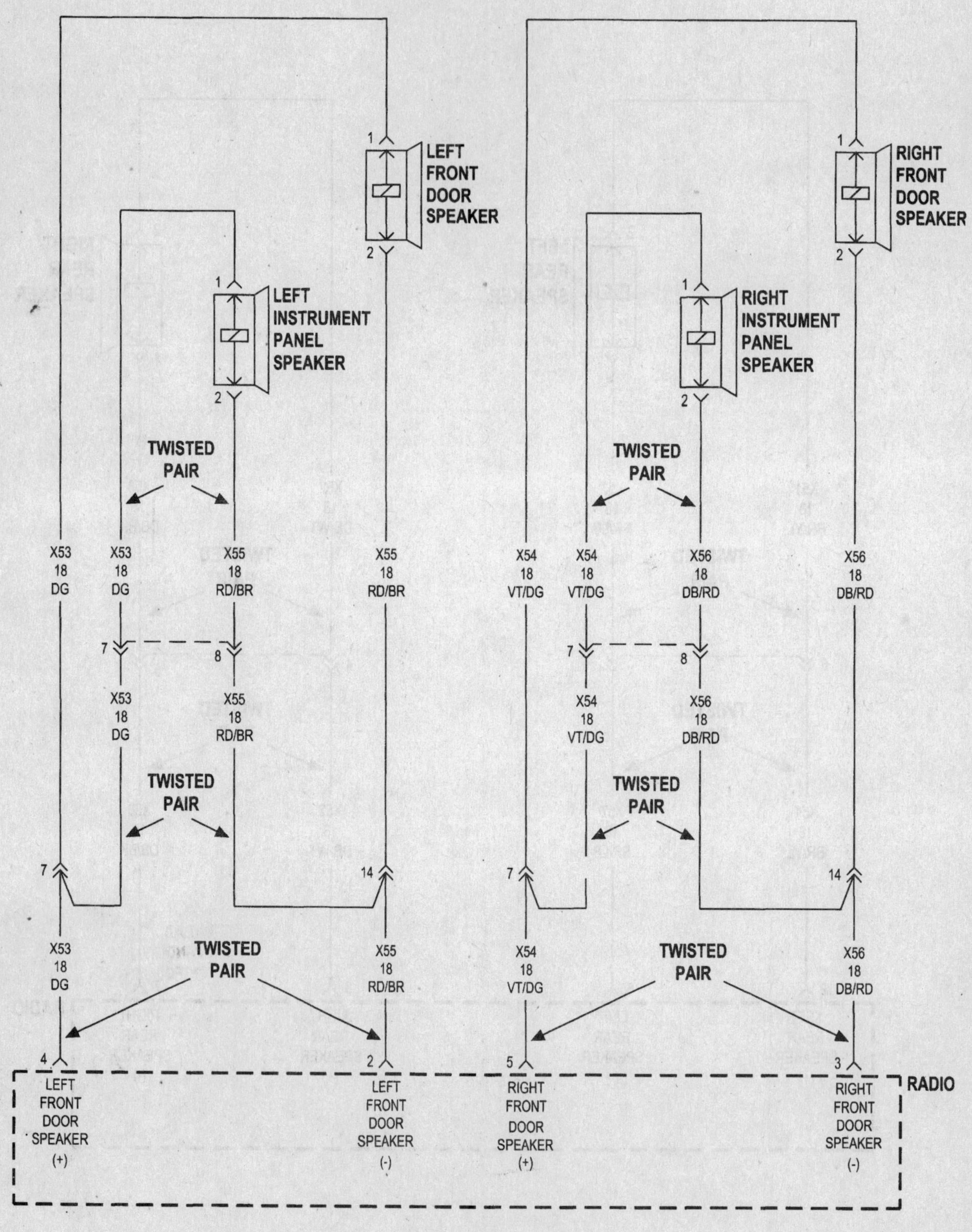


Radio system (3 of 3)

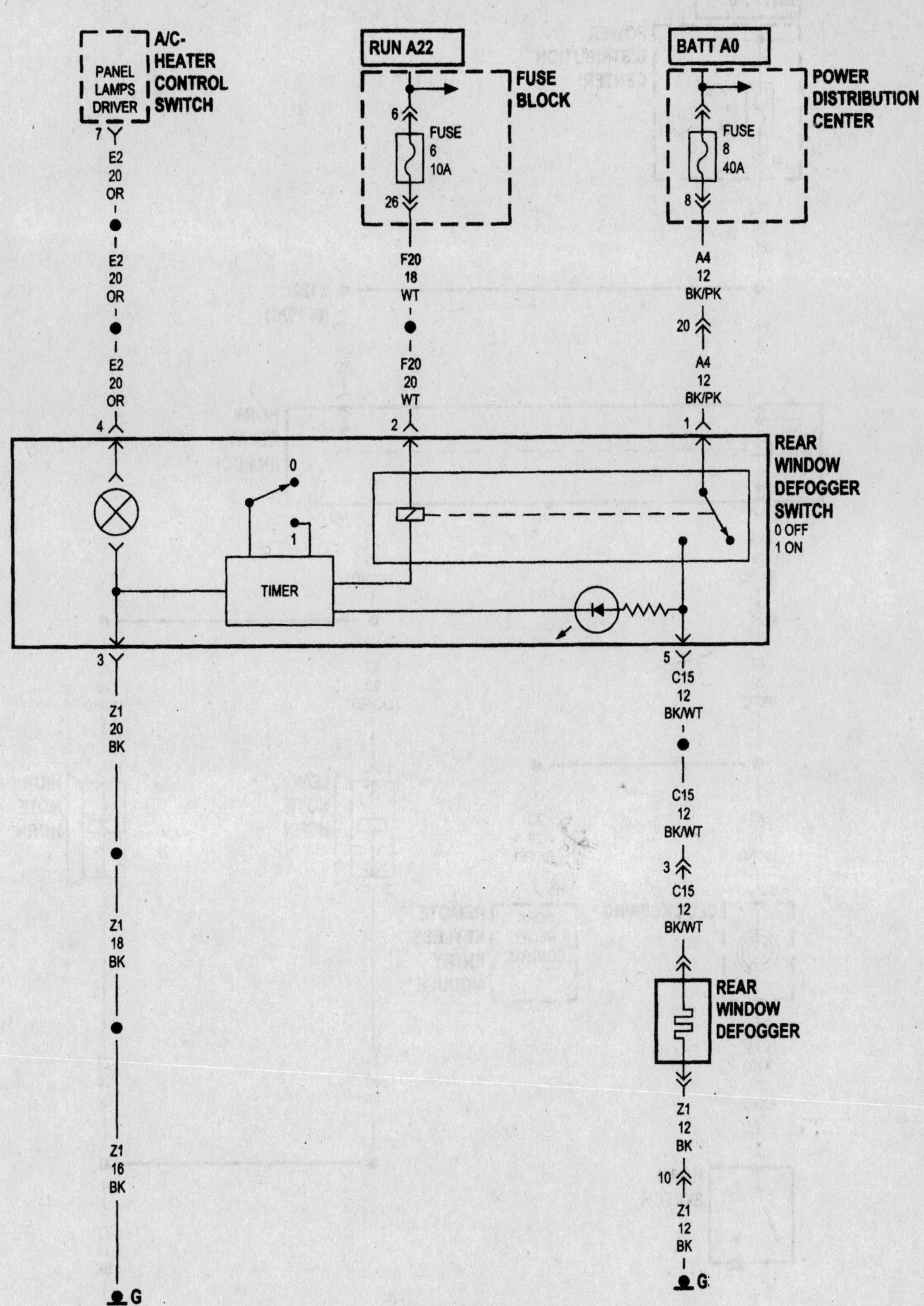


Rear window defogger system

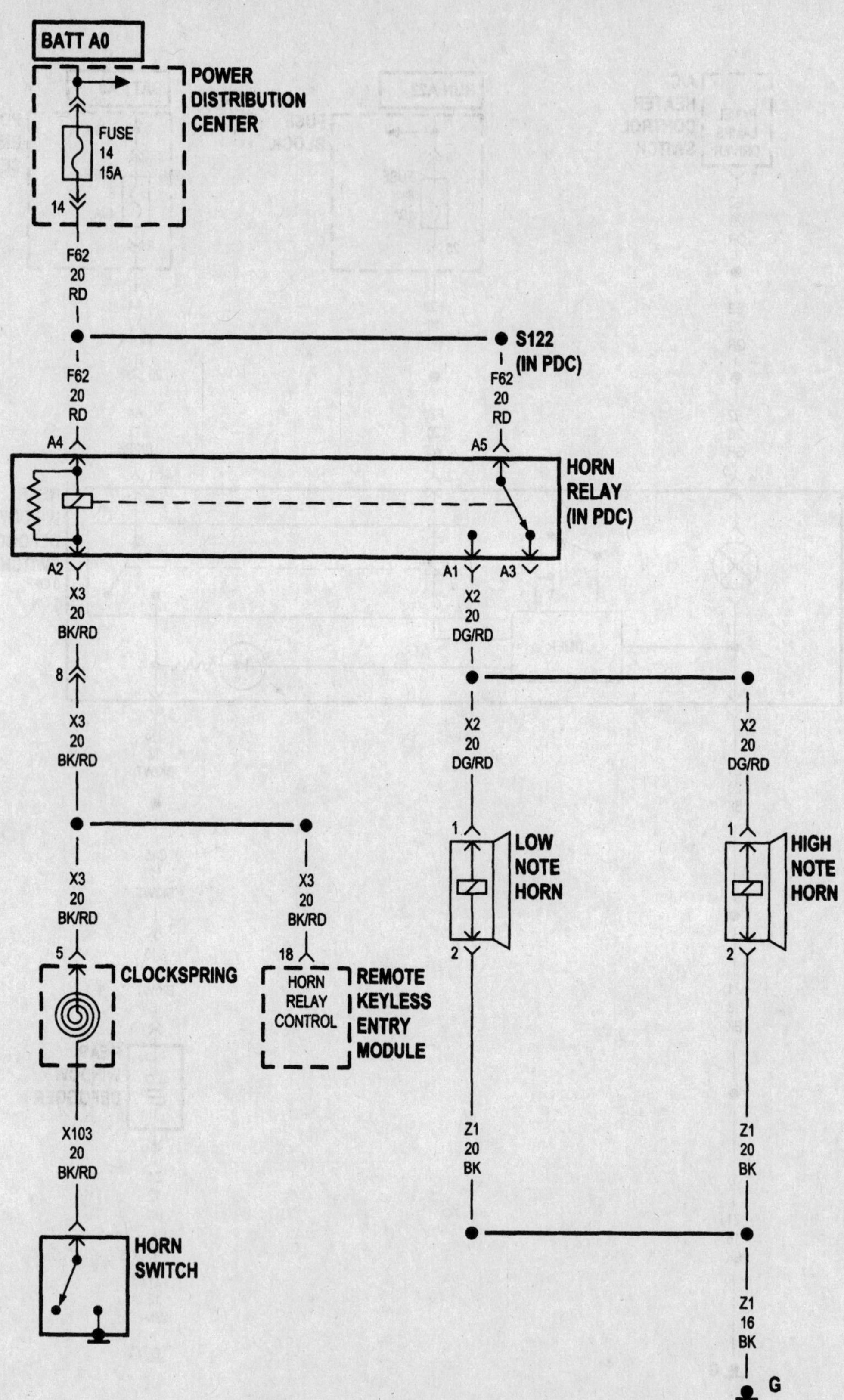


Horn and lighter power outlet (1 of 2)

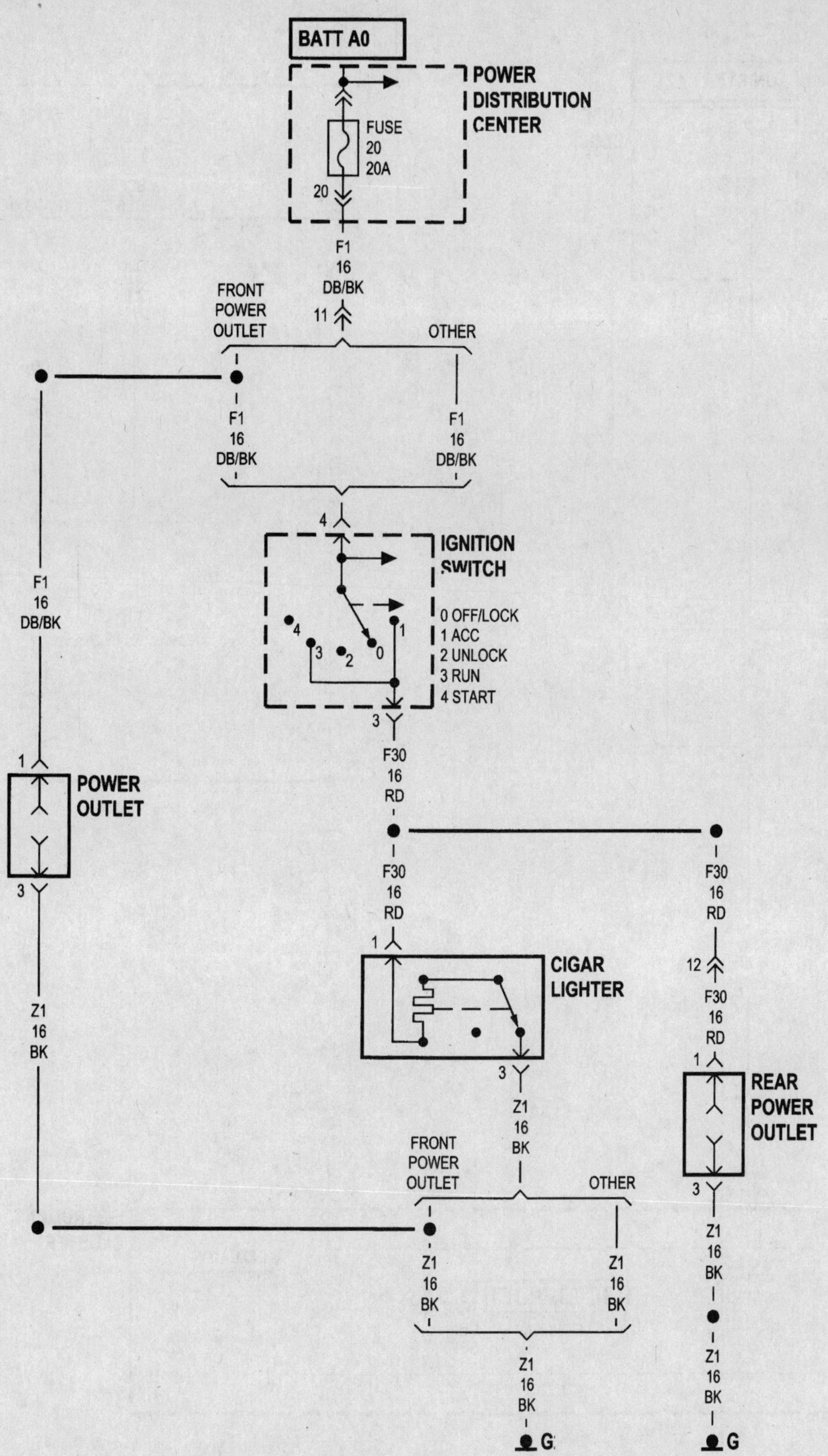


Horn and lighter power outlet (2 of 2)

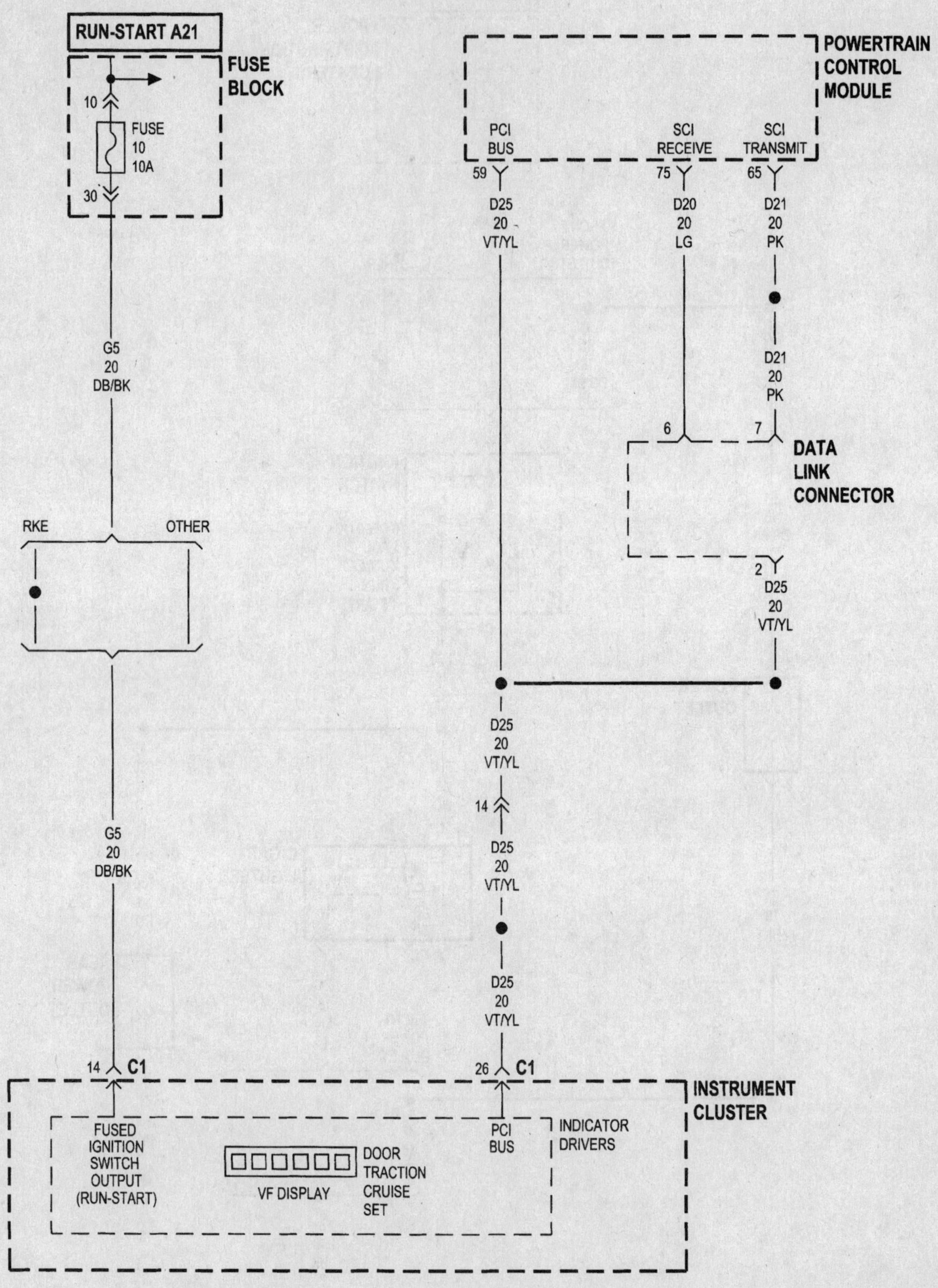


Cruise control (PCM and power circuit) - 2001 and 2002 models

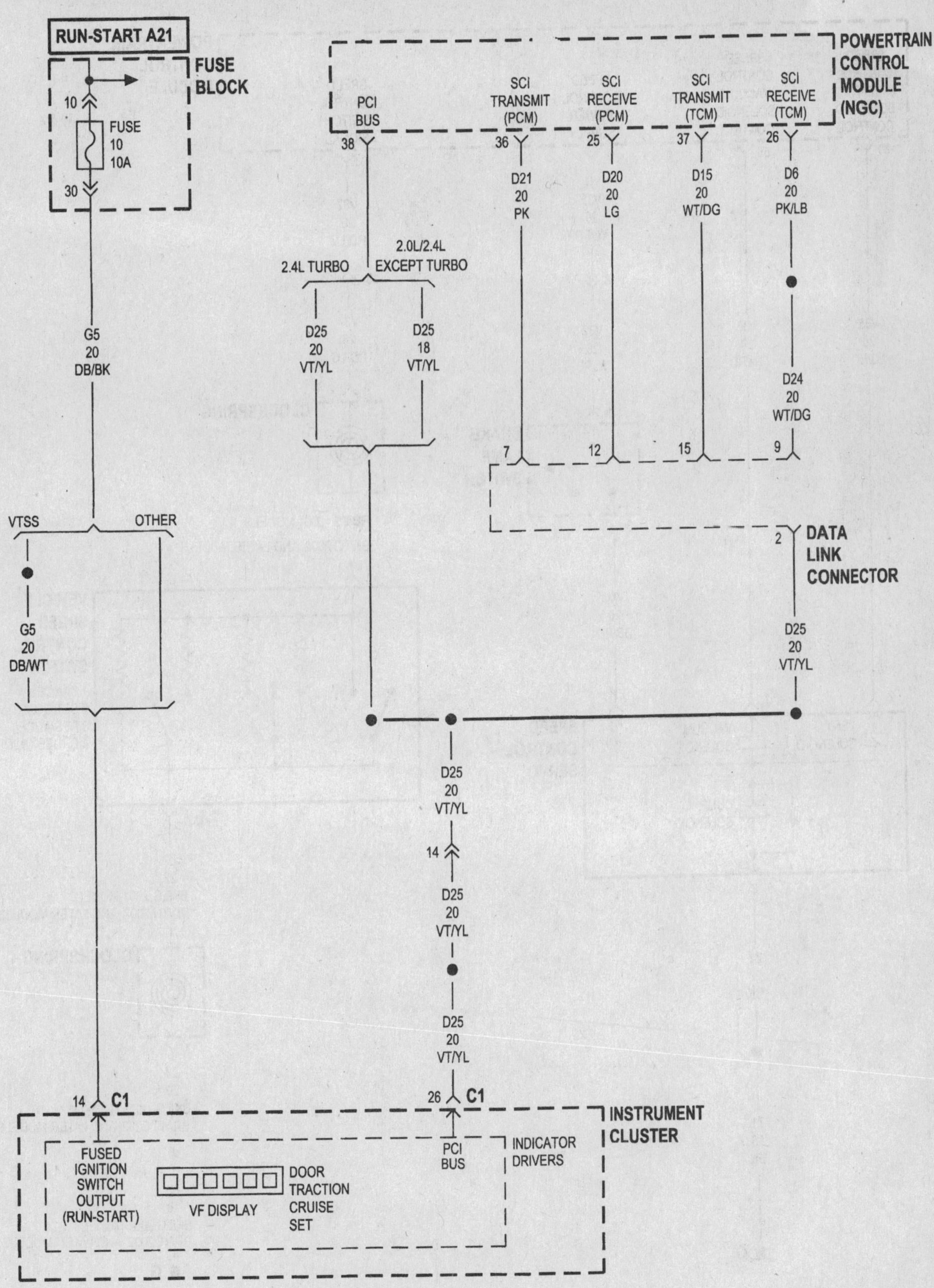


Cruise control (PCM and power circuit) - 2003 models

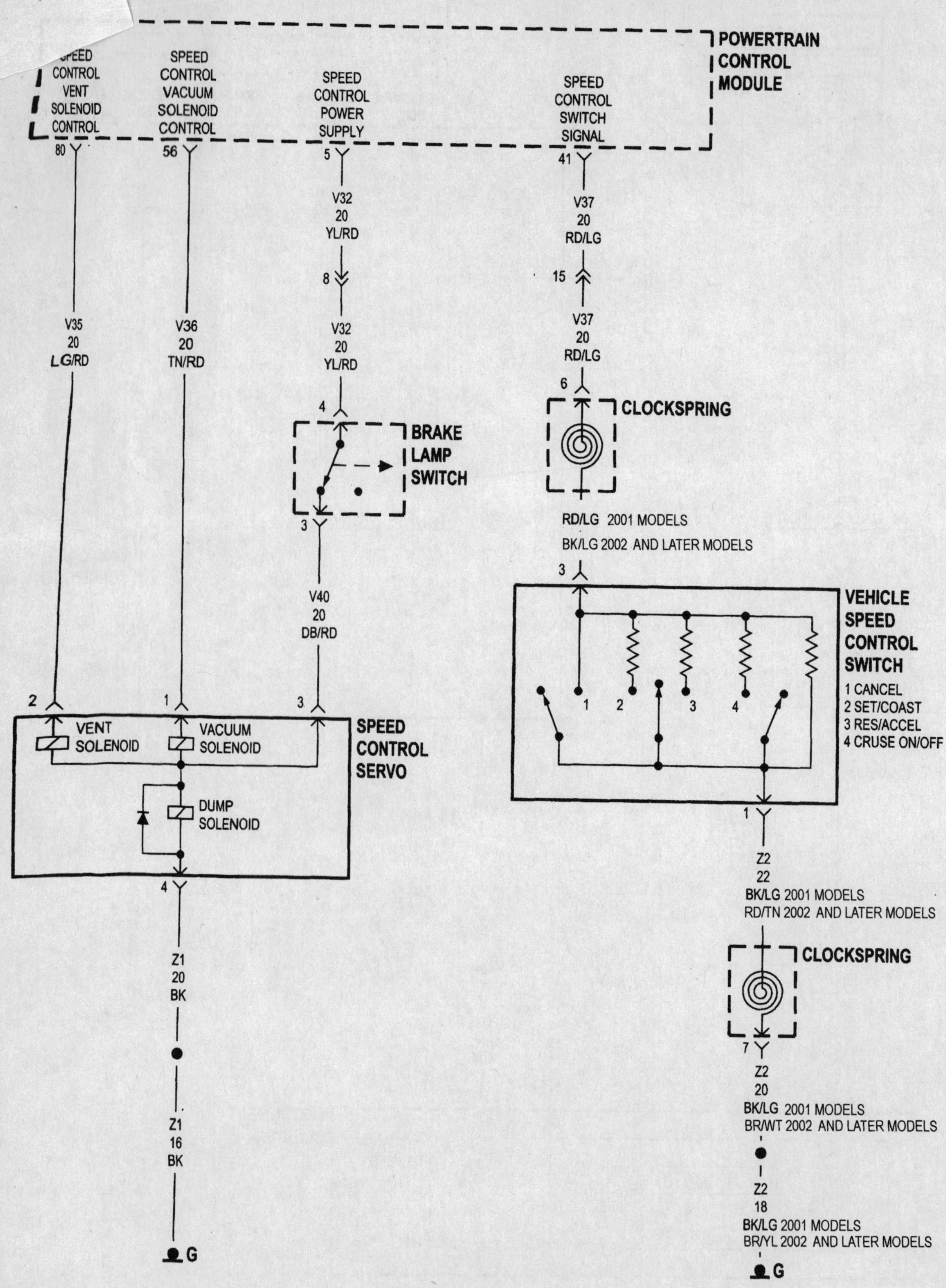


Cruise control system (1 of 2)

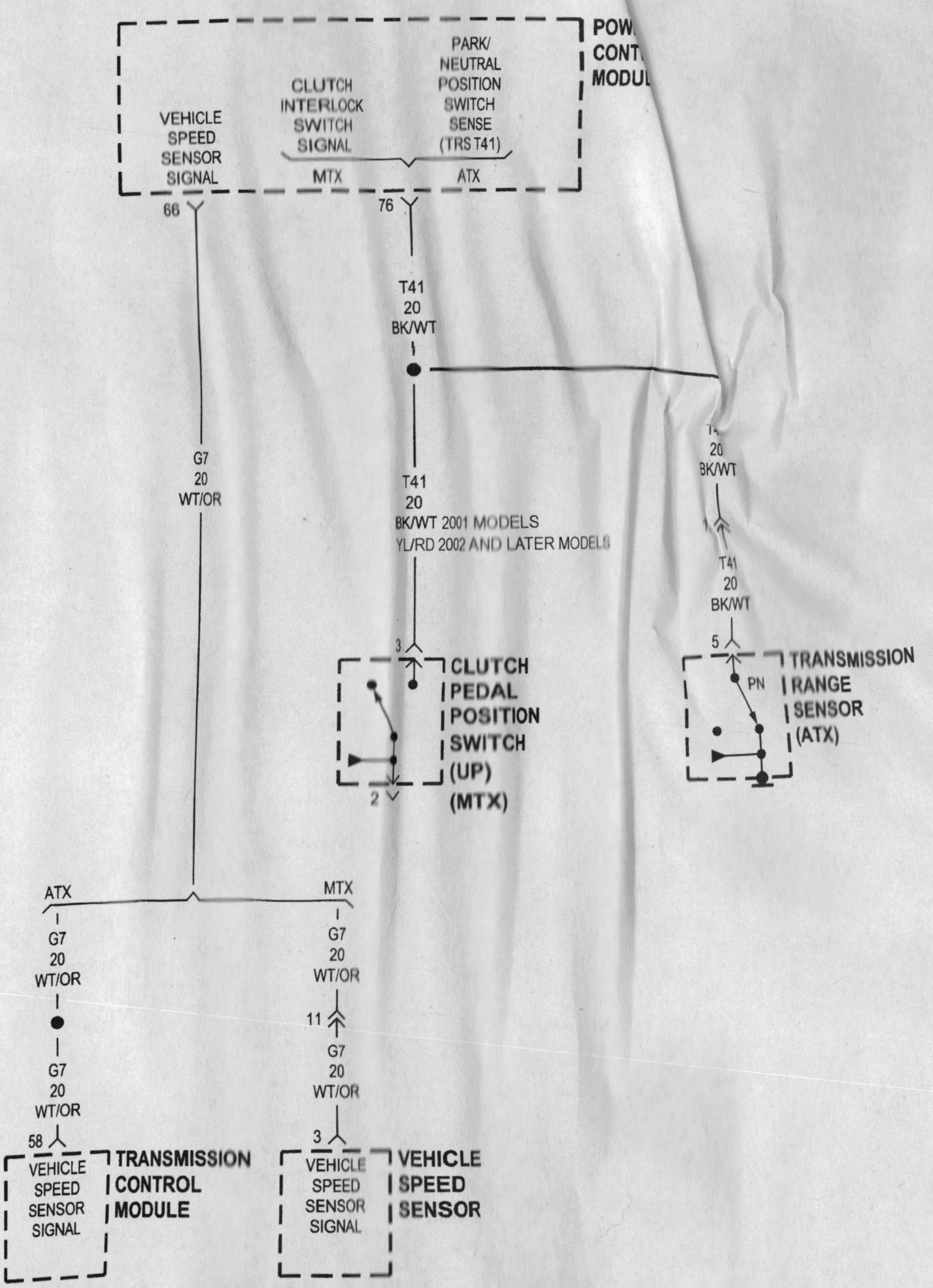


Cruise control system - (2 of 2)

## Notes

# Index

## A



## B

# C



# D

# E



# F

# T



# U

# V



# W

# Haynes Automotive Manuals

*NOTE: If you do not see a listing for your vehicle, consult your local Haynes dealer for the latest product information.*

## ACURA

12020 **Integra** '86 thru '89 **& Legend** '86 thru '90
12021 **Integra** '90 thru '93 **& Legend** '91 thru '95
**Integra** '94 thru '00 - *see HONDA Civic (42025)*
**MDX** '01 thru '07 - *see HONDA Pilot (42037)*
12050 **Acura TL** all models '99 thru '08

## AMC

**Jeep CJ** - *see JEEP (50020)*
14020 **Mid-size models** '70 thru '83
14025 **(Renault) Alliance & Encore** '83 thru '87

## AUDI

15020 **4000** all models '80 thru '87
15025 **5000** all models '77 thru '83
15026 **5000** all models '84 thru '88
**Audi A4** '96 thru '01 - *see VW Passat (96023)*
15030 **Audi A4** '02 thru '08

## AUSTIN-HEALEY

**Sprite** - *see MG Midget (66015)*

## BMW

18020 **3/5 Series** '82 thru '92
18021 **3-Series** incl. Z3 models '92 thru '98
18022 **3-Series** incl. Z4 models '99 thru '05
18023 **3-Series** '06 thru '10
18025 **320i all 4 cyl models** '75 thru '83
18050 **1500 thru 2002** except Turbo '59 thru '77

## BUICK

19010 **Buick Century** '97 thru '05
**Century (front-wheel drive)** - *see GM (38005)*
19020 **Buick, Oldsmobile & Pontiac Full-size (Front-wheel drive)** '85 thru '05
**Buick** Electra, LeSabre and Park Avenue; **Oldsmobile** Delta 88 Royale, Ninety Eight and Regency; **Pontiac** Bonneville
19025 **Buick, Oldsmobile & Pontiac Full-size (Rear wheel drive)** '70 thru '90
**Buick** Estate, Electra, LeSabre, Limited, **Oldsmobile** Custom Cruiser, Delta 88, Ninety-eight, **Pontiac** Bonneville, Catalina, Grandville, Parisienne
19030 **Mid-size Regal & Century** all rear-drive models with V6, V8 and Turbo '74 thru '87
**Regal** - *see GENERAL MOTORS (38010)*
**Riviera** - *see GENERAL MOTORS (38030)*
**Roadmaster** - *see CHEVROLET (24046)*
**Skyhawk** - *see GENERAL MOTORS (38015)*
**Skylark** - *see GM (38020, 38025)*
**Somerset** - *see GENERAL MOTORS (38025)*

## CADILLAC

21015 **CTS & CTS-V** '03 thru '12
21030 **Cadillac Rear Wheel Drive** '70 thru '93
**Cimarron** - *see GENERAL MOTORS (38015)*
**DeVille** - *see GM (38031 & 38032)*
**Eldorado** - *see GM (38030 & 38031)*
**Fleetwood** - *see GM (38031)*
**Seville** - *see GM (38030, 38031 & 38032)*

## CHEVROLET

10305 **Chevrolet Engine Overhaul Manual**
24010 **Astro & GMC Safari Mini-vans** '85 thru '05
24015 **Camaro V8** all models '70 thru '81
24016 **Camaro** all models '82 thru '92
24017 **Camaro & Firebird** '93 thru '02
**Cavalier** - *see GENERAL MOTORS (38016)*
**Celebrity** - *see GENERAL MOTORS (38005)*
24020 **Chevelle, Malibu & El Camino** '69 thru '87
24024 **Chevette & Pontiac T1000** '76 thru '87
**Citation** - *see GENERAL MOTORS (38020)*
24027 **Colorado & GMC Canyon** '04 thru '10
24032 **Corsica/Beretta** all models '87 thru '96
24040 **Corvette** all V8 models '68 thru '82
24041 **Corvette** all models '84 thru '96
24045 **Full-size Sedans** Caprice, Impala, Biscayne, Bel Air & Wagons '69 thru '90
24046 **Impala SS & Caprice and Buick Roadmaster** '91 thru '96
**Impala** '00 thru '05 - *see LUMINA (24048)*
24047 **Impala & Monte Carlo** all models '06 thru '11
**Lumina** '90 thru '94 - *see GM (38010)*
24048 **Lumina & Monte Carlo** '95 thru '05
**Lumina APV** - *see GM (38035)*
24050 **Luv Pick-up** all 2WD & 4WD '72 thru '82
**Malibu** '97 thru '00 - *see GM (38026)*
24055 **Monte Carlo** all models '70 thru '88
**Monte Carlo** '95 thru '01 - *see LUMINA (24048)*
24059 **Nova** all V8 models '69 thru '79
24060 **Nova and Geo Prizm** '85 thru '92
24064 **Pick-ups** '67 thru '87 - Chevrolet & GMC
24065 **Pick-ups** '88 thru '98 - Chevrolet & GMC
24066 **Pick-ups** '99 thru '06 - Chevrolet & GMC
24067 **Chevrolet Silverado & GMC Sierra** '07 thru '12
24070 **S-10 & S-15 Pick-ups** '82 thru '93, **Blazer & Jimmy** '83 thru '94,
24071 **S-10 & Sonoma Pick-ups** '94 thru '04, including **Blazer, Jimmy & Hombre**
24072 **Chevrolet TrailBlazer, GMC Envoy & Oldsmobile Bravada** '02 thru '09
24075 **Sprint** '85 thru '88 **& Geo Metro** '89 thru '01
24080 **Vans - Chevrolet & GMC** '68 thru '96
24081 **Chevrolet Express & GMC Savana** Full-size Vans '96 thru '10

## CHRYSLER

10310 **Chrysler Engine Overhaul Manual**
25015 **Chrysler Cirrus, Dodge Stratus, Plymouth Breeze** '95 thru '00
25020 **Full-size Front-Wheel Drive** '88 thru '93
**K-Cars** - *see DODGE Aries (30008)*
**Laser** - *see DODGE Daytona (30030)*
25025 **Chrysler LHS, Concorde, New Yorker, Dodge** Intrepid, **Eagle** Vision, '93 thru '97
25026 **Chrysler LHS, Concorde, 300M, Dodge** Intrepid, '98 thru '04
25027 **Chrysler 300, Dodge Charger & Magnum** '05 thru '09
25030 **Chrysler & Plymouth Mid-size** front wheel drive '82 thru '95
**Rear-wheel Drive** - *see Dodge (30050)*
25035 **PT Cruiser** all models '01 thru '10
25040 **Chrysler** Sebring '95 thru '06, **Dodge** Stratus '01 thru '06, **Dodge** Avenger '95 thru '00

## DATSUN

28005 **200SX** all models '80 thru '83
28007 **B-210** all models '73 thru '78
28009 **210** all models '79 thru '82
28012 **240Z, 260Z & 280Z** Coupe '70 thru '78
28014 **280ZX** Coupe & 2+2 '79 thru '83
**300ZX** - *see NISSAN (72010)*
28018 **510 & PL521 Pick-up** '68 thru '73
28020 **510** all models '78 thru '81
28022 **620 Series Pick-up** all models '73 thru '79
**720 Series Pick-up** - *see NISSAN (72030)*
28025 **810/Maxima** all gasoline models '77 thru '84

## DODGE

**400 & 600** - *see CHRYSLER (25030)*
30008 **Aries & Plymouth Reliant** '81 thru '89
30010 **Caravan & Plymouth Voyager** '84 thru '95
30011 **Caravan & Plymouth Voyager** '96 thru '02
30012 **Challenger/Plymouth Saporro** '78 thru '83
30013 **Caravan, Chrysler Voyager, Town & Country** '03 thru '07
30016 **Colt & Plymouth Champ** '78 thru '87
30020 **Dakota Pick-ups** all models '87 thru '96
30021 **Durango** '98 & '99, **Dakota** '97 thru '99
30022 **Durango** '00 thru '03 **Dakota** '00 thru '04
30023 **Durango** '04 thru '09, **Dakota** '05 thru '11
30025 **Dart, Demon, Plymouth Barracuda, Duster & Valiant** 6 cyl models '67 thru '76
30030 **Daytona & Chrysler Laser** '84 thru '89
**Intrepid** - *see CHRYSLER (25025, 25026)*
30034 **Neon** all models '95 thru '99
30035 **Omni & Plymouth Horizon** '78 thru '90
30036 **Dodge and Plymouth Neon** '00 thru '05
30040 **Pick-ups** all full-size models '74 thru '93
30041 **Pick-ups** all full-size models '94 thru '01
30042 **Pick-ups** full-size models '02 thru '08
30045 **Ram 50/D50 Pick-ups & Raider and Plymouth Arrow Pick-ups** '79 thru '93
30050 **Dodge/Plymouth/Chrysler** RWD '71 thru '89
30055 **Shadow & Plymouth Sundance** '87 thru '94
30060 **Spirit & Plymouth Acclaim** '89 thru '95
30065 **Vans - Dodge & Plymouth** '71 thru '03

## EAGLE

**Talon** - *see MITSUBISHI (68030, 68031)*
**Vision** - *see CHRYSLER (25025)*

## FIAT

34010 **124 Sport Coupe & Spider** '68 thru '78
34025 **X1/9** all models '74 thru '80

## FORD

10320 **Ford Engine Overhaul Manual**
10355 **Ford Automatic Transmission Overhaul**
11500 **Mustang '64-1/2 thru '70 Restoration Guide**
36004 **Aerostar Mini-vans** all models '86 thru '97
36006 **Contour & Mercury Mystique** '95 thru '00
36008 **Courier Pick-up** all models '72 thru '82
36012 **Crown Victoria & Mercury Grand Marquis** '88 thru '10
36016 **Escort/Mercury Lynx** all models '81 thru '90
36020 **Escort/Mercury Tracer** '91 thru '02
36022 **Escape & Mazda Tribute** '01 thru '11
36024 **Explorer & Mazda Navajo** '91 thru '01
36025 **Explorer/Mercury Mountaineer** '02 thru '10
36028 **Fairmont & Mercury Zephyr** '78 thru '83
36030 **Festiva & Aspire** '88 thru '97
36032 **Fiesta** all models '77 thru '80
36034 **Focus** all models '00 thru '11
36036 **Ford & Mercury Full-size** '75 thru '87
36044 **Ford & Mercury Mid-size** '75 thru '86
36045 **Fusion & Mercury Milan** '06 thru '10
36048 **Mustang V8** all models '64-1/2 thru '73
36049 **Mustang II** 4 cyl, V6 & V8 models '74 thru '78
36050 **Mustang & Mercury Capri** '79 thru '93
36051 **Mustang** all models '94 thru '04
36052 **Mustang** '05 thru '10
36054 **Pick-ups & Bronco** '73 thru '79
36058 **Pick-ups & Bronco** '80 thru '96
36059 **F-150 & Expedition** '97 thru '09, **F-250** '97 thru '99 **& Lincoln Navigator** '98 thru '09
36060 **Super Duty Pick-ups, Excursion** '99 thru '10
36061 **F-150** full-size '04 thru '10
36062 **Pinto & Mercury Bobcat** '75 thru '80
36066 **Probe** all models '89 thru '92
**Probe** '93 thru '97 - *see MAZDA 626 (61042)*
36070 **Ranger/Bronco II** gasoline models '83 thru '92
36071 **Ranger** '93 thru '10 **& Mazda Pick-ups** '94 thru '09
36074 **Taurus & Mercury Sable** '86 thru '95
36075 **Taurus & Mercury Sable** '96 thru '05
36078 **Tempo & Mercury Topaz** '84 thru '94
36082 **Thunderbird/Mercury Cougar** '83 thru '88
36086 **Thunderbird/Mercury Cougar** '89 thru '97
36090 **Vans** all V8 Econoline models '69 thru '91
36094 **Vans** full size '92 thru '10
36097 **Windstar Mini-van** '95 thru '07

## GENERAL MOTORS

10360 **GM Automatic Transmission Overhaul**
38005 **Buick Century, Chevrolet Celebrity, Oldsmobile Cutlass Ciera & Pontiac 6000** all models '82 thru '96
38010 **Buick Regal, Chevrolet Lumina, Oldsmobile Cutlass Supreme & Pontiac Grand Prix** (FWD) '88 thru '07
38015 **Buick Skyhawk, Cadillac Cimarron, Chevrolet Cavalier, Oldsmobile Firenza & Pontiac J-2000 & Sunbird** '82 thru '94
38016 **Chevrolet Cavalier & Pontiac Sunfire** '95 thru '05
38017 **Chevrolet Cobalt & Pontiac G5** '05 thru '11
38020 **Buick Skylark, Chevrolet Citation, Olds Omega, Pontiac Phoenix** '80 thru '85
38025 **Buick Skylark & Somerset, Oldsmobile Achieva & Calais and Pontiac Grand Am** all models '85 thru '98
38026 **Chevrolet Malibu, Olds Alero & Cutlass, Pontiac Grand Am** '97 thru '03
38027 **Chevrolet Malibu** '04 thru '10
38030 **Cadillac Eldorado, Seville, Oldsmobile Toronado, Buick Riviera** '71 thru '85
38031 **Cadillac Eldorado & Seville, DeVille, Fleetwood & Olds Toronado, Buick Riviera** '86 thru '93
38032 **Cadillac DeVille** '94 thru '05 **& Seville** '92 thru '04 **Cadillac DTS** '06 thru '10
38035 **Chevrolet Lumina APV, Olds Silhouette & Pontiac Trans Sport** all models '90 thru '96
38036 **Chevrolet Venture, Olds Silhouette, Pontiac Trans Sport & Montana** '97 thru '05
**General Motors Full-size Rear-wheel Drive** - *see BUICK (19025)*
38040 **Chevrolet Equinox** '05 thru '09 **Pontiac Torrent** '06 thru '09
38070 **Chevrolet HHR** '06 thru '11

## GEO

**Metro** - *see CHEVROLET Sprint (24075)*
**Prizm** - *'85 thru '92 see CHEVY (24060), '93 thru '02 see TOYOTA Corolla (92036)*
40030 **Storm** all models '90 thru '93
**Tracker** - *see SUZUKI Samurai (90010)*

## GMC

**Vans & Pick-ups** - *see CHEVROLET*

## HONDA

42010 **Accord CVCC** all models '76 thru '83
42011 **Accord** all models '84 thru '89
42012 **Accord** all models '90 thru '93
42013 **Accord** all models '94 thru '97
42014 **Accord** all models '98 thru '02
42015 **Accord** '03 thru '07
42020 **Civic 1200** all models '73 thru '79
42021 **Civic 1300 & 1500 CVCC** '80 thru '83
42022 **Civic 1500 CVCC** all models '75 thru '79

*(Continued on other side)*

# Haynes Automotive Manuals (continued)

*NOTE: If you do not see a listing for your vehicle, consult your local Haynes dealer for the latest product information.*

42023 **Civic** all models '84 thru '91
42024 **Civic & del Sol** '92 thru '95
42025 **Civic** '96 thru '00, **CR-V** '97 thru '01, **Acura Integra** '94 thru '00
42026 **Civic** '01 thru '10, **CR-V** '02 thru '09
42035 **Odyssey** all models '99 thru '10
**Passport** - *see ISUZU Rodeo (47017)*
42037 **Honda Pilot** '03 thru '07, **Acura MDX** '01 thru '07
42040 **Prelude CVCC** all models '79 thru '89

## HYUNDAI

43010 **Elantra** all models '96 thru '10
43015 **Excel & Accent** all models '86 thru '09
43050 **Santa Fe** all models '01 thru '06
43055 **Sonata** all models '99 thru '08

## INFINITI

**G35** '03 thru '08 - *see NISSAN 350Z (72011)*

## ISUZU

**Hombre** - *see CHEVROLET S-10 (24071)*
47017 **Rodeo, Amigo & Honda Passport** '89 thru '02
47020 **Trooper & Pick-up** '81 thru '93

## JAGUAR

49010 **XJ6** all 6 cyl models '68 thru '86
49011 **XJ6** all models '88 thru '94
49015 **XJ12 & XJS** all 12 cyl models '72 thru '85

## JEEP

50010 **Cherokee, Comanche & Wagoneer Limited** all models '84 thru '01
50020 **CJ** all models '49 thru '86
50025 **Grand Cherokee** all models '93 thru '04
50026 **Grand Cherokee** '05 thru '09
50029 **Grand Wagoneer & Pick-up** '72 thru '91 Grand Wagoneer '84 thru '91, Cherokee & Wagoneer '72 thru '83, Pick-up '72 thru '88
50030 **Wrangler** all models '87 thru '11
50035 **Liberty** '02 thru '07

## KIA

54050 **Optima** '01 thru '10
54070 **Sephia** '94 thru '01, **Spectra** '00 thru '09, **Sportage** '05 thru '10

## LEXUS

**ES 300/330** - *see TOYOTA Camry (92007) (92008)*
**RX 330** - *see TOYOTA Highlander (92095)*

## LINCOLN

**Navigator** - *see FORD Pick-up (36059)*
59010 **Rear-Wheel Drive** all models '70 thru '10

## MAZDA

61010 **GLC Hatchback (rear-wheel drive)** '77 thru '83
61011 **GLC (front-wheel drive)** '81 thru '85
61012 **Mazda3** '04 thru '11
61015 **323 & Protogé** '90 thru '03
61016 **MX-5 Miata** '90 thru '09
61020 **MPV** all models '89 thru '98
**Navajo** - *see Ford Explorer (36024)*
61030 **Pick-ups** '72 thru '93
**Pick-ups** '94 thru '00 - *see Ford Ranger (36071)*
61035 **RX-7** all models '79 thru '85
61036 **RX-7** all models '86 thru '91
61040 **626** (rear-wheel drive) all models '79 thru '82
61041 **626/MX-6 (front-wheel drive)** '83 thru '92
61042 **626, MX-6/Ford Probe** '93 thru '02
61043 **Mazda6** '03 thru '11

## MERCEDES-BENZ

63012 **123 Series Diesel** '76 thru '85
63015 **190 Series** four-cyl gas models, '84 thru '88
63020 **230/250/280** 6 cyl sohc models '68 thru '72
63025 **280 123 Series** gasoline models '77 thru '81
63030 **350 & 450** all models '71 thru '80
63040 **C-Class:** C230/C240/C280/C320/C350 '01 thru '07

## MERCURY

64200 **Villager & Nissan Quest** '93 thru '01
***All other titles, see FORD Listing.***

## MG

66010 **MGB** Roadster & GT Coupe '62 thru '80
66015 **MG Midget, Austin Healey Sprite** '58 thru '80

## MINI

67020 **Mini** '02 thru '11

## MITSUBISHI

68020 **Cordia, Tredia, Galant, Precis & Mirage** '83 thru '93
68030 **Eclipse, Eagle Talon & Ply. Laser** '90 thru '94
68031 **Eclipse** '95 thru '05, **Eagle Talon** '95 thru '98
68035 **Galant** '94 thru '10
68040 **Pick-up** '83 thru '96 & **Montero** '83 thru '93

## NISSAN

72010 **300ZX** all models including Turbo '84 thru '89
72011 **350Z & Infiniti G35** all models '03 thru '08
72015 **Altima** all models '93 thru '06
72016 **Altima** '07 thru '10
72020 **Maxima** all models '85 thru '92
72021 **Maxima** all models '93 thru '04
72025 **Murano** '03 thru '10
72030 **Pick-ups** '80 thru '97 **Pathfinder** '87 thru '95
72031 **Frontier Pick-up, Xterra, Pathfinder** '96 thru '04
72032 **Frontier & Xterra** '05 thru '11
72040 **Pulsar** all models '83 thru '86
**Quest** - *see MERCURY Villager (64200)*
72050 **Sentra** all models '82 thru '94
72051 **Sentra & 200SX** all models '95 thru '06
72060 **Stanza** all models '82 thru '90
72070 **Titan pick-ups** '04 thru '10 **Armada** '05 thru '10

## OLDSMOBILE

73015 **Cutlass** V6 & V8 gas models '74 thru '88
***For other OLDSMOBILE titles, see BUICK, CHEVROLET or GENERAL MOTORS listing.***

## PLYMOUTH

***For PLYMOUTH titles, see DODGE listing.***

## PONTIAC

79008 **Fiero** all models '84 thru '88
79018 **Firebird** V8 models except Turbo '70 thru '81
79019 **Firebird** all models '82 thru '92
79025 **G6** all models '05 thru '09
79040 **Mid-size Rear-wheel Drive** '70 thru '87
**Vibe** '03 thru '11 - *see TOYOTA Matrix (92060)*
***For other PONTIAC titles, see BUICK, CHEVROLET or GENERAL MOTORS listing.***

## PORSCHE

80020 **911** except Turbo & Carrera 4 '65 thru '89
80025 **914** all 4 cyl models '69 thru '76
80030 **924** all models including Turbo '76 thru '82
80035 **944** all models including Turbo '83 thru '89

## RENAULT

**Alliance & Encore** - *see AMC (14020)*

## SAAB

84010 **900** all models including Turbo '79 thru '88

## SATURN

87010 **Saturn** all S-series models '91 thru '02
87011 **Saturn Ion** '03 thru '07
87020 **Saturn** all L-series models '00 thru '04
87040 **Saturn VUE** '02 thru '07

## SUBARU

89002 **1100, 1300, 1400 & 1600** '71 thru '79
89003 **1600 & 1800** 2WD & 4WD '80 thru '94
89100 **Legacy** all models '90 thru '99
89101 **Legacy & Forester** '00 thru '06

## SUZUKI

90010 **Samurai/Sidekick & Geo Tracker** '86 thru '01

## TOYOTA

92005 **Camry** all models '83 thru '91
92006 **Camry** all models '92 thru '96
92007 **Camry, Avalon, Solara, Lexus ES 300** '97 thru '01
92008 **Toyota Camry, Avalon and Solara and Lexus ES 300/330** all models '02 thru '06
92009 **Camry** '07 thru '11
92015 **Celica Rear Wheel Drive** '71 thru '85
92020 **Celica Front Wheel Drive** '86 thru '99
92025 **Celica Supra** all models '79 thru '92
92030 **Corolla** all models '75 thru '79
92032 **Corolla** all rear wheel drive models '80 thru '87
92035 **Corolla** all front wheel drive models '84 thru '92
92036 **Corolla & Geo Prizm** '93 thru '02
92037 **Corolla** models '03 thru '11
92040 **Corolla Tercel** all models '80 thru '82
92045 **Corona** all models '74 thru '82
92050 **Cressida** all models '78 thru '82
92055 **Land Cruiser** FJ40, 43, 45, 55 '68 thru '82
92056 **Land Cruiser** FJ60, 62, 80, FZJ80 '80 thru '96
92060 **Matrix & Pontiac Vibe** '03 thru '11
92065 **MR2** all models '85 thru '87
92070 **Pick-up** all models '69 thru '78
92075 **Pick-up** all models '79 thru '95
92076 **Tacoma, 4Runner, & T100** '93 thru '04
92077 **Tacoma** all models '05 thru '09
92078 **Tundra** '00 thru '06 & **Sequoia** '01 thru '07
92079 **4Runner** all models '03 thru '09
92080 **Previa** all models '91 thru '95
92081 **Prius** all models '01 thru '08
92082 **RAV4** all models '96 thru '10
92085 **Tercel** all models '87 thru '94
92090 **Sienna** all models '98 thru '09
92095 **Highlander & Lexus RX-330** '99 thru '07

## TRIUMPH

94007 **Spitfire** all models '62 thru '81
94010 **TR7** all models '75 thru '81

## VW

96008 **Beetle & Karmann Ghia** '54 thru '79
96009 **New Beetle** '98 thru '11
96016 **Rabbit, Jetta, Scirocco & Pick-up** gas models '75 thru '92 & Convertible '80 thru '92
96017 **Golf, GTI & Jetta** '93 thru '98, **Cabrio** '95 thru '02
96018 **Golf, GTI, Jetta** '99 thru '05
96019 **Jetta, Rabbit, GTI & Golf** '05 thru '11
96020 **Rabbit, Jetta & Pick-up** diesel '77 thru '84
96023 **Passat** '98 thru '05, **Audi A4** '96 thru '01
96030 **Transporter 1600** all models '68 thru '79
96035 **Transporter 1700, 1800 & 2000** '72 thru '79
96040 **Type 3 1500 & 1600** all models '63 thru '73
96045 **Vanagon** all air-cooled models '80 thru '83

## VOLVO

97010 **120, 130 Series & 1800 Sports** '61 thru '73
97015 **140 Series** all models '66 thru '74
97020 **240 Series** all models '76 thru '93
97040 **740 & 760 Series** all models '82 thru '88
97050 **850 Series** all models '93 thru '97

## TECHBOOK MANUALS

10205 **Automotive Computer Codes**
10206 **OBD-II & Electronic Engine Management**
10210 **Automotive Emissions Control Manual**
10215 **Fuel Injection Manual** '78 thru '85
10220 **Fuel Injection Manual** '86 thru '99
10225 **Holley Carburetor Manual**
10230 **Rochester Carburetor Manual**
10240 **Weber/Zenith/Stromberg/SU Carburetors**
10305 **Chevrolet Engine Overhaul Manual**
10310 **Chrysler Engine Overhaul Manual**
10320 **Ford Engine Overhaul Manual**
10330 **GM and Ford Diesel Engine Repair Manual**
10333 **Engine Performance Manual**
10340 **Small Engine Repair Manual,** 5 HP & Less
10341 **Small Engine Repair Manual,** 5.5 - 20 HP
10345 **Suspension, Steering & Driveline Manual**
10355 **Ford Automatic Transmission Overhaul**
10360 **GM Automatic Transmission Overhaul**
10405 **Automotive Body Repair & Painting**
10410 **Automotive Brake Manual**
10411 **Automotive Anti-lock Brake (ABS) Systems**
10415 **Automotive Detaiing Manual**
10420 **Automotive Electrical Manual**
10425 **Automotive Heating & Air Conditioning**
10430 **Automotive Reference Manual & Dictionary**
10435 **Automotive Tools Manual**
10440 **Used Car Buying Guide**
10445 **Welding Manual**
10450 **ATV Basics**
10452 **Scooters 50cc to 250cc**

## SPANISH MANUALS

98903 **Reparación de Carrocería & Pintura**
98904 **Manual de Carburador Modelos Holley & Rochester**
98905 **Códigos Automotrices de la Computadora**
98906 **OBD-II & Sistemas de Control Electrónico del Motor**
98910 **Frenos Automotriz**
98913 **Electricidad Automotriz**
98915 **Inyección de Combustible** '86 al '99
99040 **Chevrolet & GMC Camionetas** '67 al '87
99041 **Chevrolet & GMC Camionetas** '88 al '98
99042 **Chevrolet & GMC Camionetas Cerradas** '68 al '95
99043 **Chevrolet/GMC Camionetas** '94 al '04
99048 **Chevrolet/GMC Camionetas** '99 al '06
99055 **Dodge Caravan & Plymouth Voyager** '84 al '95
99075 **Ford Camionetas y Bronco** '80 al '94
99076 **Ford F-150** '97 al '09
99077 **Ford Camionetas Cerradas** '69 al '91
99088 **Ford Modelos de Tamaño Mediano** '75 al '86
99089 **Ford Camionetas Ranger** '93 al '10
99091 **Ford Taurus & Mercury Sable** '86 al '95
99095 **GM Modelos de Tamaño Grande** '70 al '90
99100 **GM Modelos de Tamaño Mediano** '70 al '88
99106 **Jeep Cherokee, Wagoneer & Comanche** '84 al '00
99110 **Nissan Camioneta** '80 al '96, **Pathfinder** '87 al '95
99118 **Nissan Sentra** '82 al '94
99125 **Toyota Camionetas y 4Runner** '79 al '95

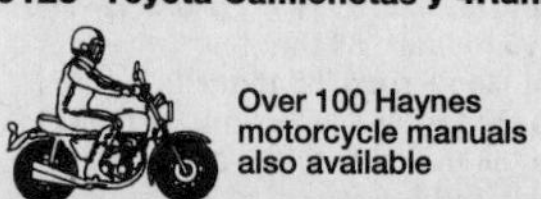

Over 100 Haynes motorcycle manuals also available

7-12